STACKS

R00207 22931

D1534803

Y

NTER

LANDOR

A Replevin

LANDOR AT SIXTY-THREE

From the portrait by William Fisher
in the National Portrait Gallery, painted
at Bath in 1838

LANDOR

A Replevin

MALCOLM ELWIN

ARCHON BOOKS, 1970

THE CHICAGO PUBLIC LIBRARY

APR JUN 11 1971 B

REF
PR
4823
.E54
1970

© 1958 by Malcolm Elwin
Reprinted 1970 with permission
in an unaltered and unabridged edition

R 821
L 236 Xe

cop.1

Hum

R0020722931

ISBN: 0-208-00990-6
Library of Congress Catalog Card Number: 75-122401
Printed in the United States of America

THE CHICAGO PUBLIC LIBRARY

APP. JUN 14 1971 B

To
EVE

CONTENTS

ILLUSTRATIONS

TOWARDS THE QUARRY

My quarry lies upon a high common a good way from the public road, and everybody takes out of it what he pleases "with privy paw, and nothing said" beyond "*a curse on the old fellow! how hard his granite is, one can never make it fit*".

—*Archdeacon Hare and Walter Landor* (1853)

The English have always preferred mediocrity and the commonplace to magnanimity and genius. Comfort is the condition most to be desired—perhaps because, as Hazlitt said, "the English are certainly the most uncomfortable of all people in themselves"—and they glance askant at the disturber of their peace. Landor therefore can never be a popular writer, for his entire life and work present a protest and a reproach to complacency.

At fifty-three he wrote:

Had avarice or ambition guided me, remember I started with a larger hereditary estate than those of Pitt, Fox, Canning, and twenty more such, amounted to; and not scraped together in this, or the last, or the preceding century, in ages of stockjobbing and peculation, of cabinet-adventure and counterfeit nobility. My education, and that which education works upon or produces, was not below theirs: yet certain I am that, if I had applied to be made a tide-waiter on the Thames, the minister would have refused me.

There he states the case against himself. A man of the people like William Cobbett, who could not aspire to membership of White's and Crockford's or to an invitation from Holland House, might be expected to express dissatisfaction with a social system from which he had derived few advantages. But Landor was a product of public school and university, who became at thirty proprietor of a large estate as head of an old family of landed gentry; party leaders were willing to guide his step upon the ladder of preferment—if he would subscribe to the conventional code of behaviour, sacrificing principle to expediency and paying lip-service to those with power to promote his interest. He declined all compromise; after a few years as a refractory and erratic pupil in the train of Charles James Fox, he chose the lonely life of one who acknowledges the discipline only of his own conscience, as he stated in the imaginary conversation, "Florentine, English Visitor, and Landor", written in his exile at Florence:

If men were to be represented as they show themselves, encrusted with all the dirtiness they contract in public life, in all the debility of ignorance, in all the distortion of prejudice, in all the reptile trickery of partisanship, who would care about the greater part of what are called the greatest? Principles and ideas are my objects: they must be reflected from high and low, but they must also be exhibited where people can see them best, and are most inclined to look at them.

His refusal to compromise denied him a platform for exhibiting his objects where many people could see them. The chief work of his youth, his epic poem *Gebir*, presented difficulties of obscurity without the challenge of eccentricity presented by a *Finnegans Wake*; it was praised publicly by Southey, privately by Coleridge, Shelley, Lamb, and De Quincey, but its readers were numbered in dozens. When Fox's private secretary published a biography of his late master and excited Landor to write a commentary on recent politics, his book proved so uncompromising in unpalatable truths that it was suppressed in proof and waited ninety-five years for publication. When one lawyer assured him that another deserved to be indicted for conspiracy, Landor saw no reason why he should not speak the truth to the latter's face; charged with libel, he preferred exile to submission under what he regarded as an unjust law and resigned his estates to be held in trust for a son then unborn!

During twenty-one years of exile he wrote and published five volumes of those *Imaginary Conversations* that he considered his title to enduring fame. As a contemporary critic[1] remarked, "the dramatic licence enjoyed by a writer of dialogues enables him . . . to exhibit to intelligent readers a more faithful portraiture of his own mind than could be given in the more usual and didactic method of composition", but while "we have fictitious letters, speeches, poems, dialogues, all written, delivered, held, by historical personages and on historical occasions . . . no narrative has awakened our interest in these persons and occasions—no train of incidents has artfully combined the inventions of the author with our old reminiscences; and the inevitable consequence is, that the whole work bears the aspect of a series of themes, and exercises, and literary imitations". Landor exhibits the same "deficiency in dramatic and narrative sense" as Mr. Edmund Wilson ascribes to James Joyce; though a supreme master of English

[1] *Quarterly Review*, February 1837.

prose, he remains in a different degree a writer as difficult of approach as Joyce, because he assumes his reader to possess a range of knowledge and an intellectual agility comparable with his own. Hence, while the five volumes of *Imaginary Conversations* excited the enthusiasm and reverence of a few readers, they found an insufficient public to justify publication of a sixth volume.

"There is one almost certain drawback on a course of scholastic study," wrote Hazlitt, "that it unfits men for active life. The *ideal* is always at variance with the *practical*." Landor's writings abound in wisdom which he failed to apply to his own life. A father so devoted that for many years he could not bear a few days' separation from his children, he abandoned home and family rather than endure the humiliation of his wife's incompatibility. He was then sixty years of age, yet he had still to live nearly thirty years in loneliness. During those years his literary reputation became so firmly established that, after his death in his ninetieth year, Swinburne wrote, "In the course of this long life he had won for himself such a double crown of glory in verse and in prose as has been worn by no other Englishman but Milton." He died in poverty, again in exile, and steadfast to the principles that he had professed throughout his life. Yet his reputation endured in spite of this steadfastness rather than from respect for that quality, owing much to the diligent publicity contrived by a man less worthy, but more worldly, and almost young enough to be his grandson.

§ 2

"Heavens preserve us from a monster of the name of Forster!" wrote a friend of Henry Crabb Robinson's in discussing possible candidates for writing Charles Lamb's biography. The task of Lamb's biographer was delicate, for Mary Lamb was still living and her brother had dedicated his life to caring for her after she had killed their mother in a fit of madness. As John Forster was only in his twenty-third year at Lamb's death in 1834, he can hardly have been considered as a likely biographer, but his personality had so far impressed members of Crabb Robinson's circle of gossips that they feared the possibility of his selection.

Forster was born at Newcastle on 2nd April 1812—when Landor was in his thirty-eighth year—of poor parents, but into an age of social change offering opportunities to enterprise. He owed his grammar-school education to the benevolence of an uncle, who sent him at seventeen to University College, London, as a law student. He read law with sufficient diligence to be called to the bar, for many years occupying the chambers in Lincoln's Inn Fields described by Dickens as Mr. Tulkinghorn's in *Bleak House*, but concentrated his abundant energy and enthusiasm on studying history and the theatre. His contributions to the college magazine impressed one of the professors, Dr. Dionysius Lardner, who commissioned a series of articles on seventeenth-century statesmen for the *Cyclopædia*—eventually completed in a hundred and thirty-two volumes—he was editing. This and other occasional work led to his appointment in 1832 as literary and dramatic critic on the *True Sun* newspaper; among the contributors he met Leigh Hunt, "the first distinguished man of letters I ever knew".

Lacking the credentials of money or influence, he sought self-advancement by cultivating friends and making himself indispensable to them. He was immediately useful to Leigh Hunt, then even more than usually oppressed by financial embarrassment, contriving the publication by subscription of Hunt's collected poems. The publisher was Edward Moxon, who had married Charles Lamb's adopted daughter; having secured an introduction to Lamb and discovered his taste for the theatre, Forster obliged him with complimentary theatre tickets obtained from such friends as Sheridan Knowles, who as a dramatist was disposed to propitiate a dramatic critic. He induced Moxon to publish a periodical called *The Reflector* with himself as editor, and Lamb promised his essay on "Barrenness of the Imaginative Faculty in the Productions of Modern Art"; before the essay could be finished, Moxon suspended publication of the paper after only three numbers, but Forster took the completed essay to Charles Dilke of the *Athenæum*, so obliging the author and at the same time impressing the editor with his possession of distinguished connections.

The process of his method of cultivating friendship may be traced in the actor Macready's diary. At Edmund Kean's funeral on 25th May 1833 Macready met Forster in the company of Sheridan Knowles and the two painters, Clarkson Stanfield and George Clint, but the actor was much in the provinces during the summer and it was after twice meeting him at the chambers of T. N. Talfourd (the lawyer and dramatist who became Lamb's literary executor and biographer) that Forster swiftly and imperceptibly engaged his intimate friendship. On 20th October Macready found Forster "quite an enthusiast; I like him"; on 9th November "Forster called, whom I have real pleasure in seeing", and eleven days later, when "Forster called, and had a long theatrical gossip", Macready's wife and sister "liked him very much". On 18th December Forster called for Macready at the theatre after the evening performance and conveyed him in a coach with Talfourd and B. W. Procter to his lodgings for "a pleasant but too indulging evening"; next morning Macready was "quite unable to get up, or to hold up my head from the effects of my facile temper last night", and "Forster called to bring my cloak, which I had left last night, and my pocket-handkerchief, which Knowles in jest had taken from me unperceived". In another ten days Macready distinguished Forster with a man who had been his intimate for seven years as "our friends" among other guests invited to dinner, and Forster confided to him that Knowles had taken offence at a critical article he had written, receiving Macready's sympathy and advice about reconciliation.

A few months later Forster was the means of reconciling a difference between Knowles and Macready, who began to depend on his advice and mediation in professional problems, particularly in difficulties with the theatre manager, Alfred Bunn. Forster persuaded Macready to sit for his portrait by the young artist, Daniel Maclise; he informed Macready that Talfourd was writing his tragedy of *Ion* and that Browning was at work on *Strafford*; he acted as intermediary between actor and author during Macready's production of Bulwer's *La Vallière* and arranged the cutting of the script.

By nature sensitive and morose, Macready was quick to take offence, and Forster was too impetuous and independent to be always tactful. When the American actor Forrest visited England, Macready was concerned that he should receive approving courtesies from the press and asked Forster's indulgence as a favour to himself; conceiving that Forrest was being praised by some newspapers to disparage Macready, Forster "was very peremptory and distinct in his expressed resolution to keep his own course"—he wrote a "slashing" criticism of Forrest, who believed that Macready had incited the attack and bore a lasting grudge on that account. On such occasions Macready decided that "Forster has not a *cool* judgment, and is certainly, though an ardent, yet a dangerous friend and ally". He could be "very indiscreet", especially when warmed by wine and argument. Habitually he dined well, and when Macready, after entertaining them to dinner, read aloud Bulwer's *Richelieu* to Forster and its author, "in the fifth act Forster was asleep". On waking, he talked volubly, but Bulwer was "chagrined, and evidently *angry*"; Forster showed due concern, but Macready felt "great pain" and considered that Forster "has warmth of feeling, but not much judgment, and wants the fine tact of good breeding".

Again, when Forster "had taken *enough* wine", Macready found him "rather exaggerating in his sensibility and praise" of his friend Browning's tragedy. Enthusiasm for his friends' work often exceeded his judgment, and mortified at having to reject a farce written specially by Dickens at Forster's instance, Macready exclaimed, "I cannot sufficiently condemn the officious folly of this marplot, Forster, who embroils his friends in difficulties and distress in this most determined manner". If his advice was not taken, he would sulk and become "most especially and conspicuously disagreeable—raising objections

B

out of mere humour and caprice and not to serve the cause or his friend." Consulted about disputes, he tended to advise aggression rather than conciliation—"he is a person of temper, therefore a bad counsellor".

As he grew more successful and influential, he became notoriously dogmatic, loudly and provocatively asserting his opinions without regard for offending or embarrassing his hearers. "Forster annoyed me by his absurd controversial spirit, which he never indulges without displaying the most vexatious casuistry", and a few months later Macready could not "help remarking upon the apparently *indomitable* bad taste which Forster continually exhibits in laying down his opinions (and upon subjects of which he, clever as he is, knows nothing) as if it were law". When "Forster displayed his unfortunate humour at dinner . . . behaving very grossly on a question which arose about a bet, in which I was deputed one of the arbiters", Macready declared "the harmony of our evening was quite destroyed, and I was made very uncomfortable by Forster's ill humour, and rude language". Next morning Macready "received a note from Forster, apologising for his behaviour, and requesting me to forget it", and was able to reply "in a very kind and cordial spirit". But sometimes Forster did not so readily repent his outbursts of temper. Dining one evening with Dickens, he goaded his host into passionate abuse; when Mrs. Dickens had left the room in tears, Macready soothed Dickens into offering an apology, but Forster "behaved very *weakly*" and ungraciously in "a very painful scene". On another occasion Browning was restrained by their host from throwing a decanter at Forster's head, and for several months in 1840 Forster and Browning were not on speaking terms, moving Macready to reflect, "Poor Forster! A little more strength of mind, and a little more judgment to bring his vanity under control, would greatly enhance his valuable qualities to himself and his friends."

As the older man by nearly twenty years, Macready felt frequent misgivings about his friend's future. "I fear he gives too much to indulgence to carve out a great reputation—'to scorn delights and live laborious days' is no more his motto than that of many others; and yet it is the only one under which to be *secure of advancing*." In 1837 (the year after his meeting both Landor and Dickens, when Forster was still only twenty-five), because "I sincerely regard him", Macready "wrote to Forster, on his intended removal to the Albany, which I am certain will bring down upon him all the fatal consequences of extravagance and rashness". In this case Forster may have responded to counsels of caution the more readily because he had recently burned his fingers in clutching at social ambition. In May 1835 he was "in a mysterious sort of uneasiness" and talked of

expecting "to 'go out' with some one"; in the following November
he confided to Macready that "he had been on the point of marriage"
with Letitia Elizabeth Landon, then fashionable in literary society
as the poetess "L.E.L.", but he had been "forced to demand explanation" from one reported circulator of scandalous gossip about Miss
Landon's reputation, and though he received a "positive and circumstantial" denial of the gossip, "it was arranged between themselves
and their mutual friends that the marriage should be broken off".
Apparently he felt the need for self-justification, as he did not scruple
to confide details of his former fiancée's indiscretions with his friend
Maclise and with Dr. Maginn—the latter a married man—so that
Macready "felt quite concerned that a woman of such splendid genius
and such agreeable manners should be so depraved in taste and so
lost to a sense of what was due to her high reputation". Forster was
then very young, but his want of sensibility and delicacy where his
own affections were engaged promised little perception in approaching
the emotional problems of others.

§ 3

Forster may have heard of Landor first from Leigh Hunt, who had
learned to reverence "that great heretic" during their friendship at
Florence between 1823 and 1825. In 1832, during his first visit to
England for nearly eighteen years, Landor called on Charles Lamb
and established a friendly correspondence with him. Forster related
that "one of the last things said to me by Charles Lamb, a week or
two before his death, was that only two men could have written the
Examination of Shakespeare—he who wrote it, and the man it was written
on". Published about two months before Lamb's death, the *Citation
and Examination of William Shakspeare* is among the least worthy of
Landor's writings, but appealed to Lamb as such literary whimsy
as he admired in his friend James White's *Original Letters of Sir John
Falstaff and His Friends*. Possibly fortified by Lamb's opinion, Forster
applauded this "book of remarkable genius" in a long article in the
Examiner, which was quoted at length a week or two later in Leigh
Hunt's *London Journal*.

Landor in Italy was delighted by what he described to his sister
as "the most eloquent piece of criticism in our language", which he
believed to have been written by the editor of the *Examiner*, Albany
Fonblanque. Less than eighteen months later, on publication of
Pericles and Aspasia, which displayed his powers to their greatest advantage, he was able to send a copy of the *Examiner* to his sisters for them
to see "how magnificently the best writer in Europe has mentioned my
Pericles". He did not in fact regard Fonblanque as "the best writer

in Europe", but at sixty-one he was still seeking to impress upon his own family an appreciation of his talents. He had returned to England in 1835, and among the inducements offered by Lady Blessington when inviting him to stay at Gore House was Fonblanque's eagerness to meet him. On meeting Fonblanque in the summer of 1836, he discovered that Forster was the author of the laudatory reviews, and was soon introduced to Fonblanque's able young assistant.

There is no reason to doubt the sincerity of Forster's admiration for Landor. As a student of history, he was impressed by the range of Landor's knowledge; as a radical in politics, he appreciated his revolutionary fervour; as a writer with pretensions to trenchancy, he recognized a master of prose. An acquaintance begun with mutual appreciation thrived on mutual usefulness. On Landor's introduction Forster advanced his social ambition by gaining access to Lady Blessington's *salon*, where he became a favoured intimate. In return he not only praised and publicised Landor's writings in print and in conversation, but provided in the *Examiner* a platform for political comment such as Landor had previously sought in vain. Soon Landor consigned to him everything he wrote, appointed him his literary executor, and had reason for gratitude to what Bulwer Lytton described as Forster's "strong practical sense and sound judgment" in managing publication of many volumes of poetry and prose, including his collected works.

When, as his literary executor, Forster became Landor's biographer, he was aware of the disadvantage—common to all biographers of subjects recently dead—that there were living relatives and friends likely to deprecate a detailed veracity. As later in his *Life of Dickens*, he therefore decided to base his narrative on his one peculiar advantage—his personal acquaintance with his subject. Both books betray the merits and defects of this approach, and his *Life of Dickens* is as much superior to his *Life of Landor* as his personal knowledge and understanding of Dickens was superior to his personal knowledge and understanding of Landor. He knew Dickens intimately for the last thirty-three of the fifty-eight years of his life; his acquaintance with Landor was limited to twenty-two of the last twenty-eight of his eighty-nine years. Dickens, moreover, was his exact contemporary; the fault of his *Life of Landor* lies in his interpretation of Landor's whole life according to an impression derived during his declining years—an impression developed in the course of friendship with a man thirty-seven years his senior, whom he regarded with the tolerance of a brisk young man of the world for the eccentricity of elderly genius.

Dickens made Landor's acquaintance about two years after Forster, but thereafter closely shared the friendship: Landor always dined at Dickens's house when in London and sometimes stayed there; Dickens

sometimes accompanied Forster on visits to Landor at Bath. Doubtless
he was recalling his first impression of Landor when he caused Jarndyce
to describe Mr. Boythorn in *Bleak House*:

with his head thrown back like an old soldier, his stalwart chest squared,
his hands like a clean blacksmith's, and his lungs!—there's no simile for
his lungs. Talking, laughing, or snoring, they make the beams of the house
shake. . . . But it's the inside of the man, the warm heart of the man, the
passion of the man, the fresh blood of the man. . . . His language is as sounding as his voice. He is always in extremes; perpetually in the superlative
degree. In his condemnation he is all ferocity. You might suppose him to
be an Ogre, from what he says; and I believe he has the reputation of one
with some people.

Young men in their twenties, Dickens and Forster regarded Landor
with the same affection and amusement as Esther Summerson regarded
Boythorn.

The dinner-hour arrived, and still he did not appear. The dinner was
put back an hour, and we were sitting round the fire with no light but the
blaze, when the hall-door suddenly burst open, and the hall resounded
with these words, uttered with the greatest vehemence and in a stentorian
tone:
"We have been misdirected, Jarndyce, by a most abandoned ruffian,
who told us to take the turning to the right instead of to the left. He is the
most intolerable scoundrel on the face of the earth. His father must have
been a most consummate villain, ever to have such a son. I would have had
that fellow shot without the least remorse!"
"Did he do it on purpose?" Mr. Jarndyce inquired.
"I have not the slightest doubt that the scoundrel has passed his whole
existence in misdirecting travellers!" returned the other. "By my soul,
I thought him the worst-looking dog I had ever beheld, when he was telling
me to take the turning to the right. And yet I stood before that fellow face
to face, and didn't knock his brains out!"
"Teeth, you mean?" said Mr. Jarndyce.
"Ha, ha, ha!" laughed Mr. Lawrence Boythorn, really making the whole
house vibrate. "What, you have not forgotten it yet! Ha, ha, ha!——
And that was another most consummate vagabond! By my soul, the countenance of that fellow, when he was a boy, was the blackest image of perfidy,
cowardice, and cruelty ever set up as a scarecrow in a field of scoundrels.
If I were to meet that most unparalleled despot in the streets to-morrow, I
would fell him like a rotten tree!"
"I have no doubt of it," said Mr. Jarndyce. "Now, will you come up-
stairs?"
"By my soul, Jarndyce," returned his guest, who seemed to refer to his
watch, "if you had been married, I would have turned back at the garden-
gate, and gone away to the remotest summits of the Himalaya Mountains,
sooner than I would have presented myself at this unseasonable hour."
"Not quite so far, I hope?" said Mr. Jarndyce.
"By my life and honour, yes!" cried the visitor. "I wouldn't be guilty
of the audacious insolence of keeping a lady of the house waiting all this
time, for any earthly consideration. I would infinitely rather destroy myself
—infinitely rather!"

Talking thus, they went up-stairs; and presently we heard him in his bedroom thundering "Ha, ha, ha!" and again "Ha, ha, ha!" until the flattest echo in the neighbourhood seemed to catch the contagion, and to laugh as enjoyingly as he did, or as we did when we heard him laugh.

We all conceived a prepossession in his favour; for there was a sterling quality in this laugh, and in his vigorous healthy voice, and in the roundness and fulness with which he uttered every word he spoke, and in the very fury of his superlatives, which seemed to go off like blank cannons and hurt nothing. But we were hardly prepared to have it so confirmed by his appearance, when Mr. Jarndyce presented him. He was not only a very handsome old gentleman—upright and stalwart as he had been described to us—with a massive grey head, a fine composure of face when silent, a figure that might have become corpulent but for his being so continually in earnest that he gave it no rest, and a chin that might have subsided into a double chin but for the vehement emphasis in which it was constantly required to assist; but he was such a true gentleman in his manner, so chivalrously polite, his face was lighted by a smile of so much sweetness and tenderness, and it seemed so plain that he had nothing to hide, but showed himself exactly as he was—incapable (as Richard said) of anything on a limited scale, and firing away with those blank great guns, because he carried no small arms whatever—that really I could not help looking at him with equal pleasure as he sat at dinner, whether he smilingly conversed with Ada and me, or was led by Mr. Jarndyce into some great volley of superlatives, or threw up his head like a bloodhound, and gave out that tremendous Ha, ha, ha! . . .

"You have brought your bird with you, I suppose?" said Mr. Jarndyce.

"By Heaven, he is the most astonishing bird in Europe!" replied the other. "He *is* the most wonderful creature! I wouldn't take ten thousand guineas for that bird. I have left an annuity for his sole support, in case he should outlive me. He is, in sense and attachment, a phenomenon. And his father before him was one of the most astonishing birds that ever lived!"

The subject of this laudation was a very little canary, who was so tame that he was brought down by Mr. Boythorn's man, on his forefinger, and, after taking a gentle flight round the room, alighted on his master's head. To hear Mr. Boythorn presently expressing the most implacable and passionate sentiments, with this fragile mite of a creature quietly perched on his forehead, was to have a good illustration of his character, I thought.

"By my soul, Jarndyce," he said, very gently holding up a bit of bread to the canary to peck at, "if I were in your place, I would seize every Master in Chancery by the throat to-morrow morning, and shake him until his money rolled out of his pockets, and his bones rattled in his skin. I would have a settlement out of somebody, by fair means or by foul. If you would empower me to do it, I would do it for you with the greatest satisfaction!" (All this time the very small canary was eating out of his hand.) . . .

"There never was such an infernal cauldron as that Chancery, on the face of the earth!" said Mr. Boythorn. "Nothing but a mine below it on a busy day in term time, with all its records, rules, and precedents collected in it, and every functionary belonging to it also, high and low, upward and downward, from its son the Accountant-General to its father the Devil, and the whole blown to atoms with ten thousand hundred-weight of gunpowder, would reform it in the least!"

It was impossible not to laugh at the energetic gravity with which he recommended this strong measure of reform. When we laughed, he threw up his head, and shook his broad chest, and again the whole country seemed to echo to his Ha, ha, ha! It had not the least effect in disturbing the bird, whose sense of security was complete; and who hopped about the table with its quick head now on this side and now on that, turning its bright sudden eye on its master, as if he were no more than another bird.

"But how do you and your neighbour get on about the disputed right of way?" asked Mr. Jarndyce. "You are not free from the toils of the law yourself!"

"The fellow has brought actions against *me* for trespass, and I have brought actions against *him* for trespass," returned Mr. Boythorn. "By Heaven, he is the proudest fellow breathing. It is morally impossible that his name can be Sir Leicester. It must be Sir Lucifer."

"Complimentary to our distant relation!" said my Guardian laughingly, to Ada and Richard.

"I would beg Miss Clare's pardon and Mr. Carstone's pardon," resumed our visitor, "if I were not reassured by seeing in the fair face of the lady, and the smile of the gentleman, that it is quite unnecessary, and that they keep their distant relation at a comfortable distance."

"Or he keeps us," suggested Richard.

"By my soul!" exclaimed Mr. Boythorn, suddenly firing another volley, "that fellow is, and his father was, and his grandfather was, the most stiff-necked, arrogant, imbecile, pig-headed numskull, ever, by some inexplicable mistake of Nature, born in any station of life but a walking-stick's! The whole of that family are the most solemnly conceited and consummate blockheads!— But it's no matter; he should not shut up my path if he were fifty baronets melted into one, and living in a hundred Chesney Wolds, one within another, like the ivory balls in a Chinese carving. The fellow, by his agent, or secretary, or somebody, writes to me, 'Sir Leicester Dedlock, Baronet, presents his compliments to Mr. Lawrence Boythorn, and has to call his attention to the fact that the green pathway by the old parsonage-house, now the property of Mr. Lawrence Boythorn, is Sir Leicester's right of way, being in fact a portion of the park of Chesney Wold; and that Sir Leicester finds it convenient to close up the same.' I write to the fellow, 'Mr. Lawrence Boythorn presents his compliments to Sir Leicester Dedlock, Baronet, and has to call *his* attention to the fact that he totally denies the whole of Sir Leicester Dedlock's positions on every possible subject, and has to add, in reference to closing up the pathway, that he will be glad to see the man who may undertake to do it.' The fellow sends a most abandoned villain with one eye, to construct a gateway. I play upon that execrable scoundrel with a fire-engine, until the breath is nearly driven out of his body. The fellow erects a gate in the night. I chop it down and burn it in the morning. He sends his myrmidons to come over the fence, and pass and repass. I catch them in humane man traps, fire split peas at their legs, play upon them with the engine—resolve to free mankind from the insupportable burden of the existence of those lurking ruffians. He brings actions for trespass; I bring actions for trespass. He brings actions for assault and battery; I defend them, and continue to assault and batter. Ha, ha, ha!"

To hear him say all this with unimaginable energy, one might have thought him the angriest of mankind. To see him at the very same time, looking at the bird now perched upon his thumb, and softly smoothing its feathers with his forefinger, one might have thought him the gentlest. To hear him laugh, and see the broad good nature of his face then, one might have supposed that he had not a care in the world, or a dispute, or a dislike, but that his whole existence was a summer joke.

"No, no," he said, "no closing up of my paths, by any Dedlock! Though I willingly confess," here he softened in a moment, "that Lady Dedlock is the most accomplished lady in the world, to whom I would do any homage that a plain gentleman, and no baronet with a head seven hundred years thick, may. A man who joined his regiment at twenty, and, within a week, challenged the most imperious and presumptuous coxcomb of a commanding officer that ever drew the breath of life through a tight waist—and got broke for it—is not the man to be walked over, by all the Sir Lucifers, dead or alive, locked or unlocked. Ha, ha, ha!"

Boythorn's exclamations—his "By Heavens" and "God bless my soul"—his violence of invective, energy of utterance, and bursts of boisterous laughter were notoriously Landor's. Knowing what Dickens and Forster expected of him, he was disposed mischievously to play up to his reputation for unorthodox opinions by plunging into paradox. An impulse of emotion excited extravagant expression; Boythorn's assurance that he would rather destroy himself than keep his hostess waiting was inspired by Dickens's recollection of Landor's dismay when Count D'Orsay pointed out the incompleteness of his dress before entering Lady Blessington's drawing-room; Boythorn's spleen against the "most abandoned ruffian" who misdirected him reflected the manner of Landor's reaction to annoyance, as in his troubles with the police at Florence.

Doubtless in much the same terms as Boythorn described his conflict with Sir Leicester Dedlock over the right of way, Landor related to Dickens some account of the litigation with his neighbour at Fiesole over the watercourse and of disputes with his Llanthony tenants. His description of the latter must have been graphic, for the correspondence with his Abergavenny attorney, Baker Gabb, shows that his Llanthony troubles followed the pattern of Boythorn's exploits more closely than Forster indicated.

Referring to the first years of his friendship with Landor, Forster remarked that "the Boythorn of *Bleak House* was the Landor of this earlier time, from a few of whose many attractive and original qualities, omitting all the graver, our great master of fiction drew that new and delightful creature of his fancy". Landor was unlikely to confide his intimate troubles to men so much his junior; probably Dickens knew little more of Landor's domestic tragedy than Mr. Jarndyce hinted of Boythorn's to Esther, when she commented on Boythorn's "courtly and gentle" manner to women by contrast with his otherwise violent expressions:

"He was all but married, once. Long ago. And once."
"Did the lady die?"
"No—but she died to him. That time has had its influence on all his

later life. Would you suppose him to have a head and a heart full of romance yet?"

"I think, Guardian, I might have supposed so . . ."

"He has never since been what he might have been," said Mr. Jarndyce, "and now you see him in his age with no one near him but his servant, and his little yellow friend."

Landor's "little yellow friend" for twelve years of his loneliness at Bath was his Pomeranian dog, on whom he lavished such tenderness and adulation as Boythorn on his canary. When Dickens first knew him, he had a tame marten, which doubtless suggested the canary; Dickens chose the canary rather than a dog because the little bird's hopping fearlessly on its master's head during Boythorn's protestations of violence offered the more picturesque antithesis. Dickens's art tended always to distort character into caricature. The portrait-painter, seeking truth to life, explores the subtle lights and shades of character; the caricaturist exaggerates the obvious to achieve immediacy in dramatic effect.

Boythorn is a caricature of Landor. As a caricaturist, Dickens depicted in Boythorn some of Landor's eccentricities at the time when he came to know him—between sixty and seventy years of age. It was a caricature readily recognisable by anybody who had a slight acquaintance with Landor at that time—who had, for instance, sat with him at dinner as Mr. Jarndyce's wards sat with Boythorn. Forster acknowledged that Dickens drew only a few of "many attractive and original qualities, omitting all the graver", but when he came to write Landor's biography, he saw Landor always in caricature as Boythorn; through all the sixty years before he knew him, he causes Landor to blunder along a turbulent, impetuous course as Boythorn. And the lovableness of Boythorn in *Bleak House* is tainted in Forster's *Landor* by the change in Forster himself during the passage of thirty years from his meeting with Landor to the writing of the biography published in 1869. Macready's ebullient young friend was hardened by materialist values into the successful careerist whom Dickens cruelly caricatured as Podsnap in *Our Mutual Friend*. Forster could no longer regard Boythorn's eccentricities with tolerant affection, for he had dedicated his own life to that materialism of Podsnappery against which Landor had revolted and protested throughout his long life.

When Landor's impetuosity involved him in a libel action six years before his death, Forster was concerned only with escaping from the embarrassment of his charge, his advice betraying the old man into a last exile of poverty and dependence. In the same year as his betrayal of Landor, he failed in his closer friendship with Dickens; his want of sympathy with Dickens in separating from his wife revealed his limited perception of spiritual and sexual problems. While he necessarily suppressed much information at his disposal because Landor's wife and children were still living when the biography appeared, he presented evidence for an assessment of Landor's reasons for leaving his wife by quoting Landor's correspondence with Charles Brown and Southey (see pages 279–280), but discounted the evidence by his own censorious interpretation.

The attitude of Landor's wife to her husband had degenerated into habitual hostility; regularly abusing him in the presence of his children and servants, she played upon the children's affections to engage their sympathies on her side and had already excited their eldest son to share her resentment against his father. Foreseeing alienation from his children, who would eventually despise their mother for having caused the alienation as much as they despised their father for tolerating the situation, Landor withdrew from his family, but Forster commented:

it was more for his own sake than for theirs the extraordinary determination was taken. He could not believe, if we are to trust the language always afterwards used by him, that, with his own mere withdrawal from his home, all indecency of language or temper was to cease there forever; and the more he condemns what had become unbearable by himself, the more he condemns himself for having left his children exposed to it.

He did not examine the alternatives to Landor's action. Presumably he would not have suggested that Landor should have taken the children away from their mother; hence he inferred that Landor should have endured the development he sought to avoid—the deterioration of his family in the unhappiness of dissension. Probably he thought that the vituperative wife should have been disciplined by masculine domination; when he himself married the wealthy widow of the publisher Colburn, their friend Clarkson Stanfield wrote to Dickens, "the depreciation that has taken place in that woman is fearful! She has no blood Sir in her body—no colour—no voice—is all scrunched and squeezed together—and seems to me in deep affliction—while Forster Sir is rampant and raging".

If Landor confided anything of his feeling for his family, Forster either misunderstood or forgot. Dickens had more perception, since he wrote of Boythorn that "he has never since been what he might have been". Having discussed Landor's separation from his family as an indiscretion to be deplored, Forster proceeded with his memories of Boythorn. The effect of his narrative upon the average reader appeared when Sidney Colvin, commenting on Forster's facts without independent research, published in 1881 his "English Men of Letters" monograph on Landor:

Did Landor then really . . . feel very deeply the breaking up of his beautiful Italian home or not? A few years before he could not bear his children to be out of his sight even for a day; did he suffer as we should have expected him to suffer at his total separation from them now?

With an academic lack of imagination, Colvin concluded from Forster's narrative that, "a wrench once made, a tie once broken, he could accommodate himself without too much suffering to the change", and "the injury done to his children by leaving them subject to no discipline at such an age and in such surroundings, would appear hardly to have weighed on Landor's mind at all, and that it failed to do so is, I think, the most serious blot upon his character".

Of the libel case that drove Landor into his last exile, Forster's statement inspired an interpretation by Colvin "which could not but make those who loved and honoured him regret that he had not succumbed earlier to the common lot"—a strangely callous conclusion for a biographer to make about his subject's attempt, however ill-advised, to expose the exploitation of a girl by a much older woman. When Forster himself died in 1876, the writer of an obituary notice in the *Athenæum* described his *Life of Goldsmith* as "an English classic", but "his *Life of Landor* was necessarily a less genial book". Among his peers there were several, like Browning and Swinburne, whose reverence for Landor remained unaltered; Augustus Hare related how, ten years after Landor's death, Thomas Carlyle "talked of Landor, of the grandeur and unworldliness of his nature, and of how it was a lasting disgrace to England that the vile calumnies of an insolent slanderer had been suffered to blight him in the eyes of so many, and to send him out an exile from England in his old age". But in general a society based on materialism self-righteously disparaged a man who had lived in contempt of its standards as a misguided victim of an ill-regulated life.

Colvin[1] ended his apology for Landor's life with the consolation that "it is the work and not the life of a man like Landor which in reality most concerns us". The fatuity of this remark by a biographer received emphasis when he proceeded to discuss the "difficulties arising from that want of consideration and sympathy in Landor for his readers" which are "the causes of his scant popularity". Obviously a man's work is the outcome of his life and character; as of cause and effect, a study of the one inevitably leads to a study of the other. Landor's work is difficult of approach because it reflects the same refusal to compromise with popular standards as directed (or misdirected) the course of his life.

It was acknowledged by Boythorn's creator, on reviewing Forster's biography in *All the Year Round*, that Landor's name was "inseparably

---

[1] It is not irrelevant to note that Sidney Colvin carried the dish of his modest talents so circumspectly that he acquired a knighthood; and that a parallel may be drawn between Sir Sidney and Lady Colvin and Mr. and Mrs. Barton Trafford in Somerset Maugham's *Cakes and Ale* (see *The Strange Case of Robert Louis Stevenson*, by Malcolm Elwin, 1950).

associated in the writer's mind with the dignity of generosity: with a noble scorn of all littleness, all cruelty, oppression, fraud, and false pretence". Those who met him found Landor one of the most attractive personalities in contemporary letters; literary historians regard him as the purest of English prose writers. But his title to recognition as one of the great thinkers of his time, denied by contemporaries to one in advance of his age, has been obscured for posterity by the Boythorn legend, masking with a motley of eccentricity the lifelong lover of liberty, the devotee of truth and beauty, the passionate assailant of injustice and hypocrisy. Unlike Boythorn's, Landor's superlatives did not "go off like blank cannons and hurt nothing".

Any reader of his prose must realise that he is in the presence of a massive intellect, with a perception sharpened and knowledge broadened by years of contemplation. But Landor assumed in his reader, not only an equivalent knowledge and perception, but also such leisure and inclination for study and contemplation as his own. Hence the average reader hesitates before the massed volumes of his works and postpones investigation to a period of greater leisure that never comes. Colvin remarked that "a selection or golden treasury of Landor's shorter dramatic dialogues", edited with occasional commentary, "would be, as was said long ago by Julius Hare, 'one of the most beautiful books in the language'." But Landor, in his prose, has been ill-served by his editors.

For many years after Colvin's monograph Landorian scholars edited tentative collections suggesting their possible progress to such a selection as Colvin proposed. Stephen Wheeler published in 1897 *Letters and Other Unpublished Writings of Walter Savage Landor*, and in 1899 his *Letters of Landor Private and Public* contained Landor's copious correspondence with Rose Graves-Sawle and a selection of his contributions to the *Examiner*. In *Walter Savage Landor: Last Days, Letters and Conversations*, H. C. Minchin presented Landor's letters to Browning during the last five years of his life; his letters to Mary Boyle were edited for a magazine by James Russell Lowell as inadequately as he handled Thackeray's letters to Mrs. Brookfield; his letters to his Rugby schoolfellow, Walter Birch, were given incompletely by the Rev. E. H. R. Tatham in the *Fortnightly Review* of February 1910. After collaborating with T. J. Wise in a valuable *Bibliography* of Landor's works, Stephen Wheeler admirably edited his English poetry, but Chapman & Hall unfortunately entrusted the editing of his prose to T. Earle Welby, a journalist of careless habits, who not only attempted no such commentary as Colvin suggested, but even ignored the guidance supplied by Wise and Wheeler towards achieving what professed to be a "complete" edition.

As the *Quarterly Review* of February 1837 remarked, "the dramatic licence enjoyed by a writer of dialogues" enabled Landor "to exhibit to intelligent readers a more faithful portraiture of his own mind than could be given in the more usual and didactic method of composition". An adequate biography is therefore an especially valuable complement to a study of his work. The present writer's research for such a biography was interrupted by the outbreak of war in 1939, and while his *Savage Landor* appeared in America in 1941, the war-time paper shortage prevented publication of such a long book in England. After the war he placed all his materials at the disposal of Mr. R. H. Super, an American scholar, who in the course of nearly twenty years published essays and pamphlets on various aspects of Landor's life and work. Eventually Mr. Super published in 1954 his *Walter Savage Landor: A Biography*—a massive work in the manner fashionable among modern American scholars, enumerating every detail that he has been able to discover about Landor in almost half a lifetime's research, with one-fifth of its 654 pages devoted to source references, including library shelf-numbers. But Mr. Super so far surpasses Forster in deprecating the eccentricities of Landor's character and conduct that his readers must wonder why he persevered so long in studying a subject with whom he felt so little sympathy.

Condescension is a disastrous attitude in a biographer, and an attitude peculiarly impertinent towards Landor; for, though the conduct of his life was unpractical according to materialist standards, few men have acted more consistently with their avowed principles. Landor's life and work require no apology; they do require sympathetic comment and explanation. This book is described as "a replevin" because it is an attempt to recover Landor's character from misrepresentation and his work from neglect. So far as possible, he is allowed to speak for himself; if there is more copious quotation than seems strictly necessary to the biographical narrative, it is because much of his work is difficult of access and examples of its quality may induce readers to seek for more.

2

THE REBEL BRED

Let the character be taken in the complex; and let the more obvious and best peculiarities be markt plainly and distinctly, or (if those predominate) the worst.

—*Walton, Cotton, and Oldways* (1829)

The most wonderful thing in human nature is the variance of knowledge and will, where no passion is the stimulant: whence that system of life is often chosen and persevered in, which a man is well convinced is neither the best for him nor the easiest. Few can see clearly where their happiness lies; and, in those who see it, you will scarcely find one who has the courage to pursue it.

—*Marcus Tullius and Quinctus Cicero* (1824).

The circumstances of his birth had especial significance in relation to the course of Landor's life; if he had not been born the heir to an independent fortune, he could not have given unbridled rein to that uncompromising conduct and opinion which became his notorious characteristic. The Landors were Staffordshire yeomen; a Landor settled at Rugeley in 1589, and his great-grandson Walter served as sheriff of Staffordshire in 1698–99. The family subsequently prospered by profitable marriages, for, after Robert Landor of Rugeley had married the co-heiress of Walter Noble of Longdon, his son and successor, Dr. Walter Landor, married as his second wife Elizabeth Savage of Tachbrook, who brought him estates estimated as worth some eighty thousand pounds.

Walter Savage Landor, born at Warwick on 30th January 1775, was the eldest child of this marriage, which produced three other sons —Charles Savage (1777–1849), who became a parson, Henry Eyres (1780–1866), a lawyer and land agent, and Robert Eyres (1781–1869), also a parson, whose little-known work as a writer has received attention only from Mr. Eric Partridge[1]—and three daughters, none of

[1] This, and all authorities subsequently cited, will be found in the Bibliography on page 471, where works are listed in alphabetical order of their authors' names. Scholars may thus trace the sources of information, while the general reader is preserved from the irritation of frequent footnotes offering nothing but references to works he is unlikely ever to consult.

whom ever married—Elizabeth (1776–1854), Mary Anne (1778–1818), and Ellen (1782–1838). Dr. Landor for some years practised medicine at Warwick; "it was, I believe, not unusual", wrote Robert Landor to Forster, "for even the eldest sons of private gentlemen to engage in some profession during their father's lifetime". From Rugby Dr. Landor went up to Worcester College, Oxford, in 1750, took his arts degree in 1754, and proceeded to a medical degree from St. Alban Hall in 1760, the year in which he married Mary, only child of Richard Wright, of Warwick. Of the children of his first marriage only a daughter, Maria, survived childhood; she married into the old family of Arden, to which Shakespeare's mother belonged. Some time after his second wife received her inheritance, he resigned his practice and divided his time between his house at Warwick and the Savage house at Bishop's Tachbrook, near Leamington, with occasional visits to Ipsley Court, near Redditch, an estate inherited by his wife in 1786 from her second cousin, John Norris.

The Norris inheritance, including much property at Tachbrook besides Ipsley, was settled in entail upon Mrs. Landor's eldest son, who was already heir to his father's Rugeley estate and thus from childhood knew himself to be destined for an ample fortune. For her younger children remained only what she could devise from her share in her father's legacy and her interest, shared with her three sisters, in the Buckinghamshire manor of Hughenden (afterwards Disraeli's home), which descended to her from a great-uncle after expiry of a life interest held by Lady Conyngham. A mother's natural affection was bound to be enlisted in the interests of the sufferers from this unjust distribution, and whatever cause for displeasure his subsequent conduct occasioned, there seem grounds for suspicion that Elizabeth Landor allowed her eldest son to realise too plainly, even from childhood, that her concern for the future of her younger children excluded him from an equal share of her consideration.

Colvin remarked that Mrs. Landor's "love for her children was solicitous and prudent rather than passionate or very tender"; presumably he judged from the evidence of her relations with her eldest son. She was a typical woman of her class and time. Women of the squirearchy in the late eighteenth and early nineteenth centuries regarded duty as the only correct guide for human conduct; any deviation from duty's narrow path, caused by whatever natural emotion or temperamental idiosyncrasy, was a weakness and a fault. The mother of Charles Reade, the novelist, was such another woman as Mrs. Landor. They devoted the best years of their lives to the bearing and rearing of large families, and having brought them to maturity, expected them to do their duty as their parents had done. The eldest son should equip himself to take his father's place as manager of the family estate; he should marry a wife whose dowry would add to the estate, and breed by her a family like his father's. The younger sons should marry as well as they could, and carve out careers according to their lights in the approved professions. The daughters should wait, unconscious of their physical potentialities, to be asked for their hands in marriage by men of such social and financial position or prospects as could be parentally approved; if no such proposals were forthcoming, they must continue unconscious of their physical potentialities, devote themselves to the comfort of their parents' declining years, and spend their own declining years in loneliness—probably in irksome dependence. A harsh but simple creed, it served England well for a century, during which sons of the squirearchy scattered wide about the world to explore, acquire, and administer the territories that became the British Empire.

Of Elizabeth Landor's children, her eldest son alone failed to sustain the traditions of his class. The daughters omitted to secure suitable husbands, but otherwise behaved fittingly, dutifully attending upon their mother, performing their functions as ladies of the manor, and wistfully watching the growth of their brothers' families. Charles Landor obediently assumed holy orders; the Landor family had the gift of a living at Colton in Staffordshire, where Charles succeeded his uncle; the Rev. John Landor, in 1806. A muscular athlete, devoted to field sports, Charles figures little in his elder brother's life, though he evidently maintained fairly close relations with his mother and sisters.

Robert, youngest of the four sons, remains a shadowy personality even after Mr. Partridge's biographical sketch. When his turn came for school, Dr. Landor felt his finances would not sustain a fourth son at Rugby, so Robert went to Bromsgrove Grammar School, whence he obtained a scholarship at Worcester College, Oxford, so enabling him to join his brother Charles at their father's old college. He also entered the Church, but after a few months as curate-in-charge of a Dorsetshire parish in 1805, appears to have performed no regular ecclesiastical function for twelve years, till, in 1817, family influence secured him a living at Hughenden. It seems that during these years he was in close touch with his eldest brother, whose literary tastes and inclinations he alone of the family shared, and their intimacy ceased— significantly—shortly before his preferment to the Hughenden living. In 1829 he obtained the living of Birlingham in Worcestershire, where he lived in seclusion for the rest of his life. Forster applied to him for assistance when compiling his biography of Landor, but either he was deliberately reticent, or Forster suppressed much information received about Landor's early life. Little known during his lifetime, Robert Landor's literary work has been examined to-day by the merest handful of students; not till twenty years after the publication of his *History of Nineteenth Century Literature* did George Saintsbury add a footnote in the ninth edition of that work to mention Robert Landor, remarking that "it may be questioned whether Robert's powers were much less—intellectually they were perhaps greater—than Walter's; but he never got them into thorough working order, and he is sometimes (in his later years especially) very obscure".

Third of the four brothers, Henry Landor had the least pretensions, but in a worldly sense proved the most successful. He followed his elder brothers to Rugby, and expected to follow them to Oxford, but when Robert won his scholarship, their father decided that he could not afford to maintain three sons simultaneously at the university and Henry entered the office of a London conveyancer. This disappointment must have awakened his mother's sympathy. Robert told Forster that, while his mother was "an anxious rather than a fond parent, she was scrupulously just". But she was also evidently both lacking in imagination and addicted to the rigidity of opinion and outlook usual in those self-consciously intent upon justice. If Henry had not been her favourite before, he became so after being excluded from sharing with his brothers the privilege of going to Oxford. Doubtless by her device, he received the bequest of a small estate at Whitnash, near Tachbrook, where he settled in professional practice as "for some forty years the busiest and most esteemed land-agent in Warwickshire". He became "the family adviser and manager", and Robert declared that, "under the guidance of my brother Henry, who managed her affairs", his mother "would give as much to any of her children as was consistent with justice to the rest". Robert added that Henry "would never accept any share in the common property", and, as Mr. Partridge observes, the little that is known of him is all to his credit, but he prospered so well that he ended his days as master of the Tachbrook home which was part of his eldest brother's birthright, and clearly he enjoyed more of his mother's confidence than any other of her sons.

From the first Mrs. Landor lavished scant maternal affection on her eldest son. In and out of child-bed to produce six children in the eight years following his birth, she had little time to watch his progress from the nursery. At the age of only four and a half he was sent away from home to school under Thomas Treherne at Knowle, about ten miles from Warwick on the Birmingham road, and from this tender age he entered the family circle only during his school holidays. Early exile from the security of home and mother-love may well encourage independence of spirit in a strong character, but this advantage accrues at the expense of such gentle manners and consideration for others as De Quincey attributed to an upbringing under the "indulgent tenderness" of women. The effect in Landor's case was

c

witnessed when Mary Martha Butt—afterwards, as Mrs. Sherwood, author of *The Fairchild Family*—was taken by her mother to visit "a Dr. Larnder at Warwick". Mary Butt was a well-behaved little girl, whose manners and good looks were a source of pride to her fond mother, and she was "amazed at the new view of domestic life which there opened to me when we arrived at the Doctor's house".

We were ushered into a parlour, where Mrs. Larnder received us very cordially; but before the fire . . . lay her eldest son Walter, a big boy, with rough hair. He was stretched on the carpet, and on his mother admonishing him to get up, he answered: "I won't," or "I shan't." She reproved him, and he bade her hold her tongue. From that day this youth became the prototype in my mind of all that was vulgar and disobedient, for I had never seen anything like family insubordination, and had hardly conceived the thing to be possible.

Mary witnessed "other specimens in this family of a thoroughly undisciplined household". She was taken to the play-room by Landor's eldest sister, Elizabeth, who said:

"I am glad you came to-day, for you have saved me from a good scolding, for my mother is out of humour"; and the poor lady, though exceedingly civil and hospitable, was in such a perpetual fume that her husband, a hearty, old-fashioned sort of man, a physician of the bygone day, kept constantly saying to her at dinner: "Come, Betty, keep your temper. Do, Betty, keep your temper."

Evidently Landor's impetuous temper was inherited from his mother, whose want of self-control encouraged a habit of defiance.

In old age, after the manner of the very old, Landor often recalled wistfully the scenes of his childhood, and though neither of his parents figured in his reminiscences, he cherished tender memories of both Tachbrook and Warwick. In 1852 he wrote to his brother Henry:

Dear old Tachbrooke! it is the only locality for which I feel any affection. Well do I remember it from my third or fourth year; and the red filberts at the top of the garden, and the apricots from the barn-wall, and Aunt Nancy cracking the stones for me. If I should ever eat apricots with you again, I shall not now cry for the kernel.

Two years later, he reminded Henry of a boyish adventure connected with a certain apple-tree, which still stood "close upon the nut-walk, and just of the same size and appearance as it was seventy years ago". When, in 1853, he stayed at Warwick as the guest of his sister Elizabeth, he picked up on the gravel-walk the first two mulberries that had fallen, and remembered having done the same just seventy-five years before. After the visit he wrote to his sister of the joy he had felt to stay again in his old home, "with its dear old mulberry-trees, its grand cedars, the chestnut-wood with the church appearing through it".

For Ipsley, close by the needle factories of Redditch, he never felt the same affection. "Never," he wrote in 1830 to his sister, "was any habitation more thoroughly odious—red soil, mince-pie woods, and black and greasy needle-makers." As evidence that Landor felt some sentiment for the place, Colvin published some doggerel verse, apparently inspired by reminiscences of later boyhood since it speaks of meeting "a maiden fair and fond"

> Expecting me beneath a tree
> Of shade for two but not for three.
> Ah! my old yew, far out of view,
> Why must I bid you both adieu.

The last execrable couplet reflects his passion for trees, which frequently inspired him to verse and—during his ill-fated venture as a Monmouthshire landowner—to extravagant outlay on the plantation of woods. To Southey in 1811 he recalled "a little privet which I planted when I was about six years old, and which I considered the next of kin to me after my mother and elder sister", and how, "whenever I returned from school or college, for the attachment was not stifled in that sink, I felt something like uneasiness till I had seen and measured it".

He loved all nature fervently. In verse he related his aversion to picking flowers, preferring

> To let all flowers live freely, and all die
> Whene'er their Genius bids their souls depart,
> Among their kindred in their native place.

It was said of him that, while at Rugby, he once pulled a boy's ears for pelting at the rooks in the School Close, and was "almost the only one of his day that never took a bird's nest". He must have been one of a mere half-dozen born and bred of the country gentry in the late eighteenth century who ventured to disapprove of field sports, on which he wrote later in life:

Let men do these things if they will. Perhaps there is no harm in it; perhaps it makes them no crueler than they would be otherwise. But it is hard to take away what we cannot give; and life is a pleasant thing, at least to birds. No doubt the young ones say tender things one to another, and even the old ones do not dream of death.

His allowance to animals of natural intelligence and a capacity for feeling comparable with humans was seen by Dickens only as an eccentricity fit for caricature in Boythorn's canary. Few men of his time loved and understood animals so well, and his devotion to dogs equalled that of Galsworthy, who has written more vividly of canine character than any other writer. "Dogs," said Landor, "are blessings, true blessings."

He never rode to hounds, even as a boy, which must alone have marked him as an oddity among the sporting gentry of Warwickshire. He once told Southey that he was "fond of riding when I was young", but gave it up when he "found that it produces a rapidity in the creation of thought which makes us forget what we are doing". But it seems more likely that his distaste for riding developed when he found himself outshone by his brother Charles, who became a brilliant horseman; it supplies the first evidence of the arrogance that cast a shadow across his character. He could tolerate no competition, must always stand out from his fellows in unchallenged pre-eminence, and so he gave up riding when his younger brother surpassed his skill as a horseman. Though at one period he kept three horses in his stables, they were only for carriage use, and his dudgeon at his lack of accomplishment nourished an unreasoning spleen against horses, the one variety of animal which escaped his affection, so that in his seventieth year he remarked acidly that, "next to servants, horses are the greatest trouble in life".

Charles Landor was a noted athlete, and Forster believed that "Rugby recollections have doubtless given to Walter many of the exploits of this younger brother". But though Charles was taller and of finer presence, "both as boy and man", the biggest and strongest are not always the most skilled at games, and Landor was so universally remembered by Rugby contemporaries as an outstanding personality that they were unlikely to confuse his physical accomplishments with those of his brother. Though the massive shoulders, thick, short neck, and leonine head, familiar from his portraits, suggest a big man, Landor was the shortest of the four brothers—all fine-looking men of constitutions commensurate with their physique, as their longevity testifies—but, though of no more than medium height, he had the square, sturdy build, swelling later to burliness, suggestive of exceptional physical strength.

He was still some months short of his ninth year when he proceeded from Knowle to Rugby in 1783. In the same batch of new boys were Henry Francis Cary, the translator of Dante, Arthur Clifton, afterwards a general and knighted, and Samuel Butler, who became Bishop of Lichfield and grandfather of the author of *Erewhon*. All were older than he, and with Clifton, he fought his first fight, of which it was written that "Landor used to say *he ought to have licked*. It is probably therefore Arthur Clifton did lick". In verse Landor said he "fought never with any but an older lad, and never lost but two fights in thirteen"; it is a tribute to his reputation that only his defeats were remembered. The other beating he received at the hands of Walter Birch, who, though as old as, or older than, Landor, came to Rugby three years later, and after the fight, became one of his closest friends.

Charles Apperley—afterwards celebrated as the sporting writer "Nimrod", who was two years younger than Landor but did not enter Rugby till the summer of 1789—relates in his memoirs that Landor "had a great name in the school as a scholar, a cricketer, a foot-ball player, and a pugilist, in all which characters he had very few equals". The official Rugbeian chronicle says "he was famous for riding out of bounds, boxing, leaping, net-casting, stone throwing, and making Greek and Latin Verses". Aggressiveness being a feature of his character all his life, his pugilism is not surprising. Nor is his riding out of bounds; his impatience of authority alone would have been an inducement to breaking bounds, but in those days it was a custom with the "bloods" of Rugby to ride over to a hostelry at Lutterworth for the indulgence of callow dissipation, and though Landor never evinced much taste for drinking, he had a healthy amorous appetite.

Of his cricket and football no details appear. His prowess at casting a net provides the sole instance of his indulgence in a sport entailing the destruction of life; perhaps he held the academic argument, often produced by fishermen, that fish lack the same feeling as birds or footed animals, but more likely he indulged the practice because his skill excited envious admiration, contributing to his reputation for brilliance. Forster, informed by Robert Landor, notes his athletic accomplishments, but adds that "he was at all times disposed rather to walk by the river side with a book than engage in such trials of strength and activity". No doubt he realised the theatrical effect of this—how the envious would marvel, after admiring his ability with the casting net, to see him carelessly leave the sport—as if he had only condescended to show them how it should be done—and wander off alone with a book.

But books early became his chief interest. Long afterwards he told Southey:

The first two books I ever bought were at the stall of an old woman at Rugby. They happened to be Baker's *Chronicle* and Drayton's *Polyolbion*. I was very fond of both because they were bought by me. They were my own; and if I did not read them attentively, my money would have been thrown away, and I must have thought and confessed myself injudicious. I have read neither since, and I never shall possess either again.

He read much in bed at night—he doubted if he "ever slept five hours consecutively, rarely four, even in boyhood"—and recalled how he "was once flogged for sleeping at the evening lesson, which I had learnt, but having mastered it, I dozed". Robert Landor said that "at school and college he had gained superiority over his companions", for "there are better scholars passing from our public schools now than were then the fellows of my college who had taken their master's degree". According to Robert, it was not till Landor went to live in Italy and began work on the *Imaginary Conversations* that he applied himself thoroughly to Greek literature, but he admitted that "Walter increased his Latin all his life long, because he had pleasure in it". Evidence of his precocious knowledge alike of English and Latin poetry appears in his having written, at sixteen, translations of Cowley into Latin verse, "correcting his extravagance".

Of arithmetic he declared himself ignorant all his life "according to the process in use"; though during his schooling at Knowle he suffered equally from the problems of grammar, his introduction to books led him to delight in the study of language, and he developed a lifelong fascination in the derivation of words, inciting him to read "the Port-Royal Grammar twice through, and Ainsworth's Latin Dictionary once". However imperfect his knowledge of Greek may have been, it was sufficiently in advance of the average to appear impressive; Landor himself declared that "Butler, afterwards bishop of Lichfield, and myself, were the first at Rugby, or, I believe, any other school, who attempted a Greek verse", and this is endorsed by Bloxam, who says that "at one period" Landor and Butler were "the only two præpostors that did Greek Verses".

His masters delighted in their pupil's brilliance. His tutor, said Forster, was Dr. Sleath, but "Nimrod" says there were two Sleaths at Rugby in his time, and if Landor's tutor was the one called "Old Bacchus", he must have been the least likely curb on his pupil's tendencies to arrogance, for he was "a very good-natured man", and allowed "Nimrod," who had no such pretensions in scholarship as Landor's, to fancy that "I knew as much Greek as he did". He tried in vain to induce Landor to compete for a prize poem, but as Landor told Southey, "I never would contend at school with any one for anything. I formed the same resolution when I went to college, and I have kept it." Few boys or men of imagination have ever tolerated with patience the pedantry of examinations, but, in Landor's case, arrogance prevented his entry into competition lest even a minor set-back might detract from the supremacy of his reputation. Just as he gave up riding when he saw that his skill could not excel his younger brother's, so he would not compete for a school prize lest he might be beaten into second place by such a rival as Butler.

Forster describes the headmaster, Dr. James, as "a scholar of fair repute, who did something to redeem the school from the effects of the long and dull mastership that preceded his". Truly James was not dull, but "Nimrod" amply illustrates his opinion that he was not "altogether the man for the situation he held". He was a type familiar among schoolmasters in valuing his wit, and "by his familiar jokes at one time —after his dinner, &c., especially, for the doctor was no teetotaller— and ill-timed severity at another, he was neither respected nor beloved. . . . The practice of flogging was unmercifully pursued at Rugby;

and it was generally believed that James—and he alone was the executioner—delighted in it. . . . He highly appreciated talent in his pupils, and certainly turned out several very clever ones into the world".

"James," said "Nimrod", "was proud of Landor, and was inclined to cultivate his friendship as well as his mind; but, to use a common expression, Landor would not have him at any price." No doubt the master made a favourite of the boy, and, in his cups, bandied witticisms with the familiarity that inspires contempt; then, when the boy presumed upon his privilege as a favourite, the doctor, in the mood of the morning after the night before, would descend on him with unexpected and seemingly unreasonable severity. So he not only lost the opportunity of securing the boy's affection or esteem, but antagonised him with a sense of grievance and injustice, while any subsequent advances of friendship, being construed as weakness, excited contempt.

As Landor came to be a senior boy and a figure of influence, the arrogance and impetuosity of his character found vent in an attitude of thinly veiled rebellion. News of the French Revolution in 1789 fired his imagination, and made him an ardent apostle of liberty, equality and fraternity. Bloxam relates that

> Dr. James, an Etonian, introduced the Eton custom of having the title of "Mister" prefixed to the sons of the nobility in the school list. . . . Præpostors then called over the names. . . . Landor, in calling over, would always omit the title of "Mister," to the great annoyance of Dr. James.

This defiance of authority must have impressed the younger boys, but Bloxam adds:

> It was not on this account, as the boy believed, that Dr. James desired his father to remove him, or because, as stated in Forster's life of him, he and Dr. James differed about the quantity of a syllable. The real reason was some of his Alcaics. In one copy he introduced allusions to the Altar of the Roman Goddess who presided over the sewers of Rome built by Tarquinius Priscus. Another Alcaic, still more gross, was "non posteris, sed post—ibus haec Landor offert."

Forster probably knew the true story, but, hesitating, with Victorian reverence for decorum, to say frankly that Landor perpetrated bawdy verses, obscured the cause of complaint and muddled the tale of its outcome.

He relates how Landor thought that "Dr. James either would not or could not appreciate what he did in Latin verse, and that when he was driven to take special notice of it, he took the worst, not the best, for the purpose". Elsewhere, referring to the Rugby custom of granting a whole day's holiday for the best exercise of the week, he mentions the awe with which a fag of the time read the notice, "Play-day for Landor's Latin verses." But "Nimrod" significantly tells that Butler was reckoned "the best scholar in the school", as "'Play for Butler' was oftener proclaimed for him than for any other boy". This surely indicates the source of Landor's resentment. He could not brook rivalry; Forster says that Landor "often generously spoke" of Birch as the best Rugby scholar, but he probably said this because he knew himself to be better than Birch, though doubting that he was as good as Butler. His arrogance would not allow that Butler was better; hence, when Butler was awarded more play-days, he decided that his work was not fairly judged. This jealousy of Butler was admitted by Landor in the account of his removal from Rugby given in a letter to Walter Birch at the time of his father's death in 1805:

You had left Rugby at the time to which I allude. It was seldom that I took the trouble to write a good, or even tolerable, exercise for myself, though I could get anyone else a shilling when I liked. But on one occasion when the subject pleased me, I was determined to try whether James would continue to treat my verses with the same indifference as had long made me insensible to his praise or censure. Butler on the same occasion wrote a profusion of verses. James extolled his. In mine he found two faults, but added that they were better than usual, and that they proved to him I had the capacity, if I had the will. They might perhaps have had two faults, while Butler's had but one; mine, however, were partial, his was total. . . . When the boys compared them—who are not, however, very nice critics—they gave mine the preference unanimously; and when James gave me the shilling, which he did, I cried aloud to my fag, "Here Blacky!" and gave it to him. This was thought an heroic action. James said I had the pride of the devil and the impudence of he did not know what. "Then, sir," said I, "Let me tell you; it is the impudence of those who say my verses are worse than Butler's." Here followed many complaints of my general negligence, and some few compliments. I was sent away soon after, and this anecdote among others was repeated to my father.

In this account Landor omits any mention of the further insolence to which Forster thus refers:

When told very graciously on one occasion to copy out fairly in the play-book verses by himself of which he thought indifferently, Landor, in making the copy, put private additions to it of several lines, with a coarse allusion beginning, "Haec sunt malorum pessima carminum quae Landor unquam scripsit." This offence was forgiven; but it was followed by another of which the circumstances were such as to render it impossible that he should continue longer in the school. The right at first was on Landor's side: for Dr. James had strongly insisted on, and the other as firmly had declined, the correction of an alleged false quantity found really not to exist. But, apart from the right or the wrong, an expression rudely used by the pupil was very sharply resented by the master, and only one result became possible.

Though he mentions it irrelevantly elsewhere, as an incident personally related to him by Landor himself, Forster does not cite the rude expression, but quotes Robert Landor's assurance that "he was not expelled from Rugby, but removed, as the less discreditable punishment, at the headmaster's suggestion. There was nothing unusual or disgraceful in the particular transgression, but a fierce defiance of all authority and a refusal to ask forgiveness". The final scene emerges from the reminiscences of "Nimrod":

Landor had provoked the doctor to that extent that it was believed he intended to expel him, and was only prevented doing so by a strong regard for his father. A thought struck him however, that he would endeavour to conciliate his compliance with the rules of the school, by reasoning with him on the subject, and accordingly he approached his study for that purpose;—"Who is there?" asked Landor, on hearing the doctor rap. "It is I," replied the doctor; "I want to speak with you." "Get thee hence, Satan!" exclaimed Landor, laying extraordinary emphasis on the last word.

Probably the doctor hesitated to expel him for fear of himself appearing ridiculous and self-confessedly incompetent of subduing insubordination, so he preferred to write, as Landor told Forster, "to my father that I was rebellious and incited others to rebellion; and unless he took me away he should be obliged ('much to his sorrow') to expel me".

§ 2

He was "within five of the head" of the school on leaving Rugby; his removal must have occurred late in 1791, when he was sixteen, since Birch, who went up to Magdalen that year, had already left. Forster says nothing of the tense atmosphere that must have greeted him on returning home, and little of Landor's father, except to emphasise the absence in the man of sixty of the failings most marked in the boy of sixteen.

The slightest symptom of arrogance or vanity none can recollect in him. He disputed no one's pretensions, and was always silent about his own. With much more than the average amount of sense and learning common to country gentlemen of that time, he made no comparisons, but took his place among them unconscious of any difference that might have placed him far above them. Social and hospitable, he never thought of rivalry.

Dr. Landor was, in fact, a praiseworthy type of country squire—well above the level of a Western, but still far short of being an Allworthy. He had done very well for himself, especially by his second marriage, and while he sufficiently sustained the responsibilities of his position, he enjoyed its privileges with a clear conscience. Obviously he belonged to the vast majority of fathers in his social class, who conceived that they fulfilled their obligations as parents if they paid handsomely for their sons' education and housed them during the school holidays.

It is unlikely that he considered his eldest son unduly remarkable. He was sufficiently a scholar to appreciate the boy's classical attainments, but while he felt these a subject for congratulation, he probably manifested more evident satisfaction in the younger son Charles's prowess as a horseman. This alone would suffice to irritate in Landor the same sense of injustice that he conceived himself as suffering at the hands of Dr. James, and to rouse his pride to antagonism. He may be pictured as normally a boy of loud and ebullient spirits, given to sudden moods of sullen resentment at ill-considered reproofs or tactless omissions of appreciation; exceptionally sensitive, he was what is called a "difficult" boy—the type requiring patient understanding and tactful management. From his father he received neither; Forster suggests that "their only point of agreement" was "an excessive warmth of temper common to both". When the boy took refuge from rebuke in defiance, the father saw him as an unlicked cub and a rebel.

A rebel Landor remained all his life. The environment of childhood can so mould a nature sensitive and impressionable as to establish the lights and shades of a lifetime's personality. Why the shy and fragile De Quincey found himself in unsympathetic surroundings during boyhood, he shrank from society in self-pity as a pariah; the proud and assertive Landor, on the other hand, became disgruntled and unmanageable, a violent antagonist of all authority. As he grew to adolescence, he must have been a disturbing youth. His enthusiasm for the cause of revolutionary France, inspired by fellow-feeling with rebellion against oppression, offended the orthodoxy of his law-abiding parent. His godfather, General Powell, subsequently a governor of Gibraltar, laughed at such boyish extravagances as the wish "that the French would invade England and assist us in hanging George the Third between two such thieves as the archbishops of Canterbury and York", but his parents looked askance at such revolutionary notions in their eldest son, fearing, not only on his own account, but lest he should infect his younger brothers with his ideas. So when he repeated his wish about the French invasion in his mother's hearing, his brother Robert remembered how she boxed his ears from behind:

They were all terrified at Walter, wondering what he might do, when they heard their mother's high-heeled shoes clattering quickly over the margin of the uncarpeted oak near the door, and saw her neat little figure suddenly disappear. "I'd advise you, mother," shouted Walter after her, "not to try that sort of thing again."

The anecdote illustrates the incapacity of his parents to manage him. Neither had any notion of making a friend of him and meeting his arguments with reason; the father stormed and talked of flogging, if he did not flog, and the mother supported him by humiliating the boy's dignity in the presence of her younger children.

When he arrived at an age to sit at table with his elders, Landor expressed such violent opinions that his father would not have him in the room when he had guests. Sir Samuel Romilly, later Solicitor-

General, frequently dined with Dr. Landor, but Robert doubted if "my brother Walter was ever present", for "he hated law and lawyers then, almost as much as he despised the church and its ministers at all times; and the gentlemanly manners by which he was distinguished thirty years later, had then no existence". Even General Powell, who had regarded with tolerance a spirited boy, felt that a wearer of his uniform could not countenance Landor's revolutionary outbursts as he grew up, and declined to dine there when he was at home.

The picture sketched by Forster, on Robert Landor's authority, presents an unprepossessingly turbulent boy, egoistically careless of the discomfort he caused to everybody about him. Yet, apart from the fact that few ever found cause for disliking Landor, there emerges even from Forster's pages a glimpse of sensibilities. When both were old men, his brother Henry, who entered Rugby five years after his eldest brother, wrote to him: "Do you think I ever forget your kindness to me at Rugby, in threatening another boy who ill-treated me if he again persisted in similar conduct? Or your gift of money to me at that time, when I verily believe you had not another shilling left for your own indulgence?" Landor himself recalled how "poor little Blacky Howard had three or four bottles to fill at the pump in a hard frost and was crying bitterly. I took pity on him and made him my fag, at three pence a week, I think. But this exempted him from obedience to others, and I seldom exercised my *vested rights*". He was always impulsively generous, always on the side of the weak against the strong, and felt the imaginative mind's horror of suffering.

"Birch and I thought ourselves men when we were only boys," he once wrote. Like De Quincey, he was impatient to grow up, to be rid of pedantic authority, to be independent and free to set out on the career of achievement dazzling his ambitious vision. He was unfortunate in encountering no such woman of charm and understanding as De Quincey's Lady Carbery, who would have encouraged him with the appreciation he craved and controlled his impulses. Always susceptible to feminine attraction, Landor was himself attractive to women. Forster quoted "a lively lady, who both liked and admired him", as saying "in his later life that the great enjoyment of walking out with him had only one drawback, that he was always knocking somebody down". The habit of railing against injustice, against some institution or person of authority—which characterised him through life and was caricatured by Dickens in Boythorn—must have struck women as attractive in a boy who was handsome, intellectually and athletically brilliant, and ready moreover to evince admiration. One woman at least interested herself in him during his Rugby days—his cousin, Sophia Venour, on whose marriage he wrote at her request, when he was fourteen, his first original verses. Possibly her marriage removed her from a sphere where she might have wielded a beneficial influence, as appears from a letter in which she wrote:

I think you are much in the right to make the most learned your friends and companions; but permit me to say, that though I think a proper spirit commendable and even necessary at times, yet, in my opinion, it is better to submit *sometimes* to those under whose authority we are, even when we think they are in fault, than to run the risk of being esteemed arrogant and self-sufficient.

Others who found him an attractive boy were the family of a fellow Rugbeian, Fleetwood Parkhurst, who lived at Ripple Court, on the banks of the Severn near Tewkesbury. Robert Landor said that his brother and Fleetwood Parkhurst "were very discordant", but they remained friends for several years, "visiting each other's friends and travelling together; but with old Mr. Parkhurst, Walter was much the greater favourite, and he had always been very happy at Ripple". Forty years afterwards, when Landor returned from his Florentine exile to live at Bath, he renewed acquaintance with the family by meeting at his brother Robert's vicarage the sister of Fleetwood Parkhurst, in whose husband, Anthony Rosenhagen, he made a friend so valued that he was moved to say "that old Parkhurst and his son-in-law Rosenhagen were the men who united most of virtue and most of politeness that he had ever met with". It was a failing of Landor's—which prompted Coleridge to wonder what he lacked to become a true poet—to insert lines of disturbing bathos among otherwise beautiful verses, and an example appears in the commonplace couplet, following graceful reference to "Malvern's verdant ridges" and "Sabrina's stream", in which he speaks of Mr. Parkhurst:

> The Lord of these domains was one
> Who loved me like an only son.

It is true that this old gentleman, who found interest and delight in the untamable spirit of an unusual boy, had not the responsibility of managing him; but the mutual respect and affection existing between Landor and a man of his father's generation indicates that the antagonism between father and son arose from parental shortcomings more culpable than the boy's waywardness. Nor did Dr. Landor make any effort to take his son in hand on his removal from Rugby. In the middle ages knights would themselves superintend their sons' progress to the winning of their spurs, but from the days when Tudor landlords took to keeping priests and parsons as pensioners down to modern times, it has been the practice of parents to leave the upbringing of their sons to paid pedagogues. As Landor was yet too young for the university, he had to be sent to one of those cynical philosophers who earn an unthankful living by undertaking troublesome or backward boys—a "crammer". He went to the vicar of Fenny Bentley, near Ashbourne, Derbyshire, the Rev. William Langley, "who had no other pupil," said Robert Landor, "and who seemed well qualified for the office by patience and gentleness"—qualities that had been notably absent in his home influences.

Besides his parish duties, Langley was also headmaster of Ashbourne Grammar School, the history of which institution shows him to have been a man of character. At the time of his appointment in 1752 the school was in a state of decay and the schoolhouse out of repair; a succession of masters had served short terms, and Langley's immediate predecessor resigned "as it is inconvenient for him to perform the duties of his office". Within two years of his appointment Langley was indicted by the governors, on the evidence of his assistant master, for wilfully damaging school property, and fined ten pounds. Apparently he declined to pay the fine, and the governors re-appointed his predecessor in his place. The official record then lapsed into discreet silence for full forty years, the next reported proceedings of the governors being their meeting in 1795 to appoint a successor to the "lately deceased" William Langley. Evidently Langley rebelled against the wretched conditions that caused the resignations of his several predecessors, and when the governors ignored his protest, he destroyed the decrepit furnishings to compel their replacement. Presumably his re-appointed predecessor declined to return under the existing conditions, so the governors had to reinstate Langley and give him what he wanted. When Landor came to him, he was an old man with only four years to live, but one who had rebelled successfully against authority could feel sympathy with the spirit of a boy like Landor.

"Though by no means ignorant, the tutor had very little more scholarship than the pupil, and his Latin verses were hardly so good as Walter's," said brother Robert, adding with unconscious significance, "Walter always spoke of him with respect." In the *Imaginary Conversations* of 1829 Landor introduced Langley as William Oldways into a dialogue with Izaak Walton and Charles Cotton, with the footnote:

I pay this tribute to my worthy old tutor, Mr. Langley of Ashbourne, under whose tuition I passed a year between Rugby and Oxford. He would take only one private pupil, and never had but me. The kindness of him and his wife to me was parental.

The relationship between tutor and pupil indicates that the undisciplined rebel of Rugby and Warwick responded readily to kindly understanding. Whatever his limitations as a scholar, Langley could ramble entertainingly about literature; the urbanity of Oldways' anecdotes about Donne to Walton and Cotton doubtless mirrored the manner of Langley in relating how he "had seen Pope when he came to visit

Oxford from Lord Harcourt's at Nuneham", and how he had a friend who, as a boy, dined at the same table with Fielding. Such reminiscences impress the imagination of a boy with Landor's reverence for the past; he remembered at Knowle an old woman who "was one hundred and two when I was four and a half", and marvelled that "she might have seen people who had seen not only Milton, but Shakespeare, Bacon, Spenser, and Raleigh".

Evidently also Langley encouraged his writing English verse and inspired the early loyalty to Pope and spleen against Warton as Pope's detractor, which lasted long enough for Landor to declare unfairly in 1800 that he had been "drawn by the Wartons" into "raptures with what I now despise". When he came to write the imaginary conversation of Leofric and Godiva, he inserted the lines to Godiva, "In every hour, in every mood", written in boyhood beside the square pool at Rugby, and related how, after showing the verses to a schoolfellow who laughed at him, he begged him "not to tell the lads". Some of his efforts at Ashbourne have also survived, like the lines to "Medea at Corinth", dated by Forster as written in 1791, and the satire, "Written in 1792", against the British tendency to wage war unthinkingly against ideas:

> He loses all his fame who fights
> Against his liberties and rights;
> Troublesome things! but soon removed
> By *our trusty* and *our well-beloved.*

He matriculated at Trinity College, Oxford, on 13th November 1792, but the college buttery books show that he went into residence in the following January, the month of his eighteenth birthday. As at Rugby, he was quickly recognised as an outstanding personality. His tutor, "dear good Benwell", delighted in his scholarship, but succeeded in influencing him no more effectively than Sleath or James. "Though I wrote better Latin verses than any undergraduate or graduate in the University," he wrote, with arrogance unmitigated by years, in 1857, "I could never be persuaded, by my tutor or friends, to contend for any prize whatever. I showed my compositions to Birch of Magdalen, my old friend at Rugby; and to Cary, translator of Dante; to none else." He still recoiled from the possibility of a rebuff to his pride, and it is evidence of his obvious brilliance, of the force of his personality, and, to some extent, of a certain likable charm, that his overbearing arrogance did not excite derision and dislike. He himself loudly expressed contempt for the abilities of others; in his first published volume of verse he scoffed at the poetical attempts of two Trinity dons, Clark and Kett—whom De Quincey remembered as "well-known in Oxford by the name of Horse Kett, from his equine physiognomy"—and not only in this volume, but in the later one of 1802, he derided the work of the Rev. George Richards, a Trinity man newly elected to a fellowship at another college, who in 1791 had been awarded the prize for an English poem offered by the second Lord Harcourt.

This talent for satire contributed to his reputation. In every generation, from Pope, through Byron and Oscar Wilde, down to our own day, appear examples of reputations for brilliance achieved by facile cleverness at the expense of others. Wilde told Frank Harris that "to write about yourself" was "the way to make yourself known", and the histories of successful men reveal the gullibility of human sheep in their readiness to accept the assertive egoist at his own assessment. Few have the knowledge to judge for themselves, fewer still the courage to abide by their own judgment, and Landor's arrogant self-confidence, supported by his facility, his ready fluency with speech or pen, and his outspoken aggressiveness, impelled a general acceptance of his own estimate of his gifts. Whatever he became during his middle-age in Italy, he was, in youth, as Robert Landor told Forster, no very profound scholar. He was not a conscientious worker. At Rugby he might have beaten Butler if he had applied himself with equal diligence to the prosaic study of syntax and kindred subjects of groundwork. But he gambled on his facility; skill and imagination enabled him to surpass the mediocre without the application necessary to lift the less talented even to the level of mediocrity. Armed with a sense of superiority he found it easy to pretend the possession of knowledge which actually he did not possess; in 1805 he professed to have read Dante's *Divina Commedia* and remarked on it contemptuously to Birch, yet years later, when writing the *Imaginary Conversations*, he confessed to having read only a fifth of the work. Like most men of imagination, he felt impatience with the academic pedantry of university educational methods, but his refusal to submit to examinations may have been inspired, not only by the possibility of wounds to his vanity by comparison with others, but by fear of exposing unexpected deficiencies. So by superficial brilliance he was content to shine above the mediocre, but because, in the days of his youthful energy, he never applied himself wholeheartedly to a task such as his genius entitled him to undertake, he failed to compete with his peers.

His reputation for brilliance was enhanced by his notoriety. He was "about the first student who wore his hair without powder", declining to receive the attentions of the college barber, whose duties included the dressing and powdering of the undergraduates' hair according to the prevailing aristocratic fashion. His tutor, awed by his temerity, warned him to take care lest they "stone you for a republican", but he continued to wear his "plain hair and queue tied with black ribbon", and soon others copied his example, among them Robert Southey.

Southey came up to Balliol the same term as Landor to Trinity; like Landor, he had been compelled to leave school, was in arms against authority, and professed contempt for Oxford's academic institutions. But he possessed a conscience and stability lacking in Landor. His impatience against Oxford arose, not from personal arrogance, but from a sense of humiliation that he should be compelled, while "Europe is on fire with freedom . . ., to sit and study Euclid or Hugo Grotius", and he sought by self-discipline to "learn to break a rebellious spirit". So, though he lived for months within a hundred yards of Landor, he never sought his acquaintance, and recalling some years later that Landor was "notorious as a mad Jacobin", added:

His Jacobinism would have made me seek his acquaintance, but for his madness. He was obliged to leave the University for shooting at one of the fellows through the window.[1]

But Southey must have heard much of Landor's "madness" before the shooting incident which ended his university career. It may be gathered that he was a leader, and his room a rendezvous, of the most violent Jacobin element among the undergraduates, that he won cheap admiration for his daring in lampooning dons like Kett, Clark, and Richards, and that he was regarded with disfavour by authority. When, in October 1894, Horne Tooke, Holcroft, Hardy, Thelwall, and others were indicted for high treason, Landor's expressions of revolutionary sentiments invoked remonstrances from his friends. But, unlike Southey, Landor felt no inclination "to break a rebellious spirit", and his "Apology for Satire", published in his first book of poems, elaborates his creed at this time. The poem, in the form of a dialogue between the poet and a friend, begins with the latter admonishing:

> Too long, my friend! hath Satire's camp confin'd
> Each active effort of thy youthful mind.
> Were it not better to have ideally roved
> Along the paths that happier poets loved.

Landor then rails against the existing state of literature, with fine scorn of Kett and Richards, till the friend—possibly his tutor Benwell—interposes:

> Hush! why complain? of treason have a care;
> You heard of Holcroft and of Tooke—beware—
> (P) I heard the whole; nor deem it a disgrace—
> (F) Tho' danger surely—(P) to lament their case.
> Without their talents I have only aim'd
> Gently to *hint* what Pope aloud proclaim'd.

[1] De Quincey, who went up to Oxford nine years after Landor went down, wrote in a letter of 1855 that Landor "began life at Trin. Coll. Oxford by firing a pistol at the Revd. Mr. Horse Kett".

Before a tyrant Juvenal display'd
Truth's hated form and Satire's flaming blade;
With hand unshaken bore her mirror-shield:
Vice gazed and trembled—shriek'd and left the field.
Shall I dissemble, then? (F) Dissemble? no.
Be silent only, and avoid the blow.

But Landor declined the counsel of caution. "I believe in God," he cried:

This only reason, courtly priest! I give.
Go, cease to moralise: learn first to live.

He himself was learning to live according to the creed summarised in the most famous lines he ever wrote—the "Dying Speech of an Old Philosopher". Throughout his life he remained an individualist. In rebellion against authority he shared none of Coleridge's and Southey's fervour for pantisocracy, for a better order of society. He always believed, as he wrote in 1850, that "democracy is the blubbery spawn begotten by the drunkenness of aristocracy", and while he sympathised with liberal reform, he expressed in an epigram his contempt for the masses:

I know not whether I am proud,
But this I know, I hate the crowd.

The success of mediocrity excited his rebellion; he despised a system that promoted meagre ability to positions of authority in legislation, and a condition of culture that mistook pretention for talent.

The incident that ended his college career was a dangerous exploit in the course of a college "binge", as he soon afterwards related to Birch. A certain Leeds, "a man universally laughed at and despised", whose Tory opinions excited Landor's scorn, was entertaining guests in rooms across the quadrangle on the same evening as Landor had a party to wine. Landor's friends apparently belonged to the "bloods", who regarded contemptuously the "servitors and other raffs of every description" comprising Leeds's party, and the rival factions soon began exchanging compliments through the open windows. When this amusement ceased on Leeds's closing his windows and shutters, Landor saw a chance of showing off. He had been out shooting and his gun lay at hand; when he proposed "to fire a volley" at the closed shutters, "it was thought a good trick"—just as his giving Dr. James's shilling to his fag had been "thought an heroic action" at Rugby.

Accordingly I went into my bedroom and fired. Soon the president sent up a servant to inform me that Mr. Leeds had complained of a gun being fired from the room in which I entertained my company, but he could not

D

tell by whom; so that he insisted on knowing from me, and making me liable to the punishment.

Sobered, he realised what he might expect from his father if he was sent down. In panic he prevaricated that no gun had been fired from the room in which his company were, and since nobody was specifically charged, he did not feel it his duty to lend himself to the identification. Loyally his friends took the same line, but they were questioned separately and inevitable contradictions enabled the president to deduce the truth.

At this point Forster condensed the narrative to Landor's detriment. In Landor's letter there is no reference to a suggestion from the president that "Landor should enable him to deal leniently by stating frankly what had occurred". Landor did, in fact, frankly confess on being found out. He was "extremely chagrined" by having humiliated himself by prevarication, and his confession to the president "painted my dissimulation in the most odious colours. For being what I never was guilty of before, it struck me with the greatest horror". He explained that he had not dissembled from "personal fear", but because, "Tho' my father had really shown me as much unkindness as was in his power, I was resolved, if possible, not to give him any further cause of complaint." The president was sympathetic; discipline demanded punishment, and the sentence was rustication for two terms, but he handsomely wrote a letter intended to mollify his father and expressed the hope that Landor would return to the college after the period of probation.

Forster implied that the letter failed to produce the intended effect, that Dr. Landor's anger was met with defiance, and that, when Landor wrote to take his name off the college books, his father concluded that he never intended to return to Oxford, whereupon—in Landor's words to Birch—"he used the most violent expressions", with the result that "I have left him for ever". But the college buttery books show that Landor went down in the week of 20th June 1794, while his name remained on the college books till 19th December, his caution money being refunded in February following. Between June and December something—of which Landor said nothing to Birch—happened to excite Dr. Landor's "most violent expressions".

3

THE PULSE OF YOUTH

> In early youth we often sigh
> Because our pulses beat so high;
> All this we conquer, and at last
> We sigh that we are grown so chaste.
> —*Lucian and Timotheus* (1846)
> I always took what Beauty gave,
> Nor, when she snatcht it back, lookt grave.
> —*Pericles and Aspasia* (1836)

On leaving Oxford, Landor spent part of the summer at the small seaside resort of Tenby in Wales. In *Dry Sticks* (1858) he published some verses on a "Voyage to St. Ives, Cornwall, from Port Einon, Glamorgan, 1794", and though, after so many years, his memory might forgivably have played him false in a date, he had reason to remember accurately in this case. For, at Tenby in that summer of 1794 he began a love affair with a golden-haired girl named Nancy Jones, whom he addressed in verse as Ione, the derivation of which name he afterwards explained.

> Sometimes, as boys will do, I play'd at love,
> Nor fear'd cold weather, nor withdrew in hot;
> And two who were my playmates at that hour,
> Hearing me call'd a poet, in some doubt
> Challenged me to adapt their names to song.
> Ione was the first; her name is heard
> Among the hills of Cambria, north and south,
> But there of shorter stature, like herself;
> I placed a comely vowel at its close,
> And drove an ugly sibilant away. . . .
> Ianthe, who came later, smiled and said,
> I have two names and will be praised in both;
> Sophia is not quite enough for me,
> And you have simply named it, and but once.
> Now call the other up. . . .

Eight years were yet to elapse before he met Ianthe, the principal
inspiration of his muse, but he may have met Nancy Jones as early as
1793, on a previous holiday at Tenby, for he dated the following lines
as written in that year:

> "Tell me what means that sigh," Ione said,
> When on her shoulder I reclined my head;
> And I could only tell her that it meant
> The sigh that swells the bosom with content.

Evidently his amour with Nancy developed in the summer of 1794, with
implications sufficiently scandalous to excite his father's "violent
expressions" when he took his name off the college books in December.
Certainly there was more than revived vituperation over the shooting
incident, which lay six months in the past, to cause Landor's leaving his
father "for ever".

Banging angrily out of his father's house, he took lodgings in London
at 38 Beaumont Street, Portland Place. Though the Ipsley and Tachbrook estates, as well as the Landor property at Rugeley, would
descend to him on his father's death, till then he had nothing beyond
what his father chose to allow him, and possibly to provide himself
with credentials for employment, he approached the reputable publishing house of Cadell & Davies with a volume of his verses to be called
The Poems of Walter Savage Landor. When the publishers required a
contribution of thirty-five pounds towards the cost of paper and
printing, Landor grandly explained that he lacked the money because
he had "spent a very considerable sum in laying in a stock of wine;
having heard that an enormous rise will take place in that article".[1]
The publishers in February accepted his promise to pay in three months,
within which time *The Poems of Walter Savage Landor* appeared, being
advertised in *The Times* of 26th May 1795 as "This Day . . . published,
in one Volume, price 4s. in Boards".

While the poems were in the press, his boyhood's horror of criticism
recurred. At school and college he had avoided competition; now he
was exposing himself as a target for the caprice of critics. Sending on
12th April an advance copy of his book to Walter Birch (with the letter
describing the Oxford shooting affair), he remarked that all the profits
were intended for the benefit of a "distressed clergyman", but the
indigent parson has never been identified and was doubtless as much a
myth as the lavish purchase of wine. To his schoolfellow he shrank
from confessing a hope of making money or reputation by his verses;
as, at Rugby, he had not troubled to work "for myself, though I could
get anyone else a shilling when I liked", so now he forestalled possible

---

[1] Details of Landor's transactions with his many publishers are collected in *The Publication
of Landor's Works*, by R. H. Super, London, The Bibliographical Society, 1954.

adverse criticism with the pretence of having graciously capitalised the scribblings of his leisure for a poor friend's benefit.

Pride prevented an overture towards reconciliation with his father. But he knew that he possessed an ardent advocate in his eldest sister Elizabeth, and must have assumed that anxiety might overcome displeasure if his parents heard of his planning such a rash project as leaving England in wartime to seek his fortune in Italy. This information he conveyed to them in correspondence with a girl whom he considered himself likely to marry.

Dorothy Elizabeth Lyttelton was the heiress of Studley Castle, an estate adjoining that of Ipsley Court, where she lived with her two uncles. Forster assumed that, as a close friend of Landor's sister Elizabeth, she may have felt for him no more than "the friendly familiarity of a good-humoured girl for the brother of her friend, a year or two younger than herself, whose cleverness she admired and whose attentions pleased her", but her letters, considered in the light of the conventional restraint imposed on girls of Jane Austen's time, suggest that she gave him ample encouragement to regard himself as a favoured suitor. Landor himself told Forster:

I should have married this lovely girl if I had been independent. My future property was equal to hers, my expectancies greater. But, having nothing, I would not ask the hand of one to whom something would be given by her uncle, who loved me heartily.

He recalled how Lady Hertford, "the best judge of beauty in the world", described Dorothy as "the most lovely and graceful creature" she knew, and how he went "every day of the vacations" to Studley. Two years after her early death in 1811, a visit to Warwickshire reminded him of their early courtship:

> Yes, in this chancel once we sat alone,
> O Dorothea! thou wert bright with youth,
> Freshness like Morning's dwelt upon thy cheek,
>
> .   .   .   .   .
>
> I know not why, since we had each our book
> And lookt upon it stedfastly, first one
> Outran the learned labourer from the desk,
> Then tript the other, and limpt far behind,
> And smiles gave blushes birth, and blushes smiles.

To this girl he wrote, soon after his arrival in London, about the quarrel with his father. She had been staying at Warwick, and her reply assured him that talking about him was the only consolation for his absence, which had diminished the happiness of her visit. He had been the "constant theme" of her conversation with his sister Elizabeth, who was much distressed at the breach with his father and to whom she asks him to write. Her next letter tells how he has charmed his sister by writing to her "and me by the compliment of attending to my request", before indulging in coquetry about sending him some coloured ribbons "to tie up for your watch-chain". With an advance copy of his *Poems* he enclosed some manuscript verses addressed to herself—possibly the lines to "Dorothea" published more than sixty years later in *Dry Sticks*:

> Stately step, commanding eye,
> Attributes of majesty,
> Others may from far adore . . .
> Adoration! mine is more
> When that stately step I see,
> Swifter now, approaching me,
> And that eye whose one command
> Is, *"Come here and take my hand."*

She assured him that she sat up into the small hours reading his verses, and could not compose herself to sleep till she had told what "exquisite delight" they had given her. How could she find words to thank him; ought she indeed to thank him for making her inordinately vain! "These verses, how could I talk of them! What I have, I can repeat as fluently as the author himself, and am longing for my memory to be farther charged."

This juncture seemed propitious for confiding—doubtless with histrionic embellishment in the manner of Goethe's Werther—his circumstances and immediate plans, and he could hardly have hoped for a response of more anxious concern. He would say that she was determined to disapprove of all his schemes, but she was adamant against his going to Italy, or anywhere else as distant. She could not "see why you should be so disgusted with people in general of your own country"; she "would have people with superior worth and abilities stay and distinguish themselves where example, in most wise and good things, is so much wanting". She had interested her uncles in his behalf, and assured him that "they talk of you much, and are ready to be mediators between you and your father". Will he tell her "on what terms and with what inducements you can be tempted to give up this voyage"?

Propose them to me, and I will commit them to my uncles, one of whom will make such proposals to your father as coming from themselves. I assure you they are bent upon restoring peace and content to you; and if they can serve you, *do* gratify their wish! Recollect in the course of nine months you will be of age. You will then have it in your power to increase your income if you do but approve of those only means to do it. *Till then,* suppose my uncle was to propose your going to Cambridge. And would you agree to giving a security to make amends to the younger part of the family if your father would allow you enough to support you in studying the law at the Temple, or living independent anywhere else in England? For I find the truth is, he cannot allow you sufficient to study the law without injuring his younger children. Three hundred a year my uncles talk of. Now this is really coming to the point. Not merely saying *don't go*, but thinking of what you are to do if you stay. Let me entreat you, then, to tell me the terms on which you will give up this melancholy scheme. Do lay them down to me, and I will acquaint my uncles of them. . . . Or, will you come down and stay a little while with them, and talk over schemes and projects to restore your happiness in England? I do hope you will take time to try if you do not find it *sufferable* to stay.

The correspondence concluded with this letter. Forster implied that Landor behaved with neither gallantry nor gratitude by stating that, "immediately after" receiving this letter, "he quitted London for Tenby in South Wales". Yet Landor himself informed Forster (in a letter of 1855) that Dorothy wrote this last letter to him "on that very night" of 17th April 1795 when she was married in Studley Church to Francis Holyoake!

How far the girl's affections were engaged may be a subject for idle speculation, but the facts surely indicate a broken romance on Landor's side. At Christmas his father had been excited to "violent expressions" resulting in Landor's banishment from home; the only obvious reason for such expressions was the scandalous connection with Nancy Jones. Like Dorothy's uncles, Dr. Landor must have welcomed his eldest son's attentions to the Studley heiress, and would be moved to "violent expressions" on discovering that Landor was offering affront to the eligible lady of "stately step, commanding eye" by indulgence in a casual amour. Rumours of Nancy Jones may have reached Dorothy's uncles, but in any case Landor's rebellious behaviour hardly commended him as a suitably stable husband for their ward. Dorothy herself had reason for pique, since Landor's pride prevented his seeking a settlement from his father to enable a proposal of marriage. So she accepted Holyoake, who, though described by Landor as "the most vulgar man alive", was a man of suitable maturity, several years Landor's senior, scion of an old family, and possessed of landed property in Staffordshire. Possibly Landor scarcely realised then or afterwards exactly how he squandered his chances with Dorothy, to whom he clearly alludes in the lines, published in *Simonidea* (1806):

> Sweet was the maid who hail'd my early lay,
>   And waited to receive my vow;
> But Love, blind Love—all hurry, for 'twas May,
>   Slipt it—my stars! I know not how.

A woman's rejection wounds a young man's self-esteem, and on hearing of Dorothy's marriage, Landor sought balm in the welcoming arms of Nancy Jones.

Forster did not attempt the task of identifying Landor's mistress among the vast clan of her name in South Wales. From Landor's verses it appears that she was short of stature, had "quivering" golden hair, and died young, at least before he wrote the moving elegy in *Simonidea* (1806):

> And thou too, Nancy!—why should Heaven remove
> Each tender object of mine early love?
> Why was I happy? O ye conscious rocks!
> Was I not happy? when Ïöne's locks
> Claspt round her neck and mine their golden chain,
> Ambition, fame, and fortune, smiled in vain.
> While warring winds with deaf'ning fury blew,
> Near and more near, our cheeks, our bosoms, grew.
> Wave after wave the lashing ocean chased,
> She smiled, and prest me closer to her waist.
> "Suppose this cave should crush us," once I cried;
> "It cannot fall," the loving maid replied.
> "You, who are shorter, might be safe," I said;
> "O let us fly!" exclaim'd the simple maid.
> Springing, she drew me forward by the hand
> Upon the sunny and the solid sand,
> And then lookt round, with fearful doubt, to see
> If, what I spoke so seriously, could be.
> Ah memory, memory! thou alone canst save
> Angelic beauty from the grasping grave.
> And shall she perish? by yon stars I swear,
> Here she shall live, though fate hath placed her there.
> The sigh of soft surrender, and the kiss
> For absence, doubt, obedience, merit this.
> Let fears, let fame, the cancel'd vow suggest,
> Love, to whose voice she listen'd, veils the rest.
> Though Nancy's name for ever dwell unknown
> Beyond her briar-bound sod and upright stone;
> Yet, in the lover's, in the poet's eye,
> The gentle young Ïöne ne'er shall die.

Knowing more than he was prepared to print, Forster remarked primly that Landor's time at Tenby "could not in any prudent or worldly sense have been very profitable", and "a part of it, including a love adventure . . . , was probably also painful"; with a nice gesture of distaste he added, "It is not necessary, however, that this should be dwelt upon"—an attitude of reticence that must have appealed to a majority of his Victorian readers who clothed their souls as respectably as their bodies, but denied biographical justice to a man of sensibility who "warm'd both hands before the fire of Life". The verses on Nancy and Ione indicate that their heroine offered tender love, of which Landor took full enjoyment and afterwards regretted nothing except loss of the happiness they had shared.

Proof of this lay under Forster's hand, for his library contained Robert Landor's marked copy of the *Quarterly Review* for April 1865, which included an obituary article on Landor. The article quotes Landor's statement in the imaginary conversation with the Abbé Delille that his "prejudices in favour of ancient literature began to wear away on *Paradise Lost*", and how "even the great hexameter sounded to me tinkling when I had recited aloud in my solitary walks on the sea-shore the haughty appeal of Satan and the deep penitence of Eve". In the margin beside this passage Robert Landor wrote:

He too should have repented then—having seduced a girl at Tenby the year before, with whom he lived at Swansea till the birth of a Child.

Discreetly Forster ignored the note, but his destructive executor, Whitwell Elwin, evidently never thought of looking for incriminating indiscretions in the pages of the periodical he himself edited, and allowed the volume to accompany the bequest to South Kensington Museum. There it was found by Mr. R. H. Super, who proceeded to consult the Swansea parish registers. He discovered no registration of a birth in Landor's name, but the registers recorded interment of a nine-month-old infant named Anne Jones on 9th May 1796 and of a twenty-two-year-old girl of the same name on 15th November 1801. If the infant was Landor's, he had good reason for hastening from London to Tenby in late April or early May of 1795.

He remained at Tenby and Swansea throughout the summer, while negotiations with his father continued along the lines indicated in Dorothy Lyttelton's letter. As late as August he was still threatening to go to Italy, for his old nurse Molly Bird (*née* Perry) wrote to him at Tenby during that month:

Honred Sir, May Health and Happiness attend you, and may I live to see you at the Head of that Family who, next to a Husband, as my Best Affections. I hope the providence of God will direct you in Every thing, but, O Sir, I hope you will Never go a Broad. My hart shuders at the thout of your leaving England Least I shud see you no more.

Probably he never seriously considered Dorothy's suggestion that he should continue his academic career at Cambridge, and as he despised the law only less than the Church, the idea of reading at the Temple was also rejected. Madden, the editor of Lady Blessington's correspondence, started a story, copied in many of Landor's obituary notices, that Landor, on leaving Oxford, lived in London with his godfather, General Powell, who urged him to enter the army. Supposing that he had given this information to Madden, Forster cited the story as an instance of Landor's defective memory, and in refutation quoted a garrulous rigmarole from Robert Landor, stating that the general never lived in London, that Walter never lived with him there or anywhere else, and that the old soldier, in view of his godson's republican opinions, "would have thought him as well qualified for the chaplaincy" as a military commission. When Madden's book appeared, Landor himself wrote in the *Athenæum* of 3rd March 1855:

I never was under the care of my godfather, General Powell, in London, nor was he ever there while I was. Out of kindness to my father, an old friend, he told him he would give me a commission in the army if I would "abstain from sporting my republican opinions". My reply was, "No man shall ever tie my tongue; many thanks to the General." He made the offer to my next brother.

The statement tallies with his brother Robert's, apart from the latter's denial that the general offered Landor a commission. Probably the general, feeling the obligation of a godfather, did make the conditional offer, which was conveyed to Landor at Tenby by his father. There is less reason for doubting the accuracy of Landor's memory than of his brother Robert's, a boy of only fourteen in 1795.

The choice of a profession and the amount of an allowance were the bones of contention between father and son. Dr. Landor considered that his eldest son, though heir to property, should qualify for a profession, as he himself had done, and literature was a pastime rather than a profession for gentlemen. Landor felt that his future prospects should relieve him from the necessity of wasting time in pursuit of a distasteful profession and that he should be granted an allowance proportionate to his expectations.

As appears in Dorothy Lyttelton's letter, Dr. Landor would not grant an allowance calculated to injure his younger children. At his father's death Landor would inherit the Rugeley estate; at his mother's death the estates of Ipsley and Tachbrook would devolve upon him. Charles, the second son, would succeed to the family living of Colton on the death of his uncle John Landor; Henry was to inherit his mother's small personal estate of Whitnash. Provision for Robert and his three sisters had to be made by saving from current income, and in his statement to Forster on family finances Robert admitted that his mother's anxiety on their behalf assumed "the appearance of too much parsimony". To Landor it seemed that he was condemned to pass his youth in penury while waiting for his father's shoes, yet his demand for an ample allowance exposed him to a charge of selfishness, since it must deplete the savings from income intended as provision for his sisters and youngest brother. This imputation of selfishness Robert recounted to Forster after sixty years, contrasting Landor's behaviour with the alleged generosity of his brother Henry, who not unnaturally identified himself with his mother's interests since he owed his fortune to her personal bequest.

Eventually his father agreed to an allowance of £150 a year; when it was spent, Landor could always resort to the parental roof. For the next three years he lived on this principle—while his money lasted, he was at Swansea; then he went home to Warwick till his next payment fell due.

§ 2

To his father Landor may well have quoted Bacon: "The illiberality of parents in allowance towards their children is an harmful error; makes them base; acquaints them with shifts; makes them sort with mean company; and makes them surfeit more when they come to plenty." Arrogance is inevitable in the intellectual young, who are intolerant of compromise and impatient that the world continues to repeat mistakes so often demonstrated by thinkers of the past.

The publication of his *Poems* offered a lesson in the hazards of impetuosity. Some satirical lines "To Dr. Warton" lamented that poetry was represented at Oxford only by such writers as "Horse" Kett and the Rev. George Somers Clark since the death in 1790 of the late Professor of Poetry, Dr. Warton's brother Thomas:

> Alas! chaotic is the dark
> 'Twixt C—— and K——, and K—— and C——.

When Clark wrote to him without resentment that "these little things promote the sale of the copies of your volume in the University", Landor felt such compunction that he tried to withdraw his book from publication. As he read more and revised his taste, he regretted that he had conducted his education in public by rushing prematurely into print, writing five years later in another suppressed work, the *Postscript to Gebir*:

Before I was twenty years of age I had imprudently sent into the world a volume of which I was soon ashamed. It everywhere met with as much commendation as was proper, and generally more. For, though the structure was feeble, the lines were fluent; the rhymes showed habitual ease, and the personifications fashionable taste. . . . So early in life I had not discovered the error into which we were drawn by the Wartons. I was then in raptures with what I now despise.

He expressed no such regret for a *Moral Epistle, Respectfully Dedicated to Earl Stanhope*, issued as a twenty-page pamphlet a few weeks after the *Poems*, though he neither reprinted nor afterwards referred to it, and Forster discovered its existence only from casual mention in a letter addressed to him at Tenby. In heroic couplets after Pope's manner the satire laments the repressive measures introduced by Pitt's government to repel the liberal influences of the French Revolution, condemns the Church for supporting war, contrasts Pitt's dissimulation at Horne Tooke's trial for treason with the independence and integrity of the seventeenth Lord Willoughby of Parham and Pope's "downright Shippen" earlier in the century, and looks forward to liberty and peace through the triumph of human brotherhood over patriotism. The third Earl Stanhope received the dedication as a noted radical who had opposed the war against the American colonies, presented a congratulatory address to the National Assembly in 1789 on "the recent glorious revolution" in France, and had been lately applauded in two sonnets by Coleridge after moving in the House of Lords the diplomatic recognition of the French Republic. Though he attacked two other ministers by name besides Pitt, William Windham and the third Duke of Portland, Landor did not shelter behind anonymity; the *Times* advertisement of the *Poems* announced that there would "speedily be published, a Moral Epistle, respectfully dedicated to Earl Stanhope, by the same Author", and the authorship is declared in the poem itself:

> Parham! and Shippon! if each honor'd name
> Be not eternally preserv'd by Fame—
> Lie tranquil in your tombs; and say " *Ye Powers*
> *Of darkness! It is Landor's fault, not ours.*"

As the dedication was dated "Feb. 25", the *Moral Epistle* was evidently sent to the printers along with the *Poems* and Landor's name was omitted from the title-page because it was intended to bind up the *Moral Epistle* with the *Poems*. Possibly it was eventually issued separately because the publishers feared an order for its suppression and would then be enabled to withdraw the *Epistle* without prejudice to the rest of the *Poems*.

During his few months in London early in 1795, Landor "accepted no hospitalities, and received few visits", being "occupied in studying Italian, and in improving my knowledge of Greek". In a letter to Forster of 1852 he declared that, in the company of his Italian coach Parachinetti, he met Alfieri "just before he left this country for ever", and hearing his enthusiasm for the French Revolution, Alfieri remarked:

Sir, you are a very young man. You are yet to learn that nothing good ever came out of France, or ever will. The ferocious monsters are about to devour one another; and they can do nothing better. They have always been the curse of Italy; yet we too have fools among us who trust them.

As Alfieri's last visit to England ended in the autumn of 1791,[1] Parachinetti must have repeated the remark to Landor, who quoted it in conversation so often as endorsing his own disgust with the French betrayal of revolutionary principles under Napoleon's dictatorship that eventually he claimed to have heard it personally from Alfieri. All his life he expressed admiration for Alfieri, who, born like Landor an heir to wealth, disdained the privileges of his position in his advocacy of republican ideals. In 1812, in his *Commentary on Memoirs of Fox*, he described Alfieri as "incomparably the greatest poet in Europe" at the turn of the century; in 1856, he stated in his *Letter to Emerson*, "I think oftener with Alfieri than with any other writer." He introduced Alfieri into two imaginary conversations, "Alfieri and Metastasio" and "Alfieri and Solomon the Florentine Jew", the former discussing "some few predudices" Alfieri supposedly brought back from England, with such quips on the English as "they think it manly to be rude, and womanly to be sensitive".

The *Moral Epistle* indicates that Landor's political views at this time coincided with those expressed by Coleridge during the same year in his *Conciones ad Populum*. As the opinions of Coleridge and Wordsworth were considered sufficiently subversive to warrant assignment of a government spy to investigate their activities in the Quantocks, Landor must soon have realised that conventional minds would follow General Powell's example in avoiding company where he was likely to be present. At Swansea, even more than in London, he must have "accepted no hospitalities, and received few visits", for there his association with Nancy Jones excluded acceptance by conventional society. Without distractions, he concentrated on intensive reading. Unlike Coleridge and De Quincey, he avowed no intention of qualifying to produce a work of philosophy as a benefaction to mankind. But he was aware that he had imposed on his tutors at Rugby and Oxford by superficial brilliance, and he now applied himself conscientiously to scholarship, improving his Greek to read Homer and Pindar.

He looked back upon this time as the happiest of his life, when— as he told Lady Blessington forty-four years later—he "did not exchange twelve sentences with men".

---

[1] As stated in my letter to *The Times Literary Supplement* of 26th February 1944, I am indebted to Sir Henry McAnally for the date of Alfieri's last departure from England. In the light of this information Mr. R. H. Super assumed in his *Walter Savage Landor: A Biography* that Landor must have spent "a short interval with a tutor in London" after leaving Rugby in 1791 and before going to study with the Rev. William Langley. But there is no evidence for this assumption apart from Landor's statement that he met Alfieri, and it is very unlikely that Landor went to London to study Italian with Parachinetti immediately after his removal from Rugby. In his letter to Walter Birch of 12th April 1795 he implies that he has only lately started his study of Italian: "I have been in London about a quarter of a year, constantly employed in studying French and Italian. The former I could read before, but not speak. The latter is extremely easy both to read and speak, and I understand it as well as French, which I have been in the habit of reading four or five years."

I lived among woods, which are now killed with copper works, and took my walk over sandy sea-coast deserts, then covered with low roses and thousands of nameless flowers and plants, trodden by the naked feet of the Welsh peasantry, and trackless.

Though indignant against social injustice, he never pretended to enjoy fraternising with his inferiors; the Welsh peasants "were somewhat between me and the animals, and were as useful to the landscape as masses of weed or stranded boats".

On one of his walks along the beaches between Swansea and Tenby he met the girl whose name lives in one of his best-known lyrics. The verses called "St. Clair", dated 5th October 1796, celebrate his first meeting with the Hon. Rose Whitworth Aylmer; on seeing her he found "my courage, voice, and memory gone", and after his first walk by her side,

> When all but lovers long had slept,
> I tost and tumbled, fretted, wept,
> To Love himself vow'd endless hate,
> Renounced my stars and curst my fate.

Long afterwards to her younger half-sister, Mrs. Paynter, Landor denied that he "ever offered a word of love" to Rose Aylmer, though he told his niece that "I was not indifferent to Rose, nor Rose quite to me", and Mrs. Paynter's daughter, Landor's "second Rose", believed her aunt to have been "his first love". Among his stars he may now have renounced his love for Nancy Jones, but he "curst" his fate for the same reason as he "slipt" his chance with Dorothy Lyttelton—he was in the same state of financial dependence.

Their acquaintance lasted only eighteen months, for in the summer of 1798 Rose sailed for India with her aunt, the wife of Sir Henry Russell, a Bengal judge. At Calcutta she died of cholera in March 1800, and the news of her death inspired Landor to write the lines that find a place in every representative anthology of English poetry—lines that had for Charles Lamb "a charm I cannot explain" and he was forever muttering, "both tipsy and sober"—

> Ah! what avails the sceptred race!
>   Ah! what the form divine!
> What every virtue, every grace!
>   Rose Aylmer, all were thine.
> Rose Aylmer, whom these wakeful eyes
>   May weep but never see,
> A night of memories and of sighs
>   I consecrate to thee.

During the eighteen months following their meeting, Landor continued to live mostly at Swansea. Rose Aylmer was just seventeen at the time of their meeting; her eldest brother, the fifth Lord Aylmer, was born in the same year as Landor; their home was with their mother and stepfather, Howell Price, at Laugharne, which Landor—who had small respect for Welsh etymology—called "Larne". A girl of seventeen, schooled in polite society of Jane Austen's generation, was unlikely to offer much intellectual inspiration. Nor could she have exercised the more mature Dorothy's feminine guile in expressing rapture at his verses, or Landor might have addressed to her more than the four lines of doggerel which he presented, not to Rose, but to a married lady in the house. The occasion was when she cut a fragment from her bonnet ribbon; Landor picked it up, and remarking that "it was too precious to be lost, or for anyone to possess it without a contest", drew lots for it with other callow youths. On such terms of sentimental gallantry he enjoyed his walks with her.

But indirectly Rose Aylmer inspired the poem on which Landor's literary reputation with his contemporaries was based. She subscribed to the Swansea circulating library, and one day lent him *The Progress of Romance* by Clara Reeve, who then rivalled Mrs. Radcliffe as a popular lady novelist. From one of the stories in this book, "The History of Charoba Queen of Egypt", Landor took the theme of his epic poem, *Gebir*.

After Langley fired the enthusiasm at Ashbourne, Pope had been established as Landor's model and master. Pope led him to Pindar, and his diligent study of Greek to Homer and Sophocles. Probably Homer led him to Milton, with the intention of measuring the greatest English epic beside the *Iliad*, and his "prejudices in favour of ancient literature began to wear away on *Paradise Lost*" as he recited its phrases "aloud in my solitary walks on the sea-shore". Hearing "the 'solemn roar' of organ under Milton's hand", he realised, with Matthew Arnold, that the soul of power in poetry and art "resides chiefly in the refining and elevation wrought in us by the high and rare excellence of the great style".

In prose more than in verse Landor was to achieve supremely this effect of refining and elevation. But such a gifted poet and critic of poetry as Swinburne declared that Landor "won for himself such a double crown of glory in verse and in prose as has been won by no other Englishman but Milton", and R. H. Horne (with whom Elizabeth Barrett Browning collaborated in the article on Landor in *A New Spirit of the Age*) thought that "his blank verse is not only the most regular that ever was written, but it is the most sweet, and far less monotonous than we should expect of a musical system which excluded occasional discords". Lamenting the absence of such discords, Sidney Colvin echoed other detractors in describing Landor's blank verse as "always too regular; it exhibits none of the Miltonic variety, none of the inventions in violation or suspension of ordinary metrical law, by which that great master draws unexampled tones from his instrument".

Colvin also acknowledged a defect of obscurity, which he ascribed to excessive condensation. "The style of *Gebir* is severe," remarked Landor to Alexander Dyce in 1850, "because when I composed it, I was fresh from repeated perusals of Pindar", and Colvin asserted that "the narrative is packed into a space where it has no room to develop itself at ease" and so "the transitions from one theme to another are effected with more than Pindaric abruptness". This criticism reflects the comments of two among the poem's earliest readers, Coleridge and Charles Lamb, to both of whom *Gebir* was commended by Southey. Lamb found "Gebor aptly so denominated from Geborish, *quasi* Gibberish", but allowed that "Gebor hath some lucid intervals"; Coleridge said, "you have eminences excessively bright, and all the ground around and between them in darkness".

Yet Coleridge, as he related in *Biographia Literaria*, detected the same defect of obscurity in Wordsworth's *Descriptive Sketches*:

there is a harshness and acerbity connected and combined with words and images all a-glow, which might recall those products of the vegetable world, where gorgeous blossoms rise out of a hard and thorny rind and shell, within which the rich fruit is elaborating. The language is not only peculiar and strong, but at times knotty and contorted, as by its own impatient strength; while the novelty and struggling crowd of images, acting in conjunction with the difficulties of the style, demands always a greater closeness of attention, than poetry—at all events, than descriptive poetry—has a right to claim. It not seldom therefore justified the complaint of obscurity.

Despite this complaint—which might well have been applied by a censorious critic to *Gebir*—Coleridge believed that "seldom, if ever, was the emergence of an original poetic genius above the literary horizon more evidently announced" than by *Descriptive Sketches*, and in reading *Gebir*, as much as in listening to Wordsworth's reading of *Guilt and Sorrow*, he might have been impressed—not merely by "the freedom from false taste"—but by "the union of deep feeling with profound thought; the fine balance of truth in observing, with the imaginative faculty in modifying, the objects observed; and above all the original gift of spreading the tone, the atmosphere, and with it the depth and height of the ideal world around forms, incidents, and situations, of which, for the common view, custom had bedimmed all the lustre".

The publication of *Gebir* was announced in the *Monthly Magazine* of August 1798, thus preceding by a few weeks the appearance in September of Coleridge and Wordsworth's *Lyrical Ballads*, with which literary historians mark the dawn of "the romantic movement" in English poetry. In 1800 Landor stated his aim in the *Postscript to Gebir*:

I have avoided high-sounding words. I have attempted to throw back the gross materials, and to bring the figures forward. I knew that people would cry out "your burden was so light, we could hardly hear you breathe, pray where is your merit". For, there are few who seem thoroughly acquainted with this plain and simple truth, that it is easier to elevate the empty than to support the full.

Two years later, in his preface to the second edition of *Lyrical Ballads*, Wordsworth stated that his "principal object . . . was to choose incidents and situations from common life, and to relate or describe them, throughout, as far as was possible in a selection of language really used by men, and, at the same time, to throw over them a certain colouring of imagination, whereby ordinary things should be presented to the mind in an unusual aspect; and, further, and above all, to make these incidents and situations interesting by tracing in them, truly though not ostentatiously, the primary laws of our nature: chiefly, as far as regards the manner in which we associate ideas in a state of excitement". Following Coleridge's exclusive adulation of Wordsworth, students of "the romantic movement" have generally ignored the relative importance of *Gebir*,[1] but it is clear that Landor at Swansea and Tenby arrived independently at much the same theories of poetry as Coleridge and Wordsworth were simultaneously discussing in the Quantocks.

There is no evidence, and it is unlikely, that Landor read either of the immature romantic poems immediately preceding *Gebir*, Wordsworth's *Descriptive Sketches* and Southey's *Joan of Arc*, but he sought to exclude suggestion of his indebtedness to these works by inaccurate statements when he reprinted *Gebir* in 1831:

Gebir was written in my twentieth year. Many parts were first composed in Latin; and I doubted in which language to complete it. I had lost the manuscript; finding it four years after in a box of letters, I reduced it nearly to half, inserting a few verses in some places to give it its proportions.

He was in his twenty-second year in October 1796 when he met Rose Aylmer, to whom he owed his introduction to Clara Reeve's story of Charoba; *Gebir* was published less than two years later—in or before August 1798. In the verse "Apology for *Gebir*" (first published in 1854) he adhered to the notion that it was "sixty the years since" he wrote the first draft of the poem, and explained how he lost the manuscript: he left it behind in North Wales on returning from a grouse-shooting expedition on the moors above Bala—where he was possibly a guest of the Price family at Rhiwlas—and "many months" elapsed before it was forwarded to him at Swansea.

[1] Professor Margaret Sherwood mentioned neither Landor nor *Gebir* in a work of 380 pages, *Undercurrents of Influence in English Romantic Poetry*, Harvard University Press, 1934. She contrived also to omit any mention of Southey, to refer only once to Coleridge's *Biographia Literaria*, to cite not a single work by Coleridge in her bibliography, and to magnify into a torrent the "undercurrent" of influence by Herder, Kant and other German philosophers without mentioning De Quincey.

He must have exaggerated the delay before his recovery of the manuscript, for it was submitted to Cadell & Davies as early as April 1797. On the 29th of that month Cadell & Davies declined the offer of "your Manuscript Poem", because Landor still owed them the cost of publishing his *Poems* of 1795 and because "the Experience we have had in Works of a similar nature convinces us that the Sale would never repay the Expences of its Publication". During a visit to Ipsley Court he commissioned a Warwick printer named Sharpe to print the poem; as he explained in the second edition five years later, "the author, from the distance of sixteen miles, and without any regular post, could not easily superintend" the proofs, and the text appeared with many errors, bound in paper covers, and bearing on its title page the imprint of Rivingtons, who undertook the London sales from their shop in St. Paul's Churchyard. Sold sometimes for half-a-crown, sometimes for two shillings, the shabby little pamphlet waited more than a year before receiving favourable notice from Robert Southey in the *Critical Review* of September 1799.

"I understand not the management of these matters," wrote Landor ruefully in the *Postscript to Gebir*, "but I find that the writing of a book is the least that an author has to do." He had no friends among fashionable reviewers, and Rivingtons, having nothing at stake, made no effort to publicise the book. Ingenuously Landor supposed that its merit must command attention; he had reason to expect that its bold liberalism might provoke controversy, for De Quincey, buying a copy as an undergraduate, admired the "audacity" of *Gebir* and "gazed with some indefinite shade of approbation upon a poet whom the Attorney-General might have occasion to speak with".

The story of *Gebir* is planned like an heroic tragedy of the Restoration stage. An Iberian prince, Gebir (of Gibraltar), invades the lands of the young Egyptian queen Charoba, who is advised by her nurse Dalica to entertain the invader with blandishments. Charoba's fears are soon dispelled by love for her conqueror, "but women communicate their fears more willingly than their love", and she omits to inform Dalica of her change of heart. Bent on securing the queen's deliverance, Dalica visits a sorceress, who gives her a poisoned mantle. This she contrives to throw upon Gebir's shoulders during his marriage ceremony, and he dies in the arms of his anguished bride. As in the conventional heroic tragedy, there is an under-plot: Gebir's brother Tamar loves a valiant nymph who defeats him in a wrestling match. Disguised as Tamar, Gebir wrestles with the nymph, subdues her, and gives her in marriage to Tamar. The nymph warns Gebir of impending danger, and after her wedding, which precedes Gebir's, she confides her forebodings to Tamar and persuades him to flee with her for safety beyond the seas.

As Landor stated in a later preface to the poem, "in the moral are exhibited the folly, the injustice, and the punishment of Invasion, with the calamities which must ever attend the superfluous colonization of a peopled country". During the winter of 1796–97 the massing of French troops at Brest excited a scare of invasion and militia volunteers were concentrated for coastal defence. Resident on the south coast of Wales, Landor was well situated to witness the excesses inspired by "alarm and despondency":

> Every-where questions, answer'd ere begun,
> Every-where groups, for every-where alarm.
>
> .　　.　　.　　.　　.
>
> Madness, which, like the spiral element,
> The more it seizes on, the fiercer burns,
> Hurried them blindly forward, and involved
> In flame the senses, and in gloom the soul.
> Determin'd to protect the country's gods,
> Still asking their protection, they adjure
> Each other to stand forward, and insist
> With zeal, and trample under foot the slow . . .

His unpopular liberalism exposed him as a victim for this "madness" of patriotic prejudice: his brother Robert informed Forster that the colonel of the Warwickshire militia proposed to offer Landor a commission, but "one of the officers present immediately objected to my brother's violent and extreme opinions, exclaiming, 'If young Walter Landor gets a commission, I will resign mine'." Such victimisation was the lot of the minority that felt the ice of truth in Godwin's *Political Justice* and followed Charles James Fox in deploring the war against republican France as a war of aggression against social revolution:

> Woe to the wiser few, who dare to cry
> "People! these men are not your enemies:
> Enquire their errand; and resist when wrong'd".

In the third of the poem's seven books Gebir descends into the bowels of the earth, and seeing his kingly predecessors doing penance for their earthly crimes, exclaims to his guide:

> "Aroar, what wretch that nearest us? what wretch
> Is that with eyebrows white, and slanting brow?
> Listen! him yonder, who, bound down supine,
> Shrinks, yelling, from that sword there, engine-hung;
> He too amongst my ancestors? I hate
> The despot, but the dastard I despise.
> Was he our countryman?"

> "Alas, O King!
> Iberia bore him, but the breed accurst
> Inclement winds blew blighting from north-east."
> "He was a warrior, then, nor fear'd the Gods?"
> "Gebir, he fear'd the Demons, not the Gods;
> Tho' them, indeed, his daily face adored,
> And was no warrior, yet the thousand lives
> Squander'd, as stones to exercise a sling!"

Forster thought that, in the event of prosecution, Landor might have pleaded that the white-browed wretch shrinking beneath the guillotine was Louis XVI, but the contemporary De Quincey found no difficulty in recognising that "*Iberia* is spiritual England; and *north-east* is mystical Hanover", and that the wretch with the eyebrows and "slanting" forehead "is our worthy old George III". The reference to the guillotine was rather to be interpreted as a bold warning that George III might share the fate of Louis XVI if his government persevered in the reactionary policy which had already lost the American colonies.

Landor at this time saw Napoleon as a soldier of the people, whose influence had stopped the excesses of the Reign of Terror and would enable the French to uphold the cause of democratic liberty in every European country. So, as Tamar and his nymph flee overseas, she points out the island of Corsica and prophesies that there

> From Tamar shall arise, 'tis Fate's decree,
> A mortal man above all mortal praise.

With the triumph of Tamar's descendants the world may look forward to liberty and peace in universal brotherhood, when

> Time,—Time himself throws off his motly garb
> Figur'd with monstrous men and monstrous gods,
> And in pure vesture enters their pure fanes,
> A proud partaker of their festivals.
> Captivity led captive, War o'erthrown,
> They shall o'er Europe, shall o'er Earth extend
> Empire that seas alone and skies confine,
> And glory that shall strike the crystal stars.

Most readers decided, like De Quincey, that *Gebir* was "too *Tom-Painish*" and seemed "up to a little treason". The *literati* prudently, like Lamb, ignored as "gibberish" the poet's thought and praised the imagery of isolated passages. Lamb particularly liked a passage near the end of the poem, where Charoba embraces the dying Gebir:

> Never so eager, when the world was waves,
> Stood the less daughter of the ark, and tried
> (Innocent this temptation!) to recall
> With folded vest, and casting arm, the dove:
> Never so fearful, when amidst the vines
> Rattled the hail, and when the light of heaven
> Closed, since the wreck of Nature, first eclipsed—
> As she was eager for his life's return,
> As she was fearful how his groans might end.

De Quincey appreciated how, watching the distant approach of Charoba's embassy in cavalcade,

> The king, who sat before his tent, descried
> The dust rise redden'd from the setting sun:

and how Tamar described his last sight of the nymph when she left after defeating him in combat,

> Restless then ran I to the highest ground
> To watch her: she was gone; gone down the tide;
> And the long moon-beam on the hard wet sand
> Lay like a jaspar column half uprear'd.

Such poetic imagery seems to have been generally admired in straightforward description, as of the workmen's operations in rebuilding the ruined city:

> Far off, at intervals, the ax resounds
> With regular strong stroke, and nearer home
> Dull falls the mallet with long labor fringed.

But charges of obscurity arose when such imagery was applied to abstract thought; when Dalica remarks,

> For, soon the sunny stream of Youth runs down,
> And not a gadfly streaks the lake beyond,

criticism impelled Landor to insert a footnote, when reprinting the poem, explaining that Dalica, an elderly woman, was reflecting how, with youth behind her, she found "nothing to break the dull uniformity of life". Frequent metaphors from moods of the sea reflect Landor's observations on his walks along the Welsh beaches: a passage in Wordsworth's *Excursion* (Book IV, lines 1132–47) seems to have been suggested by the nymph's instructions to Tamar on

> sinuous shells, of pearly hue
> Within, and they that lustre have imbibed
> In the sun's palace porch; where, when unyoked,
> His chariot wheel stands midway in the wave.

Shake one, and it awakens; then apply
Its polished lips to your attentive ear,
And it remembers its august abodes,
And murmurs as the ocean murmurs there.

§ 3

The author of *Gebir* was not called to account for treason or libel.
Pitt's government might imprison an impertinent newspaper editor
like John Walter of *The Times*; it might resort to persecution of dangerous publicists like Horne Tooke and John Thelwall; but it offered
no gratuitous advertisement to an obscure pamphlet poem unlikely to
be read by any but a few appraisers of its imagery. But churchmen
rarely turn the other cheek, and Landor attacked the established
church as a bastion of reaction. In the *Moral Epistle* the line "For
battle, parsons preach, and poets rant" carried a footnote deriding the
clergy for "calling upon us in the name of Religion to *strengthen the hand
of Government against the enemies of Church and State*" and remarking how
"among all their execrations, and all their sighs, the fate of our slaugh-
tered Countrymen seemed totally forgotten". A footnote to "The
Birth of Poesy" (in the *Poems* of 1795) observed how "The Song of
Solomon" in Archdeacon Croxal's paraphrase was "rescued from
those senseless bigots who imagined that the mistress of Solomon was
the *Church*". In the third book of *Gebir*, having seen the flaming arch
dividing the good from the wicked among the shades, Gebir receives
no answer to this appeal:

Bring me among the wonders of a realm
Admired by all, but like a tale admired.
We take our children from their cradled sleep,
And on their fancy, from our own, impress
Etherial forms and adulating fates:
But, ere departing for such scenes ourselves,
We seize their hands, we hang upon their neck,
Our beds cling heavy round us with our tears,
Agony strives with agony. Just Gods!
Wherefor should wretched mortals thus believe,
Or wherefor should they hesitate to die?

This blasphemy against orthodox theology brought a damning
notice of *Gebir* from the *British Critic* of February 1800, a periodical
ironically sponsored by Landor's own publishers, Rivingtons, but
"intended to uphold the tenets of the Established Church and the
Tory politics of the ruling government". Retorting in a suppressed
lampoon, "An Address to the Fellows of Trinity College Oxford, on

the Alarm of Invasion", Landor describes "the British Criticks" as "the hue-and-cry runners of Richards and Kett", the clerical poetasters of Trinity, but he made no personal reference to the joint-editors of the magazine, Archdeacon Nares and the Rev. William Beloe, though he may have had some knowledge of the latter. For Beloe was a pupil of Dr. Parr's, and Parr was now Landor's close friend and mentor.

At Hatton, four miles from Warwick on the Birmingham road, Dr. Samuel Parr lived at the parsonage, where he accumulated a vast library which was the wonder and envy of contemporary scholars. In appearance and personality Parr sufficiently resembled Dr. Johnson to invite comparison; both were big and corpulent, both affected oddities of dress and manner, both cultivated a reputation for dogmatism. To-day Parr survives only by Boswell's occasional references to him in the *Life* of Johnson and by De Quincey's essay on him, for though his importance was such as to invite two two-volume biographies immediately after his death, neither biographer was a Boswell. Yet while he was regarded, being a generation younger, as more or less Johnson's successor as a singular intellectual personality, most contemporaries would have rated him of greater gifts than Johnson. He was infinitely more popular, for by contrast with Johnson's irascibility, studied rudeness, and uncouth habits, Parr was genial, affable, and courtly of manners. He was a finer scholar—he used to say, "The first Greek scholar is Porson, and the third Elmsley; I won't say who the second is"—and he wielded an influence in politics to which Johnson never pretended. His home at Hatton was a shrine for pilgrimage by all the most distinguished men of the day; to have enjoyed his generous hospitality was a pleasure to remember and a privilege to be prized. His visitors were so numerous that, shortly after his death, there were lamentations locally about the decrease in revenue from turnpike tolls.

Like Johnson, Parr was born to modest circumstances, being the only son of a Harrow apothecary. He won a scholarship at Harrow, and returned there from Cambridge as head assistant master. His scholarship and personality were highly valued by the headmaster, Dr. Sumner, and on Sumner's death, Parr was generally expected to be appointed his successor. But Sumner as a schoolmaster had been in advance of his time, being a fine scholar and a just disciplinarian, and the school governors, preferring a master who would make them less uncomfortably conscious of their intellectual and moral inferiority, declined to appoint a successor of his training. As an excuse for rejection they pleaded that Parr was too young at twenty-four. He took care that youth should not again prove an impediment to preferment by making himself seem much older than his years; affecting the dress and manners of an elderly ecclesiastic, he took to wearing the huge "obumbrating" wig that became a feature of political lampoons and would have delighted caricaturists of a later age. His prematurely venerable appearance inspired from his schoolfellow, Sir William Jones the orientalist, the comment that "if you should have the good luck to live forty years you may stand a chance of overtaking your face".

Parr responded to the school governors with characteristic spirit: he resigned his post at Harrow and started a school of his own at the neighbouring village of Stanmore. Already he had achieved such esteem as a pedagogue that forty boys were removed from Harrow to continue under his care. For a further fifteen years he remained a schoolmaster, but in spite of his abilities he made little progress in his profession, and only Dr. Johnson's urgent recommendation secured for him the headmastership of Norwich Grammar School. Preferment came by patronage, and Parr not only disdained the lip-service demanded by patrons, but excited their disfavour by bold expression of enlightened opinions. Eloquence earned his popularity as a preacher, but he antagonised ecclesiastical authority by open profession of a liberal Christianity. Instead of courting the canons of Norwich Cathedral, he consorted with dissenters, supported a bill for relief of dissenting clergy, and expressed indignation at discrimination against Roman Catholics. "Alas for our church!" he said boldly. "Formerly she was the mother of all sects, now she is sectarian herself; embittered with the same spite and animosity to the sects, which the sects feel towards one another," and he warned his colleagues against a short-sighted policy "as degrading to our dignity as weakening to our strength".

He owed the gift of the perpetual curacy of Hatton to the gratitude of Lady Jane Trafford for his capable tutoring of her only son, and when he gave up schoolmastering in 1786 to live there in retirement, he took in private pupils. When Landor was removed from Rugby, there may have been no vacancy at Parr's, for he limited the number of his pupils to seven and there was keen competition for a place. But it is unlikely that Landor's father applied to Parr. Before the French Revolution Dr. Landor was a Whig so zealous that he played a leading part in sponsoring the candidature of Ladbroke and Sir Robert Lawley at the election which first exploded Lord Warwick's dominion over Warwickshire politics. But on hearing of the horrors of revolutionary Paris, he was one of the deserting Whigs who followed Edmund Burke into the Tory camp, and probably shared the popular suspicion of Parr as a dangerous firebrand, whose support of Charles James Fox excited such unreasoning prejudice that some pupils were removed from his charge by their parents.

Parr's methods may have been reckoned unsuited to a boy removed from school for insubordination. He made friends of his boys, delighting to move freely among them during their playtime; he would spend hours in the sun, puffing his pipe while watching a cricket match, and he made a practice of inviting elder boys to dinner when he had distinguished guests. They never presumed to familiarity from his freedom with them, for in school he was a strict disciplinarian and won affection and respect by his equal zeal at work and play. He admired spirit in a boy, and believed that bad blood between boys was best settled by themselves. He shocked one of his biographers, the Rev. William Field, by gleefully relating how, at Stanmore, there was a tacit understanding between him and his pupils that all fights should be staged within view of his study window; he watched, and the boys knew that he watched, but it was mutually recognised that he must be supposed ignorant of the encounters.

Parr might have been expected to admire and encourage Landor's rebellious independence, instead of effecting the chastening influence vainly hoped for by Dr. Landor. When they met during Landor's vacations from Oxford, Parr won his lasting affection and respect by favouring him for his merit. Sydney Smith remarked that Parr, in his rural retreat, enjoyed too few opportunities of entertaining his intellectual equals, and so developed a taste for easily scoring off inferior wits. But Boswell records Johnson as saying, "Parr is a fair man. I do not know when I have had occasion of such free controversy". Parr found Landor a fit match in dialectic; they shared a taste for the classics, the same revolutionary political opinions, and equal vigour in dispute.

Robert Landor believed that they "were kept from quarrels by mutual respect, by something like awe of each other's temper, and a knowledge that, if war began at all, it must be to the knife". But Robert was not an unprejudiced judge; he disliked Parr, who once treated him "more offensively than any one else ever did"—an offence which he avenged by attacking Parr in a lampoon wrongly attributed to his elder brother. There was the same mutual respect between Parr and Landor as between Parr and Johnson, and their manner of argument must have been much the same as Parr described between himself and Johnson.

"I gave him no quarter . . . Dr. Johnson was very great. Whilst he was arguing, I observed that he stamped. Upon this, I stamped. Dr. Johnson said, Why did you stamp, Dr. Parr?—I replied, Because you stamped; and I was resolved not to give you the advantage even of a *stamp* in the argument."

Between Parr and Landor there may have been much stamping, but all Parr's acquaintance agreed that, while he was opinionated and delighted to dogmatise, he diffused good humour and charmed by his courtliness. In youth Landor, always impetuous and explosive, lacked the polished courtesy of his mature years, but Parr won his life-long respect and gratitude by admitting him to argument as an intellectual equal and delighting in the violence that other elders deplored as a dangerous defect. In later years, when lionised as an eccentric genius, Landor consciously or unconsciously assumed many of Parr's characteristics.

Parr was twenty-eight years older than Landor, but the warmth of his feeling for the young man appears in the anecdote which Landor proudly told in affectionate reminiscence. Parr had one of his hospitable dinner-parties when one of the guests remarked that Landor had just arrived at Warwick, after a long absence, on a visit to his mother.

"Eat your dinner, eat your dinner," said Parr.

But as soon as the cloth was removed and the first glass of wine drunk, he laid down his pipe and said:

"Drink your wine, my friends, drink your wine; I must go and see Walter Landor."

He drove off and spent an hour with Landor, though his sense of courtesy made him decline even the offer of a cup of tea.

"No, no, Walter," he said. "I must go back to my friends; they are all at dinner."

Relating this story, Landor used to boast proudly that he was the only man for whom Parr had ever ridden half a dozen miles "with his dinner in his mouth and his pipe out of it". Such personal distinction Landor always valued beyond any other. He cared so little for popular favour that he published many of his works through obscure provincial booksellers; he never sought publicity or preferment, and disliked dining in company with more than a few personal friends. Careless of offending those who deplored his opinions, he valued above everything the affection and esteem of those for whom he felt similar regard.

He sent a copy of *Gebir* to Parr, assuring him—with the classical allusion that Parr loved—that under his criticism he would feel like Polydorus when his tomb, "new-turfed and spruce and flourishing", was plucked as a sacrifice to Æneas. As Landor once told Southey, Parr's taste in poetry was "Bromwychian", and he was concerned lest his young friend should be wasting his gifts on dilettanteism when there was useful political work for an able pen. Landor declined to allow Parr's biographer to publish his letters to Parr—he explained to one of his sisters that they were "merely notes, and of all the letter writers in the universe I am the most negligent and the very worst"—and Parr's letters to Landor were apparently among those papers of Forster's destroyed by Whitwell Elwin, but Parr evidently urged Landor to leave his Welsh retreat for London and enter party politics.

In Parr's company he attended in December 1797 a mass meeting at Warwick to protest against Pitt's budget proposals for an income tax taking a tenth of all incomes above two hundred pounds, with a modified scale of incomes between that amount and sixty pounds. "Only once in my life have I attended any publick meeting," wrote Landor in 1850. "It was fifty years ago, on Pitt's inquisitorial income-tax. This wretch was the greatest mischief our country ever endured." As the crowd proved too large for the shire hall, the meeting adjourned to the race course, where a petition to the king, stating the causes of complaint and praying for dismissal of the ministry, was moved by Sir John Throckmorton, seconded by Bertie Greatheed, and supported by Sir Francis Burdett and others. According to his biographer Field, Parr intended to deliver a written address, but was dissuaded—doubtless by representations that active participation in political agitation was unbecoming to his cloth. Either Landor drafted the intended address or collaborated in its composition, for he printed such an address *To the Burgesses of Warwick* in an eight-page pamphlet, not only stating the Whig case against taxation, but attacking the government's repression of civil liberties and the local Tory influence of Lord Warwick. Though he boldly appended his own signature to the address, the author's statement that he expected to "be abominated for this struggle by all my acquaintance here" was applicable rather to a personage of Parr's local eminence than to an obscure young man who could hardly have hoped to figure among the influential speakers at the meeting.

Parr gave him an introduction to Daniel Stuart, the proprietor and editor of the *Morning Post*, which advocated more extreme views than Perry's *Morning Chronicle*, the orthodox Whig organ, and to Robert Adair, Fox's party organiser, who became British ambassador at Vienna, and though a year or two older than Landor, died a year after he did. Over his own name or pseudonym he contributed occasional letters after the manner of Junius, to the *Morning Post*, and after 1799, when Stuart acquired the *Courier*, to that paper. Adair found him an untractable satellite. Unlike Coleridge and Southey, then employed on similar work, Landor was independent of the journalist's pittance; he wrote as his conscience dictated, regardless of editorial or party requirements. His diatribes against "the drunken democracy of Mr. William Pitt" were welcomed, but too often he strayed from the paths approved by the party machine. It happened also that Stuart's health began to fail and the control of the *Courier* came more into the hands of his partner, Peter Street, who gradually watered down the acid tone of the paper, which eventually became, in the years before Waterloo, the leading Government newspaper. Hence Adair was often obliged to devise excuses when Landor indignantly complained that a letter of his had been "edited" or omitted.

Adair cultivated him for six or seven years; they corresponded from 1800 till 1806. For Landor was a young man of talent who might have been useful as a member of Parliament in opposition; an heir to fortune, he would have money and the consequent influence necessary to secure himself a seat. So Adair frequently met him at Debrett's in Piccadilly and they went together to the House of Commons, which Landor called "the most costly exhibition in Europe". In Adair's company he once heard Sheridan, Pitt, Fox, and Burke speak at one sitting.

Pitt had a magnificent voice. Fox screeched and screamed. Sheridan was splendid. But Burke was the finest of all—yet with the House quite inattentive. Somebody said "There gets up that great fool, Wilberforce"—and he was a very mild-spoken man.

He was enabled to command a seat in the reporters' gallery when he pleased, and it seemed that he had only to write a few trenchant letters to the press and to pay court through Adair to leading Whig politicians, before he took his place on the floor of the House to pursue the career befitting a country gentleman of fortune.

Such a career, as Parr commended, seemed well suited to Landor's tastes and abilities. In Parliament he might have advanced his liberal ideas and satisfied his conscience by forcing his opinions upon the attention of legislators instead of burying them in neglected poems and pamphlets. During recess he might have divided his leisure between estate business and his taste for letters and classical study—even writing a history of England in Latin, which Parr suggested as a labour of love!

But such a career would have exacted a settled routine and a disciplined division of interests, of which he was temperamentally incapable. He was a creature of impulse; as impulse prompted his movements at a moment's notice, so he concentrated all his energies in pursuit of a momentary fancy. Want of money always sent him to Warwick; as soon as he received his allowance, he went either to London by direction of conscience, or to Wales from inclination, moving as impulsively from either place on visits to friends. Much of his correspondence bears re-directions; it is common to find letters to him with two or three postmarks.

During the four years following the publication of *Gebir*, he was much in London. He met neither Coleridge nor Southey, whose struggling circumstances excluded them from the fashionable Whig society which Landor entered with Dr. Parr's introductions. He dined regularly with the independent liberal politician, Sir Francis Burdett, "never liked him much, he being always querulous". He often met Sir James Mackintosh, most eminent of Whig journalists, then in close correspondence with Parr, and found his scholarship defective. One morning at breakfast with Parr in London, Mackintosh spoke of the *anabásis*.

"Very right, Jemmy! very right!" chuckled Parr. "It is anabásis with you, but anábasis with me and Walter Landor."

In embarrassment Landor protested (which was not quite true) "that I did not know it until then", but his courteous intention was rewarded by "a punch of the elbow under the rib, and the interjection of *lying dog*!"

At the same breakfast were a pupil of Parr's named Hargrave, and Joseph Jekyll, one of the most celebrated wits and men about town of the generation between Selwyn and Theodore Hook. Landor "went at that time into very grand company", and when he returned to Warwick with empty pockets, his family sneered at his fraternising with fashionable society. One of them who wanted "to put him down" once said:

"Well, we hear you know Tom Paine—Citizen Paine we suppose you call him with your ideas."

"To persons with *your* ideas," replied Landor, "I call him *Mister* Paine."

He met Tom Paine at a dinner, "his face blotched and his hand unsteady with the wine he took". When the host had given him a glass of brandy, "he talked very well; an acute reasoner, in fact a monstrous clever man". He met Mrs. Siddons "once or twice" at the house of the last Duchess of Ancaster; she was "a mighty pompous woman, mighty pompous—but wonderful on the stage". He knew her notoriously pompous brother, John Philip Kemble, who ruled the London stage with majesty uninspired by genius between Garrick and Kean. Through Kemble he met the great French actor, Talma, with whom he had a discussion of dramatic poetry so remarkable that, more than twenty years later, he incorporated his memories of it in his imaginary conversation with the Abbé Delille, whom he also met at this time as a political refugee from France. To Talma he remarked that "he didn't see how they managed in France to break the necks of all their verses so well, and that French poetry had a villainous metre!" Even if he knew that Talma was a fervent admirer of Shakespeare and outspoken in his preference for English blank verse to the French rhymed tragedy, the expression of this opinion to the distinguished Frenchman lacked the courtesy for which Landor was admired in later life; with youthful inexperience he spontaneously expressed his opinions and feelings, and the charm of ingenuousness was often obscured by the effect of wounding susceptibilities and seeming arrogant. Against himself he related an anecdote illustrating his regardlessness for other people's reactions. When their housekeeper at Warwick fell ill and his sister Elizabeth asked about her symptoms, the old lady replied, "Oh Lord, I've got such a beating of the heart, Miss, that I can hear it the other side of the room." His sister repeated this to Landor, who laughed uproariously and asked, "How could you keep from laughing?" "Why," she replied, "I did almost laugh out, but I don't always laugh in people's faces, as you do, Walter."

According to his brother Robert, he was as ready to take as to give offence; "some slight interruption, even a smile, was provocation enough, if there were many witnesses present at the controversy". But members of his own family were Landor's most unsympathetic critics. Robert related how Landor once rushed from Parr's table when "his anger was provoked by a Warwick physician whom he met there—a Dr. Winthrop—who felt astonished at the offence he had given", but he indicated neither the nature of the offence nor the character of Dr. Winthrop. In *The Dun Cow*—a lampoon attributed to Landor— Winthrop was satirised as too prudently respectful of Lord Warwick and as pretending to judgment of taste and manners, so possibly he had ventured to deplore Landor's taste and manners in presuming to attack Lord Warwick as the local Tory potentate.

Sometimes Landor's arrogance became insolence. As late as 1812 he informed Southey grandly, "At Parr's I converse only with Parr"; describing the Rev. Robert Fellowes as "a person I often met at Parr's", he declared, "I never exchanged a syllable with him." The genial Parr's tolerance of such discourtesy to his guests and of such disregard for his host's feelings emphasises his esteem of Landor, but Parr's esteem was unlikely to be shared by Landor's fellow-guests. If the Rev. William Beloe met Landor at Parr's, he may have had reason to welcome his contributor's attack on *Gebir* in the *British Critic*; the Rev. Robert Fellowes revealed his resentment by repeating to Anna Seward the "ill-natured gossip" that only the author of such a poem as *Gebir* could have written its favourable notice in the *Critical Review*.

Known as "the Swan of Lichfield", Anna Seward reigned as literary queen in Staffordshire society and Landor's Rugeley aunts attended her court. She praised some immature verses in Landor's *Poems* of 1795 and expressed a wish to meet their author, but Landor refused to meet her. Possibly he shrank from listening to her affected compliments in the presence of members of his family, whom he suspected of eagerness "to put him down"; at least he was proved wiser than Walter Scott, who, having been persuaded reluctantly to meet Miss Seward, received as a legacy—on her death in 1809—the "penance" of "submitting to edit her posthumous poetry, most of which" he found "absolutely execrable". Unfortunately, as Landor himself related to Southey, "in reply to her courtesy I said what she never should have heard, that 'I preferred a pretty woman to a literary one'." Somehow Miss Seward heard of the remark, and thereafter ardently repeated to others such gossip about Landor as she received from the Rev. Fellowes. Thirteen years after Landor's offence he read the tale of malice in the six volumes of her letters published in 1811; explaining its origin to Southey he remarked angrily that he was not surprised she preferred his juvenile verses to *Gebir*—"they were more like her own".

Confiding to Walter Birch in 1819 his plans for his son's education, Landor declared his intention to keep him "always among women, that he may be desirous of pleasing, and learn a gracefulness and ease of manners which few Englishmen, educated in England, can acquire". For, he said, "I remember the grossness and repulsiveness of my own manners, and am conscious how much I still retain of those truly British qualities". Intellectually precocious from childhood, in manners he matured slowly. Chivalry he learned in a hard school as lover of a married woman; his caricature as Boythorn shows that he never abated his impetuosity in expressing opinion. A friend of his youth, Major Tickell (a descendant of the poet who was Addison's friend), years afterwards wondered that Landor should have lived so long:

We were occasional guests at the same public table at Bath two winters, where there were other military men; and if I had talked as he talked, there would have been half-a-dozen bullets through my body if the first five had been insufficient.

Quoting Tickell's remark to Forster, Robert Landor commented that his brother escaped a challenge in those days of duelling only because "his character became known for extravagance, and sometimes chiefly through the interposition of such friends as the major". But Robert ignored the point of Tickell's conditional clause, "if I had talked as he talked": firstly, Tickell's brother officers would have tolerated from a civilian expressions that would have sounded unseemly from a wearer of their uniform;[1] secondly, Tickell "felt much esteem" for Landor and may have intended the inference that Landor was forgiven much on account of qualities to which Tickell himself made no pretensions.

Arrogantly ignoring people in whom he felt no interest, he generally chose his friends with discrimination, and his friendships were lasting. He was loyal, and generous in appreciation of his friends' compensating virtues. At Parr's he met at least one man besides his host with whom he condescended to converse. Bertie Greatheed, the wealthy owner of Guy's Cliff, near Warwick, was a generation older than Landor and valued by Parr as a man of parts. He wrote a play called *The Regent*, successfully produced at Drury Lane with Mrs. Siddons in the lead, but one of George III's mental lapses compelled Pitt to bring in a regency bill and it was deemed prudent in the public interest to withdraw a play on a subject too dangerously topical. An enlightened liberal, he supported the established church but advocated tolerance, including emancipation for Roman Catholics; in politics he followed Fox and Grey in sympathising with the principles of the French Revolution. He

---

[1] In his *Reminiscences and Recollections* Captain Gronow relates many anecdotes of military duelling at the period of Waterloo, but the causes of quarrels were usually women, gambling, or drunken behaviour—never in a single instance difference of opinion on politics.

was selected to second Sir John Throckmorton's motion of the Warwick-shire Whigs' petition against Pitt's budget proposals of December 1797, and apparently cherished a high opinion of his own importance locally, for Landor wrote in 1802 to correct his brother Henry's "wrong opinion of Mr. Greatheed":

> He is vain, but he is not corrupt. He has a sense of glory and a certain pride, which may make him wish to seem the rival of Lord Warwick, but would not suffer him to be the tool or even the co-partner. He is vext and he *sulks*, that is all. He could not be so silly as to imagine that Lord Warwick would bring him in. On a suspicion of such a wish, all those friends whose assistance must at last do the business, would revolt against him.

This letter was written when Landor's brother Henry, having completed two or three years in the office of a London conveyancer, was beginning practice on his own account at Warwick as an attorney and land agent. While serving his articles in London, Henry met William Rough, a young barrister who, on being appointed to the midland circuit, received letters of introduction from Henry to members of his family and to Dr. Lambe, Dr. Landor's successor in his medical practice. Robert Landor said of Rough that he "never met with any one who had so little reserve. In about an hour I had become acquainted with all his prospects, literary and professional". Ebullient and eloquent, Rough had plenty of talent, but too little sycophancy and too much humour for success in the legal profession. Prosecuting a thief who had stolen a drake, he was repeatedly corrected in court for calling the bird a duck; afterwards his junior, J. S. Copley (who acceded to the woolsack as Lord Lyndhurst), explained that there was the same difference between a duck and a drake as between a bull and a cow, and if a bull had been stolen, it would be so described and not as a cow, but Rough still maintained that there was no material difference. Robert Landor regarded such flippant perversity as "characteristic both of Rough's habits and of his future fortune". He was full of ambitious projects, but enjoyed life too thoroughly to concentrate on their fulfilment—he was always "so busy that he did nothing".

Though "he did equal justice to his own", Rough gave "ample credit to the pretensions of other people"; an "intense admirer" of *Gebir*, he wrote a tragedy, *The Conspiracy of Gowrie*, which Southey considered a "manifest imitation" of Landor's poem. "My brother repaid his admiration; for in such duties he was never ungrateful," wrote Robert Landor sourly. "Hence their very ardent friendship...." For three or four years Rough and Landor were close friends; they shared the same political views as well as literary tastes, and before his marriage with an illegitimate daughter of the demagogue John Wilkes—"attracted rather by the father's celebrity than the daughter's beauty",

according to Robert Landor—Rough also shared Landor's suscepti-
bility to gallantry, for he once proposed to travel a hundred miles by
stage coach to a Christmas ball for the pleasure of dancing with Dr.
Parr's daughter, whom he had never seen. On his marriage he wrote
affectionately to Landor, assuring him that his wife was "fully disposed
to welcome you as the most valued of her husband's friends". But the
friendship ended abruptly soon after Rough's marriage: "either Rough
had smiled at a false argument," reported Robert Landor to Forster,
"or interrupted my brother in some other way, before several guests,
whereupon Walter left his house and renounced his acquaintance."
Robert was more concerned with excusing his own quarrels with his
brother than with explaining the cause of Landor's breach with Rough,
which was momentous enough for Landor to write twenty-six years
later, in reply to his sister Ellen's news of Rough:

As for that impostor Rough, I never hear the fellow mentioned without
some fresh contempt. My friend Sir Charles Wentworth was at school
with him, and related to me many anecdotes of his shabbiness and cowardice.
However, if he had continued to cultivate poetry, instead of those thistles
called law, he would have been perhaps the best poet of the age.

While the friendship lasted, Rough often offered counsel conflicting
with the character for levity attributed to him by Robert Landor. In
May 1802, when Landor wrote from Bath of the despondency and
insomnia he was suffering as a result of a frustrated romance, Rough
replied from the Inner Temple:

Come, come, rouse yourself and write. If you must die, it is at least your
duty to leave something behind you; and though *Gebir* will do much, yet I
am persuaded it is in your power to do still more. Literature, like other
things, as often obtains the reward of praise by quantity as quality; and we
are all of us so little important to others, that unless we put them in mind
of us daily, we shall scarcely avoid being forgotten. It is strange that you
should be so insensible to the advantages you possess as you seem to be. *I* am
hourly rating my hard fate, that compels me to pursue a profession in which
Letters rather impede than assist, and in which I am forced to exert much
benevolence to save me from despising most of my co-labourers. You, on
the other hand, are at liberty to move whithersoever inclination leads—
with a more than adequate competence now, and with an assurance of a
richer fortune in years to come; with the possession not merely of the love,
but the power, of intellect; with the consciousness that you are pursuing
that which such beings as Homer, Virgil, and Milton have cultivated before
you; and with a chance of gaining the reward which they have gained.

Landor was well reminded that *Gebir* represented only a foundation
stone for a reputation still to be built. He was annoyed nearly half a
century later when De Quincey—in 1847—wrote that *Gebir* "had the
sublime distinction, for some time, of having enjoyed only two readers;
which two were Southey and myself". But, outside a narrow literary

circle, De Quincey must have sought vainly for another reader of the poem. *Gebir* enjoyed the good fortune of one favourable notice—from an anonymous writer in the *Critical Review* who proved to be Robert Southey. Though his article may have persuaded no more than half a dozen readers to look up the poem, Southey repeatedly commended it to his friends. In September 1799 he wrote to Coleridge's Bristol publisher, Cottle:

> There is a poem called *Gebir*, of which I know not whether my review be yet printed (in the Critical), but in that review you will find some of the most exquisite poetry in the language. . . . I would go an hundred miles to see the anonymous author.

Three months later he informed his friend Grosvenor Bedford, "There is a poem called *Gebir*, written by God knows who, sold for a shilling; it has miraculous beauties." He recommended it to William Taylor of Norwich as "the miraculous work of a madman", and on leaving for Lisbon in the following spring, told Coleridge that the only books he was taking to read on the voyage "were your poems, the Lyrics, the Lyrical Ballads, and Gebir", adding, "I like Gebir more and more; if you ever meet its author, tell him I took it with me on a voyage." On the boat he "read Gebir again", and found "he grows upon me"; in the preface to his *Thalaba*, he acknowledged an indebtedness to *Gebir* for a strengthening of his own verse; when Humphry Davy expressed admiration for *The Conspiracy of Gowrie*, he declared Rough's play "an imitation of Gebir", exclaiming, "How could you compare this man's book with Rough's? The lucid passages of *Gebir* are all palpable to the eye; they are the master-touches of a painter; there is power in them, and passion, and thought, and knowledge."

Southey's opinion carried weight with his friends. So did Parr's with his vast acquaintance, and Parr publicised Landor in the terms that he wrote on the fly-leaf of his copy of the Latinised *Gebir*—"the work of a scholar and a poet". Rough's advice was sound: if Landor had quickly followed *Gebir* with work of comparable quality, he might have acquired one of those little cliques of admirers that nourish the bud of reputation. Political opponents were prepared to offer publicity in abuse; he wrote to Parr when the *Anti-Jacobin Review* in February 1804 "assailed me with much virulence" as "a coward and a profligate", "Thank God, I have a mind more alive to kindness than to contumely", and consoled himself with "the example of Mr. Lemuel Gulliver, who, when the Lilliputians climbed and crept over him, forbore that contention which a more equal or a more formidable enemy would have aroused". Opposition journals might have welcomed a smart retort, but Landor neglected the publicity value of controversy.

His next publication—two years after *Gebir*—was little calculated to increase his reputation. Seeing an announcement of *Poems from the Arabic and Persian; with Notes by the Author of Gebir*, Southey remarked plaintively, "Can there possibly be Arabic and Persian poetry which the author of *Gebir* may be excused for translating?" As he stated in his preface, Landor was "ignorant of both these languages", and of translations "the few that I ever have met with are *chiefly* the odes of Hafez". These he found in the poems of Sir William Jones, a friend of Parr's who died in 1794, and in *Select Odes from the Persian Poet Hafiz*, translated into English verse by John Nott, a copy of which his father must have possessed, as the list of subscribers to that work, published in 1787, includes "Landor—M.D. Warwick". Jones's preface of 1772 declared his belief that "a writer, acquainted with the originals, might imitate them very happily in his native tongue", and when a friend remarked that "he should be glad to see how any one would succeed in an attempt to imitate them", Landor elected to imitate—not the originals—but the imitations by Jones and Nott.

His preface and notes also parodied the manner of Jones, whose preface suggested the means of passing off the poems as true imitations. Jones excused himself from citing his sources, as those ignorant of the languages might suppose that he had forged even the originals for his purpose, though "so many productions, invented in France, have been offered to the public as genuine translations from the languages of Asia, that I should have wished, for my own sake, to clear my publication from the slightest suspicion of imposture". Landor therefore implied that he was offering versions of French translations, "and as these translations have afforded *some* pleasure to those who have read them, though perhaps no language is less capable than the French of transmitting with adequate spirit the charms of original poetry", he excused himself from discussing whether they originated from Egypt or from France. His imitations successfully imposed upon Parr, and a belated notice in the *Monthly Review* of July 1804 saw "little reason to doubt that these poems are of Arabic and Persian origin".

Even this purely poetical hoax could not pass without political allusion. "At a time when the total slavery, or the total emancipation, of mankind, are the objects of cold indifference, or of mere conversational curiosity," observed Landor's preface, "it is barely possible that supineness will be awakened by the feeble echo of a foreign song." And to the poems he appended what purported to be an "Extract from the French Preface", praising the policy of Napoleon Buonaparte in encouraging the arts and science in Egypt and other countries he had conquered. "Conquerors like him, posterity will declare it, have never been the enemies of the human race"; not such commanders, but "the bestial stupidity of those, who, unfortunately for kingdoms, are exalted *above their minds*, and cannot distinguish, from their ridiculous elevation, *a battle from a review*[1] . . . should be execrated" and "extirpated". The "extract" concluded with an apostrophe bitterly ironical only two years later:

> May the general remember, in the plenitude of his power, that many have been the masters, few the deliverers of men. Who would be an imitator when he possibly might fail, instead of an original when he surely must succeed? Who would be a Cæsar that could be a Buonaparte? The republic never can suspect, that the conqueror of kings will reduce himself to their level: she relies on *his* magnanimity and does not distrust *her own*.

Landor's attitude to Napoleon as first consul may be compared with Bernard Shaw's to Mussolini at the time of *The Apple Cart* (1930) and of the *Preface on Bosses* (1936), but Shaw was writing in time of peace.

Like *Gebir*, *Poems from the Arabic and Persian* was printed by Sharpe of Warwick in a pamphlet to be sold at 1s. 6d. by Rivingtons, but apparently Rivingtons refused to handle copies containing the treasonable "Extract from the French Preface", which was omitted from copies bearing their name on the title page. Landor afterwards stated that only "a hundred copies were printed for friends".

Poems from the Arabic and Persian appeared in May or June 1800, and during the same year Sharpe printed a larger pamphlet, uniform with *Gebir*, entitled *Poetry by the Author of Gebir: and A Postscript to that Poem, with Remarks on some Critics*. Printing was delayed while Landor looked up an imitation of Montaigne which he had attributed to Pope but found in Swift, and further delayed by protests from friends who saw the proofs. "An Address to the Fellows of Trinity College Oxford, on the Alarm of Invasion" had presumably been written at the time of the invasion scare in the winter of 1796–97; Walter Birch argued that the fun at the expense of the Trinity dons had lost effect from being no longer topical, and the satire was therefore offensive without being amusing. Probably Birch also advised suppression of the satirical verses referring to Carlton House and the "comedy" of the Prince of Wales's marriage, those addressed to the Rev. George Richards and obliquely calling George III "that silly man", and the quatrain on a cleric's wedding—possibly Richards's:

> Blest idiot! with thy vicarage and thy wife,
>   Why dost thou chuckle so? come prythee say?
> Then I will tell thee—thou hast gain'd for life,
>   To be awake all night, asleep all day.

---

[1] Discussing the character of George III in his *Commentary on Memoirs of Mr. Fox*, 1812, Landor wrote: "He loved the bustle and dust of a review, and fancied a battle was quite as fine a thing"; in the imaginary conversation between Bishop Shipley and Benjamin Franklin, first published in 1837, Franklin says, "I believe *your* king . . . to be as honest and as wise a man as any of those about him: but unhappily he can see no difference between a review and a battle."

The *Postscript to Gebir* was suppressed at the request of another friend, Isaac Mocatta. This was intended mainly as a reply to the critic of *Gebir* in the *Monthly Review*, who, having shrewdly recognised the Miltonic influence, accused Landor of "borrowing the expressions" and making "the most awkward attempts to imitate the phraseology of Milton". Admitting his admiration for Milton, Landor challenged the reviewer to cite the borrowings; he pointed out that he had attempted simplicity, condensation, and "the softened air of remote antiquity, not the severe air of unapproachable sanctity" prevailing in *Paradise Lost*. Losing his dignity by inviting his critic to produce any contemporary English poem "and point out three pages more spirited, I will venture to add more classical, than the three least happy and least accurate in *Gebir*", he tried to retrieve his position by apologising that "if my rights had not been refused me, I should not have asserted my claims".

Rambling by the side of the sea, or resting on the top of a mountain, and interlining with verses the letters of my friends, I sometimes thought how a Grecian would have written, but never what methods he would take to compass popularity . . . Several of these sketches were obliterated, still more laid aside and lost; various ideas I permitted to pass away, unwilling to disturb, by the slightest action, the dreams of reposing fancy. So little was I anxious to publish my rhapsodies, that I never sate down in the house, an hour at once, for the purpose of composition . . . Far from soliciting the attention of those who are passing by, *Gebir* is confined, I believe, to the shop of one bookseller, and I never heard that he had even made his appearance at the window.

After apt comment on the "general language" of reviewers (*e.g.* "this volume possesses *considerable* merit"), he illustrated the shades of difference between plagiarism, imitation, and allusion, with examples of how Pope had borrowed ideas from Montaigne, Strada, and Phineas Fletcher, Racine from Godeau and Æschylus, and each moulded the ideas into original effects of their own inspiration. He then digressed into characteristic invective: "In France and Germany, men of talents are received with cordiality by their brethren—In England, if their brethren look upon them, it is with grudging eye. . . . There it is thought that *genius* and *wit* enhance the national glory—in England, the acquisition of sugar and slaves." Further digression led to just criticism of Johnson, whose *Lives of the Poets* include "several whose productions would hardly gain admittance in the corner of a provincial newspaper", and whose want of discrimination suggests "that, in his estimation, Collins and Gray are no higher than Addison and Pomfret". Returning to consideration of living critics, he selected for attack the then anonymous author of *The Pursuits of Literature*, T. J. Matthias, and Isaac D'Israeli. Before discussing his romances, he rebuked D'Israeli for claiming Italian descent and for taking "the greatest pains to conceal the evidence of the religion in which he was educated".

He is one of the children of Israel, nevertheless, as is also announced by the name D'Israeli. I mark this circumstance not by way of reproach, for in the number of my acquaintances there is none more valuable, there is not one more lively, more inquiring, more regular, there is not one more virtuous, more beneficent, more liberal, more tender in heart and more true in friendship, than my friend Mocatta—he also is a Jew—and . . . I see no important differences in religions if they produce the same effects.

Evidently intent upon a pretext for expressing disdain of prevailing racial and religious prejudice, Landor must have blushed in later life for the indelicacy and condescension of the reference to Mocatta. He referred the passage to Mocatta, who asked to see a proof of the whole pamphlet and persuaded him to suppress the *Postscript*, which, apart from its errors of taste, dissipated the energy of its thrusts in a discursiveness foreign to Landor's style in dialectic.

Mocatta, like Parr, provides an example of Landor's ability to inspire affection and esteem in men of an older generation. Of liberal political opinions, he neither shared Landor's republicanism nor saw the salvation of French democracy in the rise of its first consul; a refined scholar, he appreciated Landor's talents but foresaw that his work must always appeal to a limited audience. "Are you not too profound and classical for most readers?" he asked, when writing on 5th December 1800 to thank Landor for "suppressing the *Postscript to Gebir* which gave me so much pain". Probably at Rough's suggestion, Landor was thinking of writing a play, but Mocatta warned him that "a tragedy replete with sentiments such as you could not help to infuse, would not be received by the manager or sanctioned by the Lord Chamberlain"; he believed his "talents equal to the greatest undertaking", but dreaded "that impetuosity which disdains those minor niceties of language which are yet necessary to show where the narrative stands and what is going on".

Mocatta died in the summer of 1801. He left some books and a statuette of Prometheus to Landor, who endorsed the letter notifying him of the bequest, "I never knew a better or wiser man, or one more friendly."

4

THE LOVES AND THE GRACES

Ah who could believe in the days of his youth,
    When Bath was the gayest of places,
When time had not ravisht a friend or a tooth,
    And he walkt with the Loves and the Graces!—

When Tyson was ruler o'er pleasure's wide realm,
    When the sun she was warm'd by ne'er set,
And Sotheby held the poetical helm,
    Such another, as Rogers is yet—

Ah who could believe, O my dearly beloved!
    That the ardor of passion will cool,
That he ever can look upon beauty unmoved,
    Unmoved upon gooseberry-fool!
                    —High and Low Life in Italy (1837–38)

We both are young; and yet we have seen several who loved us pass away; and we never can live over again as we lived before. A portion of our lives is consumed by the torch we follow at their funerals. We enter into another state of existence, resembling indeed and partaking of the former, but another! it contains the substance of the same sorrows, the shadow of the same joys.

                        —Pericles and Aspasia (1836)

Landor lived with Nancy Jones at Swansea "till the birth of a Child". If the child was that Anne Jones who died at nine months old in May 1796, he continued to visit the mother long after her baby's death, though she reproached him for long and frequent absences.

    The poor tired bird, who fain would drink,
    But fears th' abrupt and crumbling brink,
    Sees that his weight 'twill not sustain,
    And hovers, and flies back again.
    My Nancy, thus I thirst for you,
    And he flies off, as I may do.

Nancy may not have been Neæra in the lines "To Neæra" printed in the pamphlet of 1800 with the *Postscript to Gebir*, for Nancy's poetical name of Ione would have scanned as well as Ianthe, which Landor substituted for Neæra when, reprinting the poem in 1846, he liked to nourish the illusion that all his amatory verse was inspired by Ianthe.

> Thank heaven, Neæra, once again
>   Our hands and ardent lips shall meet,
> And Pleasure, to assert his reign,
>   Scatter ten thousand kisses sweet:
> Then cease repeating, while you mourn,
>   "*I wonder when he will return.*"

Visiting Fleetwood Parkhurst at Ripple Court, he became romantically attached to a girl at Malvern, who, like Nancy, died young. He kept her letters till 1855, when he wrote, "I felt great pity, no great love, for this lady, long since dead," but the lines "Written at Malvern, June 1799" expressed more love than pity:

> If I might ask the Powers above
> One gift, that gift should be her love.
>   Hush! thou unworthy creature, hush!
> Wouldst thou not rather see her, then,
> Without her love, in health agen?
>   I pause; I bow my head, and blush.

At least once he pursued a courtship to the verge of marriage, for, at the time of Rough's wedding, he wrote to his brother Henry:

This time year, too, I was to have been married. But, after committing a piece of foolery in which I was the puppet, the farce concluded. But what can it signify? I can only be sixty thousand pounds the poorer.

He was jilted for a title—if the lady is to be identified with the heroine of verses published discreetly long afterwards in 1838:

> Now, if perchance she sees me pass,
> Raises her chin and then her glass,
> Stares at me, bows, looks gracious-grand,
> Drives on and half uncurls her hand!
> We both were younger: I am yet
> What tenderer bosoms scarce forget;
> She shines, with coronetted pannel
> And husband mummified in flannel,
> Among the haridans and hacks
> Who spread their tanneries at Almack's.

Finding among Landor's papers four lines of verse dated 1801, Stephen Wheeler wondered if they might refer to this affair:

I would not see thee weep but there are hours
When smiles may be less beautiful than tears,
Some of those smiles, some of those tears were ours;
Ah! why should either now give place to fears?

This frustrated romance seems to have followed closely upon Nancy's death, for it was in May 1802 that Landor complained to Rough of his "sleepless nights" and Rough cajoled him to rouse himself and write—"If you must die, it is at least your duty to leave something behind you."

Landor was then at Bath, but he may have courted his heiress at Oxford, for he was often there during 1801. His brother Robert was in residence at Worcester College, where he took his degree that summer and was elected to a fellowship. However little his other brothers and sisters had to thank him for, there is ample evidence that Landor behaved for some fourteen years as an affectionate elder brother to "Robin". When they eventually quarrelled, they held no communication for sixteen years and Robert displayed the capacity for nursing a grudge which he imputed to Landor as a fault. When both were elderly, Landor made a gesture of reconciliation, but Robert responded coldly; in his reminiscences of his brother quoted by Forster —though he wrote as a very old man and a parson—the quality of charity is not strained.

Robert Landor was a Jesuit lost to the army of Loyola. He was a politician by instinct, and aware of preoccupations ill becoming his cloth, conscience made him secretive about his devices. "What is Robert doing that he does not write to me," demanded Landor of their mother in 1808, and three years later he wrote to their sister Elizabeth, "Bless Robin! What is he plotting at Oxford?" In 1820 Robert contributed to the *Courier* pseudonymous letters containing a libel on Queen Caroline, and declined to come forward as the author when the newspaper was prosecuted. Hints in letters suggest that he freely practised anonymous journalism from his undergraduate days till the date of the "Laternarius" letters in the *Courier*; it is now generally recognised that he wrote in 1808 the scurrilous *Guy's Porridge Pot*, which was widely ascribed to his eldest brother. Though he assured Forster that he advised Landor against obscure publication of his work, he himself published *The Count Arezzi* and *The Impious Feast* with minor publishers, the former anonymously. In 1846 he published *The Fawn of Sertorius* anonymously, though he had previously set his name to *The Impious Feast* and *The Earl of Brecon*; when the book was praised by reviewers as the work of his famous brother, Robert avowed the authorship, the remainder of the edition bearing his name on the title-page. His biographer thought his conduct showed "that he scorned the possible advantages of silence when silence implied a lie", but the anonymity of *The Fawn of Sertorius* curiously achieved the same result as was achieved twenty-two years before by the anonymity of *The Count Arezzi*, which some reviewers ascribed to Byron—in both cases publicity accrued from speculation on the authorship.

His biographer describes Robert as "a high Tory" in politics, but Robert himself told Forster that he was known at Oxford as "Citizen Landor", while "Walter was a black Jacobin". Walter Birch was then a tutor at Oxford, and together the brothers enjoyed shocking Birch's Toryism and what Landor called his "maidenly modesty". "But Birch loved Walter and smiled at me," wrote Robert; "Birch often checked Walter's extravagant language by his laughter; and once he asked me how it could have happened that my brother should have met accidentally so many ladies, in an evening's walk or two with him and me, every one of whom was incomparably the most beautiful creature whom he had ever seen? how each of twenty fools could be by much the greatest fool upon earth? and, above all, how Mr. Pitt could be the greatest rascal living, if Mr. Canning surpassed Mr. Pitt, and Lord Castlereagh surpassed Mr. Canning, and all three were infinitely exceeded as brutes and fools by their gracious sovereign king George the Third?"

Landor's contempt for both politicians and the proletariat as "brutes and fools" intensified when he visited Paris in August 1802. After the Peace of Amiens many of the extreme Whigs took this opportunity of visiting the country which they believed—as the English Labour Party believed of Russia a hundred and twenty years later—to be practising the principles of social liberty that they themselves advocated. Charles James Fox went—to be courteously received by Napoleon and to be entertained at government direction by the beautiful Madame Tallien. Landor might have had from Adair introductions to eminent republicans, including the second consul Cambacérès and the minister of war, Berthier, but he preferred to incur no obligations.

His first impressions were not encouraging. After being delayed a day on the road, he stayed at an hotel where there was no fire in any of its sixty rooms, and he had to put on his shirt "as damp as a newspaper from the press".

Lodgings are three times as dear as in London. I give four livres a night for a miserable bedroom, besides which I have another poor brick-floor apartment for a guinea—louis—a week. It has cost me six or eight shillings a day on an average for coach hire, having been completely laid up with a swelling on the ancle, which however, I do not think was gout, & which I have now removed by bathing in cold water.

He visited Versailles and the Petit Trianon, and spent "three or four hours every day in the gallery of pictures". The Tory press had made much of Buonaparte's plundering Italy of its art treasures, but Landor assured his brother Henry that not a quarter of the pictures he saw were "the spoils of Italy".

Many were brought from the King's palace, and many were the property of rich emigrants. The number of statues brought recently from Italy does not exceed seventy four, while those belonging to the palaces and gardens are at least five hundred, not including those which are of bronze.

He found that the pillaging of mansions by the mob had been much exaggerated; "the religious houses alone have suffered by the revolution and these in general not much".

In a letter to his sister Elizabeth on 13th August he described his first sight of Buonaparte.

I stood within six or eight yards of him nearly a quarter of an hour. His countenance is not of that fierce cast which you see in the prints, & which perhaps it may assume in battle. He seems melancholy and reserved, but not morose or proud. . . . He rode a little white horse, about the size of my father's, and cantered up and down six or eight lines of military drawn out in the Court of the Tuileries, which is about the size of Lincolns-Inn-fields. Each line lowered its colours as he passed and he took off his hat in return. The French are not mightily civil, and one cannot much wonder, but I got an admirable place by a piece of well-timed flattery. After I had seen Bonaparte canter by me, at the distance of about a dozen yards, I left my situation at the window, and went down close to the gate of the palace. Presently came the Chief Consul & half a score generals. The people made room, thro fear of the horses, which indeed were fierce enough, being covered with blue or red velvet, one half of which was hid with gold lace. Instead of going with the crowd, I pushed forward & got by the side of Buonaparte's Mamalouk, in a place where there were none but soldiers. There was a very tall fellow just before me. I begged him to let me see Buonaparte, and observed that probably *he* had seen him often and shared his victories. The youth was delighted. Ah le voila, Monsieur, said he and in a moment there was nothing between me and this terror of Europe, but the backs of two horses over which I could see him as distinctly as I see this paper.

This was the occasion he remembered sixty years later, when he told Kate Field that Buonaparte "was exceedingly handsome then, with a rich olive complexion and oval face, youthful as a girl's", and how "near him rode Murat, mounted upon a gold-clad charger; and very handsome he was too, but coxcombical".

He saw Buonaparte again a few days later, on "the most important day since the commencement of the revolution".

The palace of Government, the Metropolitan church, the arches of the bridges, the bridges themselves and all the public edifices were illuminated most magnificently. In the garden of the Tuilleries there were several hundred pyramids of wood, about twenty-five feet high covered with the most brilliant lamps . . . There was not a statue nor an orange tree of which you could not distinguish the minutest part.

He noted that, in spite of all this lavish display by the authorities, "the private houses were no more illuminated than usual" and shops lighted merely with two lamps instead of one. When Buonaparte appeared on the palace balcony, beside his wife and the other two consuls:

I expected that the sky would have been rent with acclamations; on the contrary he experienced such a reception as was experienced by Richard the Third. He was sensibly mortified. He bowed, but he waved to & fro, and often wiped his face with his handkerchief. He retired in about ten minutes.

Witnessing the scene, Landor recognised the sham of a ruthless autocracy masquerading as representative of the will of the people; realising that all his beliefs since boyhood were illusory, he felt hatred for the nation which had betrayed his ideals and for the militarist who sponsored the betrayal. In the *Commentary on Memoirs of Mr. Fox* he wrote:

The French lately were free, as much as any people so light and ignorant can ever be. Two men of transcendent abilities, Cambacérès and Talleyrand, men unrestrained by any sense of religion or any principle of morality, have instructed a soldier of fortune how to govern and keep that people in subjection. Under his vast encampment—such is France—these harpies devour the prey they have collected. . . . No man ever was so well formed to govern France as Bonaparte. He had associated in person with the vilest, the most unprincipled, and the most turbulent. He was chosen to fill his office as thief-takers are chosen for theirs: from knowing the haunts and habits of the abandoned and desperate.

Henceforth he echoed Alfieri's maxim that "nothing good ever came out of France, or ever will", and his loathing of Napoleon was unabated in his old age when he felt the same loathing for his nephew. When he was annoying Mrs. Browning in 1859 by his vituperation of Napoleon III, he described "this wretch and his uncle" as "the two greatest scourges of Italy".

Returning from the Tuileries to his lodgings, he vented his feelings in a letter to his brother Henry.

Doubtless the government of Buonaparte is the best that can be contrived for Frenchmen. Monkeys must be chained, tho it may cost them some grimaces. If you have read attentively the last senatus consultum, you will find that not an atom of liberty is left. This people, the most inconstant, and therefore the most contemptible in the world, seem'd to have recovered their senses when they had lost their freedom. The idol is beyond their reach, but the idolatry has vanished. . . . A consul of so great a genius will make the nation formidable to all the earth but England, but I hope there is no danger of any one imitating its example. As to the cause of liberty, this cursed nation has ruined it for ever.

He did not prolong his stay at Paris. Long afterwards, he said he returned home "at the end of the year", and he remembered Madame Tallien, Madame Récamier, and Napoleon's sister Pauline as three of the most beautiful women he saw at Paris. Most of his letters to his brother Henry relate to money matters, and he had previously written to ask his brother to undertake the delicate business of requesting their father "to advance me twenty pounds of my next quarter's revenue".

"My pocket begins to wax feeble. One cannot travel in France or live at Paris for a little. They know an Englishman every where. . . ."

Verses "To Antinöe in Paris, 1802" suggest some such adventure in Paris as befalls bachelors of twenty-seven less susceptible than Landor. Antinöe came from the Auvergne, and Landor informed his brother Henry that he wished to join some friends who were travelling next month from Paris to Switzerland—"if my mother would lend me a hundred pounds, this would make all the difference between travelling comfortably and uncomfortably". Apparently his mother refused the loan, for, on collecting his Latin poems in 1847, Landor thus described how he completed the Latin version of *Gebir*:[1] "On the day after that on which Bonaparte was proclaimed *Consul for Life*, I withdrew from Paris to the *Petit Trianon*, and lived for two months in that part of the house where the unhappy queen had lived, walking in the gardens of which I finished the little work begun long before."

§ 2

On his return to England, Landor finally abandoned any idea of adopting a political career. If his impressions of France and its first consul left him with any hope of honesty in politics, such hope was finally dispelled when war was resumed after the short-lived Peace of Amiens. He had followed Fox as leader of the opposition against the war with France from 1793 to 1802—which he described as "a court war . . . necessary to create that danger in the midst of which all clamours for reform were to be stifled". But he never admired Fox and characteristically declined opportunities to meet the leader of his party; when Fox's biographer wrote, "The passions of the vulgar made and kept Mr. Pitt minister," Landor commented, "No, no; the vices, the profligacy, the perfidy of Mr. Fox made Mr. Pitt minister." Pitt's "court war"—as stated in the *Commentary on Memoirs of Mr. Fox*— "succeeded in nothing but in preventing the demolition of the French monarchy", since "a sense of common danger united all parties in France" under the "more formidable dynasty" of Napoleon. On the resumption of war a similar "sense of common danger" united Whig and Tory against the threat of Napoleon's military despotism; even

---

[1] Postridie ejus diei in quo Bonaparta *Consul Perpetuo* nuncupatus est, a Parisiis in *Trianonem Minorem* secessi, et eam aedium partem per duos menses habitavi quam habitaverat infelix regina, cujus deambulans in hortis opusculum diu antea inchoatum absolvi.—*Poemata et Inscriptiones*, 1847.

revolutionaries like Coleridge and Southey, who had opposed Pitt's war, now subscribed to the national emergency—though Coleridge, aware that he was sacrificing principle to support an expedient, withdrew from active political journalism. Landor also ceased to write for the Whig press and allowed his correspondence with Adair to languish, but while he hated Napoleon, he was not prepared to ignore social evils in concentrating on fear of the enemy. "Woe betide the government," he wrote in the *Commentary*, "that forces men to deliberate whether it be the more disgraceful to admit a new dynasty, with economy and peace, or to support an old establishment in irremediable corruption and in hopeless war"; and when Fox combined with Pitt in 1804 to defeat Addington's ministry—as Landor stated long afterwards in the imaginary conversation, "Florentine, English Visitor, and Landor"—"I detested his abandonment of right principles in a coalition with a minister he had just before denounced."

To state unpopular opinions in time of war is quixotry inviting persecution; to hold them with discretion exacts patient fortitude. Pride rather than prudence may have dictated Landor's measure of discretion. He would neither invite rebuffs from fools nor inflict embarrassment on friends, so he kept aloof from the fashionable world in which Parr urged him to seek a career. He did not exaggerate when stating in the *Commentary*, "No person mixes in general society so little as I do; no man has kept himself so totally detached from all factions."

In Oxford lodgings he worked on a revised edition of *Gebir*, which was printed by the Oxford firm of Slatter & Munday in 1803. *Poetry by the Author of Gebir*—omitting the *Postscript to Gebir* and the lampoons to which Walter Birch objected—was published under Rivingtons' imprint in the autumn of 1802 and noticed in the *Annual Review*, a short-lived periodical, published by Longmans and edited by Arthur Aikin. Though attributed by Landor to Aikin, the article was written by Southey. Still an admirer of *Gebir*, Southey was troubled by the comment of William Taylor of Norwich, to whom he had commended the poem: "There are exquisitely fine passages, but they succeed each other by such flea-skips of association that I am unable to track the path of the author's mind, and verily suspect him of insanity." Citing this criticism of the "flea-skips", Southey attributed the defect of obscurity in *Gebir* to excessive compression, but considered that poem lucid by comparison with *The Phocæans*—which, though only the fragment of an intended epic, was the longest poem in *Poetry by the Author of Gebir*—and concluded therefore that the author's taste had not matured in the years since publication of *Gebir*.

But *The Phocæans* was evidently written before *Gebir*. At Oxford Landor read of the Phocæans in the eighth book of Justin, and having further studied their story in Herodotus, he designed an epic on the adventures of a people who preferred to leave their native land and seek a new settlement in freedom rather than to live in subjection under their Persian conquerors. "Before the year's end I did what you see," he told Robert Browning, "and corrected it the year following." The first fragment tells how the Phocæans fled from the Persians to Iberia, seeking aid from the king of Tartessus, at whose direction a minstrel relates the history of the Tartessians as a moral example; in the second fragment the leader of the Phocæans relates their defiance of the Persian king. The story was to be completed with the Phocæans' settlement in Gaul and their foundation of the city of Marseilles—according to Landor's manuscript notes in his own copy of *Poetry by the Author of Gebir*:

> There would have been a second part of this poem, narrating a sea-fight with the Carthaginians, recorded in history; then conflicts with the natives. The main difficulty was to devise names for them. An approximation was attempted from the Welsh and Irish, many of which are harmonious in the termination, an essential in poetry. Druids, Druidesses, Bards, old oaks and capacious wicker baskets were at hand.

These materials—and the druidical atmosphere—were at hand on the beaches of South Wales, where he was pondering the problems of completing *The Phocæans* when Rose Aylmer lent him Clara Reeve's *Progress of Romance* and he saw in the story of Gebir and Charoba a more dramatic medium for the same theme—the futility of military conquest.

Probably the chief problem in finishing *The Phocæans* was how far he might safely venture in satirical allegory, for another manuscript note in his copy of the book stated that, in describing the proposed "conflicts with the High Priest of the Druids and the priests and people under his influence . . . the main difficulty lay in the fabrication of proper names for these impostors and barbarians. Anagrams would look like satire". The names of such "impostors and barbarians" as Pitt, Windham, and Archbishop Moore did not lend themselves to anagrams! In the two existing fragments parallels with contemporary politics are vague to trace, and a footnote points the sharpest stab. When an ambassador from the Chians explains that, as a subject people under the Persians, they cannot offer asylum to the fugitives, one of the Phocæans exclaims:

> Go, tell thy master, go, thou self-bound slave,
> Thou subject! soon his dreaded foe departs.

Lest the reader should suppose "that, after calling any one a *self-bound slave*, the word *subject* could hardly be used as a term of severe reproach", Landor explained, "Subjects are by convention what slaves are by compulsion: slaves are unwilling subjects, subjects are willing slaves."

In the *Story of Crysäör*, the longest complete poem in *Poetry by the Author of Gebir*, Crysäör blasphemes against the gods and is duly smitten by Neptune at Jove's behest. Following Crysäör's punishment, the final apostrophe begins:

> Nations of fair Hesperia! lo o'erthrown
> Your peace-embracing war-inciting king!
> Ah! thrice twelve years, and longer, ye endured
> Without one effort to rise higher, one hope
> That heaven would wing the secret shaft aright,
> The abomination!

In the "Advertisement" to the poem Landor declared that it was written when he diverted his attention from *The Phocæans*—in the autumn of 1796, when George III had reigned just "thrice twelve years". This identification lends point to Jove's description of Crysäör:

> Crysäör, Sovereign of the golden sword,
> Still hails as brethren men of stouter heart,
> But, wise confederate, shuns Phlegreean fields.
> No warrior he, yet who so fond of war,
> Unfeeling, scarce ferocious; flattery's dupe
> He fancies that the gods themselves are his;
> Impious, but most in prayer. . . .

On Jove's deprecating ambition as unworthy of gods, Neptune deplores the plight of mortals ruled by avarice:

> What is Ambition? What but Avarice?
> But Avarice in richer guise array'd,
> Stalking erect, loud-spoken, lion-mien'd,
> Her brow uncrost by care, but deeply markt,
> And darting downwards 'twixt her eyes hard-lasht
> The wrinkle of command. . . .

The identification of ambition with avarice bears upon Crysäör's defiant address to the gods:

> Tell me, and quickly, why should I adore,
> Adored myself by millions? why invoke,
> Invoked with all thy attributes? men wrong
> By their protestations, prayers, and sacrifice,
> Either the gods, their rulers, or themselves:
> But flame and thunder fright them from the *Gods*,
> *Themselves* they cannot, dare not—they are ours,
> *Us*—dare they, can they, *us*? but triumph, Jove!
> Man for one moment hath engaged his lord,
> Henceforth let merchants value him, not kings.

To the last line Landor appended a footnote explaining the obscure allusion to the slave trade, against which William Wilberforce and Thomas Clarkson agitated for twenty years before securing its abolition in 1807:

This poem describes a period when the insolence of tyranny and the sufferings of mankind were at the utmost. They could not be so without slavery; and slavery could not generally exist without some sort of barter. Merchants then were necessary. It appears that Crysaor, wicked as he is represented, had no personal share in its propagation. He encouraged it. But, a Sovereign who is powerful enough, either by the fears or affection of his people, to abolish from amongst them this inhuman traffic, and who makes not one effort, uses not one persuasion, for the purpose, deserves the execration which followed, and the punishment which overtook Crysaor. Every man, instead of waiting with awe for some preternatural blow, should think *himself* a particle of those elements which Providence has decreed to crush so abominable a monster.

However obscure the allusions to George III in the body of the poem, this footnote plainly indicated the parallel intended in the *Story of Crysäör*; while therefore Southey had reason to criticise the obscurity resulting from excessive condensation in expression, he unjustly implied a want of courage in Landor by remarking that, "while the poet involves his meaning in such allegory and such language, he may continue to publish without danger of comments by the Attorney General".

Revising *Gebir* for its second edition of 1803, Landor was so far influenced by Southey's criticism in the *Annual Review*—which endorsed Isaac Mocatta's private criticism—that he expanded some passages to make an addition of nearly fifty lines to the original. He also added numerous explanatory footnotes, some of which reflected change of opinion effected by subsequent political events. On the line describing Napoleon as "a mortal man above all mortal praise", he commented:

Bonaparte might have been so, and in the beginning of his career it was augured that he would be. But unhappily he thinks that to produce great changes is to perform great actions. To annihilate ancient freedom and substitute new; to give republics a monarchical government, and the provinces of monarchy a republican one; in short, to overthrow by violence all the institutions and to tear from the heart all the social habits of man, has been the tenor of his politics to the present hour.

The comment expressed the changed view of many liberal thinkers, including Coleridge, Wordsworth, and Southey, on witnessing the eruption of a military dictatorship above the chaos of the French Revolution. But it also drew attention to the presence of allusions to contemporary politics in *Gebir*, reminding such Tory patriots as the contributors to the *Anti-Jacobin Review* that the obscurity noticed by Southey might be a mask for treasonable subtlety. So, when *Gebirus*, the Latin version of *Gebir*—also printed at Oxford by Slatter & Munday

—was issued later in 1803, it seemed that Landor was resorting to the
subterfuge of scholarship as a means of escaping his deserts for dissemi-
nating seditious literature and the *Anti-Jacobin Review* condemned its
author as "a coward and a profligate". The charge of profligacy may
have been suggested by Landor's private circulation of some Latin
verses called *Iambi* in a pamphlet lacking a publisher's imprint,[1] for
some of which he apologised as emulating the licentiousness of Catullus.
As in *Poems from the Arabic and Persian*, he pretended that the contents
of *Iambi* proceeded from an unidentified continental source—a device
inviting the charge of cowardice from his political opponents, though
such accusations were common currency under the prevailing conditions of anonymous and pseudonymous journalism.

§ 3

Robert Landor was deputed to superintend his brother's printing
commissions with Slatter & Munday, and it was probably Robert who
employed a Christ Church scholar named Dovaston to correct the
proofs of *Gebirus* at £2 a sheet. Oxford was a convenient port of call
on the way to or from Warwick, but Landor's visits to Warwick became
less frequent as he developed the habit of securing advances on his
allowance, either through his brother Henry or through his father's
Rugeley agent Hicken.

Do not be in any alarm [he wrote to his brother Henry in February
1805] lest I should write to Mr. Hicken for money. I have more than I shall
spend before the next quarter. Had I written to him at all it would not
have been for more than ten pounds, and now the necessity is over.

The necessity was over till the next dunning tradesman's letter arrived,
when he would again appeal to Henry or to Hicken. His father gave
him some property—only a few months before his death the old man
conveyed to him the house in Rugeley market-place where his uncle
lived—but Landor made no effort to live within his income, satisfied
that all his debts could be settled when he inherited the estate.

Expensive and fashionable Bath became his favourite resort. His
"earliest Bath friend", he said, was the brilliant and beautiful Bess
Caldwell, who lived with her sister, Lady Belmore, the young widow
of the first earl.

Bess Caldwell was a well-known and loved Mrs. Malaprop [he wrote in
1840]. Sir William Gell, when they were at Naples, compiled—and I believe

[1] In my American edition of 1941 I followed Wise and Wheeler's *Bibliography* in assuming
that *Iambi* was privately printed at Frome or Oxford in 1800, as the paper used for the
pamphlet bore the watermark of Cobb, a Frome printer, dated 1800. But Mr. R. H. Super
(*The Publication of Landor's Works*, 1954) has pointed out that the same watermark appears
on the errata leaf of *Gebirus*, so the *Iambi* pamphlet was probably printed by Slatter & Munday
about the same time as *Gebirus*.

published—a book called "Caldwelliana" of her remarkable sayings. Hayward's very clever essay mentions her as having said, "She had been to see the house where Ariosto lived with the widow of Charles the First" [meaning Alfieri and the widow of Bonnie Prince Charlie]. She was a very intimate friend of my mother's.

She was an old lady when Landor published *Pericles and Aspasia* in 1836 and exclaimed on meeting him in London, "Sure, Landor, it is a beautiful book, your 'Periwinkle and Asparagus'; but faith! I've no time to read it." Once, about the same time, he described himself as having been "half baked at a dull and stupid party", which "even the brilliancy of Miss Caldwell could not render . . . supportable". His admiration lasted till her death fifty years after he first knew her. Her sister, Lady Belmore, made a favourite of him, and when she died thirty-seven years later, he wrote in a reminiscence to Lady Blessington:

I liked her frankness so much, that I overcame my abhorrence of routs, and went at her desire to hers, although to no others. But then her small Sunday parties, never exceeding fourteen, and from which all but those whom she thought the pleasantest or the prettiest were excluded! Ah, then, indeed, was I devout, and offered my little taper offerings up at shrine after shrine. Bath, in those days, was frequented for a few weeks by many persons of high rank, and there was none of that familiarity, even among themselves, which people now indulge in with their superiors of all sorts.

His professed contempt for balls suited a pose of masculine contempt for frivolity, but he was always an indifferent dancer, and as his vanity impelled him to give up riding as a boy because his brother Charles rode better, so he avoided dancing lest he appeared at a disadvantage with other men under feminine appraisal. "Not dancing well!" he exclaimed to Lady Blessington nearly thirty years later. "I never danced at all; and how grievously has my heart ached when others were in the full enjoyment of their recreation."

Lady Belmore was a leading hostess to fashionable youth at Bath. At her house Landor met young Lord Mountjoy—fresh from Oxford and "somewhat fat for so young a man"—whom he was to know better more than twenty years later as Lord Blessington. Probably at Lady Belmore's he first met "Ianthe". She was Sophia Jane Swift, daughter of an Irishman whose great-grandfather was uncle of the author of *Gulliver's Travels*. She married a distant cousin, the head of her family, Godwin Swift, of Swiftsheath, County Kilkenny, and Lionsden in Meath. Her second son, William Richard Swifte (her children restored the old spelling of the family name with the final *e*), her "third child of a family of seven", related that his father was "a delicate man, and died when I was in my sixth year"—in 1814.

After my mother's acute grief for him which brought on brain fever, had worn itself out, she began once more to see her neighbours. She was a most humane and tender-hearted person, not only towards humanity in general, but also towards every species of living thing. . . . She was kept, during the assizes, in a constant state of fever, when unfortunate culprits had to stand their trial for their lives.

Often she succeeded in persuading the judge to mitigate a sentence. She would invite the judge and jury to dinner and a dance, and appeal to the judge when he was "in the height of good humour with wine and dancing". By this method she succeeded with the formidable Lord Norbury, who was heard to exclaim that he would "dance with the fascinating young widow as long as he had a leg to stand on". She stayed little more than a year in Ireland after her husband's death; though left comfortably off, she was extravagant, and having been persuaded to make her children wards in chancery, she spent a season in London, where she married in 1816 the Comte Lepelletier de Molandé, then attached to the Prince Regent's household.

Landor's earliest verses to Ianthe suggest that she was not yet married when they first met; family tradition ascribes her marriage to 1803, so they probably met in the early part of that year. It was at Bath—her son relates—that Landor

became acquainted with two young ladies, sisters of great beauty. The *naiveté* and sprightliness of their disposition attracted him, perhaps, as much as their personal advantages. He constantly sought their society, and although neither of them admired his *exterieur*, yet both delighted in his company, particularly as he bore remarkably well being made a butt of by them, which their natural wit often furnished occasion for, and which he encouraged.

Though betrothed, Jane Swift was well inclined to a final flirtation before subduing her careless gaiety as a sedate matron. No harm appeared in accepting a gift of Petrarch's sonnets with some apt verses ending in amorous compliment, but danger developed when they lingered together in the twilight, listening for the first notes of the nightingale, and her escort broke the stillness by surreptitiously dislodging a crumbling part of "the turfy mound" they leaned against

> To make her arms cling round me, with a start
> My bosom must assuage.

Dismay came with the discovery that Landor was seriously in love with her:

> *Ask me not* . . . a voice severe
> Tells me . . . *for it gives me pain.*
> Peace! sweet maid! the hour is near
> When I cannot ask again.

The hour came for her return to Ireland. The Swifts evidently married by family arrangement; like his father, grandfather, and great-grandfather before him, Godwin Swift was to marry "his cousin of the half-blood". Jane's troth could not be broken, and Landor was left to brood:

> I often ask upon whose arm she leans,
>   She whom I dearly love;
> And if she visit much the crowded scenes
>   Where mimic passions move.
> There, mighty powers! assert your just controul,
>   Alarm her thoughtless breast;
> Breathe soft suspicion o'er her yielding soul—
>   But never break its rest.
> O let some faithful lover, absent long,
>   To sudden bliss return;
> Then Landor's name shall tremble from her tongue,
>   Her cheek through tears shall burn.

His poems suggest that he soon sought and found consolation. He spent these years of his vigorous youth mainly in pursuit of pleasure, occasionally visiting London and staying a few days with Robert at Oxford, but spending most of his time at Bath, Clifton, and other watering places. For Landor pleasure meant the society of women. He never indulged to excess in wine or food. He disliked dinner parties, eating and drinking only to suit his appetite, and became almost a water drinker as years advanced. "However active at dinner," wrote his brother Robert, "he was always temperate after it; and I never saw the smallest sign of excess, though he greatly enjoyed three or four glasses of light wine." Unlike his father and three younger brothers, he never suffered from gout—mercifully, for he could not endure physical pain; when, at twelve years old, he was attacked by what was doubtless wrongly diagnosed as a "violent fit of the gout", "his imprecations, divided equally between the gout and his nurses, were heard afar". Memory of that affliction may have determined his temperate habits, which so fostered a sturdy constitution that he never suffered any serious illness throughout his long life.

He may have been as fastidious in choosing as he was chivalrous in concealing his amours. To Robert Browning he admitted "numerous flirtations & love-makings . . . in the spiritual & sentimental way", though "never but once in his life . . . had he sinned otherwise", and Mrs. Browning primly commented in 1859, "I am afraid this is very peculiar among men of his time & stamp". After twenty-two years of Victoria's reign, an old man was unlikely to confide in the uxorious Browning a catalogue of his youthful indiscretions; nor does a man of ardent temperament remain a bachelor till thirty-six and write so much amatory verse without amorous experience. There was more than one successor to Nancy Jones and Neæra; though Landor flattered Ianthe by grouping thirty-one love poems under her name in his volume of 1831, there is reason to suppose that some owed their inspiration to others besides Jane Swift.[1] Though Ianthe held his heart, he admitted infidelities to her:

> Circe, who bore the diadem
>   O'er every head we see,
> Pursued by thousands, turn'd from them
>   And fill'd her cup for me.
>
> She seiz'd what little was design'd
>   To catch a transient view;
> For thee alone she left behind
>   The tender and the true.

Bath was his favourite resort for several years following his meeting with Ianthe, as he wrote afterwards to Southey:

You remind me of Bath! if not a delightful, a most easy place. . . . The South Parade was always my residence in winter. Towards spring I removed into Pulteney Street—or rather towards summer, for there were formerly as many nightingales in the garden, and along the river opposite the South Parade, as ever there were in the bowers of Schiraz. The situation is unparalleled in beauty, and is surely the warmest in England. I could get a walk into the country without crossing a street, which I hate. These advantages often kept me in Bath till the middle of June, and I always returned in the beginning of November. . . . I always hated plays and playhouses, and in the nine first years I was only once at the Bath Theatre.

Nightingales annoyed him by waking him at night; years later in Italy when he read Byron's *Bride of Abydos* and came upon the lines, "Know ye the land &c., where the citron and olive are fairest of fruit, And the voice of the nightingale never is mute", he exclaimed, "who indeed does know where the nightingale never is mute?" Nightingales may have reminded him too poignantly of enchanted hours spent with Ianthe in listening to their song.

---

[1] "Thank Heaven, Neæra," of 1802, was reprinted as "Thank Heaven, Ianthe," in 1846, and though Landor included a revised version of "Darling Shell" in the Ianthe poems of 1831, Stephen Wheeler prudishly declined to admit the original version of 1806 among the Ianthe poems in the *Collected Works* because it contains expressions of passion "altogether inadmissible in a poem about Ianthe". Commenting on Mr. Robert Gittings' suggestion (in *John Keats: The Living Year*, 1954) that Keats's "Bright Star" sonnet was inspired by Isabella Jones and afterwards addressed to Fanny Brawne, Mr. Middleton Murry (in his *Keats*, 1955) finds "something very repugnant in the idea that Keats should have written an impassioned and immortal sonnet about one woman and touched it up for another". Yet a young man's fancy for one woman may be as ardently engaged for another the next springtime; Coleridge addressed his verses on "Kisses" to Fanny Nesbitt in 1793, to Mary Evans in 1794, and to his wife in 1796. Landor adapted most of his amatory verse to Ianthe, partly in gallantry to his only enduring love, partly to erase traces of past indiscretions.

§ 4

When his father died on 3rd November 1805, Landor wrote to Walter Birch:

It was an event for which we were long prepared by a most tedious and excruciative malady, a species of cancer. It was what he most earnestly & incessantly desired, and what on that account we the less bitterly regret. My fortune, as you may suppose, will be much increased, but I had always enough for my expences. After paying the younger children's fortunes, and some other incumbrances, I shall have about eleven hundred a year, my mother about fourteen hundred, from estates which are entailed on me, and which may be greatly increased when the leases have expired.

If he had always had enough for his expenses, it was not by suiting his expenditure to his pocket or without frequent subsidies to his income, and he now increased his scale of living without worrying how much was within his means. His brother Robert, visiting him at Bath soon after their father's death, found him credited "with the reputation of very great wealth, and the certainty, at his mother's death, of still greater. A fine carriage, three horses, two men-servants, books, plate, china, pictures, in everything a profuse and wasteful outlay, all confirmed the grandeur".

Whether or not the young man of twenty-five regarded his brother's "profuse and wasteful" establishment with the same eyes as Forster's sour old correspondent, he readily enjoyed Landor's hospitality. In reading his uncharitable reflections on his brother's conduct, it is not irrelevant to remember that Robert achieved materially less in his life than Landor did. Without any apparent fervour for religion, he took orders in 1804, and for a few months at the beginning of 1805, he acted as curate-in-charge at Wyke Regis in Dorsetshire during the Rector's illness. This move from Oxford to Dorset inspired the Latin verses, "Ad Fratrem", in *Simonidea*. His biographer says he resigned his Worcester fellowship "(presumably in 1804) when he was left a small independent income by a relative". But the identity of the generous relative does not appear.

Forster says that Landor's father "had to sell some property in discharge of debts contracted by him; and in return he had undertaken to present his brother Charles to the family living of Colton, in the event of its not falling vacant before his father's death". This promise for Charles—fulfilled in 1806, when Charles succeeded his uncle John Landor as rector at Colton—seems a slight demand for the father to have made upon the prodigal son; more likely, in return for settling Landor's debts, the old man demanded concessions enabling him to make the provision for all his younger children desired by himself and their mother. Landor's generosity in consenting to such a proposal—

for he never considered the future in purchasing the solution of a present difficulty—was so far recognised by his father that he made a voluntarily generous gesture in return, for the conveyance of the Rugeley house was neither requested by Landor nor required by his creditors, since Landor wrote to his brother Henry in February 1805 that he did not "see the necessity of any such conveyance".

Robert Landor may have resigned his Worcester fellowship on his father's death. His biographer could not find that, during the ten years between November 1805 and his continental trip of 1815, Robert performed any clerical duty or otherwise earned a regular living, but after his eldest brother had gone abroad to live on an allowance from the administrators of his estate, he obtained through family influence in 1817 a living at Hughenden and continued thereafter in clerical practice. It seems therefore a reasonable inference that Landor to some extent subsidised his favourite brother during the years he remained master of his own money.

Forster spoke of Landor's "gaieties and follies" in the first years following accession to his inheritance, but his gaieties seem to have been governed by the folly of his passion for Jane Swift. To Walter Birch on 20th November 1805 Landor wrote from Clifton, "My books are just come out, Walter, and I hasten to send you the *literal errata*". His books were the first copies of *Simonidea*, printed at Bath by W. Meyler and published early in 1806 by G. Robinson of Paternoster Row, of which he wrote to Southey five years later:

> There are many things of which I am ashamed in the *Simonidea*. I printed whatever was marked with a pencil by a woman who loved me, and I consulted all her caprices. There is a sneer, of which I am heartily ashamed, at Mr. Grant, Mr. Heber, and Lord Strangford. But is it not a cursed galling thing to hear a woman (who is soul and senses to one) tell me to write like these? She had read no better and few other poets. I added some Latin poetry of my own, more pure in its Latinity than in its sentiment. But the *Pudoris Ara*[1] is incomparably the best poetry I have been able to write."

Jane Swift was the only woman ever "soul and senses" to Landor, and the contents of *Simonidea* indicate the dictation of her caprices.

The volume contained six Latin and twenty-five English poems. Four of the first six poems were elegies, "a species of composition in which Simonides excelled". The first elegy was addressed to Mrs. Lambe, wife of the doctor who succeeded Dr. Landor in his Warwick

---

[1] Landor included an English version of this poem in his *Hellenics* of 1847 as "The Altar of Modesty", revising and improving it for the new edition of 1859. "Is *The Altar of Modesty* too much 'calculated to bring a blush to the cheek' of the virgin votaries of that goddess?" wrote Swinburne to Lord Houghton; "I only ask for 'information'—but I fear it must be, tho' certainly one of his most perfect pieces." The poem may be no more suitable reading for blushing virgins than Shakespeare's "Lover's Complaint" or Dryden's "The Flower and the Leaf", but Mr. Super's taste is surely at fault in describing as "impudicity" the grace and wit of suggestive whimsicality in Helen's account of how she preserved her virtue when abducted by Theseus.

practice; she died in 1804 from a fever caught in nursing one of her children. There followed the famous lines on Rose Aylmer and the elegy on Nancy Jones; the sixth poem, "Come back, ye Smiles", was described as "Written at Malvern" and evidently inspired by the death of the Malvern girl addressed in 1799, though reprinted among the Ianthe poems of 1831. Of the remaining twenty-one English poems, no fewer than fifteen were reprinted as addressed to Ianthe in 1831— though one of these, "She leads in solitude her youthful hours", must have been originally addressed to the Malvern girl.

Even the one narrative English poem, *Gunlaug and Helga*, begins, "Sophia, pity Gunlaug's fate".[1] Landor owed the story of this poem to the Hon. William Herbert's *Select Icelandic Poetry*, which was published in 1804 and brought to his notice by Walter Birch in a letter of April 1805. Scott's *Lay of the Last Minstrel* was published in January 1805, and—no doubt at the suggestion of the lady who "had read no better and few other poets" than Grant, Reginald (later Bishop) Heber, and the sixth Viscount Strangford, translator of Camoens—Landor wrote his ballad in the iambic tetrametre of that popular success. In love with Helga, Gunlaug is bidden by the girl's father to serve three years abroad and then return to claim the girl if he is still of the same mind; on his return he injures his leg in a wrestling match, and while he is lying crippled, his rival Rafen informs Helga's father that Gunlaug is delayed in dalliance with light women, with the result that Helga is married to Rafen. It may be no more than curious coincidence but, just before hearing the news of his father's death in November 1805, Landor was laid up at Clifton with a wound in his leg; he told Birch that he expected to be "well in a fortnight" but was condemned to a "course of medicine which will deprive me of the pleasures of Bath for many weeks". He thus had a personal reason for asking, "Sophia, pity Gunlaug's fate".

Pinned inside the lid of his writing-desk was found, after Landor's death, an engraving of the view from Clifton Church. The Ianthe poem beginning "Clifton, in vain thy varied scenes invite", dwells on the beauties of this view before proceeding:

> What voice can charm us, or what view can cheer,
> Removed from her the restless heart holds dear!
> Ah why then, self-tormenter, why removed?
> Say, thou who lovest, art thou not beloved?
> Resume thy courage, give thy sorrows o'er—
> Will not her bosom press thy bosom more!

[1] Without any authority Wheeler (*Complete Works*, vol. xiii) asserted that *Gunlaug and Helga* was addressed to Sophia Shuckburgh, the cousin to whom Landor wrote his earliest verses, "To a Lady Lately Married". In the Huntington Library Mr. Super has seen an undated letter from Landor to the printer of *Dry Sticks* (1858) definitely stating that the Sophia addressed in *Gunlaug and Helga* was Jane Sophia Swift.

> Her clasping arms around thy neck entwine,
> Her gentle hand be linkt again in thine!
> Will not her lips their honied dews impart,
> And will not rapture swell her answering heart?
> Soon shall thy exile and thy grief be closed,
> By whom but thee, for whom but her, imposed!
> Through seven days, imperfect, waste and wild,
> In seven days the whole creation smil'd.

This seven days' self-banishment at Clifton happened some time before illness or injury threatened in November 1805 to prevent his return to Bath for several weeks, but not so long before as 1803, when his passionate addresses gave pain to the girl already promised in marriage. He is now beloved in return by the woman he loves, and they are on terms of passionate intimacy; their amour has inspired whispers of gossip in Bath, and for the sake of his mistress's reputation Landor has voluntarily withdrawn from her society for a week.

Landor and Ianthe lived in the world of Jane Austen, where a girl prudently preserved her value in the marriage market till she was settled with a suitable husband; they lived in the world also of Byron's Lady Oxford, who presented her husband with a numerous family of which only "the law gave him the right to be called father", and of Georgiana, Duchess of Devonshire, who bore a child to an eminent statesman while her husband was keeping a mistress under the same roof. A married woman might indulge indiscretions impossible to an unmarried girl, and unless she was his mistress, only a heartless coquette could have behaved with the abandon of Ianthe in the poems. So, far from being heartless, Jane Swift was emotionally impulsive; her son relates how, when visited by her children for the first time after her second marriage, she was excited to such transports that she was prematurely confined of a daughter the same evening. A volatile temperament is suggested by the miniature cherished by Landor, which portrays a lively brunette with expressive eyes, a ripe mouth, dark ringlets, and vivid complexion.

Many of the Ianthe poems refer to stolen blisses, impossible in the courtship of a reluctant girl and suggestive of clandestine meetings with a married woman. A spray of myrtle, taken from Ianthe's bosom, thus replies when asked why it must fade and die:

> Remember then the guilty night
> You snatcht and seized me pale with fright,
> At every swell more close I prest
> With jealous care that lovely breast:
> At every tender word you said
> I cast a broader, deeper shade;

> So trembling, that I fell between
> Two angel-guards the rose unseen:
> There, pleasures, perils, all forgot,
> I clung and fainted—who would not?

As a keepsake Ianthe presented her lover with the shell on which she
cut her infant teeth, and the *Simonidea* version of "Darling Shell"
contains these lines:

> Earlier to whose aid she owes
> Teeth like budding snowdrop rows;
> Teeth, whose love-incited pow'rs,
> I have felt in happier hours.
>
> On my shoulder, on my neck,
>   Still the cherisht mark remains,
> Well pourtray'd in many a speck
>   Round thy smooth and quiet veins.

For obvious reasons Landor consulted their married heroine on which
of the poems might be safely printed at that time. With pencil poised,
she struck out the poems too plainly indicating her identity, like that
lamenting her decision to rejoin her husband in Ireland:

> Ianthe! you resolve to cross the sea!
> A path forbidden *me*!

They must have found amusement in devices of deliberate mystification,
interposing the verses addressed to the Malvern girl and some inspired
years before by Nancy Jones, and Landor in the preface of *Simonidea*
confidently warned the reader to "beware of hoping he can trace, to
any object within his view, the source of those affections he may
discover there and here. He will be wrong; that is certain". Faithfully
he maintained the mystification through the lifetime of her first husband: in 1831 he could group a selection of the love poems under
Ianthe's name without embarrassment to the Comtesse de Molandé,
and add still more in 1846 when she was an old lady; after her death
in 1851 he addressed her in her own name and printed an anecdote of
their youthful love so immodest as "The Primrose-Bank"; in his last
year of life he proclaimed the history of their secret,

> Ianthe took me by both ears and said
> You are so rash, I own I am afraid.
> Prop, or keep hidden in your breast, my name,
> But be your love as lasting as your fame.[1]

[1] This quatrain was probably written at the time of Ianthe's injunction; on sending it to
the printer he added a couplet as comment:
> All men are liars, said a sage of old:
> One was not, he who this sad tale hath told.

Following the practice of Irishwomen in her social position, Jane Swift probably spent some six months of the year in England. When her children accompanied her, she must have established her own household at Bath and Landor doubtless indulged in the extravagance of keeping a carriage—with his pair of horses, Frolic and Favourite—as much for her convenience as for his own.[1]

The poems show that his happiness with her was haunted always by the need for subterfuge and the sorrow of their partings when she returned to Ireland. An undated letter to his sister Elizabeth reveals that, on at least one occasion, he threatened to follow Ianthe to her home in Ireland. He sent his sister a song of which he wrote an Italian translation, thinking "the English would be less proper for music".

It was written when I first had thoughts of going into Ireland, and when I was—as we all of us are, some time or other—so foolish as to be in love. . . . Here are the words

> In vain, O Love my steps you guide
> To shores for which I've often sighed!
>   No longer is Ianthe mine!
> On whom so blest as once were we
>   While I lov'd her and she lov'd me
> Did evening close or morning shine?
> Could I then ask my heart, if this
> Were sure repose and lasting bliss!
>   Could I then wish to change my lot!
> I fancied Pleasure was untrue
> But I have lived to learn and rue
>   Alas that Grief is not.

He may have sought to persuade Ianthe to defy convention by leaving her husband and children and by living openly with him till divorce freed her to marry him. But only the essentially chaste or the desperately unhappy woman leaves her husband for a lover, and divorce was then a difficult process. Ianthe preferred such a discreet *liaison* as society tolerated at Bath and Brighton under the Prince Regent. Assured that he would have been the husband of her free choice, he must rest content with clandestine favours; if he could not refrain from fretting, he might seek happiness elsewhere—to which he replied bitterly:

[1] On 20th December 1828 Landor wrote to Lady Blessington, when asking her interest in support of a claim to the viscounty of Carlingford by Ianthe's eldest son, Godwin Swift: "I never saw him since he was a baby, but I hear he is a most amiable and gentlemanly person." Ianthe's second son relates in his memoirs that his mother had a dog named Frolic when she visited Landor at Florence in 1829.

> Bid my bosom cease to grieve!
>   Bid these eyes fresh objects see!
> Where's the comfort to believe
>   None would once have rival'd me?
>
> What, my freedom to receive?
>   Broken hearts, are they the free?
> For another can I live
>   If I may not live for thee!

Sometimes she seemed to waver, feigning compliance with his plans in happy times together; when she returned to Ireland, she left him with the sad solace of her tears:

> Flow, precious tears! thus shall my rival know
>   For me, not him, ye flow.

Often he felt bitterness in jealousy and loneliness, but tenderness for her immediately tempered the wish that she might feel afflicted in conscience as the cause of his unhappiness:

> So late removed from him she swore,
>   With clasping arms and vows and tears,
> In life and death she would adore,
>   While memory, fondness, bliss, endears . . .
>
> Can she forswear? can she forget?
>   Strike, mighty Love! strike, Vengeance! . . . soft!
> Conscience must come, and bring Regret . . .
>   These let her feel! . . . nor these too oft!

His sister Elizabeth was troubled by what she heard of his devotion to a married woman and urged him to find a suitable wife.

Birth and fortune are not requisite, but good disposition and good understanding are; and how many innocents, only for being pretty, have you all your life been thinking sensible!

Again she wrote:

I hope to God your choice may be a fortunate one, for I never was and never shall be happy when you are otherwise. You are not just to me. I *do* wish you to be married; but I am sure the common sort are not calculated for you.

Shaken by his sister's appeals, he began to think of settling in a home of his own. He did not by choice attend the "routs, plays, concerts, and balls", of which he spoke in a letter to Dr. Parr; his inclination lay always to the retreat from society he had enjoyed in South Wales.

Forster stated that Landor's extravagance compelled his "selling the old paternal estate in Staffordshire, and reinvesting in other land at greater profit". But neither of the estates Landor thought of buying could compete in value per acre with the well-cultivated land of Staffordshire or Warwickshire. Feeling no desire to settle within the social circle of his family's friends, he sought solitude in such picturesque surroundings as at Swansea and Tenby. His fancy turned first to the Lakes, which he visited in the summer of 1807, only a few months before young De Quincey accompanied the Coleridge family to Grasmere. He carried a letter of introduction from Dr. Parr—a generous tribute from one who had known him intimately for twelve years and whose own character commanded the respect of all who knew him:

In the course of the summer you will be called upon by Mr. Walter Landor, who is going on a tour to the lakes. He is my particular friend. He is impetuous, openhearted, magnanimous; largely furnished with general knowledge; well versed in the best classical writers; a man of original genius, as appears in his compositions both in prose and verse; a keen hater of oppression and corruption; and a steady friend to civil and religious liberty. I am confident you will be much interested by his conversation; and it is my good fortune to know that his talents, attainments, and virtues amply compensate for all his singularities.

He met none of the Lake celebrities on his tour, and expressed regret to his sister that he had missed an introduction to Southey. Attracted by an estate at Loweswater, he made an offer but negotiations for purchase broke down. Within a few months he was in treaty with Sir Mark Wood for the wild Monmouthshire vale enshrining the ruins of Llanthony Abbey; his brother Henry made a tour of inspection, reported favourably on the prospects of improving the property, and arranged the sale of the Rugeley estate, about four-fifths of which had been owned by the Landor family for more than a century.

The sale of Rugeley realised £35,715, leaving a further £14,000 to be raised by two mortgages. To pay off the mortgages Landor proposed to his mother the sale of the Savage estate at Tachbrook, which would have descended to him by entail at her death. He wrote to her on 16th June 1808:

I have just returned from Monmouthshire and find here two letters from Henry. It is impossible for me to express how sensible I am of your goodness in consenting to clear and complete the purchase of Lanthony, by selling the property at Tachebrook.

But his mother took counsel with her son Henry to safeguard the interests of her younger children, and on receiving "Henry's very extraordinary letter", Landor replied with acid remarks on his brother's advice. When his mother ignored this letter, he wrote again

on 30th June to propose that they should agree to accept the opinion
of an independent arbitrator, adding:

It would certainly save me at least a thousand pounds if I were able to
make my bargain with the freeholders at Lanthony before the road is
finished. I cannot do this, until we have agreed to sell. But surely the sale
of Tachebrook will not alter your intentions in regard to the timber. Your
accommodation to me is an act of kindness, and my giving up Colton to
you is to make amends for any advantages (in timber or otherwise) that
might arise to you from keeping the estate in your own hands.

His mother replied that she would sell her land at Tachbrook if he
agreed to pay her an annuity of £450 for life, she would sell him her
share on adjoining property for £2,000, and she would only consent to
cutting down timber to raise money for his Llanthony expenses if he
would secure the full value of the timber to her executors. She thus
excused her hard bargaining:

as I think your Sisters & Robert will have very small fortunes, I certainly
aught to make up as much for them as I can, & there is no other way than
falling of Timber at Ipsley. . . . Their whole fortunes will not in all prob-
ability exceed £3000 each, while at my Death you will have more per
annum; now ask your own heart if I am doing wrong by endeavouring to
make them in a comfortable situation for Life, & their health may occasion
expences we little now think of.

Landor replied on the 7th July: "I return you a thousand thanks for
your very kind letter, and perfectly agree to all your proposals. Nothing
can be more just than that I should pay the full value of the timber . . ."
A few days later he wrote again, emphasising that "I shall want all the
money I can raise to pay off the incumbrances on Lanthony and to
purchase the remainder of the manor": as to cutting the woods at
Ipsley, "as I shall never see the place again, I am not quite so anxious
as I might be about any havoc that may be made".

§ 5

While writing to his mother in June and July 1808, Landor was
moving about between Clifton, Worthing, Brighton, and Bath. Presumably he had returned from Monmouthshire to pursue Ianthe, again
over from Ireland, for he sent Southey some Latin elegiacs, of which he
said that Ianthe had "held me by both ears till I gave her the English":

> Soon, O Ianthe, life is o'er,
>   And sooner beauty's playful smile!
> Kiss me, and grant what I implore,
>   Let love remain that little while.

Through the mediation of a mutual friend at Clifton, Mrs. Carrick, he had met Southey in April, for on the 26th of that month Southey wrote to his old friend Grosvenor Bedford:

At Bristol I met with the man of all others whom I was most desirous of meeting,—the only man living of whose praise I was ambitious, or whose censure would have humbled me. You will be curious to know who this could be. Savage Landor, the author of *Gebir*, a poem which, unless you have heard me speak of it, you have probably never heard of at all. I never saw any one more unlike myself in every prominent part of human character, nor any one who so cordially and instinctively agreed with me on so many of the most important subjects. I have often said before we met, that I would walk forty miles to see him, and having seen him, I would gladly walk fourscore to see him again. He talked of Thalaba, and I told him of the series of mythological poems which I had planned,—mentioned some of the leading incidents on which they were to have been formed, and also told him for what reason they were laid aside;—in plain English that I could not afford to write them.

Landor's reply was, "Go on with them, and I will pay for printing them, as many as you will write and as many copies as you please."

Southey told Walter Scott that, though he had not "the least thought of accepting this princely offer, it has stung me to the very core", and on his return home to Keswick, he sent Landor all that he had written of *The Curse of Kehama*, saying, "You offered to print it for me; if ever I finish the poem it will be because of that offer, though without the slightest intention of accepting it."

The friendship between Landor and Southey continued unbroken till the latter's death. Byron called Southey "the only existing entire man of letters"; he was also the most completely admirable man as a personality in the history of English letters. Five months older than Landor, he too had been a rebel and a Jacobin; at Oxford he despised the "pedantry, prejudice, and aristocracy" of the university, and shocked authority by refusing to have his hair dressed and powdered by the college barber, wearing his hair in its natural state. The ardent apostle of pantisocracy, he was the recognised leader of the little circle which planned a miniature Utopia; the brilliant, wayward Coleridge followed obediently the lead of his strong and serene personality. He may be blamed for having urged Coleridge into incompatible marriage with Sarah Fricker, but he himself sought escape from the disturbance of amorous desires in early marriage with his Edith and he had reason to hope that the susceptible Coleridge might find similar security with her sister. He married without a penny, and after a wry grimace at the necessity, settled to earn a living as "hireling writer to a newspaper". A hireling writer he remained all his life; year after year, with tireless regularity, he produced leading articles, long reviews, biographies and historical works of wide research, till the trained machinery of his brain gave way.

LANDOR
aged
twenty-nine

From the portrait by George Dance R.A., painted in 1804

SOPHIA JANE SWIFT

From the miniature of Ianthe possessed by Landor, believed by T. J. Wise to be the work of Horace Hone

Dowden said truly that "there is not perhaps any single work of Southey's the loss of which would be felt by us as a capital misfortune". But he condescended unduly in saying "the more we consider his total work, its mass, its variety, its high excellence, the more we come to regard it as a memorable, an extraordinary achievement". More than merely memorable, it was a magnificent achievement. Through years of ceaseless labour he gave of his best, not only in the quality of his work, but in the generous goodness of his daily life. Nobody appealed to him vainly for comfort or advice; when Coleridge's productive ability foundered on the shoals of despondency and drugs, Southey assumed his responsibilities in addition to his own. Nobility was the keystone of his character. If men received their just deserts, Southey should have achieved affluent ease and lasting fame; the sorrows and sufferings that rewarded his virtue offer a problem to believers in a benevolent deity. During his life continuous and conscientious toil earned him a reputation of dignity, but of even this he was deprived after death by the malice of Wordsworth, and posterity accepted his value at the assessment of that man of genius whose selfishness had shrivelled his soul.

His brother Robert remarked that Landor was never ungrateful in repaying admiration; when he liked anybody, he was ready to believe their work as good as he hoped it might be. Stoutly Landor persisted in proclaiming Southey as the greatest poet of his time, for he assessed him at his true value as a man. Long after Southey's death, he expressed the hope that he and Cowper had met in heaven, for "two such men have seldom met on earth". He declared that Southey's *Roderick*, *Thalaba*, and *Curse of Kehama* surpassed any three poems by Wordsworth, who lacked Southey's diversity and invention as well as his humour. But he emphasised his love for the man; "if his elegant prose and harmonious verse are insufficient to incite enthusiasm, turn to his virtues, to the ardour and constancy of his friendship, to his disinterestedness, to his generosity." Southey's regard for Landor was similar. At the time he publicly admitted the influence of *Gebir* on his own verse, and long afterwards told Bowles that the "three contemporaries, the influence of whose poetry on my own I can distinctly trace", were "Sayers, yourself, and Walter Landor". But while men like Browning and Forster cherished Landor's friendship because he was a man of genius, Southey, like Parr, valued him for his own sake. "Never did man," he wrote, "represent himself in his writings so much less generous, less just, less compassionate, less noble in all respects than he really is. I certainly never knew anyone of brighter genius or of kinder heart."

After he had been Landor's friend for sixteen years, Southey wrote to Caroline Bowles, who became his second wife, "Differing as I do from him in constitutional temper, and in some serious opinions, he is

yet of all men living the one with whom I feel the most sympathy in
heart and mind." The feeling of mutual confidence began with their
first meeting, for they discussed freely their most intimate problems,
Southey writing, "I wish you were married, because the proverb about
a rolling stone applies to a single heart, and I wish you were as much a
Quaker as I am"—plainly inferring that Landor confided his love for
Ianthe.

Contact with Southey must have pointed the contrast between
Southey's disciplined diligence and his own motiveless drifting. Possibly
at this time he brought his affair with Ianthe to a crisis, demanding that
she must either throw in her lot with him or make a break, and on her
persistence in evasion he wrote:

> O fond, but fickle and untrue,
> Ianthe take my last adieu.
> Your heart one day will ask you why
> You forced from me this farewell sigh.

A situation dramatically suited to his farewell lay at hand. Spain
was suffering a tragedy curiously like that repeated a century and a
quarter later. King Charles IV had been compelled to abdicate in
favour of his son Ferdinand, who, after a brief reign as Napoleon's
puppet, placed his crown at the disposal of the conqueror, who be-
stowed it upon his brother Joseph. When the Spaniards thereupon
revolted, there were expressions of warm sympathy in England.
Southey saw "more public virtue in Spain than in any other country
under Heaven", and in the revolt "a spirit of patriotism, a growing
and proud remembrance of the past, a generous shame for the present,
and a living hope for the future", which might yet inspire England to
something better than the degrading policy of "appeasement" towards
Napoleon. Coleridge related how he and Wordsworth walked at two
in the morning to meet the Keswick carrier with the newspaper,
and their neighbour, John Wilson—then, like Landor, a wealthy
young man of literary inclinations—thought of going to Spain as a
volunteer.

The idea may have occurred to Wilson when he heard from Southey
of Landor's example, for Landor wrote to Southey on 8th August from
Falmouth:

Nothing I do, whether wise or foolish, will create much surprise in those
who know my character. I am going to Spain. In three days I shall have
sailed.

One evening at Brighton, to two of Ianthe's countrymen named Fitzgerald and O'Hara, he "preached a crusade" in terms of invective at

which he expected Southey's "gentler and more benevolent soul" would shudder:

May every Frenchman out of France perish! May the Spaniards not spare one! No calamities can chain them down from their cursed monkey-tricks; no generosity can bring back to their remembrance that a little while since they mimicked, till they really thought themselves, free men. Detestable race, profainers of republicanism,—since the earth will not open to swallow them all up, may even kings partake in the glory of their utter extermination!

Napoleon's contempt for the independence of weaker nations excited in liberal minds the same indignation as the misfortunes of Spain, Abyssinia, Austria, and Czecho-Slovakia in the nineteen-thirties. Convinced by his rhetoric, the two Irishmen accompanied Landor to Falmouth where, missing the packet-boat by two hours, they had to wait till the following week for another sailing.

Landor employed the days of waiting in learning the Spanish language, which "appears to me such as I should have expected to hear spoken by a Roman slave, sulky from the bastinado". "I hope to join the Spanish army immediately on my landing," he wrote to Southey, "and I wish only to fight as a private soldier," adding a remark indicative of the extent to which he had confided in Southey his emotional entanglement, "There is nothing in this unless it could be known what I have left for it, and, having left, have lost." During the voyage to Spain, or soon afterwards, he explained the significance of this remark in verses that deserve to be more widely known:

> Against the rocking mast I stand,
>   The Atlantic surges swell
> To bear me from my native land
>   And Psyche's wild farewell.
>
> From billow upon billow hurl'd,
>   Again I hear her say,
> "Oh! is there nothing in the world
>   Worth one short hour's delay?"
>
> "Alas, my Psyche! were it thus,
>   I should not sail alone,
> Nor seas nor fates had sever'd us . . .
>   But are you *all* my own?"
>
> Thus were it, never would burst forth
>   These sighs, so deep, so true!
> But . . . what to me is little worth,
>   The world . . . is much to you.

And you shall say, when once the dream
(So hard to break!) is o'er,
My love was very dear to him,
My fame and peace were more.[1]

He was hardly at sea before Southey hailed him as a hero, writing on 16th August to his brother in the navy:

Landor has gone to Spain! to fight as a private in the Spanish army, and he has found two Englishmen to go with him. A noble fellow! This is something like the days of old, as we poets and romancers represent them; something like the best part of chivalry: old honours, old generosity, old heroism, are reviving, and the cancer of that nation is stopped, I believe and fully trust, now and for ever. A man like Landor cannot long remain without command; and, of all things in this world, I should most rejoice to hear that King Joseph had fallen into his hands;—he would infallibly hang him on the nearest tree, first, as a Buonaparte by blood; secondly as a Frenchman by adoption; thirdly as a king by trade.

Like Henry Crabb Robinson, who had left for Spain three weeks earlier as war correspondent for *The Times*, Landor had a rough voyage; "the vessel received some material damage" from violent winds while it stood "two whole days within sight of Corunna". He made a friend of the ship's captain, who wrote in November to thank him for the gift of a compass, which would remind him always "of the many pleasant and instructive hours passed with the giver, notwithstanding the prevalence of many adverse gales in a very leaky ship".

On landing at Corunna, Landor lost no time in introducing himself to the British envoy, Charles Stuart (who was subsequently British ambassador in Paris and raised to the peerage as Baron Stuart de Rothesay). On August 24th Stuart presented him to the governor of Corunna, to whom Landor proposed "a small offering of 10,000 reals for the unfortunate town of Venturada", which had been sacked by the French; announcing his intention of enlisting under General Blake,

[1] First published in the *Examiner*, 23rd September 1838, these verses were reprinted in *The Book of Beauty* for 1842 under the title, "To Zoë . . . June 1808," with the name Zoë substituted for Psyche. As he sailed for Spain in early August, Wheeler thought that a lapse of memory caused Landor to date the poem "more than a month too early", but the poet evidently intended to remind his mistress—not of the time when he stood "against the rocking mast"—but of the date of her "wild farewell". Addressing her as Psyche and Zoë instead of as Ianthe, he intended the same mystification as in *Simonidea*: like the heroine of the Ianthe poems, she was not "*all* my own", she enjoyed the pleasures of society, and she compelled him to sacrifice their love to her reputation and comfort. Mr. Super (*Walter Savage Landor: A Biography*) sees here "a suggestion of an affair of the heart" with an unidentified woman. As Landor and Jane Swift destroyed their correspondence, Mr. Super finds "no evidence whatsoever" that Ianthe "ever became Landor's mistress", and though he assumes without evidence that Landor "eagerly romanticized his acquaintance with every girl he knew", he thinks it "not inconceivable" that Ianthe should have disturbed her lover's peace of mind for more than five years "without dragging on the flirtation beyond a season". He therefore ascribes no fewer than seventeen of the Ianthe poems—including "Darling Shell" and "Remember then the guilty night"—to the brief period of their acquaintance before Ianthe's marriage to Godwin Swift.

an Irish soldier of fortune who held a command in the Spanish army under Cuesta, he declared that, if any volunteers wished to accompany him, "though their number should amount to 1,000", he would "with much pleasure pay the expenses of their journey, travel with them on foot, and fight along with them . . . in defence of religion and liberty". Speaking in French, Stuart interpreted his offer to the governor, and hearing the words, *Il est fou, il n'a pas l'argent*, Landor concluded that Stuart was referring to himself. Having "the highest and most inviolable respect for whatever (*sic*) is in office under the king and constitution of my country", he refrained from immediate protest and proceeded to carry his proposals into effect. Two days later he secured from the governor a written receipt for the payment of ten thousand reals and the copy of a letter forwarding his further proposal to the Supreme Council of Castile, which documents were published in *Saunders' Dublin News-Letter and Daily Advertiser* of 3rd October 1808, with the statement that the Council had accepted the gift for the people of Venturada and complimented "Mr. Landor and the two Irish gentlemen" on "their generosity, valour, and honourable enthusiasm".

His troop soon enrolled, he marched with it by way of Lugo to Villa Franca, where he found time to record his adventures and observations. At Lugo, when a magazine of stores caught fire, with no water available, he prevented the spreading of the fire by ordering dust to be flung upon the flames. At one place he ate bread "indebted for its whiteness to the sand with which it was mixed". He described crops and scenery with the trained eye of a countryman. On 1st September he saw barley "only six or seven inches high" and standard peaches "laden with unripe fruit"; the season in that part of Galicia was later than in England, but "the fruit more rarely fails and grows in more abundance". In well-wooded country he was surprised to see neither elm nor ash, and remarked the value of ash "in an elevated situation, for which it is peculiarly adapted by the toughness and flexibility of its branches".

Also from Villa Franca he addressed a complaint about Stuart's conduct to the envoy's colleague, C. R. Vaughan, who had been a schoolfellow at Rugby: "the forbearance I have shown, and even the letter I am writing, will controvert the charge of imbecility," while payment of the gift for Venturada and "a daily allowance of full pay to every soldier I am leading to the armies, together with some occasional gratuities to keep up their spirits on the march", afforded "proof that the calculations of Mr. S. are groundless, frivolous and false". Vaughan forwarded the complaint to Stuart, who replied that a member of the Galician junta would "certify that Mr. Landor must have misunderstood me". On 1st November Vaughan assured Landor that if Stuart "made use of those expressions in your hearing it must have been with respect to some other person". Later Stuart wrote a full apology to Landor for having "had the misfortune unintentionally to offend you at Corunna", though he now asserted that "I do not recollect the conversation you state to have passed". Landor accepted the apology: "Mr. Stuart has declared that he never could apply those expressions to me which I resented, and offers peace," he informed Southey; "I always accept this offer."

Stuart found it necessary to remind Vaughan of circumstances at both Corunna and Lugo that "would not permit me to show" Landor "the civilities I desired", and his demeanour at Corunna must have suggested to Landor an inclination to disparagement. Landor's arrival to set an example of energy to the Spaniards may well have embarrassed the official policy of *laissez-faire*. Sir Arthur Wellesley—soon to be celebrated as Duke of Wellington, but then reputed only an able officer distinguished on active service in India—arrived in Spain little more than a fortnight before Landor, but he was subordinate to an unsuccessful veteran, Sir Harry Burrard, who could be relied upon to accept guidance from the governor of Gibraltar, Sir Hew Dalrymple. After the action at Vimeiro in August, Wellesley assured Burrard that Lisbon might be taken in three days, but Burrard preferred to await instructions from Dalrymple. Negotiations drifted into an "imperfect armistice" which proved the prelude to the unpopular Convention of Cintra.

With Blake's army "sometimes at Reynosa, sometimes at Aguilar", Landor waited fretfully for a decisive action, seeing little but sniping and guerilla skirmishing. He told Southey that he wished to have seen Madrid, but feared to go lest the long-expected battle might be fought in his absence. Late in September he was present at the occupation of Bilbao, where "I had the satisfaction of serving three launches with powder and muskets, and of carrying on my shoulders six or seven miles a child too heavy for its exhausted mother". He "was near being taken the following day" when the French re-occupied the town, escaping with the aid of "Juan Santos de Murieta, a poor man of Castro". During September and early October he beguiled his leisure in writing three letters to Riquelme, the brigadier commanding his division under Blake—the first on a "means of supplying an adequate force of cavalry", the second "a view of parties in England, their errors and designs", the third, dated from Santander on 3rd October, a review of "our conduct at Ferrol, at Buenos Ayres, and at Cintra". In a preface to the letters—which were printed on his return to England by Meyler, the publisher of the *Bath Herald*—Landor related how Riquelme, with whom he formed "a sincere friendship", was mortally wounded at Espinosa and died at Santander on 10th November.

The Convention of Cintra excited demonstrations of protest in

England, and Wordsworth denounced the principles of the treaty in a pamphlet which De Quincey prepared for press. The government took refuge in a board of inquiry, which reprimanded Dalrymple and deprived him of his governorship, but continued the vacillating policy that induced in January the disaster of Sir John Moore's retreat to Corunna. Landor joined with those who blamed John Hookham Frere, the British minister in Spain, for having misled Moore by failing to furnish accurate information of the French movements. His charges of "vanity and incapacity" rankled so long in Frere's memory that, after the publication of the *Imaginary Conversations*, he vented his spleen in the satirical verses to be found in his collected works.

Landor had left Spain before Moore's disaster. He returned to England late in November 1808, feeling shame for the disgrace of Cintra and—as Coleridge,[1] informed by Southey, reported on 4th December— "cut at heart by the questions and remarks of the Spaniards, who, he says, are the noblest people on earth, and will finally succeed in spite of their allies". The Supreme Junta published its thanks for his "gallant personal service" and for a donation of twenty thousand reals, and King Ferdinand's minister sent him a commission as honorary colonel in the Spanish army. When, some years later, Ferdinand restored religious intolerance and subverted the constitution, Landor returned his commission to the minister, saying he had served in the cause of Spanish liberty against Napoleon, but would have "nothing to do with a perjurer and traitor". Publishing in 1829 the satirical imaginary conversation, "Ferdinand and John-Mary-Luis", he said of Spain, "Legitimate government and catholic religion are maintained by a mob of plunderers and assassins, with a fugitive, perjurer, and parricide at the head of them."

---

[1] Soon after his return from Spain, Landor received from Southey a prospectus of Coleridge's periodical, *The Friend*, and wrote immediately to Coleridge from 9 South Parade, Bath, on 14th December:

Sir,
    I beg permission to be a subscriber to the publication you announce. Mr Southey sent me the Prospectus. It followed me from Warwickshire to Clifton, and from Clifton to Bath. Hence arises my delay in acknowledging the pleasure I received from it and in offering the congratulations it gives me the liberty to make.
I am Sir
Yours very respectfully
W. LANDOR

Coleridge forwarded the note to his wife with the endorsement, "Send it back: as I should like to have a specimen of the Handwriting of so remarkable a man, and of a Genius so brilliant and original." The note lay unnoticed in the Wordsworth Museum at Dove Cottage, Grasmere, till printed by Mr. Super in his "Landor's Letters to Wordsworth and Coleridge", *Modern Philology*, November 1957.

5

MARRIAGE

I never will ask for anything except for heaven and a wife.

—Landor to Southey, March 1810

On last Wednesday I was present at a wedding, the only one I ever was at, excepting my own. I wish it had been the first.

—Landor to Lady Blessington, 23rd December 1839

On his return from Spain in November 1808, after a visit to his mother at Warwick, Landor settled at Bath for the winter. He was full of plans for development of his new estate at Llanthony, and letters from his agent indicated need of his presence to superintend the building operations in progress. But all the farms at Llanthony were occupied, there was no house for the owner, and the privations of campaigning must have left little appetite for wintering in the rooms of the Abbey ruins furnished by his predecessor as a shooting-box.

The Tachbrook estate being entailed, an act of Parliament was necessary before its sale to the Earl of Warwick could be effected. Informed by Landor in January 1809 that he had a bill coming before the House of Commons, Southey offered him an introduction to his friend John Rickman, who was secretary to the Speaker; though he went to London in late April, it does not appear that Landor took advantage of the introduction. The act was passed on 20th May, and the estate subsequently realised twenty thousand pounds, of which legal expenses absorbed rather more than five per cent.

Between visits to Llanthony from his headquarters at Bath, Landor resumed his excursions to Clifton and Brighton. Deeply concerned with the state of Spain, he wrote to Southey, "I believe no breed of people to be so good; but they have nothing to fight for, and nobody to lead them if they had." Following his *Letters to Riquelme*, he wrote a pamphlet or letters called "Hints to a Junta"; Southey was impressed by its arguments, particularly by the proposal that Spanish and Portuguese should unite in a federal republic, but Landor questioned "if any bookseller would print the thing if I gave it him".

With Napoleon's conquests spreading all over Europe, liberal opinion became virulent in its criticism of the government's hesitant policy, and like all harassed rulers, the government retaliated with repressive measures against freedom of speech. Gale Jones, a radical surgeon, was imprisoned for an alleged breach of parliamentary privilege, and Sir Francis Burdett was committed to the Tower for protesting against the illegality of Jones's conviction; William Cobbett was committed to Newgate as "a common sower of sedition"; Leigh Hunt and his brother were charged on the same grounds as Cobbett and escaped his fate only by Brougham's eloquence; even the respectable Perry of the *Morning Chronicle* was prosecuted for "seditious libel". On the news of Burdett's imprisonment in April 1810, Landor told Southey that he devoted "five long hours' work" to addressing an open letter to Burdett, but apparently he found no newspaper willing to print it. As newspaper contributors resorted to the anonymity that the *Edinburgh* and *Quarterly* reviews adopted as their rule, editors and publishers grew increasingly careful of their responsibility and an unhealthy timidity prevailed.

Landor resorted to his former method of expressing in Latin views considered unprintable in English, addressing *Ad Gustavum Regem* and *Ad Gustavum Exulem* to Gustavus IV of Sweden, whose hatred of Napoleon led in 1809 to his dethronement and replacement by an uncle, who ruled under the direction of Napoleon's marshal, Bernadotte. Some letters of Landor's may have found their way into the anonymity of newspaper columns, but he already had reason to regard the practice of anonymity with suspicion. In 1808 gossip caused him annoyance by attributing to him authorship of a lampoon on Dr. Parr and his friends called *Guy's Porridge Pot*. Hearing of the rumours from his sister, he immediately assured Parr that he was innocent of such treachery; as he told Southey, "Parr believed me instantly", for Parr wrote on 21st June 1808:

My excellent and dear friend, how could you give yourself the trouble of defending yourself to me against a Warwick rumour; or for one moment suppose me so completely sottish as to believe such an imputation against Walter Landor.

Probably on the authority of Robert Landor, Forster denied definitely that Landor wrote the lampoon. Robert may have confessed to Forster that he himself was the author, for in the catalogue of Forster's library *Guy's Porridge Pot* is listed under Robert's name, and in a letter from the continent in 1816 Robert wrote to his brother Henry: "I am sorry for what you tell me about Shuckburgh; as to Jack Venour, I will finish Guy's Porridge Pot on my return for his sake."

Robert disliked Parr and bore him a grudge; he had also suited his political colour to the changing tone of the *Courier*, which by 1808 had assumed support of the government. The reasons why rumour attributed *Guy's Porridge Pot* to Landor were, firstly, he was not included among the victims of the satire, and secondly, the lampoon was printed at Oxford by Slatter & Munday, printers of the revised *Gebir* and the Latin *Gebirus*—in preparing which for the press Landor had been helped by Robert. The printers may have hinted that the anonymous author's name was Landor, whereupon everybody thought of the better-known brother, just as years afterwards Robert's *Fawn of Sertorius* was ascribed to him.

More than probably Robert Landor wrote *Guy's Porridge Pot*; it seems only less likely that his eldest brother wrote the anonymous reply, *The Dun Cow; An Hyper-Satirical Dialogue in Verse with Explanatory Notes*. In the catalogue of Dr. Parr's library *The Dun Cow* was listed as Landor's, doubtless on the authority of a manuscript note by Parr; it contains a satirical passage on the Warwick physician Winthrop, with whom Landor had a score of long standing to settle.[1] He never otherwise employed the London printers of *The Dun Cow*, W. and T. Darton, but as Slatter & Munday's imprint was the main reason for rumour's ascribing *Guy's Porridge Pot* to him, he would naturally seek—writing his reply in annoyance during May or June 1808—to secure his anonymity by employing printers with whom his name was not associated. Published in 1808, *The Dun Cow* evoked a reply called *The Warwickshire Talents, alias Guy's Porridge Pot, with The Dun Cow Roasted Whole*. The balance of honours rested with the *Porridge Pot*, but while Landor bore a redoubtable lance in the lists of scholarly controversy, he always uneasily condescended to scuffles in journalism.

On his return from Spain concern with high politics left him no taste for local bickering. "As I never drink wine," he told Southey, "I am forced every now and then to write half a dozen verses, that I may forget what is passing round about." Southey counselled him to "Christian stoicism"; "were I your confessor, I should enjoin you to throw aside Rousseau, and make Epictetus your manual". He begged him to "write in English, because it is a better language than Latin":

Literary fame is the only fame of which a wise man ought to be ambitious, because it is the only lasting and living fame. Bonaparte will be forgotten before his time in Purgatory is half over, or but just remembered like Nimrod, or other cut-throats of antiquity, who serve us for the commonplaces of declamation. If you made yourself King of Crete, you would differ from a hundred other adventurers only in chronology, and in the course of a millennium or two, nothing more would be known of your conquest than what would be found in the stereotype Gebir prefixed as an account of the author. Pour out your mind in a great poem, and you will exercise authority over the feelings and opinions of mankind as long as the language lasts.

[1] Curiously Mr. Super (*The Authorship of* Guy's Porridge Pot *and* The Dun Cow, *The Library*, June, 1950) interprets the satirical passage on Winthrop as praise of him.

Having finished *The Curse of Kehama*—dedicated "to the Author of *Gebir*, Walter Savage Landor"—Southey was writing his *Roderick* and regularly sending instalments for Landor's criticism. Early in 1809 Landor was "reading what I had not read before of Euripides" and finding "in most of his tragedies . . . more preachment than poetry"; he was also reading Aristotle's *Poetics* in Twining's translation. With the current news of the war in Spain daily in his thoughts and his experience of the country and its people fresh in his memory, the reading of Southey's *Roderick* inspired the idea of writing his own version of the theme as a tragedy in verse.

Count Julian, a noble Spanish general, assists the Moorish enemy to conquer his country as vengeance against his king Roderigo for the seduction of his daughter. The actual unfolding of this story would have furnished the action of a heroic tragedy in Dryden's style, but such is the situation at the opening of Landor's tragedy, which develops the consequences of Julian's indulgence of personal revenge—by Moor and Spaniard alike he is regarded as a traitor whose treachery was inspired only by ambition—he brings sorrow and evil upon all he loves and suffers remorse for having betrayed his country and his religion. As De Quincey wrote:

The story is wrapt in gigantic mists, and looms upon one like the Grecian fable of Œdipus . . . it is the most fearful lesson extant of the great moral that crime propagates crime, and violence inherits violence;—nay, a lesson on the awful *necessity* which exists at times that one tremendous wrong should blindly reproduce itself in endless retaliatory wrongs. To have resisted the dread temptation would have needed an angel's nature: to have yielded is but human; should it, then, plead in vain for pardon?—and yet, by some mystery of evil, to have perfected this human vengeance is, finally, to land all parties alike, oppressor and oppressed, in the passions of hell.

As early as July 1810, when Southey first mentioned his plan of *Roderick*, Landor professed that he had written "about the third of a tragedy, the subject of which is Count Julian"; but he then intended to present Julian "as the most excellent and the most patient of all earthly beings, till the violation of his daughter". Suspicion arises that he had not in fact started the tragedy, but wished to forestall Southey's possible resentment at his writing about the same subject. In the following November he wrote to Southey from Bath:

One evening, as I returned from the concert, I wrote down a speech for my tragedy of *Count Julian*. I am happy we take such opposite, or rather such distant ground. . . . My magnificent plan is now totally changed. I had made some fine speeches, really and truly; but, alas, I rejected them all because they *were* fine speeches. I am a man who *semper ad eventum festinet*; and although I have not more than about four hundred verses that will remain . . . yet I have finished the last scene.

He enclosed a draft of the last scene, where Julian is told of the deaths of his wife and son.

"I work with great rapidity on what interests and excites me," he remarked to Lady Blessington in 1838, and so, once started, he worked on *Count Julian*. In one burst of forty hours he wrote a thousand lines. Normally his hours of work "were four or five together, after long walks, in which I brought before me the various characters, the very tones of their voices, their forms, complexions and step. In the daytime I laboured, and at night unburdened my mind, shedding many tears". In December he reported completion of the first act. On 21st January 1811 he wrote, "I have finished *Count Julian* this evening." He thought "it cannot be well done, written with such amazing rapidity", but on 5th February he sent a fair copy to Southey, having "laboured days and nights, without intermission almost, in correcting".

Seeking an explanation why *Count Julian* never achieved production on the Victorian stage, Sidney Colvin damaged its repute with the opinion—reflecting his own want of feeling—that the characters "fail to convince or carry us away"; he thought "this effect is partly due, no doubt, to defect of dramatic construction", as "the scenes of the play succeed each other by no process of organic sequence or evolution". Landor had no knowledge of contemporary stagecraft—"you would hardly imagine it", he confided to Southey, "I have not seen a play acted a dozen times in my life". He sent to the library for a volume of Racine, "for the sole purpose of counting what number of verses was the average of a tragedy"; when it came, "I turned over his messieurs and mesdames with a vacant stare, and sent the volume away in a passion without the least idea what had induced me to order an author I dislike so much." Too closely he followed Aristotle's precepts on classical drama: the models he cited to Southey were Sophocles and Euripides, and he congratulated himself on achieving unity of action— "the events of the first act lead naturally to the last, and every scene is instrumental to the catastrophe". As soon as he read the play, Southey remarked, "it is too Greek for representation in these times".

For many years a practising dramatic critic, Forster thought "too little is left for the art of the actor, and too much for the imagination of the audience". "I will cut all my figures out of one block," Landor told Southey, "under one conception of their characters." All the characters are pre-conceived, and with all the action happening off-stage, each is the mouthpiece of thoughts and emotions reflecting on the central theme; they are not permitted to develop their characters by their conduct in circumstances visually presented before the audience. As Forster said, the audience is presented with "results too quickly, when all the little intermediate steps have been overlooked".

"I delight in the minute variations and almost imperceptible shades

of the female character," Landor told Southey in 1812, "and confess
that my reveries, from my most early youth, were almost entirely on
what this one or that one would have said or done in this or that
situation. Their countenances, their movements, their forms, the
colours of their dresses, were before my eyes." He was in fact a potential
novelist, but *semper ad eventum festinat*—he was always hurrying to the
crux of the situation, without pausing to portray the setting or to
convey to his reader the appearances so vividly before his own eyes.
The *Imaginary Conversations*, like *Count Julian*, reveal that Landor
possessed both the original creativeness of the novelist and the imaginative re-creativeness of the biographer in drawing character. He wrote
neither novels nor biography, because he lacked the self-discipline to
acquire the art of either; he chose the form of dialogue as the most
direct means of presenting his imaginative conceptions.

Count Julian is not a play in a theatrical sense, but a series of imaginary
conversations in verse. Recognising the limitations of his art, De
Quincey alone among Landor's critics appreciated the power of his
genius in presenting his conceptions in spite of self-imposed handicap.
Possessing equally the gift of imagination without the self-discipline of
the novelist or the biographer, he expressed in his "ecstasies" that which
Landor expressed in dialogue. Like Landor he could see the people and
their setting without having them described for him. Comparing *Count
Julian* with Shelley's *Prometheus Unbound*, he wrote:

After all has been done which intellectual power *could* do since Æschylus
(and since Milton in his Satan), no embodiment of the Promethean situation, none of the Promethean character, fixes the attentive eye upon
itself with the same secret feeling of fidelity to the vast archetype as Mr.
Landor's "Count Julian". There is in this modern aërolith the same
jewelly lustre which cannot be mistaken, the same *non imitabile fulgur*, and
the same character of "fracture" or *cleavage*, as mineralogists speak, for its
beaming iridescent grandeur, redoubling under the crush of misery. The
colour and the coruscation are the same when splintered by violence; the
tones of the rocky harp are the same when swept by sorrow. There is the
same spirit of heavenly persecution against his enemy,—persecution that
would have hung upon his rear, and "burnt after him to the bottomless
pit" though it had yawned for both; there is the same gulf fixed between the
possibilities of their reconciliation, the same immortality of resistance, the
same eternity of abysmal sorrow. Did Mr. Landor *consciously* cherish this
Æschylean ideal in composing "Count Julian"? I know not: there it is!

If *Count Julian* is read as De Quincey read it, there is no room for wonder
that Landor shed tears over its writing. He not only so absorbed himself in his hero that he felt his emotions, but in Julian's nightmares about
the ruin of his race mirrored his own despair at the current plight of
humanity. There was a parallel between Roderigo's proposal to put
away the barren Egilona for marriage with Covilla and Napoleon's

recent divorce from Josephine to marry the youthful Marie-Louise.
Then as now Spain faced the choice:

> Whether we live beneath a foreign sway—
> Or under him whose tyranny brought down
> The curse upon his people.

And Julian apostrophises Spain as Landor thought of England as well as
of Spain:

> Unconquerable land! unrivalled race!
> Whose bravery, too enduring, rues alike
> The power and weakness of accursed kings.

Julian counsels his daughter to seek refuge in scenes visited by Landor
himself:

> Whether where Castro from surrounding vines
> Hears the hoarse ocean roar among his caves,
> And, thro' the fissure in the green church-yard,
> The wind wail loud the calmest summer day;

or

> in Aguilar—
> Impenetrable, marble-turreted,
> Surveying from aloft the limpid ford,
> The massive fane, the sylvan avenue—
> Whose hospitality I proved myself,
> A willing leader in no impious war
> When fame and freedom urged me—or mayst dwell
> In Reynosa's dry and thriftless dale,
> Unharvested beneath October moons,
> Amongst those frank and cordial villagers.

The Metropolitan of Seville reproaches Julian for involving the innocent in war:

> If only warlike spirits were evoked
> By the war-demon, I would not complain,
> Or dissolute and discontented men;
> But wherefor hurry down into the square
> The neighbourly, saluting, warm-clad race,
> Who would not injure us, and could not serve;
> Who, from their short and measured slumber risen,
> In the faint sunshine of their balconies,
> With a half-legend of a martyrdom
> And some weak wine and withered grapes before them,

Note by their foot the wheel of melody
That catches and rolls on the sabbath dance.
To drag the steddy prop from failing age,
Break the young stem that fondness twines around,
Widen the solitude of lonely sighs,
And scatter to the broad bleak wastes of day[1]
The ruins and the phantoms that replied,
Ne'er be it thine.

Julian's remarks on patriotism reflected Landor's own affliction in contemplating his country's misgovernment:

All men with human feelings love their country . . .
'Tis the old mansion of their earliest friends,
The chapel of their first and best devotions;
When violence, or perfidy, invades,
Or when unworthy lords hold wassail there,
And wiser heads are drooping round its moats,
At last they fix their steddy and stiff eye
There, there alone—stand while the trumpet blows,
And view the hostile flames above its towers
Spire, with a bitter and severe delight.

Its topical allusions suggested a possibility of popular success for *Count Julian.* "I confess to you," Landor had confided to Southey a few months before, "if even foolish men had read *Gebir*, I should have continued to write poetry;—there is something of summer in the hum of insects." His fears of disparagement revived on sending the script of *Count Julian* to Southey: "Do not whisper to any one that I have written a tragedy," he begged; "my name is composed of unlucky letters." But, encouraged by Southey's praise, he began to build hopes on the suggestion that the notorious vanity of John Philip Kemble might be tempted by the part of Count Julian. He disliked the theatre: "I am not remarkably pure or chaste; but to hear generous and pathetic sentiments and to behold glorious and grand actions amidst the vulgar hard-hearted language of prostitutes and lobby-loungers, not only takes away all my pleasure by the evident contrast, but seizes me with the most painful and insuperable disgust." He thought "Kemble may be tried", though "if Kemble will not act it, I would not submit it to inferior actors". "I think now of the public taste precisely as I did

---

[1] Here, Landor told Southey, he intended to insert the line, "Spectres of bliss and avenues of hope"—"the meaning being—and destroy all those scenes of privacy and retirement in which the wretched raise up those illusions which reply and are correspondent with their distempered imagination". While impressed by "the thought and feeling which you have frequently condensed in a single line", Southey cited this passage among those marred by obscurity resulting—as in *Gebir*—from excessive condensation.

when I wrote the first preface to *Gebir*," he said; "if *Count Julian* is endured, it will be because it is different from anything of the day, and not from any excellence."

When, in May 1811, proposing to show the script to Kemble during a visit to London, Southey hinted a tactful warning against too hopeful expectation, Landor recoiled from the indignity of possible rejection.

Count Julian shall never lie at the feet of Kemble. It must not be offered for representation. I will print it, and immediately. Give me your advice how this is to be done.

Evidently he hoped that Southey might suggest an approach to his own publishers, Longmans; he did not realise that Longmans were unlikely to consider a dramatic poem on the subject of the epic they were expecting from Southey. Ignoring the hint, Southey chose to suppose that Landor intended to print at his own expense, and advised: "Print the tragedy in a volume with boarded covers, not as a pamphlet to be dog-leaved." Foolishly Landor sent the manuscript to Longmans, explaining that Southey "thought not unfavourably of it". Longmans refused it, and added to his mortification by still refusing to publish when he offered to pay for the printing. On 25th June he wrote to Southey from Llanthony:

On receiving the last letter of Mr. Longman to this purport, I committed to the flames my tragedy of *Ferrante and Giulio*, with which I intended to surprise you, and am resolved that never verse of mine hereafter shall be committed to anything else. My literary career has been a very curious one. You cannot imagine how I feel relieved at laying down its burden, and abandoning this tissue of humiliations. I fancied I had at last acquired the right tone of tragedy, and was treading down at heel the shoes of Alfieri.

Southey replied from London on 15th July:

It is utterly unaccountable to me why you of all men should care either for good or evil report of your poems, certain as you must be of their sterling value. I look upon Gebir as I do upon Dante's long poem in the Italian, not as a good poem, but as containing the finest poetry in the language; so it is with C. Julian, and so no doubt it was with the play you have so provokingly destroyed.

He sought to soften the blow of Longmans' rejection by explaining that "the people at that house know nothing about books except in the mere detail of trade; and the only thing which they would think of was, that single plays did not sell unless they were represented". Landor reassured him that "portions" of *Ferrante and Giulio* had been saved from the flames; he was not normally careless with his compositions, as appears in the many poems of his youth preserved in manuscript for half a century to be published in the last eleven years of his life.

In August 1811 Southey visited Llanthony. Asked to suggest a bookseller who would print *Count Julian* on commission, he wrote in October

RUINS OF LANDOR'S HOUSE AT LLANTHONY
Known locally as "The Sharple"
From a drawing by James Wood about 1940

that John Murray would publish the poem if Landor paid for the printing; he recommended an edition of only two hundred and fifty copies, "because the play would be highly admired by the few, but probably not popular, being too good for the many". Murray published *Count Julian* in the spring of 1812 at 5s. 6d.,[1] without the author's name. "I hear that Southey has criticised it in the Edinburgh Review, and Mr. Gifford in the Quarterly," wrote Landor from Llanthony to Walter Birch on 11th May 1813; "I never read Reviews. A man who has a taste for them, must have a taste for gaols and lazarettos." Southey's review appeared in the *Quarterly* of September 1812; he said of his script that the editor, William Gifford, "so completely knocked its brains out" that he never mentioned it to Landor. The tone is much less flattering than that of his letters. It is pointed out that the author interprets the characters of Julian and Opas differently from approved historians, though "the purposes of the dramatist have certainly been served by this departure from historical verity and received tradition". Six pages relate the action of the play, quoting eight extracts displaying "a rich vein of poetry" and "containing parts in as deep a tone of passion as can be found in English poetry". The conclusion may well be the result of clumsy condensation by Gifford:

As a drama, it is evident that it has not been intended for representation,— so little is it addressed either to the eyes or the ears of the multitude. The fable is not always sufficiently clear; in a few instances the language, which is occasionally laboured into stiffness, borders on obscurity, and the verse is everywhere epic rather than dramatic.

We should have no hesitation in ascribing Count Julian to the author of a narrative poem of which the story is strange and unprepossessing, and the diction obscure, but in which the higher requisites of poetry are incidentally displayed in an eminent degree. The same powers are exhibited here so strikingly, and the defects which exist partake so much of the same character, that the internal evidence secures decision; but when an author has not thought proper to affix his name, the critic who gives it publicity assumes an authority to which neither the laws of courtesy nor of his profession entitle him.

If the last sentence did not exceed in obscurity anything of Landor's, its rebuke to anonymity might seem ironical in a periodical insisting upon anonymity in its contributors.

§ 2

Landor interpreted in *Count Julian* his personal feelings not only on politics. The anguish of Covilla's lover, Sisabert, in believing her

---

[1] The price was first announced as 5s., as in the *Edinburgh Review*, July 1812, but in the *Edinburgh*, July 1813, the volume appears as "Foolscap, 5s. 6d. boards" and the price is 5s. 6d. in the *Quarterly Review* of December 1812 and July 1813, described in the latter as 8vo.

I

faithless reflects the emotions inspired by Ianthe's refusal to sacrifice her reputation for their love:

> Fear me not now, Covilla! thou hast changed,
> I am changed too—I lived but where thou livedst,
> My very life was portioned off from thine.
> Upon the surface of thy happiness
> Day after day I gazed, I doted—there
> Was all I had, was all I coveted;
> So pure, serene, and boundless it appear'd:
> Yet, for we told each other every thought,
> Thou knowest well, if thou rememberest,
> At times I fear'd; as tho' some demon sent
> Suspicion without form into the world,
> To whisper unimaginable things;
> Then thy fond arguing banisht all but hope,
> Each wish, and every feeling, was with thine,
> Till I partook thy nature, and became
> Credulous, and incredulous, like thee.
> We, who have met so alter'd, meet no more.
> Mountains and seas! ye are not separation;
> Death! thou dividest, but unitest too,
> In everlasting peace and faith sincere.
> Confiding love! where is thy resting-place!
> Where is thy truth, Covilla! where!—go, go,
> I should adore thee and believe thee still.

Absorbed in plans for a model estate at Llanthony, he now wished to marry and settle in a home of his own. On his return from Spain in November 1808, he confided to Southey:

I believe I should have been a good and happy man if I had married. My heart is tender. I am fond of children and of talking childishly. I hate to travel even two stages. Never without pang do I leave the house where I was born. Even a short stay attaches me to any place. But, Southey, I love a woman who will never love me, and am beloved by one who never ought. I do not say I shall never be happy. I shall be often so, if I live; but I shall never be at rest. My evil genius drags me through existence against the current of my best inclinations. I have practised self-denial, because it gives me a momentary and false idea that I am firm; and I have done some other things not amiss, in compliance with my heart; but my most virtuous hopes and sentiments have uniformly led to misery, and I have never been happy but in consequence of some weakness or some vice.

His biographers have remained content to be baffled by the statement that he loved a woman who would never love him and was "beloved by one who never ought".[1] Yet it is surely plain that, while he wished to confide his predicament to Southey, he was intent on guarding Ianthe's reputation. He therefore implied that he was implicated with two women, though the situation of both was Ianthe's—she would never love him as he wished, by sacrificing her reputation and leaving her husband to live with him; though as a married woman she "never ought", she wished to continue their illicit affair clandestinely.

Tactfully ignoring Landor's dilemma, Southey counselled him from his own experience:

> Find out a woman whom you can esteem, & love will grow more surely out of esteem, than esteem will out of love. . . . *Rest* is the object to be sought: there is no other way of attaining it here where we have no convents, but by putting an end to all the hopes & fears to which the best hearts are the most subject.

To Southey marriage was a refuge from disturbing desire—from such desire as Landor was suffering for "a woman who will never love me". If he remembered that his advice had proved disastrous in Coleridge's case, he may have reflected that Landor was not, like Coleridge, a victim of both physical affliction and addiction to drugs. Landor was physically normal and tender of heart; married to a woman whom he esteemed, he would shrink from wounding her by infidelity and therefore secure the requisite "rest" by banishing the possibility of pursuing desire.

Southey's advice coincided with that of Landor's sister Elizabeth, and after his return from Spain he earnestly sought a suitable wife. He continued at Ianthe's feet when she was in England, for he told Elizabeth that "the *heart* has had her picture taken", and though the portrait was "not half so beautiful as she", he was moved to write the verses beginning, "O thou whose happy pencil strays". In the same letter of 1809 he wrote to Elizabeth from Bath, "I believe I am more in request here then I have ever been, not for myself—we are not like wine, improvable with age—but for Frolic and Favourite, and Lanthony." But, he added, "Frolic and Favourite look prudent, and Lanthony is jealous of everything I *could* admire"—implying that expenses at Llanthony left no margin for other extravagance. Again:

> I went to Mrs. Wells's Ball and Supper. We had pines, peas, sparagus, strawberries, and at least sixty other good things! There were two tables.

[1] Mr. Super ungenerously remarks that "since the original letter does not survive we may be dealing not with what Landor actually wrote but with what Forster partly invented"; he does not explain why Forster should have invented a statement on which he offered no comment. Colvin followed Forster, but assumed that Landor's "flirtations were numerous and were carried far. There is even not wanting, in his dealings with and his language concerning women during this brief period, a touch of commonplace rakishness, a shadow of vulgarity nowhere else to be discerned in the ways of this most unvulgar of mankind". Declining to identify Jane Swift with the "woman who will never love me" or the "one who never ought", Wheeler decided that Ianthe was not the woman who selected the love poems in *Simonidea*.

The ladies sat down first, the men attending them. When the ladies rose, they fell to—remember it was past one o'clock. They danced till six. Tell Robin—whom God preserve—that—God forgive me—there was ice enough to cover the Nieper and beauty enough to thaw it all, had any remained uneaten.

He kept Elizabeth informed of his matrimonial prospects; in letters to his mother he included such messages as "tell her that at present there is nothing interesting, not a soul".

At the end of January 1811—when he was revising *Count Julian*— he made his choice, which he announced to Southey in April:

I have found a girl without a sixpence, and with very few accomplishments. She is pretty, graceful and good-tempered—three things indispensable to my happiness. Adieu, and congratulate me. I forgot to say that I have added thirty-five verses to scene ii of act 3.

About the same time he wrote to his mother:

The name of my intended bride is Julia Thuillier. She has no pretensions of any kind, and her want of fortune was the very thing which determined me to marry her. I shall be sorry to leave Bath entirely, but when I have completed my house I must remain there.

After a four months' courtship the wedding took place at St. James's Church, Bath, on 24th May 1811. Few of Landor's friends were present; several heard of it only after the event. Dr. Parr wrote his congratulations on 7th June:

My heart would leap for joy if I saw both of you at my parsonage gate. . . . God bless you both! Walter, your genius and talents, your various and splendid attainments, your ardent affections, your high and heroic spirit, will ever command my admiration, and give me a lively interest in your happiness.

Fearing lest the marriage might have been an impetuous decision, Walter Birch offered diffident advice, "Do not smile at me; but it is my belief that an excellent wife is seldom made perfect to our hands, but is in part the creation of the husband after marriage, the result of his character and behaviour acting upon her own." Landor may have uttered his boisterous laugh, thinking this admonition characteristic of the friend known at Rugby as "Sancty", but he immediately acknowledged Birch's "very kind & sensible letter, not only because it was written by one of the wisest & best among my friends, but by the earliest of them all".

I often feared I should be tempted to marry a woman of fortune, & particularly as my expenses in planting & other things have lately been very great. I have preserved so far the consistency of my character in this important point—it is uneven in others, but those are only the edges & extremities. You are right,—that the character of women depends very much upon ourselves. We also, tho' of firmer texture, are moulded by others more than we are willing to allow. More people are good because they are happy, than happy because they are good. This is not however, the highest kind of goodness but it wears passably well, and always looks sleek.

Forster repeated an anecdote—apparently gleaned after the first edition of his biography had been published in 1869—that, on first seeing Julia Thuillier as he entered a ballroom, Landor exclaimed, "By Heaven! that's the nicest girl in the room, and I'll marry her." The story can be believed neither of "this most unvulgar of mankind" nor of one with a horror of seeming foolish, who believed that his name was "composed of unlucky letters". Clearly Landor was not such a fool as Forster inferred. Having decided to follow Southey's advice—to marry without passion, in the hope that affection would grow out of esteem—he did not delude himself that he desired in a wife no more than an accommodating housekeeper. As he remarked in reference to Miss Seward, he "preferred a pretty woman to a literary one", and he expressed the opinion to Southey in February 1811—within three or four weeks of meeting Miss Thuillier—"that it is the highest of all virtues to choose such a woman as may confer a good form and good dispositions on her progeny".

"I have been told," wrote Robert Landor sardonically to his brother, "that notwithstanding your indifference about everything else besides good temper, you have contrived to get a great many other qualities into the bargain." Julia Thuillier came of good stock. The Thuilliers left France during the persecution of the Huguenots and settled at Geneva, and her grandfather—according to Landor—was a general in the Austrian service. Her father—"a republican and *ultra* even at Geneva"—came to England and married a Miss Burrow of Exeter, one of whose brothers became vicar of Bampton in Oxfordshire. Apparently for some time a banker at Banbury, Thuillier invested in a business at Cadiz, which naturally suffered vicissitudes during the Peninsular War; he was absent at Cadiz, recouping his losses, at the time of his daughter's marriage to Landor.

Julia was one of ten children; her mother gave birth to an eleventh in 1813. She was attractive, with hair as golden as Nancy Jones's, and only seventeen years old. With a seniority of nineteen years, Landor may well have expected to "mould" her character. Her youth and financial dependence offered claims to his chivalry—a quality he always required in the conduct of men towards women. Nearly half a century later, in August 1859, he told Kate Field, "I never loved but *twice*. I married to get rid of love, but found *this did not answer at all*".

6

BOYTHORN AT LLANTHONY

Homeward I turn: o'er Hatteril's rocks
I see my trees, I hear my flocks.
Where alders mourn'd their fruitless bed,
Ten thousand cedars raise their head;
And from Segovia's hills remote
My sheep enrich my neighbour's cote.
The wide and easy road I lead
Where never paced the harness'd steed;
Where scarcely dared the goat look down
Beneath the fearful mountain's frown,
Suspended, while the torrent's spray
Springs o'er the crags that roll away.
But Envy's steps too soon pursue
The man who hazards schemes so new;
Who, better fit for Rome and Greece,
Thinks to be—*Justice of the Peace*!
— Landor to Southey, October 1812

The French laws, if they are observed, are incomparably better than ours, which are calculated only for the rich and the crafty. A man in France cannot be ruined by pursuing his rights. In England he unquestionably may.

— Landor to Southey from Tours, 8th May 1815

Landor's letter to Birch on his marriage was dated from Llanthony on 25th June 1811. Having wasted no time on a travelling honeymoon, he wrote to Southey soon after his arrival at Llanthony:

After my marriage I stayed at Rodboro' and Petty France for three weeks, intending to spring upon you on your way to London. There was a disinclination in my wife either to remain at Bath or visit Clifton. She wished to escape from visits of ceremony and curiosity, and I would not hint to her any reason why I should be happy to pass a few days at Bath.

Is it too "imaginative" to suppose that Landor's wife had heard in Bath of his long attachment to Ianthe and prudently resolved to avoid meeting her?

His house, as Landor told Birch, was not yet finished:

My house here has once been taken down, and has once fallen down of its own accord. I am building it again, and hope to complete it before the end of September. It is situated on the edge of a dingle, in which is a little rill of water, overshadowed by a vast variety of trees. I have a dining-room 28 by 22 and 14 feet high, drawing-room & library 18 square, six family bedrooms & six servants; but in the abbey—which is a quarter of a mile off, however—I can make up a few more beds, and there I intend to have all my offices. I shall live on very little—I should even if I were not obliged —I planted last year three hundred acres, and shall plant as many this.

The ruins of the house still stand, beside the little rill tumbling down the hillside, past the Abbey, to join the river Honddy in the valley. Locally it is known as the Sharple, or Sharpll, though this name does not appear to have been used by Landor; its back premises, deep in mud, have served as a cattle hovel. Behind the building runs a grass-grown road, crossing the rill by a bridge; the road leads nowhere, for it is the road begun and unfinished by Landor, which he apparently intended should run down from his house to the village of Cwmyoy, and above his house over the hill to the Herefordshire village of Longtown. Nobody will deny that he knew how to select the site of a house. The ruins stand at the foot of a steep fall of the Hatterell Hills, on the slope of which the little farmstead of Loxidge perches perilously. From his front door Landor commanded a view across the whole of the vale, and beyond the vale, through a gap in the mountains, far into the mists above the Usk valley.

Visitors to Llanthony will realise how the sombre grandeur of its wild scenery appealed to Landor's imagination, to his morose moods and his craving for solitude. Except that the winding lane to the Abbey, which leaves the Abergavenny-Hereford road by the ancient Skirrid Inn, now possesses a tarmac surface, the place is little altered from Landor's day. The Vale of Ewyas forms a narrow peninsula of Monmouthshire at the extreme north of the county; on the west the first ridge of the Black Mountains rises steeply to form the bleak boundary of Brecknockshire, on the east the more richly tinted Hatterell Hills loom equally high to cut off the vale from Herefordshire. At the foot between the hills—running for several miles beside the lane, which continues past the Abbey to the hamlet of Capel-y-ffin, and thence becomes a mere track over the hills to the market town of Hay—rush and tumble the curiously dark though clear waters of the little river Honddy (Welsh *Honddu*, or black water), which swells to flood rapidly after rain, and is reputed one of the richest trout streams in Wales. It is about six miles from the Skirrid Inn to the Abbey; two miles after passing Llanvihangel Court the impressive splendour of the vale appears, with the village of Cwmyoy close by the river on the right. The Queen's Head Inn, at the

threshold of one of the two by-lanes running down to Cwmyoy, provided one of the many causes of friction between Landor and his tenants.
Soon the site of Landor's bridge at the Henllan is reached, shortly
before passing the entrance gate of Maes-y-berin farm (which Landor,
who had his own way of spelling Welsh names and usually wrote
"Lantony" with one *l* and no *h*, called "Marybaren"); little more than
another mile brings the traveller to the handful of cottages comprising
Llanthony village.

The name of Llanthony is corrupted from *Llan-Honddu*, or, according
to Giraldus Cambrensis, *Llan-Ddewi-Nant-Honddu*, "the Church of St.
David on the river Honddu", as St. David, the patron saint of Wales,
built a chapel there, to which he retired for periods of fasting in contemplation and quiet. At the Conquest the manor came to a Norman,
Hugh de Lacy, a kinsman of whom was moved by the valley's sombre
beauty to reflect upon "the vanity and transience of the human life",
to renounce the world, and to settle at Llanthony as a hermit. This Lacy
built the Abbey—more properly, a priory—which was completed by
1120, so narrowly preceding the building of Llandaff Cathedral.
Subsequently the Bishop of Hereford found difficulty in persuading
monks to accept exile at Llanthony, "for they used to say there was
much difference between the City of Gloucester and the wild rocks of
Hatyrel; between the river Severn and the brook of Hodeni; between
the wealthy English and the beggarly Welsh; there fertile meadows;
here barren heaths". In a Latin manuscript one of the monks, while
praising the natural beauty of the Abbey's surroundings, condemns the
local peasantry as "savage, without religion, thieves, and vagabonds,
who viewed the establishment of a religious community with suspicion,
and delighted more in feuds among themselves than in the practice of
the arts of peace". The lawlessness of its natives earned for the vale the
name of Ewyas, or Gwyas, meaning in Welsh "a place of battle". The
Monk of Llanthony records an occasion when a peasant and his family
took refuge in the Abbey from their neighbours, who pursued them into
the sanctuary; after a fight in the outer court, the women seized the
monks' refectory, and were "not ashamed to sing and to profane that
place with their light and effeminate behaviour". The monks appealed
against their exposure to such lawlessness, and their bishop secured a
grant for the building of another priory near Gloucester.

At the dissolution of the monasteries Henry VIII granted Llanthony
to Sir Nicholas Arnold. The Arnolds were active persecutors of Roman
Catholics, and in 1680 John Arnold, M.P. for Monmouth, escaped
assassination by a native of Usk. John Arnold's son Nicholas sold the
Llanthony and Llanvihangel estates in 1720 to Edward Harley, Earl of
Oxford, son of Queen Anne's minister, who suffered vexatious litigation
for several years after his purchase. The Harley family retained the

estates till October 1799, when the manors of "Cwmyoy, Lantony, Stanton, Redcastle, Oldcastle, and Triley" were offered by auction in forty-six lots at Abergavenny. Llanvihangel Court was purchased by Hugh Powell, an Abergavenny attorney, but bidding was insufficient for the Cwmyoy and Llanthony lots, which were subsequently sold by private treaty to Colonel (later Sir) Mark Wood, M.P., of Gatton in Surrey. Presumably Wood bought them as a speculation, for he never lived there, and he sold them, doubtless at a handsome profit, to Landor in 1808.

Landor thus entered upon an inheritance of strife, and his experience proved not unlike that of the monks who built the Abbey. On acquiring the estate, he pursued energetically plans for its improvement. Lodging in the "offices" adjoining the Abbey that now comprise the Llanthony Abbey Hotel, he began the building of his house two fields away. He built a bridge over the Honddy to connect the farms on the Black Mountains' side with Cwmyoy village, and started to make a new road. He planted hundreds of acres of woods, including a plantation of cedar of Lebanon, which, he told Southey, "will look magnificent on the mountains of Llanthony, unmixed with others; and perhaps there is not a spot on the earth where eight or ten thousand are to be seen together". On his return from Spain he brought over Merino sheep to infuse a new strain into the local stock.

The rustic mind resents innovation, especially by a "foreigner",[1] and the character of the Llanthony peasantry was little changed through the centuries since the flight of the mediaeval monks. "My people are idle and drunken," Landor told Southey in April 1809: "Idleness gives them time, and drunkenness gives them spirit, for mischief." Thus early he recognised the quality of his tenants, of whom he was to write to Birch in 1813 with a bitterness reminiscent of the monk's nearly seven centuries before:

These rascals have as great a hatred of a Saxon as their runaway fore-fathers had. I never shall cease to wish that Julius Cesar had utterly exterminated the whole race of Britons. I am convinced they are as irreclamable as Gypsies or Malays; they show themselves, on every occasion, *hospitibus feros*.

He received no sympathy from his family, who assumed that his troubles arose from his own difficult temper. "I think Walter a subject of great pity," wrote his half-sister Maria Arden to Robert Landor; "for he does not seem at all inclined to conciliate the peasantry about

[1] The late Dr. Paterson of Cardiff—with whom I first visited Llanthony—remarked that, after forty years' practice in South Wales, he was still regarded as a foreigner by many of his rural patients. Some years ago in North Devon, when I suggested that it was sad for a farmer of sixty-five to be selling the farm where he was born and worked all his life, the local publican protested, "But he's not a local man; his dad was a foreigner—come from somewhere over Dulverton way not more than seventy years since."

Lantony but on the contrary—therefore he must expect to be plagued." Yet, however aggressive his attitude towards persons in positions of authority, Landor was always courteous and considerate towards his social inferiors; his brother Robert remembered "the joyous greeting" —at Tours in 1815—"that broke forth from all the market-women successively as he came into view, and his laughing word of jest or compliment for each that had given him universal popularity".

Nor does his brother Henry appear to have offered even professional advice. Henry had surveyed the estate and been associated in transacting the purchase with Charles Gabell, a solicitor of Crickhowell, yet he seems to have made no protest when Landor entrusted to Gabell the management of the estate. Though not legally a rogue, Gabell was a type of the predatory lawyer that regards his clients as defenceless game. The correspondence preserved by Baker Gabb, his successor as Landor's legal adviser, shows that Gabell made contracts without securing estimates, that he neglected to collect rents (in one case owing to his tender relations with a tenant's daughter), and that he was curiously evasive in reluctance to take proceedings against malefactors. If he did not actually accept commission percentages, he must have profited handsomely in presents from grateful contractors and tenants.

Long afterwards Landor told Forster, "I lived there little more than eight months altogether"; his frequent and prolonged absences encouraged Gabell and other malefactors in their depredations. On his return from Spain Landor was annoyed to find that many well-grown trees had been cut down without authority. He regarded wanton cutting of trees as the worst of crimes: "We recover from illness, we build palaces, we retain or change the features of the earth at pleasure —excepting that only! The whole of human life can never replace one bough." He found also that part of the Abbey ruins had been pulled down in his absence, though he had ordered only the removal of some new building distastefully erected beside the ruins by Sir Mark Wood. He told Southey in March 1809:

I am about to remove an immense mass of building which Colonel Wood erected against the abbey, and with which he has shamefully disfigured the ruins. I would live on bread and water three years to undo what he has done, and three more to repair what he has wasted.

Afterwards he was reproached locally for neglecting preservation of the ruins, though he seems to have been the first owner to care for them; Sir Richard Colt Hoare, the antiquary, related that the abbey's eastern front, still standing in 1777, had fallen before 1800, and while the western front then "still retained its exterior elegance . . . in 1803 I was a mournful eye witness of the total downfall of the three windows which then composed the principal ornament of that front".

Disgusted by the "chapel of ease"[1] that served as a place of worship for the Llanthony villagers, Landor proposed a remedy in August 1809 to the Bishop of St. David's. Having received no reply to his letter, he wrote again October:

I wished to restore to its former state and uses an edifice which I believe to have been the original chapel, no less from its internal and external structure than from the field in which it is situated being called the Chapel-field. The ruinous place which receives the few people who attend divine service in the summer months was not originally built for any such purpose; and your lordship is best able . . . to discover whether it ever has been consecrated. If it has, it is the only instance of an ancient chapel in which I ever saw a chimney. It is under the same roof with oxstalls, and surrounded by a farmyard. My intention is to remove instantaneously the buildings on which it leans; and it declines so greatly from the perpendicular that its fall is certain. I had hoped for permission to construct from the materials a school and a receptacle for the poor. I have conversed with the lower ranks of more than one nation in Europe, and last of all with those who have generally been considered the most superstitious and most barbarous. But if drunkenness, idleness, mischief, and revenge are the principal characteristics of the savage state, what nation, I will not say in Europe, but in the world, is so singularly tattooed with them as the Welsh? Had I never known how to appreciate the sacrifice your lordship makes, voluntarily and silently and alone, turning away your eyes from the most perfect models of the most polished ages on a country which at no period of its history hath produced one illustrious character, most certainly I should not have requested your assistance in forwarding its interests. God alone is great enough for me to ask anything of twice. I wished to repair some monuments of antiquity, and to rescue some others from the injuries of time . . . While Scotland and Ireland have been producing in every generation historians, philosophers, and poets, the wretched Welsh repeat their idle legends from first to second childhood, bring forward a thousand attestations to the existence of witches and fairies, boast of their illustrious ancestors and of the bards more illustrious who have recorded them, and convert the tomb of Taliessin into a gate-post.

This time the bishop replied promptly, though studiously avoiding comment on the Celtic character; in view of "the liberality of your offer to exonerate the parish from all charges in the improvement . . . I should be very glad if my consent would be sufficient", but "an act of parliament would be necessary for the removal of a place of public worship". Landor replied that, having recently presented a parliamentary bill, he would be slow to repeat that experience; he had read in Plot's *History of Staffordshire* that a Mr. Chetwynd of Ingestre had received permission from an archbishop of Canterbury to take down a parish church and build another—"I should not have ventured so far, in reply to your lordship's condescension, if I had been aware that parliament had ever taken away or lessened this power in the bishop or the primate".

---

[1] Forster was "startled" by the "rudeness" of this structure when he saw it some sixty years later.

The first architect employed on building his house dawdled through a summer and autumn till the winter gales destroyed part of the unfinished structure. Landor engaged another architect to pull down what was left and begin again, but in the summer of 1810 he informed Southey:

In architects I have passed from a great scoundrel to a greater, a thing I thought impossible; and have been a whole year in making a farm-house habitable. It is not half finished, and has cost already two thousand pounds. I think seriously of filling it with chips and straw and setting fire to it. Never was anything half so ugly, though there is not a brick or tile throughout . . . The earth contains no race of human beings so totally vile and worthless as the Welsh. I doubt whether they will allow me to make improvements, I am certain they will not allow me to enjoy them. I have expended in labour, within three years, eight thousand pounds amongst them, and yet they treat me as their greatest enemy.

The house was still only half finished when he brought his bride to Llanthony in June 1811, and they lodged in the rooms adjoining the Abbey. "I live among ruins and rubbish," he wrote, "and, what is infinitely worse, band boxes and luggage and broken chairs."

His wife cannot have been happily impressed by her new home, but during the summer Landor found satisfaction in showing the beauties of the valley to visitors. His mother and sisters came, and Southey and his wife stayed three nights in August. After nearly thirty years Southey recalled his visit as "a joy for memory", and Landor wrote of it after Southey's death:

> Along Lantony's ruined ailes we walkt
> And woods then pathless, over verdant hill
> And ruddy mountain, and aside the stream
> Of sparkling Hondy. Just at close of day
> There by the comet's light we saw the fox
> Rush from the alders, nor relax in speed
> Until he trod the pathway of his sires
> Under the hoary crag of Comioy.
> Then both were happy . . .

One of the largest farms wanted a tenant, and Landor looked for a "foreigner" as an ally against "the rascally Welsh". Southey remembered that Mrs. Wordsworth's brother, Thomas Hutchinson, was looking for a farm—"an illiterate man, but a very worthy one, and a thoroughbred farmer, with money at command". Hutchinson came to look at Llanthony, but, while he admitted that the soil was "the best possible", he objected that the vale was "too narrow, the hills too steep", and that Landor would have trouble in building farm-houses.

Southey then introduced another candidate. Among his correspondents was Matilda Betham, a bluestocking assiduous in cultivating himself, Coleridge, and Charles Lamb. She was the eldest of a Suffolk parson's family of fourteen—"the measureless Bethams" Lamb called them in referring afterwards to Landor's "Welsh annoyancers". One of her eight brothers had returned from service in the East India Company, married a Norfolk farmer's daughter, and was looking for a farm in which to invest his wife's small capital. Southey wrote to her, quoting a letter in which Landor said:

I have several hundred acres to let instantly for a pound an acre, tithe free, extremely small parochial rates, a lease for twenty-one years, and after the first ten a rise of four shillings per acre. Many thousands of land to be enclosed at three shillings for the first 10 years, six for the remaining. A rail now forming [the Llanvihangel Railway, a horse tramway, was built in 1811–12] within a mile along a level to the market town. . . . I hope to get a scientific tenant for about 1600 acres. He shall have every encouragement, but he should have £6 or 7000.

Warning her that Hutchinson had declined the tenancy, Southey told Miss Betham that, if her brother was interested, he might use his name as an introduction to Landor.

Charles Betham's tenancy at Llanthony began in January 1812. Landor wrote of him so enthusiastically that Southey felt it prudent to deny personal knowledge of him. "Your tenant Charles Betham is of an excellent stock," he wrote:

I have a great respect for one of his sisters, both for her genius and her goodness, both of which are soon discoverable thro a most unprepossessing exterior, & a nervousness of manner which gives at first an appearance of silliness. She happened to say in writing to me that her brother wanted a farm, as little expecting that I should direct him where to find one, as I was of such an enquiry from her. He has probably to learn farming; & in this respect is not so desirable a tenant as Mr. Hutchinson would have been: in others he is more so.

Betham's advantages over Hutchinson were social; he had a gentleman's manner and appearance, and his young wife might have been an eligible companion for Landor's wife. In spite of Southey's caution, Landor received Betham as a friend, and behaved with the generosity of friendship. Betham wanted new outbuildings; having no ready money, Landor told him to deduct the cost from his rent. He gave Betham some of his own stock, and allowed him use of his own labourers. In his pleasure at having an ally against the Welsh, he proposed that Betham's father should accept the livings of Cwmyoy and Llanthony, which were in his gift and then held by old clergymen on the verge of retirement.

§ 2

Despite his assurance to the Bishop of St. David's, Landor was compelled to repeat the expense of presenting a private bill to Parliament.

After the successful experiment at Holkham by Coke of Norfolk and the establishment of the Board of Agriculture in 1793, enclosure of waste land became inevitable. Even Cobbett, the most militant opponent of land enclosure, admitted that land should be enclosed where cultivation could be improved without prejudice to the interest of resident labourers—a condition that applied to Landor's thinly-populated valley. Delaying the necessary legislation, the government continued to subsidise legal parasites with the expensive anomaly of requiring a parliamentary petition for every enclosure, and Landor wrote indignantly to Southey on 12th February 1812:

What think you of our detestable villains of *the House*? While the people are starving for want of food and employment, those infamous scoundrels reject an act for the enclosure of waste lands. So the attorneys and the commissioners will eat up two-thirds of the scanty allotments which would otherwise be the portion of the poor . . . Three pounds of miserable bread costs two shillings at Abergavenny. The poor barbarous creatures in my parish have actually ceased to be mischievous, they are so miserable. We can find them employment at present, and four-and-sixpence a day; yet nothing can solace them for their difficulty in procuring bread. All my hay is spoilt. This is always worth a day's meal to them, but it can happen only once in the season. The poor devils are much to be pitied, for they really look now as if they hardly enjoyed it. It is their moulting time, and they cannot crow.

By his house-building, road-making, draining, planting, sheep-breeding, he created employment to relieve local distress—to the extent, as events proved, of ruining his fortune. He was also prepared to risk imprisonment as a critic of the government—if he could have achieved publication.

Fox's secretary, J. B. Trotter, had written his memoirs of his former employer—with such misrepresentation as usually appears in reminiscences of recently defunct statesmen. From his association with Adair and Parr, Landor knew much of Fox's life and character; he wrote a commentary on cited passages in Trotter's book, added a preface and a postscript, and sent his manuscript to John Murray, as the publisher of *Count Julian*. As the publisher of Trotter's book, Murray was not unwilling to advertise it by publishing a pamphlet to be printed at Landor's expense. The *Quarterly Review* of December 1811—the issue in which Canning and his friend Ellis reviewed Trotter's book—announced among forthcoming publications an anonymous *Appendix to Mr. Trotter's Memoirs of Mr. Fox* as an eightpenny pamphlet. Murray had not examined the manuscript; he was unaware that the pamphlet was dedicated to President Madison of the United States—who was to declare war against Britain in the following June—as "the wisest and most dignified chief magistrate that presides in the present day over the destinies of a nation, because on his humanity and power, the little freedom that remains among his fellow-creatures now principally depends." He was therefore appalled on receiving a report on the proofs from William Gifford, his literary adviser and the editor of the *Quarterly*:

I never read so rascally a thing as the Dedication. It is almost too bad for the Eatons and other publishers of mad democratic books. In the pamphlet itself there are many clever bits, but there is no taste and little judgment. His attacks on private men are very bad. Those on Mr. C. are too stupid to do much harm, or, indeed, any. The Dedication is the most abject piece of business that I ever read. It shows Landor to have a most rancorous and malicious heart. Nothing but a rooted hatred of his country could have made him dedicate his Jacobinical book to the most contemptible wretch that ever crept into authority, and whose only recommendation to him is his implacable enmity to his country. I think you might write to Southey; but I would not, on any account, have you publish such a scoundrel address.

Execrated as the most malignant of contemporary critics and the most bigoted of reactionaries, Gifford is now mainly remembered as a subject of Hazlitt's indictment in *The Spirit of the Age*; his remarks on Landor indicate that, if not—in Hazlitt's phrase—"the tool of a crooked policy," he wore blinkers as a party hack.

Following Gifford's advice, Murray appealed to Southey, who wrote to Landor on 10th February 1812:

About an hour ago came a parcel to me from Murray, containing among other things an unfinished commentary upon Trotter's book. Aut Landor, aut Diabolus. From the manner, from the force, from the vehemence, I concluded it *must* be yours, even before I fell upon the passage respecting Spain which proves that it was yours. I could not lie down this night with an easy conscience if I did not beseech you to suspend the publication till you have cancelled some passages: that attack upon Fellowes might bring you into a court of justice; and there are some others which would have the more painful effect of making you regret that you had written them. . . . Tomorrow I will point out every passage which is likely to inflict unde-served pain upon others, and therefore to recoil upon yourself. It would equally grieve me to have the book supprest, or to have it appear as it is. It is yours and yours all over. . . .

Landor responded by promising to "do precisely as you recommend", but, though prepared to delete personalities, he maintained the grounds of his thesis:

I praised Hastings, and drew a comparison between him and Fox; but, said I, possibly this great ruler may have been deaf to the voices of misery and of justice. I drew a comparison also between Lord Peterboro' and Lord Wellington, in which I *proved* the latter to be equal to the other. In short, with reference to the military administration, I preferred the present to every other in this reign except Lord Chatham's. But I asked myself what source of corruption these Percevals and people had cut off? What protec-tion they had given to freedom or to literature? After all, who will read anything I write? One enemy, an adept in bookery and reviewship, can without talents and without industry suppress in a great degree all my labours, as easily as a mischievous boy could crush with a roller a whole bed of crocuses. . . . I am surprised that Murray should object to publish my dedication to the president of the United States. It is very temperate, and, I believe, not ineloquent. War is not declared; and I earnestly point out the mischief it would do America; how deplorable that freemen should contend with freemen, and diminish a number already so reduced! I never wrote anything better.

Southey's reference to the "attack upon Fellowes" indicates how troubled he was to find reasons for justifying his support of Murray; the contempt for "this reverend gentleman having settled religion to his mind, but unhappily", was exceeded eleven years later when Landor wrote, in the first imaginary conversation between Southey and Porson, of "poor Robin Fellowes, whose pretensions widen every smile his imbecility excited". When he wrote again, in his concern with exculpating the government by blaming its misfortunes upon its predecessors, he seems to be rather defending his own political persuasions than condemning Landor's:

The dedication and the postscript are so full of perilous matter that it will be difficult to weed them clean. And there is this objection to both, that they, far more than the Commentary itself, tend to produce that state of feeling which such wretches as Cobbett are continually labouring to excite and inflame for the worst purposes. We are suffering for the antijacobin war,—the sins of the fathers are visited upon the children,—now it seems as if you designed to represent that the sins were our own. That we are not in peace and abundance and security, is the effect of *that* war,—*this* is unavoidable, and so are the expenses which it necessitates . . . I have no doubt that what you recommend, America is looking to; but I have as little doubt that it is under the direction of Bonaparte, who keeps the American government in pay. They dream of conquering Canada on the one hand, and Mexico on the other . . .

Southey provided a common example of how intelligent men sacrifice reason to patriotic fervour in time of war. After more than half a century Forster could deprecate Southey's readiness "to give credit to any absurdity that might help to put a wider breach between us and our transatlantic kinsmen", but he was so determined to recognise only "startling paradoxes" in Landor that he ignored equally his magnanimity and his courage in expressing unpopular opinions. Landor replied to Southey:

I never can be induced to believe that Madison is in the pay of Bonaparte, or that an American wants any pay to make him resent the indignities and privations he endures from our maritime laws . . . So tyrannical a system never existed; nor one which could so certainly throw America into a confederacy with France. Why could we not have revoked our orders in council, and left nothing to the French but her hatred and vengeance?

On the contrary, we resolve to seize American vessels so long as Napoleon perseveres in his system; as if the Americans could alter it, as if they could hinder him from doing what he chooses to do on the Continent . . . Whichever Power was inclined to relax first from its pretensions, was certain of conciliating the Americans, and of directing all their animosities against the Power that persevered in its injustice. Napoleon saw this, and his pride and hatred yielded to his policy. I pray fervently to God that no part of America may be desolated; that her wildernesses may be the bowers and arbours of liberty; that the present restrictions on her commerce may have no other effect than to destroy the cursed trafficking and tricking which debases the brood worse than felonies and larcenies . . . To accomplish this end I would throw myself at the feet of Madison, and implore till I were hoarse with imploring him.

As history has shown, Landor's was the voice of humanity and reason— no less so in the remarks on the government's repression of Ireland and Roman Catholics with which he concluded his preface to the pamphlet:

If the clue of those measures which they are now pursuing in Ireland were traced to its utmost extent, it would lead us through a labyrinth of defilement so dark and horrible that, even with broad daylight before us, we should almost doubt the practicability of escape. Of what consequence is it to us if the Irish choose to worship a cow or a potato? Is there any danger that the purity of our religion should be contaminated by it, or that the purity of our parliament should be sullied by their admission? If all the members returned were Catholics, still what harm could they do?

It was Landor's misfortune that the morality of his arguments was invulnerable, just as his exposure of government policy was disconcertingly incisive. As the publisher of the *Quarterly Review*, which depended largely upon the support of Canning and other Tory ministers, Murray could not possibly publish Landor's commentary.

"I perceive that Murray is disposed to suppress the Commentary," wrote Landor; "whether for pay, or prejudice, or fear, I cannot tell." Southey assured him that Murray's attitude was "a matter of feeling and not of fear", as he was "under obligations to Canning". At first Murray proposed to find another publisher to assume his obligation, but quickly withdrew this offer—probably recognising the impossibility of persuading another to undertake what he was himself afraid to publish—for Landor wrote to him, "The fault was not mine that you first undertook it yourself; that you next proposed to find another who would undertake it; and that at last you relapse even from this alternative." As he had readily agreed to delete the personalities to which Southey objected, he not unreasonably concluded that Murray had "been persuaded, either by Canning or some other scoundrel whom I have piquetted in the work, to withdraw from the publication of it; although I have soaped all the bristles that could have been clutched by the foul hand of our attorney-general".

K

Concluding that his *Commentary* was "condemned to eternal night",[1] he declared himself in favour of two immediate reforms: "perfect equality in all religionists as to their competency in civil employments, and an acknowledgment of the principle . . . that there is no libel without falsehood".

> Unless these rights are admitted and established, I think it a matter of utter indifference who governs. I confess I care not how fast that system runs to ruin which opposes them.

To establish these rights, to embarrass both Whig and Tory, "to uphold the cause of Lord Wellington" (whose conduct of the war in Spain was being attacked in both parliament and the press), and to recommend the revolutionising of South America,

> I think of employing my time in proving that neither war nor ministers are formidable; that nothing is very much so but poverty, which strips us of all resistance when the enemy comes to close quarters . . . I am about to borrow five thousand pounds that I may establish a press for this purpose, and may have the glory, at much private loss, disquiet, and danger, of setting the public mind more erect, and throwing the two factions into the dust.

This announcement excited anxiety in Southey, whose party associations informed him of the government's measures to repress criticism under the pretext of prosecuting the war against Napoleon. Within a few months Shelley's publisher suppressed a pamphlet attacking Chief Justice Ellenborough's sentence on Eaton for printing Tom Paine's *Age of Reason*, and a Barnstaple billposter, whom Shelley employed to distribute a leaflet of his "Declaration of Rights", was sentenced to a fine of two hundred pounds or six months' imprisonment. Popular opinion compelled the release of Sir Francis Burdett, acclaimed as "Westminster's pride and England's hope", but the government renewed their repressive measures after the assassination of the prime minister, Perceval, in May 1812, and Leigh Hunt and his brother were soon editing the *Examiner* from the gaol in Horsemonger Lane. Sydney Smith wrote in the preface to his collected works:

> From the beginning of the century . . . to the death of Lord Liverpool, was an awful period for those who had the misfortune to entertain liberal opinions, and who were too honest to sell them for the ermine of the judge, or the lawn of the prelate:—a long and hopeless career in your profession, the chuckling grin of noodles, the sarcastic leer of the genuine political rogue —prebendaries, deans, and bishops made over your head—reverend renegadoes advanced to the highest dignities of the Church, for helping to rivet the fetters of Catholic and Protestant Dissenters, and no more chance of a

---

[1]Southey preserved his copy of *Commentary on Memoirs of Mr. Fox*, which passed into the hands of Monckton Milnes and provided copy for the reprint in 1907, edited by Stephen Wheeler and ironically published by the house of John Murray. Historically valuable, as well as a brilliant example of Landor's political dialectic, this work was inexplicably omitted by T. Earle Welby from what he called Landor's "Complete Works".

Whig administration than of a thaw in Zembla—these were the penalties exacted for liberality of opinion at that period ... the man who breathed a syllable against the senseless bigotry of the two Georges, or hinted at the abominable tyranny and persecution exercised upon Catholic Ireland, was shunned as unfit for the relations of social life.

Inability to raise the necessary loan, rather than Southey's admonitions, must have prevented Landor's establishment of a seditious press at Llanthony. Local malefactors were conspiring to render his position untenable. Lifeholders encouraged their tenants to cut timber, but refused to allow Landor a tree and offered violence to his servants as trespassers. He found it impossible to collect his rents; those who had pleaded poverty, and successfully appealed to his generosity for delay of payment, continued to owe, and their neighbours imitated their successful imposition. Architects, masons, and carpenters, employed by Gabell without preliminary estimates on the plea of fluctuating wartime prices, presented enormous bills and demanded immediate payment. Understandably Landor became infuriated by his anomalous position in being dunned while he could not obtain his dues, especially as both debtors and creditors pleaded the same excuse of poverty for their conduct. After behaving with generous sympathy in deferring payment of rents, he found himself accused of heartlessness in delaying settlement of blatant overcharges; one solicitor wrote unctuously that "by withholding payment from a labouring man who has a family in these dear times you must be sensible of his privation". While Gabell procrastinated and counselled leniency, other attorneys readily accepted fees for prosecuting claims against Landor.

Exasperated by Gabell's evasions, Landor attempted reprisals on his own account. One of the persecuting attorneys, John Price, was the local surveyor of taxes; notorious for favouring his patrons, he levied surcharges on those who failed to defer to his powers with offers of suitable perquisites. Landor was told that "if I would invite Mr. Price to dinner, and send him occasionally some game, I should not find him troublesome"; as he disdained thus to encourage dishonesty in a public official, he found in Mr. Price an active champion of his "annoyancers". In the summer of 1812 he discovered that Price had been guilty of sharp practice in dealing with a tenant farmer, and being sworn a member of the grand jury at Monmouth assizes, he interpreted the oath literally—adjured to lay before the seat of justice any felony of which he had knowledge, he cited his charge against Price. The judge, Baron Thompson, ignored the breach of decorum, but Landor persisted by having the evidence of his charge attested by a local magistrate, the Rev. J. W. Davies, of Court-y-Gollen, and enclosing it with a letter to the judge. When that dignitary refrained from reply, Landor wrote again:

Among the things that I should have fancied could never be, is a judge refusing to investigate a felony when a grand juror, whom he had commanded to lay such matters before him, states the fact, and a magistrate brings the evidence. I acknowledge my error, and must atone for my presumption. But I really thought your lordship was in earnest, seeing you, as I did, in the robes of justice, and hearing you speak in the name and with the authority of the laws.

Unable to move the judge and declining to leave the matter to be lost in a pigeonhole of Gabell's desk, he sought counsel's opinion as to whether he could indict his fellow jurors for not supporting his charge against Price, of which they all knew the facts as well as he did. After six weeks he received a reply from Mr. Henry Clifford, of Lincoln's Inn, acknowledging his letter "on the subject of a felony stated to have been committed on John Lewis of Coedypain".

I am at a loss to discover from that statement what blame attaches to the Grand Jury. It appears that no indictment was preferred and I do not conceive that they are bound to notice any charge unless brought before them by indictment supported upon oath. I know of no mode of proceeding now but by indictment at the sessions or assizes if you shall think either advisable. But it is impossible for me to interfere as this is the business of an attorney in its present stage not of a Barrister.

For this useful contribution to the game of legal finesse, Landor paid Mr. Clifford three guineas.

As a lawyer and a pillar of conventional society, Forster thought Landor was "not so much wrong as wrong-headed" in this matter, which to Landor must have seemed evidence of that "amalgam of rottenness and soundness" in public life described in his suppressed *Commentary* as "a much greater curse than all the poverty and distress arising from ministerial profusion". Further evidence followed. As related in the imaginary conversation, "Florentine, English Visitor, and Landor", "in the county where my chief estate lies, a waste and unprofitable one, but the third I believe in extent of any there, it was represented to me that the people were the most lawless in Great Britain; and the two most enlightened among the magistrates wished and exhorted me to become one". The two magistrates—the Rev. J. W. Davies and Hugh Powell, the Abergavenny lawyer who owned Llanvihangel Court—made the suggestion when Landor consulted them about his charge against Price. He accordingly applied to the lord-lieutenant of the county, the sixth Duke of Beaufort—the duke soon to figure without dignity in Harriette Wilson's *Memoirs* when extricating his heir from that lady's embraces. Besides his unconventional behaviour as a grand juror, his radical opinions were unlikely to recommend him to the Tory duke, who replied tersely from Badminton on 28th August 1812, "I beg leave to acknowledge the receipt of your letter, and to express my regret that at present it is not in my power to comply with your request." Pointing out that it was necessary for a magistrate to reside within ten miles of Llanthony, Landor replied with temperate irony that, since it was not the duke's pleasure to appoint himself, he might nominate another of more information and of more independence, "qualities which no one can better appreciate, and which are so abundant in all parts of the county, particularly the magistracy". The duke did not reply, so Landor begged "leave to enclose some testimonies of his fitness for the office which, in furtherance of the public good, he was willing and desirous to undertake".

When the lord-lieutenant sees them coming from persons of experience and virtue, it is much to be hoped that he will approach one step towards wisdom by taking some advantage of theirs. By generous and elevated minds many deficiencies are overlooked on a little relaxation of arrogance, and many follies are pardoned for retracting one. This observation is made by Mr. Landor in the same spirit of pure benevolence as constantly and zealously animates him in the guidance of weaker intellects, which are always in the more danger the higher the station is; and he entreats that it may not be considered as a reflection, much less as a reproach . . . Never will Mr. Landor be induced to believe that a person invested with authority (which however, as a stronger safeguard against revolutionary principles, is more often conferred on rank than on information, and on subservience than on integrity) would, for the indulgence of an irrational prejudice, or the gratification of an unmanly resentment, render himself an object of detestation to the honest or of ridicule to the wise.

As he warned the duke, he wrote also to the Lord Chancellor, reporting that the reason for the lord-lieutenant's rejection of his application was locally rumoured to be because "I preferred a charge of felony against an attorney who is said to have been very serviceable in elections". No acknowledgment came from the Lord Chancellor, who was John Scott, first Earl of Eldon, of whom Hazlitt wrote in *The Spirit of the Age*, "On all the great questions that have divided party opinion or agitated the public mind, the Chancellor has been found uniformly and without a single exception on the side of prerogative and power, and against every proposal for the advancement of freedom."[1] After waiting more than a month Landor composed an address to the Chancellor, given at length in Forster's biography. After repeating the circumstances of his application, he stated why he had believed himself qualified to be a magistrate:

I have constantly endeavoured, from my earliest youth, to acquire and disseminate knowledge. My property in the county is little short of 3000£ a year, and capable of improvement to more than double that amount. . . .

---

[1] Sydney Smith described Eldon as "the most heartless, bigoted, and mischievous of human beings, who passed a long life in perpetuating all sorts of abuses, and in making money of them." Landor satirised his sycophancy and notorious parsimony in the imaginary conversation, "Eldon and Encombe" (1836); asked to pay a gambling debt, Eldon commends to his son the examples of George III and George IV and refers him to "the authority of your sovran for denying the validity of lawless obligations".

I have planted more than 70,000 oaks, and 300,000 other forest trees; and I shall not leave off till I have planted one million. . . . I have, at my own expense, done more service to the roads in a couple of years than all the nobility and gentlemen around me have done since the Conquest.

He thought that "what honour it will confer on the lord-lieutenant to have rejected the public and gratuitous services of such a man is worth his consideration rather than mine", and declared that he would never in future accept "anything whatever that can be given by ministers or by chancellors, not even the dignity of a country justice, the only honour or office I ever have solicited". He did not profess to possess the qualities "which have adapted the great statesmen of the day for the duties they so ably and disinterestedly fulfil", but study of philosophers and historians from Demosthenes to Locke

may console me for the downfall of my hopes from that bright eminence to which none of them, in these times and in this country, would have attained; and for which my pursuits equally disqualify me. Here I have only occupied my hours with what lie beneath the notice of statesmen and governors: in pursuing, with fresh alacrity, the improvement of public roads, of which already I have completed, at my own expense, more than a distance of seven miles over mountains and precipices, and have made them better and much wider than the turnpike roads throughout the country; in relieving the wants and removing the ignorance of the poor; and in repressing, by personal influence rather than judicial severity, the excesses to which misery and idleness give rise. These things appear of little consequence to the rich and prosperous, but they are the causes why the rich and prosperous cease to be so; and if we refuse to look at them now, in the same point of view as humanity and religion see them in, they will have to be looked at hereafter from a position not only incompatible with leisure and quiet, *but far too close for safety*.

Resentment inspired a final effort in the general election of October 1812. "I was guilty of offering a subscription of £1,000 to whatever association might be formed in Monmouthshire in opposition to the Duke of Beaufort," he informed Samuel Carter Hall many years later. "At the same time, I never asked one of my sixty-four tenants at Lantony for his vote, but told them all to act according to their conscience." The sitting members were Sir Charles Morgan and Beaufort's brother, Lord Arthur Somerset, who had been foreman of the grand jury that failed to support the charge of felony against Price; in a published address to the freeholders of Monmouthshire Landor wrote:

We often find throughout whole families as lifeless an equality of mind and soul as the revolutionists of France would have established in rank and property. . . . Let us prove that the race of country gentlemen is not yet extinct, and that some one of this order can be found in the county of Monmouth whose character for probity and intelligence renders him worthy to be the colleague of Sir Charles Morgan.

There was small chance of unseating the Beaufort interest in a rural constituency when such a centre of trade depression as Liverpool rejected Brougham, not only for Canning, but as second member for a military nonentity with no better credentials than being a supporter of the policy which had implemented the town's unemployment. Lord Arthur Somerset returned to Westminster with Sir Charles Morgan, and Landor relieved his feelings in a poetical epistle to Southey, part of which appears at the head of this chapter.

§ 3

These rebuffs from authority stimulated Landor's resentment of injustice. He resolved to end his exploitation by Gabell, from whom he demanded a statement of accounts and immediate action against debtors and malefactors.

Tombes of Trodrumon, the tenant recommended by Gabell, had paid no rent. Landor sent a servant to demand it, with instructions not to leave without satisfaction. Tombes assaulted the man, and locked him up till he was glad to escape with his bruises. Landor then called himself on Tombes, to say that he intended to sue him for arrears of rent and to prosecute him for "assault and false imprisonment" of his servant. Tombes was out, but his wife greeted Landor's ultimatum with a "torrent of abuse" and subsequently asserted that he had forced an entry into her house during her husband's absence, breaking the lock on the door to do so. Vainly Landor called the testimony of his servant and two carpenters working at the farm that he "knocked on the door twice", that he "never attempted to open it, much less to break it", and that he could not have opened the door, as he had his hat in one hand and his umbrella in the other. The foreman of the jury at the quarter sessions asked if he "had not levied a distress on Tombes, & on hearing the answer, he smiled to the others, who immediately made up their minds. . . ." In disgust Landor wrote to Baker Gabb, "I presume it will be doing no good for *me* to proceed against Tombes . . . unless there is a special jury. . . . It will be in vain to prosecute Price, until an oath has any sanctity here."

The Tombes affair was the first transaction undertaken by Baker Gabb on Landor's behalf. When recommending Tombes, Gabell had promised to engage that his brother-in-law, one Gough, the manager of the Brecon Bank, would join with him as surety for Tombes, but Landor had never received any such guarantee; realising the futility of expecting Gabell to secure any satisfaction from his *protégé*, he sought another attorney. The Gabbs were an old family of repute in Abergavenny; besides their hereditary practice as attorneys and stewards to the barony of Abergavenny, they were considerable landed proprietors in the

district. The reigning Baker Gabb (1756–1821) resided over his office
in Monk Street House in Abergavenny; with him, possibly on his friend
Davies's introduction, Landor at first corresponded. But, after the first
four months, the elderly gentleman handed over Landor's complicated
affairs to the conduct of his son, Baker Gabb Junior (1785–1858), who
had become his father's partner in 1807 and lately managed promotion
of the Llanvihangel Railway. With young Gabb, Landor developed a
friendliness impossible with the elderly father. After 5th April 1813—
when he hoped "I shall have the pleasure of your company at dinner;
we can give you a bed"—Landor's letters ceased the formality of beginning "Sir" and ending "Yr. very obedt. Servt."; they began "My
dear Sir" and ended "Yrs. very truly", or even "Yrs." and "Yrs. very
sincerely". The correspondence preserved by the Gabb family begins
with a note about Tombes on 27th November 1812 and ends with a
letter from Swansea postmarked 31st March 1814. Before the latter
date nothing had happened to disturb their cordial relations; it was
after Landor left England that he accused Gabb of misconducting his
affairs, and after more than thirty years he wrote in September 1846:

> If the Devil, a mighty old Omnibus driver,
> Saw an Omnibus driving downhill to the river,
> And saved any couple to share his own cab,
> I do really think 'twould be Gabell and Gabb.

By his negligence, evasions, and talent for perquisites, Gabell deserved
Landor's indignation, but Gabb was a man of repute. The very qualities that commended him to Landor may have limited his competence
to deal with Landor's litigious difficulties. Being young, he was eager
to please and loth to offend; a gentleman by breeding, he was more
suited to the leisurely business of a family lawyer than to outwitting
the shrewd sharp practice of Landor's tormentors.

To Gabb on 29th December 1812 Landor enumerated the lawsuits
accumulated in Gabell's flaccid hands. He declared that he had "in-
variably sought a compromise, where the aggression had not been
violent or repeated":

> My business having been so procrastinated is the reason why I have a
> mess of it on my hands, which, to persons who do not know the reason, must
> make me appear very litigious or very oppressive. Yet every one of these
> cases will prove both my forbearance, & (if a man may say it of himself)
> my liberality.

Plenty of evidence supports this claim. A small freeholder named
Nicholas Hopkins had made an agreement to sell his holding to Sir
Mark Wood, who assigned to Landor his rights in the contract. Plead-
ing that he had been "taken unawares" by Wood, Hopkins begged
Landor not to compel completion of the agreement, and Landor agreed

to submit to an arbitration by two separate valuers. Gabell allowed negotiations to continue for three years, during which Hopkins successfully appealed to Landor that, pending the settlement, his tithes should not be increased. When Landor at last pressed for a settlement, Hopkins, on the advice of an Abergavenny attorney named Hugh Jones, renounced his contract.

Several suits arose from the vague titles of lifeholders and copyholders on the estate, which Gabell neglected to investigate at the time of Landor's purchase. A man named Prosser held his farm without better title than having taken "possession on the death of another person of the same name". A notorious ruffian named Thomas refused to pay rent for the blacksmith's shop at the Henllan and the public house called the Queen's Head, impudently presuming on the lawyers' bungling over the changes of ownership to assert that the properties were his own freeholds. Two farmers, Lewis Parry and David Powell, admitted breach of covenant in their leases and agreed to resign their farms, but when Gabell, with characteristic negligence, allowed the date for their surrender to pass unnoticed, they sought advice from an attorney named Spencer—"who", said Landor, "gains, as I understand, the best part of his livelihood from the poor ignorant people of this parish" —and were persuaded to resist Landor's claims.

Harassed by these irritations, Landor conceived a grievance against Sir Mark Wood for having sold him properties to which he had indistinct title. Wood met him fairly. In December 1812 he assured Gabell that he would "have no objection to give Mr. Landor all the power and authority which I possess to compel Hopkins to perform his undertaking, but I will not myself engage in litigation respecting a property so long ago disposed of". In the matter of the lifeholds, he agreed to the appointment of an independent arbitrator, though warning Gabell that "it is merely involving Mr. Landor and myself into legal discussions from which neither of us can ever be benefited one shilling". When, in May 1813, Landor submitted the name of a barrister as arbitrator, Wood appealed to him personally to settle their differences by direct correspondence, as "I have a very great dislike to lawyers, provided they can be possibly dispensed with, and of all the pickpocket business of the profession, should we be so unfortunate as to fall into bad hands, a reference to a Lawyer is the very worst". Landor immediately responded to this appeal and ceased to press his claims against Wood.

He had reason to endorse Wood's opinion of lawyers, for the hostilities of John Price, Hugh Jones, and Spencer raised most of the neighbourhood against him. He was pursuing the policy approved by the Board of Agriculture and its secretary, Arthur Young—absorbing unprofitable smallholdings into large farms capable of producing more from the same land by means of capital outlay and organised labour. Inevitably the policy was unpopular because it entailed dispossession of the peasant farmers, who, as Young observed, "work like Negroes and do not live so well as the inhabitants of the poor house; but all is made amends for by possessing land". As an innovator, Landor was labelled an oppressor by Price, Jones, and Spencer, who posed as champions of the oppressed and encouraged the peasants to believe that, if such cases as those of Hopkins, Prosser, Parry, Powell, and Thomas could be defended, any fantastic claim might be prosecuted against the unpopular "foreigner".

A man less proud than Landor might have hesitated to go about without a bodyguard. He was warned by Betham and other tenants that Tombes, under notice of eviction from Trodrumon, was uttering murderous threats against him; when a local gunsmith reported that Tombes had inquired for a pistol and bullets, giving "an evasory and suspicious answer" when asked what he wanted them for, Landor asked Gabb if there was sufficient evidence "to punish him". He refrained from exercising his right to have a distress warrant served on Tombes, waiting to dispossess him at the end of his year's tenancy and resigning himself to the loss of the rent. After his eviction Tombes proclaimed his grievances in the taverns of Abergavenny till, within a few months, he drank himself to death, whereupon Landor was said to have caused his untimely end.

John Thomas, the publican, was a type of the worst pest among the labouring classes—the mean and truculent illiterate who commits petty annoyances out of bravado to brag of his boldness in the taproom. An inveterate poacher, he supplied tackle to others for poaching. One night Landor followed him through the woods into the enclosures.

He broke down the fence of my wood, & was in no foot-path. He stood before me with his arms folded & told me I had better not touch him. I instantly took him by the arm & swung him thro the hedge. I know not whether this is an assault—but if I catch him in my woods again, there shall be no doubt about the matter. . . . I have watched him every night since, and court an attack that I may have a memorable example. I trust I can punish the rascal for having a net. . . .

Thomas seized this occasion for instituting a suit for assault against Landor, who retaliated by prosecuting him for poaching. Landor had long vainly urged Gabell to demand rents from Thomas for the public house and the blacksmith's shop, but "Mr. Gabell did not proceed against him", Landor told Gabb, "because, he said, it was a pity; the daughter is a very pretty girl". On 29th June 1813 Landor wrote: "After a thousand searches for the memorandum of Col. Wood, which I mentioned to you as containing his acknowledged right to the Black-smith's shop & the Public House, I have discovered it among some old papers which I threw aside . . . I pray to God my right to seize these two houses may be decided this term."

Apparently Gabb took no action in the matter, and more than a century and a quarter later the signed agreement between John Thomas and Colonel Wood was found among the Gabb papers, wrapped in a cover endorsed by Gabb on receiving it from Landor. This may afford an instance of the negligence afterwards imputed to Gabb, for as late as January 1814 Landor was asking if he had "given notice" to Thomas for the blacksmith's shop and public house. Gabb may have neglected Thomas for more pressing business on Landor's behalf.

During his first year as tenant, Betham had been Landor's friend and partisan; he sympathised with Landor in the matter of Price and the grand jury, and warned him of Tombes's threats. Their first difference occurred when Betham bargained with Tombes for taking over the tenancy of Trodrumon; Landor afterwards told him that "on his leaving the farms, I did expect that you would apply to me about the terms of the lease, instead of holding it in spite of me". Tombes left in February 1813; a month later, instead of receiving as expected the balance of Betham's rent less a sum spent on repairs, Landor was presented with an account showing that he was indebted to Betham, who had lavished his landlord's credit to a sum far exceeding that of his annual rent. Gabb was sent for on 5th April to examine the account, with the result that Landor upbraided Betham for abusing his confidence.

Thereafter Betham became Landor's chief tormentor. Pressed for money in the previous autumn, Landor had cut down timber on Betham's land; as Betham proposed to plough the land, he asked that Landor should require the purchasers of the timber to grub up the roots instead of merely cutting down the trees. Landor made the request, but the purchasers had not complied, and Betham now refused to allow removal of the fallen timber till the roots had been grubbed up. When Landor sent his servants to seize the timber, Betham "met his hosts with very inferior numbers, armed as I could provide them, and maintained my ground". Landor brought an action to compel Betham's release of the timber, but meanwhile the purchasers withheld payment.

To preserve the natural beauty of the estate Landor cherished his meadows only less than his woods, and inserted a clause in the tenancy agreements that no pasture should be broken up without his permission. Betham had subscribed to the agreement, but now ploughed up his meadows. Landor asserted "that you ploughed up the meadows for no other purpose than to break the covenant, and that you threatened to plough up others to force me into some accommodation", but Betham argued that his covenant required him to manage his farm according to the rules of good husbandry, and "such meadows as I have ploughed up . . . should be ploughed".

Betham had neglected requests to repair his hedges, so allowing his beasts to wander at large, and Landor lamented to Gabb on 23rd April that "I must bring an action at last."

A whole year together he has neglected to repair the fences against 2 of my woods. 30 acres of thriving timber have in consequence been much injured; & will be ruined unless I make the fence. If I do, it appears, according to him, that I am liable to do so always. Yet, if I do not, I lose many thousand trees—more than *his* whole property will pay for.

When Betham drove sheep to graze on an adjoining farm, Landor put up a notice threatening action for trespass. Betham promptly tore down the notice, but Landor erected another before evening. Years later he must have related to Dickens these exchanges much as Boythorn relates his warfare with Sir Leicester Dedlock.

Following the example of his Welsh neighbours, Betham contrived that his annoyances should be of a nature defensible by legal chicanery, but he could not curb the excesses of his younger brother Frederick, aged twenty-one, who had sailed under the flag of the East India Company—the Betham family historian dignified him with the rank of midshipman, without explaining how such an officer belonged to the merchant service—and left the sea to learn farming with his brother Charles. In zealous support of his brother's quarrel this young man committed misdemeanours to which Landor referred with dignity in a letter to Charles Betham of 30th July 1813:

I should be happy if I could acquit you of the disgraceful and scandalous act, of having my fences and trees destroyed. I can make suitable allowances for youth, for a limited understanding and a neglected education. But you appear to have enjoyed advantages in which your brothers have not partaken, and you are therefore without excuse. . . . The inconveniences you can make me suffer are small & temporary: those which you are bringing on yourself are ruinous and for life. I must not conceal from you that this breaking down of the fences and of the trees and the attack on the woman in the [word illegible] Hills is known to the chairman of the East India Company, & that circumstances are now in full proof which a little while ago were but suspected. No difference in respect to the tenure of the farm could authorise the rude and unmanly conduct of your brother, not only to me but to Mrs. Landor, who has always treated him as if he were a gentleman. His education and rank in life do not permit me to chastise this insolence, but it is made known to those who will not suffer it to be forgotten. Nothing but a just indignation at such baseness would force me to remind you of those actions of mine which, from any man of honorable sentiments, would excite some sentiments of gratitude. You ought to remember that I always treated you with kindness till you ploughed up my meadows, after repeated expostulations—that, as you wished to have your family about you, I offered your father the next presentation to my two livings, after the decease of two men of seventy. . . . In fact, you cannot dissemble with yourself, whatever you may attempt with others, that the ploughing of the meadows was the first act of difference, & that I entreated you not to commit it—& that I cut down my woods that I might be able to accommodate you.

Unhappily Landor failed to sustain this dignity under the irritation of young Betham's conduct. Charles Betham disputed Landor's right to plant on one of his holdings; when Landor planted fir-trees there and Fred Betham pulled them up, Landor issued this handbill:

FELONY! *Fifty Guineas Reward.*—

Whereas Frederick Betham, late an inferior mate in a merchant ship in the East India Company's service, did threaten, in the presence of several persons, at several times, that he would root up some fir trees in the plantation of W. S. Landor Esq.; and was seen, in the evening of Saturday the 15th of May, followed by a person with a spade or shovel; and the said trees were found about twenty minutes afterwards rooted up. Whoever will give such evidence against this F. Betham as may lead to his conviction, shall receive 50 Guineas as reward from me,

W. S. Landor

Llanthony Abbey, May 28, 1813.

According to Fred Betham's counsel in the libel suit brought on account of this handbill, Landor "condescended to become a bill-sticker", and was seen with one of his servants posting up the bill in the streets of Usk! He also, "in the Company of his amiable and elegant wife (walking with her whose presence ought to have softened his malice), distributed these bills about the streets of Monmouth—this, too, at the time of the Assizes, as the time of the Quarter Sessions had been chosen at Usk, merely because on these occasions the greater publicity could be given to the libel".

Meanwhile the web of his tangled finances tightened about him. On 7th May he forwarded to Gabb a notice he had received from Mr. Jones of Leethroy, holder of the £10,000 mortgage raised on the estate, saying, "The fellow has been so impudent, I shall be glad to have nothing more to do with him. I hope 10,000£ can be procured in London, as the security is founded on Act of Parliament." Next day he sent a hurried scrawl—much blotted and unsigned but bearing the Abergavenny postmark—to his brother Robert:

Tomorrow I go to prison, because [words illegible] chose rather that the 2,000 should remain in the hands of a Banker than pay off a mortgage, of which notice was given six months ago. . . . I have no method but giving a draft for the money. Neither the one nor the other will accept it. The whole parish knowing that I could pay the money.

On 13th May, in reply to a further demand from the mortgagee's attorney, he argued that the interest was not yet due, concluding, "I request, Sir, you will not have the assurance to write me any more letters, as I wish to have as little to do as possible with people in the lower classes of your profession." Unable to obtain his rents or payments for timber and farm produce, he had no cash to meet his liabilities, and the small private banks were reluctant under wartime restrictions to allow overdrafts. In January 1814 he accepted from a firm of Swansea bankers, on the security of his mortgaged estate, the offer of a loan of £2,800, on which he was to pay interest of £400 a year.

By August 1813 his creditors and tormentors together had rendered untenable his residence at Llanthony. "I never can be happy here, or comfortable, or at peace," he told Southey.

I live in my house merely to keep it dry, just as a man would live in a dog-kennel to guard his house. I hate and detest the very features of the country, so much vexation have I experienced in it. I wish to God I could exchange it for a house in Bath, or anywhere.

He afterwards declared that he lived only five months in the house he built at Llanthony, and these must have covered the summer of 1813, for he wrote in May to Walter Birch:

I have not completed my poor miserable house yet, but I have a spare bed, or shall have till the second of August [Southey was then to have paid a second visit to Llanthony, but was prevented by family bereavement]. If his Lordship should come afterwards, I have only an attic for him. In fact I built my house as a batchelor. I have half a dozen rooms which grouse shooters could sleep in, & two large & handsome ones for Company. As I think no company better than a wife, I surrender one to her, reserving as is done in all leases, a right of entry.

"His Lordship" was the son and heir so eagerly anticipated that, when he realised the impossibility of remaining at Llanthony, he proposed, as soon as peace was concluded, to live in France for economy's sake and allow his fortune to accumulate for his children. On 1st August his brother Robert wrote to dissuade him from this idea. Asking how he could "voluntarily become the Subject of such a Tyrant" as Buonaparte, he pointed out how people would sneer at "this Apostle of Liberty, who passed so much of his life in praising it, who not only talked of it & wrote for it, but who gave his money, & risked his person to defend it, he has left his connexions, his property, his Country, & chosen to live under the most arbitrary Government in Europe". To this Landor might have replied, as he had written some months before to Southey, that he hated Buonaparte, "I execrate him: but I detest our own government worse", believing that the European "kings and governments are such fools and rascals that I wish from my soul Buonaparte may utterly extinguish all of them". But the rest of Robert's argument was irrefutable.

Why not enjoy yourself now? Why look so far forward & that for those, who at present are not in existence? It is making money of too much consequence, & time of too little. You will leave as good a fortune as you received, without anxiety or deprivation. Instead of shutting myself up at Lantony, I would take a pleasant House in a good neighborhood and live, after setting apart a quarter of my income for repairs, on the remainder. A Man, & particularly a Married Man risks everything by determining on solitude. Solitude influences the temper in one year, more than Society can in twenty, it creates habits and feelings the most dangerous, particularly to a warm & sensitive character. The Melancholy man becomes infinitely more Melancholy, & the proud man more proud, that which was at first a rill, becomes a torent. . . . The more I observe, the more I am convinced that everything in life which is singular, is dangerous. You have now the happiness of others to consider, so take the safest road, which is the commonest. . . .

The worldly cleric must have known that this prudent advice would be wasted on Landor, who had never shown any inclination to seek safety in the common road. His young wife can hardly have welcomed the prospect of leaving her family and friends for exile in France, though that project was inevitably deferred while the war continued. But he had to leave Llanthony. Not only was he harassed by importunate creditors, but he found it expedient to hide his whereabouts to escape the service of a summons.

He feared the hostilities of the attorneys, John Price and Hugh Jones, throughout the summer. Price had sponsored the cause of Tombes, and after the latter had "killed himself by drinking brandy", on seeing Landor in the streets of Abergavenny, he asked loudly of a companion if he was "the person who murdered poor Tombes". On the advice of the friendly magistrate, Hugh Powell, Landor brought an action against Price, but "the jury were unanimously of opinion that he asked only for the sake of information, and found him not guilty". In spite of this, Landor told Gabb he was "resolved to prosecute Price out of the county", and on their meeting in Gabb's office, he so excited Price that Price "assaulted" him. This would seem to have supplied a sound case, but for some reason Gabb neglected to proceed for some months, and as late as the following January Landor wrote in a tone of query:

Of course you have long ago taken the necessary steps for the prosecution of Mr John Price for the attack on me in your office. This will go a good way in my favour, as a defence in the business of Mr Hugh Jones. . . .

Jones was a more subtle rogue than Price. He had managed the case of Hopkins, and when he took up the defence of John Thomas for poaching, he so instructed Thomas that Henry Price, the Hereford barrister employed by Landor, remarked that he ought to be indicted for conspiracy. Landor rashly repeated his barrister's remark to Jones's face, "treated him as he deserved", and had to face a criminal action.

"The grand jury of course brought in a true bill," Landor told Southey, for, as he observed bitterly to Gabb, "Any bill brought against me would be found a true bill in this county, whatever might be the character of the accuser." Worried over the consequences of this action, Landor was instructing Gabb to exercise all possible means to appease Jones, when, late in September, he left Llanthony forever.

On 3rd October he wrote to Gabb from "Myrther-Tidvill"; on the 19th he wrote from Swansea, and the eighteen letters to Gabb between that date and 31st March 1814 bear the Swansea postmark. None bears any more definitive address than "Swansea", and it does not appear whether he and his wife stayed with friends or in lodgings. Mostly the letters deal with money matters. Jones of Leethroy threatened to recall his mortgage, and Landor's big worry was to raise another mortgage on Llanthony of £10,000. He was pestered by a Bristol mason for a debt of £35, "which is so little I do hope to contrive to send it directly". On 2nd November he wrote, "I am now so totally without money that even if a letter comes I have not enough to pay the Postage"; asking Gabb to instruct one of his smaller tenants to bring over to Swansea his arrears of rent, he added, "Tell him if he will bring me five pounds I will excuse him all the remainder of the half year's rent." Gabb replied by sending two five-pound notes, and with characteristic carelessness of whence the money was forthcoming, Landor soon began to use him as a cashier. "You will oblige me if you can send me two or three pounds to go on with," he writes once; and again, "Pray send me 5 £ as I have only 2 £ left". His naivety in business appears when, remarking that his rent day will be the most convenient for him to pay the mortgage interest, he writes with an air of business-like decision:

In future I must insist on my tenants paying their rents on the day due. It is just as easy, when they know it is to be done.

Within a month of writing this, he was suggesting that one of his few promptly paying tenants should be persuaded to pay part of his rent a few weeks in advance—"he would probably do it for two or three guineas, which I would gladly give, for I have no money."

§ 4

Though frequently worried for want of a few pounds in his pocket, he never thought of supplying the deficiency by literary earnings. Yet in the throes of financial worry and litigation he still found time to write. He re-drafted his comedy of *Ines de Castro* as *The Charitable Dowager* and told Southey that he wished it to be "both printed and acted", because, "if I can make my comedy worth ten pounds, I will send the money to an honest and generous man named Juan Santos de Murieta, whose property was destroyed by the French at Castro"; Murieta, "who received me hospitably when I found Bilbao in occupation of the French, is perhaps ruined by those barbarians", and "I see no speedier way, little speed as there is in this, of sending him some money".

He also projected a volume of Latin verse, of which he wrote to Southey:

Valpy the printer, the greatest of all coxcombs, very much wished to print my Latin poems; but I have an intention to print them at Oxford, under the title of *Idyllia Heroum atque Heroidum*, in a size like the sixpenny books of children. It will cost me 35 *l*; and I intend to give whatever they sell for, which may amount to about half the money, to the poor of Leipzig . . . My head rises to the shoulder of Robert Smith, and every other of the modern Latin poets is below my knee.

The Leipzigers had to wait for his charity, for it was not till 1815 that the Oxford printers, Slatter & Munday, issued *Idyllia Nova Quinque Heroum atque Heroidum*.

A new session of Parliament opened on 4th November 1813 with the announcement of negotiations for peace with France, and Landor, under the pseudonym of Calvus, addressed three letters to the *Courier* protesting against negotiations with Napoleon. Like the *Times*, the *Courier* opposed the policy of peace with Napoleon, both papers being reviled by the *Morning Post* for "existing only on the misery and quarrels of mankind". But the *Courier* hesitated to publish unexpurgated such bold expressions from an anonymous writer, and on 28th November Landor wrote anonymously to the publisher Henry Colburn (the Mr. Bacon of Thackeray's *Pendennis*):

I am desirous of publishing as many letters, as will amount to about 50 pages in octavo . . . I send only the first. The principal part of the others I directed to the Editor of the Courier . . . I shall write, in this, a request that the Editor will return it, and entrust it to you. It is very desirable that they should be printed *quite* correctly. If you do not think proper to undertake the printing, pray inform me, by the name or rather the signature of C. in the Courier, and the expense of the advertisement shall be paid by my order. Rather than that they should not appear, I would myself become the publisher, if I fancied that you would have reliance enough on the honesty of a stranger, and without a name. In that case I would have only 300 copies printed, and sold at such a price as would not exceed in profit the expenses of publication . . . From an extreme desire of correctness in the printing, and from a wish to remain unknown, I have contrived that letters shall reach me within a few hours, if directed to Miss Rose

Mount Pleasant
Swansea

and shall rely on your delicacy in destroying this part of the letter immediately.

L

Colburn agreed to publish, for Landor wrote again in an undated letter:

I send all the other letters that I have finished. The one addressed to Ld. Liverpool comes first: *then* those which I now include, according to their series: *lastly* the three which you received from the Editor of the Courier. I am about more . . . The last letter ends with this sentence.

Sovereigns of the Earth, if you prolong the existence of this miscreant, this accursed of God and man, declare at once that you have drawn the Sword only to divide dominion with him; that you have brought nations to fight one against another, only that you might at last be admitted to peace and amity with him; go, and the blood of extinguished and of unborn generations be upon your heads, the scorn of your contemporaries, the reproaches of your posterity, and the vengeance of your Almighty Judge.

Colburn printed and published expeditiously, for *Letters Addressed to Lord Liverpool, and the Parliament, on the Preliminaries of Peace,* a four-shilling pamphlet, was advertised in the *Courier* of 17th December and reviewed in its issue of 12th January with the remark that the letters were "originally sent to *The Courier* for insertion, and were only delayed by the pressure of parliamentary and foreign intelligence". The publisher prudently expurgated the letters without consulting "Calvus", for Landor told Southey that "the evil genius to whom I committed the manuscript has printed what he chose and omitted all the best". Two further letters from Calvus appeared in the *Courier* of 19th January and 21st April 1814.

Landor's trend of thought during the Napoleonic terror ran curiously parallel with that of intellectual opinion in England during the years 1935 to 1939. He had always been an advanced Liberal. He loathed war, but had voluntarily taken up arms in the cause of the Spaniards against oppression. He now appealed against the futility of a treaty with Napoleon. "To engage in war," he wrote, "with so futile a design as merely to bind at last an atheist with an oath, and an assassin with a piece of red tape, is as foolish and as wicked as to discharge a cannon into a crowded market place for a jubilee." He demanded the continuance of the war to effect the extinction of "the monster" Buonaparte, and addressed his demand as a private person entitled to justice and reason from the nation's rulers.

I never wrote a pamphlet: I belong to no party, no faction, no club, no coterie; I possess no seat in Parliament, by brevet or by purchase; I can afford to live without it; but I cannot afford that accumulation of taxes which will arise from another war, if after our experience we conclude another probationary peace.

He did not consider that the French were to be pitied as dupes of a megalomaniac and that the removal of Napoleon would alone procure peace. Quoting Castlereagh's statement that "we are not to meddle with that great and powerful country itself", he asked, "Why not? Has not that great and powerful country meddled with every other? Is she not great and powerful because she has done so?"

Southey warmly agreed with Landor, writing to his brother:

You have seen the letters in the *Courier* with the signature of Calvus? Landor is the writer. I entirely agree with him that this is the time for undoing the mischief done by the Peace of Utrecht. France was then made too strong for the repose of Europe, and she ought now to be stript of Alsace, Lorraine and Franche-Comté.

Prudent regard for the policy of the government to which he owed his appointment as Poet Laureate compelled Southey to suppress reference to Buonaparte in his official ode in celebration of the new year, but he salved his conscience by publishing in the *Courier* the lines beginning, "Who calls for peace at this momentous hour?" And he reminded Landor how for five years he had been "preaching the policy, the duty, the necessity of declaring Bonaparte under the ban of human nature"; he believed that, if the government had openly avowed such a policy, other countries would have followed the lead, and the French themselves would by then have cast out the tyrant.

The government's vacillations and vicissitudes between 1808 and 1814 find reflection in events of 1935 to 1939 with the derisive mockery of a distorting mirror. Complaining that rulers would endure any insult rather than listen to those who entreat them to look to history for a guide, Calvus gibed, "History would lead them into that chilly and awful chamber in which, under the suspended armour, they might read their own destinies."

§ 5

While writing the Calvus letters from Swansea, Landor was impatiently urging Gabb to obtain a loan of £3,000 to relieve his immediate difficulties. His concern "to remain unknown" in correspondence with Colburn was inspired less by fear of government proceedings against Calvus than by need of hiding from his creditors. Remembering the handsome fortune left by his father, his family and friends had difficulty in understanding how he had arrived in such straits. Such minor extravagances as his carriage and pair were well within his means; apart from a handsome collection of books and pictures, he had nothing to show for his vanished fortune. Everything had been spent on Llanthony; "all the money I ever spent beyond my income was spent upon that," he told his brother Henry more than twenty years later—"my own expenses never amounted in any year to a thousand pounds." After forty years his prodigal outlay in planting showed signs of earning its reward, and Landor must have felt grim satisfaction when his brother

Henry assured him in 1855 that "I do not know so desirable a property for investment & extension, & which if now sold would to your Successor's son (if he should have one) be a very great sacrifice of Property". But meantime for two decades the estate was burdened with the penalty of his misplaced confidence and unwise generosity. As late as 1834 Gabell, of whose negligence there is plenty of evidence, and Francis Robbins, who became Landor's trusted agent after the dismissal of Henry Williams along with Gabell in 1812, were still receiving payments of interest on debts which they held to be owing to them.

Gabb's negotiations with a Mr. Moore for a loan broke down after more than three months, and in January 1814 Landor himself secured a loan of £2,800 from his Swansea bankers. The rate of interest was typical of his other financial transactions—"for 700 £", he told Gabb, "I pay 100 per ann." He advertised for sale in the *Bath Herald* the next presentation to the perpetual curacies of Cwmyoy and Llanthony, and proposed to ask £1,200 for the two livings, which he reckoned to be worth £300 a year. These monies, with £1,500 which Gabb assured him he would get from Betham, would clear his immediate necessities, which included instalments of purchase money on several farms he had bought to enlarge the original estate.

But apparently there were liabilities of which he omitted to notify Gabb till unpleasant reminders arrived. In February he received from Henry Price, the Hereford barrister, a lengthy account of expenses incurred between September 1812 and April 1813 in securing the act of parliament to enclose the waste land and commons at Llanthony— an illuminating document, revealing the law as a luxury tax on capital. Price and his clerk spent "36 days in London attending Parliament to get the bill passed" at "2½ guineas per day exclusive of expenses"— for himself £94 10s. and two guineas for the clerk, £75 12s; expenses for each at another guinea a day made another £75 12s. Price's junior and his clerk then spent another twenty-four days waiting for the bill to receive the royal assent at a cost of £163 16s. The statement shows that Landor had already paid £850, but there still remained a balance due of £196 15s. 2d. Explosively Landor wrote to Gabb:

He [Price] said that six hundred or perhaps less would do, provided no opposition was made & no counsel employed. He also promised me that he would engage to do it on as easy terms as any one could, and that he could do so, by saving me the expense of a solicitor. This being the case, unless I am obliged by a court of justice, I will not pay him one farthing more.

He did, however, send Price a further hundred pounds, remarking acidly that he "thought 2 guineas a day very handsome pay for his young man, as a gentleman of high rank in the army had not so much".

Litigation, like a spider, held him in its web. He was still urging Gabb to proceed against Thomas for possession of the blacksmith's shop and the Queen's Head tavern, as well as "in the business of the Bethams and of John Price, the one in the Exchequer, the other in the Ct. of Kings Bench". His friend Davies, of Court-y-Gollen, sent him a list of poachers supplied by the gamekeeper at Llanthony, and recommended him to "order them all in the Crown Office for the pursuit & killing of game", as "the only way of insuring you *your Prerogative* and *a future Peace* on that Head". The names of John Thomas and Charles Betham appeared on the list, but Landor was disappointed "not to observe the name of Frederick Betham".

Davies wrote in sincere terms of cordial friendship. "You seem," he said, "to be encircled with Enemies, who, I shall hope, will yet be defeated by Perseverance, Caution, & Prudence." He and Hugh Powell, the squire of Llanvihangel, seem to have been the only inhabitants of Monmouthshire whom Landor had reason to remember without regrets. The last of his letters to Gabb expressed his obligation to the kindness of Powell and his brother in their efforts on his behalf to effect a compromise with Hugh Jones. This letter was posted from Swansea on 31st March 1814, by which time he recognised his financial position to be much more precarious than he had supposed in January, though he still hoped to resolve its difficulties. If, he told Gabb, he could obtain the agreed price for the timber which Betham had wrongfully withheld from removal, "and sell the oaks, my books, wine and part of the furniture, *as well as the livings*, I shall not want above 1200£—and surely the Joneses wd. let that remain upon annuity". He had not been able to transfer the mortgage from Jones, but he now planned to sell his life interest in Llanthony—a Quaker was going over in a few days to look at the estate.

Apparently the Quaker was insufficiently impressed. The anticipated sale of the livings also fell through, and it appears from correspondence twenty years after that Landor actually sold the presentation to Llanthony for only £75. The purchaser of the timber backed out of his bargain. Finally, as Landor reminded Gabb in his letter, in calculating his assets he reckoned on securing his rent from Betham, and this proved to be not forthcoming.

In April the Bethams presented two libel suits against him at Monmouth assizes before Mr. Justice Dallas and a special jury. In the first Fred Betham was awarded damages of a hundred pounds for Landor's publication of the felony handbill. Landor himself did not appeal, and his counsel, Dauncey, admitted the handbill to be libellous, though he proposed that, "in the absence of his client and exercising no judgment of his own, he should, in compliance with his client's instructions, state and prove the circumstances under which it was published". Charles Betham sued for damages for a libel "in the form of a written order, given by Mr. Landor to a constable, he not being a magistrate, to apprehend the plaintiff, on a charge of felony and theft". The constable gave evidence that he never executed the order, but the judge ruled that, while "the publication of this libel appeared to have been very limited . . . at the same time a charge of felony was conveyed by it, without excuse or explanation", and the plaintiff received the verdict, with damages of forty shillings.

Stung by the injustice of both verdicts, Landor smarted still more from the derisive eloquence of Fred Betham's counsel, Thomas Jervis, who described him as "condescending to become a bill-sticker" and hawking his handbills about the Monmouth streets "in the company of his amiable and elegant wife". He accordingly published as a leaflet a *Letter from Mr. Landor to Mr. Jervis*, stating his case against the Bethams and demanding an apology from Jervis for his language; failing such apology, he would consider Jervis a calumniator wherever they might meet, except in those courts miscalled of justice, "where calumny is sanctioned by custom, and insolence has the protection of the laws". He concluded the letter by stating the result of his proceedings against Betham in the Court of Exchequer, which had "overruled the whole of their exceptions, dissolved the injunction, and awarded me every farthing of my demand, to the amount of £1,968 17s. 6d."

On 16th May Landor announced to Southey his intention of leaving England. The brothers Powell had failed to conciliate Hugh Jones, and Landor was cited to be tried at Monmouth. "As I certainly shall not appear," he said, "I shall be outlawed." Before going he intended to spend three weeks with his mother at Warwick and Ipsley; he hoped to delay long enough for Jervis to decide whether or not to reply to his letter, and for Slatter & Munday to finish printing his Latin poems, which were to contain a chastisement of W. E. Taunton, who, as Charles Betham's counsel, had treated him "with much more violence than any criminal". But on 27th May he was about to embark from Weymouth when he wrote to Southey:

The Court of Exchequer has decided in my favour; but Betham has been able to promise bail and a replevy, so that the ends of justice are defeated. Nearly three years' rent will be due before I can receive one farthing from him; and all my timber is spoiled. I shall be utterly ruined. Not being able to pay the interest of 10,000 £ debt on the Llanthony estate, the mortgagee will instantly seize on it until he has paid himself the whole of the principal. The laws of England are made entirely for the protection of guilt. A creditor could imprison me for twenty pounds, while a man who owes me two thousand, and keeps me from the possession of two thousand more, can convert wealth and affluence into poverty and distress,—can, in short, drive me for ever from my native country and riot with impunity on the ruins of my estate. I had promised my mother to visit her. I never can hope to see her again. She is seventy-two, and her sorrow at my overwhelming and most unmerited misfortunes will too surely shorten her days. My wife, when she married, little thought she should leave all her friends to live in obscurity and perhaps in want. For my sake she refused one of the largest fortunes that any private gentleman possesses, and another person of distinguished rank. Whoever comes near me is either unhappy or ungrateful. There is no act of forbearance or of kindness which Betham did not receive from me. . . . I go to-morrow to St. Malo. In what part of France I shall end my days, I know not, but there I shall end them; and God grant that I may end them speedily, and so as to leave as little sorrow as possible to my friends. No time will alter my regard and veneration for you; nor shall anything lessen the kind sentiments you entertain for me. It is a great privilege to hold the hearts of the virtuous. If men in general knew how great it is, could they ever consent to abandon it? I am alone here. My wife follows me when I have found a place fit for her reception. Adieu.

§ 6

Jervis did not reply to Landor's letter, but Charles Betham's long statement of his disputes with Landor was dated from "Lantony Abbey, June 23rd 1814" and published in the *Gloucester Journal* of 4th July. As Landor had left England some weeks before, he probably never saw the letter, which was unknown to Forster and first reprinted in the Betham family chronicle, *A House of Letters*, in 1905. Betham's self-righteous explanations were unquestioningly accepted by this chronicler, who used Forster's conception of Landor as an irresponsible eccentric to suggest that Betham was the victim instead of the victimiser.

Landor's letters to Baker Gabb[1] reveal that Forster was less than just to Landor in attributing his troubles rather to his own incompetence and impetuosity than to misplaced confidence and unwise generosity. Betham took every advantage of Landor's friendliness till, at the year's end, when Landor expressed anger on realising from the accounts how his confidence had been abused, he condescended to the same weapons as the meanest of the peasantry—a campaign of petty harassments, backed by the chicanery of shady attorneys. Legally he was much in the right—apart from non-payment of his rent, which was the root of the trouble. For instance the law, as he relates, was on his side in the dispute about the timber:

The assertion that the Timber, which I prevented him from removing, was cut down to enable him to grant me indulgences, has already been made in a Bill of Equity against me and denied on my oath; I solemnly repeat that denial. I had consented to the trees being grubbed up, that I might plough the land; and when Mr. Landor cut them down, and refused to grub up the

---

[1] These letters were first examined when I was preparing my *Savage Landor*, 1941. Subsequently they were examined by Mr. Super, but while the coherence of his analysis suffers from division between a summarised narrative and a commentary in notes at the end of his book, his attitude to Landor is even less sympathetic than Forster's. Commenting, for instance, on Landor's indignation against John Price's dishonesty as a public servant, Mr. Super remarks that "Landor undertook a course which was utterly naïve in its failure to perceive how useful such a man must have appeared to the larger part of the propertied gentry".

roots, I refused my permission to their being removed . . . by the same order
which authorizes him to remove the trees, he is directed, without delay, to
cause the roots and stools to be properly and effectually grubbed up; and I
was awarded costs.

But the moral, apart from the legal, aspect of his conduct appears in
Landor's letter to him of 30th July 1813:

> I have forborn, Sir, on all occasions to harass you; it was not harassing
> you to abstain from rent last September at your own request, in the presence
> of Mrs. and Miss Betham, the want of which money obliged me to cut down
> the great wood and the Grove, together with a view to your further advan-
> tage in allowing it (as I should have done) to be ploughed. You yourself
> admitted the great importance it would be of to the farm, & happily you
> admitted it in the presence of a person who will give the fullest evidence
> of the fact, and *after a part of the Great Wood was cut down.* You requested me
> to apply to the purchasers of both woods to negotiate with them for grubbing
> up the trees instead of cutting them. I did so. . . .

Betham, in fact, begged the double favour of a postponement of his
rent and an increase of his farm's arable value, and then used the law
to compel Landor to pay for the labour of clearing the soil for him.
Landor's letter of 30th July 1813, already quoted in relation to Fred
Betham's exploits, was written primarily to warn Betham against breaking a lock on his garden gate, Betham claiming a right of way through
the garden apparently for the purpose of annoying Landor and his
wife. "The act of violence you now threaten can do me no great
injury," the letter ended, "it is however, a violation of the law, which a
copy of this letter, attested as it will be, must prove that I warned you
not to commit." The copy, attested by a Llanthony tenant named
Matthews, was lodged with Gabb, who preserved it with Landor's
letters to him.

Betham's avoidance of any mention of this letter destroys his slight
claim to ingenuousness. Relating how he filed a bill in Equity, offering
to pay what he owed after a ruling on the accounts and meanwhile
restraining Landor by injunction from suing him, he declared:

> This bill was filed on the 30th of June, and Mr. Landor served about the
> same time with a subpoena to appear and answer to it. No answer was
> given until February last. In the meantime, in November, I had offered
> to refer all the accounts to private arbitration. . . . Mr. L. declined this,
> unless I would also refer the action brought by me against him for a libel
> on my character . . . conditions obviously inadmissible.

He did not mention that Landor had made an offer of arbitration some
six months before his, as appears from the same letter of 30th July:

> To prove my sincere desire of justice, and nothing more, I stated all the
> circumstances to your friend and patron Mr. Adair, and left him sole arbiter
> of *all* the differences. I offered to bring affidavits of *all* the facts, & of course
> he is able to judge of the truth or untruth, the fairness or unfairness of all

when they should come before him. If he declined it, perhaps I need not hint the reason.

Betham's statement studiously avoids noting the date of Landor's offer:

Mr. Landor states a proposal made by him to Mr. Adair . . . to appoint that gentleman judge of our differences. This it would be difficult to reconcile with the refusal which my offers to refer have met with. But when it is considered that Mr. L. was not known to Mr. Adair, and that it was made without purporting to be with my concurrence, I think little doubt will be felt that he expected Mr. Adair would decline it, and that it was hazarded for the purpose of giving to his proceedings an appearance of candour which did not really belong to them.

Apart from leaving unexplained why his own friend and patron should have declined the opportunity of arbitration, Betham imputes to Landor a cunning or talent for "sharp practice" ludicrously incompatible with his character. But Betham himself was capable of sharp practice, as in the matter of the timber. He does not explain why, after Landor had offered arbitration before July, he himself waited till the following November to make a similar offer. It seems that he waited till he had instituted proceedings for libel, knowing that Landor would then refuse to submit one case to arbitration without the other, and so achieved the purpose which he impudently imputed to Landor—"of giving to his proceedings an appearance of candour which did not really belong to them".

His failure at Llanthony was a lasting humiliation to Landor's pride. After six years he wrote to Wordsworth from Pisa on 23rd September 1820:

A desire of covering with forest-trees many thousand acres, induced me to settle in a country the most lawless and faithless in Europe. To enjoy, as I hoped, these occupations of retirement & solitude, I fancied I had nothing to do but to sacrifice a few unworthy prejudices. I sold the estates of my father's family, and the only remaining one of my mother's, which had remained in it little short of seven hundred years—a family which had given to the house of commons the greatest & best of its speakers, the man to whom England is indebted for the truest and plainest declaration of its freedom, Sir Arnold Savage. Something, if I remember, is said of him in Hakewell de modo tenendi parliamenti. And something is said of him to me and against me every day and every night of my existence. Your poem on Repentance has harmonised all this, and I feel a pleasure in touching the quiescent points of weapons that have so often wounded me.

He could take comfort that he did not merit the reproach in Wordsworth's "Repentance" against the "ill-judging sire of an innocent son Who must now be a wanderer", for henceforth he lived frugally so that his heirs should not suffer from his folly.

7

FIRST YEARS OF EXILE

Ought I to be indignant that my country has neglected me? Do not men in all countries like those best who most resemble them? And would you wish me to resemble the multitude who are deluded? or would you rather that I were seated among the select who are in a situation to delude? My Gemma! I could never, by any knowledge or discipline, teach foxes to be honest, wolves to be abstemious, or vipers to be grateful... Let us love those who love us, and be contented to teach those who will hear us. Neither the voice nor the affections can extend beyond a contracted circle. But we may carry a wand with us and mark out with it that circle in every path of life. Never in future will I let men approach too near me.

—Dante and Gemma Donati (1846).

Southey urged Landor against selling his life interest in Llanthony and against permanently settling abroad. "I grant there is vexation enough in our laws; but take it for all in all, there is no country in which a man lives with so little annoyance from the government." If financial trouble necessitated exile for the present, let him go—said Southey—"not as an emigrant, but as a guest or stranger". Writing before he had received Landor's letter of 27th May from Weymouth, Southey addressed his letter to Warwick, whence Robert Landor wrote to him on 27th June:

My brother was indeed expected at Warwick. He is in France. I feel no hesitation in communicating what we are anxious to conceal from every other person, that he left this country under circumstances the most perplexing to his family, and with feelings the most unhappy for himself.

Landor considered that he was compelled into exile by contemporary English law. His creditors might have secured his imprisonment for debt, and failing his collection of debts due to him, he must have submitted to a forced sale of much of his property. A shrewd business manager might have accommodated the creditors and disembarrassed a residue of the estate, but meanwhile Landor would have faced the humiliation of examination by lawyers and of condescension from his creditors. With his pride already sufficiently wounded and his sense of justice affronted, he preferred exile; having made up his mind, he could bear no argument on the subject, which he sought to banish from his mind and conscience.

He left England alone, but was soon joined in Jersey by his wife and one of her sisters. Julia Landor was still only twenty, and her three years of marriage must have rudely disappointed expectations on marrying a rich husband. With her husband alternately shut up with his writing or raging about vexatious business, she can have felt little love for the loneliness of Llanthony, and after residing only a few months in the newly-built house, she accompanied Landor's flight to Swansea and the desolation of a small seaside resort during winter months. With dismay and despair she now heard Landor's resolution to live permanently abroad; not only vanished were her dreams of the gracious life of a squire's lady, but she was to be banished from Bath, from her family and her friends.

As appears from his letter to Southey from Weymouth on 27th May, Landor sympathetically recognised that "my wife, when she married, little thought she should leave all her friends to live in obscurity and perhaps in want". A wise or a loving woman would have refrained from reminders of her disappointment, but, as Landor related to Southey on 2nd October 1814:

Julia had long shown a disinclination to quit this country, and hardly a day elapsed without some expression, more or less energetic, of her sentiments. I subdued my temper—the worst beyond comparison that ever man was cursed with—remembering the rank and fortune she had refused for my sake, and the content and moderation she had always preserved in the midst of privacy and seclusion. . . . A thousand times have I implored her not to drive me to distraction; to be contented if I acknowledged myself in the wrong; to permit me to be at once of her opinion, and not to think a conversation incomplete without a quarrel. The usual reply was, "A pleasant sort of thing truly, that you are never to be contradicted!" As if it were extraordinary and strange that one should wish to avoid it. She never was aware that more can be said in one minute than can be forgotten in a lifetime.

The crisis came when they "had passed above a month at Jersey, and in another day were about to sail for France". Julia's recriminations, "with a thousand variations, both of anger and mockery, and all of them turning upon what she declared to have been her own fault in marrying such an old man, made her little sister burst into tears".

Julia told her not to be such a fool as to cry; that if *she* cried, it certainly should not be about me. I endured all this a full hour and a half without a syllable of reply; but every kind and tender sentiment was rooted up from my heart for ever . . . No woman could or ought to live with a man by whom such language was merited: nor could any man support life with a woman from whom it fell undeserved. I remained broad awake, as I firmly believe, and yet I had a succession of dreams, rapid, incoherent, and involuntary. I rose at four. I walked to the other part of the island, and embarked alone, on board of an oyster-boat, for France. It was this very day month. I am resolved to see her no more. I wish to have only 160*l.* a year for myself. It is enough. I have neither wife nor family, nor house nor home, nor pursuit nor occupation.

If Landor had loved his wife, he could not have written thus of their quarrel to a friend; if in so writing he seems to have stumbled from dignity, he had sufficient reason for despondency without abuse from his wife. He was not of those who can find solace for wounded feelings and vanity in casual amours: he wrote to Southey after a few weeks in France, "I wish I could acquire all the heartless profligacy of this people—that I could be anything, good or bad, dead or alive, but what I am." His confidence in his friend was not misplaced, for he wrote to Southey from Tours on 4th November, "There is more kindness in one sentence of your letter than I have received from all quarters of the world from my birth to the present hour."

Soon after hearing from Southey he received a letter from his wife's eldest sister, "dated so early as the middle of September".

It acquainted me with her extreme grief, and of an illness which threatened to be fatal. This banished from my mind all traces of resentment, and I wrote instantly to comfort and console her. My one fear is, that I shall never be able to keep my promise in its full extent, to forgive humiliating and insulting language. Certainly I shall never be so happy as I was before; that is beyond all question. If there is a pleasure in pardoning, there is a proportionate pain in doubting whether we possess the power. Julia has not yet recovered her health entirely, but expresses a wish to join me.

If by then he had heard that Jane Swift was a widow—Godwin Swift died in 1814—he can have felt no great happiness in their reconciliation when, in February 1815, he travelled from Tours to meet Julia at Dieppe.

The following month Napoleon escaped from Elba. English residents in France took fright; four thousand, according to Landor, hurriedly applied for passports, by one of whom he sent a letter to Southey on 8th May:

I have applied to Fouché for permission to remain in France, and he has granted it. Whether our countrymen in general will be molested or not depends, I presume, in great measure, on the future conduct of our government. I should rather have said, of *your* government; for with me they have nothing more to do than to despoil me of my property to support their stupendous folly. What has happened was quite certain to happen from the beginning. Can anything be more clear than the prediction of Calvus?

Throughout the Hundred Days he remained at Tours. After Waterloo, when English residents were warned to leave, he wrote to Carnot, the

Minister of the Interior, that, while he felt "no confidence in the moderation or honour of the Emperor", he preferred to stay where he was because there might be greater danger in the midst of a broken army. When Napoleon's army occupied Tours, Landor's—"a cheap house for Tours . . . the only sitting-room looks into a pretty little garden"—was the only house in the town without a billet, a consideration owed to Carnot's courtesy. One day seeing a horseman dismount in the courtyard of the prefect's house, he believed that he recognised the traveller as the fugitive emperor.

On 2nd October Robert Landor arrived at Tours and found his brother on friendly terms with all about him. Among the English colony Landor started a close friendship with Francis Hare, who had come to Tours in April to visit his dying father; he was intimate with Arthur Clifford, a brother of the barrister consulted over the matter of Price and the grand jury, and with Roderick Murchison, the geologist, a friend of Hare's, whom he addressed in verse nearly fifty years later:

> Upon the bank
> Of Loir thou camest to me, brought by Hare
> The witty and warm-hearted, passing through
> That shady garden whose broad tower ascends
> From chamber over chamber; there I dwelt,
> The flowers my guests, the birds my pensioners,
> Books my companions, and but few beside.

Robert accompanied him on shopping excursions in the market place —"Walter says that he rather saves than not, but I suspect there must be some mistake in the calculation"—and remarked the joyous greetings he received from the market women, whose hearts he had won by his laughter and compliments. He was friendly even with the prefect— a rare instance of his amiable relations with authority.

Robert came as a disturbing influence. He brought deeds for Landor's signature, assigning management of his estate to his brothers Charles and Henry as joint trustees, and news that the Swansea bankers were threatening his arrest for debt. Landor suffered from his reputation in the family as difficult of temper, impetuous, unreasonable, careless of money; apparently his family were persuaded that his enemies were in the right and he uniformly in the wrong. During the sixteen months since his leaving England little accurate information had been extracted from Gabb and the other Welsh attorneys. As holder of the annuity reserved to her under the act of parliament required for the sale of Tachbrook, his mother claimed priority among his creditors, and in return for his agreeing to appoint Charles and Henry administrators of his estate, proposed to make him an annual allowance.

Robert came like a priest to shrive a convicted sinner, but found that he had heard only one version of the story. Apparently Landor was believed by his family to have raised the loan at Swansea to finance himself on the continent; Robert was surprised to learn that "of the £3000 paid by the Swansea Bankers, Walter reserved to himself but £200; the rest was sent to the Banker at Abergavenny & to Mr. Gabb, for the payment of different Debts". He heard for the first time of "many large sums paid into Mr. Gabb's hands for particular purposes to which they have never been applied", and, "as for Mr. Gabell, Walter swears that Mr. G. owes him more than a thousand pounds and that he lent him £50 at a time". He began to realise "how wretchedly everything has been managed, both by him and his agents". In a long letter from Tours to his brother Henry, Robert wrote on 4th October:

Walter appears to be very much altered in disposition & I never felt so sorry for him before. This threat of the Swansea Bankers hangs upon his Mind, which might otherwise be cheerful enough. He has made a solemn resolution never to spend more than £450 a year, even after my Mother's death, till every guinea is paid off & his wife joins him in this determination. . . . I am delighted with the conduct of Julia, who appears quite indifferent about her mode of life. She is, however, very much affected by the situation, for Tours is between two rivers on a dead level, which runs sixty miles, & by the dread of public outrage. How much I wish that it was in Mrs. Landor's power to relieve them from this apprehension of arrest, & pay the Swansea Bankers. I know the difficulties & I have made Walter quite sensible of them, but I am fully persuaded that his intentions are now quite honourable, & that nothing would be lost ultimately. When I told him of his Servants & the Tradesmen's debts or rather dues, & represented the state of his property, he seemed quite confounded & overwhelmed, he had heard of them before, but not understood them, his Mind seemed quite bewildered & he only perceived things by piecemeal. Sometimes he is very cheerful, & at others, languid & miserable. Since I came he has not slept half an hour, & today he is quite unwell.

Within a few days of his brother's arrival, Landor decided to leave Tours. "I quite agree in thinking that Tours is a very unsafe residence indeed," wrote Robert to Henry; "all the English Families are gone, excepting four or five out of 300 and every hour there are reports that one party or the other will rise." Apart from the danger of political unrest and the change required by Julia's health, there was a possibility, with France under allied occupation, that the Swansea bankers might secure Landor's extradition. The cheap rate of living at Tours enabled him to keep his own carriage, and "after contests with his landlady of a most tremendous description", they set out through German-occupied territory on the east of the Loire, travelling post, "Walter and myself on the dicky, his wife and her maid within". Landor had thought of settling at Chambéry in Savoy, but arriving there "he was too restless" and "we agreed with a voiturier; a man who undertakes to conduct you with his horses and carriages to any given distance for a certain sum, and to pay for your eating, drinking, and lodging".

Walter gave him his carriage on condition that he would carry him free of expense first to Milan and afterwards to Como, twenty-five miles farther, where the princess of Wales resides.

During the journey, with nights spent at "miserable inns", tempers frayed and Robert became less sympathetically disposed. Evidently Julia had been chastened in spirit by Landor's leaving her in Jersey; possibly her mother had shown no enthusiasm for the liability of a daughter living apart from her husband. Seeking to recover her husband's confidence by submissive behaviour, she was at pains to impress his brother favourably, and Robert became resentful on her behalf against Landor's irritability.

He is seldom out of a passion or a sulky fit excepting at dinner, when he is more boisterous and good-humoured than ever. Then his wife is a darling, a beauty, an angel, and a bird. But for just as little reason the next morning she is a fool. She is certainly gentle, patient, and submissive. She takes all the trouble, is indeed too officious, and would walk on foot most willingly if he wished it, and she were able. If he loses his keys, his purse, or his pocket-handkerchief, which he does ten times in an hour, she is to be blamed; and she takes it all very quietly.

By the time they reached Milan, Robert had lost all patience with his brother:

If he is ever really unhappy, it is because the cook has put oil or garlic into the soup. Give him a good dinner well cooked, and he is happier than an emperor. He writes and reads all the day besides. As for his creditors, he cares no more about them or his own concerns than about Bonaparte's. He has plenty of money for this country; lives as well as ever he did in his life; and at Tours had even saved five-and-thirty pounds. He has one entire quarter in his banker's hands at present, after travelling so far.

They parted at Milan, Landor and his wife proceeding to Como, Robert to Rome. Robert told Forster that he left Julia with "regret and pity", but between the brothers there was no regret at parting.

At Como Landor fell into trouble. Caroline of Brunswick was living there and had reason to suspect that spies had been deputed to report on her conduct to the Prince Regent as evidence for divorce proceedings. As Landor and his wife sought privacy to avoid possible pursuit by the Swansea bankers, their conduct invited suspicion and Robert reported from Rome to Henry Landor on 1st January 1816:

I have heard from Walter, who has got into hot water about the Princess of Wales; they seem to have taken him for a Spy on her Conduct, which, as

all Italy knows, & I suppose all the world must know, is infamous & profligate to such a degree that the Prince can find no difficulty whatever in
getting a Divorce.

Relating (as Landor himself later told Southey) how Lady Cumming,
daughter of a former lady-in-waiting on the Princess, had been "obliged
to leave the house abruptly through the indecencies she had witnessed",
and how the Princess could now obtain no reputable English ladies to
attend her, Robert exclaimed, "But yet what had Walter to do with
all this? He has a most surprising alacrity in getting into Scrapes."

Robert's letters show that he was adopting an attitude of impatience
towards his eldest brother as an irresponsible eccentric—an attitude in
which he persisted for the rest of his life and impressed upon Forster.
"Walter has been imploying Slatter & Munday to print Latin Poetry,"
he told their brother Henry, "which no one ever reads or even hears of
—perhaps the books will not pay the expenses of publication—there is
nothing left you but patience and, if possible, indifference." Talking
of the danger of arrest—"it is impossible to conceal Walter's place of
residence", he said, "as he has proclaimed it everywhere". He failed
to recognise that Landor, indignant at the imputation of being a spy
on a woman's misconduct, would inevitably sacrifice considerations of
personal safety to disprove the libel. Gossip soon speculated on the
reason for his exile; a dozen years later popular rumour at Florence
credited him with "some offence against police regulations" and with
having "threatened to pull the judge by his throat down from his
judgment seat".

On his way homeward Robert called at Como in June 1816. Finding
Landor and his wife installed in a "comfortable house", he "observed
all due caution about the state of his Spouse" but remarked:

Julia looks thin, but not pale; talks much of dying, and of returning to
Bath, preferring the latter a little . . . Walter is much as usual; that is, in
very unequal spirits; fretful, gloomy, absent, and very gay by turns. Unfortunately the latter is not frequent, and I believe that I saw him to the greatest
advantage.

Contrary to his belief, he probably saw his brother to the worst advantage, for Robert's presence must have served, as at Tours, to remind
Landor of his financial troubles and of the Llanthony nightmare.

§ 2

Landor now cultivated the habit of detachment that prevailed
throughout the rest of his life. His closest rival as a writer of gorgeous
rhetoric in prose, De Quincey listed in his youth the "constituents of
happiness" necessary in the life of a man devoted to intellectual pursuits. De Quincey lacked the tenacity to acquire all the constituents;

Landor lacked the self-insight to recognise their necessity, but acquired all by instinct or by accident. Briefly De Quincey's list was: 1. A capacity of thinking—of abstraction and reverie. 2. Interest in human life and nature. 3. Fixed, and not merely temporary, residence in some spot of eminent beauty. 4. Interchange of solitude and interesting society. 5. Books. 6. Some great intellectual project. 7. Health and vigour. 8. A sense of moral elevation and purity. 9. A vast predominance of contemplation. 10. Emancipation from worldly cares, anxieties, and connections, and from all that is comprehended under the term business, so that time, thoughts, and feelings may be unfettered by petty considerations. 11. The education of a child. 12. A personal appearance tolerably respectable, which, if lacking, may be compensated by dignity of demeanour bespeaking a mind at peace with itself, or by acquiring a high literary name.

Landor cultivated the first constituent as a young man walking the beaches of Swansea and Tenby, but in the habit of "abstraction and reverie" he now acquired "a vast predominance of contemplation" (9); in later years he would sit for hours lost in meditation, and resent interruption by those who supposed that he was doing nothing. Of the second, he delighted more in the study of animal life, flowers, and plants, than of human personality; "I love to enter into the thoughts of animals", he told Southey, "and contract a friendship with them whenever they come in my way". The third he had always sought— at Swansea, Clifton, Llanthony, Como, and soon at Fiesole. Of the fourth, he had long appreciated the value of solitude, and exchanged it only for the company of chosen friends. Fifthly, though he never collected books after the sale of his library at Llanthony, he always obtained those he wanted, stored their pith in his exceptional memory, and gave them away. Sixthly, his great intellectual project, as he confided to Southey, was the writing of a history of his own times that would not confound him "with the Coxes and Foxes of the age". Seventhly, he possessed exceptional health and physical strength. Eighthly, he indulged no vices, disdained the petty preoccupations of self-advancement, and nourished his mind by studying the humanities. The ninth he acquired by cultivating the first; he was to delight in the eleventh when his wife bore children.

As to the tenth and the twelfth—the latter De Quincey, a man of small appearance and timid demeanour, might have esteemed him to possess. But by this constituent De Quincey implied a sufficient consciousness of well-being to warrant a feeling of serenity and confidence. This Landor lacked through the first forty years of his life. Since his boyhood at Rugby only a few friends like Parr and Southey had offered the encouragement of praise, and he had worn a mask of arrogance to hide a conscience troubled by inadequate achievement. More men are

M

spoiled than improved by success, but Landor needed prestige for his finest qualities to flourish; when fame came, he wore it fittingly as his due. Meanwhile he developed the serenity of self-possession. Since boyhood his self-esteem had suffered from his family's attitude that he over-valued his powers; it sustained a heavy blow in the humiliation of his failure at Llanthony. In Italy for the first time his self-esteem was flattered by a sense of superiority. With a philosophy foreign to the fortitude of the English public-school class, the impoverished Italian nobility cynically paraded their poverty. Contemptuously Robert Landor wrote from Rome:

> I have just dismissed an Italian Nobleman, who calls me Milord & accepts a Crown for the Compliment. He adds in such Italian as I can understand that a pair of old Shoes or an old Shirt would contribute to his comforts, he kisses hands, he bows to the Earth & retires. These are the descendants of Romulus & Remus!

Landor found such humility in men of birth and culture a gratifying contrast with the boorishness of the Welsh peasants, who reluctantly touched their forelocks even to a lady. Landor's spirit was heartened by homage; thirty years later, noting how many sycophants surrounded Landor at Bath, young Augustus Hare shrewdly observed how, "though he despised the persons, he did not always dislike the flattery". Nor did he neglect to learn a lesson from these ruined Italian aristocrats. Their polished courtesy, despised by Robert as servile, Landor recognised as a mark of caste of which misfortune could not deprive them; significantly all who met him from this time remarked the courtliness of manner for which he was admired in old age.

In assimilating the twelfth of De Quincey's constituents he was helped by acquiring the tenth. The humiliation of his Llanthony failure oppressed him so that he could not bear its mention by his wife at Jersey; his letters to Southey show how he brooded upon it alone at Tours, and Robert's arrival re-opened the wound. Robert recognised only irony and eccentricity on finding that, "when we supposed him to be so miserable at Tours after parting with his wife, he was busy about a long Latin poem on the Death of Ulysses!" Obviously Landor sought refuge from sorrow in the distraction of composition. Continuing this habit in the following years, though soon he ceased to dread every recall from study as a reminder of anxiety, he came to resent as an intrusion any consideration of practical business.

Without complaint he accepted his mother's terms by which his brothers Charles and Henry administered his estate as trustees and she paid him an annual allowance on condition that the money so advanced should be repaid to her younger children on his inheriting Ipsley at her death. A sense of grievance at her severity may have inspired his writing so rarely and reservedly to his mother in the first years of his exile. His effects at Llanthony were sold, and some handsome bargains secured at the remote country auction—Henry Landor bought for ten pounds a Titian valued at twelve hundred guineas. The house was not let, though it was occupied by somebody six months after Landor left England, for the manuscript diary of Captain Thomas Morgan, of the Monmouth and Brecon Militia, records on 28th October 1814, "Went to Llanthony coursing, kill'd 2 hares, had 5 courses dined at Mr. Landor's new home". Some seventeen years later the house was demolished.

After the birth of a son and heir to Landor in 1818, his mother relented so far that, on his undertaking not to fell any timber at Ipsley during his lifetime without his brother Henry's consent, she resigned to him all arrears of the Llanthony rent charge of £450 a year due to her. Thenceforward, throughout the ten years preceding her death in 1829, she enjoyed with him a regular and affectionate correspondence; in 1825, having arranged her affairs so that her younger children lost nothing by the concession, she secured their consent to an agreement that Landor should not be required to repay, at her death, the sum of her annual allowances to him.

§ 3

Landor lived nearly three years at Como—from the end of November 1815 to September 1818. During these years he published nothing; he wrote to the famous printer Bodoni, inviting him to publish his Latin poem on the death of Ulysses, but Bodoni's widow replied that her husband had died in 1813 and she could accept no new commissions. He read much for his projected history of his own time, but kept in touch with current English literature through Southey, who sent him recent publications in return for rare editions of the classics or French and Italian books. Without professional envy, he praised contemporary poetry with more enthusiasm than discrimination, as appears in a letter to Walter Birch of 27th November 1818:

Do not let us be so unjust to our own age as to compare any other with it in genuine poetry. If the whole of the *Excursion* is equal to this portion of it, I do not hesitate to assert that all the productions of the Augustan age put together fall greatly short of it—Wordsworth, Southey, Miss Bailie, what a class! Even the breakfast-table poets—Campbell, Lord Biron, Scott, Crabbe, Rogers—put all the continent to shame.

In June 1817, during the course of a continental holiday taken after the death of his eldest son, Southey spent three days with him at Como:

> ... Came
> Southey, a sorrowing guest, who lately lost
> His only boy. We walkt aside the lake,
> And mounted to the level downs above,

Where if we thought of Skiddaw, named it not.
I led him to Bellaggio, of earth's gems
The brightest. *We in England have as bright,*
Said he, and turn'd his face toward the west.
I fancied in his eyes there was a tear,
I knew there was in mine: we both stood still.

They talked much of poetry, especially of Wordsworth, to whom Landor subsequently enclosed one or two books in his parcels to Southey, so opening an occasional correspondence with the recluse of Rydal. Southey was also entertained with the scandalous tales of the Princess of Wales, and on his return home, he warned Landor that, in consequence from the death of the Princess Charlotte, leaving no heir of the younger generation to the throne, "the amusements of Como may very probably become the amusements of England ere long".

At Como, on the 5th March 1818, Landor's eldest son was born. He waited a month before writing to his mother, "knowing the accidents to which such events are liable", especially to women in his wife's "very delicate and feeble state of health". Contrary to expectation, the child "was remarkably strong and healthy, and Julia has not enjoyed such health and spirits for these last five years". This seems remarkable, as "she was bled seventeen times in six months". Landor admitted that such treatment "in England would be considered as imprudent", but otherwise the physician had assured him "she never would have a child born alive", and he reckoned this man's skill to be "totally unexampled in Italy, where to say nothing of ignorance, slovenliness & negligence, particularly among the medical men, are almost universal".

He decided to call the boy Arnold Savage, after Sir Arnold Savage, a Speaker of the House of Commons whom he believed to have been of his mother's family. He read that this legislator was "the first who declared that grievances should be redressed before money should be granted", and "I have so much respect for a person of this stamp that I should be likely to name a son after him, even if I had no connection with his family or name". His wife's sister Laura was godmother, and General Meyrick one of the godfathers, but Landor added:

He will be christened again in England, if we should return within the next twelve or fourteen years, but on this subject, I am doubtful, or rather, I am indifferent. I have learned that it is possible to live out of England, and that a person, who hates all society, can do without it here full as well as there.

In May 1818 Landor told Southey that he planned to leave Como for Genoa in September, but he left only after trouble with the local authorities.

A scoundrel, one Monti, wrote a most violent invective in the form of a sonnet against England . . . I answered it in Latin, and attempted to print my poem, with an epigram on Voltaire and four others, in which no name whatever was employed. The censor declared that they were six libels . . . I informed him, for I had consulted a sensible jurist, that censors never refused their license to Latin compositions unless sovereigns or their alliances, or religion or morals, were attacked. [1]

As a result he was bidden to an interview with the *regio delegato* of the province, who proceeded with officious pomposity till he referred to Landor's "insolent" letter and Landor "stopped him quietly", saying, "Sir, the word *insolent* is never applied to a gentleman . . . and if you had dared to utter it in any other place you would have received a *bella bastonata*." Calling his guards, the outraged official proposed to send him under arrest to Milan unless he retracted his words; Landor refused to "retract any word of mine" and invited him to proceed with his threat, "if you are not afraid of exposing yourself still more than you have done". When the man declared that "if it was not for his high office he would settle the business with his sword in the square", Landor "laughed in his face; and the rascal had the baseness to offer his hand in token of reconciliation, and to tell me what a friend he had always been of the English". "My time expired on the 19th of September," wrote Landor, but "rather wishing to be sent for to Milan, . . . I protracted my stay till the 28th, and no attempt was made to assassinate me".

In leaving Como he regretted the loss of his intimacy with an Italian scholar, "the calm philosophical Sironi", and remembered with affection "the little turreted city" as the scene of visits from Southey and from "the learned and modest" Immanuel Bekker. At Albaro near Genoa he rented for a few weeks the palace of the Marchese Pallavicini, in an imaginary conversation with whom he recorded comments that may have been recollections of an actual interview. "No city in the world," he told Walter Birch, "except Rome (when it was rebuilt by Nero) and Corinth, ever equalled the magnificence of Genoa." Bath, he thought, came next, "but immense the distance", though "nothing in the world equals the Circus at Bath". Nervi, four miles from Genoa, had "probably the best climate in the world", and "if the Genoese state was still in the enjoyment of its freedom, I could live and die at Nervi". At Genoa he visited the veteran statesman Gianni, to whose character he paid tribute in the imaginary conversation, "Peter Leopold and President Du Paty": "I was refreshed and comforted by the calmness and simplicity of this venerable old man,"

[1] Vincenzo Monti (1754–1828) was one of the most distinguished contemporary poets and sculptors. For his *Bassvilliana* he was compared with Dante, his translation of the *Iliad* was praised for its Homeric feeling, and his sculpture was rated with Canova's. In politics he would have been a Fascist a century later; he opposed the French Revolution, attacked the Papacy, and applauded the victories of Napoleon.

who "enjoyed good health from good spirits, and those from their only genuine source, a clear conscience".

Hearing that "it was a cheap place", he moved to Pisa, whence he wrote to Birch on 27th November:

Pisa has the advantage of a river, 200 feet wide, running through its principal street; but it is infested with English and Irish and moschitos. I pay a guinea a week for my lodgings, without linen and plate, and everything is a third dearer than Genoa, except game. I am anxious to visit Rome to see the Pope and Consalvi and Canova. Curious, and rather a pity, that the only three great men in Europe should be within the same walls.

To Southey he wrote in the following April, "When my spirits wax faint I say to myself, I have yet to see Rome and Southey." Before he saw Rome seven years later Pope Pius VII and his secretary of state, Cardinal Consalvi—whom he admired for their defiance of Napoleon and their liberal measures after the Congress of Vienna—as well as the sculptor, Canova, were dead.

In the spring of 1819 he retired from Pisa to spend the summer in the coolness of the mountains at Pistoia.

He rented a villa at the recommendation of the proprietor, who assured him that the walls were dry, although built recently. Within a few days it rained, and the bedchambers were covered with drops. His wife and child suffered in their health: he expostulated: he offered to pay a month's rent and to quit the premises, insisting on the nullity of an agreement founded on fraud. The proposal was rejected: a court of judicature declared the contract void. The gentleman, to prove that there was nothing light or ungenerous in his motive, gave to his banker, M. Cassigoli, the amount of the six months' rent, to be distributed among respectable families in distress.

After circulating a report "that the gentleman might well throw away his money, having acquired immense sums by piracy", the disgruntled landlord appealed to a local tribunal, which referred the dispute for arbitration to the local commissary. This official, like John Price at Llanthony, was disposed to oblige those from whom he received material expressions of gratitude, and Landor had to appeal to the *Presidente del buon Governo*: he "stated his case fully to the president, from whom he obtained no redress, no answer, no notice". These circumstances he related in "Peter Leopold and President Du Paty" as having befallen "a literary man of a life extremely retired", but his complaints against the commissary Fantoni are preserved in the state archive at Florence.[1]

At Pistoia he was occupied with Latin composition. Besides verse, he wrote a Latin prose essay "concerning the cultivation and use of the Latin language, why modern Latin writers were not more widely read", and the advantages of using Latin in writing works of culture

[1] Mr. Super (*Walter Savage Landor: A Biography*) quotes from the complaints without relating them to Landor's statement in "Peter Leopold and President Du Paty".

and imagination. For a prize offered by the Stockholm Academy he wrote an ode to Bernadotte on his accession to the Swedish throne; he printed at Pistoia in 1819 *Sponsalia Polyxenae*, of which he wrote an English version, "The Espousals of Polyxena," for his *Hellenics* of 1847; with his prose essay and the five idyls printed by Slatter & Munday, he included five new idyls and some fifty hendecasyllabics in *Idyllia Heroica Decem*, published at Pisa in 1820. "Oh that you would write in English," wrote Southey in February 1820; "I can never think of your predilections for Latin verse but as a great loss to English literature." On 4th August following Robert Landor wrote to his brother Henry:

I have received two or three Letters lately from Walter about some Latin Poems, which have been printed at Pisa, and sent to Longman for publication. Here is another foolish expense without the chance of sixpence in return! Who reads Latin Poems written in these days!

Though protests repeated for years by Southey and Robert Landor had failed, a single letter from Wordsworth sufficed to divert Landor from Latin composition. His letters to Southey frequently contained courteous messages to Wordsworth and applause of his poetry. "In thoughts, feelings and images not one amongst the ancients equals him," he wrote of *The Excursion*; "I hope Wordsworth will write no more short poems until he has finished his Recluse." When Southey announced that Wordsworth wished to send him a copy of *Peter Bell*, he replied, "The present of a book from W. will be one of the three or four eras in my life." On receiving *Peter Bell* he was not uncritical and wished the first 120 lines of the Prologue had been omitted, but "in whatever Wordsworth writes there is admirable poetry . . . The first poet that ever wrote was not a more original poet than he is, and the best is hardly a greater".

In return for Wordsworth's gift he sent a copy of *Idyllia Heroica Decem*, together with the manuscript of a second Latin essay, supplementary to the first, discussing aspects of poetry and criticism treated in Wordsworth's prefaces, and "saying in the preface that I had taken whatever I wanted from him, with the same liberty as a son eats and drinks in his father's house". Apologising for delaying his reply, due to trouble with his eyes, Wordsworth assured him that "it could not but be grateful to me to be praised by a poet who has written verses of which I would rather have been the author than of any produced in our time". But he could not agree with Landor's plea for the use of Latin and his "frequent infirmity" of sight gave him "an especial right to use this argument", for "had your Idylliums been in English, I should long ere this have been as well acquainted with them as with your *Gebir* and with your other poems; and now I know not how long they may remain to me a sealed book". If Wordsworth, baited by praise of himself, could not be tempted to read Latin verses, Landor must have recognised that he was knocking on a sealed door. He published no more Latin verse before his collected *Poemata* of 1847.

§ 4

From Pistoia Landor returned to Pisa in the autumn of 1819. He had intended to go to Florence, but firstly, the Austrian Emperor was there on a visit, and "these people produce no other effect by their visits than degradation and dearness"; secondly, he was disappointed in negotiations for a house there. From Pisa, on 6th March 1820, he wrote to his mother:

I am happy to inform you that Julia was safely delivered of a girl, about nineteen minutes after seven this morning. She suffered very little, and has been laughing and talking with the nurses ever since. . . . It is the custom here to carry the children to be baptised the very day of their birth. I shall not pay any attention to such foolery.

Doubtless in order that his wife should remain near her doctor, he stayed at Pisa throughout the following summer.

In the autumn he heard that his amusements of Como, as Southey had prophesied, were become the amusements of England, Caroline being used by the Whigs as an instrument of attack on the government and George IV. At Como in 1817 one of his English neighbours had been Sir Charles Wolseley, who had married a sister of Landor's friend Clifford. As a radical reformer Wolseley shared Landor's impetuosity and quixotry; on his return to England he was prominent in the agitations culminating in the Peterloo riots and imprisoned in 1819 for sedition. When Queen Caroline's trial divided popular opinion, he wrote from prison to the *Times* that, if released, he would "undertake to be of the utmost service to her Majesty in the pending prosecution against her, by going from hence to Como, where, during the year 1817, I lived several months with my family; and from that circumstance, and being acquainted with several people who were employed by the queen, I have an opportunity of getting at evidence that would be of the greatest consequence, that no Englishman but myself and a Mr. Walter Landor, who is now in Italy, can have had the same opportunity of knowing".

"Sir Ch. W. must be half crazy," wrote Southey to Landor; "we may judge how capable he is of forming a sane opinion upon any subject when he has so topsy-turvy a recollection of your knowledge upon this." Landor had, indeed, no first-hand knowledge of the Queen's conduct, for she had left Como in the month of his arrival. But the suggestion of his being a spy upon her had so annoyed him that he listened readily to gossip about her and her friends. To Southey he had reported, as Robert Landor had written to their brother Henry, the indecencies committed by Caroline and her Italian chamberlain, Pergami, in the presence of Lady Cumming. On the occasion of Caroline's later visit to Como, he gleaned further gossip, which he confided to Walter Birch in a letter from Pisa on 27th November 1818.

You have probably heard of the misfortune that has befallen the Princess of Wales. The physician who attended her at Pisa, and who left her—with anger on both sides—because his return to Milan was indispensable, told Cavalier Morosini, who informed my friend Sr Sironi, that he was called in too late to perform a speedy cure, that the P. and five of her stallions had the syphilis, the men probably knew what was the matter, but the P. gave it out everywhere that she was poisoned by the English, hinting that her husband was the author of the attempt, and hiring a rascally advocate to write a book, in which he declares literally that the Prince had tried to do the same thing in another manner, both at Como & at Genoa. It was reported at the former place that she actually was dead, poisoned by the English. . . .

Such evidence as Landor could have given, therefore, was the reverse of favourable to Caroline, but while he lamented to Southey that "Parr should take so active a part in favour of that woman", he felt disgust with the scavenging of the informers:

Never did I entertain a doubt of her guilt and infamy; but those wretches are more guilty and more infamous who employ false keys in bedrooms and escritoires . . . Had Brougham's brother entered my house, the interview would have been short, and both standing. I admire the impudence of Wolseley. He attempted to defend the doings of the princess; but never hinted a thought of her innocence when I constantly represented her what all Italy knows her to be, not indeed with legal proofs (such are almost impossible in similar cases), but according to all appearances year after year. Yet if a court of justice called on me to give evidence, I should give my evidence according to the orders and spirit of our laws, and say that, not knowing her guilty, I am not authorised to prejudice her: proofs alone constitute guilt.

In similar terms he addressed a letter to the *Times*: "the secrets of the bedchamber and the escritoire have never been the subject of my investigation . . . I desire that in future the name of *a Mr. Walter Landon* may not be united with *a Sir Ch. Wolseley.*"

Robert Landor read with disgust his brother's letter to the *Times*. From the security of his Hughenden parsonage he was writing pseudonymous letters to the *Courier* so savagely vituperating the Queen that the newspaper was indicted for libel. To his brother Henry—who generously offered to go to prison in his place if the identity of the letter-writer was revealed—he wrote on 11th December 1820:

Elizabeth will tell you of Walter's letter in the Times, if you have not already heard of it. He is the most whimsical creature upon earth, since the times of Puck. His indignation against the government is so great that it has half consumed his former hatred for the Queen, as a fire is supposed to burn out a scald. But, however, his letter is just what one could have wished in one respect, it is too magnificent to be intemperate.

Again he interpreted only eccentricity in a sense of honour he was unable to appreciate.

Landor contemplated England's internal troubles with detachment. On his forty-fifth birthday he told Southey, "I think of England as if I were in another world and had lost all personal interest in it." With the balance of his thought unbiassed by patriotism, he developed a cosmopolitan ability to debate a cause on its own merits, so that his statements of political philosophy remain apposite with the permanence of wisdom. The trial of Queen Caroline, dividing England in faction, inspired him only to reflect on "the moral character of the English aristocracy" that "their two most memorable acts are their opposition to the repeal of the slave-trade, and their miserable weakness and indecision in the affair of the queen". He cited this reflection as a warning to the Neapolitans in their demands for representative government. "I have written three orations," he informed Southey on 12th March 1821, "exposing the duplicity of the *Alleati Santi* (as the Neapolitans call them), the danger to which all constitutional governments are exposed, and the inexpediency, not to say impossibility, of forming a house of lords." He shared Brougham's view of the Holy Alliance as "a sinister combination of the despots of Europe against the liberties of free peoples". "I wish I had some thousand pounds to spare," he wrote of the revolution at Naples, "as I had when the Spaniards rose against Bonaparte, that what I offered to them I might offer to the Neapolitans." Having no money to help their cause, he published his "orations" as *Poche Osservazioni ... di Walter Savage Landor, gentiluomo inglese, signore di Lantony*; he sent an English version of the pamphlet to Longman, but later told Southey that the publisher had "not thought it worth his while to give me any information about the little work I sent to be printed".

On 22nd April 1821, he wrote to his mother from Florence, where he had gone to look for a house. "Julia," he said, "is thin and weak, but is without any particular complaint, and is recommended to change the air for the summer, as Pisa lies low, and is abandoned by all the inhabitants in the warm season." His mother had been ill, and writing to inform him of the arrangement she had made to relieve him of the arrears of the Llanthony rent charge, hoped "in time you will come and spend the remainder of your life in this country where you have many well-wishers, which some time or other you will be convinced of". After expressing concern for her health, he replied:

The misery of not being able to see you, is by far the greatest I have ever suffered. Never shall I forget the thousand acts of kindness and affection I have received from you, from my earliest to my latest days.

I have deferred the christening of my little daughter, because I wished to have one to be named after you, and to whom I might request you to be godmother. As perhaps I may never have another, I shall call my little Julia by the name of Julia Elizabeth Savage Landor, and, with your permission, will engage some one of Julia's English friends to represent you. This is the first time I was ever a whole day without seeing Arnold. I wonder what his thoughts are upon the occasion. Mine are a good deal more about him than about the house I must look for.

He is of all living creatures the most engaging, and already repeats ten of the most beautiful pieces of Italian poetry. The honest priest, his master, says he is a miracle and a marvel, and exceeds in abilities all he ever saw or heard of. He turns into ridicule every person that speaks bad Italian. What a pity it is that such divine creatures should ever be men, and subject to regrets and sorrows.

This last reflection has pathos in the light of later events; Landor could not foresee the tragic destiny of his passionate love for his children, though, with that wise philosophy contrasting so oddly with his mismanagement of his own life, he was always aware, even in moments of doting fondness, that he could not expect unalloyed delight in his children to last beyond their childhood. Telling his sister Ellen four years later how he wished never "to be a day without any of them, while they are children", he added, as if with foreboding, "they are different creatures when they grow up".

8

FLORENCE: FIRST *IMAGINARY CONVERSATIONS*

Those who are born for the benefit of the human race, go but little into it: those who are born for its curse, are crowded.
—Diogenes and Plato (1829)

To be wise indeed and happy and self-possessed, we must often be alone: we must mix as little as we can with what is called society, and abstain rather more than seems desirable even from the better few.
—Epicurus, Leontion, and Ternissa (1829)

Poetry was always my amusement, prose my study and business. I have publisht five volumes of *Imaginary Conversations*: cut the worst of them thro the middle, and there will remain in this decimal fraction quite enough to satisfy my appetite for fame. I shall dine late; but the dining-room will be well lighted, the guests few and select.
—Archdeacon Hare and Walter Landor (1853)

Some three months after her arrival in the city with Shelley and his wife, Claire Clairmont recorded in her journal on 5th May 1820 some "account of the odd English at present in Pisa": "Walter Savage Landor who will not see a single English person—says he is glad the country produces people of worth but he will have nothing to do with them." This reputation was unlikely to commend Landor to official representatives of his country, and soon after his arrival in Florence he became on hostile terms with the British minister's entourage.

As his first residence in Florence, he rented furnished apartments in the palazzo of Count Lozzi in the Via della Scala ("A palace here is different from a house," explains Mr. Stivers in *High and Low Life in Italy*, "by having a barn-door for the entrance, and room enough for horses and mules to stand against the staircase"). Lozzi was an invalid, and one evening when Landor was walking with a guest on the terrace, he called from a window that their conversation was disturbing his rest. Landor was not unnaturally annoyed by this discourtesy in the presence of his guest, but his reactions were extravagant: he challenged Lozzi to a duel and wrote a complaint against him to the Grand Duke of Tuscany. The Grand Duke's secretary referred him to the police, who invited him to state his case to the *presidente del buon governo*. Having recited evidence of Lozzi's eccentricity, Landor explained, "I have a wife, young, frail in health, timid, who has been insulted by him: I have young children who could be poisoned," and therefore demanded "that this miscreant be placed where he can do no harm to my family— or that the money which I have paid in advance on my lease be restored to me". As Lozzi—who was known as de Lootz in his native Palatinate —had been previously in trouble with the police, he was bound over to keep the peace and apparently compelled to accommodate Landor by remitting the lease agreement.

The violence of Landor's spleen suggests that Lozzi's act of discourtesy was the climax in a series of offences, chief of which was his behaviour to Landor's young wife. Punctilious in chivalry towards women, Landor cannot have approved the freedom of Italian gallantry towards married women, and he was the more susceptible to offence owing to the disparity in age, his wife's reminder of which had caused him to leave her in Jersey. Gossip must have assumed that Lozzi's behaviour to Mrs. Landor was the reason for Landor's challenge, and the character of a jealous husband invited the more derision as Lozzi was an antagonist commanding little respect.

Soon Landor reported that the British minister's secretary, "one Dawkins, the most consummate scoundrel in Italy, was so insolent that I requested him to mention any place in England or France where we might become better acquainted in a few minutes". To Southey he complained of Dawkins:

To show his courage, whenever he meets my wife in the streets he walks up and sings or whistles. This has affected her health, and I am afraid may oblige me to put him to death before we can reach England. Is it not scandalous that our ministry should employ such men? I have a presentiment that you will hear something of me which you would rather not hear, but my name shall be respected as long as it is remembered.

The minister, Lord Burghersh, intervened pacifically, but finding that Dawkins remained unpunished, Landor informed the minister "that he had neglected his duty and forgotten his promise, which was to see an injury done me redressed". Indignantly he wrote to Birch:

The only Englishman in Italy who does any credit to his country is the only one who receives from its ministers and their dependents and visitors every mark of insolence and injustice. I have collected anecdotes of those who have been employed by our government on the Continent, and will publish them at some future time.

Anecdotes of "the sieur Dorcas, . . . a necessitous and uneducated young person", appeared in the imaginary conversation, "Peter Leopold and President Du Paty"; an account of how the secretary was fooled by a woman of fashion to whom he paid impertinent addresses was repeated of "Sieur Dorkins" in "Florentine, English Visitor, and Landor". Landor's resentment endured beyond the years of the secretary's stay in Florence, for he wrote to Lady Blessington on 28th November 1834 of "the insolent adventurer Dawkins . . . now minister in Greece", who "had profited so little by living in such intimate familiarity with all the swindlers, spies, and jockeys in Tuscany" that he had provided "abundant proofs . . . of his negligence and stupidity", though he was so "much improved" that, "if he has not clean hands, he has clean gloves".

From Lozzi's house Landor removed to a palazzo of the Medicis;[1] informing Birch that he had taken the house for three years and a half and "it is perhaps the best in Italy that is ever let", he gave a glimpse of the last representatives of this ancient family, indicating the straits to which the Italian aristocracy had been reduced by the Napoleonic wars:

The old man has two sons, excellent young men, one of whom is married, but has only a daughter. I told the marchesa, his wife, that I hoped she would have a son. She replied that she was contented without one, and the husband said, "It is time that our family should be extinct." The head of a family the most illustrious on earth possesses about £700 a year, which will be divided between his sons according to the laws established by Napoleon.

To a friend of Southey's, Mrs. Hodson, who asked his advice on taking a house in Florence, Landor wrote in 1835:

there were more unfurnished apartments than furnished . . . It then was expedient, for any family wishing to reside in Florence even two years only, to furnish them. Furniture is very cheap in Italy, and sells for above two-thirds after much using. I furnished the Palazzo Medici, fourteen rooms, for about six hundred pounds—there were however the carpets and giran-doles—and my dinner service cost seventy. There were three or four rooms remaining which were left bare. Every thing is cheaper here than in England except the wages of servants. I pay my coachman nearly the same as at Lanthony and the maids are paid more. Hay and corn are brought from a distance and by land-carriage, and are dearer than with you. Without a carriage, you may live very handsomely on less than four hundred a year, supposing you pay fifty for your house, ready-furnished. For that sum, renting it for two years first, you may have a convenient and handsome one on the sunny side of the Arno. I do not mean on Lung' Arno, which is extremely unhealthy, both in winter and summer.

[1] Mr. Super's researches have revealed that the Medici-Tornaquinci family owned four such houses in Florence; the "Palazzo Medici" occupied by Landor from 1822 to 1825 was one of two in the Borgo degli Albizi.

At Florence, Landor settled to enjoyment of that interchange of solitude and interesting society which De Quincey had earlier secured at Grasmere. He had now abandoned financial cares; he was in regular affectionate correspondence with his mother and, thanks to the low cost of living in Italy, his expenses rarely exceeded his annual allowance. In the intervals of his absorption in study, he received and entertained a few chosen friends. "There are few foreigners of learning who do not come to see me," he said in 1823, though he received less English, owing to friction with the minister. Two years later, he said, "Here in Florence I have two or three friends, a manageable number, and some dozens who call on me, but whom I cannot receive."

The dearest of his friends was Francis Hare. Like Landor, who was eleven years his senior, Hare was an eldest son and heir to a large fortune; he likewise possessed brilliant intellectual gifts, and as a boyhood friend of the future Lord Palmerston, discussed with him such subjects as *Don Quixote* in the original, marriage, and the less conventional classics. After his father's death he "kept horses and resided much at Melton Mowbray, losing an immense amount of money there". He lost so much that his career as a Regency buck lasted only three years before he was compelled by debts and reduced income to reside on the continent, mostly in Florence and Rome, where he accumulated amorous affairs. The acquaintance begun at Tours was renewed at Pisa, and rapidly ripened into affectionate friendship when Landor came to Florence. Each found a match in the other as equally well read, equally extravagant in opinions, and equally excitable in argument.

"It was a constant struggle of competition and display between them," said their friend Seymour Kirkup; "both often wrong, although men of strong memory. They used to have great disputes, mostly on questions of history. . . . Hare was often astounded at being corrected. He was thought infallible; and I remember our consul-general at Rome calling him a monster of learning."

Hare had an "excited, spluttering manner", and received the nickname of "The Silent Hare", from his extreme loquacity; the society anecdotist, Captain Gronow, described him as "remarkable for his leanness, his appetite, and his conversational powers".

He could not only speak every European language, but all the various *patois* of each tongue, with a rapid and effervescent utterance that reminded one of the rushing of some alpine torrent. . . . His memory was as surprising as his loquacity; he could repeat whole pages from almost any book that was mentioned in his presence, and "come down" with effect on any unlucky wight who had made an incorrect quotation from some rare or obsolete volume.

His taste in practical jokes led him to enter a confessional box at Pisa, there to draw upon his picturesque imagination for such a narrative of crime and vice that the simple priest at length put his fingers in his ears and fled in horror from the building. Hare also shared Landor's independence of spirit; like him, he refused to leave France during the Hundred Days, and actually contrived to attend a levée held by Napoleon at the Tuileries, where Gronow reports the following conversation to have taken place:

"Well, sir," asked Napoleon, "what has kept you in Paris when your countrymen have all left?"

"To see the greatest man in Europe, sir."

"Ah, it is, then, your opinion, having seen and conversed with me, that I am not that wild beast I am represented to be by your ministers and the members of your Houses of Parliament?"

"Oh no, sir," replied Hare, "it cannot be the opinion of the English ministers; but I blush when I call to mind the manner in which your name has been traduced by our garrulous members of both Houses."

Two years younger than Hare, Seymour Kirkup arrived in 1816 in Italy, where he lived, mostly at Florence, till he died, aged ninety-two, in 1880. He was reckoned a gifted painter, but Leigh Hunt aptly said that he was "not poor enough, either in purse or accomplishment, to cultivate his profession as he ought to have done". "A man of a more cordial generosity," added Hunt, "with greater delicacy in showing it, I never met with," and that Kirkup deserved such praise is witnessed by the firm friendships of his long life—with William Blake and Haydon, Landor and Browning. His intimacy with Landor began in 1824; forty years later he was among the last faithful friends to visit him.

Through Browning, Kirkup supplied Forster with fifty letters written to him by Landor, which Forster never returned to him, as well as some notes of his personal recollections. From these it appears that Kirkup met Landor through Charles Armitage Brown, whom he described as "the most intimate and confidential friend of Landor for many years". Remembered as the friend of Keats and the editor of Trelawny's *Adventures of a Younger Son*, Brown is a figure of intriguing mystery. The same age as Francis Hare, being born the son of a Scottish stockbroker in 1786, he went to Russia when little more than a boy to act as agent to his elder brother's business. He returned to England in 1810, when the business failed, and for some time struggled on the verge of destitution until another of his brothers came to his rescue. From this brother he derived a sufficient income to live comfortably and pursue a taste for letters. He wrote the libretto of an opera, which was successfully produced at Drury Lane, and when Keats met him in 1817, he was occupying the smaller of a pair of semi-detached houses on Hampstead Heath called Wentworth Place from a name hereditary in the family of his next-door neighbour, Charles Wentworth Dilke. With his small son he emigrated to Italy in 1822, arriving at Pisa a month after Shelley's death.

Keats's mock Spenserian stanzas on Brown as "a melancholy carle, thin in the waist, with bushy head of hair", were ironical. He was bald, bespectacled, and stout, with the heart and humour of the Rabelaisian lover of food, wine, and a wench. Keats was warmed by his geniality and sensual gusto, and the sturdy loyalty of his friendship with Keats he gave freely to Landor for nearly twenty years. Confessing that he had fallen into a habit of "looking towards you as a help in all difficulties", Keats once told him that he was "living for others more than any man I know". He loved the conviviality and the company of his friends too well to concentrate on any substantial work; he sketched a little, wrote a little, spent years collecting materials for a biography of Keats and for his book on *Shakespeare's Autobiographical Poems*, which, on its publication in 1838, he dedicated to Landor as the best lover of Shakespeare and the best living writer of English. Generously he resigned his own interests for the sake of others; having got an Irish servant girl into trouble, he married her, and so devoted himself to his son by her, that he sacrificed a peaceful old age to seek in New Zealand better prospects for him. His implacable spirit and outspoken honesty appealed to Landor. Having quarrelled with Dilke on Keats's financial affairs, he felt such resentment after twenty years that he instructed his son, "If he should accidentally meet with you and civilly accost you, spit in his face." When his son fell in love, he bluntly stated his disapproval of the girl—"She is sadly deficient in common sense; I never met with a more affected fool—ugly to boot."

Brown had been intimate with Leigh Hunt at Hampstead, and when, in the early autumn of 1823, Hunt and his wife came to live at Maiano near Florence, Brown soon introduced him to Landor. At Maiano, the scene of Boccaccio's *Decameron*, Brown was then living, "with all the joviality of a comfortable natural piety", in a convent.

The closet in his study, where it is probable the church treasures had been kept, was filled with the humanities of modern literature, not the less Christian for being a little sceptical; and we had a zest in fancying that we discoursed of love and wine in the apartments of the Lady Abbess.

Francis Hare doubtless shared the zest more than Landor, for while he had no patience with "any kind of romish idolatry or superstition", Landor's sense of chivalry would have blushed for ribaldry in even the imagined presence of a lady. It is unlikely that Brown invited him, as he invited Hunt, on such occasions as the visit of the beautiful Mrs. W., and more often at the Palazzo Medici than at Brown's convent Hunt must have heard Landor's boisterous laughter resounding "in peals, and climbing; he seemed to fetch every fresh one from a higher story".

N

Hunt was as impressed with the depths of Landor's scholarship, which enabled him to "fancy and feel with, as well as read, Ovid and Catullus", as with his odd contrasts of manner and temper. In his conversation, as in his writings, "after indulging the partialities of his friendships and enmities, and trampling on kings and ministers, he shall cool himself, like a Spartan worshipping a moonbeam, in the patient meekness of Lady Jane Grey". Remarking that he had never known one of such a vehement nature with so great delicacy of imagination, Hunt likened him to "a stormy mountain-pine, that should produce lilies". He was impressed when Landor told him how "he had shot at a pheasant, and *many hours afterwards* found it where it had fallen, not dead, and in manifest torment. Since then he has never drawn a trigger".

At their first meeting Hunt showed Landor a hair from Lucrezia Borgia's head given to him by Byron, and published in 1825 the quatrain written on the occasion by Landor:

> Borgia, thou once wert almost too august,
> And high for adoration;—now thou'rt dust!
> All that remains of thee these plaits infold—
> Calm hair, meand'ring with pellucid gold!

Wordsworth's damping letter had turned him from Latin composition to a renewed interest in English verse, and his friendship with Hunt and Brown encouraged this development by bringing him acquaintance with the work of Shelley, Keats and Byron. Shelley he had seen at Pisa, and seems to have had a nodding acquaintance with him from the lines in *Last Fruit*:

> Shelley! whose song so sweet was sweetest here,
> We knew each other little. . . .

Shelley had sought his acquaintance, but Landor said, "I refused his proffered visit" because "his conduct towards his first wife had made me distrustful of him". Leigh Hunt corrected this false impression of Shelley's character, and Landor made amends by writing thus of Shelley in the imaginary conversation, "Florentine, English Visitor, and Landor", of 1828:

Innocent and careless as a boy, he possessed all the delicate feelings of a gentleman, all the discrimination of a scholar, and united, in just degrees, the ardour of the poet with the patience and forbearance of the philosopher. His generosity and charity went far beyond those of any man (I believe) at present in existence. He was never known to speak evil of an enemy, unless that enemy had done some grievous injustice to another: and he divided his income of only one thousand pounds, with the fallen and the afflicted. This is the man against whom such clamours have been raised by the religious à la mode, and by those who live and lap under their tables: this is the man whom, from one false story about his former wife, I had refused to visit at Pisa. I blush in anguish at my prejudice and injustice, and ought hardly to feel it as a blessing or a consolation, that I regret him less than I should have done if I had known him personally. As to what remains of him now life is over, he occupies the third place among our poets of the present age—no humble station—for no other age since that of Sophocles has produced on the whole earth so many of such merit.

The poets rated above Shelley were of course Southey and Wordsworth. Unfortunately Landor omitted this generous panegyric on reprinting the imaginary conversation in his collected works, because Southey thought that it was less merited by Shelley's character than by his poetry.

"It has been my fortune to love in general those men most who have thought most differently from me," wrote Landor in a footnote to his "Southey and Porson" dialogue. He was thinking perhaps of his brother Robert and Dr. Parr, who were of the opposite faction over Queen Caroline's trial; of Walter Birch, an orthodox Tory; but most particularly of Southey, who, as befitted a Poet Laureate and a trusted contributor to Murray's *Quarterly Review*, abandoned his early liberalism for rigid allegiance to Church and State. Friendship with Leigh Hunt taught him that he would have found more sympathy in thought and feeling with Shelley, Byron, and their circle, than with their opponents. "I regret all enmities in the literary world," he wrote, "and particularly when they are exercised against the ornaments and glories of our country, against a Wordsworth and a Southey." Southey's influence shared responsibility with scandalous gossip for preventing his acquaintance with Byron.

"Lord Byron is here with his Physician, they keep a Mistress each," wrote Robert Landor from Geneva on 26th July 1816. A few weeks earlier the physician Polidori had recorded the arrival in Geneva of "the author of Queen Mab"—"bashful, shy, consumptive; twenty-six; separated from his wife; keeps the two daughters of Godwin who practise his theories; one L.B.s." Shelley was not yet married to Mary Godwin, though she had an infant son by him; Claire Clairmont was pregnant by Byron. Though brought up together, Mary and Claire were not sisters—Mary was William Godwin's daughter by his first wife, Mary Wollstonecraft, Claire the daughter of Godwin's second wife by a previous marriage—but others besides Polidori supposed them to be so, especially as Shelley generously sheltered Claire as Mary's sister. In December 1816 came news that Shelley's first wife Harriet had drowned herself in the Serpentine; in March 1817 Lord Chancellor Eldon refused to Shelley the custody of his children by her. Three months later Southey passed through Lausanne and Geneva on his way to visit Landor at Como.

Eighteen months after Southey's excursion Byron wrote to his publisher, John Murray, "I understand the scoundrel said, on his return from Switzerland . . ., that 'Shelley and I were in a league of Incest, etc., etc.' He is a burning liar!" Within a few weeks he sent to Murray the first two cantos of *Don Juan*, with a satirical dedication to Southey, saying that he had explained to his friend Hobhouse "why I have attacked that Scoundrel". Murray and his advisers were afraid for the effect of the poem on Byron's reputation; the dedication was suppressed till after Byron's death, and the two cantos appeared the following July without the names of author or publisher.

Whether or not Southey repeated the gossip as Byron supposed, in discussing modern poetry with Landor he must have mentioned both Byron and Shelley, and could hardly have done so without reference to the scandalous tattle about them. Southey had met both Shelley and Byron personally; Landor saw Byron "once only . . . at Smith's the perfumer's in Bond Street", where he saw a fellow customer buying attar of roses and was told that it was "the young Lord Byron". As Byron informed Lady Blessington, some kind friend at Pisa told him that "Landor had declared he either would not, or could not, read my works." Probably Landor declared that he would not read *Don Juan* when he heard that Wordsworth and Southey were crudely abused, as in the lines:

> Thou shalt believe in Milton, Dryden, Pope;
> Thou shalt not set up Wordsworth, Coleridge, Southey;
> Because the first is crazed beyond all hope,
> The second drunk, the third so quaint and mouthy.

Previously he had read no more deeply in Byron's work than enabled him to endorse Southey's opinions in writing to Birch early in 1819:

> Biron is incapable of continued and strenuous exertion. A mind of his structure is radically weak . . . B. has done at thirty all that he can do at forty . . . Between genuine poetry and that of Biron there is the same difference as between roses and attar of roses. He smells of the spirit, not of the flower; you are overpowered and not satisfied.

From Pisa on 30th January 1820 he wrote again to Birch:

> I do not think I could have been explicit in my last about Byron . . . My opinion is this, that a man of a heart so rotten, and a mind so incompact, was never formed for more than temporary greatness. *If* he would do this, *if* he would do that, should not be said; it is not his nature.

Repeating no personal gossip to Birch, he confined criticism of Byron to his writings, though he resorted to *ifs* in admonishing, without naming, Byron in the Latin essay published in *Idyllia Heroica Decem*:

When they come upon somebody distinguished by vices of style and morals, but not without wit nor sparing in production of books, they crowd about him, applauding, absorbing, fawning. If he would somewhat correct his morals, pay a little attention to his style, curb his impetuous temper, pause for a little deliberation, then he might fashion, by the time he is forty, something remarkable and truly epic.[1]

Byron might never have seen the Latin essay if Southey had not quoted the relevant passage in support of his priggish attack on Byron in the preface to his *Vision of Judgment*, published in April 1821. "Of its author (the author of *Gebir* and *Count Julian*)," wrote Southey, "I will only say in this place, that, to have obtained his approbation as a poet, and possessed his friendship as a man, will be remembered among the honours of my life, when the petty enmities of this generation will be forgotten, and its ephemeral reputations shall have passed away." Byron's first reply to Southey's "cowardly ferocity" appeared in the third canto of *Don Juan* the following August; a second reply—in the Appendix to *The Two Foscari*, December 1821—commented on Southey's reference to his friendship with "a Mr. Landor, the author of 'Gebir'":

I for one neither envy him "the friendship", nor the glory in reversion which is to accrue from it ... This friendship will probably be as memorable as his own epics, which ... Porson said "would be remembered when Homer and Virgil are forgotten, and not till then".

After Murray had refused to publish it, Byron's *Vision of Judgment* appeared in *The Liberal*, the short-lived magazine published by Leigh Hunt's brother; in a note to the Preface, published in January 1823, Byron shrewdly observed Landor's difference from Southey's attitudes to politics and prudery:

Mr. Southey laudeth grievously "one Mr. Landor", who cultivates much private renown in the shape of Latin verses: and not long ago the poet laureate dedicated to him, it appeareth, one of his fugitive lyrics, upon the strength of a poem called *Gebir*. Who could suppose, that in this same *Gebir* the aforesaid Savage Landor (for such is his grim cognomen) putteth into the infernal regions no less a person than the hero of his friend Mr. Southey's heaven,—yea, even George the Third!

After quoting the passage where Gebir, viewing the royal shades in the infernal regions, asks, "Aroar, what wretch that nearest us?" Byron concluded:

---

[1] Quum aliquem inveniunt styli morumque vitiis notatum, nec infacetum tamen nec in libris edendis parcum, eum stipant, prædicant, occupant, amplectuntur. Si mores aliquantulum, vellet corrigere, si stylum curare paululum, si fervido ingenio temperare, si moræ tantillum interponere, tum ingens nescio quid et vere epicum, quadraginta annos natus, procuderet.—The quarrel between Byron and Southey, and Landor's part in it, is fully examined by Prothero in the sixth volume of Byron's *Letters and Journals* and by Mr. Super in his essay on *Landor and the "Satanic School"*.

I omit noticing some edifying Ithyphallics of Savagius, wishing to keep the proper veil over them, if his grave but somewhat indiscreet worshipper will suffer it; but certainly these teachers of "great moral lessons" are apt to be found in strange company.

Either Shelley or Leigh Hunt informed him, not only of Landor's "ithyphallics" in *Iambi*, but of the "sinuous shells" passage in *Gebir*, for a couplet in the second canto of *The Island*, published in June 1823,

> The Ocean scarce spoke louder with his swell,
> Than breathes his mimic murmurer in the shell,

occasioned this note:

If the reader will apply to his ear the sea-shell on his chimney-piece, he will be aware of what is alluded to. If the text should appear obscure, he will find in *Gebir* the same idea better expressed in two lines. The poem I never read, but have heard the lines quoted, by a more recondite reader— who seems to be of a different opinion from the editor of the *Quarterly Review*, who qualified it in his answer to the Critical Reviewer of his *Juvenal*, as trash of the worst and most insane description. It is to Mr. Landor, the author of *Gebir*, so qualified, and of some Latin poems, which vie with Martial or Catullus in obscenity, that the immaculate Mr. Southey addresses his declamation against impurity!

Byron's final shot was fired in the eleventh canto of *Don Juan*—written at Genoa in October 1822 and published in August of the following year—when discussing claimants to the title of the "greatest living poet":

> Some persons think that Coleridge hath the sway;
> And Wordsworth has supporters, two or three;
> And that deep-mouth'd Bœotian "Savage Landor"
> Has taken for a swan rogue Southey's gander.

"Bœotian" was a neat insult to a classicist; "deep-mouth'd" indicates that Byron had discussed Landor with personal acquaintances like the Marquis Pallavicini and Gould Francis Leckie, a student of diplomatic history who became a friend of Landor's at Florence.

After Southey had publicly refuted the charges in the appendix to *The Two Foscari*, Landor wrote to him on 21st June 1822:

I saw with pleasure your victory over Lord Byron. I have no right to complain of him. I had thrown slight upon him by avoiding him, and I had pointed him out to contempt in my Dissertation. You will find some ridicule on his poetry, and a severe sarcasm on his principles, in two different parts of my dialogues.

In the imaginary conversation "Abbé Delille and Walter Landor", facetious comment on *The Bride of Abydos* is followed by a remark reminiscent of Landor's association of Byron with attar of roses, "Our poems must contain *strong things*: we call for essences, not for flowers." In "Bishop Burnet and Humphrey Hardcastle" the bishop exclaims, "Who would have imagined that the youth who was carried to his long home the other day, I mean my Lord Rochester's reputed child, Mr. George Nelly, was for several seasons a great poet?" Nelly is described as insulting Milton and seeking to show him "a rogue and a liar" on the evidence of *Comus*, "which was composed for the entertainment of Lord Pembroke, who held an appointment under the king, and this very John hath since changed sides, and written in defence of the Commonwealth". The bishop continues:

Mr. George began with satirizing his father's friends, and confounding the better part of them with all the hirelings and nuisances of the age: with all the scavengers of lust and all the link-boys of literature . . . Afterward, whenever he wrote a bad poem, he supported his sinking fame by some signal act of profligacy, an elegy by a seduction, a heroic by an adultery, a tragedy by a divorce. On the remark of a learned man that irregularity is no indication of genius, he began to lose ground rapidly, when on a sudden he cried out at the Haymarket, *there is no God*. It was then surmised more generally and more gravely that there was something in him, and he stood upon his legs almost to the last.

Unfortunately Landor could not command such prompt publication as Byron. The *Imaginary Conversations* were published only a few weeks before Byron was "carried to his long home" following his death in the cause of Greece's liberty on 19th April 1824. Landor was not aware that his book was published when he wrote to Southey that he was "deeply affected" by Byron's death:

All his little impertinences against me only made me smile; and they were all provoked. His exertions in favour of the Greeks incited me to send, immediately on hearing of his death, a note to be added (I forget whether to the character of Mr. George Nelly, in case of a new edition, or to the last pages) in the forthcoming volume.

Too late for inclusion in the first edition, the note on Mr. George Nelly appeared when the book was reprinted in 1826:

Little did I imagine that the extraordinary man, the worst parts of whose character are represented here, should indeed have been carried to the tomb so immaturely. If, before the dialogue was printed, he had performed those services to Greece which will render his name illustrious to eternity, those by which he merited such funereal honours as, in the parsimony of praise, knowing its value in republics, she hardly would have decreed to the most deserving of her heroes, if, I repeat it, he had performed those services, the performance of which I envy him from my soul, and as much as any other does the gifts of heaven he threw away so carelessly, never would I, from whatever provocation, have written a syllable against him. I had avoided him; I had slighted him; he knew it; he did not love me; he could not. While he spoke or wrote against me, I said nothing in print or conversation: the taciturnity of pride gave way to other feelings, when my friends, men so much better, and (let the sincerity of the expression be questioned by those who are unacquainted with us) so much dearer, so much oftener in my thoughts, were assailed by him too intemperately.

Later he enlarged upon the note in "Florentine, English Visitor, and Landor", where, describing Byron as "the keenest and most imaginative of satirists", he remarked perceptively, "he had drawn largely from his imagination, penuriously from his heart".

§ 2

Obviously "*a* Mr. Landor" did not become "*the* Mr. Landor" merely as a result of his implication in the controversy between the Poet Laureate and the most discussed poet of the age. There was no immediate reassessment of Landor's reputation as the author of *Gebir* and *Count Julian*. But the publicity of the dispute happened opportunely before publication of *Imaginary Conversations* in the spring of 1824, insuring the attention of reviewers who might not otherwise have noticed a work appealing only to minds accustomed to reflection.

Writing *Count Julian* and *Ferrante and Giulio* in 1811, Landor realised his facility in the composition of dialogue. In 1820 he sent to Southey two new dramatic scenes in verse, *Ines de Castro* and *Ippolito di Este*, the latter a re-written version of *Ferrante and Giulio*. In August 1820 Southey confided that he was projecting "a series of Dialogues, upon a plan which was suggested by Boëthius;" two months later he explained that his dialogues would be "speculations upon the progress of society". Preoccupied with more urgent work, he published his *Colloquies on the Progress and Prospects of Society* in 1829.

As Landor admitted to Southey when announcing on 9th March 1822 that he had completed fifteen dialogues, "I began to do the same thing after you," though he had "formerly written two or three about the time when the first income-tax was imposed". Of these one "between Lord Grenville and Burke, the other between Henry the Fourth and Sir Arnold Savage, were written more than twenty years ago, which no person would believe of the former; but I gave the substance of it to Robert Adair to get inserted in the *Morning Chronicle*, and a part of it (now omitted) was thought too personal, and it was refused". In Southey's *Colloquies* the shade of Sir Thomas More appears to Southey in his study, and discussion of "the progress and prospects of society" develops from comparison between conditions in More's time and in the present. Sometimes, as in "The Abbé Delille and Walter Landor", Landor was content to follow Southey's device of identifying himself with one of the speakers, but the range of his imagination and variety of his thought and reading demanded wider scope; by means of his familiarity with the lives and works of his characters—his ability, in

Hunt's phrase, to "fancy and feel with" them—he was enabled to recreate their personalities in combining the functions of the dramatist and the biographer.

Sometimes the reader may suspect that one character or another is merely a mouthpiece for the author's own opinions. But Landor was sincere—not merely seeking a lawyer's safeguard—in warning his readers to "avoid a mistake in attributing to the writer any opinions in this book but what are spoken under his own name". Inevitably his own opinions are expressed, since the author selected the subjects and directed their discussion, but they are coloured, qualified, or exaggerated according to the character of the speakers. Just as some aspect of their creator's personality may be detected in the characters of John Cowper Powys's novels, so the protagonists of Landor's dialogues express themselves with his eloquence and force, because in either case the author has succeeded by a feat of imagination in projecting himself into the skin and spirit of his created character.

But the background of Landor's stage is no more than the black curtain of Shakespeare's theatre, and the actors wear no costume to indicate their period. Projecting his people as they appear to himself, Landor provides no introductions. His own familiarity with his subjects enabled him to visualise every gesture of his speakers, and the reader's imaginative faculty is strained for similar vision. For appreciation of the dialogues some foreknowledge of their characters is necessary—for their full enjoyment, some semblance even of their author's scholarship—and their appeal was therefore limited to students of the humanities.

Soon after writing to Southey on 9th March 1822, Landor dispatched the fifteen dialogues to Longmans by a "Captain Vyner of the lifeguards". The manuscript should have arrived by 18th April; hearing nothing by 3rd June, he was suffering the anxiety of impatience. Asking Southey to retrieve the manuscript from Longman and to offer it to Joseph Mawman, whom he had once visited with Dr. Parr, he wrote:

This disappointment has brought back my old bilious complaint, together with the sad reflection on that fatality which has followed me through life, of doing everything in vain. I have however had the resolution to tear in pieces all my sketches and projects, and to forswear all future undertakings. I try to sleep away my time, and pass two-thirds of the twenty-four hours in bed. I may speak of myself as of a dead man. I will say, then, that these *Conversations* contained as forcible writing as exists on earth. They perhaps may come out after my decease, and the bookseller will enrich some friend of his by attributing them to him, and himself by employing him, as the accredited author of them, on any other subjects. If they are not really lost, or set aside for this purpose, I may yet have the satisfaction of reading them here at Florence, and perhaps they may procure me some slight portion of respect.

Eagerly waiting from day to day, he was haunted by the possibility of failure; disappointment darkened into depression as he feared repetition of the frustration suffered when Longman declined to publish *Count Julian* and Murray suppressed the *Commentary on Fox*. Was he now to disappoint Hare and Brown and Southey as, years before, he had disappointed Serjeant Rough and Dr. Parr? He had asked Wordsworth's permission to dedicate the book to him; how could he ever write again to Wordsworth if Longman ignored this manuscript as he had ignored the Latin poems and the translated *Osservazioni*?

So far from sleeping away his time, he seems to have allowed himself no rest from agitation, according to his letter to Southey of 21st June:

> I shall request a friend of mine to demand the manuscript; and shall try some other means of having it printed next year. I have passed the last eighteen days and nights in trying to recover all parts of it. I am afraid I have lost several, as a great deal was written on scraps of paper. I have lost my patience at all events, and the remainder of my health by it.

The guardsman had merely dawdled, for news came that Longman received the manuscript only on 19th August, by which time Francis Hare had written to his brother Julius entrusting him "with the care of delivering it to Mawman for printing". Landor's impatience revived: "If Mawman begins to print on the 5th of October (he will receive the ms. on the 1st), they will be finished by the end of the month." He thus allowed four days for reading the manuscript and about three weeks for setting, printing, and binding. In fact Mawman declined to publish the book.

Landor was too busy to indulge another passion of despair. From the "scraps and projects" destroyed in vexation survived "a couple of sheets (I think)" of a dialogue between Southey and Porson, and "an old letter" contained "some remarks on Wordsworth's poetry": together these formed the nucleus of one of the most quoted conversations. By the spring of 1823 the number of dialogues was "more than doubled" to thirty-three—enough for two volumes instead of one. He was so absorbed in his work that, as he told Southey in March, "it is not improbable that I forgot to tell you I had another son born about five months ago". Even the news that three publishers, Martin, Valpy, and Ridgway, had successively followed Mawman in declining the book, failed to disturb his concentration. Informing Southey that he would undertake "half the loss, provided that only three hundred and fifty copies were printed in octavo", he expressed arrogance only in the remark, "It will vex me if I am at last obliged to employ a printer who publishes only pamphlets for the mob, conscious as I am that in two thousand years there have not been five volumes of prose equal in their contents to this."

His temper was curbed by Julius Hare's example of generosity and patience.

I have wearied my excellent friend Mr. Hare to death with perpetual corrections and insertions. He never even saw me. He does not complain of his trouble, occupied as' he is in other literary labours: but reproves my attacks on Catholicism, to which he appears more than moderately inclined.

He had given Julius Hare a letter of introduction to Southey, who co-operated in seeking a publisher for the book. Becoming a contributor to the *London Magazine*, Hare asked John Taylor, of Taylor & Hessey, the magazine's proprietors, to publish the *Conversations* under the usual profit-sharing agreement. On 4th March 1823 Taylor replied:

I shall be glad to see Mr. Landor's Ms. and to publish it on the Terms you propose, if it answers the Expectations I am lead to form of it, both from your Description and from the acknowledged Ability of the Author. I have often heard my Friend Mr. De Quincey speak of him in such Terms for his extraordinary Powers of Mind, as surpass even the Estimation in which he is generally held.

As Taylor "found some Difficulty in reading Mr. Landor's writing", it was not till 16th April that he announced, "it would suit us to publish it, if certain Passages or the Conversations in which they occur were omitted". Fearing Landor's anger at a publisher's presuming to censor his work, Hare put forward Landor's offer to bear any financial loss sustained. But, as Charles Brown remarked during negotiations after Keats's death, Taylor was "somewhat vain of his talents, and consequently self-willed"; he valued his literary pretensions with the unbending solemnity of the self-educated.

If I looked only as a Man of Business on the speculation of publishing Mr. Landor's Work, I could not hesitate after his liberal Proposal to bear the Loss; but that has not been in my thoughts . . . I am averse to become instrumental to the appearance of such of these Conversations, or such Parts of them, as I cannot honestly approve . . . I must therefore decline the Publication.

Hare invited him to cite the objectionable passages and persuaded him to agree that the proofs should be submitted to Wordsworth and Southey, Taylor promising that "if they approve what I condemn, I will consent to forego the Right of private Judgment, and be bound by their Decision". Hare then insured Wordsworth's co-operation by giving Taylor the dialogue between Southey and Porson, flattering Wordsworth's poetry, for publication in the July number of the *London Magazine*. To Landor he wrote the warning that Taylor was "the most honourable man in the trade; and after no small difficulties, arising however altogether from conscientious scruples and in no degree from considerations of profit, we came to an agreement; or I ought rather to say, I was so weary of soliciting publisher after publisher . . . that I forced Taylor to undertake it".

Southey wrote on 8th May, endorsing Hare's estimate of Taylor and assuring Landor that, Wordsworth being then abroad, he "would most willingly take upon myself this responsibility" of arbitration, and "act for you as you would act by me,—taking care that wherever there was an omission the place should be marked". Ironically Landor suggested some annotation drawing attention to a passage "liable to do mischief, if general principles are drawn from it unwarily, and if it is not considered as the fancy of the individual who utters it, rather than as a theory laid down for establishment by the writer". More practically he argued that Taylor would not expect "Demosthenes should talk like Canning", as "the language of the ancients is suitable to them, and can do no more harm than their works, which I presume he would not hesitate to print if a new edition were called for". Knowing Southey's orthodoxy, he was prepared for worse than any alterations either Hare or Southey contemplated, for he told Birch on 20th June that his *Conversations* would be "published in another month, but some of them will not appear". In fact the Grenville-Burke dialogue was suppressed in deference to Taylor's objection that "it gives the popular Account of the Cause of Burke's Change of Party, but I think not the true one"— surely an impertinent objection by a publisher, but the concession may have been made because omission was preferable to mutilation.

Southey proved a loyal friend in performing a delicate task. He declined to alter the poem read by Cecil to Queen Elizabeth, in which Taylor objected that the line, "Too late the goddess hid what hand may hide", was "an excellent Picture, but done with a Freedom almost beyond the Era of Elizabeth". Taylor objected to the "Elizabethan" frankness of Oliver Cromwell's exclamation to Walter Noble, "I must piss upon these firebrands, before I can make them tractable"; but Southey acknowledged the justice of Landor's plea that "no other mode of expression would be so characteristic", though Taylor informed Hare that retention of the expression would make the difference between his printing a thousand copies or two hundred and fifty less. Apparently the publisher was unmoved by the anecdote related by Porson to Southey illustrating the trend to squeamishness since the eighteenth century:

I then understood for the first time that *neck* signifies *bosom* when we speak of women, though not so when we speak of men or other creatures. But if *bosom* is *neck*, what, according to the same scale of progression, ought to be *bosom*? The usurped dominion of neck extends from the ear downward to where mermaids become fish. This conversation led me to reflect that I was born in the time when people had *thighs*; before your memory, I imagine. At present there is nothing but leg from the hip to the instep.

For months Taylor argued. He suggested Simpkin & Marshall as publishers who might not share his scruples; he even offered to have the book printed while Hare sought another publisher. Most persistently he objected to the dialogue in which Conyers Middleton—the eighteenth-century divine who sought to extricate Christian doctrine from the embellishments of ecclesiastical ritual—disputed with the Florentine Magliabechi on the efficacy of prayer. As Middleton died in 1750 and his *Letter from Rome showing an exact Conformity between Popery and Paganism* was published in 1729, his opinions might have been supposed sufficiently historical to escape topical controversy, but Taylor was prudently orthodox with a publishing list always containing a proportion of theological works. Landor's defence of the dialogue, written to Southey on 2nd July 1823, expressed the religious opinions that he held all his life:

It appears to me that I have acted fairly. I have given the known sentiments of both parties. The fabricators of religions for state purposes found the pure and simple doctrines of Jesus Christ unfit for them. . . . In regard to prayer, if ever I prayed at all, I would not transgress or exceed the order of Jesus Christ. In my opinion all Christianity (as priests call their inventions) is to be rejected excepting His own commands. There is quite enough in these for any man to perform; which he will be best induced to do by reading His life and reflecting on His sufferings. His immediate followers were, for the greater part, as hot-headed fanatics as Whitfield and Wesley, and probably no less ambitious . . . To increase the sum of happiness, and to diminish the sum of misery, is the only right aim both of reason and of religion. All superstition tends to remove something from morality, and to substitute something in its place; and is therefore no less a wrong to sound probity than to sound sense.

Southey did not understand why Taylor should object to opinions for which the author, not the publisher, would be held responsible. But Hare feared lest refusal to accommodate Taylor might result in his declining to publish the book; on his own responsibility he therefore deleted the most offending passages, including the subsequently added footnote ridiculing Italian superstitious belief in the miraculous powers of Saint Maria Bagnesi. "I had agreed to print what Southey sanctioned," he wrote in justification, "but of course this . . . could not oblige Taylor to print what he thought morally wrong."

More reasonably Taylor objected to Landor's attacks on contemporary politicians. Defending to Southey his bitterness against the Tory government of Liverpool and Canning, Landor cited his maltreatment by the British legation at Florence:

Why have these rascals suffered me to be insulted by their agents? . . . Out of four thousand English here I was selected for slight and contempt! the only man in all the four thousand who ever acted with disinterestedness for the public good, or who will be remembered a year after his death. . . .

It could not have happened in Russia or in Turkey. In those countries men who are superior to others in virtue and intelligence are promoted and rewarded. I wanted neither. . . . I would only have avoided disrespect, disdain, and insult. So long as such wretches are in power and employment, I am the avowed and unmitigable enemy of those who countenance them, and of the government that allows it.

In Lord Liverpool he recognised a mediocrity who excluded men of talent from his government lest their brilliance might by contrast display the limitations of their colleagues. "Our affairs," he wrote to Birch in May 1823, "are now under the direction of a fellow who has no sense of honour, public or private; so ignorant that he did not know that Walcheren was pestilential, and France perfidious." In the dialogue between Pitt and Canning, Pitt advises the junior statesman:

Employ men of less knowledge and perspicacity than yourself, if you can find them. Do not let any stand too close or too much above; because in both positions they may look down into your shallows and see the weeds at the bottom.

In the last of his preserved letters to Walter Birch, received on 16th December 1823, Landor wrote: "We are now living, politically, from hand to mouth, as the people say—upon shifts and expedients, and the people of England has no more a representation than the people of Turkey." Yet he built no hopes of betterment on the possibility of such parliamentary reform as came in 1832. For, says Pitt to Canning, "the most honest and independent members of Parliament are elected by the rotten boroughs", because "they pay down their own money, and give their own votes: they are not subservient to the aristocracy nor to the treasury".

The Pitt-Canning dialogue was not published till 1829, two years after Canning's death had removed the possibility of prosecution for libel. But its ideas so closely reflect Landor's letters of six years earlier that the dialogue may have been rejected by Taylor—like that between Grenville and Burke—as politically too prejudiced. Recognising the unpopularity of his opinions, Landor cancelled the proposed dedication to Wordsworth; "as the political opinions of many characters introduced are widely different from those in fashion," he explained to Southey, "I feared lest anyone should attempt to wrong him by presuming that he favoured the opinions by accepting the dedication".

While the Middleton debate progressed, Taylor sought counsel's opinion "on the propriety and safety of publishing those Passages which were considered libellous". Brougham "refused to pronounce upon it in the present State of the Law of Libel"; James Scarlett, soon to be Attorney-General, was then approached, and Taylor transcribed his opinion for Hare:

It is really impossible to affirm that any Composition which is not a Hymn or a Prayer may not be deemed a Libel. I entertain no Doubt but that if any one of the Passages referred to were indicted the Judge would give his Opinion to the Jury that it was a Libel. Yet I think they are not Passages which any Attorney General would prosecute, and that they are above the Comprehension of those who manage the affairs of the Constitutional Association.

With a flash of humour Taylor remarked that "this opinion is itself more libellous than any thing in the Work", and he ventured to publish the two volumes of *Imaginary Conversations*, at twenty-four shillings a set, in April 1824.

§ 3

A letter from Southey of 29th February 1824 accompanied Landor's advance copies of the book:

In looking over your volumes, you will, I think, wherever you perceive that a passage has been struck out, perceive at the same time for what reason it was omitted. The reason for every omission was such that, I am persuaded, you would, without hesitation, have assented to it, had you been on the spot. A most powerful and original book it is, in any one page of which—almost in any single sentence—I should have discovered the author, if it had come into my hands as an anonymous publication. Notice it must needs attract; but I suspect that it will be praised the most by those with whom you have the least sympathy, and that the English and Scottish Liberals may perhaps forgive you even for being my friend.

Having done his best to preserve Landor from the editorial scissors, Southey thus sought to prepare him for the poisoned darts of reviewers. He had no influence to insure favourable notice in the *Quarterly Review*, being on terms of mutual dislike with William Gifford, who would not entertain the possibility of Southey's succession to his editorial chair, as "the gentleman in the North would, in a few numbers, ruin the *Review* if *he* had the management". If Gifford had not been so ill that the *Quarterly* for January 1824 appeared only in the following August, he might himself have scourged the *Imaginary Conversations*; instead he delivered the book with instructions to a novice, Henry Taylor, who confessed many years later that his article "was written in the arrogant and malapert vein of review-writing prevailing in those days, when I knew no better, and was quite prepared to insult my superiors". This twenty-three-year-old civil servant affected surprise that "eminent individuals" like Southey and Porson "meet only to agree upon the merits of Mr. Wordsworth's poetry" and "talk as if they were writing commentaries and tired of it"; he professed to "know, somewhat better than Mr. Landor does, the incurable infirmities of French verse", but allowed that Landor "by some accident" had "come to a just conclusion"; "in noticing the absurdities and perversities of this author", he was "far from denying that he is a man of knowledge and abilities, which nothing but his singular deficiency of judgment could have rendered useless", and concluded that, "whatever measure of absurdity there may be in Mr. Landor's work . . . there is also in it a good deal to be admired, and some little to be approved". Informing the young reviewer that in his article "upon Landor, I liked every thing that had no reference to him, and nothing that had", Southey wrote, "The general tenour I should, no doubt, have liked better, if Gifford had not struck out the better parts; but nothing could have reconciled me to anything like an assumption of superiority towards such a man."

Leigh Hunt's friendship insured a favourable review in the *Examiner*, and Julius Hare wrote in the *London Magazine* an imaginary conversation with an adverse critic, by which device he was enabled to rebut the objections of reactionary opinion by enlarging upon the merits of a work that would "live as long as English literature lived". In the Tory *Blackwood's Magazine* Christopher North used the Southey-Porson dialogue as an excuse for one of his outbursts of personal spleen against Wordsworth, but the most important notice came from Hazlitt in the *Edinburgh Review*. Though he did not fail to mock Landor's extravagances, he praised his "power of thought", his "variety and vigour of style", and especially the excellence of the classical dialogues. His praise might have been less qualified if his editor, Francis Jeffrey, had not altered his script to admit animosities against Southey and Wordsworth. Hare reported to Landor that Hazlitt was "among the greatest admirers of the *Conversations*", and Hazlitt himself sought the earliest opportunity of making Landor's acquaintance.

The early notice in the *Edinburgh* insured that the *Imaginary Conversations* was not among the review copies that left editorial offices for the second-hand booksellers. By July Taylor announced that "the Trade are beginning to send for more Copies of the Work, which shews that it is moving", and Hare was soon able to inform Landor that a second edition might be called for: was he to reserve the additional dialogues to supply a third volume in the second edition the following year, or should he prepare a third volume for separate publication at Christmas? Unluckily he added that he hoped to "persuade Taylor" to reinstate the Middleton omissions in the new edition; "as so much has come out without offending, he will perhaps not be quite so scrupulous next time".

If Landor saw any of the reviews, he made no comment. "I never ask what is the public opinion of anything I write," he told Southey on 4th November; "God forbid it should be favourable; for more people think injudiciously than judiciously." But he exulted in the praise of his peers. Southey told him no more than he said to others; he wrote in June to Caroline Bowles, "I wish Landor's book may fall in your way; still more do I wish that you could see Landor himself, who talks as that book is written, as if he spoke in thunder and lightning." In December he told Landor that "the book is making you known, as you ought to be; and it is one of those very few which nothing can put aside". On the same paper Wordsworth sent a message: he had not written before owing to his eye trouble, but he now assured Landor that "your dialogues are worthy of you, and a great acquisition to literature". Like Hazlitt, he liked the classical dialogues best—"most of all that between Tully and his brother"—and he looked forward to the third volume. Landor received this double letter of congratulation with "incredible delight"; "never", he exclaimed, "did two such hands pass over the same paper, unless when Barrow was solving some problem set before him by Newton."

Praise by two such eminent writers encouraged his resentment against his publisher's presuming to censor his work. He was less concerned with the Middleton omissions than with passages that Southey thought "would either have given most offence here, or endangered his personal safety where he is". In the dialogue between the Cavaliere Puntomichino and Mr. Talcranagh—which, as Landor remarks, "is reported in a manner differing from the rest", with himself as compère commenting on the characters and behaviour of the Italian and his young Irish guest—Southey deleted an attack on Prince Borghese's callous treatment of Napoleon's sister, the "once lovely, generous, and confiding" Pauline, and of a poor peasant family. He reproached Southey for suppressing this passage "lest I should be assassinated"—"had I my choice of a death, it should be this, unless I could render some essential service to mankind by any other".

Taylor proved obdurate about Middleton on prayer: "I refused Lord Byron's *Vision of Judgment,*" he told Hare, "yet I did not think *that* a Production so likely to prove pernicious as the Article in Question." Proofs of the new edition were ready in November, but publication was delayed by Landor's continual dispatch of dialogues as he finished them—one, between Bloody Mary and Philip of Spain, was lost in transit. "Julius Hare assures me that the third volume of my *Conversations* will come out at the end of January," he told Southey on 6th January: "He however had not then received two sheets closely written on a conversation between the late Duc de Richelieu and others." Soon after this Hare wrote, "You had better let us stop the printing off until I ascertain more clearly how far the dialogues I have will extend."

During the consequent delay Landor was reminded that he had received no money from his publisher. He had developed a habit of speculation in buying pictures—"if I had had 3,000£ eight years ago", he told his sister Ellen in 1828, "I could have cleared 12,000 in the first two years"—and now lamented his lack of funds for that purpose

o

in conversation with Hazlitt, who visited Florence in the spring of 1825. When Hazlitt expressed surprise that he had received no proceeds from the sale of his book, the spectres of Gabell and Betham suggested to Landor that he was again the victim of a rascal. From Brown and Hunt, as well as from Hazlitt, he heard nothing in Taylor's favour; they agreed in thinking that Taylor had behaved badly in attempting to appoint himself as Keats's biographer immediately after Keats's death, and Taylor had refused an advance of fifty pounds to Hazlitt on account of articles to be written for the *London Magazine* during his visit to Italy.

On hearing from Landor, Hare tactfully informed Taylor that Landor "has been buying some pictures, and perhaps, in the state of his property, would find a little help in paying for them convenient; and it is unpleasant for anybody, even without Landor's pride, to speak twice on such subjects". Instead of continuing to communicate through Hare, Taylor wrote directly to Landor. He began unfortunately by expressing regret for the omissions he had caused to be made in the dialogues; apologising for being guilty of a further omission in having neglected to place at Landor's bankers the half-profit of the first edition, he facetiously suggested that he might be excused for the neglect, as the cost of the second edition might absorb the profit of the first and leave Landor in his debt.

As Hazlitt pointed out, Taylor was thus assuming that Landor intended to allow publication of the second edition on the same terms as the first, and Hare had so far conceded no such agreement. Taylor might have argued that, as Landor, on first offering the book, had proposed to bear any loss on the publication, he was justified in supposing Landor to be little interested in the matter of profit, but he could not exculpate himself from having neglected prompt payment or from having intended to take advantage of Landor's unbusinesslike carelessness. "He knows very well what I hear from Mr. Hazlitt," wrote Landor to Hare on 1st April 1825, "that these booksellers who engage to take half the profits never take only half the risk."

Greatly do I regret that I have had anything to do with so insincere a man, with such an impudent coxcomb. . . . Does he consider himself as a man of business? or (as these people in our days are apt to do) as a gentleman? In either case his conduct seems to me inexplicable. . . . To delay the payment of what is due, on the plea that I may hereafter be indebted to one for something not ordered, nor contemplated by me, is the conduct of a scoundrel. I shall consult Mr. Leigh Hunt, and other English authors now at Florence, on what is best to do or say in this business.

With this letter he enclosed a copy of what he had written to Taylor, who wrote indignantly to Hare on 19th April "to keep my Place in your good opinion", though "I cannot condescend to justify myself to ·

the Writer". Landor's "whole Letter is in fact Contemptible", and "Perhaps the Presence of Hazlitt may help to explain the Mystery": "the Notion he has taken up that I had any sinister End or selfish View in the reprinting of the Work" he described as "absurd", but in his anger saw no absurdity in suggesting "that Landor desired to find an Excuse for breaking with me". Within three days he recognised the weakness of his position, admitting on the 22nd that Hare was "probably right in thinking that I should have attended sooner to Landor's wish to have the Balance of his Account paid to his Banker". He now paid £89. 17s. 8d. to Landor's bankers, Herries & Co., offering the lame excuse for not having done so before that his partner "Mr. Hessey pays and receives everything". In his anger with Landor's letter he asserted that "I renounce him and all his Works with the greatest Willingness", but maturer reflection developed regret with settlement of all blame upon Hazlitt.

> With such an honest Iago as Hazlitt at his Elbow I don't wonder at the consequences. . . . What there is good in him may be said to be of the Devil. How different from the Genius of Landor.

Sadly he declared himself "compelled to decline all future Interest in Landor's Works", though the decision placed him in a position of anxiety. Having printed only 750 copies of the first edition, a thousand copies of the second edition were now being printed and fifteen hundred copies of the third volume were "provided". Besides facing a loss on these preparations, he feared a lawsuit from "the Blindness of Landor's Fury" and felt uneasy on receiving a formal communication from Landor's cousin and agent, Walter Landor of Rugeley.

Landor fairly stated to Southey his case against Taylor. He had sanctioned the printing of the third volume, but was then unaware that the second edition had gone to press. He had not intended that the second edition should be published on the same terms as the first, and reasonably deduced that Taylor's ordering double the number of copies of the third volume indicated an intention to take advantage of the original agreement that Landor should bear any loss.

> I was advised to demand a fixt sum in ready money. . . . He might print a second edition, and then a third, and then a fourth, and say after all, who knows whether the next edition I print may not leave you in my debt!

Having expressed himself thus far reasonably, he flew into such a passion of petulance as when the original *Conversations* were delayed in delivery.

> His first villainy in making me disappoint the person with whom I had agreed for the pictures, instigated me to throw my fourth volume, in its imperfect state, into the fire, and has cost me nine-tenths of my fame as a

writer. His next villainy will entail perhaps a chancery suit on my children—for at its commencement I blow my brains out. . . . Mr. Hazlitt, Mr. Leigh Hunt, Lord Dillon, Mr. Brown, and other authors of various kinds, have been made acquainted, one from another, with this whole affair; and they speak of it as a thing unprecedented. . . . This cures me forever, if I live, of writing what could be published; and I will take good care that my son shall not suffer in the same way. Not a line of any kind will I leave behind me. My children shall be carefully warned against literature. To fence, to swim, to speak French, are the most they shall learn.

Southey commiserated tactfully but expressed vexation—as he had fourteen years before when Landor announced his burning of *Ferrante and Giulio* on Longmans' rejection of *Count Julian*—that such a writer should destroy a single line, or forbear writing one, because a bookseller showed himself to be no better than the spirit of trade had made him. Probably Landor destroyed no more of value than during his previous frenzy. The fourth volume was in an "imperfect state"; listing its proposed contents on 4th November 1824, he confessed that he had only "composed parts". "Hardly anything was done" of "Cornelia and Caius Gracchus", and though he had then drafted a conversation between Tiberius and Agrippina, he was dissatisfied with his interpretation of Agrippina's character, and when in the following April he "wrote a new conversation between her and Tiberius" as "Tiberius and Vipsania", he "could not recollect one sentence of the old". During the winter he had suspended work on the projected fourth volume, as he thought "three are enough".

Apart from acknowledging his culpability in neglecting correspondence and accounts, Hare loyally defended Taylor's conduct and character, reminding Landor of "what you make Cicero say, that neither to give nor take offence are surely the two things most delightful in human life". Taylor's clumsiness caused further offence when he sent a presentation copy of the book to the Spanish general Mina without explaining that it was sent at Landor's direction, and the general wrote a letter of thanks to the publisher without mentioning the author. In reply to Landor's complaint that Taylor had crept into Mina's notice under his skirts, Hare could only plead for forbearance; quoting Landor's own words in "Florentine, English Visitor, and Landor", "lose nothing, as you hope for heaven, of that which may give you a better opinion of your fellow-creatures", he exclaimed, "O that you yourself would more regularly act according to this principle, and believe, when you see something that appears not quite right, that it may as often be a mistake as a misdeed!" Landor accepted the rebuke in silence; he was grateful to Hare—as he acknowledged in the dedication of his *Works* in 1846—and had no wish to lose such a valued agent. Already he had written three letters about further publishing plans, but "As your second letter contradicts the first, your third says you will have nothing to do with either Longman or Constable, and I fear a fourth may come with a new scheme," Hare asked what he was to do, for "after having failed once so egregiously, I do not like trusting anything but your express desire". Landor responded generously: Hare had full authority to act for the best according to his own judgment. Forster failed to appreciate this consistency in Landor: when he confided his trust, it was without reserve.

9

FLORENCE AND ROME

Children are not men nor women: they are almost as different creatures, in many respects, as if they never were to be the one or the other: they are as unlike as buds are unlike flowers, and almost as blossoms are unlike fruits. Greatly are they better than they are about to be, unless Philosophy raises her hand above them when the noon is coming on, and shelters them at one season from the heats that would scorch and wither, and at another from the storms that would shatter and subvert them.

—*Epicurus, Leontion, and Ternissa* (1829)

From my earliest days I have avoided society as much as I could decorously, for I received more pleasure in the cultivation and improvement of my own thoughts than in walking up and down among the thoughts of others. Yet, as you know, I never have avoided the intercourse of men distinguished by virtue and genius; of genius, because it warmed and invigourated me by my trying to keep pace with it; of virtue, that if I had any of my own it might be called forth by such vicinity.

—*Southey and Landor* (1846)

Throughout this time, while he wrote and published the first two volumes of *Imaginary Conversations*, Landor lived at the Palazzo Medici in Florence, where his second son, Walter Savage, was born on 13th November 1822. During the heat of the summer months he usually rented a furnished house in the hills outside the city; he spent the summer of 1822 or 1823 at the Villa Catani, "just behind Poggio Imperiale", and "the greater part of two months" in the autumn of 1824 at Castel Ruggiero, "the villa of the commissary-general here, Buccellato". In September 1825 he took a three years' lease of the Villa Castiglione, "two miles from Florence out of the Porta San Niccolo". The move to a country home was dictated by his wife's health and his own melancholy, "to which", he told his sister Ellen on 21st November 1825, "I am sometimes very much disposed".

To relieve this, and to improve the health of Julia, I have taken a country-house for three years. Of which 2 months only are expired. . . . I wish Julia would consent to live entirely in the country, but she cannot live without some company in the evening, one or two, old or young. For my part, I could live and even enjoy life, if I never were to see any other face, or hear any other voice, than those of my children.

He had never liked town life and resorting to the country in the summer months must have emphasised his dissatisfaction with residence in the city; "I never write under a roof anything but letters," he said in remarking how "the last three" volumes of *Imaginary Conversations* "were composed in a little wood below my Villa, on the left, where my children made a pond to swim in".

To satisfy his wife's social inclinations he continued to spend some part of the winter months in Florence. He stated that he "resided six years" at the Palazzo Medici, but apparently the winter of 1825–26 was his last in the Borgo degli Albizi and he moved for the following winter into another of the Medici houses in the Via Pandolfini. His tenancy ended after a dispute with the owner, amusingly described by Seymour Kirkup. Landor had written to the old marquis, accusing him of having seduced away his coachman.

The marquis enjoyed no very good name, and this had exasperated Landor the more. Mrs. Landor was sitting in the drawing room the day after, where I and some others were, when the marquis came strutting in without removing his hat. But he had scarcely advanced three steps from the door when Landor walked up to him quickly and knocked his hat off, then took him by the arm and turned him out. You should have heard Landor's shout of laughter at his own anger when it was all over, inextinguishable laughter which none of us could resist. Immediately after he sent the marquis warning by the hands of a policeman, which is reckoned an affront, and quitted his house at the end of the year.

Edward Willson Landor, a young cousin who visited Landor at Florence, remarked that such exhibitions of arrogance resulted, not from a sense of self-importance as an English gentleman, but from "the vast ever-present conviction of the infinity of his mental superiority". Landor never forgot the Duke of Beaufort's slight in declining to make him a magistrate at Llanthony; he despised all rank—especially official rank—and allowed distinction only to aristocracy of intellect. "The smallest unintentional appearance of slight from a superior in rank," said Edward Landor, "would at any moment rouse him into a fury of passion, never thoroughly allayed till its last force had spent itself in an epigram."

For many years at Florence he continued hostile to the British legation because he conceived that the minister treated him with insufficient deference; exaggerating as insults every omission of what he considered the courtesy due to him, he regarded himself as a victim of official persecution. "The learned languages will be of little or no use to my children," he told Southey: "They and my latest descendants will be excluded from every kind of preferment in the state. I am no contemptible man who have insured all this."

Some imagined slight doubtless inspired the attack on Prince Borghese in the Puntomichino dialogue. His strained relations with the legation closed the doors of fashionable society against him, and visitors to Florence had to seek him with letters of introduction. "I have never been tempted to dine from home these seven years," he tells Puntomichino, and he wrote in *High and Low Life in Italy*:

> I take no interest whatever in the affairs of Italians:. I visit none of them: I admit none of them within my doors. I never go to the gaming house, to the coffee house, to the theatre, to the palace, or to the Church.

In "Florentine, English Visitor, and Landor" he admitted that he had exchanged courtesies with the Grand Duke's librarian Nicolini, but as to the "Granduke", he described himself as "the only Englishman in Florence who did not attend his court, and the only one he ever omitted to salute". Except Medici's daughter-in-law and his own daughter's music master, "I never let any of the natives enter my doors", he wrote as late as 1831.

The Florentines were "beyond all others, a treacherous, tricking, mercenary race". When the painter Middleton came to Florence in 1827 with an introduction from his sisters, he hastened to recommend him to three specific places of lodging, in case he "may not know what scoundrels the greater part of the Florence innkeepers are, not to say thieves and assassins". He had incessant trouble with his domestic servants. To his sister Ellen he wrote in 1833:

> I wish it was possible to get servants from England; I would not have one Italian. I am well convinced that, in 18 months, I should save greatly more than the expense of bringing them over. No woman will cook here, nor open a door. . . . Every Italian is a thief by nature, and no foreigner can gain the slightest redress.

More than once servants excited him to passion resulting in legal proceedings. A footnote to "Peter Leopold and President Du Paty" relates how a maidservant, under notice of dismissal, spilt boiling water on one of the children, and "the father . . . pushed her out with some violence, and, as it appeared, not without a bruise on the face", with a resulting suit in the police court. On another occasion a carpenter complained to the police that Landor had angrily aimed to kick him when he arrived late at his work.

To the charge that he was "prejudiced against the Tuscans in general, the Florentines in particular", Landor retorted that he had met within "twenty miles from Florence some of the best people I have ever yet conversed with".

The country folks are frank, hospitable, courteous, laborious, disinterested, and eager to assist one another. I have sat among them by the hour, almost the only company in the nation I could ever endure half so long; and, at the first time of seeing me, the whole family has told me its most intimate concerns.

He won the confidence and affection of simple folk with the same charm that delighted the market women at Tours—with the natural ease of manner and the "swift genius for grasping earthbound essentials" that John Cowper Powys envied in his brother Llewelyn and that enabled Coleridge to win devotion wherever he wandered in misfortune.

He was a more familiar figure at the public library and at shops of second-hand booksellers and picture-dealers than in the villas and palaces of Florence. Once or twice a year Southey and Wordsworth sent him parcels of books, mostly their own latest works or those of leading contemporaries; in return Landor sent rare old volumes he had picked up. Sometimes his gifts suffered in transit from ship rats or salt water; Wordsworth wrote lamenting the condition of a valuable *De Re Rustica* and a venerable Bible "sorely damaged, the binding detached from the book, the leaves stained and I fear rotted".

In *High and Low Life in Italy* Landor relates some of his experiences, not only with dealers, but with impoverished aristocrats like Medici-Tornaquinci (the Marchese Scampa arraigned before the Cardinal-Legate) who traded their heirlooms. From Medici he obtained a half-length portrait of Marie de Medici, which he sent to his sister Elizabeth. His interest in pictures dated from his visit to Paris in 1802, when he studied at the Louvre the Italian masters plundered by Napoleon. Before his father's death he had purchased a Titian and a Hogarth; by the sale at Llanthony he lost a rare and valuable collection. "Florence," he wrote near the close of his life, "is richer in works of art than any other city in the world"; there, besides filling his house with purchases, he learned much about Italian painting. Forster disparaged Landor's knowledge of art, inferring that he indulged an amiable eccentricity by making presents of pictures which he had been deceived into believing the work of old masters. But Landor's knowledge ranged beyond the scope of Forster's appreciation. In art, as in literature, he was an unconventional critic. He esteemed a work for its originality and historical value, often without due regard for its execution. Visiting him at Bath in 1852 Lowell saw a room full of early Italian paintings, which he pronounced "nearly all aggressively bad". This was the time when Forster knew him well, and most of the pictures Lowell saw were the fruits of bargains with Bath dealers, who offered no such prizes as the dealers of Florence. The best of his Florentine collection were given before he left Florence to friends and to his sisters and his brother Henry. "Landor anticipated the public taste in the admiration of the early

Italian schools," wrote Monckton Milnes, who saw his collection in 1833; "thus amid some pretenders to high birth and dignity, his walls presented a genuine company of such masters as Masaccio, Ghirlandaio, Gozzoli, Filippo Lippi and Fra Angelico."

Landor forestalled by a generation the Pre-Raphaelite taste introduced by Rossetti and Holman Hunt. Raphael was for him the greatest of painters. "I delight in Titian, I love Correggio, I wonder at the vastness of Michel-Angelo," he wrote; "I admire, love, wonder and then fall down, before Raffael." Pietro Perugino "was worthy of leading him by the hand"; though he told his sister that Perugino "comes immediately after Raffael & Frate Bartolommeo". He was annoyed when his friend Middleton, in 1828, "could not be prevailed upon to buy a Raffael for 500£. It is worth 2,000, and will bring it ere long". But he was the means of Middleton's buying a Perugino for £70—"I could have had it, if I had had the money, for 15 pounds. It is worth about 300." Later on, he purchased old paintings taken from suppressed monasteries at Pistoia. Writing in 1833 to his brother Henry, he offered him, as "an admirer of old workmanship", "about one hundred pictures, from the restoration of painting in Italy down to 1500". The Kings of Prussia and Bavaria were "the only two men, who ever made so large a collection of these interesting things". He himself was "the only private man, who possesses a Cimabue, the restorer of that art". He offered them to his brother because they had been put up in his children's bedroom, but his wife "either feared or pretended to fear, that they might fall upon their heads and knock their brains out, so she threw them into a closet pêle mêle, where nobody can ever see them".

They cost me hardly anything, some of them only a few shillings each, so that you, who have paid so much for me, cannot hesitate on that score. They are such things as ought to be in Warwick Castle. There are some things in them, which it is evident that Raffael copied.

This was a value which Forster failed to appreciate. Landor was a true enthusiast; he would hang the ancient, blackened daub of some forgotten painter beside the work of a genuine master to show how genius had perfected an idea derived from a lesser predecessor.

Relating how Landor "lived economically and dressed very shabbily", Kirkup mentioned his "buying a number of very ancient pictures which were not esteemed at that time" as his only indulgence. Nor was it an expensive hobby with him, for his values remained those of the Florence bargainers. Visiting the National Gallery with him in 1836, Crabb Robinson was "amused" by "his odd judgments"—"a small Correggio, with the frame, he valued at 14s.". Kirkup shared Landor's enthusiasm for old pictures, and in 1839 made the discovery at Florence of Dante's portrait by Giotto. In the *Examiner* of 16th August 1840, Landor applauded the discovery, praising Giotto as "the most illustrious of the Italians, their earliest great painter", though at the same time he annoyed Kirkup by giving all credit for the find to a fellow-researcher, Aubrey Bezzi. Francis Hare was also an enthusiast, and when he bought a Raphael for four hundred louis, Landor described it as "a Raffael, indeed, but a copy from Pietro Perugino".

Pictures remained Landor's hobby, but his children dominated his emotions in these years at Florence. Like all his emotions, his love for them was extravagant, consuming, agonising, and he allowed it unbridled rein. From the first he recognised that his delight in them would be limited to duration of their childhood; referring to his fiftieth birthday on 30th January 1825, he wrote to Southey, "We may both reasonably hope to see our children men, but I would rather see mine a child than lord chancellor." He seems never to have entertained the illusion that, by sympathy, understanding, and devotion, he might win his children's abiding confidence to attain that rarest of human relationships—affectionate companionship between father and son. Landor often knew himself better than his friends realised. An egoist by instinct, an enthusiast by nature and habit, he was at fifty enjoying a measure of self-fulfilment beyond his earlier experience, and he recognised that pursuit of self-fulfilment would not admit the self-discipline required to win the questioning confidence of adolescence. Within the dominant features of his arrogance lurked wrinkles of wry humility; while he lavished caresses on the child in his lap, he recognised that he was indulging a pleasure in possessiveness limited to the period of childhood's dependence. He was an egoist, but also a philosopher who neither shed tears over departed joys nor wore sackcloth in the ashes of a lost romance.

In his adoration of his children he lived in a fool's paradise with small thought of the future. Leigh Hunt related how he played with his children like "a real schoolboy; being as ready to complain of an undue knock as he was to laugh, shout, and scramble himself". He was their Babbo, his daughter was "my Julietta", and the youngest boy's affectionate diminutive was "Carlino". "To see the happiness of children was always to me the first of all happiness," he wrote to Southey. "How pure and brilliant is it in them! how soon it runs over the brink, and among what shouts and transports!"

His mode of bringing up his children was a characteristic mixture of wisdom and impracticality. To Birch he wrote in April 1819, when his eldest son was little more than a year old:

I smile at your idea that four or five years hence I shall be deep in plans of education. My plan is to have no plan at all. I shall teach my son Latin and Greek, as I teach him Italian and English, by practice. One year is enough for a language, if the mind is never puzzled by grammars. . . . Facciolati, the purest of modern Latinists . . . banishes grammar from education. I had fixed my intention before I read his oration on this subject, from observing that all well-educated persons speak grammatically without grammar, and that all learned persons write ungrammatically with it. To swim and fence and love cleanliness are the three things to be taught first. I intend to keep him always among women, that he may be desirous of pleasing, and learn a gracefulness and ease of manners which few Englishmen (educated in England) can acquire. . . . There are three places which my son shall never have my consent to enter—gaming-houses, brothels, and colleges. I hope he will be habitually fond of gardening—a great preservation from mischief and conductor to health. I shall repress too evident a desire for study, if he should have it. Health, good humour, and the habitude of pleasing are the only objects I keep constantly in view.

These designs Landor carried out in the years which followed. His children were the chief topic of his letters to his mother, who, as the tenth year since her son's departure from England approached, began to wish for his return. Her hints were the more pathetic in being veiled by apparent carelessness—Landor inherited pride from his mother as well as from his father—and she sought to devise his return by urging the needs of his eldest boy's education. Thanking her for her "kindness in offering to place him in some English school", Landor wrote on 2nd December 1824:

At present he is not quite seven years old. . . . I do not think I could live a single month without him, and it is not my intention to send him ever to any school where I cannot see him every day. We have in Florence an excellent schoolmistress, who takes ten or twelve young scholars, none above eight years old. Here they learn English, Italian, French and dancing, as well as drawing and accounts. . . . Latin and Greek I can teach him myself, and intend to do so in the spring. . . . If he ever goes to any public school, it shall be Eton, and that five or six years hence, for about three years.

He did not exaggerate his horror of even the shortest separation from his children, for, though he had longed to see Rome ever since his arrival in Italy, he remarked to his sister Ellen in February 1825, "As for sending Arnold to England, I refused an invitation to Rome last year, because I could not leave him." About the same time he confided to Southey his anxiety over his wife's proposal to accompany her brother on a visit to England. His favourite sister-in-law, Laura Thuillier, had lately married Colonel Edward Stopford, to whom he dedicated the first volume of *Imaginary Conversations*; another of his wife's sisters was about to leave for India to be married. His wife hesitated between leaving her two-year-old son Walter, and her desire to revisit her family circle. "I neither persuade it nor oppose it," said Landor, "but I shall be very unhappy without the two children she takes with her." She did not go, however, for she found herself pregnant of her fourth and youngest child, Landor's third son, Charles, born 5th August 1825.

His wife's fragile health after this fourth childbirth was the motive for removal to the Villa Castiglione. In November 1825 the children were "all in excellent health and the baby promises to be one of the strongest of the party". Expressing satisfaction that his family had escaped contagion from a recent epidemic of small-pox, Landor confided to his sister Ellen one of his many opinions far in advance of his time: "In my opinion every child ought to be inoculated with the vaccine at three months by order of the magistrates, and every parent who resists it to be imprisoned for a year, and in case another catches the distemper, for fourteen." With the move to the Villa Castiglione, he dispelled his mother's hopes of his return to England by telling his sister:

I shall pass my life upon the continent, having met with so many acts of injustice and unkindness in England. Eleven years have domesticated me; and the children may live together after my death.

§ 2

Landor continued to see with pleasure many faces besides his children's, though inevitably new friends replaced the old. Dr. Parr died in March 1825; Landor had not seen him since the visit after his marriage in 1811, but a few weeks before his death he heard from his sister Ellen that the old man, proud to see his faith in his former *protégé* justified, felt sad at receiving no word from him. "How is Walter?" he asked. "I hope he is well. O, he has shown a mighty mind—a mighty mind." Not knowing then whether Taylor had actually published the third volume of *Conversations*, Landor sent an addition to his sister with the instruction, "Pray send it immediately to Dr. Parr, *unless* the book is actually out." The addition was the handsome expression of gratitude to Parr for his friendship and encouragement that appeared in the preface to the fourth volume of *Conversations*. His sister Elizabeth made him a present of Parr's portrait, which reached him in 1827; "he had not exactly that expression when I saw him last", but "it brings back to me the features of my delightful old friend".

Walter Birch died in 1829. The last of Landor's preserved letters to him discussed the imminent publication of the first *Imaginary Conversations*—some thirty-five years after their friendship began at Rugby. Their correspondence sometimes lapsed for long intervals, but each wrote always with affectionate intimacy and with enthusiasm for discussion of classical scholarship.

Charles Brown, Francis Hare, and Seymour Kirkup continued his

closest intimates. Another friend was Byron's acquaintance, Gould
Francis Leckie, whom Kirkup remembered as "elderly . . . very jocose
and satirical, whom Landor liked as much as his wife disliked him".
With Francis Hare and his brother Augustus, who became an equally
close friend, Landor met their cousin Anna Maria Dashwood, a charming widow whom he hoped Francis might marry. "Landor was much
attached to Lord Dillon," wrote Kirkup, whose description of Dillon
combines with Leigh Hunt's to suggest a personality peculiarly sympathetic to Landor. "The gallant Viscount was a cavalier of the old
school of the Meadowses and Newcastles, with something of the O'Neal
superadded; and instead of wasting his words upon tyrants or Mr.
Pitt, ought to have been eternally at the head of his brigade, charging
mercenaries on his war horse, and meditating romantic stories."
Hazlitt was taken to dinner with Dillon at Florence: "It was the first
time I had dined with a lord; and by gad, sir, he had all the talk to
himself. He never waited for an answer. He talks as much as Coleridge;
only he doesn't pump it out." Dillon had pretensions to poetry; "he
was always reciting, and people laughed at him".

Not so Landor. He showed the most courteous attention; and often gave
him a word of advice, so gently as never to offend him. He used to say that
Lord Dillon's smiling handsome fair face was like a ray of sunshine in Florence.

This tenderness for the eccentric Dillon indicates the change in Landor
since his sister Elizabeth rebuked him for laughing in people's faces;
he had learned how tolerance and consideration won confidence, so
that people showed him the best in themselves. "He had the reputation of being a violent man, and no doubt was so," said Kirkup;
"but I never saw anything but the greatest gentleness and courtesy in
him, especially to women. He was chivalresque of the old school."
Such dialogues as Washington-Franklin and Puntomichino-Tal-
cranagh suggest that Landor derived much of his understanding of
Ireland from Dillon. Washington emphasises the merits of the Irish,
and the "centuries of misrule" which brought them to a condition
more hopeless than any other nation or tribe upon the globe; Franklin
demands the abolition of tithes and that, "to pacify and reclaim the
people, leases to middlemen must be annulled". At Dillon's house
Landor met Lamartine, then attached to the French Legation at
Florence; as a poet he pronounced him "a mere versifier, fantastically
grave, and epigrammatically devout", and the Lamartine-Thiers
dialogue, written twenty years later, implies that, while he respected
Lamartine's politics, he was alienated by his personal ambition.
These were the "two or three friends, a manageable number",
whom he mentioned to his sister Ellen in 1825. There were "some

dozens who call on me, but whom I cannot receive". Recalling Hazlitt's arrival at Florence in March 1825, Kirkup said:

He wished to pay Landor a visit, but was advised not, unless he was well introduced. Armitage Brown, who was Landor's greatest friend here, offered him a letter; but Hazlitt said he would beard the lion in his den, and he walked up to his house one winter's morning in nankeen shorts and white stockings; was made much of by the royal animal; and often returned—at night; for Landor was much out in the day, in all weathers.

Hazlitt's attire—qualified by Mrs. Landor as "a dress-coat and nankeen trousers halfway up his legs, leaving his stockings well visible over his shoes"—was unnoticed by Landor, who "would not know whether he was dressed in black or white"; Kirkup said that Landor himself was often so "shabbily dressed" that "I have known servants offend him by taking him for a beggar". The best hated writer of his day, Hazlitt held strong opinions and maintained them fiercely; he and Landor found much in common and developed mutual respect and liking. Friendliness, rather than genuine admiration for his work, inspired insertion of a note in the second edition of "Southey and Porson" that in Hazlitt's *Table Talk* "there are strokes as vivid and vigorous as in any work edited these hundred years"; for long afterwards he informed Forster that, while Hazlitt's books were "delightful to read", he would not "get much valuable criticism out of them—Coleridge was worth fifty of him in that respect".

Besides advising him on details of his dispute with Taylor, Hazlitt entertained Landor with the dry humour of his comments on life and people. When Landor expressed admiration of Wordsworth and eagerness to meet him personally, Hazlitt said, "Well, sir, you never saw him then? But you have seen a horse, I suppose? Well, sir, if you have seen a horse—I mean his head, sir—you may say you have seen Wordsworth." Kirkup recalled how Hazlitt related to himself, Landor, and Brown the story of his collusion in securing divorce from his first wife.

They took the steamboat to Leith, provided themselves each with good law advice, and continued on the most friendly terms in Edinburgh till everything was ready: when Hazlitt described himself calling in from the streets a not very respectable female confederate, and, for form's sake, putting her in his bed, and lying down beside her. "Well, sir," said Hazlitt, turning more particularly to Landor, who had by this time thrown out signs of the most lively interest, "down I lay, and the folding-doors opened, and in walked Mrs. H. accompanied by two gentlemen. She turned to them and said: 'Gentlemen, do you know who that person is in that bed along with that woman?' 'Yes, madam,' they politely replied, ''tis Mr. William Hazlitt.' On which, sir, she made a curtsey, and they went out of the room, and left me and my companion *in statu quo*. She and her witnesses then accused me of adultery, sir, and obtained a divorce against me, which, by gad, sir, was a benefit to both."

Landor greeted this exposure of legal vanities with "irrepressible delight".

From Rome Hazlitt wrote to Landor on 9th April 1825, describing his travels and expressing himself "much gratified that you are pleased with the *Spirit of the Age*". Calling at Florence on his homeward journey, he visited Landor, Dillon, Kirkup, and Brown. He recalled conversations with Landor in the *New Monthly Magazine* of November 1827 and contributed an appreciation of the third volume of *Imaginary Conversations* to the *London Weekly Review* of 14th June 1828. They never met again; when Landor returned to England, Hazlitt—three years his junior—was dead.

In the autumn of 1825 Francis Hare was with Landor when a Mr. Hogg sent in his card with a note of introduction from Landor's old Warwick friend Dr. Lambe; Landor joked that "I now thought myself La Fontaine, with all the better company of the beasts about me." The visitor was Shelley's friend, Thomas Jefferson Hogg, who related how Shelley at Oxford used to read *Gebir* aloud "with a tiresome pertinacity"; once "I went to his rooms to tell him something of importance, but he would attend to nothing but *Gebir*" till "I snatched the book out of the obstinate fellow's hand, and threw it through the open window into the quadrangle." "Well," said Landor "with his hearty, cordial, genial laugh", "you must allow it is something to have produced what could please one fellow creature and offend another so much." Hogg, like Hazlitt, was much disliked, but Landor agreed with Leigh Hunt that he had "a good heart as well as wit". Regretting that Landor and Shelley never met, Hogg wrote in his *Life of Shelley*, "If I would confer a real benefit upon a friend, I would procure for him, if it were possible, the friendship of Walter Savage Landor!"

§ 3

In January 1826 Francis Hare persuaded Landor to accompany him to Rome. He spent each day "from nine til five, in looking at the antiquities and the churches", though "Rome is certainly the finest city in the world, exclusive of the antiquities". "As I have only one room," he wrote to his mother, "I admit no one, but I meet every evening the best and most splendid society in the place." Hare introduced him to the genial gossip and lover of good living, Sir William Gell; to Lord Ward, soon to be Earl Dudley and British Foreign Secretary; to the Archbishop of Tarentum; and to the British ambassador, Sir William Drummond, who soon afterwards told Lady Blessington that he regarded Landor as "one of the most remarkable men of our time". All were dead when Landor recalled their talk of poetry:

CHARLES BROWN

From the bust
by Andrew Wilson,
done at Florence
in 1828, now at
Keats House,
Hampstead

LANDOR
aged fifty-one

From the drawing
by William Bewick,
"Done at Florence
Sept. 12, 1826"

Gell, Drummond, Hare, and wise and witty Ward
Knew at first sight and sound the genuine bard,
But the street hackneys, fed on nosebag bran,
Assail the poet and defame the man.

When Dickens visited Italy in 1844, Landor recalled nostalgically his pleasure there:

I miss the tales I used to tell
With cordial Hare and joyous Gell,
And that good old Archbishop whose
Cool library, at evening's close
(Soon as from Ischia swept the gale
And heav'd and left the darkening sail),
Its lofty portal opened wide
To me, and very few beside.

Yet at the time such pleasure "only makes me melancholy, for I think incessantly of Arnold, and of the greek he is learning, many sentences of which he speaks correctly", he wrote to his mother on 8th February:

All the wonders of Rome do not console me for the absence of Arnold and Julia; and, tho I promised to remain here three weeks, I shall return within the fortnight. This is the first time in my life that I have ever been twelve hours without seeing Arnold, and he is now eight years old within a month. He has written me a letter, which came together with yours, and which I must not lose a post in answering.

Forty years later among his papers Forster found the childish note to "My dearest Papa", and Landor's reply:

My dearest Arnold, I received your letter today, much too late to answer it by the post; but you will see that I was thinking of you and Julia yesterday by the verses I send you on the other side. I am very much pleased to observe that you write better than I do; and if you continue to read the Greek nouns, you will very soon know more Greek, unless I begin again to study it every day. When I was a little boy I did not let any one get before me; and you seem as if you would do the same. I promised you a Greek book, but I will give you two if you go on well, and next year two others, very beautiful and entertaining. I shall never be quite happy until I see you again and put my cheek upon your head. Tell my sweet Julia that, if I see twenty little girls, I will not romp with any of them before I romp with her; and kiss your two dear brothers for me. You must always love them as much as I love you, and you must teach them how to be good boys, which I cannot do as well as you can. God preserve and bless you, my own Arnold. My heart beats as if it would fly to you, my own fierce creature. We shall very soon meet. Love your Babbo.

The tender sympathy between parent and child reflected in this letter contrasts with Landor's own loveless upbringing and with the convention then coming into vogue, according to which children were

P

expected "to be seen and not heard", to address their parents as "sir" and "ma'am", and to pass from the care of servants to that of school teachers.

The visit to Rome was important to Landor. His welcome by men like Gell and Drummond assured him that he was at last recognised as a man of genius and achievement. He was no longer conscious of being regarded askant as a man of unproved possibilities when applauded by those, like Parr, who believed in his quality. Feeling no longer the need for self-assertion, he discarded the armour of aggressive arrogance deplored by those who knew him in earlier life, and impressed with admiration for his impulsive charm and gracious courtesy of manner. At home he remained difficult of access, for he cherished solitude for study, but he no longer disdained the pleasures of society. On 1st December 1826 he wrote to his mother:

We are very gay here at Florence. Last night we were at a private play, given by Lord Normanby. He and Lady Normanby act admirably. Arnold was very much flattered by being invited, and the more as he was the only one of his age who received an invitation. . . . Julia is less proud, tho the Duchess of Hamilton gave her a thousand kisses and played to her on the pianoforte an hour together. They are both in excellent health—I wish I could say as much for the infant who has been christened by the name of Charles, after my grandfather. Last night is the only one that Julia has left him a single hour for three months. He continues to suffer extremely by his teeth, four of which are cutting at once. . . . Walter is troubled with chilblains. . . . I have improved my digestion by the use of cayenne pepper and never was so little bilious these last twelve years.

Rather than to cayenne pepper, he owed the improved condition of his liver to banishment of melancholy by enjoyment of recognition.

Drawn at this epoch in his life, his portrait by William Bewick offers curious interest. In September 1826 Bewick spent a fortnight in Florence on his way to Rome. One morning he called upon Charles Brown, whom he knew through his fellow-painters Haydon and Severn,

and a gentleman sitting at a desk, whom I had never seen before, joined our conversation about trees, their beauty, character, &c. I was very much astonished at the powerful language he used, and the knowledge he possessed of the subject. He went into the planting, the growth, the proper soil and situation of every kind of tree, and its particular capabilities and uses. His whole bearing struck me as being that of no common man, and afterwards I took care to inquire who he was, and Mr. Brown told me he was one of the most remarkable and talented men of the age, and was the author of *Imaginary Conversations of Great Men*, &c., Walter Savage Landor. I afterwards made my drawing of him, and he very good-naturedly gave me as many sittings as I required.

Bewick took his drawing with him to Rome, where he showed it to David Wilkie, who exclaimed, "Like! it is more than like—it is the

man and his character."[1] The unlikeness between the several portraits
of Landor suggest that painters found difficulty in assessing the character
of their sitter; while Bewick conveys the impression of a character
formidably massive, with a stubborn firmness about the mobile lips,
with sadness as well as serenity in the contemplative eyes, he suggests a
quizzical humour and capacity for deep emotion lurking close to the
surface of present repose.

Landor recognised his debt of gratitude to Francis Hare. Though
four more years elapsed before its publication, he now began to prepare
a volume of his collected poems, with a dedication to Hare dated 1st
January 1827, in which he wrote: "It was at your persuasion, and
through your attention, that I publisht my Imaginary Conversations;
most of which, unless you had animated and excited me, would have
remained for ever unfinisht."

While he now enjoyed social functions at which he was a celebrity
to be pointed out with confidential whispers, he remained a difficult
capture for hostesses. Marguerite, Countess of Blessington—not yet
celebrated as the bluestocking hostess of Gore House, but already
"gorgeous" in the wealth of her devoted husband and in the flower of
her stately beauty—spent the spring of 1826 in Florence without meeting Landor, though she knew Francis Hare, Lord Dillon, Lord Normanby, and other friends of his. It was in June 1827 that she recorded
in her journal:

Made the acquaintance of Walter Savage Landor, ten days ago, and have
seen him nearly every day since. There are some people, and he is of those,
whom one cannot designate as "Mr." I should as soon think of adding the
word to his name as, in talking of some of the great writers of old, to prefix
it to theirs. Of Walter Savage Landor's genius, his "Imaginary Conversations" had, previously to our meeting, left me in no doubt: of the elevation
of his mind, the nobleness of his thoughts, and the manly tenderness which
is a peculiar attribute of superior men, and strongly characterises him, I
had learned to form a just estimate; but the high breeding and urbanity
of his manners, which are very striking, I had not been taught to expect;
for those who spoke of him to me, although sincere admirers of his, had not
named them. His avoidance of general society, though courted to enter it,
his dignified reserve when brought in contact with those he disapproves,
and his fearless courage in following the dictates of a lofty mind, had somehow or other given the erroneous impression that his manners were, if not
somewhat abrupt, at least singular. This is not the case, or, if it be, the only
singularity I can discern is a more than ordinary politeness towards women
—a singularity that I heartily wish was one no longer. The politeness of
Landor has nothing of the troublesome officiousness of a *petit-maître*, nor the
oppressive ceremoniousness of a fine gentleman of *l'ancien régime*; it is grave and
respectful, without his ever losing sight of what is due to himself, when most
assiduously practising the urbanity due to others. There is a natural dignity

---

[1] Landor must have met Wilkie during his visit to Rome, where he called on the painter
Joseph Severn with an introduction from Charles Brown, and also met Bertel Thorwaldsen
the sculptor.

which appertains to him that suits perfectly with the style of his conversation and his general appearance. His head is one of the most intellectual ones imaginable, and would serve as a good illustration in support of the theories of phrenologists. The forehead broad and prominent; the mental organs largely developed; the eyes quick and intelligent; and the mouth full of benevolence. The first glance at Landor satisfies one that he can be no ordinary person; and his remarks convince one of the originality of his mind, and the deep stores of erudition treasured in it. It is not often that a man, so profoundly erudite as Landor, preserves this racy originality, which . . . gives a colour to all that he has acquired. He reads of the ancients, thinks, lives with, and dreams of them; has imbued his thoughts with their lofty aspirations, and noble contempt of what is unworthy; and yet retains the peculiarities that distinguish him from them, as well as from the common herd of men. These peculiarities consist in a fearless and uncompromising expression of his thoughts, incompatible with a mundane policy; the practice of a profuse generosity towards the unfortunate; a simplicity in his own mode of life, in which the indulgence of selfish gratifications is rigidly excluded; and a sternness of mind, and a tenderness of heart, that would lead him to brave a tyrant on his throne, or to soothe a wailing infant with a woman's softness. These are the characteristics of Walter Savage Landor, who may justly be considered one of the most admirable writers of his day, as well as one of the most remarkable and original men.

Much of this extract was doubtless written when the journal was published as *The Idler in Italy* in 1839, after twelve years of friendship. But, if written *con amore*, the sketch faithfully presents an impression of Landor in his first years of celebrity by an accomplished woman of the world who maintained with him a disinterested friendship to the end of her life.

Seven years younger than Landor, Lord Mountjoy—apparently for no other reason than his possession of great wealth—had been created Earl of Blessington in 1816, two years before he married the beautiful and gifted Marguerite as his second wife. Widow of an army officer, she was the kept mistress of a rough-spun Hampshire squire before Blessington married her, and in spite of her beauty and her husband's wealth and title, she was excluded from fashionable London society. For the past six years they had travelled about the continent, attended by a retinue so expensive and extensive that it was called "the Blessington Circus", and accompanied everywhere as their inseparable companion—so adding scandal to the Countess's name—by the handsome young dandy, Count Alfred D'Orsay.

Aware that her reputation and her husband's eccentricity must thwart her ambitions as a political hostess, Lady Blessington developed designs on the less censorious world of letters. She published three books, she pursued Byron's acquaintance at Genoa, gathering materials for her *Conversations of Lord Byron*, she knew men like Gell and Hare and Drummond. Francis Hare was staying with the Blessingtons when he heard that Landor was laid up with quinsy, and made his excuses to go and see his friend. Blessington knew it would please his wife to add this latest literary lion to her acquaintance, and called on Landor. When his card was brought in, Landor was denying all knowledge of him, but Blessington followed in behind the servant, saying, "Come, come, Landor! I never thought you would refuse to see an old friend. If you don't know Blessington, you may remember Mountjoy."

Landor afterwards confessed that he did not remember Mountjoy, who had been "somewhat fat for so young a man" but was "now become emaciated"; he nevertheless enjoyed recalling old times at Bath with the genial Irishman. "In a few days he brought his lady 'to see me and make me well again'." Lady Blessington immediately won his respect and admiration, as he wrote to his mother a year later:

Lady Blessington is, without any exception, the most elegant and best-informed woman I ever conversed with; but, as she is accused of some incorrectness in early life, the ladies (at least the English ladies) do not visit her. In France she enjoys the first society, and admits *only* the first. Never was there woman more generous or more high minded.

He also liked and admired Count D'Orsay, on whose death twenty-five years later he wrote:

With many foibles and grave faults he was generous and sincere. Neither spirits nor wit ever failed him, and he was ready at all times to lay down his life for a friend.

Of all their acquaintance Landor seems to have been the only friend to appreciate Lord Blessington as his wife appreciated him. Blessington's first wife was his mistress before marriage; his second he was said to have purchased from her keeper; he was now regarded as a complacent husband who made a friend of his wife's lover. Early inheriting great wealth, he had attempted no ambition; though prodigally extravagant, he achieved no reputation even for vice. He was considered a harmless eccentric, rather foolish and pathetically uxorious. Most people derided his indignation at the state of his native Ireland, contrasting his mode of life with his opinion that the nobility and gentry should be made to "live on their estates or sell them". But Landor appreciated that his advocacy of liberal ideas was endorsed by many private benefactions. Though "we thought differently on many points, particularly on the political abilities and integrity of Canning", wrote Landor on Blessington's death, "our opposition in sentiment did not alter or diminish our mutual esteem".

With these new friends Landor was quickly on terms of intimacy, writing to his sister Ellen from the Villa Castiglione at the beginning of August 1827:

I am always at the Blessingtons' from eight to eleven, I mean when I am in Florence. At present I do not go over to them more than once or twice a week, the distance being three good miles.

In the same letter, he recorded "a very pressing invitation from Lord Blessington to accompany him in his yacht to Naples". The previous winter he had been flattered by an invitation from Lord Guilford, to whom he dedicated the fifth volume of *Conversations*, "to visit him in the Ionian Islands". Devoted to the cause for which Byron died, Guilford had established a university at Corfu. Perhaps Landor was unduly flattered by the invitation, for, remarking that "never was mortal man so devoted to one pursuit, as this estimable creature is to the restoration of literature in Greece", Lady Blessington regarded a similar invitation as "not so much, I verily believe, for the sake of our society, as for the purpose of showing us his literary establishments". Landor, however, declined Guilford's invitation, saying, "I do not think I shall ever move farther than a morning's walk from the table where I am writing."

But Blessington's offer tempted him. "As I have never seen Naples," he wrote to his sister, "and never could see it to such advantage, as in the company of a most delightful well-informed man, and as four hundred a year do not afford all the facilities and *agréments* of forty thousand, you may be assured I was not very reluctant to accompany him." Arnold had been ill of a fever, and Landor waited to be satisfied of his convalescence before sailing. He was to be away for twenty-five days.

Afterwards he recorded his impressions of Naples. He was "in raptures with the bay", though "these roads are dustier than any other in the world & noisier".

La Cava is one of the most beautiful places in the world. . . . The ruins of the temples here, if ruins they can be called, are magnificent; but Grecian architecture does not turn into ruin so grandly as gothic. York cathedral, a thousand years hence, when the Americans have conquered and devastated the Country, will be more striking.

"The Lucrine lake is a poor pond", and though he had imagined that Lake Avernus would be "terrific", he found "on the contrary it is a pretty little round lake, with groves full of birds all round". The island of Capri was among the sights he regretted missing owing to the agony of anxiety he suffered on receiving no letter from Arnold.

Not receiving any letter at Naples, I was almost mad, for I fancied his illness had returned. I hesitated between drowning myself and going post back. At last I took a place—the only one, for one only is allowed—with the post man in what is called the diligence. Meanwhile Lord Blessington told me he would instantly set sail, if I wished it, and that I could go quicker by sea. I did so, and we arrived in four days at Leghorn.

There he gave me a note, enclosed in a letter to him, informing me that Julia had been in danger of her life, but was now better. I found her quite unable to speak coherently, and unhappily she was in the country. Nevertheless the physician, who sometimes passed the whole day with her, and once slept at the house, never omitted for forty-three days to visit her twice a day. . . . The complaint was a malignant fever of the very worst kind. She took three emetics in one day, and in the first two of her illness she was bled twice in the arm, and in the succeeding days with leeches. Besides all these tortures, she had mustard, and God knows what, applied to her feet and legs. All this began the day after I left Florence for Naples.

Charles, the youngest child, caught the infection from his mother, but, although "for three days it was thought he had no chance of his life, he made a rapid recovery in sixteen days". Little Julia and Walter were saved from infection by Lady Blessington, who drove out from Florence and took them home with her. Towards the end of September, his wife was well enough to be moved to the city; Landor "brought her part of the way by means of oxen on the sledge, and upon two mattresses". On 1st October, when she had "begun to take a new preparation of bark, and can walk about the room", the physician attended her for the last time, and Landor wrote to his sister Elizabeth:

These afflictions have turned the rest of my hair white, after taking off what was refractory and would not turn. However it has left me strength and spirits better than ever. No man was ever so near to losing three of his family without at last losing one.

The Blessingtons were the main source of his good spirits. He was, as long afterwards he told Mrs. Story, "quite the *ami de la maison*". They remained at Florence till November, when they visited Rome, and returning in the spring, continued at Florence till the late autumn of 1828. Landor said he went "every evening from my villa and spent it in their society", and Lady Blessington noted in her journal:

The shades of night send us home to enjoy iced tea and sorbetti in our charming pavilion overlooking the Arno, where a few friends assemble every evening. Walter Savage Landor seldom misses this accustomed visit, and his *real* conversations are quite as delightful as his imaginary ones. In listening to the elevated sentiments and fine observations of this eloquent man, the mind is carried back to other times; and one could fancy oneself attending to the converse of a philosopher of antiquity, instead of that of an individual of the nineteenth century; though, to be sure, one of the most remarkable persons of this, or any age.

At the Blessingtons' he met Henry Hallam the historian—to whom he took one of his rare dislikes, describing him ten years later as "that surly, ill-conditioned prig, Hallam"—William Richard Hamilton, formerly British minister at Naples, the Duc de Richelieu, and the Count di Camaldoli, of whom he wrote to his sister in November:

I never met with a graver or sounder man than the Count di Camaldoli, who was minister to the King of Naples in the time of the Constitution. In these last six weeks I have seen him most evenings, and conversed with him the greater part of them, unless when his daughters sang, which they do divinely.

He also met D'Orsay's sister, the Duchesse de Guiche, "retaining a part of her bloom and all her graces", and Blessington's daughter, Lady Harriet Gardiner, of whom he afterwards said that he could not promise much "if you converse with her more than once".

Lady Harriet's wedding to D'Orsay was the cause of the Blessingtons' departure from Florence to Rome in November. The licence of the British minister had to be obtained, and Lord Burghersh, believing the popular scandal about D'Orsay and Lady Blessington, was accordingly revolted by the proposed marriage, used every available obstacle to prevent the ceremony, and finally spoke his mind in undiplomatic language to both Lady Blessington and her stepdaughter. Landor never believed that Lady Blessington was D'Orsay's mistress—"I disbelieve in the tales of her last friendship," he announced in a public letter after her death, and "No truth at all about D'Orsay and Lady B. All a complete lie," he told Mrs. Story—and his old indignation against Burghersh was revived by this affront to his friends. He wrote to Lady Blessington:

I believe I may have said on other occasions that nothing could surprise me, of folly or indecorum in Lord Burghersh. I must retract my words: the only ones he will ever make me retract. That a man educated among the sons of gentlemen could be guilty of such incivility to two ladies, to say nothing of condition, nothing of person, nothing of acquaintance and past courtesies, is inconceivable, even to the most observant of his behaviour throughout the whole period of his public life. From what I have heard and known during a residence of six years at Florence, I am convinced that all the ministers of all the other Courts in Europe (I may throw in those of Asia and Africa) have never been guilty of so many unbecoming and disgraceful actions as this man. . . .

He urged that Burghersh's conduct in refusing "to sanction a father's disposal of his daughter in marriage with almost the only man who deserves, and certainly the very man who deserves her most" should be represented "to the Administration at home; without which it cannot fail to be misinterpreted here, whatever care and anxiety the friends of your family may display, in setting right the erroneous and malicious". D'Orsay wrote to him from Rome that he hoped Burghersh would take offence at a letter he had written to him, as he would have pleasure in cutting off the minister's nose. But no official complaint appears to have been presented, and as Landor foresaw, gossip decided that Burghersh had reason for his decision. Possibly Landor alone entirely believed in the propriety of the marriage.

10

MOVE TO FIESOLE

Six years the Medicæan palace held
My wandering Lares; then they went afield,
Where the hewn rocks of Fiesole impend
O'er Doccia's dell, and fig and olive blend.
There the twin streams in Affrico unite,
One dimly seen, the other out of sight,
But ever playing in his smoothen'd bed
Of polisht stone, and willing to be led
Where clustering vines protect him from the sun,
Never too grave to smile, too tired to run.
Here, by the lake, Boccaccio's *Fair Brigade*
Beguiled the hours and tale for tale repaid.
—"My Homes" (1858)

After Landor's six years as a tenant of the Medicis ended in the autumn of 1827, he lived for a short time at the Casa Cremani, by the Croce al Trebbio—he was at that address when the carpenter complained to the police of Landor's attempt to kick him. By February 1828—when Landor himself complained to the police that a picture stolen from him was being offered for sale in the shop of a dealer named Ussi—he had moved to the Casa Castellani in the Via dei Banchi. The following autumn, after spending the summer as usual in the country, he settled at the Palazzo Giugni in the Via degli Alfani.

On 25th April 1828 he wrote to his sister Elizabeth:

... Some friends of mine, I am told, are going to Lemington; one is Mrs. Dashwood, daughter to the late Dean of St. Asaph, the best man in England. If by chance you should see her, I hope you will make much of her! She is cousin to Francis Hare, my particular friend. I believe a Mrs. Young is with her. This lady is sister to Mrs. Ablett, from whom and her husband I and my family have received a thousand acts of Kindness. Ablett is the kindest and most generous man in existence, and particularly attached to me. ... My children are all well, but Julia within these two days has begun to complain a little. I hope there is no danger of such an illness as that of last year. ...

Yet another whose acquaintance he owed to Francis Hare, Joseph Ablett proved a devoted admirer and munificent friend. With wealth acquired from Manchester trade he cultivated an estate in North Wales and a taste for the arts. Despite his interest in painting, Landor's frugal economy did not allow many commissions to painters. In April this year Middleton had "half finished a most beautiful drawing of Arnold and Julia", which Landor sent to his mother; sometime earlier Trajan Wallis, a friend for several years at Florence, painted a portrait of Landor's wife with two of her children. Landor sat to Bewick at the request of the artist, who took his drawing away with him; before Bewick's the only surviving portrait of Landor is that painted by George Dance in 1804. Now Ablett asked him to sit for a bust by John Gibson, the pupil of Canova and Thorwaldsen, who came from Rome to execute the commission, as Landor informed his sister Ellen on 19th June:

> Gibson came to me the very day Colonel Ackelon brought me Robert's poem, and I give him two sittings, one in the morning, one in the evening. There have been three days, and there will be four more, before he takes the cast in plaster of Paris. I am told that Chantry is equal to him in busts, but very inferior in genius. The one is English upon principle, the other Attic.
>
> On Sunday I redd Robert's Preface, which is well written. I shall not begin the poetry, til I can give it an undivided attention, which will be when I get into the country, and be under the vines all day.
>
> I hope to begin this mode of life on the first of July. I am very much obliged to Henry for his kind offer of letting me have the legacy now. I do not want any money for myself, but shall be very happy to pay off *one hundred pounds*.
>
> The mine of wealth derived from my Conversations brought me three hundred and seventy two pounds, the two Editions. One hundred & seventy two the first, 200 the second.
>
> Mr. Burrow Julia's unkle, lent me 400 £ before I left England, with which I paid my silversmiths bill. I have returned him only 100 £ and this from the last Edition. 68 £ more went in payment of what was given to Julia, but which I insisted should not be given. I laid out nearly 100 in pictures, part of which I sold again for 180, and the *better* part is left yet. If I had had 3,000 £ eight years ago, I could have cleared 12,000 in the first two years.
>
> The dealers here know only the Florentine school, and one of them, the best and most honest, often asks my opinion even on this. I have put a few hundred pounds into his pocket.

Robert Landor's book was *The Impious Feast*, an epic poem in blank and rhymed verse on the fall of Babylon; his anonymous tragedy in verse, *The Count Arezzi*, had appeared four years earlier. The legacy, according to Forster, was a small bequest from the estate of Landor's half-sister, Maria Arden. Though Robert still felt coolness to his eldest brother, Landor was now on cordial terms with his brother Henry, having ended the resentment he had felt since Henry's reluctant part in the purchase of Llanthony by writing on 19th December 1825:

Dear Henry My cousin W. Landor has informed me how very kindly and nobly you have acted in regard to me, and I cannot do so great a violence to my heart as to suppress the declaration of my gratitude for it. I hope the manner in which I propose to live abroad will enable me to indemnify my family for any losses they might have sustained by the arrangements made in my behalf. . . .

The second edition of the first two volumes of *Imaginary Conversations*, after being withdrawn from Taylor & Hessey, was published by Henry Colburn in May 1826, but the third volume, though set up in type, waited two years before publication by Colburn in May 1828. Ten years later Harrison Ainsworth described Colburn as "a sad shuffling fellow", and so he seems to have proved in this case. Before Richard Bentley started in business, Colburn was the most successful of London publishers; he was the Bacon, and Bentley the Bungay, of Thackeray's *Pendennis*. While he published mainly fiction and memoirs assured of topical popularity, he was reluctant to lose the credit of publishing a work of literary merit, if limited sale. But, lacking the publishing philosophy which allows that a season's best-sellers must balance the losses on literary works of limited appeal, he was not prepared to lose money; he paid an advance of two hundred pounds on the second edition of the first two volumes and the third volume, and refused to publish the third volume till the sales of the second edition could be assessed.

Urged by Francis Hare to bring the number of dialogues to a hundred, Landor had meanwhile written enough for two more volumes. "Whether they will ever be printed I know not, and never will inquire," he told Southey; "this is left with Julius Hare." Exasperated by Colburn's delay, Julius Hare took the fourth and fifth volumes to young Harrison Ainsworth, who was making a short-lived venture into publishing before starting his career as a novelist. At this stage Landor wrote to his sister Ellen on 18th November 1827:

I heard yesterday, for the first time, that the three last volumes of my Conversations are printed or printing, and will come out early in the ensuing year. The third Vol. has indeed been printed these ten or eleven months, but Colburn has been *persuaded* to delay, and if possible to prevent, its publication. Another publisher has undertaken the fourth and fifth. I am sick of writing. Never will I write any thing more. I have burnt all the things I had begun, and many that I had nearly completed. I was very much grieved to hear of poor Lord Guildford's death. I had dedicated the last volume to him; and the dedication shall hold its place, together with some words preceding it, regretting his loss and Parr's. . . .

To his sisters' suggestion that Colburn's hesitancy might be due to fear of trouble from his outspoken opinions, he retorted on 4th February 1828:

Southey and Hare have full power to erase whatever they think proper to erase from my Imaginary Conversations. At present, so far as I know, they have exerted their authority over only two paragraphs, which they thought *actionable*. As for the rest, they would, as they will tell you, as soon think of cancelling a scene of Shakespear. Doctor Wade and Doctor Innes would be braver. . . .

Despite his momentary distaste for writing, he continued to send more dialogues, and in March 1828 Julius Hare reported that the publisher was objecting to the bulk of the volumes: "one of between 500 and 550 pages makes a very good octavo", but the last calculation "gives us 1,500 pages for the fourth and fifth volumes, and I think therefore you must determine on having a sixth".

Landor heard no more from Hare for more than a year, though in the following November he told Southey that he had received the third volume and proofs of the fourth. By the time the fourth and fifth volumes were in type, Ainsworth had abandoned his publishing business to his father-in-law, John Ebers, and having been recently bankrupt, Ebers felt no enthusiasm for a publication of doubtful profit. "The *Conversations* are too classical and substantial for the morbid and frivolous taste of the English public," wrote Hare, "and few publishers, except my friend Taylor, look beyond the saleableness of a work." The fourth and fifth volumes eventually appeared in the spring of 1829 as *Imaginary Conversations of Literary Men and Statesmen, Second Series*, the publisher being James Duncan, who agreed to a profit-sharing basis. The sixth volume never appeared; some of its intended contents appeared in periodicals during the following seventeen years, but several dialogues awaited publication till the *Works* of 1846.

§ 2

During the summer of 1828 Landor's children suffered in health, and he thought of leaving Italy for a more temperate climate, as he wrote to his sister Elizabeth on 12th July:

I do not remember whether I am a letter in your debt, but suspect I may be. In a little while you will see Colonel Ackelon, who carries one for my mother. I saw but little of him; he appears a strange foolish creature. His daughter is a very amiable girl.

But of all the delightful and sensible girls I have seen for many years and indeed almost at any time, Miss Middleton is the most so. Her father has made a very beautiful picture of Arnold and Julia. . . . It is not unlikely that in another year I may remove to the borders of the Rhine, on account of the general badness of the climate in Italy. I should very much regret to leave Florence, where I have several friends, excellent and well-informed men, English you may suppose; for none such are to be found among the natives. The greatest loss after this would be the public library, and then the picture gallery. But the children cannot resist the heat, and I am in danger every summer of losing one or other of them. . . . My bust is finished, or rather the mould for it. Never was anything in the world so perfectly like. Gibson is the sculptor; and I doubt whether any modern one excells him. . . .

On 19th August he wrote to his mother:

. . . The children and myself have all had the whooping cough, and have it stil, altho much more lightly. Nothing is absurder than that certain disorders can come only once. In the same country they may never return, but a new climate makes a new creature. Besides the whooping cough, we have all been covered with nettle rash, which I am sorry for, as I believe it to be an incurable disease, and likely to return every year. It has ruined the skin of my hands.

In this country a warm bath is requisite from the beginning of April to the middle of October. Without it there is no health or comfort.

I have received an invitation from Lord Blessington to stay with him at Paris, or rather with his family, and remain until he returns from England. This would delight me, if I could leave the children. . . .

He declined the Blessingtons' invitation, though it was endorsed in September by Count D'Orsay, who sent him a sketch of Prince Borghese, the suppressed passage about whom in the "Puntomichino and Talcranagh" dialogue had been restored in the second edition. Established at the Palazzo Giugni, he sent news to his sisters on 8th December:

. . . I hear from Rome that the cast for my bust is very much admired. Mr. Ablett has given me leave to have one taken for my mother and another for my wife. . . . This morning I met Sir Robert Lawley, who walked with me for half an hour, and made many inquiries about the family. He had taken it ill that I had declined two or three of his invitations to dinner parties; but I told him I never intended to be at one anywhere all the remainder of my life. . . . My friend Hare has married Miss Paul, the daughter of Sir John Paul, and has 20,000 £ with her. His brother Augustus writes me word that he follows the good example in the summer, and that Lady Jones gives him 400 £ a year. She is his aunt, and the widow of Sir William. Have you redd Southey's Vindiciae Ecclesiae Anglicanae? He has sent it me; it contains the highest eulogy on me I ever received or ever shall. . . .

An old Warwickshire friend of his family, soon to be raised to the peerage as Lord Wenlock, Sir Robert Lawley was to prove a useful friend. Criticism of Italy in the *Imaginary Conversations* had not endeared Landor to the Florentines; as he informed Southey—who had attempted to protect him by suppressing such passages in the first edition—"my note on Corsini selling his wife's old clothes before she had been dead a fortnight; that on Borghese; that on our patriots, &c; leave me none but enemies". In April 1829 he was robbed of seventeen pieces of silver plate and had reason to suppose that the thief was a discharged servant. In reporting the theft to the police, he reminded them of their failure to recover his picture from the dealer Ussi in the previous year, saying he therefore had no hope of their "recovering my silver, because

I am quite certain that the Police will do nothing about the matter, it being their policy when thefts are committed against Foreigners to act so as to protect the thieves". He cited the case of his friend Captain Guyon, who had recently suffered robbery without redress, and declared, "In Tuscany there is no such thing as Justice" and "I speak in this manner because I am not afraid of anyone". Thus insulted, the police collected all the evidence they could extract from servants and tradesmen with grievances against Landor to show that he "was in constant danger of committing some act of violence in the grip of rage", with the result that he was ordered to leave Tuscany within three days.

Landor thereupon addressed an expostulation to the Grand Duke, pointing out the impossibility of settling his affairs in so short a period; he published a translation of his letter in *High and Low Life in Italy*, beginning:

Highness! I am by the direction of my studies, unable to write a *Supplication*, and, were I able, I would rather die. I ask for justice; and under the son of Ferdinand, and the grandson of Peter Leopold, I am sure to find it.

The situation was patently absurd. There was no reason for Landor's banishment except his expressed contempt for the police and the judicature, and there was no justification even for that. On the other hand, the police had to save their faces, and this Landor seemed likely to prevent by announcing his intention of resisting expulsion. His friends saw that they must save him from himself.

First Charles Brown's friend, Charles Wentworth Dilke, then visiting Florence, pointed out to Landor that he had been wrong to blame the president of the Buon Governo for the matter of Ussi and the picture, as another president had been in office at that time. Immediately Landor agreed that "I am bound, as a gentleman, to write and beg his pardon", and did so. Then Lord Normanby, Sir Robert Lawley, and a Mr. St. John appealed to the Grand Duke's secretary of state, Prince Neri Corsini; not unnaturally, in view of what Landor had written about him, they found him "exceedingly incensed" against Landor, but he agreed to extend by eight days the period of grace before banishment, already extended by three days after Landor's letter to the Grand Duke.

After thirteen days Landor was persuaded to retire to the Baths of Lucca for a month, while his friends sought to procure the lifting of the ban. There he received news of Lord Blessington's death in Paris from apoplexy and wrote to the widow in condolence on 6th June:

The whole of this day I have spent in that stupid depression which some may feel without a great calamity, and which others can never feel at all. Every one that knows me knows the sentiments I bore towards that disinterested and upright and kind-hearted man, than whom none was ever dearer or more delightful to his friends. If to be condoled with by many, i f to be esteemed and beloved by all whom you have admitted to your society is any comfort, that comfort at least is yours. I know how inadequate it must be at such a moment, but I know too that the sentiment will survive when the bitterness of sorrow shall have past away. You know how many have had reason to speak of you with gratitude, and all speak in admiration of your generous and gentle heart, incapable as they are of estimating the elevation of your mind.

Evidently feeling too depressed to remain longer alone, he next day returned unbidden to Florence. Knowing that ministers were still protesting to the Grand Duke against his recall, an official "looked amazed" on meeting him in the street and asked who had recalled him. "My family," replied Landor. Apparently the Grand Duke had expressed the opinion that the matter was a *mésintelligence* which might have been avoided, and as Landor had obeyed the order to leave Florence, he should now be allowed to return. Without Landor's knowledge his wife was required to petition both the Grand Duke and the president of the Buon Governo "to grant me the recall of my Husband"; this enabled Prince Corsini to sign an order graciously permitting Landor's return.

Any idea of removal to the Rhine or elsewhere was now abandoned. Hearing of his narrow escape from expulsion, Francis Hare wrote in August from Cambridge—where he was staying with his brother Julius —reminding Landor of the good times they had enjoyed together in Florence and begging him to avoid further scrapes that might drive him out of the city, which he believed to be "the best and fittest abode" for him. Landor needed no such persuasion; as he wrote to Southey, it was enough that the Florentines had tried to expel him:

Such being the case, I resolved to pitch my tent in the midst of them; and have now bought a villa, belonging to the Count Gherardescha, of the family of C. Ugolino, and upon the spot where Boccaccio led his women to bathe when they had left the first scene of their story-telling. Here I shall pass my life, long or short, no matter; but God grant without pain and sickness, and with only such friends and such enemies as I enjoy at present.

He had neither the intention nor the money to buy a villa when he went house-hunting to Fiesole. Escape from the summer heat in Florence was necessary for the health of his wife and children, so he went to look at "a small cottage with about twelve acres of land", which was to be let. He was accompanied by his friend Joseph Ablett, who liked the cottage well enough, but "preferred another house very near it, with a much greater quantity of ground annexed". Landor tried to persuade him to become his neighbour.

He said little at the time, beyond the pleasure he should have in seeing me so pleasantly situated: but he made inquiries about the price of the larger house, and heard that it was not to be let, but that it might be bought for about two thousand pounds. He first desired me to buy it for him: then to keep it for myself: then to repay him the money whenever I was rich enough —and if I never was, to leave it for my heirs to settle. In fact, he refuses even a farthing of interest. All this was done by a man with whom I had not been more than a few months acquainted. It is true his fortune is very large; but if others equal him in fortune, no human being ever equalled him in generosity.

Thirteen years later, Ablett was repaid his two thousand pounds out of a sum raised by a mortgage on Ipsley; he never accepted any interest.

Landor entered upon possession of the Villa Gherardescha in the autumn of 1829. In mid-October he wrote to his sister Ellen: "I am living in the country, where I intend to pass the remainder of my life." His letter was in reply to one from Ellen, acknowledging receipt of Ablett's gift of the bust by Gibson and conveying disquieting news of their mother's health. "Your letter would have given me the greatest pain, if you had not consoled me with the idea that my mother's disorder is but weakness," he wrote. "At her age we cannot expect any great renovation of strength, but God grant her many days yet of health and happiness." As he wrote, the old lady was already dead; she died on 8th October, within a month of her eighty-sixth birthday. Her pride denied expression of sentiment, but during the past five years she had repeatedly hinted hopes of a visit from her eldest son. She would have gladly exchanged his accession to celebrity for a sight of him and his children. He must have recalled his exasperation in boyhood at being "put down" by his family when his mother wrote on the publication of *Imaginary Conversations*, "For God's sake do not hurt your eyes, nor rack your brains too much, to amuse the world by writing: but take care of your health, which will be of greater consequence to your family." Later she "heard your late publication highly spoken of by many; but as I am no judge, I shall say nothing relating to it. I wish you to take care of your eyes and health, and let the world go on as it has done". Having thus rebuked his ceaseless rebellion against established institutions, she reflected, "I think of the fate of Lord Byron, and that those who have the greatest abilities have the greatest misfortunes—because they have, more than others, mortifications and disappointments."

Despite her age, his mother's death came as a shock; though he spoke of being settled forever in Italy, he had not realised that he would never see his mother again. He wrote to his sister Elizabeth:

' Tho' Ellen's letter gave me much uneasiness, yet I did not apprehend at present the sad loss we have all sustained. My mother's great kindness to me, throughout the whole course of her life, made me perpetually think of her with the tenderest love. I thank God that she did not suffer either a painful or a long illness, and that she departed from life quite sensible of the affectionate care she had received from both her daughters. I am not sorry that she left me some token of her regard; but she gave me too many in her lifetime

LANDOR AT FIFTY-THREE

From the bust by John Gibson, R.A., in the National
Portrait Gallery, completed in July 1828. "Gibson is the
only man who has not either flattered or abused me"—
Landor to Lady Blessington, 18th September, 1838

for me to think of taking any. You and Ellen will retain, for my sake, the urn and the books. I wish to have her little silver seal in exchange for an oriental cornelian, which you and my brothers gave me, belonging to my father. I have his arms, which is enough. The one I mean is pretty in its setting, and contains the word "Leitas" in persian letters. My brother Henry was so kind as to purchase two Venetian paintings, once mine and to place them at Ipsley. I thanked him at the time and thank him again; but I am resolved to accept nothing whatever from any of my relatives. If my mother's picture was purchased at Lantony, I would buy it gladly. Pray let me hear about it. I remember it at my grandmother's fifty years ago. Adieu. I am ill-disposed for writing more. Yours affectionately, W.L.

Though he knew that his mother's personal fortune was left among her younger children, he conceived that his inheritance of the entailed Ipsley estate would again raise him to affluence. By declining to benefit by his mother's death, he believed that he was abjuring wealth when he wrote to his cousin and agent:

I propose that my net income be divided into three equal portions; two for my Creditors, and one for my family.

Revd. Mr. Burrow of Bampton near Witney, my wife's Uncle, lent me 400 £ and he should be paid first. Perhaps you might propose to pay him 100 £ half yearly, beginning at the next rent day. Jones, and the person from whom Gabell borrowed for me, should be paid in equal proportions and equal degrees.

You will remember that I lose my right to the inclosure unless it is carried into effect within 20 years. This is in the Agreement, any kind of Inclosure will preserve my rights, but I would gladly see 100 £ laid out as soon as possible in this and planting, particularly near as possible to the Abergavenny road, for exporting the timber.

Neither in this nor anything else do I consult my own interest, but my Son's. Ipsley Court will, of course, be lett, together with the Manor &c.

I shall never see it again.

Hare has lent me this month another hundred pounds. If it is not inconvenient to give him a Draft payable to Drummond at 3 months after date, and dating it the first of January, I should be glad. I owe him one hundred and six pounds nine shillings for he sent me the value of the odd money in books.

The only other debt I have here is my grocers: It will be about 40 £ by Christmas.

Receiving this letter, Walter Landor of Rugeley wrote on 16th November to Landor's brother Henry:

Wr. evidently knows little of the income he proposed to divide, & would find it difficult to manage with one third of it. I doubt the sum from Lanthony will be very trifling, indeed none if times do not quickly improve.

Advised by Henry, Landor's cousin paid him six to seven hundred a year, reserved several hundred annually for estate expenses, and continued to pay only the interest on the principal debts. For five years, however, Landor believed that he was sacrificing two-thirds of his income to his creditors.

The shock of his mother's death was softened by the reappearance of Ianthe. Telling his sister Ellen in October that he was dividing much of his time between two or three families of friends, he wrote:

> You may well image that I divide it somewhat unequally when you know, unless you have first seen it in the papers, that the Countess de Molandé is come to Florence.

Perhaps tho you may never have heard that the dearest of all the friends I ever had or ever shall have, Mrs. Swift, accepted the Count de Molandé for her second husband. He died about two years ago, and the succession was disputed by many, but the only two anything like competitors were the Earl of Bective and the Duc de Luxembourg. The first, tho the younger and the handsomer man, was rejected, because the Countess thought that a woman who had sons & daughters grown up, never should contract a second marriage, much less a third. The same reason was given to the Duke; but he has shown such constancy, such resolution both against his relations and the King averse to the match from her being a protestant, that she has told him it would be better for both parties to be absent from each other for one winter, and to consider the matter a little more calmly. She has given him *no* promise: he has sworn to her that, if *ever* she will accept him, he is her husband. I have advised her to accept him, as adding a fresh splendour to her lovely daughters, and very sure to conduce to their more desirable establishment in life. Her fortune, from several relations, is become very large, and she has no ambition. I doubt whether she will do what I think most advisable.

Probably he was well pleased that this charming widow in her late forties disregarded his advice. He had reason to congratulate himself that she would have more willingly resigned widowhood if he had been free to be her suitor, for when one of her daughters married in the following year he wrote:

> Maria! I have said *adieu*
> To one alone so fair as you;
> And she, beyond my hopes, at last
> Returns and tells me of the past;
> While happier for remembering well
> Am I to hear and she to tell.

And he added, as his advice to insure the girl's happiness in her married life,

> Remember one command of mine:
> Love with as steddy love as e'er
> Illumed the only breast so fair.

After twenty years, romance thus re-entered Landor's life to make an idyl of his first months at Fiesole. Her son relates how Landor came every second day to breakfast at Ianthe's, while her family dined occasionally at Fiesole. "Reciprocal entertainments were of the most hilarious and delightful character"; Ianthe's children by her second marriage were of an age with Landor's eldest, and his fun must have been at its most boisterous in seeing his own adored children laughing with those of the woman he loved. "With Landor for our cicerone," Ianthe's family found Florence "extremely gay"; they visited the amateur theatricals of Lord Normanby, "who delighted in Landor", and it appears that Ianthe's company tempted Landor not only to the "Granduke's" balls, but even to the opera ball of the loathly Burghersh. Ianthe, too, shared his now absorbing hobby of planning the garden at his villa. To his sisters, who sent him mulberries and grass seed—his worst failure in his efforts to create a garden like that of his Warwick home was the raising of turf—in exchange for the rich fruits of Fiesole, he wrote that "I have four mimosas ready to place round my intended tomb, and a friend who is coming to plant them." This occasion inspired him to write his epitaph:

> Lo! where the four mimosas blend their shade,
> In calm repose at last is Landor laid;
> For ere he slept he saw them planted here
> By her his soul had ever held most dear,
> And he had lived enough when he had dried her tear.

Ianthe revived his mood for poetry. His dialogues were laid aside; his literary occupation was the collecting and revising of his verse for the representative volume suggested by Francis Hare. Hare had brought his bride to Florence, and theirs was the house most frequented by Landor after Ianthe's. John Kenyon, who had first come to him in 1827, bearing an introduction and a parcel of books from Southey and Wordsworth, was one of his earliest guests at Fiesole. Nine years younger than Landor, Kenyon had both wealth and generosity like Ablett's. He had written enough verse of sufficient merit to be accepted for his literary pretensions, and his wealth and good nature won him popularity as a host and patron of literary men. The oldest of his literary friends, Southey, justly said of him that everybody liked him at first sight, and liked him better the longer he was known. Stout and hearty, he had "the face of a Benedictine monk, and the joyous talk of a good fellow". Perhaps he was not, like Hare or Southey or Charles Brown, a friend to turn to in unhappiness or adversity; shrewdly Crabb Robinson remarked, "He is more bent on making the happy happier, than on making the unhappy less unhappy." He loved life in its richness—good food, fine wines, laughter, the company and conversation of men he liked and admired. He so delighted in entertaining at his table "every variety of literary notabilities" that he was called a "feeder of lions". He was an epicure, and as he studied how best to relish the flavour of a dainty and the bouquet of wine, so he sought to draw the best out of his friends. His pleasure was to give pleasure to others, to see them on good terms with themselves, and he delighted in Landor for his spontaneous response. He had only to give Landor his head, to let him explode one of his furious tirades against stupidity or injustice, and then catch the infection of his uproarious laughter. Their friendship continued unabated for twenty-six years after this stay at Fiesole—till Kenyon's death in 1856; when it had lasted sixteen years, one of their joyous meetings inspired some of Landor's better occasional verse:

> So, Kenyon, thou lover of frolic and laughter,
> 　　We meet in a place where we never were sad.
> But who knows what destiny waits us hereafter,
> 　　How little or much of the pleasures we had!
> The leaves of perhaps our last autumn are falling;
> 　　Half-spent is the fire that may soon cease to burn;
> How many are absent who heed not our calling!
> 　　Alas, and how many who can not return!

　　Henry Crabb Robinson, the diarist, a retired barrister and journalist, who lived for the society of men of letters, also came to Fiesole with an introduction from Southey and Wordsworth. On 14th August 1830 he met "the one man living in Florence whom I was anxious to know". Sententiously he described Landor as "a man of unquestionable genius, but very questionable good sense; or rather, one of those unmanageable men—

> 　　Blest with huge store of wit,
> 　　Who want as much again to manage it."

He noted that he was shunned by the Italians, who said, "Everyone is afraid of him."

　　Yet he was respected universally. He had credit for generosity, as well as honesty; and he deserved it, provided an ample allowance was made for caprice. He was conscious of his own infirmity of temper, and told me he saw few persons, because he could not bear contradiction. Certainly, I frequently did contradict him; yet his attentions to me, both this and the following year, were unwearied.

Robinson liked himself not a little, and failed to appreciate that Landor's chivalrous loyalty demanded his utmost exertion for a friend of his beloved Southey, whatever he thought of Robinson personally. The diarist was, therefore, enabled to record, "To Landor's society I owed much of my highest enjoyment during my stay at Florence," adding:

He was a man of florid complexion, with large full eyes, and altogether a *leonine* man, and with a fierceness of tone well suited to his name; his decisions being confident, and on all subjects, whether of taste or life, unqualified; each standing for itself, not caring whether it was in harmony with what had gone before or would follow from the same oracular lips. But why should I trouble myself to describe him? He is painted by a master hand in Dickens's novel, Bleak House. . . .

Robinson, like Forster, was a man of the world, with more common sense than imagination; in Landor's contempt for orthodoxy, for popular applause, for material honours and self-advancement, in his passionate loyalties and loathings, he saw no defiant consistency in self-fulfilment—only eccentricity. For Robinson, as for Forster, Landor was Boythorn. On his side, Landor liked Robinson well enough, though long afterwards he remembered how "Crabb Robinson bored me to death with his German talk."

I said I hated the language, and he said that if I knew it and understood it I should be delighted with it. Goethe alone, he said, would repay me for the trouble of learning it. "His epigrams," says he, "you're fond of epigrams." I told him I didn't care a farthing for 'em. I said I knew many Latin and Greek ones—also many French ones that were better by far than either. He repeated to me one of Goethe's, saying it was wonderful. When he had finished I said "Where's the epigram?" "What, don't you see it?" says Crabb. "Well then, here's this one"; and he tried me with another. "I don't call *that* an epigram either," said I. "No? Good Lord, then I've done." "Thank God," said I.

In Robinson himself there was much of the humourless Teuton, which Landor thus delighted in baiting. But with a shrewdness unsuspected by Forster or Robinson, he accurately valued the latter's virtues to a friend at Rome, when Robinson moved on to that city—"He was a barrister, and, notwithstanding, both honest and modest—a character I never heard of before: indeed, I have never met with one who was either."

§ 3

Landor had the same feeling for plant life as John Cowper Powys, who annoyed his brother Llewelyn by refusing to rest in a hedgerow lest he should crush the wild flowers growing there. In "Fæsulan Idyl", written during his first year at Fiesole, he tells of his love for flowers:

> They bring me tales of youth and tones of love,
> And 'tis and ever was my wish and way
> To let all flowers live freely, and all die,
> Whene'er their Genius bids their souls depart,
> Among their kindred in their native place.
> I never pluck the rose; the violet's head

Hath shaken with my breath upon its bank
And not reproacht me; the ever-sacred cup
Of the pure lily hath between my hands
Felt safe, unsoil'd, nor lost one grain of gold.

Again owning a garden, he renewed his countryman's delight in planting. "I spend in improvements what I used to spend in house-rent:
that is, about 75£ a year," he told his sisters; "I have planted 200
cypresses, 600 vines, 400 roses, 200 arbutuses, and 70 bays, besides
laurustinas . . . and 60 fruit-trees of the best qualities from France."
He had not had a moment's illness in his first two years at Fiesole,
he said, "nor have the children", and he had "the best water, the best
air, and the best oil in the world".

His water supply caused trouble with his neighbour, a Frenchman
named Antoir, "formerly a vendor of prints and sea-shells, now an *attaché*
to the French Legation". Antoir's property received its water supply
by a stream overflowing from the fountain of the Villa Gherardescha.
Owing to Landor's prodigal watering of his garden there was often
no overflow, and the stream dried up in summer. Antoir lodged a
claim, "which led to some depositions on oath, contradicted by six
witnesses on oath, before a notary public". According to Landor's
account in *High and Low Life in Italy*, Antoir then sent him a challenge,
though Seymour Kirkup told Forster that Landor challenged Antoir
when the Frenchman accused him of prevarication in denying that
he had stopped the flow of water.

The law against duelling was strictly enforced in Tuscany, and
Landor received an order "to leave Tuscany within an hour, though he
had violated no law, and no order of the Government". He believed
that the order was issued in malice by Prince Corsini and the president
of the Buon Governo, smarting from their previous failure to expel him.
Fortunately the French minister, the Count de Garay, recognising the
possibility of diplomatic complications since his subordinate was
involved, informed Prince Corsini "that if Mr. Landor was sent out
of Tuscany, he would accompany him". The order was withdrawn,
and the duel was averted when the Count de Garay sent for Kirkup—
who had agreed to act as Landor's second—and proposed to answer for
Antoir's pacification if Kirkup would undertake Landor's. Landor
agreed to preserve the peace when he found Kirkup had pledged his
responsibility, and Kirkup mentioned the story to Forster "as a curious
proof of our friend's docility and confidence in others". But Antoir's
lawsuit about the watercourse dragged on for years, to be finally settled
in 1842 at a cost to Landor of between two and three hundred pounds.[1]

[1] Some account of the litigation, based on papers in the state archives at Florence and on
Antoir's diary, appears in *The Golden Ring: The Anglo-Florentines 1847–1862*, by Giuliana
Artom Treves, 1956.

Writing to his sisters in February 1831 of his being "tormented by a rascal about a watercourse", Landor explained that "I must resist, as without the water I lose the produce of nearly a hundred lemon-trees, each at least a century old", which "have enjoyed this water unrestricted for above forty years". In the same letter he mentioned the publication of his collected poems—"Lady Mulgrave sent me the *Court Gazette*, in which a flaming panegyric is lavished on them, preparatory, I presume, to announcing my appointment to the see of Canterbury." *Gebir, Count Julian, and Other Poems* was published on commission at half-a-guinea by Edward Moxon, the expenses being guaranteed by Julius Hare, who told Crabb Robinson some months later that fewer than forty copies had been sold. One discerning review, praising much of the occasional verse in preference to the more pretentious poems, appeared in *Fraser's Magazine* for July 1831—a periodical recently established under the editorship of the much maligned Dr. Maginn. The reviewer took a tone of graceful appreciation towards a writer of established eminence: "His *Imaginary Conversations* are known to every reader as being among the most original and powerful productions of modern times; and the poems now given to the world are, though not likely to enjoy extensive popularity, replete with proofs of force and elegance of mind." If Maginn did not write the whole review, he was evidently responsible for its last paragraph, remarking that Landor was unlikely ever to become a popular poet, "but in whatever way a man of genius may please to pour forth the treasures of his mind, they should be received with reverence and gratitude", and such reception he would ever meet with from *Fraser*. Persisting in his old illusion, Landor told his sisters, "My Latin poetry is thought better than my English."

When not occupied with gardening, he amused himself by satirising the Florentines in *High and Low Life in Italy*. The idea of using the form of the epistolary novel may have been suggested by his memory of *Sir Charles Grandison* from the days when he borrowed novels from the Swansea circulating library, for Richardson satirically defines his characters in that novel as "men, women, and Italians". Pidcock Raikes and his secretary Stivers are supposed to have arrived in Italy in 1824; a semblance of story is built up in developing their characters and circumstances and those of their correspondents, but the fiction serves only as a device for satirical relation of all the anecdotes to the disadvantage of the Italians that Landor could remember from his experiences of the past decade.

His mood of contempt for the Florentines inspired temporary despair of the Italians' achieving national independence. The recent revolt of the French to instal Louis-Philippe as their "citizen king" suggested to Southey that "Italy cannot be long inactive in the day of regeneration", and remembering Landor's enthusiasm for the Neapolitans ten years before, he feared his becoming involved in probable disturbances. But Landor recognised no such spirit as Mazzini and Garibaldi were to inspire in the years following 1848:

Be assured there is not a patriot in Florence who would have a single pane of glass broken in his window to bring about any change whatever. At my time of life, and with my utter indifference what befalls so rascally a race, you need not apprehend that, in case of a bustle, I should take any part in it . . . The principle of honour and virtue was extinct in Tuscany long before the Romans appeared. They once had an idea of independence, but never of liberty; and the spirit of petty personal revenge is the only spirit they show now, and almost the only one they ever showed. Lombards are sprung from better blood, and possess both sounder minds and stronger bodies.

Having finished *High and Low Life in Italy* in the autumn of 1831, he sent the manuscript to Crabb Robinson in London by the hand of the painter Trajan Wallis. He asked Robinson to sell the copyright outright, as "I will never more *go halves* with anybody". He also wished that his authorship should remain secret—"If my name were prefixt I shd be driven out of Tuscany—but they may suppose what they please" —though he virtually signed his name to the book by including the dialogue between "The Cardinal-Legate Albani and Picture-Dealers", which had been designed for the sixth volume of *Imaginary Conversations*.

His correspondents in England found him unusually equable on the subject of home politics. When his sisters wrote in gloomy foreboding about conceding the popular demands for parliamentary reform, he replied on 20th May 1831:

You are a little too melancholy in regard to the times. Whatever is happening and about to happen was foreseen by me in the period of Pitt's war against France. He squandered the nation's wealth with more imprudence than the most wanton youth ever squandered his new inheritance; and the facility he found in raising supplies from a venal parliament shows the necessity of changing the system. The misfortune is that the change had not taken place fifty-five years earlier. Then we should not have lost America, except as a colony and a dependant, and by no means as a confederate and friend. But above all we should have had a debt of about 40 instead of 800 millions.

Thirty years earlier he had blamed the Whig leadership of Fox for not insisting on religious toleration, abolition of the slave trade, and parliamentary reform; now all three changes were being reluctantly conceded by those who had derided his opinions as eccentric and impracticable. He did not fail to remind his sisters of this when, in reply to their further lamentations, he wrote on 29th December 1831 to wish them "many happy new years":

When the good people of England helped Pitt to gamble in war, and to run the nation in debt beyond the value of all the money in Europe, we might easily have foreseen the result. I did see it, and tried to prevent it, in my remonstrance against the income-tax.

Sir Robert Lawley, now Lord Wenlock, shared his political sympathies; though "nearly blind", he kept "in good spirits" and predicted that the flame of liberalism would blow towards Italy.

Another liberal sympathiser at hand was E. J. Trelawny, the friend of Shelley and Byron. After Byron's death Trelawny had remained in Greece to play his part in the war of liberation and to marry as his third wife Tersitza, half-sister of the Greek leader Odysseus, but Odysseus died by treachery, Tersitza entered a convent, and Trelawny passed through Italy on his way to England in the summer of 1828. Apparently he was introduced to Charles Brown by Joseph Severn as "a mad chap" who "comes as the friend of Shelley, great, glowing and rich in romance", and Landor was so impressed by his personality and the story of his adventures in Greece that he wrote—in time for publication in the fourth volume of *Imaginary Conversations*—the conversation between Odysseus, his mother Acrive, Tersitza, her brother Leonides, and Trelawny. Based on Trelawny's own spoken narrative as a tribute to his friend Odysseus, this conversation has curious interest as a historical document in conjunction with Trelawny's memoirs.

In the spring of 1829 Trelawny returned from England to Florence, where he shared lodgings with Charles Brown and wrote his *Adventures of a Younger Son*. "Brown and Landor are spurring me on," he wrote to Mary Shelley, "and are to review it, sheet by sheet as it is written." When Mary Shelley read the completed manuscript and complained that "certain words and phrases pardoned in the days of Fielding are now justly interdicted", he retorted that "Landor, a man of superior literary acquirements: Kirkup, an artist of superior taste: Baring, a man of the world and very religious: Mrs. Baring, moral and squeamish: Lady Burghersh, aristocratic and proud as a Queen, and lastly, Charles Brown, a plain, downright Cockney critic . . . have read and passed their opinions on my narrative". Landor afterwards described the book as "like nothing but the *Iliad*". He enjoyed Trelawny's company and celebrated his amorous exploits in doggerel:

> It is not every traveler
> Who like Trelawny can aver
> In every State he left behind
> An image the Nine Months may find.

> Considerate, he perceived the need
> Of some improvement in the breed,
> And set as heartily to work
> As when he fought against the Turk.

Persuaded by a fellow Cornishman, Sir William Molesworth, that he might stand for parliament as a Radical after the passing of the Reform Bill, Trelawny left for England in the spring of 1832. Lord Wenlock returned about the same time, and these departures may have influenced Landor in following their example. In his letter of new year greetings he said nothing to his sisters of an impending visit, but in February he wrote that Joseph Ablett had been pressing him, and in view of his obligations to him, he could not persist in refusal.

With an effort he parted from his children:

I promised my dear Arnold to bring him with me, but his mother would not let him go. He was grieved at the disappointment, but bore it heroically. Dear good divine creature! Poor Julietta cried and hung about me and told me not to go away. If she had told me only once more, I could not have left her.

He chose the same means of transport as in the year of Waterloo; he "would not travel by any public conveyance, but purchased a horse and phaeton expressly to convey him across the Continent, and sold both at the French port of embarcation".

I went safely thro France in the midst of the cholera, and reached Dieppe the very day after the steam vessel had departed for England. In consequence of this mishap I was detained a whole week at Dieppe, with nothing to see or read and nobody to converse with.

After an absence of almost exactly eighteen years, he returned to England early in May 1832, at the height of public excitement over the passing of the Reform Bill.

11

ENGLAND AFTER EIGHTEEN YEARS

> Lord of the lovely plain
> Where Celtic Clwyd runs to greet the main!
> How happy were the hours that held
> Thy friend (long absent from his native home)
> Amid those scenes with thee! how far afield
> From all past cares, and all to come!
> —"Ode to a Friend (Joseph Ablett, 1834)"

Ablett's urging was not the only inducement to visit England, and Landor had a motive in sailing from Dieppe rather than from Calais or Boulogne. Brighton lay on the way to London, and he wrote to his sisters on Monday 14th May:

At Brighton I stayed two days with the Countess de Molandé and her family, in the midst of music, dancing, and fashionable people turned radicals. This amused me highly. Lady Bolingbroke told me that her husband would never enter the House of Lords again.

Yesterday I dined with our good old friend Lord Wenlock and this morning the people were half mad about the King and the Tories. My excellent Mr. Abblett will take me first to see Cambridge, for a single day, because Julius Hare came over here to see me, having heard from him that I should be here on the first or second of the month.

I stay in London til after Saturday, because on that day I must be at the soiree of the Duke of Sussex, by his invitation. I have one invitation for the beginning of the next week, but on Wednesday we shall set out for Warwick.

In London he called on Crabb Robinson, with whom he had "a long and interesting chat on English politics"; he learned that *High and Low Life in Italy* had been vainly offered to Baldwin, Cradock & Joy and to John Murray, and hearing of Leigh Hunt's poverty, he made him a present of the manuscript. Hunt also failed to secure its publication till, five years later, he became editor of the *Monthly Repository*, in which *High and Low Life in Italy* appeared serially from August 1837 to April 1838.

Having awaited Landor's arrival in London for nearly a fortnight, Ablett was impatient to return home, so, after a day at Cambridge with Julius and Augustus Hare, Landor accompanied his host directly to Denbighshire without making the promised call at Warwick. From Llanbedr Hall he wrote to his sisters on 6th June:

In another week we are leaving this place for Lancashire and Cumberland, where I propose to spend a day or two with Southey, & then about as much time with Wordsworth.

Llanbedr is really in all respects the most delightful place I ever was in. Magnificent trees, the richest valley in the world and the most varied hills, with lofty mountains not too near nor too distant, but just as great folks should be. . . . Every cottage is more habitable than the best house on the continent; every one has a patent oven and a clock and is surrounded by a garden. Mrs. Ablett is extremely fond of flowers, and I understand their gardens cost them three hundred a year. This morning we are going to visit . . . a most polished and highly informed woman, a friend and correspondent of mine, Mrs. Dashwood, niece of Sir William Jones and Hare's cousin.

I fear I shall not have the pleasure of seeing you at Warwick before the beginning of next month.

Mr. Ablett will spend perhaps four days with you. Of all men living he is the very best, the most modest and sober minded. He is very religious, and reads prayers to his servants on the Sunday evening, and one before they go to church. He has set up a gravestone for himself on the north side of the churchyard, to induce other people to overcome their prejudices against this situation. On this gravestone I wrote some verses . . .

With Ablett he travelled by steamer from Liverpool to Whitehaven, where they heard that Wordsworth was visiting his son at Moresby. There they met, and next day visited Wordsworth's friend Rawson at Wastwater. Wordsworth wrote to Crabb Robinson that Landor "appears to be a most warm-hearted man, his conversation very animated, and he has the heartiest and happiest laugh I ever heard from a man of his years". Little addicted to laughter, Wordsworth was impressed by Landor's laugh; he wrote in another letter, "His conversation is lively and original; his learning great, tho' he will not allow it, and his laugh the heartiest I have heard for a long time."

A year later Landor asked Crabb Robinson to tell Wordsworth "how often I think of the delightful hours I passed with him at Wastwater", but this courteous message seems to have been his only contemporary reference to the meeting. As he usually expressed enthusiasm on making new acquaintances and had so eagerly looked forward to meeting Wordsworth, his reticence suggests such disappointment as De Quincey had felt at his first sight of Wordsworth twenty-five years before. Recalling his impressions in his *Letter to Emerson* of 1856, he remembered Wordsworth as "extremely civil".

There was *equinity* in the lower part of his face: in the upper was much of the contemplative, and no little of the calculating . . . he spoke contemptuously of Scott, and violently of Byron. He chattered about them incoherently and indiscriminately. In reality, Scott had singularly the power of imagination and of construction: Byron little of either; but this is what Wordsworth neither said nor knew. His censure was hardened froth. I praised a line of Scott's on the dog of a traveller lost in the snow (if I remember) on Skiddaw. He said it was the only good one in the poem, and began instantly to recite a whole one of his own upon the same subject. This induced me afterwards to write as follows on a fly-leaf in Scott's poems,

> Ye who have lungs to mount the Muse's hill,
> Here slake your thirst aside their liveliest rill:
> Asthmatic Wordsworth, Byron piping-hot,
> Leave in the rear, and march with manly Scott.

Of Landor's visit to Keswick Southey wrote to Caroline Bowles on 4th July:

Last week I was most delightfully surprised by the apparition of Landor from Italy, whom I had not seen since I was at Como in 1817. He remained two days here, and holds out a hope of coming again to England three years hence, which to him seems not so long a time to look forward to as it does to me, for he has had no home-proofs of the uncertainty of human life.

Though Landor wrote in August to Mrs. Hodson of his pleasure at finding Southey "in the full enjoyment of his health and spirits", he sadly recognised how sedentary labour and family bereavement had aged him during the past fifteen years, as appears in the ode he wrote "To Robert Southey" a few months later:

> Alas! that snows are shed
> Upon thy laurell'd head,
> Hurtled by many cares and many wrongs!
> Malignity lets none
> Reach safe the Delphic throne;
> A hundred kennel curs bark down Fame's hundred tongues.

Both Southey and Wordsworth, thirty-five years before enthusiasts for the principles of the French Revolution, viewed with gloom the reform agitation, and Landor wondered if he might have offended Wordsworth by vigorous argument of his liberal opinions, for Julius Hare—who soon afterwards visited Wordsworth—wrote in reassurance, "Your politics did *not* alarm him."

Back at Llanbedr, Landor wrote to his sister Elizabeth on 14th July:

It was my intention to have left Llanbedr the beginning of this month, but my hospitable friends would not hear of it. I should however have left them yesterday, if we had not met Lord Bagot, who very civilly invited me to spend a day in the coming week with him at Pool Park in this neighbourhood.

I am grieved that my excellent friend Ablett has given up all idea of coming with me to Warwick. You and Ellen would have been delighted with him.

The only coach going from any part of this neighbourhood to Warwick goes (I believe) thro Rugeley: at all events thro Birmingham. This induces me to make Charles a visit at Colton, on my way to you. I write to him by the present post telling him of my intention to be with him at dinner on Friday next, I think the twentieth, as well as I can count. I shall spend a week there.

While staying with his brother Charles at Colton, he made an excursion to the upper Trent Valley with his cousin and agent, Walter Landor of Rugeley, and was moved by the beauty of the scenery to exclaim, "Why the deuce did not I buy this place and build my house here, instead of at that confounded Llanthony?" Drily his cousin replied that the scene he admired had been his property and that of his ancestors before him, being part of the family estate sold for the purchase of Llanthony.

He did not visit Llanthony. The house was tenantless, and he instructed his cousin to pull it down and sell the building materials. "I never think of it without thinking of the ruin to which it has brought me," he told his sisters, "leaving me one of the poorest Englishmen in Florence, instead of one of the richest."

From Colton he must have arrived at Warwick about 27th July; he was still there when he wrote to Mrs. Hodson on 13th August. Naturally his sisters had felt some grievance at his long delay before visiting them, and evidently confided their feeling to their brother Robert. But once he arrived, their umbrage was forgotten and they welcomed him affectionately, as did their brother Henry; it was Robert who cherished the grievance and wrote after his brother's death more than thirty years later, "Walter came from Italy—not to see his Brothers and Sisters—but to visit Wordsworth."

Landor's stay at Warwick was enlivened by the presence of Kenyon and his wife at Leamington. He marvelled at Leamington's development as a spa, for he remembered it as having "only two tenements that joined each other, and in the whole village only six or seven of any sort, besides the squire's, one Prew, who was the uncle of my grandmother". Everywhere he saw changes since he left England; railways were still in their infancy and the penny post was yet to come, but the spreading smoke of the towns indicated the progress of the industrial revolution.

Leaving Warwick for Bath, he "had the good fortune to meet" his brother Robert "before the Inn at Evesham, where his carriage and my coach had stopped. He promised me that, if possible, he would come and see me at Bath, and I waited there a day longer than I proposed". His sisters—not Robert—wrote to explain that he had been prevented from coming to Bath by an attack of gout, which Landor curiously believed likely to improve his general health, though he assured his sisters of his "regret that either this or any other incident has deprived me of the satisfaction I should have had in seeing him again".

From Bath he went again to Ianthe at Brighton, before staying a few days with his wife's family at Richmond. He arrived "in Upper Brook Street" about 22nd September, "having left the Thuilliers with some regret, they were so kind and attentive to me". Writing to his sisters a letter received at Warwick on the 24th, he mentioned a letter of theirs forwarded from Brighton; with the forwarded letter was evidently a message from Ianthe which caused him to urge Crabb Robinson on the 24th to accompany him on a visit to Brighton. That day he introduced Robinson to Trelawny—whom Robinson was surprised to find "quite human" and "amiable as well as handsome"—and accompanied him to the sculptor Flaxman's, where "Landor was most extravagant in his praise". Apparently he then travelled alone to Brighton, reappearing to breakfast with Robinson and a Cambridge friend of Julius Hare's, Thomas Worsley, on the 28th, before visiting Charles and Mary Lamb at Enfield. They "had scarcely an hour to chat" and Robinson "thought Lamb by no means at his ease, Miss Lamb quite silent", but Landor was delighted with them both and with their adopted daughter, Emma Isola, to whom he afterwards addressed some verses at Lamb's request. Lamb "did not think it worth his while to put on a fine new coat to come down and see me, as poor Coleridge did, but met me as if I had been a friend of twenty years' standing", Landor told Lady Blessington. "Indeed, he told me I had been so, and shewed me some things I had written long ago and had utterly forgotten."

Landor had read *The Essays of Elia*, and when Robinson at Florence lent him *Mrs. Leicester's School*, he thanked him for "many hours of exquisite delight"—"Never have I read anything in prose so many times over, within so short a space of time, as 'The Father's Wedding-day'." This simple story of a stepmother's tender understanding of a child's emotions must have appealed to him as a revelation of the possible effect on his own children if they lost either parent; three years later he told Lady Blessington how the story so affected him that "I pressed my temples with both hands, and tears ran down to my elbows". In his admiration of this story—"with the sole exception of the *Bride of Lammermoor*, the most beautiful tale in prose composition in any language"—he rated Mary Lamb as her brother's equal in genius; when he heard of Charles Lamb's death, "no thought took possession of my mind except the anguish of his sister", and as an "attempt at consolation to the finest genius that ever descended on the heart of woman", he wrote the verses of sympathy that appeared in Leigh Hunt's *London Journal* of 13th June 1835. "Never did I see a human being with whom I was more inclined to sympathise," he wrote of Charles Lamb:

Once, and once only, have I seen thy face,
Elia! once only has thy tripping tongue
Run o'er my heart, yet never has been left
Impression on it stronger or more sweet.
Cordial old man! what youth was in thy years,
What wisdom in thy levity, what soul
In every utterance of that purest breast!
Of all that ever wore man's form, tis thee
I first would spring to at the gate of Heaven.

"I say *tripping* tongue, for Charles Lamb stammered and spoke hurriedly," he explained in sending to Lady Blessington these "Lines on the Death of Charles Lamb" on 25th April 1835.

Probably because the volume was published by his friend Moxon, Lamb had been one of the few readers of Landor's poems the year before, when Robinson reported that "tipsy and sober he is ever muttering 'Rose Aylmer'". But he forgot to tell Landor of his admiration at their meeting. Evidently they spoke of Shakespeare—perhaps Landor mentioned his idea of introducing Shakespeare into an imaginary conversation—for Lamb gave him a copy of *Original Letters of Sir John Falstaff and His Friends*, by his schoolfellow James White. He was touched when Landor sent him the verses for Emma Isola: "I do not know how to thank you for attending to my request about the Album," he wrote; "I thought you would never remember it."

Many things I had to say to you, which there was not time for. *One* why should I forget? 'tis for Rose Aylmer, which has a charm I cannot explain. I lived upon it for weeks. Next I forgot to tell you I knew all your Welch annoyancers, the measureless Beethams. I knew a quarter of a mile of them, 17 brothers and 16 sisters, as they appear to me in memory. . . . The shortest of the daughters measured 5 foot eleven without her shoes. Well, some day we may confer about them. . . .

With his letter he enclosed a copy of *The Last Essays of Elia*, and later lamented to Samuel Rogers the punctilious promptness of Landor's acknowledgment: "It was a little tantalizing to me to receive a letter from Landor, *Gebir* Landor, from Florence, to say he was just sitting down to read my 'Elia', just received, but the letter was to go out before the reading."

Crabb Robinson failed to recognise the mutual liking between Lamb and Landor, and recorded "nothing in the conversation recollectable". He slightly preferred his entertainment the next day, when he called with Landor on Coleridge at Highgate.

We sat not much more than an hour with him. He was horribly bent and looked seventy years of age—nor did he talk with his usual fire but quite in his usual style. A great part of his conversation was a repetition of what I had heard him say before—an abuse of the Ministry for taking away his pension. . . . He spoke only of Oriental poetry with contempt, and he showed his memory by alluding to Landor's juvenile poems. . . . Landor and he seemed to like each other. Landor spoke in his dashing way, which Coleridge could understand and he concurred with him.

On the subject of Coleridge's pension Landor expressed himself to Lady Blessington nearly a year later:

George IV, the vilest wretch in Europe, gave him £100 a year, enough, in London, to buy three turnips and half an egg a day. Those men surely were the most dexterous of courtiers, who resolved to show William that his brother was not the vilest, by dashing the half egg and three turnips from the plate of Coleridge. No such action as this is recorded of any administration in the British annals, and I am convinced that there is not a state in Europe, or Asia, in which the paltriest minister of the puniest despot would recommend it.

He remembered how Coleridge "put on a bran-new suit of black to come down and see me, and made me as many fine speeches as he ever could have done to a pretty girl"; he was "very infirm . . . but he retained all his energy of mind, and all his sweetness, variety, and flexibility of language". When Coleridge died, he described the previous deaths of Byron and Scott as "only the patterings of rain before the storm", and "my heart aches at the thought that almost the greatest genius in the world, and one so friendly to me, is gone from it". On reading De Quincey's recollections of Coleridge, he wrote to Lady Blessington:

The Opium-eater calls Coleridge "the largest and most spacious intellect, the subtlest and most comprehensive that has yet existed among men". Impiety to Shakespeare! treason to Milton! I give up the rest, even Bacon. Certainly, since their day, we have seen nothing at all comparable to him. Byron and Scott were but as gun-flints to a granite mountain; Wordsworth has one angle of resemblance; Southey has written more, and all well, much admirably.

Other contemporaries he regarded as "ground ivy".

On the evening between the calls on Lamb and Coleridge, Landor introduced Robinson to Lady Blessington. In reply to Landor's letter of condolence on Blessington's death, Lady Blessington had begged him to write again—"It will be a pleasure to me to hear from you, as, independent of my own feelings of friendship for you, I well know that there was no man breathing for whom my ever to be lamented husband entertained a higher opinion or felt a warmer regard." After a brief courtesy call, he had apparently explained that his journey to Brighton would cut short his stay in London, for she wrote to reproach him "that in your sojourn in London, you do not give me a single day", though "you promised to stay a week, and that of that week I should have my share".

R

He had another motive for introducing Robinson to Lady Blessington besides returning courtesy for his introductions to Lamb and Coleridge. D'Orsay's young wife had left him, and gossip attributed the separation to his adulterous relations with his wife's stepmother. Ostracised by fashionable society, Lady Blessington bravely set out to establish herself as hostess to the less conventional literary world, and Robinson's influence might be useful among men of letters. Landor assured him that she was "the most devoted wife he ever knew", that "she was by far the most beautiful woman he ever saw", and that she was now "about thirty"—though Robinson noted, "I should have thought her older", and she was in fact forty-three. Robinson went again on the evening of 29th September to see Landor at her house, and "my two interviews have left a delightful impression".

Landor returned to Italy with the gift of an engraving of Lady Blessington's portrait, "that it may sometimes remind you of the original", and she asked that they should "by letters keep up our friendly intercourse"—"you will tell me what you think and feel in your Tuscan retirement, and I will tell you what I do, in this modern Babylon, where thinking and feeling are almost unknown".

§ 2

Julius Hare and his friend Worsley accompanied Landor when he left England, crossing by steamer to Rotterdam, at the beginning of October 1832. Having travelled through Belgium and up the Rhine, they visited Hare's half-sister Georgiana at Bonn. There August Wilhelm von Schlegel was invited to meet Landor and presented himself in full dress, wearing orders. "Among other novelties, he remarked that Niebuhr was totally unfit for a historian." This Landor considered an affront to Julius Hare as Niebuhr's translator, and retorted, "Perhaps Mr. Schlegel, who has found out that Shakespeare is a poet, may discover that Niebuhr is a historian." Writing to Robinson from Frankfort on 20th October, he likened Schlegel to "a little pot-bellied pony tricked out with stars, buckles, and ribands, looking askance from his ring and halter in the market, for an apple from one, a morsel of bread from another, a fig of ginger from a third, and a pat from everybody". His meeting next morning with the patriot, Ernst Moritz Arndt, "settled the bile this coxcomb of the bazaar had excited". On Arndt's death in 1860 he wrote:

> Arndt! in thy orchard we shall meet no more
> To talk of freedom and of peace revived.
> We stood, and looking down across the Rhine
> Heard fifes and choral voices far below.

At Frankfort he lifted his hat in passing the house where Goethe was born; in the following week he passed through Nuremburg, Augsburg, and Munich.

In going thro the Tyrol, the snow fell upon us furiously, and we were in danger of passing the winter at Innspruck. I conversed with several of the companions of Andrew Hofer, and received from one of them a narration of his death. Nothing was ever more heroic, not even his life. He said "I pray God to protect my children and their mother, and to pardon her brother, and to let his *fault* be forgotten". Now what do you think his *fault* was? Betraying to the French this brave and righteous man.

Already he had portrayed Hofer heroically in an imaginary conversation, and he contributed "The Death of Hofer" to Ablett's *Literary Hours* in 1837.

In Venice and Padua he was a "delightful and instructive" companion in looking at pictures, and Hare was impressed by his "inimitable skill in bargaining" when Landor bought for him a Giovanni da Udine and a head of St. Cecilia, which he inclined to think an early Raphael though perhaps a Perugino. They reached Fiesole, after a journey of two months, on 30th November, but Hare and Worsley were Landor's guests for three weeks before proceeding to Rome for Christmas.

On 22nd January following, Landor wrote to thank Georgiana Hare for successfully engaging a German tutor for his children, and concluded with reference to his stay at Bonn:

I hope the good and cordial Arndt is well. The other gentleman I met at Bonn I do not quite remember, excepting the little person, or rather pony, in ribbands—apparently for fair or market—and for which (had I any superfluous money) I might have offered three dollars. I have not however so easily forgotten the frank and military and gentlemanly manners of your brother, whom I should have liked at first sight, even if he had not been a Hare.

12

DOMESTIC BREACH

When the mimosas shall have made
(O'erarching) an unbroken shade;
And the rose-laurels let to breathe
Scarcely a favourite flower beneath;
When the young cypresses which now
Look at the olives, brow to brow,
Cheer'd by the breezes of the south
Shall shoot above the acacia's growth,
One peradventure of my four
Turning some former fondness o'er,
At last impatient of the blame
Cast madly on a father's name,
May say, and check the chided tear,
"I wish he still were with us here."
—(1846)

There were changes at Fiesole after Landor's return from England. His eldest son Arnold, now fifteen, showed signs of being "spoiled" and in need of discipline, as Landor wrote to Lady Blessington on 14th March 1833:

Arnold is idle. A German tutor is coming to manage him within a few days. I can hardly bring him to construe a little Greek with me; and, what is worse, he is not always disposed to fence with me. I foresee he will be a worse dancer than I am, if possible. In vain I tell him, what is very true, that I have suffered more from my bad dancing than from all the other misfortunes and miseries of my life put together.

To his sisters a few days later he showed himself tolerant though aware of Arnold's faults:

Good Arnold is inclined to be idle. His new tutor will have more authority with him than I have & he is now coming to an age, when ambition will begin to operate a little. But let him be healthy, honorable & well-bred, & I care little about his learning & not much about his accomplishments.

To Georgiana Hare, who engaged the tutor, he outlined what was required:

I shall be most happy to see Mr. Schiems in March, and hope he will be contented to remain with us for several years. My children of course speak perfectly well their native language, the Italian; the English nearly as fluently; and Arnold and Julia are near proficient in the French. I hope M. Schiems will allow Julia to benefit by his lessons. She and Walter are more studious than Arnold, tho certainly not more acute. Habits of regularity are what they all want most. I shall not pretend to interfere with whatever system Mr. Schiems may deem proper.

The tutor remained for rather more than a year, but apparently declined responsibility for Julia as well as for the boys, and within a few months a German governess, the Countess von Schaffgotsch, was added to the household.

Lord Burghersh had been succeeded as British minister at Florence by George Hamilton Seymour, who subsequently rose to high rank in the diplomatic service. With this "unaffected, good, sensible man", whose wife was "as beautiful and as good as an angel", Landor became on terms of friendly intimacy, and his complaints to the president of the Buon Governo were now respectfully received on being officially presented and endorsed by the British minister. Lord Normanby had returned to England, but Lord Wenlock came regularly to Florence, and "nothing can be more friendly", wrote Landor in July this year, "than he has always been to me".

Charles Brown and Kirkup were still at Florence. A young clergyman named Hutton, introduced by Landor's sisters, became a regular guest at Fiesole; Landor was "quite delighted with his society", as he was "everything that an English Clergyman should be" and "very fond of the children, which alone would win my heart". He introduced Hutton "as an exemplary man" to Lord Wenlock, who promised "that he would give £50 yearly to the English church here".

Five years before he had complained to his mother, "there are so many people in Florence who bring me letters of introduction, that I have hardly an hour to myself", but now he seems to have accommodated his habits to frequent visitors. Early in the year came Sir George Phillips, a wealthy industrialist and munificent patron of art, of whom the painter Haydon wrote that "a more benevolent man never lived". Commiserating with his sisters over the result of the Reform election, Landor sought to dispel their fears of the tradesmen and manufacturers returned to Parliament:

I assure you there is not a more honorable, a more generous, or a more rightly-minded man than Sir G. Philips. I once dined with him in London; he heard I was in Florence, and came to visit me after thirty years. He is highly educated and well connected. Even the most excellent of all earthly beings, Ablett, is the son of a Manchester tradesman, and the father was as irreproachable as the son.

His old schoolfellow, Henry Francis Cary, came for three days in early May, and was taken to see a Correggio owned by Trajan Wallis. Landor remembered this visit when writing *Letters of a Conservative*:

When I was a member of the university, I remember at Christ-church two gentlemen of the name of Carey: one was called the Dean's Carey; the other had no patronymick. He however was considered as among the best scholars in Oxford, although young, and was remarkable for the simplicity of his manners, the mildness of his disposition, his thoughtful and religious turn of mind, his gentleness and his modesty. The two in fact were not easily mistaken. At the present time, one receives, as bishop of Saint Asaph, what is called only eight thousand pounds a year, but has often been ten thousand; the other, as librarian to the British museum, I know not exactly what, but certainly a good deal less than Crockford and Lord Sefton pay their cooks.

A few days later, when Julius Hare and Thomas Worsley were in Florence on their return journey to England, Ralph Waldo Emerson dined with Landor in their company, having obtained an introduction through the American sculptor, Horatio Greenough. Earnest and humourless as any of his countrymen at thirty, Emerson was pleasantly surprised on meeting Landor; from gossip as well as from his books he had derived "an impression of Achillean wrath—an untameable petulance", but found that "his courtesy veiled that haughty mind, and he was the most patient and gentle of hosts".

He praised the beautiful cyclamen which grows all about Florence; he admired Washington; talked of Wordsworth, Byron, Massinger, Beaumont and Fletcher. To be sure, he is decided in his opinions, likes to surprise, and is well content to impress, if possible, his English whim upon the immutable past. No great man ever had a great son, if Philip and Alexander be not an exception; and Philip he calls the greater man. In art, he loves the Greeks, and in sculpture, them only. He prefers the Venus to everything else, and, after that, the head of Alexander, in the gallery here. He prefers John of Bologna to Michael Angelo; in painting, Raffaelle; and shares the growing taste for Perugino and the early masters.

"Sir James Mackintosh he would not praise, nor my Carlyle . . . He pestered me with Southey; but who is Southey?"

Two days later, on Friday 17th May, Emerson and Greenough breakfasted with Landor.

He entertained us at once with reciting half a dozen hexameter lines of Julius Cæsar's!—from Donatus, he said. He glorified Lord Chesterfield more than was necessary, and undervalued Burke, and undervalued Socrates . . . I had visited Professor Amici, who had shown me his microscopes, magnifying (it was said) two thousand diameters; and I spoke of the uses to which they were applied. Landor despised entomology, yet, in the same breath, said, "the sublime was in a grain of dust". I suppose I teased him about recent writers, but he professed never to have heard of Herschel, *not even by name.* One room was full of pictures, which he likes to show, especially one piece, standing before which, he said "he would give fifty guineas to the man that would swear it was a Domenichino".

Weary of the "cloud of pictures", Emerson wished to see his library, but Hare "told me that Mr. Landor gives away his books, and has never more than a dozen at a time in his house". At home Emerson summed up for judgment:

> Mr. Landor carries to its height the love of freak which the English delight to indulge, as if to signalise their commanding freedom. He has a wonderful brain, despotic, violent, and inexhaustible, meant for a soldier, by what chance converted to letters, in which there is nor a style nor a tint not known to him, yet with an English appetite for action and heroes. The thing done avails, and not what is said about it. An original sentence, a step forward, is worth more than all the censures. Landor is strangely undervalued in England; usually ignored; and sometimes savagely attacked in the Reviews. The criticism may be right, or wrong, and is quickly forgotten; but year after year the scholar must still go back to Landor for a multitude of elegant sentences—for wisdom, wit, and indignation that are unforgetable.

Unabashed to find this impression of a long-forgotten conversation published after twenty-three years in *English Traits*, Landor replied in the autumn of 1856 with a brilliant exposition of dialectic in a *Letter from W. S. Landor to R. W. Emerson*. Softening the reproof with graceful compliment, he rebuked the growing fashion for interviewing: "The short conversations we held at my Tuscan Villa were insufficient for an estimate of my character and opinions." He related the education of his taste in pictures—"my Domenichino, about which I doubted, has been authenticated by M. Cosveldt; my Raffaelle by M. Dennistoune"— but "curious as I was in collecting specimens of the earlier painters, I do not prefer them to the works either of their nearer successors or to those of the present day".

> I am sorry to have "*pestered you with Southey*", and to have excited the inquiry, "*Who is Southey?*" I will answer the question. Southey is the poet who has written the most imaginative poem of any in our own times, English or Continental; such is *The Curse of Kehama*. Southey is the proseman who has written the purest prose; Southey is the critic the most cordial and the least invidious. Show me another, of any note, without captiousness, without arrogance, and without malignity.
>
> *Slow rises worth by poverty deprest.*

But Southey raised it.
> Certainly you could not make me praise Mackintosh. What is there eminently to praise in him? Are there not twenty men and women at the present hour who excel him in style and genius?

He discussed Carlyle, with whom by then he was personally acquainted, and digressed into trenchant statement of political opinions. He compared his own with Carlyle's "despairing or satirical views of literature at this moment":

I am little fond of satire, and less addicted to despair. It seems to me that never in this country was there a greater number of good writers than now; and some are excellent. Our epic is the novel or romance.

After discussing Scott and Wordsworth:

I never *glorified* Chesterfield; yet he surely is among the best of our writers in regard to style, and appears to have formed Horace Walpole's and Sterne's, a style purely English. His Letters were placed by Beresford, Archbishop of Tuan, in the hands of his daughters . . . perhaps the neglect of them at the present day is one reason why a gentleman is almost as rare as a man of genius.

I am not conscious that I underrate Burke: never have I placed any of his parliamentary contemporaries in the same rank with him . . .

I do not "undervalue Socrates". Being the cleverest of the Sophists, he turned the fraternity into ridicule. . . . To compare his philosophy (if indeed you can catch it) with the philosophy of Epicurus and Epictetus, whose systems meet, is insanity.

I do not "despise entomology". I am ignorant of it; as indeed I am of almost all science.

I love also flowers and plants; but I know less about them than is known by a beetle or a butterfly.

I must have been misunderstood, or have been culpably inattentive, if I said "I knew not Herschell even by name". The father's I knew well, pernicious madman who tore America from England, and who rubbed his hands when the despatches announced to him the battle of Bunker's Hill, in which he told his equerry that his soldiers had "*got well peppered*". Probably I had not then received in Italy the admirable writings of the great Herschell's greater son. . . .

I make no complaint . . . that "Landor is strangely under-valued in England". I have heard it before, but I never have taken the trouble to ascertain it. Here I find that I am "savagely attacked in the Reviews". Nothing more likely; I never see them; my acquaintances lie in a different and far distant quarter. Some honors have, however, been conferred on me in the literary world. Southey dedicated to me his *Kehama*; James his *Attila*: he and Dickens invited me to be godfather to their sons. Moreover, I think as many have offered me the flatteries of verse as ever were offered to any but Louis the Fourteenth.

Emerson was young and unknown when he was entertained at Fiesole; in the following month came an even younger man, Richard Monckton Milnes, just down from Cambridge and bearing an introduction from his former tutor, Julius Hare. Immediately after his arrival at Florence, Milnes fell ill with an "intermittent fever", not then diagnosed as malaria, and Landor insisted that he should leave his hotel "to come and stay at his beautiful villa as long as I liked". He stayed some weeks, for, as he wrote to his mother, "Mrs. Landor was as attentive to me and kind as if I had been at home," and "I have my books, and Mr.

Landor's delightful conversation, and my whole day to myself, and a carriage at my orders whenever I want to drive out."

To a young man feeding his ego on the grist of experience, Landor was a fortunate accident; Milnes gleaned a few ideas from him and proudly quoted his approval of his compositions. He possessed a good memory, which was stimulated by Forster's biography to embellish the most discerning monograph written by any of Landor's friends. His prolonged visit enabled him to observe the household with a familiarity available only to close friends, like Brown and Hare, who left no written record. Like Ianthe's son, he had heard much of Landor's local notoriety for "a supposed eccentricity of conduct and violence of demeanour"—he had been expelled from school after thrashing the headmaster, sent down from the university for shooting at a fellow of the college, and outlawed from England for "felling to the ground" a cross-examining barrister. He found in fact an elderly gentleman of "stately and agreeable presence", whose guests "spoke of his affectionate reception, of his complimentary old-world manners, and of his elegant though simple hospitality". He delighted to discuss his pictures, and Milnes noted that those sold at Manchester in 1836 "in no way represented the value of his collection", the best remaining in possession of his family. He liked plenty of space in a room, despising what he called "carpentry" and the English notion of "comfort"—"there is something smothering in the very word", he said; "it takes the air from about one". Mirrors and lustres were "only fit for inns". He disliked dining out—"I cannot bear to be from home a single evening," he wrote this year to his sisters, "and I hate everything public, even music" —preferring to choose his own food and to have it cooked to his liking. "His highest luxury was dining alone, and with little light, and he would often resort to Florence for that purpose." He said "a spider was a gentleman—he eats his fly in secret".

Boythorn is credited with a passionate love of animals and birds, and Milnes remembered how, while his relations with his neighbours were "friendly without familiarity", Landor's favourite companion was his dog. He was never without a dog of some sort—in his later Bath days, his pugnacious Pomeranian called Pomero was well-known; lastly he had another of the same breed named Giallo; now it was Parigi, a splendid mastiff. He would take Parigi's head between his knees, and say, "Ah, if Lord Grey (or any other notoriety of the hour) had a thousandth part of your sense how different would be things in England!" He despised fear of dogs; "when a dog flies at you, reason with it", he said, and "remember how well-behaved the Molossian dogs were when Ulysses sat down in the midst of them as an equal".

Milnes, who knew all the famous talkers of his day, rated Landor's conversation highly; "so affluent, animated, and coloured, so rich in

knowledge and illustration, so gay and yet so weighty—such bitter
irony and such lofty praise, uttered with a voice fibrous in all its tones,
whether gentle or fierce— it equalled, if not surpassed, all that has been
related of the table-talk of men eminent for social speech". He liked
open discussion, frank in argument and statement of opinion, as Mrs.
Battle liked her whist, with "a clear fire, a clean hearth, and the
rigour of the game". He had no use for masculine bawdry over port;
"I enjoy no society," he said, "that makes too free with God or the
ladies."

Landor developed an affection for Milnes, who was the first of the
rising generation to win his friendship. "I am grieved that my good
Milnes, so pure-hearted, so affectionate, should mix with the busy
adventurers of either faction," he wrote in 1839 to Lady Blessington;
"his genius is so very far above them, and his fortune so independent."
Since Milnes was wealthy, Landor deplored his active participation in
politics, believing that a man possessed of both the necessary means
and talents demeaned his dignity by pursuing personal ambition, and
wasted his opportunity of self-dedication to philosophy and letters. His
judgment as usual prejudiced by affection, he over-estimated Milnes's
talent, and five years later Crabb Robinson disgustedly recorded of a
breakfast party "a great deal of rattling on the part of Landor",
who asserted that Milnes was "the greatest poet now living in
England".

Apart from the satisfaction of shocking Robinson, Landor had no
other motive for this exaggerated opinion than amiable sponsorship.
He introduced Milnes to Charles Brown, who was persuaded to present
him with his material for Keats's biography, so that Milnes's *Life,
Letters, and Literary Remains of John Keats* became the first official tribute
to the poet. Perceiving that the surest way to his host's heart lay in
attentions to his children, Milnes addressed verses to the two younger
boys, Carlino, "a child with black eyes and golden hair", and the
eleven-year-old Walter, "sweet, serious child,—strange boy", who so
impressed his father with "a most wonderful taste and facility in
drawing" that "he goes to Florence to take lessons".

Short of sending the boys away to school, Landor was doing his best
with tutors and teachers to educate his children. "It was a kind of
pride with him that all children loved him," wrote Milnes, but "in his
demeanour to his own his tenderness was excessive". "He was always
drawing analogies between children and flowers," and Milnes noticed
how "in his garden he would bend over the flowers with a sort of worship, but rarely touched one of them". Landor was a devoted and
indulgent but unwise parent, and his children were growing beyond the
age to be tended like flowers. Milnes saw no reason to "detail the
miserable domestic tumults" that developed after the time of his visit;

he remarked discreetly, "At that time his domesticity, though not cheerful, was not angry."

More casual visitors naturally noticed nothing wrong between Landor and his wife. Among such visitors in the autumn of 1833 were Captain Basil Hall, a minor celebrity as a writer of travel adventures, and Bulwer Lytton, who came with an introduction from Lady Blessington and wrote to her his impressions of Landor. As the author of *Pelham* and *Eugene Aram*, Bulwer wrote with the self-conscious affectation of a newly-arrived fashionable novelist:

> One is at home instantly with men of real genius: their oddities, their humours, don't put one out half so much as the formal regularity of your half-clever prigs. But Landor, thanks to your introduction, had no humours, no oddities, for me. He invited me to his villa, which is charmingly situated, and smoothed himself down so much, that I thought him one of the best-bred men I ever met, as well as one of the most really able: (pity, nevertheless, so far as his talent is concerned, that he pets paradoxes so much: he keeps them as other people keep dogs, coaxes them, plays with them, and now and then sets them to bite a disagreeable intruder).

Though Bulwer described Landor as "particularly kind to me", neither he nor his beautiful but vulgar wife much impressed Landor; the dandified young novelist was too absorbed in worldly ambition to win his sympathy, and Rosina Bulwer was to be one of the few women who asked anything of him in vain. He esteemed Bulwer's novels slightly till, more than twenty years later, he compared *The Caxtons* with Sterne.

Landor referred to Bulwer's recent visit when writing to his sisters early in November 1833:

> I and all the children, and Julia too, have had the grippe . . . I am expecting every day my friend Augustus Hare and his brother Marcus, who has just now married a daughter of Sir John Stanley. The Hares are beyond all comparison the most pleasant family *of men* I ever was acquainted with. Francis wants me to dine with him at Rome on Christmas day, Sir John Paul's birthday, when a dozen or two of both families will meet at his house. But I have old recollections, and old feelings about Christmas day, and never will dine from home again on that day.

This was Augustus Hare's last visit, for Landor wrote to Lady Blessington the following April:

> The death of poor Augustus has grieved me very much. He promised to spend a few days with me on his return. Were I certain of seeing my departed friends in another life, I know not anything that would detain me in this. Pazienza! Those who hope much fear something.

He continued to make new and lasting friendships. William Sandford— addressed in verse as "Sandford! the friend of all the brave"—became a frequent guest at Fiesole at this time, and remained an unobtrusive but staunch friend till Landor's death. The novelist G. P. R. James made a practice of wintering at Florence for several years after the publication of his most successful novel, *Richelieu*, in 1829, and was renting the Villa Palmieri at Fiesole when Mary Boyle, a daughter of Admiral Sir Courtenay Boyle, met Landor at his house early in 1834. Young enough to be Landor's son, James shared few qualities in common with him except a preference for country life, freedom from jealousy of his fellow writers, and a vast knowledge of history; he kept aloof from literary society and few seem to have penetrated his quiet reserve. Yet a sincere affection grew between them. "You cannot overvalue James," wrote Landor to Mary Boyle after knowing him nearly ten years. "There is not on God's earth (I like this expression, vulgar or not) any better creature of his hand." To the same correspondent he wrote again: "Literary men in general are the vilest of the human race; happy we, who enjoy the friendship of one incomparably good and great in all his works, words, and thoughts." Affection as usual prejudiced his judgment; magnifying James's talent, he preferred his historical romances to Scott's. James was stimulated by Landor's conversation; "I stagnate when I do not see you", he wrote when inviting him to stay at the Hampshire home where he lived from 1837 to 1839. Landor was godfather to James's son born in 1832, and James dedicated to him his novel *Attila* in 1837.

§ 2

Landor told Southey in November 1824 that he was writing an imaginary conversation introducing Shakespeare, but this must have been laid aside or destroyed when he quarrelled with the publisher Taylor. Apparently the idea was revived by reading Lamb's present of the *Letters of Sir John Falstaff*, for he wrote to Lady Blessington on 8th April 1834:

For some time I have been composing *Citation and Examination of Wil. Shakespeare, Euseby Treen, Joseph Carneby, and Silas Gough, before the Worshipful Sir Thomas Lucy, Knight, touching deer-stalking, on the 19th day of September in the year of grace 1582, now first published from original papers.*
This is full of fun, I know not whether of wit. It is the only thing I ever wrote that is likely to sell. It contains about 300 pp. If I send it, will you have the kindness to offer it to Colburn, not as mine—though probably he may recollect my handwriting. If he prints it, he shall give me two hundred pounds for it. No other publisher can give it so extensive a circulation, otherwise I would rather burn it than he should have it. I hope to send it you by Marcus Hare, who returns to England shortly.

Within a few days Horatio Greenough introduced a literary countryman contrasting with the earnest Emerson. Having "covered" the Mediterranean countries, N. P. Willis was now hurrying to England to write notes on literary London for a work called *Pencillings By the Way*, distinguishing him as an early exponent of the gossip journalism that attached the stigma of vulgarity to the American national character during the following century. Without confessing that he was a "gentleman of the Press", he presented himself as "an attaché to the American Legation, a poet and literator"; Crabb Robinson described his appearance as "that of a dandy—one who strives to be genteel". He successfully imposed upon many less gracious than Landor; even a lady so formidable as Harriet Martineau allowed that "there was something rather engaging in the round face, brisk air and *enjouement* of the young man". Landor himself related of Willis:

He expressed a wish to reprint in America a large selection of my *Imaginary Conversations*, omitting the political. He assured me they were the most *thumbed* books on his table. With a smile at so energetic an expression of perhaps an undesirable distinction, I offered him unreservedly and unconditionally my only copy of the five printed volumes, interlined and interleaved in most places, which I had employed several years in improving and enlarging, together with my manuscript of the sixth, unpublished.

At the same time he gave Willis letters of introduction to Crabb Robinson and Lady Blessington, writing to the latter:

This will be presented to you by Mr. Willis, an American gentleman attached to the Legation at Paris. It is not, however, in this character that I introduce him to you; but in that of the best poet the New World has produced in any part of it.
He will bring you the Examination of Shakespeare. If you offer it to Colburn, pray do nothing more. It is the only thing I ever wrote that ever can be popular. I will venture a wager that two thousand copies are sold in six months.

Having paused suitably for copy at Milan, Geneva, and Paris, Willis fulfilled his mission to Lady Blessington on the second day after his arrival in London. "I have received your ms., and am delighted with it," she wrote on 9th June; "Mr. Willis delivered it to me with your letter, and I endeavoured to shew him all the civility in my power, in honour of his recommendation."

Without approaching Colburn, she immediately secured an advantageous offer from Saunders & Otley, a firm which had just succeeded in enticing her own novels away from Bentley. By the time Landor received this information on 7th July, he was no longer concerned with profit from the publication:

My zeal is quite evaporated for the people I hoped to benefit by the publication of 'The Trial of Shakespeare.' I find my old school-fellow (whom, by-the-bye, I never knew, but who placed enough confidence in me to beg my assistance in his distress) has been gaming. Had he even tried but a trifle of assassination, I should have felt for him; or, in fact, had he done almost anything else. But to rely on superior skill in spoliation, is less pardonable than to rely on superior courage, or than to avenge an affront in a sudden and summary way.

Now a thousand thanks for the trouble you have taken. MM. Saunders and Otley ought to hazard nothing by me. . . . It would be dishonourable in me to accept all they offer. I will not take the entire profits. I will take half and shall be glad if they begin to print the volume as soon as they conveniently can.

Five days later he wrote again, enclosing "A Conference of Master Edmund Spenser . . . with the Earle of Essex, touching the state of Ireland", to be added to the *Examination*—an imaginary conversation germinated in a letter written to Southey ten years before:

In Ireland the errors of many centuries are to be corrected. The worst of these was omitting to extirpate Romish influence when it could be extirpated easily, as in England and in Scotland. The death of Cromwell, usurper as he was, was by far the greatest misfortune that ever befell the English nation, not excepting the ministry of Pitt. How very interesting even still, is the account your 'Master' Spenser gives of Irish affairs in his times! I have often turned to it, when I could not go on with the *Faery Queen*.

Mr. Otley, of Saunders & Otley, expressed himself "sensibly touched" by Landor's generosity, and lost no time over the printing. The book was published anonymously in October at 9s. 6d. It was reviewed in the *Examiner* of 30th November with extravagant praise as "a book of remarkable genius—an honour to the age"—later more critically in the *Quarterly Review*. The reviewer in the *Examiner* was John Forster, then a young man of twenty-two, who maintained his opinion thirty-five years later with a lengthy eulogy in his biography of Landor. It was ironical that, having received such rare and reluctant approval over so many years, Landor should have first experienced unstinted praise for his most worthless work to date, which was thus briefly analysed by Crabb Robinson:

It is a sort of semi-poetical and semi-humorous account of the examination of Shakespeare for deer-stealing. He wins the heart of the magistrate, Sir Thomas Lucy, whilst he offends the clerk, the Rev. Silas, by his sarcasms against the Church. The magistrate has manifested a determination to forgive him, but wants him to give up his love to Anne Hathaway, on which the young poet *bolts* and flies to London, where he becomes the great poet. . . . I cannot conceive who is the author.

Later Robinson admitted, "I did not recognise it as Landor's; perhaps I was unwilling to ascribe to him anything I so little liked." Too successfully Landor imitated the archaisms of Elizabethan expression, dissipating his normal force of style and degenerating into what Stevenson called "tushery"; too extravagant for an illusion of reality, the treatment is too erudite and elaborate for burlesque.

Landor was less concerned with its reception than with the appearance of the book. Though he deprecated with gallant diffidence that she should "have really taken the trouble to overlook the sheets", Lady Blessington insisted on entrusting the proof-reading to nobody else, and she neglected to compare the proof with the copy, as appears from Landor's letter to Southey:

I hope my publisher sent you the *Examination of Shakespeare*—alas that I should say it! the very worst-printed book that ever fell into my hands. "*Volubly* discreet"! "slipped into" for "stripped unto"! "Sit mute" for "stand," with many others! And then there are words I never use: such as "utmost"; I always write "uttermost". In fact the misprints amount to 40 of the grosser kind, and I know not how many of the smaller!

Chivalry forbade a hint of his disappointment to Lady Blessington, but a few months later, on sending her a contribution to the annual she was editing, he wrote:

Let me entreat of you to retain my orthography in the poem I send you, lest I should appear to countenance any violation, any innovation, of our language. There never was, and never could be, such a word as cherish'*d,* as clasp'*d,* as shriek'*d,* as cross'*d,* as dropp'*d,* as press'*d.* And if you insert the *e,* you had destroyed the verse. I would retain both cross*ed* and cro*st,* dropp*ed* and dro*pt* &c. But we ought to use in writing the words we use in speaking, and we should write them as we speak them, consistently with analogy. I write as Englishmen wrote before literary men courted the vulgar, or gentlemen were the hirelings of booksellers; and I have not altered any word whatever; I have restored the rights of many.

His correspondence with Gabb reveals that, as early as 1813, he wrote *exclame* and *proclame* as true to Latin derivation, *favor* and *honor, fulfill* and *compell*; in a note to the revised *Gebir* of 1803, he cited the authority of Milton for spelling *therefor* and *wherefor* without the final *e,* and asked "why *preceed* and *exceed* are spelt differently in their termination from *recede*". But he had not then begun to insist that *til* should be written as in *until,* and many of the notions in his Tooke-Johnson dialogue— which he considered "highly necessary for the restoration of our language"—derived from learning Italian and renewed classical studies on his first coming to Italy. In *Tait's Magazine* for March 1847 De Quincey challenged Landor's spelling theories in an essay on "Orthographic Mutineers"; he mocked Landor's "caprice" in calling Aristotle Aristoteles, because Empedocles must then be called Empedocle, arguing that, as he says Virgil for Virgilius, "he ought to say Valer for Valerius; and yet again he ought *not*; because, as he says Tully and not Tull for Tullius, so also he is bound in Christian equity to say Valery for Valer", and as he says Ovid for Ovidius, "he must call Didius Julianus by the shocking name of *Did,*—which is the same thing as Tit, since T is D soft".

§ 3

The German tutor procured by Georgiana Hare proved "a very good quiet man, who makes no noise in the house, and is likely to make as little in the world at large", but after fourteen months—in May 1834—the Prussian law required his recall to his native country. Lord Wenlock had died the previous month, and his secretary Mac-Carthy was engaged for the duties of the German tutor, who was expected to return after complying with Prussian regulations. Hearing of this engagement, Henry Landor wrote to warn his brother that Lord Wenlock had latterly expressed dissatisfaction with his secretary, and Landor replied in June:

I also believe that Lord Wenlock became but little fond of Macarthy, but Dr. Barkhead *knows* that he promised him an encrease of salary. At Lord Wenlock's death he was forced to borrow 8 dollars. During the absence of Arnold's tutor, I took him into my house in that capacity, hearing that he was absolutely destitute. I find him attentive to his duties.

The German tutor duly returned but "obtained a good situation at Rome", and MacCarthy continued in Landor's employment. During that summer the Countess von Schaffgotsch, a loud-voiced woman of voracious appetite, departed unregretted, and was satisfactorily replaced by "the governess of Mrs. Colingwood's daughters, Miss D'Arville".

On 17th November 1834 Landor replied to a letter from his sister Elizabeth saying that "Mrs. Southey is quite deranged & in an Asylum at York":

I had heard from Mrs Hodgeson (*sic*), whom you remember as Margaret Holford, a deplorable account of Mrs Southey and it totally deprived me of rest. Poor good Southey! What must be his sufferings! . . . Arnold has the finest voice I ever heard. He is more shy than he was and has less manner, but never was there a more perfect being in temper and principle. He takes too little pains to be pleasing, and yet he pleases everybody . . . I received a letter last week from my friend Ablett. He reminds me of the promise I made him to renew my visit in three years. Certainly I shall see you next April or May. Julia will go to her mother, and take the two youngest. I will make my first visit to you, with Arnold and Julia, and after a week or fortnight procede to Denbighshire.

Still he persisted in praising Arnold, now nearly seventeen, though he recognised his faults of manner; he deluded himself that Arnold "pleases everybody", for Monckton Milnes told Crabb Robinson that he was "a wicked boy", and Milnes's last opportunity for observing Arnold was during his visit to Florence in February 1835. On this occasion Landor gave Milnes a letter to carry to Southey:

LANDOR'S WIFE AND TWO ELDER CHILDREN

(*Julia on her knee, and Arnold*)

From a painting by Trajan Wallis about 1825

I need not tell you that I have grieved, and not for an hour or two, at your afflictions. Nor did it satisfy my mind, nor can it yours, that you still have more reason for contentment, and higher sources both of consolation and delight, than any man on earth. The human heart was never made for listening, and even this truth will find but tardy admittance into yours. I am so disgusted with politics and politicians that I never read a newspaper, but I hear that some respect has been shown to the services you have rendered the country by your writings. Poor Coleridge has not lived for the restoration of what was taken from him. I wish he had indulged less in metaphysics. Had I seen him a second time, I would have asked him whether the principal merit of the Germans does not consist in nomenclature and arrangement. . . . My friend Mr. Robinson has not told me whether Charles Lamb has left any writings behind him. . . . He was a most affectionate creature, pleasurable and even-tempered. Him too I saw but once, and yet I think of him as if I had known him forty years. . . . Is there anything yet left upon the earth? or is there only a void of space between you and me. . . . I began a conversation between Pericles and Aspasia, and thought I could do better by a series of letters between them, not uninterrupted; for the letters should begin with their first friendship, should give place to their conversations afterwards, and recommence on their supposed separation during the plague of Athens. Few materials are extant: Bayle, Menage, Thucydides, Plutarch, and hardly anything more. So much the better. The coast is clear: there are neither rocks nor weeds before me. But I am writing as if I had not torn to pieces all their love-letters and orations! Few were completed.

This letter's tone of sombre reflection harmonised with the mood prevailing in *Pericles and Aspasia*, on which he worked during the following months.

Soon after Milnes's visit Mrs. Sophia Paynter, half-sister of Rose Aylmer, came to Florence with an introduction from her half-brother, Lord Aylmer. When Landor had last seen her, she had been a little girl in pigtails, walking on the Swansea sands with her hand in that of her half-sister. "Give me Swansea for scenery and climate," he had written a few years before to his sister Ellen. "If ever it should be my fortune, which I cannot expect, and do not much hope, to return to England, I shall pass the remainder of my days in the neighbourhood of Swansea, between that place and the Mumbles." In Mrs. Paynter's younger daughter Rose he recognised a resemblance to her long-dead aunt.

Moving from Florence to Rome, Mrs. Paynter carried introductions to Francis Hare—"certainly the best informed as well as the best natured man you will meet in Italy"—and to Miss Mackenzie of Seaforth, with whom Landor had corresponded since his visit to Rome with Hare. He wrote to her on 3rd April:

Since you left Florence I have rarely gone within the gates. Yesterday I finished the planting of two thousand vines, and in the autumn I shall plant as many more, besides seventy olives. I did think of going to England, but if I do, I shall return by November. . . . I am losing all my friends. Mr.

s

Brown, an intelligent and most friendly man, is gone to England with a resolution never to return to Italy. Mr. James goes to-morrow with the same resolution. I cannot bear the idea of seeing anything for the last time. There is something in those two monosyllables that weighs very heavily on the heart; more heavily than volumes of school divinity. *Coragio, coragio.* We must not talk in this manner.

For four years past politics had failed to excite the stimulus of rebellion. While he did not share the horror of reform expressed by his sisters, Southey, and Wordsworth, he felt no enthusiasm for its changes. "I hate Tory principles and Whig practices," he wrote to Lady Blessington in 1833, and to the same correspondent on 28th November 1834:

I would not live in London the six winter months for a thousand pounds a week. No, not even with the privilege of hanging a Tory on every lamp-arm to the right, and a Whig on every one to the left the whole extent of Piccadilly. This goes sadly against my patriotism. Do not tell any of the radicals that I am grown so indifferent to the interests of our country.

Despondency he had experienced before—often in youth. But rarely before had he expressed indifference; never before had he been so indecisive as on this projected visit to England.

His state of indecision derived from his "domesticity", which had deteriorated since the summer of 1833, when Milnes thought it "not cheerful", but "not angry". Like Coleridge before him, he had discovered the fallacy of Southey's advice, "Find out a woman whom you can esteem and love will grow more surely out of esteem, than esteem will out of love." Like Coleridge, Wordsworth, and Southey himself, he had embraced marriage as a makeshift, because "*Rest* is the object to be sought"—rest from the emotional stress he suffered in his passion for Ianthe. When, at thirty-six, he chose a girl of seventeen "with very few accomplishments," and her sister Lucy Thuillier apparently queried the wisdom of his choice, he replied in verse:

> In Clementina's artless mien
>   Lucilla asks me what I see,
> And are the roses of sixteen
>   Enough for me?
>
> Lucilla asks, if that be all,
>   Have I not cull'd as sweet before . . .
> Ah yes, Lucilla! and their fall
>   I still deplore.
>
> I now behold another scene,
>   Where Pleasure beams with heaven's own light,
> More pure, more constant, more serene,
>   And not less bright. . . .

> Faith, on whose breast the Loves repose,
>   Whose chain of flowers no force can sever,
> And Modesty who, when she goes,
>   Is gone for ever.

When Walter Birch warned him, "An excellent wife is seldom made perfect to our hands, but is in part the creation of the husband after marriage, the result of his character and behaviour acting upon her own," he replied, "You are right—that the character of women depends very much on ourselves." It was reasonable to suppose that a girl might be more easily moulded than a mature woman, and Julia Thuillier was "pretty, graceful and good-tempered—three things indispensable to my happiness".

The vexations and anxieties at Llanthony created unpropitious circumstances in the first years of the marriage; a girl of twenty might well have felt cheated in her expectations of marriage with a man of fortune. Dismay at banishment excited recriminations, and he left her in Jersey when she referred, in her sister's presence, to "her own fault in marrying such an old man". He may have left her the more readily from having heard of Jane Swift's recent widowhood; however that may have been, after their reconciliation his wife must have known that he had never loved her.

Subduing resentment at this knowledge, she assembled her defences. Finding that Landor, like most physically strong men, was deeply moved by sight of pain, she assumed a habit of querulous indisposition as a weapon of reproach. At Como in June 1816 Robert Landor, a sympathetic witness, remarked that she "looks thin, but not pale; talks much of dying, and of returning to Bath, preferring the latter a little". After the birth of her children she became a hypochondriac; Landor's letters to his mother and sisters refer frequently to her ailments, and her health required resorts to the country from the summer heat of Pisa and Florence. The account of the dispute with Antoir in *High and Low Life in Italy* states that she was "subject to convulsions from the slightest cause, and suffering from an affection of the nerves, which endangered her existence, and for which alone Mr. Landor was induced to purchase his residence in Tuscany". Estimating his expenses in 1834, Landor informed his cousin, "My wife has a Doctor in the house at least a hundred days in the year & a nurse at least fifty."

Her portrait by Wallis, painted when she was about thirty, shows beauty and grace, but her expression suggests a peevish temper, unhappiness, and ill health. She was not a delicate woman; she bore her four children without trouble and lived to be eighty-five. Crabb Robinson in 1830 found her "a beautiful woman still, though the mother of four very fine children". After calling at the Villa

Gherardescha in 1853, Dickens told Landor how she was "walking with a rapid and firm step, had bright eyes, a fine fresh colour, and looked animated and agreeable".

Landor checked off each clause of the description, with a stately nod of more than ready assent, and replied, with all his tremendous energy concentrated into the sentence: "And the Lord forbid that I should do otherwise than declare that she always was agreeable—to every one but *me*!"

There is a north-country saying that "all can deal with the Devil but those who have him". Many of Landor's friends, finding his wife attractive and agreeable, wondered that he did not find her so; a man of sixty might consider himself fortunate in possessing a wife still beautiful and little over forty. It seems reasonable to suppose that Mrs. Landor herself took this view. Sex is an impenetrable jungle through which no two people ever with certainty tread the same path, but Mrs. Landor's case was fitted by Congreve's lines,

> Heav'n has no Rage, like Love to Hatred turn'd,
> Nor Hell a Fury, like a Woman scorn'd.

If there is no evidence of her jealousy, it may be because Landor was for many years careful to offer no reason for jealousy. Though he had always enjoyed feminine society, he formed no friendships with women during the first sixteen years of his married life; his friendship with Lady Blessington then developed as a consequence of her husband's friendship with him, and about the same time he became friendly with Mrs. Dashwood through her cousins, the Hares. Mrs. Landor shared in neither friendship, and Lady Blessington's letters contain no messages of courtesy to her.

When the Countess de Molandé came to Florence in 1829, Landor can hardly have been so tactless as to inform his wife—as he reminded his sister—that she was "the dearest of all the friends I ever had or ever shall have," but he must have offered some explanation for Ianthe's writing to him after a lapse of nearly twenty years and for his eagerness in making arrangements for her reception. Her son's memoirs record Landor's assiduous attentions during the stay of Ianthe and her children at Florence, but it does not appear that Mrs. Landor shared their pleasures. Less than eighteen months later, in the spring of 1831, Landor's volume of poems was published, with thirty-one poems grouped in a section headed "Ianthe". Apart from the lines on "Clementina's artless mien", no verses were addressed to his wife.

As Milnes remarked, "it is small reproach to any woman that she did not possess a sufficient union of charm, tact, and intelligence to suit Landor as a wife." He freely admitted the violence of his temper, and Milnes recorded the legend—repeated in various forms—with which the Florentines celebrated his reputation for violence and for love of flowers: "he had one day, after an imperfect dinner, thrown the cook out of the window, and, while the man was writhing with a broken limb, ejaculated, 'Good God! I forgot the violets.'" Emphasising that Landor's temper was more formidable in popular repute than in the estimation of his friends, Milnes cited Augustus Hare's reply to an expression of surprise that his brother Julius should have selected a travelling companion of such uncertain temper for his journey from England to Italy in 1832:

I cannot regret that he should travel with Landor, though I do regret the abuse I hear of the latter. I wish that I could speak publicly in defence of a man whose heart I know to be so large and overflowing; though much of the water, from not having the branch which Moses would have shown him thrown into it, has unhappily been made bitter by circumstances. But when the stream gushes forth from his natural affections, it is sweet and plentiful, and as strong almost as a mill-stream. For his love partakes of the violence of his character; and when he gives it a free course, there is enough of it to fill a dozen such hearts as belong to the ordinary man of pleasure, and man of money, and man of philosophy, and to set the upper and nether mill-stones in them a-working.

The other quality that made Landor difficult to live with was his arrogance and intemperate response to contradiction—described by his young cousin Edward Landor as "the vast ever-present conviction of the infinity of his mental superiority". Yet Milnes justly remarked, "If a woman could have forborne, and swayed herself according to the vacillations of his temper, his whole character might have been modified, and his happiness saved in his own despite." By contrast Landor's wife behaved with neither intelligence nor tenderness; as Milnes told Mrs. Lynn Linton, she "would never learn the art of silence and letting things alone . . . and she never failed to contradict him flatly before folk, if she had a mind that way".

Lawyers argue that children provide a bond to hold together an ill-assorted couple; more often they supply a bone of contention. Because Landor in 1824 declined his mother's offer to pay for Arnold's education at an English school, pointing out that "he is not quite seven years old". Forster unjustly attributed the children's defective education to their father's doting fondness in refusing to be parted from them. When, in 1825, he wrote, "I do not even wish to be a day without any one of them, while they are children," he added, "They are different creatures when they grow up." In declining his mother's offer for Arnold, he wrote, "If he ever goes to any public school, it shall be Eton, and that five or six years hence, for about three years"; two years later he declared that "nothing but the education and settlement of my children would make me at all desirous of seeing England again". His visit to England in 1832 separated him from his children for eight months; he had promised "my dear Arnold to bring him with me", and the boy was "grieved at the disappointment"—it was his mother who "would not let him go".

Perhaps Mrs. Landor feared to let any of the children accompany their father to England lest he should remain there with them. For she knew that he now continued to live with her only for the children's sake. After interviewing her in 1837, Crabb Robinson wrote, "unless I am strangely mistaken she said that they had lived together as brother and sister ever since she was thirty-six years old!" Landor himself told his brother Henry in June 1836, "I have found her bedroom locked and all the doors leading to it, more than once. Many years ago!" Robinson—a bachelor who had never experienced revulsion from the nagging of a jealous woman—thought that abstinence from his wife's bed would seem "strange and incredible . . . were Landor not a very strange man". There is nothing strange in such abstinence by a man of Landor's pride: if he was induced by tearful repentance to overlook the first experience of a locked door, he would remain adamant after a second resort to such reprisal. To such resort she may have been moved in resentment of her husband's attentions to Ianthe; she was about thirty-six years old when Ianthe came to Florence in 1829.

In accordance with his remark that "the spider was a gentleman—he eats his fly in secret", Landor disclosed few suggestions of his domestic unhappiness as it developed. When he took the Villa Castiglione for the sake of his wife's health in 1825, he implied only difference of opinion and taste in remarking, "I wish Julia would consent to live entirely in the country, but she cannot live without some company in the evening." But in 1831, telling his sisters of the excellent health enjoyed by himself and the children since coming to Fiesole, he added a note of asperity, "My wife runs after colds; it would be strange if she did not take them; but she has taken none here; hers are all from Florence." In July 1833, "the Granduke is married again, and fireworks, balls &c empty all the world into Florence", he wrote; "I alone stay in the Country, having been in the town only once in a fortnight, and that was to dine in a family party at the Seymour's, our excellent highminded minister." Of Lord Wenlock he wrote in the same year, "Nothing can be more kind than he always is to me and all my family, offering his box at the opera, beds at his house &c. These things I do not accept." But it appears that Mrs. Landor accepted the box at the opera if not the beds, and as Lord Wenlock was ailing and infirm, it is not unlikely that his secretary MacCarthy was frequently her escort.

Landor's friends observed the loyalties of friendship; few dropped hints of the discord they must have witnessed. Remarking to Crabb Robinson in April 1834 that Mrs. Landor "did not appreciate her husband", Lady Blessington "mentioned the finding of Wallis at her house when she was ill and Landor was away"—on his visit to Rome with Lord Blessington; "I know not whether she meant anything," recorded Robinson, but as she had remembered the incident for more than six years, Lady Blessington's meaning seems obvious. Eight years after his stay at Fiesole in December 1832, Julius Hare remarked that John Sterling's engraving of Michael Angelo's Jeremiah reminded him of "Landor scolding his wife". In July 1833 Landor asked his brother Henry to accept "about one hundred pictures, from the restoration of painting in Italy down to 1500"—"These were put up in the children's bedchamber," but "my wife either feared or pretended to fear, that they might fall upon their heads and knock their brains out, so she threw them into a closet pêle mêle, where nobody can ever see them," though "they are such things as ought to be in Warwick castle."

Evidently his unusual state of indecision about the projected visit to England in 1835 was due to his wife's changes of mood. He was unwilling to make the visit again alone, and knowing his unwillingness, though she was persuaded in November 1834 to take the two youngest to her own family while the elder pair travelled with their father, she threatened to withdraw from this arrangement whenever he excited her antagonism. The climax came at the end of March 1835, when Charles Brown was invited to dinner before leaving Florence for England and Mrs. Landor made a scene before him and the elder children. Asked by Landor afterwards to describe her expressions, as evidence that he was justified in leaving her, Brown wrote from Genoa on 4th April:

It commenced by upbraiding you for conduct excessively bad towards herself; but her own statement, as well as your answer, certainly proved that you were blameless, and I ventured to point out her mistake. Unfortunately no attention was paid to either of us. . . . I am ashamed to write down the words, but to hear them was painful . . . [passage here omitted by Forster, who apparently destroyed the original letter] . . . I am afraid my patience would have left me in a tenth part of the time; but you, to my astonishment, sat with a composed countenance, never once making use of an uncivil expression, unless the following may be so considered, when, after about an hour, she seemed exhausted: "I beg, madam, you will, if you think proper, proceed; as I made up my mind, from the first, to endure at least twice as much as you have been yet pleased to speak." After dinner, when I saw her leave the room, I followed, and again pointed out her mistake; when she readily agreed with me, saying she was convinced you were not to blame. At this I could not forbear exclaiming, "Well, then?" in the hope of bearing back to you some slight acknowledgment of regret on her part: but in this I was disappointed. You conclude your letter with "I feel confident you will write a few lines, exculpating me if you think I have acted with propriety in very trying circumstances; and condemning me if I acted with violence, precipitation, or rudeness." For more than eleven years I have been intimate with you, and, during that time, frequenting your house, I never once saw you behave towards Mrs. Landor otherwise than with the most gentlemanly demeanour, while your love for your children was unbounded. I was always aware that you gave entire control into her hands over the children, the servants, and the management of the house; and when vexed or annoyed at anything, I could not but remark that you were in the habit of requesting the cause to be remedied or removed, as a favour to yourself. All this I have more than once repeated to Mrs. Landor in answer to her accusations against you, which I could never well comprehend. When I have elsewhere heard you accused of being a violent man, I have frankly acknowledged it; limiting however your violence to persons guilty of meanness, roguery, or duplicity; by which I meant, and said, that you utterly lost your temper with the Italians.

The passage omitted by Forster may have contained reference to the conduct of Arnold, who was now of an age to take sides in his parents' disputes; some years afterwards Carlyle—informed perhaps by Milnes or Julius Hare—related that Landor "was about to remove his children that they might be properly educated, a task for which he esteemed her [his wife] in no way fit; but the eldest son snatched up a gun, and declared that he had come to a time of life to form an opinion on this question, and by G— he would shoot any one who attempted to separate his mother and her children".

　　Landor wrote later to Southey:

　It was not willingly that I left Tuscany and my children. There was but one spot upon earth on which I had fixed my heart, and four objects on which my affection rested. That they might not hear every day such language as no decent person should ever hear once, nor despise both parents, I left the only delight of my existence.

By the time he received Brown's letter from Genoa, he had left home for Florence, where he remained till some time after 18th June. He then waited at the Baths of Lucca while Francis Hare, Mrs. Dashwood, and Miss Mackenzie tried to persuade his wife to allow the two elder children to accompany him to England. Once their persuasions succeeded so far that arrangements were made for Arnold and Julia to meet him at Verona—"Verona! loveliest of cities, but saddest to my memory!" he wrote in *The Pentameron* a year later—but Mrs. Landor changed her mind before they could leave. Resigning hope after five months, he travelled alone to England, where he arrived late in September 1835.

13

CELEBRITY AND SOLITUDE

Tears, O Aspasia, do not dwell long upon the cheeks of youth. Rain drops easily from the bud, rests on the bosom of the maturer flower, and breaks down that one only which hath lived its day.

—Pericles and Aspasia, Letter xxviii

How much fondness, how much generosity, what hosts of other virtues, courage, constancy, patriotism, spring into the father's heart from the cradle of his child! And does never the fear come over him, that what is most precious to him upon earth is left in careless or perfidious, in unsafe or unworthy hands?

—Pericles and Aspasia, Letter cxxxiii

Is it not in philosophy as in love? the more we have of it, and the less we talk about it, the better. Never touch upon religion with anybody. The irreligious are incurable and insensible; the religious are morbid and irritable: the former would scorn, the latter would strangle you. It appears to me to be not only a dangerous, but, what is worse, an indelicate thing, to place ourselves where we are likely to see fevers and phrenzies, writhings and distortions, debilities and deformities. Religion at Athens is like a fountain near Dodona, which extinguishes a lighted torch, and which gives a flame of its own to an unlighted one held down to it. Keep yours in your chamber; and let the people run about with theirs; but remember, it is rather apt to catch the skirts. Believe me, I am happy: I am not deprived of my friends. Imagination is little less strong in our later years than in our earlier. True, it alights on fewer objects, but it rests longer on them, and sees them better.

—Pericles and Aspasia, Letter clxxiv (1836)

On reaching England, Landor seems to have gone almost directly to his friend Ablett at Llanbedr. From there he wrote on 28th September to Lady Blessington, explaining that, while passing through London, he had called at her house in Seamore Place and found her out of town. She replied on 1st October, but his next letter was posted on 31st December:

Since I had the pleasure of reading your last kind letter, I have been travelling about occasionally, and hoped to spend my Christmas at Clifton.

There are some old thoughts resting upon Bath; but Bath is no longer what it was to any one, and least of all to me. Clifton is the best climate on this side of Nice, and climate is everything to so Italianized a piece of machinery as I am. . . . You ask me how Wales appears to me after Italy. My house is the most delightfully situated of any in Tuscany, and contains the greatest number of good pictures after Palazzo Pitti, yet the vale of Clewyd also has its charms. My old abbey at Llantony, which I never think of visiting again, has scenery about it equal to any of the Appennines, but, alas! it has also fogs, snows, and Welshmen. When April comes, I hope to make my bow in Seamore Place.

When not "travelling about", he was hard at work, seeking incessant activity to escape reflection on his domestic troubles. Ablett encouraged him by projecting a symposium of prose and verse, *Literary Hours, by Various Friends*, which was privately printed at Liverpool in 1837, but he was busily occupied besides writing some of his contributions to this volume.

He brought with him to England the manuscript of *Pericles and Aspasia*, which he had finished in July, and offered the book to Saunders & Otley. Perhaps to avoid a repetition of Lady Blessington's proof-correcting, he asked G. P. R. James—who was himself then publishing with the same firm—to act as his agent. "When I offered my Pericles to MM. Saunders & Otley," he wrote to James, "I did not suppose there was more than enough for one volume, the size of the Examination of Shakespeare." As a professional novelist, more shrewd in bargaining than either Hare or Lady Blessington, James secured an agreement by which the publishers promised a hundred pounds for a book of that size, but on receiving the manuscript, they found it too long for a single volume and Landor proposed to lengthen the book to fill two volumes. When he supplied another hundred pages and the publishers advised him that the second volume would still make no more than 175 pages, he wrote to James:

In reply to their letter I have said that, if they will give me fifty pounds more, I will send one hundred more pages, 50 within three weeks, 50 more in the three following; and if this does not appear equitable to them, I leave it entirely to you. I shall then have given them 200 pp. for fifty pounds, when I offered them only 285 for a hundred.

The publishers agreed, and Landor more than fulfilled his contract; besides lengthening the text of *Pericles and Aspasia*, he added some "Reflections on Athens at the Decease of Pericles"—introducing arguments for disestablishment of the Irish Church and reform of the House of Lords—and a "Letter to an Author", containing remarks on orthography recollected from an imaginary conversation among those sent to America by N. P. Willis.

"The first of Feb. I set out for Clifton," he wrote from Llanbedr to James on 18th January 1836. He was delayed a few days, doubtless by finishing *Pericles and Aspasia* before he left, for he wrote to Southey from Llanbedr on 4th February:

> Pray tell me whether there is any certainty of your being in London soon. I abhor the very name, but I will meet you there if you will let me. But I am afraid you will hardly have patience with a man so obstinate and incorrigible in his politics. I detest the trickery and sheer dishonesty of many of the whigs as much as you do; but I am convinced that we must yield to the impulse that has been given to men's minds, and that we must remove (since we cannot cure) what works upon their envy and malice. . . . I am now on my way to my favourite Clifton, where my intention is to remain a month at least; for the fogs of London make my heart quite flabby, to say nothing of quinsy.

At Clifton—"within sight of the city in which Robert Hall was preacher"—he wrote *The Letters of a Conservative*, arguing, as Hall and Milton had argued, "that the union of Church and State is injurious, not only to civil liberty but to pure religion".

In Letter X he tells how he began to recognise the urgency of the need for church disestablishment:

> During several months which I spent in the principality of Wales, indeed all the autumn, I was chiefly occupied in inquiries relative to the political opinions of the people, in the midst of the changes and innovations which were taking place. I found that these opinions were formed, as they are in Ireland, as they are wherever the clergy is not quite inoperative, by those of their religionary instructors. In every small town, in every village, I saw a building, often more than one, remarkable for the ugliness of its structure, and announcing by that ugliness its destination. These are the *meeting-houses* of dissenters.

In Wales he saw the established church almost entirely supplanted by nonconformity; in Bath and Bristol he noted the advance of Roman Catholicism during the forty years since his youth. "Why," he asks, "is the Church of England the only national Church in Europe that is in a minority?" and answers, "Why, it happens because the spiritual wants of the people were insufficiently supplied by the pastors engaged to tend them." He denied the right of bishops to sit in the House of Lords or to own great wealth "while clergymen of equal merit . . . live curates and die paupers." Asserting that "the whole service of the church is education", he predicted with excess of optimism that "the time will come when every church in the world will be a school-room".

For a lifelong rebel and Radical to write as a "Conservative" might suggest irony or paradox, but Landor declared himself a true Conservative since he was showing "the only means of saving what is left of the English Church". Twenty years later, when Emerson in *English Traits* quoted Carlyle's remark that "Landor's principle is mere rebellion", he replied:

Quite the contrary is apparent and prominent in many of my writings. I always was a Conservative; but I would eradicate any species of evil, political, moral, or religious, as soon as it springs up, with no reference to the blockheads who cry out *"What would you substitute in its place?"* When I pluck up a dock or a thistle, do I ask any such question? . . . It is worse than mere popery that we should be encumbered by a costly and heavy bench of Cardinals, under the title of Bishops, and that their revenues should exceed those in the Roman States.

His was the isolation of the independent mind in a two-party democracy; he hated equally Tory principles and Whig practices, because, while he revolted from the reaction of the people he personally liked, he resented the manners and motives of reformers. He condemned a system sustained by a contrast of evils when he wrote, "Democracy is the blubbery spawn begotten by the drunkenness of aristocracy." The system's weakness appeared in its attitude to church reform, for neither party would advocate a policy of embarrassing some of its own supporters. Yet Landor remained always hopeful of applause; he wrote from Clifton to his sister Elizabeth on 31st March 1836:

At present I am printing the *Letters of a Conservative*. Henry will applaud this. Good Aunt Eyres would have given me her blessing for trying to save the clergy.

Twelve days before—on the 19th—he had written in despondent mood to Lady Blessington:

Your letter, with all its kindness on its wing, followed me from Denbighshire to Bath, and from Bath to Clifton, where I am. Really I do not know whether I shall have the courage to make a visit to London. What would charm everybody else, disheartens me. I am not indifferent to grace, to wit, to friendship, more than formerly—but I tremble at literary men. I am inclined to believe that I can have the best of them to myself for as little as a plate of strawberries at this season, and can avoid the dust of the little skirmishes in which they are perpetually engaged. They do not like one another, they would dislike me. Beside, I am out of spirits at dinner, if there are more than five or six people. To confess the truth, I like best dining quite alone, taking my glass of water, my coffee, and my siesta— uniting as much of the Christian as I remember with as much of the Turk as I can. There may be something wolfish in this solitariness—I cannot help it—I acknowledge that when I look at myself I seem rather too like little Red-Ridinghood's grandmama. Cleverness, learning, eloquence, are capital things. When they are brought round to me, I take my spoonful, but I do not desire the fumes of them at table.

Yet "you cannot doubt how happy and proud I shall be to be your guest", he wrote again only ten days later: "If you should not have left London in the beginning of May, do not be shocked at hearing that a *cab* is come to the door with a fierce-looking old man in it." The reason for his change of mood appeared in the opening of his letter to his sister on 31st March: "I send you the Examiner, in which you and

Ellen will be pleased to find how magnificently the best writer in Europe has mentioned my Pericles." Even before he had received his own copies of the book, *Pericles and Aspasia* had been lavishly praised in the *Examiner* of 27th March by the reviewer who had applauded the *Examination of Shakspeare*; Landor believed that his admirer was the editor, Albany Fonblanque, and discovered only during his London visit that "the best writer in Europe" was his future biographer, a young man of twenty-four.

Forster had better reason for enthusiasm in *Pericles and Aspasia* than in the *Examination of Shakspeare*. It was unfortunate for Landor that Hazlitt was dead and that De Quincey omitted this work when discussing a selection of Landor's writings in his three essays on "a man of great genius" who "has *not* been read", for appreciation by an eminent critic might have gained for *Pericles and Aspasia* at least as many readers as the novels of Peacock and Pater have attracted. Nowhere is his quality of prose and profundity of thought more impressively sustained than in this romance related in 237 letters, which alone among his works achieves, without flaw from haste or from excess in condensation, complete fulfilment of design.

The story opens with Aspasia's arrival at Athens, where she attracts Pericles' attention by swooning with emotion at a performance of *Prometheus Bound*. She relates the development of her romance with Pericles and the incidents of her life as his mistress and confidante in a series of letters to her friend Cleone, who hopelessly loves Xeniades, a rejected lover of Aspasia's. Other correspondents intervene: Pericles writes to Aspasia in moments snatched from the business of public transactions and planning campaigns; later the philosopher Anaxagoras—closely identified with Landor himself—becomes Aspasia's correspondent from exile, while the young Alcibiades writes confidential reports to Pericles, receiving in reply the admonitions of his guardian. In the exchange of familiar letters within an intimate circle the history of the time, enlivened with anecdotes of character and incident, is traced in dramatic glimpses against a background of personal emotions. Ending with two letters from Alcibiades describing to Aspasia the deaths from plague of Pericles and Cleone, the narrative follows the design of classical drama in the mounting solemnity of its foreboding of impending tragedy, gathering momentum from the measured dignity of expression, with its wealth of epigram in philosophical reflection.

Sidney Colvin sought a facile explanation of the failure of *Pericles and Aspasia* to secure popular recognition as a masterpiece by suggesting that it "has the misfortune of being weighted with disquisitions too learned for the general reader, and not sound enough for the special student". Yet Landor expressly denied in his brief "Advertisement" to the book any intention of addressing himself to students:

He who opens these Letters for a History of the Times, will be disappointed. Did he find it in a Montague's or a Walpole's?

In a letter of 27th April 1836 he wrote:

In writing my *Pericles and Aspasia* I had no books to consult. The characters, thoughts, and actions, are all fictions. Pericles was somewhat less amiable, Aspasia somewhat less virtuous, Alcibiades somewhat less sensitive; but here I could represent him so, being young, and before his character was displayed.

Seeking escape from brooding over his domestic troubles, he projected himself in imagination into the surroundings of ancient Athens, drawing upon all he could recollect from his reading of the period and allowing his characters to develop from the circumstances in which they started. He wrote as a novelist, exercising the function of what Coleridge called "the secondary Imagination", which "dissolves, diffuses, dissipates, in order to recreate". "It is easy to throw pieces of history into letters," he said, "but there is no species of composition so remote from verisimilitude." Too successfully he achieved verisimilitude; his letters are such as Aspasia and her correspondents might actually have written, assuming in the recipients of their letters a knowledge of contemporary circumstances impossible in the general reader. As in the *Imaginary Conversations*, he asked too much knowledge and imagination of his readers, forgetting the art of distortion in dramatist and novelist, who draw their characters imperceptibly larger than life.

Following the praise in the *Examiner*, Lady Blessington wrote "to thank you for the very highest intellectual feast I have ever enjoyed".

Yes, your "Aspasia and Pericles" are delicious, and reflect everlasting honour on you; never was there so beautiful a mirror of wisdom and tenderness; the book continually filled my eyes with tears, and my heart with gentle and generous emotions. I am proud of, and for you, and repeat frequently to myself—*he is my friend*. How delightful, yet how rare is it, when our friends make us feel proud of them! every one talks of your book, and every one is loud in its praises. . . . Never was there such a triumph as you have achieved by this book!! Mr. Fonblanque is impatient to shake you by the hand. . . . I shall be at Gore House the whole season, and charmed to see you; come and take possession of your room in it—why can you not come before May?

This letter came from London's leading literary hostess, a fashionable novelist and the editor of a popular annual; to Landor it meant much besides—for, as Milnes remarked, "his feeling for female beauty was intense"—that Lady Blessington was a beautiful woman. Throughout the first half of his long life he had hungered vainly for recognition and appreciation. During the past ten years at Florence praise from correspondents and homage from visitors had appeased his grievance and mellowed his character, though he still sought to impress his sisters by quoting what others said of him. Now he was at last receiving his deserts.

Arriving on 2nd May, he was one of Lady Blessington's earliest guests in her splendid new home at Gore House, to which she and Count D'Orsay moved in March from Seamore Place; he delayed till then because he had promised to await Mrs. Paynter's return to Bath after the serious illness of one of her daughters. His hostess was unexacting: "I never saw Lady Blessington until dinner-time," said Landor of his visits to her; "She always breakfasted in her own room, and wrote during the morning." He therefore spent many of his days with Crabb Robinson, who noted on 3rd May:

I had a call from Landor just as I was going out. He was in excellent spirits and laughed as heartily as ever; yet I was sorry to learn that he does not mean to return to Italy. He says he will give four-fifths of his income to Mrs. Landor for herself and the three children and will live on the one-fifth himself. He says that for years Mrs. Landor has been making him ridiculous in the eyes of the servants and that he cannot possibly live with her.

On the 5th Landor and Kenyon "breakfasted" with Robinson, and "we did not break up till past two". Landor amused Robinson "by his odd judgments" during a visit to the National Gallery, and at the Academy praised pictures by Landseer, Eastlake, and Etty.

The following week Wordsworth arrived in London, and Kenyon—doubtless at Robinson's suggestion—urged Landor to remove to his house from Lady Blessington's, as Wordsworth "might not like to visit him at *Gore House*". In fact Robinson reveals that Wordsworth was instructed by his daughter Dora "that he was not to visit Landor at Lady Blessington's", and her letter was actually read aloud to Landor, who "only laughed at it" though—as Robinson realised after several months of reflection—"he may after all have felt it". No doubt Robinson was also sufficiently tactless to convey to Landor a message in Wordsworth's letter announcing his arrival in London:

If you see Landor, thank him for Pericles & Aspasia, but tell him to leave the Church alone. He has lived too long in Italy to know how the Church of England is now working, & what it stands in need of.

Without the comment on the Church, the acknowledgment of a presentation copy through a third person was enough to remind Landor of Wordsworth's lukewarm reception of his complimentary ode three years before.

When they met at Robinson's on 13th May for "an agreeable chat" of two hours, Robinson remarked, "Wordsworth and Landor agree on poetry better than on other matters, and where Wordsworth finds conformity in this he will be tolerant even of religious and political differences." Two days later they met at breakfast, but Robinson

recorded nothing of their conversation, being out of humour because
"Wordsworth beset me with his church-building solicitations". With
his conviction that England was trembling on the brink of revolution
and his concern with ecclesiastical conventions, Wordsworth was
socially tolerated only for his reputation: after Sydney Smith satirically
remarked, "I never saw Wordsworth look so well, so *reverend*. And yet
one fancies a poet should be always young," even Robinson noticed that
Sydney Smith spoke to Wordsworth "in a tone of exaggerated and
affected respect". After "a long morning of gossip" on 18th May,
Wordsworth declared himself "not up to" inspecting the Elgin Marbles;
Landor by contrast became so absorbed in examination that Robinson
left him there.

However Landor excused his removal to Kenyon's house, Lady
Blessington evidently divined the reason, for Robinson was displeased
with her manner to him when he spent an evening at her house with
Landor; he was annoyed that Landor supported the playwright
Planché in defending the stage presentation of "angels, devils, the
Virgin Mary, etc." in Dumas's new play, *Don Juan de Marana*. On 19th
May Kenyon gave a large dinner-party, but "Landor was put out of
humour by the number there, and Wordsworth was not in spirits".
Among the guests were Kenyon's cousin, Elizabeth Barrett, and Mary
Russell Mitford, neither likely to appeal to Landor's taste in feminine
beauty. Miss Mitford informed her father that Landor was "as splendid
a person as Mr. Kenyon, but not so full of sweetness and sympathy".
Landor talked with Miss Barrett "only for about ten minutes": "hearing that she was an excellent Greek scholar, I gave her a few Greek
verses, which I happened to recollect at the moment." He was so
little impressed that a few weeks later he promised only with reluctance
to invite from her through Kenyon a contribution to Lady Blessington's
annual.

For Miss Barrett the evening was an event: "I never walked in the
skies before; and perhaps never shall again, when so many stars are
out!" Landor—"in whose hands the ashes of antiquity burn again—
gave me two Greek epigrams he had lately written . . . and talked
brilliantly and prominently" till her brother—a young man of unhappy manners—"abused him for *ambitious* singularity and affectation". Determined to be "not at all disappointed in Wordsworth,
although perhaps I should not have singled him from the multitude as
a great man", she remarked "a *reserve* even in his countenance, which
does not lighten as Landor's does", and comparing him with "Landor
—the brilliant Landor!"—she "*felt* the difference between great genius
and eminent talent". After she became the wife of Robert Browning,
this early prejudice survived to prevent her sharing her husband's
devotion to Landor; though she unwillingly liked him, she admitted in

THE COUNTESS OF BLESSINGTON

From the portrait by Sir Thomas Lawrence, P.R.A.,
exhibited at the Royal Academy of 1822 and now in
the Wallace Collection

the last year of her life that Landor was always "unsympathetical to me . . . in his *morale*".

Thomas Noon Talfourd, the friend and biographer of Charles Lamb, met Landor at both Robinson's and Gore House; apart from his literary connections, he was a distinguished barrister and member of Parliament, and Macready's production at Covent Garden of his tragedy, *Ion*, on 26th May was an event of that London season. Wordsworth and Landor dined at his house before the play, which they saw from Crabb Robinson's box, and Landor apparently observed that Wordsworth failed to join in the enthusiastic applause, as he afterwards wrote,

> Amid the mighty storm that swell'd around,
> Wordsworth was calm, and bravely stood his ground.

After the play they were entertained to supper at Talfourd's, where Macready "met Wordsworth, who pinned me; Walter Savage Landor . . . whom I very much liked". Always ready to take offence if he felt his importance insufficiently recognised, Macready found himself "very happily placed between Wordsworth and Landor, with Browning opposite, and Mrs. Talfourd next but one—Talfourd within two". He "talked much with my two illustrious neighbours", and Landor "promised to send me his play of *Count Julian*, and expressed himself desirous of improving his acquaintance with me".

Further down the table sat the dramatic critic of the *Examiner*, John Forster, who thus recalled his first sight of the writer he had so recently praised:

He was not above the middle stature, but had a stout stalwart presence, walked without a stoop, and in his general aspect, particularly the set and carriage of his head, was decidedly of what is called a distinguished bearing. His hair was already silvered gray, and had retired far upward from his forehead, which, wide and full but retreating, could never in the earlier time have been seen to such advantage. What at first was noticeable, however, in the broad white massive head, were the full yet strangely-lifted eyebrows. . . . In the large gray eyes there was a depth of composed expression that even startled by its contrast to the eager restlessness looking out from the surface of them; and in the same variety and quickness of transition the mouth was extremely striking. The lips that seemed compressed with unalterable will would in a moment relax to a softness more than feminine; and a sweeter smile it was impossible to conceive. . . . It was altogether a face on which power was visibly impressed, but without the resolution and purpose that generally accompany it.

Finding that Forster, not Fonblanque, was his reviewer in the *Examiner*, Landor naturally welcomed the attentions of this young admirer. On 30th May he was at Forster's chambers when Macready through indisposition "lost the pleasure of again seeing Landor", and he introduced Forster—as well as his other young friend, Milnes—to Lady

T

Blessington. Writing on Talfourd's *Ion* in the *New Monthly Magazine* for July, Forster digressed into praise of "The Shades of Agamemnon and of Iphigeneia"—the dramatic scene in verse included in *Pericles and Aspasia*—and the unpublished "Death of Clytemnestra", which Miss Mitford found Landor writing "one fine June morning, seated on a garden-roller in the court before Mr. Kenyon's house in London".

<h2 style="text-align:center">§ 2</h2>

Landor left London in the first days of June, spending "a day at Oxford, and another at Cheltenham" on his way to Clifton, whence he wrote on 6th June explaining to Lady Blessington how he had "lost one more delightful walk with you round your gardens" through his seat having been booked on the morning instead of on the afternoon coach. He travelled to Oxford by coach but from Cheltenham by train: "The rattle of carriages is still sounding in my ears, and my brains are floating in the fumes of a coal-pit, with no Davy-lamp to save me."

For nearly two years he had tried to recover the manuscripts and corrected volumes of his *Imaginary Conversations* from N. P. Willis, who had entrusted them to his colleague on the *New York Mirror*, Theodore Sedgwick Fay, for transport to America by a third person. In the spring of 1835 Landor discovered that "Mr. Willises friend never consigned them to the person he mentions"; though he accordingly assumed that "the corrected Imaginary Conversations, and the unpublished volume, are irreparably lost", he expressed no anger against Willis, but in the same letter to Lady Blessington declared himself "very happy to hear of Mr. Willises new poems". On his return to England he found that many people were annoyed at Willis's abuse of hospitality in making copy of them in his *Pencillings by the Way*. In the "Letter to an Author" at the end of *Pericles and Aspasia* he therefore explained how Willis had imposed on him, and remarking that "I regret the appearance of his book more than the disappearance of mine", he owned the responsibility of having introduced him to Lady Blessington and to Robinson, through whom Willis had met Charles and Mary Lamb. Robinson deplored Landor's "injudicious" comment more than Willis's offence and was the more annoyed when Albany Fonblanque told him he "ought to be pleased with" Landor's notice of him, but the publication caused Willis to write an apology and to restore the books and manuscripts. These Landor now unpacked at Clifton after his London visit, finding such "sad confusion" that "it would be an easier and a pleasanter business to write fresh ones, than to arrange and decipher these".

He had thought of accepting "a very kind and flattering invitation to Ireland" from Lord Normanby—now Lord Lieutenant and Earl of

Mulgrave—to whom he had dedicated *Pericles and Aspasia,* but his plans were altered by news of his family. On leaving Florence he had allotted nearly three-quarters of his income to his family, retaining himself about two hundred pounds a year. On 10th March 1836 he wrote to his brother Henry that "my kind friend Mrs. Dashwood" offered to pay off the £5,000 annuity debt on his mother's estate, "on no other security than my honour and Arnold's", but his cousin Walter Landor informed him that the debt was already provided for by insurance. Hearing of his arrival in England, his Llanthony creditors—notably his former agent Robbins—pressed for settlement of their claims. While he represented to the lawyers "the propriety & expediency of trying to separate the just claims of Robbins from the usurped ones", he proposed to make an interim payment of a hundred pounds to Robbins by selling the pictures he had brought over from Florence. A few pictures were sold in London "by Christie for less than twenty pounds, the expenses of transport alone were eleven pounds eight", so "with packages & auction business I may put about four in my pocket". He directed the bulk of the pictures to "be sent to any respectable auctioneer in Manchester, where I understand there is always a ready sale". Encouraged by Saunders & Otley's agreement for *Pericles and Aspasia,* he informed his brother, "I entertain no doubt that I shall be able to pay all my own expenses without one shilling from my property"; he therefore proposed to allow his family £480 a year, besides "50 for the boys tutor, MacCarthy", and to surrender the rest of his income to his creditors.

From Clifton on 12th June he enclosed to his brother Henry a letter just received from William Sandford at Florence:

He does not say perhaps all that he knows why Mr. Macarthy should no longer be the tutor of my children. When I was in London, I think I could have obtained a situation for Arnold, but he has been persuaded by his mother that he stands above all authority of mine. I wish you would advise me what should be done, or *can* be. When I think of my family it almost drives me mad, for whatever I have at any time projected or ordered has been systematically overthrown. I have been obliged to give Sandford the most convincing reasons that I never can in future live under the same roof with my wife.

She knows that it was out of consideration for my children, Julia in particular, that I endured her conduct so long, and might (she thought) do so longer. However it suited her purpose to render my home intolerable, and she fancied my extreme love to the children would bring me back again at any convenient season.

I am sorry that Julia has observed what it was impossible she should not observe, sooner or later. My friend Hare and his wife have also written to me, and have done everything in their power to save my family from utter destruction. But their mother will not allow Julia to go to Mrs. Hare, because Mrs. H did not think it proper to invite her too. . . . I hope it may be thought expedient to pay Macarthy 25 £ for his half year and dismiss him at once. Arnold can grow no worse with him or without him. But I distrust my judgement in every thing, and indeed have none left.

Apparently Henry advised him to go to Florence and offered money for the journey, for Landor wrote again on Wednesday 15th June:

When I wrote to you I was resolved to take your advice and not to take any other assistance you might offer: I have a hundred and seven pounds, which is more than enough for my voyage. This however is certain. My wife will not give up the children, she swore she never would. Otherwise I should have taken them out of Italy some years before.

I have found her bedroom locked and all the doors leading to it, more than once. Many years ago! She has called me for an hour together, twice or thrice a week, villain, coward, &c. &c. *always* in the presence of my servants. She never in her life expostulated with me on any thing that displeased her, but always waited to abuse and insult me in the presence of others. You have seen what Mr. Brown wrote. Mr. Hutton once took me by the hand and said he did not believe I had so much patience &c. &c., yet he had often seen me *nearly* equally insulted. Nothing was ever so much my desire as to conceal the misconduct of my wife, for the sake of my children.

To have removed them would have exposed her at once, yet their good seemed to require it. The only favor I ever asked of her was, to treat me with as much gentleness as the lowest of the servants, and to tell me when I had offended her, without unbecoming language, and without their presence.

On Thursday (tomorrow sennight) I will go to London, and set out for the continent within two or three days after. Never will I venture into Tuscany, nor see her face again if I can help it.

I have written to Johnstone the banker to devise some means of conveying the children to me without her, and not to furnish her with the means of molesting me. I suspect at last she will keep my children from me, and the winter will whiten my bones among the Alpes. . . . If you would write a few lines to my dearest Julia, telling her how necessary and how desired her presence is in England, she would leave Italy with less regret, and would not have to hear that it is all my madness, the usual expression, and not always so far from the truth.

The last was added in consequence of a letter from G. P. R. James, who wrote: "I wish to Heaven Julia were with you. It would be a comfort to you and a blessing to her; for Italy, and Italy without a father's care, is a sad land for young fair woman."

To Lady Blessington he wrote after a hurried visit to Bath, "You will see me again in eight days, for one or two, if you have room for me." On arrival at Gore House he was "a week laid up"—apparently with erysipelas resulting from agitation. He asked Crabb Robinson to accompany him on his journey, but Robinson thought "he is so excessively capricious that it would be difficult to manage with him. Quarrelling would be inevitable". So he travelled alone, writing to Henry from Heidelberg on 15th July:

Mr. Ablett has heard quite sufficient of the irregularities of my wife and the ingratitude and wickedness of her son, to leave nothing to the justice of such persons. He would never have accepted from me one farthing of principal or interest, but he has no reason, now I am driven out of my house, to leave it in the possession of the present occupants.

I have written to my cousin Walter to advertise the house, furniture and pictures. To sell the pictures, the finest collection any Englishman ever made in Italy, breaks my heart. But go they must. I gave Arnold all that was mine, I could not give him what is anothers. The residue may go to the creditors. I do not want anything. I can live on bread and milk, and could be contented to see no other face upon earth than my childrens.

As he asked his cousin to communicate his instructions to his wife, the threat of selling the house was designed to alarm Mrs. Landor into compliance with his plans for the children, but he waited for weeks at Heidelberg without word from his family.

"Nothing can exceed the civilities I met with in Germany among the learned," he afterwards told Southey. To Dr. Brabant—who visited him at Florence in 1823 as the bearer of a letter from Walter Birch[1]— he owed introductions to university society at Heidelberg, notably to the rationalist professor of theology, Dr. Paulus, who reviewed his *Letters of a Conservative*. As in the previous winter, he escaped from his troubles by writing. Before leaving England he had disposed of two of the unpublished imaginary conversations recovered from Willis: for her annual, *The Book of Beauty*, Lady Blessington accepted the dialogue between Colonel Walker and the Hindu woman Hattaji and her daughters on infanticide and vaccination, and Forster published "Eldon and Encombe" in the *Examiner* of 21st August. At this time Landor revised the unfinished conversation, "Andrew Marvel and Bishop Parker", in which Marvel (so Landor spelt Marvell) defends Milton against the bishop's denigrations, remarking of Milton's *Treatise on Divorce*:

He proved by many arguments what requires but few: that happiness is better than unhappiness; that, when two persons can not agree, it is wiser and more christianlike that they should not disagree; that, when they cease to love each other, it is something if they be hindered by the gentlest of checks, from running to the extremity of hatred; and lastly, how it conduces to circumspection and forbearance to be aware that the bond of matrimony is not indissoluble, and that the bleeding heart may be saved from bursting. . . . He proceeds to demonstrate that boisterous manners, captious contra-dictions, jars, jealousies, suspicions, dissensions, are juster causes of separation than the only one leading to it through the laws. . . . Let it also be remem-bered that marriage is the metempsychosis of women; that it turns them into different creatures from what they were before. Liveliness in the girl may have been mistaken for good temper: the little pervicacity which at first is attractively provoking, at last provokes without its attractiveness: negligence of order and propriety, of duties and civilities, long endured, often depre-cated, ceases to be tolerable, when children grow up and are in danger of following the example. It often happens that, if a man unhappy in the

[1] As a practising physician at Devizes, Brabant attended Coleridge at Calne in 1816. Walter Birch held the living of Stanton St. Bernard, near Devizes, from 1813.

married state were to disclose the manifold causes of his uneasiness, they would be found, by those who were beyond their influence, to be of such a nature as rather to excite derision than sympathy. The waters of bitterness do not fall on his head in a cataract, but through a colander; one however like the vases of the Danaides, perforated only for replenishment. We know scarcely the vestibule of a house of which we fancy we have penetrated into all the corners. We know not how grievously a man may have suffered, long before the calumnies of the world befell him as he reluctantly left his house-door. There are women from whom incessant tears of anger swell forth at imaginary wrongs; but of contrition for their own delinquencies, not one.

As Forster recalled how Landor showed him this passage a few months after his return from Heidelberg, it is curious that he should have considered Landor's objections to living with his wife as "very far from insuperable"—unless it is remembered how, more than twenty years later, his insensitive attitude towards Dickens's marital problems provoked the caricature of Podsnap in *Our Mutual Friend*.

On 1st September Landor sent to Forster from Heidelberg the first dramatic scene in the Clytemnestra sequence, in which Electra thus exhorts her brother Orestes to vengeance against their adulterous mother:

> Pass on, my brother! she awaits the wretch,
> Dishonorer, despoiler, murderer . . .
> None other name shall name him . . . she awaits
> As would a lover . . .
> Heavenly Gods! what poison
> O'erflows my lips!
> Adultress! husband-slayer!
> Strike her, the tigress!
> Think upon our father . . .
> Give the sword scope . . . think what a man was he,
> How fond of her! how kind to all about,
> That he might gladden and teach *us* . . . how proud
> Of thee, Orestes! tossing thee above
> His joyous head and calling thee his crown.
> Ah! boys remember not what melts our hearts
> And marks them evermore!

He soon had reason to reproach his own son's fickle memory of former happiness. Mrs. Dashwood was trying to persuade the two elder children to join their father: "the concern she takes in my family is infinitely greater than that of all the rest of the world", he told Forster, "and the last thing I forget will be that". He was receiving regular reports from Mrs. Dashwood, for he wrote to Lady Blessington from Mannheim on 12th September how "my good and sensible friend Mrs. Dashwood" had rebuked him for writing the "Eldon and Encombe" dialogue, "as poor Lord Eldon is no longer a public man, and eighty years old", to which "My answer was, the devil is older". On 17th September he heard from the banker Johnstone "that Arnold was much affected by the remonstrances of Mrs. Dashwood, who ordered Johnstone to supply him with whatever money he wanted for his journey". On 2nd October he received from Arnold a letter "doing me the favor to invite me back to Italy". He replied immediately:

Arnold, I would not be thought so unpolite as to defer the expression of my gratitude, for your permission to return to what was formerly my home, and for your promise that every thing shall be forgotten. Alas, Arnold, too much has been forgotten. Do you hate a father because he cannot bear the dishonour of his family? do you despise a gentleman because he avoids the endurance of worse language than the vilest rabble indulge in? I do not appeal to your justice; I appeal to your memory. Have I not often been obliged to leave the room rather than reply however moderately? You may dislike Mr. Leckie: but he may reasonably be expected to speak rather in another's favour than in mine, I having written, as you know, most bitter things to him, and having shewn them to persons whom he would least wish them to be shown—to Mr. Seymour and Lord George and Hare. Yet he told your Aunt Rose that he would not have born for half an hour what I have been bearing for a quarter of a century. And did not Mr. Hutton say 'I really give you credit: I did not believe you had so much patience'? I have Mr. Brown's testimony, and some others. Is it not strange that the only person that treats me with indignity, is the person who made oath in the presence of God, to treat me very differently? And is this the worst? I shall leave behind me proofs to the contrary. I shall show that I shut my eyes, not because they were blind or weak, but from tenderness to my family. The man who is living in health and hope may write and speak rashly, but he who knows he is going before God, will not go before him with falsehood and malice. I have loved all of you most fondly, and without distinction. Some of you may be taught that you have no right or reason to treat me as a father. I have every day of my life wished to see my family and have now made one last effort to save it. I am incapable of more. Two painful and violent disorders the eresypelas and cholera, came rapidly over me. Either of them, at my age, would be enough to prepare me for the inevitable hour. God grant it may come soon. My bagage is taken on board the steamer, and I find myself strong enough to undertake the voyage. I do not desire you to return me any part of the love I have incessantly borne toward you, nor to observe the courtesies of society in my favour. But I think it is my duty to recall your attention to what you must have observed in me, and to consider how moderate a share of human infirmities are attributable to me, when rancour is forced back half a lifetime for some trivial subject of invective. At last I was accused of vile hypocrisy in *seeming* kind and attentive at the bed of sickness, I whom the cry of any animal pierces with pity! Arnold, permit me to call myself, perhaps for the last time, your affectionate father W. S. Landor.

Enclosing a copy of this letter to his brother Henry, to whom he wrote on Sunday 9th October after his return to Clifton, he related the sequel:

Finding my disappointment, my forehead felt again the same pains, as when my eresypelas first came on. I took a large dose of physick and went to bed, until a hot bath could be prepared. I then remained perspiring violently and no return of eresypelas. However I kept my bed, without eating, til the steamer was about to leave Manheim. I went aboard and grew much better. I could not however carry my sadness into Lady Blessington's so I slept at Ibbotson's Hotel, and sett out for this place in the morning.

The verses, "Written on the Rhine", published the following year in Ablett's *Literary Hours*, include the lines:

> Fresh blows the gale, the scenes delight,
> Anear, afar, on plain, on hight;
>   But all are far and vast:
> Day follows day, and shows not one
> The weary heart could rest upon,
> To call its own at last.

From Ibbotson's Hotel he wrote to Lady Blessington on the evening of 6th October:

I arrived here in such disarray, and so vilely out of spirits, in the dark, that I could not in my conscience present myself at Gore House. . . . Early to-morrow morning I must go to Clifton, where I have been expected these last four days. Sadness ought never to be where you are, and yet I must have brought it. I return quite alone—the cholera is the plea why none of my children were allowed to meet me in Tyrol. To-morrow I shall roll myself up like a hedge-hog for six months. . . . This melancholy weather would certainly make me throw myself into the Thames, if I were to remain near it; and yet the throw is an idle one, for the air itself is a Thames.

Settling for the winter at Penrose Cottage, Clifton, he continued to seek forgetfulness of trouble in work. Thinking no more of selling the house at Fiesole, since the threat had failed as a stratagem, he was now concerned that his family should have no grievance in a reduction of income as a result of his living apart, as he wrote to his brother Henry:

I do not know whether I am capable of writing long together, but I think I can get about a hundred pounds a year by it, or more, so that in future, indeed always from this time forth, I shall want nothing from my estate.

Would it not be well to put into the *tontine* for the 3 younger children, 100 a year each? I saw a woman of about my age, living now at Frankfort and keeping her carriage, who had done so.

800£ were allowed me. Now, if my family have 450, and 300 are thus laid out yearly, each will become rich at thirty years of age.

From Mannheim on 12th September he wrote to Lady Blessington that he was transcribing "the last sheet of my third and final interview of Petrarca and Boccaccio." These interviews became *The Pentameron*, and besides dramatic scenes and occasional verse he had written some "Audiences granted by the Emperor of China to Tsing-ti", in which

English society and especially conventional religion were satirised in their interpretation by an oriental traveller, as in Tom Brown's *Amusements Serious and Comical*, Montesquieu's *Lettres Persanes*, and Goldsmith's *Citizen of the World*. In view of the advance of £150 on *Pericles and Aspasia* he thus had reason to suppose that he might earn a hundred a year from his writing, but the illusion was dispelled within a few days of his letter to his brother, for he informed Lady Blessington on 21st October:

Yesterday I had a letter from Saunders and Otley, to whom I had sent another volume for publication. They decline it, telling me that they are losers of 150 by the Pericles. A young author would be vexed. I wrote them by this post as follows:

"Gentlemen, you judge very rightly in supposing that nothing of mine can be popular. I regret that for the present you are subject to a considerable loss by the Pericles. I never can allow any one to be the loser by me, on which principle (if on no other) I would never play a game at cards. Perhaps a few more copies, though probably very few, may be sold within another year. At all events, at the end of the next, I will make good your loss. I am also in your debt for the 'Letters of a Conservative,' which have lately been reviewed in Germany by Dr. Paulus. But in England they do not appear to be worth the notice of the learned world, or the political. Be pleased to let me know what I am in your debt for the publication and the books you sent me, that I may discharge this portion of it immediately."

I now rejoice that I reserved for my own expenditure only 200 a year, and that I have not deprived my wife of her horses, nor my sons of theirs, nor of anything else they had been used to. I never feel a great pleasure in doing what anybody else can do. It would puzzle a good many to save 50 out of 200 in one year. The rest must come out of my estate, which I am clearing of its encumbrances very fast.

Within twelve days he thus forgot his plan of living by his writings and taking nothing from his estate, and four years later his brothers Charles and Henry were still consulting with their Rugeley cousin about reducing encumbrances on the estate.

Forster recorded as "among the curiosities of literature" that "what was here threatened was soon afterwards actually done, and the hundred pounds which Mr. James had obtained for the ms. of *Pericles* was paid back by Landor to its publishers"! He was still more astonished when, three years later, having "forgotten, not merely that anything had ever been paid him for the book, but, more marvellous still, that he had himself sent the money back", Landor insisted that "I published *Pericles and Aspasia* on my own account" and "was sending farther remittances in satisfaction of the supposed loss, when I stopped him by a statement from Mr. Saunders himself". Having known him only since his sixty-second year, Forster attributed this lapse of memory to infirmity of age, but Landor's simple explanation, "Never in my lifetime have I kept any accounts," was an understatement, for his troubles at Llanthony show that he had never troubled to remember money transactions. De Quincey was equally careless of money, and for the same reason—"emancipation . . . from all that is comprehended under the term business, so that time, thoughts, and feelings may be unfettered by petty considerations".

§ 3

During recent months *Blackwood's Magazine* had been publishing a series of papers called "Alcibiades the Young Man", and the September number included an epistle taunting Landor with "developing under a plurality of names the uniform material of a very peculiar idiosyncrasy" in his "clever monopolydialogues" and with actually borrowing ideas from the magazines that he affected not to read. Asked by Mrs. Dashwood if he proposed to retort, Landor wrote, "Do you think it possible I should abase myself to notice any witticisms in Blackwood's Magazine? . . . I never read criticisms upon me unless to acknowledge an obligation, when I hear of it." The more indignant at the attack on her friend in her sympathy with his domestic trouble, Mrs. Dashwood interpreted this comment as a crushing reply to the magazine's aspersions and quoted it in a protest of her own, which appeared in *Blackwood's* November number with derisive editorial comment.

However he deplored Mrs. Dashwood's indiscretion, Landor now felt forced into reprisal, as he informed Lady Blessington on 13th November:

I do not like to write anything satirical. But Blackwood, among other impertinences, has declared that I read his publication. If as Byron thought, and Byron was not *over nice*, a gentleman could not write in it, how can a gentleman be supposed to read it? I never ran over a single number in my whole existence, though something was once shewn to me as very clever; and it was so. I should have thought it criminal to give half-a-crown to a murderer of Keats, to say nothing of scurrilities.

In the same letter he remarked:

I have added a good many verses to those your Ladyship saw about the impudence of Wordsworth to Southey. Good Southey has been a week here. What delight to see him in tolerable spirits.

Southey arrived on the 3rd November to stay at the Bedminster house of Joseph Cottle, who had published the *Lyrical Ballads* almost forty years before. With him travelled his son Cuthbert, the main object of the visit being to show his son the haunts of his youth and to introduce him to his few remaining friends in the west country. Chief of these was Landor, "in whose society we spent several delightful days", wrote Cuthbert Southey: "He was one of the few men with whom my father used to enter freely into conversation, and on such occasions it was no mean privilege to be a listener." On Tuesday the 8th "we walked with Landor about the finest parts of the neighbourhood", wrote Southey; "but the house which I inhabited for one year at Westbury, and in which I wrote more verses than in any other year of my life, has been pulled down." The next day they visited Southey's old school at Corston.

There was pathos in Southey's eager revisiting of his distant past, sharpened by the knowledge of his sorrow under his wife's affliction and by awareness—as he told Cottle—that his "powers of exertion" were failing. Yet "he manifested the same kind and cordial behaviour", said Cottle, "which he had uniformly displayed for nearly half a century", and Landor must have contrasted his manner with Wordsworth's frigidity and self-centredness. As Cottle discussed his reminiscences with Southey, he may have remarked in Landor's presence how Coleridge praised Wordsworth at the expense of his own reputation and how Wordsworth ascribed the failure of *Lyrical Ballads* to Coleridge's "Ancient Mariner". It was on the day after Southey's departure from Bristol that Landor told Lady Blessington how he had "added a good many verses" to those she had already seen "about the impudence of Wordsworth to Southey"; eleven days later, on 24th November, he told her that "my satire cost me five evenings, besides the morning (before breakfast), in which I wrote as much as you have about Wordsworth", and "the whole will be out in another ten days"; on the 26th he wrote to Milnes:

The worthies of Edinburgh have been attacking me. I never read a number of *Blackwood* in my life; this was told the editor, who has ragged me in some passages which were sent to me. Within next week you will have a copy, not of my answer, for I answer no man, but of a satire on these people and others somewhat better.

Crabb Robinson received a presentation copy of *A Satire on Satirists, and Admonition to Detractors* on 6th December—a thirty-eight-page pamphlet in paper wrappers, published by Saunders & Otley—and "thought it right to remonstrate with Landor". He admitted that Wordsworth "does not appreciate other poets as they deserve", but declined to acknowledge "the justice of its being imputed to him as a crime"—what did it matter if Wordsworth was insensible to others' merits.

He is, after all, Wordsworth. In all cases I care little what a man is *not*; I look to what he *is*. And Wordsworth has written a hundred poems the least excellent of which I would not sacrifice to give him that openness of heart you require.

In convicting Landor of citing Wordsworth's remarks in private conversation as examples of his depreciation of other writers, he indicated the source of Landor's irritation at one of their meetings during the previous summer.

I have had the pleasure of enjoying the company of both of you together, when I remarked nothing but cordiality between you; and now I receive from you a very bitter attack, not upon his writings, but upon his personal character,—a portion of the materials being drawn, unless I deceive myself, from opinions uttered by him in the freedom of unpremeditated conversation in my presence.

Respecting the dignity of Robinson's protest, Landor replied with a reasoned "defence" of his attitude, and in deference to Robinson's remark that Byron had failed in his intention "to cause a breach between Southey and Wordsworth by what Coleridge happily terms 'an implement, not an invention, of malice'", he asked Robinson to countermand the copy of the satire which he had ordered Saunders & Otley to send to Southey. To Lady Blessington he wrote:

I wish our friend Robinson would shew you my *defence*, for I never make any note of what I write. . . . Wordsworth, no doubt, has a thousand good reasons why there is not a poet upon earth; but as there are many who have given me pleasure, I love them for it; some of them perhaps a little more than they deserve. All men are liable to error. I particularly, who believe that there may be criticism without sarcasm, and Christianity without deans and chapters. The surface of Wordsworth's mind, the poetry, has a good deal of staple about it, and will bear handling; but the inner, the conversational and private, has many coarse, intractable, dangling threads, fit only for the flock-bed equipage of grooms and drovers. I am glad I praised him before I knew more of him, else I never should: and I might have been unjust to the better part had I remarked the worse sooner. This is a great fault, to which we are all liable, from an erroneous idea of consistency.

Unfortunately Robinson was not content with his remonstrance and Landors' friendly response. He acknowledged that "nothing can be more civil than his letter to me", but "nothing more vain and arrogant than what he says of himself", and "I care not if I never see him again". Even when he wrote a second letter to Landor, pointing out "that his lampoon against Wordsworth is but a repetition of Lord Byron", he acknowledged that Landor "answered my letter very kindly as far as I am concerned". Yet he lost no time in calling on Samuel Rogers, reputed the most malicious gossip in London, for no better reason than Rogers' having been "at the bottom of the worst part of the poem, the allusion to the words said to be used by Wordsworth of Southey"— presumably he knew that Rogers had tattled to Byron. He was satisfied when Rogers declared Landor "an *unsafe* man", though he later regretted that "of Wordsworth he spoke with less cordiality than I could have wished". When he met Southey a few weeks later, he told him how he had prevented a copy of the satire from reaching him: Southey "expressed his great regret at the publication, was sure it was founded on mistake, viz. the anecdote of what Wordsworth said of him; that Landor was always doing things he was sorry for afterwards; that people thought him crazy, or he would have been killed before now". The last remark seems more likely to have been suggested by Robinson than offered by Southey; only eight months earlier Robinson thought N. P. Willis "must be the meanest of men" because he had not called Landor out for writing the letter appended to *Pericles and Aspasia*. Discussing the subject with Kenyon, whose acquaintance he owed to Landor, he found "Kenyon only thinks better of the talent of the *Satire* than I do, but of the moral there can be no difference", and "he, too, says there must be a touch of insanity in Landor".

Thereafter for many years Robinson habitually imputed "madness" to Landor, though he affected cordiality towards him. In March 1837 Julius Hare told him that Landor remarked to Mrs. Dashwood, in reference to Robinson's correspondence on the satire, "he is my friend, but more the friend of Wordsworth, and it probably put an end to our acquaintance". Yet Robinson thereupon wrote to Landor, offering to call on his family in Florence.

Wordsworth heard of the satire from Edward Quillinan, who was soon to be allowed to marry Dora Wordsworth after a courtship of thirteen years, but told Robinson that "he never saw nor means to see the *Satire*". He denied that he had ever said he would not give five shillings for all Southey had ever written, and "acknowledged no obligation to Landor's *Gebir*" for the image of the sea-shell used in *The Excursion*—"from his childhood the shell was familiar to him"—though Landor, in a note to the satire, had quoted the passage as proof of his unacknowledged debt.[1]

Landor never again met Wordsworth, whose conduct during Southey's last illness deepened his dislike. Discussing the defects of Wordsworth's poetry in the second imaginary conversation between Southey and Porson, published in *Blackwood's Magazine* for December 1842, his criticism carried the more conviction in also weighing its merits. But such was the change in the popular estimate of Wordsworth that Landor's criticism in 1842 was accounted as extravagant as his praise in 1823. When Forster protested against his hostility to Wordsworth, he wrote in 1845:

No writer . . . has praised Wordsworth more copiously or more warmly than I have done; and I said not a syllable against him until he disparaged his friend and greatest champion, Southey. You should be the last to blame me for holding the heads of my friends to be inviolable. Whoever touches a hair of them I devote *diis inferis, sed rite*.

[1] Probably neither Wordsworth nor Landor remembered a curious example of his self-complacency when he wrote to Landor on 20th April, 1822: "In your *Simonidea*, which I saw some years ago at Mr. Southey's, I was pleased to find rather an out-of-the-way image, in which the present hour is compared to the shade on the dial. It is a singular coincidence, that in the year 1793, when I first became an author, I illustrated the sentiment precisely in the same manner." Byron acknowledged his borrowing of the sea-shell image from Landor (see pages 69–70 and 198).

The Southey-Porson dialogue inspired a malicious skit in *Blackwood* by Quillinan, for which Robinson "supplied the materials", but Landor's only comment was a pun: "I am told a Mr. Quillinan has been attacking me," he wrote to Kenyon; "His writings, I hear, are *Quill-inanities.*" His dislike did not detract from his appreciation of Wordsworth's poetry; he privately praised *The Prelude* as "the Eikon Basilike of poetry" and defended his estimate of Wordsworth in the imaginary conversation between Julius Hare and himself:

Discriminating praise mingled with calm censure is more beneficial than lavish praise without it. Respect him; reverence him; abstain from worshipping him.

In the same imaginary conversation he claimed no more than his due in believing "there are few, if any, who enjoy more heartily than I do, the best poetry of my contemporaries, or who have commended them both in private and in public with less parsimony and reserve". In *A Satire on Satirists* "the one-spurr'd critick begs to ask",

> Hath Sheffield's glorious son the genuine vein?
> Did *Paracelsus* spring from poet's brain?
> When all expect it, *yes* will never do,
> The cautious and the business-like say *no*.

Footnotes to this passage praised the sonnets of Ebenezer Elliott, "the Corn-law Rhymer", and remarked, "*Paracelsus* has found a critick capable of appreciating him. It is not often that the generous are so judicious, nor always that the judicious are so generous." On reading Forster's appreciation of Browning the previous autumn, Landor wrote to him:

When you told us that the author of Paracelsus would be a great poet, you came rather too late in the exercise of prophecy—he was one already, and will be among the greatest. I hope he does not relax in that sirocco of faint praise which brother poets are fond of giving. Such as yours will brace him against it.

This passage survived from one of Landor's earliest letters to Forster because Forster cut it out and sent it to Browning, who cherished the fragment and recalled as late as 1881 that Landor's "praise was prompt, both private and public—(in his Satire on Satirists)".

§ 4

In his letter of remonstrance on *A Satire on Satirists*, Crabb Robinson told Landor that he had also "received or suspected I received an amusing memorial of your enviable faculty of contemplating the follies of life with a free and cheerful aspect". Three months before, on 9th

September (when Landor had been for two months at Heidelberg), Robinson noted in his diary:

At the Athenaeum I found three copies of a very small poem, *Terry Hogan*, a *Schwanke*, gross and not very clever, with notes of burlesque criticism. It may be by Landor; he is a very unequal writer; Collier would not waste money in that way (the thing is not published) and Kenyon is too moral.

Terry Hogan is described on its title page as "An Eclogue; Lately discovered in the Library of the Propaganda At Rome, And now first translated from the Irish", with "A Dissertation By the Editor, Phelim Octavius Quarle, S.T.P." The poem begins:

> Terry Hogan, who married Teresa Magrath,
> Met Phin Malahide in the mass-house footpath . . .
> Phin scratch'd both his shoulders as those who condole—
> "'Tis pity! 'tis pity! it goes to my soul!
> It goes to my soul and touches my heart
> That a couple so lately united must part.
> A couple on earth never saw I so proper,
> The one to knock under, the other to top her.
> With book and with cruet, too surely 'twas she
> That Father Macreagh in such haste went to see.
> Run back, Terry, quickly run back! crave a blessing!
> For may-be you'll come rather late for her kissing."

It is sheep-shearing time, and Terry runs back carrying his "shears of Tralee", with which he wreaks drastic vengeance on the priest discovered in the most compromising of postures.

Landor was hardly in the mood for such amusement when he left England for Heidelberg, nor did he either before or afterwards employ the services of the printers of *Terry Hogan*, J. Wertheimer & Co., of Circus Place, London Wall. On the other hand, it is such fooling as he and Charles Brown might have enjoyed together; the device of the fictitious editor is the same as in *Citation and Examination of William Shakspeare* and *The Pentameron*; the editor declares himself "indebted to . . . an English gentleman, long resident in Italy", who objects to the writing of "the name of Shakspeare with an *e* between the *k* and *s*", which "reminds us of a silly young coxcomb, who wrote 'procede' because we write 'recede'"—in a note to the 1803 edition of *Gebir* Landor asked "why *preceed* and *exceed* are spelt differently in their termination from *recede*, and why they are not both spelt after the manner of the latter?"

Landor never reprinted *Terry Hogan*; Forster did not mention it in his biography or include it in his edition of Landor's works, but preserved a copy in his library; Colvin described it as "an Irish squib in verse, of which the less said the better, directed against the morality of the priesthood"; accepting Colvin's dismissal, Wheeler excluded *Terry Hogan* from his edition of Landor's poems, but acknowledged that Landor's authorship "can be supported, if not proved beyond question, by passages in the text". In *The Publication of Landor's Works* Mr. Super thinks *Terry Hogan* "shows something of Landor for which the biographer must be very grateful", but no reason for such gratitude emerges in *Walter Savage Landor: A Biography*. With his opinion of priests, freely expressed elsewhere, Landor must have been amused at their ridicule by Boccaccio; if humour is rare in his writings, he always had a sense of fun. It is true that MacCarthy was an Irishman, but many of Landor's friends were Irish, and so was Ianthe.

§ 5

"To-day is my birthday, and never on my birthday was I happy," wrote Landor on 30th January 1837, sending to Lady Blessington the verses:

The day returns, my natal day,
　　Borne on the storm and pale with snow,
And seems to ask me why I stay,
　　Stricken by Time and bowed by Woe.

Many were once the friends who came
　　To wish me joy; and there are some
Who wish it now; but not the same;
　　They are whence friends can never come;

Nor are they you my love watcht o'er,
　　Cradled in innocence and sleep;
You smile into my eyes no more,
　　Nor see the bitter tears they weep.

His anxiety about his daughter was now intensified by a letter from Arnold, informing him that their cousin, Edward Willson Landor, was making advances to her. A somewhat unsatisfactory young man of twenty-six, Edward had stayed at Fiesole in 1835, when he was so attracted to Julia that, as he explained to Landor in a long letter pleading his suit on 4th February 1837, "notwithstanding the warmth of friendship I met in your house, I resolved to quit it hastily".

I should probably have continued to obey the dictates of prudence, & for ever have shunned her society, had not the most horrible thoughts been excited in my breast & in those of most of your relations by your reports of the disorderly conduct of your wife and family during your absence. I conceived with others, that your daughter though untainted herself was living within the sphere of contamination and who is there so ungenerous, so contemptible that would not make every effort to withdraw purity from the foul atmosphere, which I was led to believe she inhaled? Your two younger sons were absolutely running wild, uncontrolled, & uninstructed in the necessary lesson of self-government; and no one could see a whole family so left to themselves, & left to ruin, without striving in some way to aid them, however dangerous might be the essay to himself. I went to Florence & did all in my power to induce your family to repair to England.

He enclosed a girlish letter from Julia, asking her father's consent to her engagement—"do not think that time can alter my sentiments", she warned him; "when once I have given my whole heart unreservedly, neither time nor distance can make me change"—and he promised, if Landor agreed to the engagement, he would undertake not to see her for two years.

Edward Landor was not a suitor to be welcomed. Three years before, his uncle, Walter of Rugeley, had generously given him a junior partnership in his attorney's practice, not because he was greatly disposed in his favour, but because "by the time my eldest boy is Edward's age, I shall be in my dotage or my grave". Sarcastically he told Henry Landor that he had doubted the young man's acceptance of the offer, since he had "a mind much superior to that of a 'Country Attorney' & a most independent spirit", and was "in great danger of becoming a scribbler for magazines". But Edward had shown gallantry and initiative in going to Florence, and Landor might have been well advised to consent to a provisional engagement as a means of conveying his daughter to England. Unluckily, before Edward could approach him, he was informed of the affair by Arnold, who evidently disapproved of his cousin's attentions to his sister, and pathetically eager to see cause for applauding some conduct of his eldest son, he exclaimed enthusiastically at Arnold's dutiful conduct and accused Edward of "baseness" in tampering with Julia's affections in her father's absence. Edward's "independent spirit" prompted a tactlessly aggressive tone, which ruined his chances. He did not persevere in his profession, but sometime later emigrated to Australia, whence he wrote to Forster thirty years afterwards. Not yet seventeen, Julia was unlikely long to repine, but even an early and unwise marriage would have been better than her actual unhappy fate.

The incident inspired renewed efforts by Landor to bring his children to England, but not all his agents had the same understanding of the situation as Francis Hare and Mrs. Dashwood. Travelling with Wordsworth to Italy, Crabb Robinson was disinclined to sympathy with Landor and immediately became Mrs. Landor's partisan when he called on her. He decided that "Mrs. Landor is certainly a very weak woman, but I think respectable in her conduct"; his "suspicions on this head" were removed, though MacCarthy was then still a member of the

U

household and Landor afterwards informed him, "The fellow would not take the dismissal I gave him, and remained in the house after my return to England, in spite of me." He thought Mrs. Landor's "provocations have been very great indeed: she complains of personal violence, even beating, and I can believe such things". She told him how Landor "ran away from her" in Jersey "a short time after their marriage" and confided details of their marital relations; "notwithstanding all this, she allowed me to say that she should be happy to see him". The daughter "cried several times" while he spoke of her father, and he enclosed a note from her in writing to Landor: "I am sure you are wanted at home, and that your presence might have the happiest effect on the character of your children. It might be decisive as to the happiness of your daughter." As Landor had told him more than a year before why he could not possibly live with his wife, Robinson can hardly have thought that he was serving any useful purpose. Only a few weeks earlier, when Trelawny sent a message through Lady Blessington that their mutual Florence friend Macdonell was visiting England, Landor replied that he was "afraid I shall be unable to meet him in England, and Italy is quite out of the question".

Landor was adamant in declining to live again with his wife. When his brother-in-law Ravenshaw appealed to him to return to her, he replied so that Forster recorded Ravenshaw's "frank admission of the strength of the grounds on which his refusal to comply was based". As all witnesses agreed that the children were backward in education, it was obvious that they should have come to school in England, but Mrs. Landor refused to be separated from them. To meet her objection Francis Hare persuaded Landor to agree to his wife's accompanying the children to England, and in November 1837 Mrs. Dashwood wrote to Landor's sister Elizabeth that a house was being taken for the family at Plymouth, where Charles Brown was living, and Landor would occupy lodgings close by. Landor wrote to Mrs. Dashwood: "I shall tell him (F.H.) that they may all come next April, on condition that I never see her." Apparently this condition provided an excuse for retraction, Arnold resenting the slight to his mother. In reprisal Landor deducted a hundred pounds from the family's annual allowance, but so far from reverting to his threat of selling the Fiesole house, he assigned the property to Arnold immediately on his coming of age in 1839. Following this generous gift, Arnold and his mother again intimated through Kenyon and Aubrey Bezzi that they would welcome Landor's return: urging the advantage to the children, Bezzi wrote, "Their mother, as you well know, does not, perhaps cannot, exercise any wholesome control over them; she plainly admits this, and adduces it as a reason, among others, why she wishes and hopes you will return." If, as Mrs. Landor assured Robinson, Landor was guilty "of beating her and of making himself an object of terror to the children", it is difficult to understand why she urged that his return would benefit the children.

Nor did Arnold's repeated truculence indicate a feeling of terror towards his father. After the failure of the Plymouth project, Landor addressed to him the verses published in the *Examiner* of 14th October 1838, beginning "Arnold! thou wert a lovely child!" and ending;

> Arnold! thy breast was tender then!
> Ah why, so slightly verst with men,
> Avoids it now the holy ties
> Of all our early sympathies?
> I am not cross, I am not cold,
> My heart . . . it never can grow old. . . .
> The tears fast falling from my cheek
> Are signs for words I will not speak.

"I was moved to tears the other day, on reading in 'The Examiner' your lines to Arnold," wrote Lady Blessington: "If he reads them, how can he resist flying to you?" In a letter of the same year to Lady Blessington, Landor wrote:

I heard from Florence not long ago, but nothing from that quarter is likely to give me pleasure or composure. I wish I could utterly forget all connected with it. But the waves of oblivion dash against my Tuscan terraces, and the spray reaches my family, and blinds the eyes that should be turned towards me, for other waters fill my heart with bitterness.

14

SETTLEMENT AT BATH

I hardly know which is most afflicting; to hear the loudest expression of intolerable anguish from the weak who are sinking under it, or to witness an aged and venerable man bearing up against his sufferings with unshaken constancy.

—Galileo, Milton, and a Dominican (1839)

Before we go into another state of existence, a thousand things occur to detach us imperceptibly from this. To some (who knows to how many?) the images of early love return with an inviting yet a saddening glance, and the breast that was laid out for the sepulchre bleeds afresh. Such are ready to follow where they are beckoned, and look keenly into the darkness they are about to penetrate.

—Vittoria Colonna and Michel-Angelo (1841)

"By living at Clifton, I am grown as rich as Rothschild," wrote Landor to Lady Blessington in December 1836; "if Count D'Orsay could see me in my new coat, he would not write me so pressingly to come up to London." Still seriously trying to live on two hundred a year, which his trustees soon increased to four hundred, he became notorious for the shabbiness of his snuff-coloured clothes. "He never bought any new clothes," said Francis Hare's son Augustus, "and a chimney-sweep would have been ashamed to wear his coat, which was always the same as long as I knew him, though it in no way detracted from his majestic and lion-like appearance." Lady Bulwer, however, remarked that Landor in the daytime, wearing "his old gabardine of a brown surtout, shining at the seams, and often minus some buttons", looked very different from "the thoroughbred, noble-headed, distinguished-looking man . . . when dressed for dinner".

At Clifton he became intimate with Charles Elton, a man three years his junior, who succeeded to his father's baronetcy in 1842, and with whom he had been acquainted in their youth. Elton was a classical scholar of distinction, and they "delighted in reciting alternate stanzas from Homer" together. Elton had a large and merry family of children, three boys and eight girls, and more for their society than their father's Landor went so often that, writing their news to their eldest brother, the girls would note, "nothing occurred—only Old Landor called oftener than ever". "He would come in at about dinner time, six o'clock, when he would ask leave to sit in the room, without dining, as he preferred to go home to a later dinner," and taking an easy chair, would "talk delightfully without causing the least restraint or inconvenience". He chose as his favourites the two youngest girls, who were most nearly the age of his own daughter, and Jane Elton wrote:

He was most kind and sympathetic to us all though he singled out me and my sister Mary at that early age to tell us he had troubles. One day he said he had left a drawer full of Southey's letters at home—letters he had treasured and intended to keep, but "My wife has been so good as to burn them," and he gave the loudest burst of laughter I ever heard.

When one of the girls consulted him about a short story she had written, he obtained for her five pounds for it from Lady Blessington, who published it in the *Book of Beauty*.

The Eltons moved their home from Clifton to Southampton in the autumn of 1837, and Mary Elton wrote to her sister: "Mr. Landor says it will make him melancholy to pass by our terrace, so he will not return to Clifton." But the absence of a dearer friend than the Eltons inspired Landor's sudden distaste for Clifton, of which he had written to Southey on his return from Heidelberg, "here I think I shall finish my days; the climate suits my health so perfectly". Ianthe was living at Clifton when he went there from Llanbedr early in 1836; it was she by whom he had "been expected these last four days" when he paused only one night in London on his return from Heidelberg, and to whom he hurried for comfort in his wretchedness. For the rest of her life, Landor contrived to live near her whenever she was in England, first at Clifton, then at Bath. This intimacy he sacredly kept from most of his friends, but he referred to her when writing to Forster how "every autumn I save something, because, in the months of December and January, I give to poor families half the income of those two months. A person unerring in her judgment and boundless in her goodness helps me to find them out". Throughout the twenty-two years of his residence at Bath, he practised a habit of unobtrusive charity. At Christmas 1844 he asked Rose Paynter:

Have you any old pensioners who are looking out for you? If you have, appoint me your almoner. I have kept some money on purpose. This month and the next, I am resolved to spend on myself only half my large income. My heart sinks and aches every time I go out of doors, such is the misery of the poor.

Always he had felt sympathy with the sufferings of the poor. In 1812 when wartime prices were at their height and he informed Southey that "three pounds of miserable bread cost two shillings at Abergavenny", he was touched by the distresses of the Llanthony peasantry in spite of their malicious treatment of himself—"the poor barbarous creatures in my parish have actually ceased to be mischievous, they are so miserable". Forty-two years later, in 1854, he excused himself to Forster for visiting London more rarely: "I too often think at night of what I had been seeing in the morning, poor mothers, half-starved children, and girls habitually called unfortunate by people who drop the word as lightly as if it had no meaning in it. . . . So many heartaches always leave me one."

If, as Forster recorded, Landor visited Ablett at Llanbedr and his sisters at Warwick in 1837, the visits must have occurred between February and April, when he was troubled by Edward Landor's suit to his daughter—a matter on which he consulted both Ablett and his brother Henry. In reply to Lady Blessington's invitation to repeat his visit to Gore House, he wrote on 12th May from Clifton Hill Cottage, "I have been unwell for some time, indeed never very well since I went to Germany"; in the same month Monckton Milnes reported, "Landor is at Clifton, eating up his own heart, with no better relish than the bitter herbs of world-contempt and self-exaltation." Apparently Milnes read "self-exaltation" in Landor's self-praise of his "Death of Clytemnestra", though he wrote in the same letter of the previous November, complying with Milnes's request for a contribution to a volume published for charity by Lord Northampton:

> As for my contributions of poetry, they are utterly worthless, and I seldom keep anything. What I do keep I send to Lady Blessington, having told her long ago that I would never publish anything before she had judged whether it were worth a place in any of her publications.

This promise—made when Lady Blessington undertook the editorship of Heath's *Book of Beauty* with its issue for 1834—he so faithfully fulfilled that every volume of the annual for fourteen years from 1834 to 1847 contained contributions from him in verse or prose.

To another charity volume, sponsored by Lady Mary Fox, he sent three contributions at the request of G. P. R. James, including "Death of Clytemnestra" and the lines addressed to his friend Charles Elton. Asked in January by Samuel Carter Hall for "some memoranda, out of which to form a brief page of biography, to accompany specimens of modern Poets", he was unimpressed by this mark of celebrity and asked Lady Blessington, "Is it possible that any one, excepting Southey, Forster, and James, can believe that I myself am a poet?" Later in the year, when Leigh Hunt's editorship of the *Monthly Repository* enabled him at last to make use of *High and Low Life in Italy*, he supported Hunt's brief venture by adding numerous verses to the prose narrative and asked Lady Blessington to "take in poor Leigh Hunt's Monthly Repository; not because there are some trivial things of mine in it, but because he wants encouragement and assistance". Forster's friendship opened to him the columns of the *Examiner*, in which extracts from the "Audiences granted by the Emperor of China to Tsing-ti" in December and January were followed by a series of "Mr. Landor's Conservative Epistles on the Church".

"My eyes are in a miserable plight from the influenza," he wrote to Lady Blessington in May:

I sat up all last night to read James's *Attila*, not greatly to the benefit of my eyes or the credit of my prudence. But I never can leave off a book that interests me until I have gone thro' it. . . . I have received more honour than Augustus, or Mecenas, or Louis Quatorze, or any other man, living or dead, for to no one were ever inscribed two such works of imagination as the *Curse of Kehama* and *Attila*.

Influenza induced such despondency that he felt "more than half inclined to look a peep's depth under a turf", and in June he accepted an invitation from Kenyon to recuperate at Torquay, where he completed the interviews between Boccaccio and Petrarca, as he told Lady Blessington on the 25th:

This very evening I sent off to Saunders and Otley the last of my last book. Instead of calling it *Certaldo*, I now entitle it "The Pentameron"—the *five* days' interview of Boccaccio and Petrarca. . . . I am now at Torquay, formerly the most beautiful and retired bay in England, covered with woods all round, and containing but six or seven thatched cottages. At present it is filled with smart, ugly houses, and rich, hot-looking people. It is however still the most beautiful watering-place in the British dominions, but deprived of its ancient refinement. I remember it more than forty years ago.

As explained in the Introduction, the publishers advised the change of title from *Certaldo*—the name of the site of Boccaccio's villa—to *The Pentameron*, "unless I would return with nothing in my pocket". "Of course I must publish it at my own risk," said Landor, "for any publisher would be a fool to undertake anything of mine at his."

With Kenyon at Torquay was a friend from Florence, Aubrey Bezzi, and Landor also met Sheridan Knowles the dramatist, Andrew Crosse the scientist, and Theodosia Garrow, afterwards Tom Trollope's first wife. Charles Brown came to stay for a week, and when Landor accompanied him to his home near Plymouth for a few days, he asked Mrs. Dashwood to correct the proofs of *The Pentameron* while he made another "visit or two in the rest of Devonshire and Cornwall". Returning to Torquay, he lingered, reluctant to spend the winter at Clifton without Ianthe, who had gone to stay at Vienna with her Austrian daughter-in-law. "I have a great love for Clifton," he wrote to Southey on 18th September, "yet I cannot endure the sight of flowers or fields where I had ever spent pleasurable hours. So, instead of Clifton, I think I shall go to Bath in the middle of next month."

His departure from Torquay was delayed till the middle of November, for he wrote on the 25th to Lady Blessington from new lodgings at 35 St. James's Square, Bath, that he left Torquay only "in the beginning of last week":

I pass my time between Bath and Clifton. I forgot to give up my lodgings at Clifton the six months I have been away. In fact I intended to spend only so many weeks at Torquay, but I found there some old friends, and made some new ones. . . . In the beginning of April I hope to enjoy once more the splendid hospitalities and charming conversation of Gore House. There I shall find no alteration. Alas! how great have I found here at Bath. Most of my old acquaintance are dead, most of my younger married and gone elsewhere. Poor Lady Belmore, whom I have known the longest of any, is totally blind. Her sister, Miss Caldwell, still sings and plays on the guitar, but like Anacreon, she has changed all the strings. Two or three people have recollected me, whom I had utterly forgotten, not that I am less changed than they are, but because my memory of faces is a most unloyal one. I may converse a whole evening with a person and forget both his features and his name before the next.

Lady Belmore and Miss Caldwell still "presided over the dances" at the Assembly Rooms, where he now saw Rose Paynter enjoying such admiration as Ianthe had received more than thirty years before. Reminding him of her aunt Rose Aylmer, Rose succeeded the Elton sisters as substitute for the daughter he had lost. He became the privileged intimate of the Paynters' family circle, and Rose's visit to Paris in the following year began a correspondence lasting through the remainder of his life.

Through the Paynters he found a friend in Colonel William Napier —later knighted as a general—who was then writing his *History of the Peninsular War*. Married to a niece of Charles James Fox, Napier disagreed with Landor's estimate of that statesman, but shared most of his political views. "You don't draw your ale mild, any more than I do," Napier wrote to him in later years, "but if Pam or Johnny (Lord John Russell) call you out, I will be your second". With his usual prejudice in friendship, Landor reckoned Napier "the greatest historian of our age" and remarked in 1855 that he had "never known more than two *great* men, although many good ones—Napier and Kossuth." He idolised as a hero William Napier's elder brother, Sir Charles James Napier, the conqueror of Sind, rating him above Wellington as "the only truly wise general of our times" and expressing indignation at the difference over military reform with the viceroy Dalhousie that caused Napier's retirement as commander-in-chief in India:

> If thou wert only foul and frowsy,
> If only itchy, only lousy,
> Bold men might take thy hand, Dalhousie!

Among many verses addressed to the Napier brothers, the least elegant but most descriptive appeared in *Dry Sticks*:

> One brother closed the Scindian war,
> The other the Peninsular:
> One bore his painful wounds few years,
> The other his thro' fifty bears.
> Each, who abroad had overcome
> His foes, encountered worse at home.
> England! are such rewards for these
> Who won and wrote thy victories?

When William Napier left Bath in 1842 to become lieutenant-governor of Guernsey and one of his attractive daughters wrote to him affectionately, Landor remarked with pleasure, "I do really think one or two of them would even give up a flirtation for five minutes to write to me or converse with me."

Neither the Paynters nor the Napiers could compensate for Ianthe's absence, and when, in May 1838, she deferred her return from Austria, he appealed to her in verse:

> Ianthe! since our parting day
> Pleasure and you were long away.
> Leave you then all that strove to please
> In proud Vienna's palaces
> To soothe your Landor's heart agen
> And roam once more our hazel glen?
>
> .   .   .   .   .
>
> You sate beside me on that stone,
> Rather (not much) too wide for one:
>
> .   .   .   .   .
>
> Ianthe, come! ere June declines
> We'll write upon it all these lines.

§ 2

Saunders & Otley issued rather than published *The Pentameron and Pentalogia* in December 1837: "I have given express orders that no copies be sent to such people as the editor of the *Athenæum*, &c., who cannot understand it, and have always been ill-disposed towards me," wrote Landor; "I will not even allow it to be advertised." The

Pentalogia comprised five dramatic scenes in verse added as an after-
thought, probably for the purpose of paying a compliment to Southey;
besides "The Death of Clytemnestra" and "The Madness of Orestes",
in "Essex and Bacon" Essex disdains Bacon's suggestion that he should
plead for pardon, in "Walter Tyrrel and William Rufus" Tyrrel kills
the king after vainly appealing against an order for callous destruction,
in "The Parents of Luther" the parents discuss the future of their
unborn son. Remarking that "you and two others will read these
dramatic scraps with pleasure", the dedication "To Robert Southey"
continued:

> You are almost the only public man, of either party, whom I would give
> a farthing to please by anything I write. But never shall I cease to eulogise
> those of either, who are friends to liberal economy, fair conciliation, and
> watchful peace.
> I publish no more in my lifetime. I may, however, throw off my fingers'-
> ends a few drops to lay the dust; a few to make the point-lace lie closer on
> the lawn, which others must wash and mend. As you will not enter the
> laundry or tire-room with me, pray accept these lumps of sugar-candy, to
> remove any bitterness left in the mouth by the astringency of my conservatism.

Clearly the dedication was intended to affirm that the friendship of
thirty years was unaffected by divergence of opinion.

In *The Pentameron* Boccaccio, ailing in his last years of retirement at
Certaldo, receives a five days' visit from his old friend Petrarca, and
from Petrarca's remark that "little more than a tenth of the *Decameron*
is bad: less than a twentieth of the *Divina Commedia* is good", they proceed to desultory discussion of Dante's work. Landor might well have
agreed with John Cowper Powys's assertion that "you cannot become a
disciple of Dante in the metaphysical sense without becoming a
Catholic; but you *can* become a disciple of Dante as a poet and lover and
as the representative of a particular kind of imaginative response to
life". Landor's two protagonists allow to Dante the beauties of the
poet and the lover: the story of Paolo and Francesca is the "perfection
of poetry", "all the verses that ever were written on the nightingale are
scarcely worth the beautiful triad of this divine poet on the lark", "the
little virgin Beatrice Portinari breathed all her purity into his boyish
heart . . . and if war and disaster, anger and disdain, seized upon it in
her absence, they never could divert its course nor impede its desti-
nation". But the occasional beauties of the *Inferno* are "streaks of light
in a thunderstorm"; Boccaccio and Petrarca, like Landor himself,
were repelled by Dante's cruelty, by "his harshness and meagreness
and disproportion", by the sadism of frustration and repression, and
Petrarca remarks,

> Lucretius, in his vituperation, is graver and more dignified than Alighieri.
> Painful; to see how tolerant is the atheist, how intolerant the catholic: how

anxiously the one removes from among the sufferings of Mortality, her last and heaviest, the fear of a vindictive Fury pursuing her shadow across rivers of fire and tears: how laboriously the other brings down Anguish and Despair, even when Death has done his work. How grateful the one is to that beneficent philosopher who made him at peace with himself, and tolerant and kindly toward his fellow creatures! how importunate the other that God should forego his divine mercy, and hurl everlasting torments both upon the dead and the living!

Elsewhere the pair debate the views on religion that Landor propounded in *Letters of a Conservative* and in many of the imaginary conversations:

Petrarca. What Dante saw in his day, we see in ours. The danger is, lest first the wiser, and soon afterward the unwiser, in abhorrence at the presumption and iniquity of the priesthood, should abandon religion altogether, when it is forbidden to approach her without such company.
Boccaccio. Philosophy is but the calix of that plant of paradise, religion. Detach it, and it dies away; meanwhile the plant itself, supported by its proper nutriment, retains its vigour.
Petrarca. The good citizen and the calm reasoner come at once to the same conclusion: that philosophy can never hold many men together; that religion can; and those who are without it would not let philosophy, nor law, nor humanity exist. Therefore it is our duty and interest to remove all obstruction from it; to give it air, light, space, and freedom; carrying in our hands a scourge for fallacy, a chain for cruelty, and an irrevocable ostracism for riches that riot in the house of God.

It is perhaps indicative of the obtuseness of orthodoxy that Leslie Stephen, who said of Landor's work that "probably the highest triumph is in the Pentameron", concluded that "his religious principles are . . . little more than the assertion that he will not be fettered in mind or body by any priest on earth". Landor's warning was uttered also by Coleridge—the apostle of the Broad Church movement—when he said, "whenever religion excludes philosophy, or the spirit of free inquiry, it leads to wilful blindness and superstition". As a Hellenist, Landor agreed also with Coleridge that, after its development by the Greek philosophers, "the measure of human philosophy was thus full, when Christianity"—meaning of course the teachings of Christ and not of the churches—"came to add what before was wanting—assurance".

What Leslie Stephen admired in *The Pentameron* was less the major arguments of debate than their setting. For, by contrast with all the other imaginary conversations, Landor here supplies a background. Writing at Heidelberg and Clifton, he transported himself among the familiar scenes of Fiesole; as they digress into reminiscence and reflection, Boccaccio and Petrarca condescend to gossip of the maidservant Assunta, introducing a contrast of levity and mundane triviality with the preoccupations of philosophy and poetry, and the details of Petrarca's Sunday morning ride vividly depict the scene in village and countryside. The fifth day's interview ends with the allegory of

Petrarca's dream, in which the spirits of Love, Sleep, and Death appear to him, and this conclusion emphasises that the whole work is itself an allegorical dream of life, for the two friends, so near the end of living their full lives, though they debate poetry, philosophy, politics, with all the meaning and wisdom of life's experience, still turn aside in tender regard for Assunta's ingenuous youth and in pleasure at the kindliness of simplicity. "Alas, alas! the time always comes," says Petrarca, "when we must regret the enjoyments of our youth"; and Boccaccio, the life-lover, comments tersely, "If we have let them pass us."

§ 3

Near the end of *The Pentameron* Boccaccio invites Petrarca to read him some "verses written by a gentleman who resided long in this country, and who much regretted the necessity of leaving it":

> Carlino! what art thou about, my boy?
> Often I ask that question, though in vain,
> For we are far apart: ah! therefore 'tis
> I often ask it; not in such a tone
> As wiser fathers do, who know too well.
> Were we not children, you and I together?
> Stole we not glances from each other's eyes?
> Swore we not secrecy in such misdeeds?
> Well could we trust each other. Tell me then
> What thou art doing. Carving out thy name,
> Or haply mine, upon my favourite seat,
> With the new knife I sent thee over sea?
> Or hast thou broken it, and hid the hilt
> Among the myrtles, starr'd with flowers, behind?
> Or under that high throne whence fifty lilies
> (With sworded tuberoses dense around)
> Lift up their heads at once, not without fear
> That they were looking at thee all the while?

From such nostalgic reflections he escaped, according to habit, in work, the progress of which appears in his letters to Lady Blessington. "I am employed in adding to my Imaginary Conversation between Horne Tooke and Johnson," he reported on 13th January 1838. "When I come to London, I intend to bring my revised and enlarged copy of Conversations with me, and make a present of them to Forster, one among the few who think that they are worth a farthing." He had "quite enough" for a sixth volume, "on the whole, quite as good as the former . . . but never will I consent to publish anything more in my lifetime".

This resolution was qualified in the course of a few weeks. On 11th February:

Here in Bath I am leading a quiet and therefore pleasant life. . . . The revisal of my "Imaginary Conversations" has cost me more time than the composition. For this, after all, is my great work; the others are but boudoir-tables to lay it on.

A week later:

When you do me the favour of writing to me again, pray give me Forster's address, for I want to send him the corrected addition of my "Imaginary Conversations". I have finished all the volumes excepting the dialogue between Johnson and Horne Tooke, which I have enlarged prodigiously, and which I once thought of reprinting separate. But neither in my lifetime nor afterwards shall anything more of mine be published, excepting such few matters as have been completed long ago, and are sufficient to form another volume of "Imaginary Conversations".

On 4th March:

. . . it was suggested to me by my sensible friend Mrs. Dashwood, that although my "Imaginary Conversations" were unpopular, yet that if I would consent to publish those containing female characters separately, the case might be somewhat different. . . . I do not care a fig either for popularity or profit, for if ever I am popular I shall never know anything about it; and if ever I get money I shall neither spend nor save it! I have already more than I want. But I really should like to make a pretty present of such a volume as no other man living can write, embellished with worthy engravings. If you can manage this affair, I am confident you will.

Proposing that the book should be called "Landor's Female Characters Illustrated", after the style of Mrs. Jameson's *Shakespeare's Female Characters*, he listed seventeen dialogues for inclusion. But Lady Blessington soon replied that her publishers were not interested in the proposition, whereupon Landor consoled himself on 15th March, "I myself have always had a great dislike to engravings in books, and must confess I am rather glad at the failure." "This last week I have sent Saunders and Otley a hundred and forty pounds as a fine for committing the folly of authorship," he added. "Next year I shall pay them eighty more."

Kenyon stayed four days with him in April, immediately after the publication of his poems: "he was obliged to print them at his own expense; and his cousin, Miss Barrett, who has also written a few poems of no small merit, could not find a publisher". Landor proposed to go to Gore House by the end of April, but delayed his arrival till 11th May in awaiting the arrival of a consignment of pictures from Italy—"which, if they are unpacked in my absence, will probably be ruined". His hostess was as accomodating as two years before: "I told Lady Blessington I should not let any of her court stand at all in my way," he wrote, inviting Forster to call one evening. "When I am tired of them, I leave them."

Twice he breakfasted with Milnes, on the second occasion in distinguished company:

Carlyle is a vigorous thinker, but a vile writer, worse than Bulwer. I breakfasted in company with him at Milnes's. Macaulay was there, a clever clown, and Moore too, whom I had not seen till then. Between those two Scotchmen he appeared like a glow-worm between two thistles. There were several other folks, literary and half literary, Lord Northampton, &c., &c. I forgot Rogers.

There was no liking between Landor and the little banker-poet; Crabb Robinson, who was among the "half literary" etceteras present, noted, "Rogers angry with being forced into Landor's company." Robinson had received a presentation copy of *The Pentameron* and been "glad of the opportunity of praising with sincerity this delightful book"; he had therefore invited Landor to breakfast two days before, and considered that he was "rattling" when he "maintained Blake to be the greatest of poets". But at Milnes's, where the talk was "very good, equally divided" and "Talleyrand's recent death and the poet Blake were the subjects", he remarked that "Tom Moore had never heard of Blake— at least not of his poems", and "even he acknowledged their beauty". Landor must have been one of the first to recognise the greatness of Blake as a poet.

At Gore House Landor met the Hon. Grantley Berkeley, a "half literary" man of fashion who fought a duel with Dr. Maginn when his novel was attacked in *Fraser's Magazine*; finding that Berkeley was one of the members of Parliament for West Gloucestershire, Landor "told him a bit of my mind" because he had not been invited to be one of the deputy lieutenants for Monmouthshire, though "my estate there is larger than the Lord Lieutenant's".

Henry Fothergill Chorley, who made a reputation for taste and judgment as art and music critic of the *Athenæum*, frequently met Landor at Gore House, and one evening this month recorded "a very rare treat":

A dinner at Kensington *tête-à-tête* with Lady Blessington and Mr. Landor; she talking her best, brilliant and kindly, and without that touch of self-consciousness which she sometimes displays when worked up to it by flatterers and gay companions. Landor, as usual, the very finest man's head I have ever seen, and with all his Johnsonian disposition to tyrannise and lay down the law in his talk, restrained and refined by an old-world courtesy and deference towards his bright hostess, for which *chivalry* is the only right word. There was never any one less of "a pretty man;" but his tale of having gone from Bristol to Bath, to find a moss-rose for a girl who had desired one (I suppose for some ball), was all natural and graceful, and charming enough.

Later in the evening Isaac D'Israeli came in; "as of course they talked and I heard", Chorley "had the luxury of undisturbed leisure wherein to use eyes and ears". He noticed that D'Israeli affected "a rather *soigné* style of dress for so old a man, and a manner good-humoured, complimentary (to Gebir), discursive and prosy, bespeaking that engrossment and interest in his own pursuits which might be expected to be found in a person so patient in research and collection"; he also detected "a tone of the *philosophe* (or I fancied it), which I did not quite like", and when D'Israeli "advanced a theory about Shakespeare's having been long in exciting the notice he deserved, as compared with Ben Jonson and other dramatists", Chorley was pleased with Landor's rejoinder, "Yes, Mr. D'Israeli, the oak and the ebony take a long time to grow up and make wood, but they last for ever!" Apparently D'Israeli had forgotten or never read Landor's reference to him in the *Postscript to Gebir*, for soon after this meeting he wrote his congratulations on reading *The Pentameron*:

I have been your constant reader. I have never turned over a page of your works but with a pause of reflection. . . . All that you have written has been masterly, and struck out by the force of an original mind. You have not condescended to write down to the mediocrity of the populace of readers. You will be read hereafter. I know not whether you have written a century too late or too early: too late, if the taste for literature has wholly left us; too early, if the public mind has not yet responded to your sympathies.

There was shrewdness in this comment by the compiler of *Curiosities of Literature*: in the time of Swift, Pope, and Addison, when books were published in small editions by subscription, Landor's works would have been studied and collected by leisured scholars, just as in the nineteen-twenties they might have been the subject of such a cult as George Moore's later work enjoyed, but in his own day he was too profound and too scholarly for the half-educated reading public born of the industrial revolution.

The manners of a young American, Charles Sumner, were inferior to Chorley's in deference to an older man; he was shocked when Landor "called Napoleon the weakest, littlest man in history", and "we crossed each other several times". He described Landor as "dressed in a heavy frock-coat of snuff colour, trousers of the same colour and boots", with "an open countenance, firm and decided, and a head grey and inclining to baldness"; his talk was "animated and energetic in the extreme".

Not surprisingly, in view of his tactless interference in Landor's domestic affairs, Crabb Robinson found Landor indisposed to talk of his family on the only occasion they were alone together; he was "most uncomfortable and unhappy and it is painful to be *tête-à-tête* with him". Though he remained always cordial when they met, Landor no longer called on Robinson uninvited. After a stay of about three weeks at Gore House, he was back at Bath by 27th May, when he wrote his bread-and-butter letter to Lady Blessington and sent her the verses he had just addressed to Ianthe in Vienna, but he returned to London for Queen Victoria's coronation at the end of June, apparently as the escort of Rose Paynter and her sister. When Robinson called at Gore House on 6th July, he was relieved "to hear that Landor had left London" after being "rampant" at the coronation, for though "I can justify apparent neglect, I am not anxious to do it".

Apparently owing to the death of his sister Ellen on 17th July, Landor deferred an intended visit to Ablett in North Wales. In August he visited the Eltons at Southampton and the Paynters in the Isle of Wight; in September he stayed a week or ten days with "my excellent friend James" at Fair Oak Lodge, Petersfield, where he "was happy to find the two Miss Boyles".

Soon after his return to Bath he was "laid up a whole fortnight" in October "with a sprained ancle"; "a fool of a mason dropt some mortar in Milsom Street; I sett my foot in it and twisted my foot almost round". The next day he sent to the library for Mrs. Jameson's *Memoirs of Female Sovereigns*, and "on Sunday after tea I began a drama on Giovanna di Napoli (God defend us from the horrid sound, Joan of Naples!); and before I rose from my bed on Monday morning, I had written above a hundred and seventy verses as good as any I ever wrote in my life excepting my Death of Clytemnestra". Encouraged by Forster's conviction that he possessed a dramatic gift, he may have felt inclined to emulate Browning's feat in completing his *Strafford* in ten days; though interrupted by callers inquiring about his accident, he sent the tragedy of *Andrea of Hungary* to Forster by 2nd November, "conceived, planned, and executed in thirteen days; transcribed (the worst of the business) in six". Forster wrote his congratulations on 3rd November and was astonished to hear about a week later that Landor had surpassed his own and Browning's achievements in speed of composition by writing *Giovanna of Naples*—which became the second play of a trilogy—in no more than eight days:

Your praises, which came this day se'nnight, created the last drama I shall ever write. . . . I only write now to tell you that I completed (just before dinner) the second of my trilogy. I will not ever write the third, tho' I have a scrap or two for it.

In the first play, Andrea brought up ignorant under his monkish mentor, Fra Rupert, is married to the spirited Giovanna, and seeing that he is falling under the influence of his wife, Rupert contrives his death; in the second Giovanna, falsely accused of her husband's murder, is acquitted of the crime by the tribune Rienzi and returns in triumph to marry her first lover; in the third Giovanna is forced to abdicate by the man on whom she lavished a mother's love when her own son was taken from her, and Fra Rupert stabs himself on being convicted of his crime. To Rose Paynter, citing the authority of the anti-papal historian

Giannone, Landor defended his presentation of Giovanna "as an amiable and virtuous woman", but confessed to Forster, "I am a horrible confounder of historical facts. I have usually one history that I have read, another that I have invented." Evidently he had not read Bulwer's recent novel, *Rienzi*; he complained that he had no life of Rienzi at hand, and though he had read an Italian biography, he could not remember the name of Rienzi's wife.

After Landor's death Robert Landor tried to suggest to Forster that Landor owed the suggestion of *Andrea of Hungary* to his own play, *Count Arezzi*. Relating that Landor was astonished when he pointed out to him the resemblance between the plays, Robert remarked that "my brother indeed would never have borrowed consciously from any man, and least of all from me", but "possibly he may have read this tragedy of mine, without any remembrance afterwards that he had seen it; or met with a review of it without knowing who had written either the tragedy or the criticism, for at that time we had no correspondence or communication: and so, many years after, he may have mistaken memory for invention". *Count Arezzi* was published anonymously in 1824 and attributed by rumour to Byron; in December 1836 Landor told Lady Blessington that he had never read any of Byron's dramas, "nor anything beside 'Don Juan,' and some short pieces". As Robert admitted, the brothers did not correspond for years before and after 1824, and Landor rarely saw reviews, especially in Italy, so it is unlikely that he had ever seen *Count Arezzi* before Robert asked him to compare it with *Andrea of Hungary*. At the time of writing *Andrea of Hungary* he told Forster that years before he had written "a good many scraps of two Imaginary Conversations in which Giovanna is a speaker"; possibly he had discussed the subject with Robert in the days of their intimacy, and also that of Sertorius, who was the theme of an imaginary conversation mentioned to Southey in 1824, as well as of *The Fawn of Sertorius*, published by Robert in 1846.

He seems to have been thinking of his son Arnold in drawing the character of Andrea:

I have made Andrea rather tolerable: at last rather interesting: quite uneducated: ductile: but gentle-hearted, compliant, compassionate, and, above all, a graceful rider. These qualities, taken together, are enough to make a sensible woman of great generosity *love him even*. Such a woman would be more likely than another. I never knew a very sensible woman, once excepted, love a very sensible man. There never was one who could resist a graceful and bold rider, if there was only one single thing about him which would authorise her to say, "It was not merely for his horsemanship."

"In the characters generally I have avoided strong contrasts," he remarked to Forster. "These are the certain signs of a weak artist." As in *Pericles and Aspasia*, concerned with verisimilitude, he disdained the

x

distortion necessary for dramatic effect; Fra Rupert wears the mask of hypocrisy as naturally as priest or politician in real life, without the emphasis of caricature dramatising a Pecksniff or a Uriah Heep. The most dramatic scene occurs in *Giovanna of Naples*, where Rienzi is urged by his wife to administer justice regardless of political interest; when he exclaims indignantly at the suggestion that he might be corrupted by money, his wife rejoins:

> Who scorns the ingot may not scorn the mine.
> Gold may not move thee, yet what brings gold may.
> Ambition is but avarice in mail,
> Blinder, and often weaker. Is there strength,
> Cola! or speed, in the oblique and wry?
> Take heed thou turn not water into blood
> And show the pure impure. If thou do this,
> Eternal is the stain upon thy hand;
> Freedom thro' thee will be the proud man's scoff,
> The wise man's problem; even the slave himself
> Will rather bear the scourge than trust the snare.
> Thou hast brought large materials, large and solid,
> To build thy glory on: if equity
> Be not the base, lay not one stone above.
> Thou hast won influence over potent minds,
> Relax it not. Truth is a tower of strength,
> No Babel one . . . it may be rais'd to heaven
> And will not anger God.

In first mentioning *Andrea of Hungary* to Forster, Landor wrote:

My drama will never do for the stage. Besides, why should I make so many bad men worse? Is there any poet, beside Southey and perhaps our Paracelsus, who would not suffer from blue devils at any success of mine? The best of our living dramatic writers, Sheridan Knowles, gets grudgingly praised.

On 13th November he suggested, "you might ask Macready whether he thinks it adapted to the stage, and whether *he* can suggest any improvement". When Forster expressed doubts of theatrical production, he agreed at once:

You are right in what you say of the theatre. I shrink from the acting. We will give up that idea, both for one and other of the dramas; and as to printing, you know I said openly I would publish no more.

On 23rd December he informed Lady Blessington, "Yesterday I requested Forster to order my drama to be printed at my own expense."

As chief reader to Richard Bentley, Forster entrusted the plays to that publisher, and Macready had a proof copy when he noted in his diary on 10th March 1839, "Read passages from a play of Landor's *Giovanna of Naples*—of great beauty." He made no offer to produce either play, probably for the reason contained in his later judgment on *Fra Rupert*, "which I like, as a thing of character and picture without design or construction".

Publication was delayed owing to Bentley's dispute with Dickens and Forster resulting in Dickens's withdrawal from the editorship of *Bentley's Miscellany*. Apparently Dickens and Forster used Landor as an instrument to embarrass Bentley, for Dickens wrote on 20th March to Harrison Ainsworth, his successor as editor:

Forster, acting for Mr. Savage Landor, arranged with Mr. Bentley for the publication of two tragedies by that gentleman, which were proceeding rapidly through the press when these matters occurred, and have since been taken from the printers by Mr. Bentley—not published, though the time agreed is long past; not advertized, though they should have been long ago—their existence not recognized in any way. . . . Mr. Landor, who . . . is violent and reckless when exasperated, is as certain by some public act to punish the bookseller for this treatment (if he be not prevented by an immediate atonement) as the sun is to rise to-morrow. This would entail upon me the immediate necessity, in explanation of the circumstances which led to it, of laying a full history of these proceedings before the public.

On 22nd April Landor explained to Lady Blessington how he had been disappointed in the failure to publish "my Giovanna" that month:

Mr. Bentley, after he had printed all but the three last sheets, stopt suddenly, two months ago. No doubt, he received a valuable consideration (as the price of roguery is called) for this dexterity. Forster, Dickens, and James are up in arms against him. James has put him into the Court of Chancery. Dickens had advised me to write him a contemptuous letter. To write at all to people of that description is not sufficiently contemptuous. I have ordered the printing to be begun by another publisher, at my own expense, leaving the edition now ready for sale, on this worthy's hands.

No doubt he was dissuaded by Forster from this independent course, which would have served no purpose in the dispute between Dickens and Bentley, now reaching a compromise. Bentley fulfilled his agreement to publish, though with little effort at publicity, but Landor was personally unconcerned with the financial result, having announced that the author's profits were intended for Grace Darling, the lighthouse-keeper's daughter whose heroism had rescued the survivors from a wreck in the previous September. He was well content when he received his author's copies—apparently in late April, promptly after his threat to seek another publisher—and was enabled to write to Rose Paynter, "At last I am able to send you a little book." The pleasure of distributing presentation copies among his friends was now his main object in publishing his work.

§ 4

Landor felt no disappointment at the failure of his drama. He might have been forgiven a pang of jealousy that *Strafford*, the work of a poet so much his junior, succeeded in achieving stage production, but, on the contrary, though some coolness had come between Browning and their mutual friend Forster, his friendship with Browning steadily developed from March 1840, when he received a presentation copy of *Sordello* with a request for his opinion, and replied, "You much overrate my judgment: but whatever it is, you shall have it, before I have read it so often as I read *Paracelsus*." He had no ambition as a poet or dramatist. "With the exception of my 'Agamemnon' and my 'Orestes'," he wrote in June 1839 to Procter, another poet with whom he exchanged the courtesy of presentation copies, "my poetry in no part satisfies me." As he confessed to Lady Blessington, he had rather shamefacedly consented to Forster's proposal of publishing the first two dramas, for "I said, in my last publication, that I would publish nothing more". To the end of his life he went on writing and publishing, and not unnaturally Forster regarded with tolerant amusement as eccentricity his repetition that each succeeding publication must be his last. Within three months of his seventieth birthday, he wrote to Lady Blessington:

Once beyond seventy, I will never write a line in verse or prose for publication. . . . The wisest of us are unconscious when our faculties begin to decay. Knowing this, I fixed my determination many years ago.

He went on writing, because his loneliness could not tolerate idleness, and he continued to publish in the hope of achieving some benefit to society; daily his indignation was roused by some injustice, and he resorted to his pen to register protest.

From his retreat in Italy he had viewed contemporary politics with detachment; his absence abroad of twenty years, during the period of reconstruction after the Napoleonic war, had made him immune from the influences that subverted the liberalism of men like Southey, and he retained unimpaired the fervour of his early beliefs. This stalwart tenacity contributed to his popularity with his juniors. Nearly all the rising generation of writers—Carlyle, Thackeray, Forster, Dickens, Browning, Mill—favoured liberal reform, and it was refreshing to find in a veteran who remembered the French Revolution, not merely no senile reactionary, but the advocate of radicalism more robust than their own.

His return to England revived his intimate concern with politics. When he asked, in advocating reform of the House of Lords, "Why should not gentlemen distinguished by wealth and *abilities*, and possessing hereditary landed property to the low amount of only a hundred thousand pounds, be called, or stand in a position to be called, to the high council board of their country," he must have reflected on Dr. Parr's unfulfilled hopes of his political future. In the imaginary conversation, "Florentine, English Visitor, and Landor", he had commented on his political qualifications before relating the Duke of Beaufort's refusal to make him a magistrate,[1] and in *Pericles and Aspasia* he recalled his *Calvus* letters in these words of Anaxagoras:

Before I left my country, I offered some brief observations on important matters, then in discussion, to persons of authority. Do I much over-estimate my solidity of intellect, my range of comprehension, or my clearness of discernment, in believing that all these qualities in me, however imperfect, are somewhat more than equivalent to theirs? . . . They rewarded me by suffering me to depart in peace, unanswered and unnoticed.

Following his *Letters of a Conservative*, he used the pulpit of the *Examiner* and his prestige as an elder man of letters for outspoken comments on current affairs.

His labelling himself a Conservative was a paradox credited to his reputation for eccentricity. "You know I am a Conservative," he insisted to Rose Paynter in 1839, "and wish things to continue as they are." But his notions of conserving existing institutions entailed reforms such as few avowed radicals ventured to advocate. To Mary Boyle— with whom he began correspondence after she was his fellow-guest at G. P. R. James's in September 1838—he stated his political faith:

My "Letters of a Conservative" were written to bring the apostate Bishops back to Christianity; to make them useful as teachers; that the indignation of the people might not rise up against the only unreformed Church in Christendom. It would grieve me to see religion and education taken out of the hands of gentlemen, and turned altogether, as it is in part, into those of the uneducated and vulgar. I would rather see my own house pulled down than a cathedral. But if Bishops are to sit in the House of Lords as Barons, voting against no corruption, against no cruelty, not even the slave-trade, the people ere long will knock them on the head. Conservative I am, but no less am I an *aristocratic radical* like yourself. I would eradicate all that vitiates our constitution in church and state, making room for the gradual growth of what altered times require, but preserving the due ranks and orders of society, and even to a much greater degree than most of the violent tories are doing.

After his philippics on church reform, he wrote to the *Examiner* on the subject of Canada; "what a deplorable thing! that the only man in England capable of governing a country, has thrown up his powers", he exclaimed when Lord Durham, finding his reforms obstructed, resigned the governor-generalship. In September 1838 he addressed an open letter to Daniel O'Connell—which evoked a reply—exposing the iniquities of Irish peers, demanding the sale of church lands to establish schools, and urging the means of assisting Irish emigration to

[1] Quoted on page 13.

Canada and Australia. In the following year, the *Examiner* published his "Petition to Parliament concerning Copyright", advocating reforms for which Charles Reade was still agitating nearly forty years later, and two letters on the political situation in the Near East, counselling support of the Egyptian dictator, Mehemet Ali, in opposition to Palmerston's policy of assisting France to make mischief against Russia—wise advice in the light of the Crimean War fifteen years later.

The same year he began a vendetta against Lord Brougham with a merciless exposure of his "hastiness and inaccuracy" in *Sketches of Statesmen in the Reign of George III*. He abominated Brougham, of whose notorious ugliness he wrote to Rose Paynter, "it is quite the worst, and very nearly the ugliest physiognomy in existence. It has, however, one advantage over its proprietor—it does not lie". Infuriated when Brougham, in opposing the government's Irish policy, attacked his friend, Normanby, "the first Governor of Ireland who had pacified, by pacific means, that abused and indignant nation", he wrote in the *Examiner*:

I dare not say that I never found in any other author, ancient or modern, so much of insincerity and falsehood: I dare not say it, for Lord Brougham is a very great and a very choleric man; and I am a very humble and a very timid one: but I will venture to affirm that in none whatever have I found so much which I am unable to reconcile, by any process of ratiocination, with what I believe to be sincerity and truth. Again, I dare not say I never saw in any one so much of arrogance, impudence, and presumption: but . . . never have I descried what *appeared* to me so extremely like them. I may be asked if I think myself capable of setting right so great a personage. No, indeed. Great personages are never to be set right. This is the only criterion I know of greatness.

Four years later, when Brougham threatened a libel action against the *Examiner*, Landor gleefully entered the lists, inviting Brougham to turn his lance against himself with a scathing summary of his career—when Brougham and his "confederates" controlled the *Edinburgh Review*, "more falsehood and more malignity marked its pages than any other Journal in the language"; "what other man within the walls of Parliament, however hasty, rude and petulant, hath exhibited such manifold instances of bad manners, bad feelings, bad reasonings, bad language, and bad law?"

Most of his campaigns in the *Examiner*, a liberal paper, consorted oddly with his professions of conservatism. He exposed the vicious government of Otho of Bavaria as King of Greece, rejoiced in the revolution at Athens, and recalling his friend Guilford's establishment of a university at Corfu, recommended Greece to a trusteeship of the powers, which would save the country from the barbarism of imperialist Russia and "restore a little of Hellenism". The erection of the Nelson monument inspired the protest that "no such monument has been raised to Blake, because he fought for a country without a king at the head of it"; the absence of a suitable memorial to Cromwell in the Houses of Parliament derived from "antipathy to republicanism". He protested against "the injustice and jealousy which withholds from General Napier his reward" for the conquest of Scinde:

> To swagger and sweat for a paltry fee in a law court, to make common cause with the criminal, to insult the seeker of justice, is enough to obtain the Peerage, by people whose manners and conversation scarcely fit them for the most ordinary society. . . . Unbelief in public virtue is accompanied by indifference to public interests. And surely both parties in Parliament are exerting the little energy that is in them to spread this unbelief and inculcate this indifference.

"Neutrality has not usually any advantage", he wrote to Rose Paynter during the general election of July 1841, but "in these days of political excitement I have reason to be gratified that all factions are as civil and courteous to me as before". Anticipating the defeat of Melbourne's administration by Peel, he wrote sardonically to Lady Blessington:

> Perhaps you may have interest enough with the Tories, now they are coming into place, and I am growing old, to obtain me the appointment of road sweeper from Gore House across to Hyde Park. You can present them a proof in print that I avowed myself a Conservative. . . . Be particular in saying, that the place I wanted was for *removing* dirt, or else there may be some mistake.

Apparently the incoming Tapers and Tadpoles decided that "something should be done" for Landor, for he informed Rose Paynter on 25th September 1841, "Neither party can ever be of the slightest use or advantage to me; and I was not very highly pleased when I was desired and invited to ask for something."[1] Southey declined a baronetcy; as a republican, Landor must have declined the offer of any title. The invitation "to ask for something"—which may have come from Milnes —was an affront to his life-long principles; only four months before, while staying at Gore House, he had deferred calling on his old friend Lord Normanby, the Colonial Secretary, till he received news of Melbourne's resignation, as "I will never pay a visit to a man in office".

---

[1] In January 1839 Lady Blessington applied to the Duke of Wellington, as Chancellor of the University, for the appointment of the Rev. Whittington Landon (brother of the poetess, "L.E.L.") as Provost of Worcester College. Printing the Duke's reply in his *Literary Life and Correspondence of the Countess of Blessington*, Madden misread Landon for Landor—an error inspiring the inference in *Count D'Orsay*, by Willard Connely, 1952, that Lady Blessington made the application on Landor's behalf (*cf. The Blessington Papers*, edited by Alfred Morrison, 1895).

15

FAMILY AND FRIENDS 1839-43

Dickens! how often, when the air
Breath'd genially, I've thought me there,
And rais'd to heaven my thankful eyes
To see three spans of deep blue skies.

. . . . .

Ah! could my steps in life's decline
Accompany or follow thine!
But my own vines are not for me
To prune, or from afar to see.
    —"To Charles Dickens" (going to Italy, 1844)

The nights had now grown longer, and perhaps
The Hamadryads find them lone and dull
Among their woods; one did, alas! She called
Her faithful bee: 'twas when all bees should sleep,
And all did sleep but hers. She was sent forth
To bring that light which never wintry blast
Blows out, nor rain nor snow extinguishes,
The light that shines from loving eyes upon
Eyes that love back until they see no more.
    —"The Hamadryad" (1842)

It is better to repose in the earth betimes than to sit up late; better, than to cling pertinaciously to what we feel crumbling under us, and to protract an inevitable fall. We may enjoy the present while we are insensible of infirmity and decay: but the present, like a note in music, is nothing but as it appertains to what is past and what is to come. There are no fields of amaranth on this side of the grave: there are no voices, O Rhodopè, that are not soon mute, however tuneful: there is no name, with whatever emphasis of passionate love repeated, of which the echo is not faint at last.
    —*Æsop and Rhodopè* (1844)

Landor never had the erratic habits of the eccentric; his life was always ordered with the regularity of the egoist who resents disturbance of his privacy. As a young man he had wintered at Bath and travelled about the country during the summer; for many years in Italy he had wintered in Florence and taken a house in the hills for the summer months; now he resumed the habit of his youth, residing at Bath from September till May, when he went up to London and thence on visits to friends in the country. He broke his habit for the sake of Francis Hare, with whom he stayed a few days in the new year of 1839 at Westwood Hay House in Berkshire, an old house built by Inigo Jones, which he said "would have done passably well for Naples, and better for Timbuctoo"—"the cold was intense, and I slept in a bed large enough for a company of comedians".

Having finished *Andrea of Hungary* and *Giovanna of Naples*, he became preoccupied with "an ill-tempered and captious article in the *British and Foreign Review* on my *Pentameron*". When the *Quarterly Review* for February 1837 paid him the unusual honour of reviewing his complete works at length, he did not even read the article, but wondered "where they found their telescope". Somebody told him that this reviewer was Henry Hallam. He disliked Hallam, whom he had met ten years before at Florence and again at Clifton with Charles Elton, whose sister was Hallam's wife, but he allowed that "unless he talks of poetry, he is not likely to talk like a blockhead". He therefore composed a long commentary on the review and sent it to Forster, who "with great difficulty" dissuaded him from printing it, arguing that Hallam was improbably the reviewer, though apparently he was still unaware that the reviewer was in fact William Bodham Donne when he printed the commentary in his biography of Landor. Landor contented himself with an epigram on Hallam as

> Snappish and captious, ever prowling
> For something to excite thy growling,

and with relating to Forster how Lord Dudley had described to Francis Hare a dinner with Hallam and his son, when "it did my heart good to sit by, and hear how the son snubbed the father, remembering how often the father had unmercifully snubbed me".

A more personal complication distracted his attention from Forster and Dickens's dispute with Bentley. In February of the previous year he had informed Lady Blessington:

A few days ago Mrs. Bulwer came to Bath. As she had done me the honour to look in at my villa in Italy, I thought it a duty to wait on her, and she received me with great politeness. She is staying with the (Irish) Bagots, whom I meet occasionally at Lady Belmore's.

He had formed no very favourable impression of Bulwer, and as Rosina Bulwer was a beauty as well as graciously disposed, he listened sympathetically to the tale of injuries she professed to have suffered from her husband. Against prudence and his own inclination he had conceded custody of his own children to their mother; he was therefore the more sympathetic with Mrs. Bulwer in her indignation at being deprived of her two children, and as Lady Blessington and Count D'Orsay were close friends of Bulwer's, he agreed to attempt mediation during his visit to Gore House in May 1838. On 19th May he met Bulwer at Albany Fonblanque's in the company of D'Orsay, Forster, Macready, and Lord Nugent, and on his return to Bath he wrote to Lady Blessington that "Poor Mrs. B, who is nearly out of her senses at her sufferings, begs me to express her gratitude for the interest you have taken in her behalf".

At this time Landor was a helpful patron to the young painter, William Fisher, who painted three portraits of him, one each for Mrs. Paynter, Rosina Bulwer, and Kenyon—of the last Southey said "the picture was as good as the likeness", though Landor himself thought "its colour too like a dragon's belly". Fisher also painted Kenyon and Rose Paynter, whose portrait Landor persuaded Lady Blessington to reproduce in *The Book of Beauty* for 1840 with appropriate verses of his own. Rosina Bulwer consented to Landor's request that she should sit for Fisher "upon the express proviso that he should always be there at the sittings, so that I might either listen or talk during the penance, and not die of ennui". Their friendship had lasted almost exactly a year when Lady Bulwer—her husband received a baronetcy from the Melbourne administration in 1838—proposed to dedicate to him her first novel, *Cheveley, or The Man of Honour*.

Such a compliment was no novelty to Landor; as he remarked with characteristic prejudice, "the best poem and almost the best novel of our days, were dedicated to me—'Kehama' by Southey and 'Attila' by James", and he was gratified in the summer of 1838 by Charles Brown's dedication to him of *Shakespeare's Autobiographical Poems*. But he explained his present embarrassment to Lady Blessington on 8th February 1839:

Lady B. is about to publish a novel. I have not seen it, nor heard the title, but was told by her a week ago that she intended to inscribe it to me. This is an honour I could not decline at all, or receive in any way but with profound respect. Yet, as I *know* that it contains allusions either to Sir Ed. B. or his mother, it will pain me. She was by no means satisfied with the service I attempted to render her, and said it saved Sir Ed. B. instead of exposing him. My reply was, very meekly, that what I undertook was to conciliate and not expose, and that the only result I expected or hoped was to obtain her children for her. I hope her book will bring her money, for she is generous and charitable to an extreme, added to which, I fear her health has very much suffered by her vexations and anxieties.

Apparently Lady Blessington consulted Forster, who had heard of the contents of the novel when it was submitted to *Fraser's Magazine* and wrote to warn Landor that the story was primarily an attack on Bulwer, with Lady Blessington and Forster himself satirised under thin disguises, and Lady Bulwer obviously intended that the dedication should excite gossip by the analogy of her separation from her husband to Landor's from his wife.

Landor therefore wrote to Lady Bulwer "to entreat your patience", explaining how "I have been *implored* by those whose happiness and contentment I feel myself most especially bound to consult, 'never to allow my name to be implicated in matters of such delicacy'." Relating that he "had destroyed, with my own hands, the most elaborate of my works"—this being his political history of his own times, begun at Florence, which he records, in *Letters of a Conservative*, having destroyed because his exposure of living statesmen might "serve for the indulgence of ill-humour and the excitement of malignity"—"lest it might disquiet the peace of my mother, then in perfect health", he declared that he was now concerned "not to give intolerable pain to a sister, grievously afflicted by a hopeless malady of many years", and concluded: "Do not imagine, dear Lady Bulwer, that I consider the expression of your friendship as a light and valueless distinction: I trust I shall be worthy of retaining it, and not the less for the sacrifice of my pride to the sacredness of my affections." The reply was tersely feline:

Dear Mr. Landor, You need not fear. The Dedication shall be with pleasure withdrawn, as I dislike Dedications at all times, and should be sorry to compromise you, even in the moral and virtuous atmosphere of Gore House. I remain (privately)
Your sincere friend,
R. Lytton-Bulwer.

"For the remainder of my life I will keep aloof from the concerns of others," wrote Landor, enclosing the correspondence in explaining to Rose Paynter "Lady Bulwer's declaration of hostilities against me". "The little good I can do without effort and without inconvenience I will do—nothing more." He had reason to feel rueful, for Bulwer never forgave his well-intentioned efforts on Lady Bulwer's behalf: in 1841 Count D'Orsay found it necessary to assure Bulwer that Landor had never countenanced the attack on Bulwer and his mother in *Cheveley*, and as late as 1847 Bulwer annoyed Lady Blessington by absenting himself from her party in honour of Hans Andersen because he always "staid away from Gore House when he thought Landor was there".

Lady Bulwer soon left Bath to live abroad, but her malice survived into old age, for she published a flippant article of "reminiscences" in *Tinsley's Magazine* of June 1883, discreetly omitting reference to the intended dedication but depicting Landor as a talented buffoon who delighted to exercise his wit on dullards. Mrs. Paynter appears as "Mrs. Avenel, who had two beautiful daughters, and a hobbledehoy of a son", and Landor's favourite butts are said to have been the son, Fred Paynter, and a poet engaged on a work which "had taken him twenty years to *conceive*". Her anecdotes had sufficient foundation in fact to lend venom to their malice. Informing Lady Blessington that the poet, John Edmund Reade, was "about to publish a drama on the Deluge, on which he tells me he has been engaged for twenty years", Landor wrote, "you cannot be surprised that he is grievously and hopelessly afflicted, having had water on his brain so long". But his mention of Reade—for many years his neighbour in St. James's Square —to Lady Blessington was consequent upon an attempted kindness in introducing him as a possible contributor to *The Book of Beauty*, and in July 1842 he anonymously reviewed Reade's *Record of the Pyramids* in *Blackwood's Magazine*—a notice, though satirical, which must have gratified Reade by contrast with the silence that normally greeted his work. Probably he was also the good-natured means of introducing Reade to Macready, who expressed indignation when "that ludicrously wretched fellow, Mr. E. Reade . . . endeavoured to *bribe* me, by a promise of dedicating his miserable play to me, to act it".

Obviously Landor would not have commended himself to Rose Paynter's friendship by making a butt of her brother. Indulging the histrionics of adolescence, Fred Paynter caused concern to his mother and sisters, and Landor laughed him out of his moods with amiable cajolery. To Rose, absent in Paris, he reported progress in January 1839:

Fred has come sometimes to visit me in the evening. You will be delighted, on your return, to find him so improved. He is extremely amiable as well as clever, and is only in want of occupation. I am convinced he will be distinguished, and particularly if his profession should be the army.

His prediction had no chance of fulfilment, as Fred Paynter died young on active service in India; meanwhile he humoured the young man's poetic ambitions, congratulating him six years later on losing "a little of his admiration for Byron", in whom "there is much to admire, but nothing to imitate".

§ 2

"A little of the influenza" was Landor's excuse to Lady Blessington for delaying his visit to Gore House in 1839 beyond the beginning of May, but a stronger reason appeared in the verses he enclosed with a letter of 14th May announcing his arrival on the 18th:

> Sweet was the song that Youth sang once,
> And *passing* sweet was the response;
> But those are accents sweeter far
> When Love leaps down our evening star,
> Holds back the blighting wings of Time,
> Melts with his breath the crusty rime,
> And looks into our eyes, and says,
> "Come, let us talk of former days."

According to the verses entitled "What News"—beginning, "Since you, my true love, went abroad", and sent to Lady Blessington on 21st July following—Ianthe "went abroad" about the middle of May.

At Gore House he again met Carlyle, sat one evening next to Lady Blessington's brother-in-law Lord Canterbury—a former Speaker of the House of Commons as Charles Manners-Sutton—and enjoyed his first meeting with Prince Louis Napoleon only a few days after the *Examiner* of 19th May had published a letter "in which I brought down Bonaparte from the stilts on which our traitors have placed him".

> Prince Louis Napoleon, Montauban, and Persigny had been conversing with me in admirable good humour, when something was said by Lady Blessington about an article in I know not what paper. "*Apropos*," said Louis, "I owe many thanks to the author of the *Examiner* for his notice of the Emperor." Luckily he had forgotten that my name was at the bottom. I could not help smiling. They say he is no fool—he looks like one, which is unusual in that family.

Wordsworth was in town but their meeting was avoided, though Crabb Robinson one morning accompanied Landor to the diorama and to the Academy, and had him to breakfast a few days later with Kenyon and others, admitting that "Landor entertains by his wild talk at all events".

Immediately after arrival at Warwick on 2nd June, Landor wrote his thanks to B. W. Procter for a copy of his *English Songs*, which he made the subject of congratulatory verses published in the *Examiner* the following December. Explaining to Rose Paynter why he was concerned lest his sister Elizabeth should suffer "intolerable pain" from the implications of Lady Bulwer's proposed dedication, he revealed that he had felt some grievance against his sister because she had not offered the inducement of hospitality to persuade his daughter to come to England:

> If she has not shown the same kindness to my family as she always did to me in our early days, that is only a reason the more with me for showing my compliance with her wishes. And indeed I now find that if she had invited Julia to her house it would have been painful to them both.[1]

---

[1] This evidence conflicts with Crabb Robinson's statement that Landor's wife "showed me a letter from Landor's sister offering her an asylum".

Presumably he now recognised that the invitation was withheld owing to the state of Ellen Landor's health before her death the previous summer. Friendly relations with his family were resumed, and the interest of this stay was enlivened by a visit from his cousin Sophia Shuckburgh, whom he had addressed in verse on her marriage in 1788.

From Warwick he intended to go to the Eltons at Southampton, but in July he was back at Bath, receiving a visit from Monckton Milnes and his sister and brother-in-law, Lord and Lady Galway. He took lodgings at Clifton for a week, but stayed only two days, as "the place is utterly ruined" by the erection of "that detestable" suspension bridge. He visited Mary Boyle and her sister at Marston, near Ilchester, but the wet summer caused him to defer a proposed excursion into Devon till it was finally abandoned in late September when he heard that Francis Hare and Kenyon, whom he was to have met at Torquay, had both left for the continent. During September he received a visit from Forster.

In these months he contributed to the *Examiner* letters of warning against Russian imperialism and against Palmerston's policy towards Egypt and Turkey that laid the train for the Crimean War. In writing to his correspondents he frequently enclosed verses; to Theodosia Garrow he sent the dream in verse, "A voice in sleep hung over me", to Lady Blessington the prose dreams of "Youth and Beauty" and "Pleasure, Youth, and Age". Some of the verses were published from time to time in the *Examiner*, but among those that remained in manuscript was the quatrain sent to Lady Blessington after he attended the wedding of Sophy Paynter and Henry Caldwell on 18th December:

> Directed by the hand of Fate,
>   May Love inscribe your lot;
> And, Sophy, be your wedded state
>   All that my own is not.

Apparently the wedding so unsettled him that he overcame his distaste for London in winter and wrote to Lady Blessington on 23rd December that he would arrive at Gore House on 2nd January. Henry Reeve, afterwards editor of the *Edinburgh Review* and the Greville *Memoirs*, who shared rooms with H. F. Chorley, called after dinner on the day Landor arrived:

His face reminds me a little of Michael Angelo's. We were talking of that brilliant society of Leo X's Court . . . and I could not help thinking how truly Landor belongs to those scholarlike gentlemen in tastes and tone, and even in his whimsical faults. There is something of perpetual youth in his age; and he has that clear spirit of thought in him which shines like the eye of some large bird in the twilight. I anticipate much pleasure from his visit.

A week later Reeve found dinner at Gore House "very good fun . . . Landor rode several fine paradoxes with savage impetuosity; particularly his theory that the Chinese are the only civilised people in the world". He added that Landor "is quite as vain of not being read, as Bulwer is of being the most popular writer of the day. Nothing can equal the contempt with which he treats anybody who has more than six readers and three admirers".

In Forster's company Landor met Richard Hengist Horne, who was impressed by his "grand breadth and ease of manner", and saw much of Dickens. As they corresponded in the spring of 1839 over the Bentley dispute, Dickens must have met Landor at Gore House in 1838, but it was now that affection, based on mutual admiration, developed between them. "Tell him," wrote Landor to Forster while *Nicholas Nickleby* was appearing serially, "he has drawn from me more tears and more smiles than are remaining to me for all the rest of the world, real or ideal"; asking Rose Paynter at Christmas 1844 if she had enjoyed *The Chimes*, he exclaimed, "Wonderful man! Everything he writes is in the service of Humanity. His Genius was sent from Heaven to scatter good and wisdom upon the earth." Though Dickens had only twelve years to live when Landor last saw him and was then prematurely aged by overwork and unhappy marriage, he remained for Landor the charming, buoyant young man self-described in *David Copperfield*.

When Landor left London, it was with a promise that Dickens and Forster would soon visit Bath, and on 27th February 1840 they travelled down by coach together to stay at the York House Hotel. After an evening at 35 St. James's Square Dickens was somewhat surprised that he was "not bored" by Landor; the young men enjoyed their evening, "although desperately learned and frequently first-person-singular-ish", and Forster formed his condescending opinion of Landor's taste in pictures when they were shown "a fine Rubens—a lion", which Landor had acquired a few months before; "as they walked back to their hotel, at midnight, the usually quiet streets of Bath rang with their inextinguishable laughter, with which were mingled 'Roars for the lion!'" The idea of Little Nell and *The Old Curiosity Shop* occurred to Dickens during this visit, and when Landor heard of this some years later, "he broke into one of those whimsical bursts of comical extravagance, out of which arose the fancy of Boythorn", declaring "with tremendous emphasis" that "he meant to have purchased that house, 35 St. James's Square, and then and there to have burned it to the ground, to the end that no meaner association should ever desecrate the birthplace of Nell". Having said this, becoming "conscious of our sense of his absurdity", he broke into "a thundering peal of laughter". By that time he must have grown well aware that Dickens and Forster were entertained by extravagance and he played up accordingly; Forster so much enjoyed this and subsequent visits to Bath that he saw them in retrospect as more frequent and regular than they were in fact, for he claimed to have passed with Landor at Bath "his sixty-third birthday, and with hardly an intermission for the next twenty years we dined together on that memorable 30th of January".

Late in March Crabb Robinson came to Bath, called on Landor, and took him to meet the novelist Sarah Burney. Next morning he "breakfasted self-invited with Landor" and "afterwards took him out with me" to call on "Manning, the Chinese traveller and friend of Charles Lamb". Manning "seemed glad to engage Landor to renew his call", and as Robinson decided that Landor "wants occupations and objects of interest", he thought "they are likely to relish each other's conversation". Some time afterwards he had reason to "suspect that neither introduction had any material effect" on Landor, as "it is the beauty of early youth that attracts him". A paralytic invalid between two and three years older than Landor, Manning died the same year; Miss Burney died in her seventies about four years later. Neither was likely to provide enlivening company for an elderly man living alone.

Robinson found Landor "as usual wild in his talk", but "when alone, he inquired with feeling about his children" from Robinson's recollections of his visit to Fiesole in June 1837. Landor now had hopes of a visit from two of his children. "Julia is my darling and delight", he told Rose Paynter in April on receiving "a long letter" from his daughter describing the parties she was attending; hearing that she was to be bridesmaid at a fashionable wedding, he ordered his agent to send her pin-money. Then he heard that his sons Arnold and Walter would come to England; he went to Warwick to await their arrival, writing from there on 5th June that he expected them on the 20th for two months.

On the first of July I am engaged to my friend Ablett in Denbighshire, where we spend all that month, so that I have scarcely a fortnight for them to stay with my sister, and another fortnight to divide among my other relatives who have invited them. Arnold says he cannot stay above two months in England, since it grieves him to leave his mother for a longer time. I cannot blame him nor argue with him on that point. It shows an affectionate heart which I am pleased at finding, although I may grieve in secret that it does not lean a little more toward me. I shall ask him only one favour; which is that he will allow me to show him Bath . . . I think I am destined to spend there all the remainder of my days, living on recollections—which, however, are more likely to wear out life than to nourish and support it.

His sister Elizabeth, afflicted by asthma, was confined to her room, with one of her nieces (Charles Landor's daughter) "very kind and attentive to her". Though he then felt "but little inclined to go beyond the garden", he thought "perhaps I may go up the Rhine with my sons":

They shall have their own way. Indeed one of them in this respect seem resolved to leave me no alternative. Well, if he pleases himself, I am satisfied.

Three weeks later, still at Warwick, he explained bitterly to Rose Paynter that he was cancelling engagements to stay with relatives and friends "because my sons do not come to England".

They had reached Bologna, when poor Walter felt suddenly ill after his late meazles. Arnold either felt the same, or pretended it. Walter, in spite of his severe fever would have proceeded, but Arnold was resolved to return, and, after much difficulty prevailed on the good and affectionate Walter to abandon his determination of going onward. He, I mean Walter, expresses the deepest regret at it, and trusts he shall be more fortunate another time. Arnold on the contrary tells me at the close of his letter that he never comes to England at all unless with his mother and the whole family. He has not the humanity to express the slightest regret at my disappointment nor to defer to another moment the resolution he announces. If you live long in the world you will find perhaps many such instances of hardness and ingratitude, but I hope it may be in persons not quite so near to you as this is to me . . . I will see none of my friends while there is any weight of sadness on me. I will walk it and reason it away. There is only one thing on earth worth an effort from me, and that is to grasp back again the senses that seemed for an instant resolute to leave me.

In August and early September he went to Devon, visiting Theodosia Garrow and her father at Torquay and spending some time at Exmouth, "taking my long solitary walks over the cliffs or along the shore". Here he expressed his mood in the lines, "A Sea-Shell Speaks", imagining himself addressed by a shell thrown up among the rocks:

> Both are deprived of all we had
> In earlier days to make us glad,
> Or ask us why we should be sad.

"I am by no means tired of the world, and never am likely to be sentimental," he wrote about this time to Rose Paynter, "but I have sometimes hours of deep seriousness, as far removed from sadness as possible." Late in September he made his postponed visit to Ablett at Llanbedr, and "having scarcely had a day without rain since my arrival", he wrote, "I am never tired of solitude where there is sunshine, but sometimes this gloom is rather more than external with me."

Leaving Llanbedr on 14th October, he spent a few days at Cheltenham on his way to Bath, apparently to visit the sister of his old schoolfellow Fleetwood Parkhurst. Her husband, Anthony Rosenhagen, was a retired civil servant, who had been private secretary to the assassinated Prime Minister, Spencer Perceval. Sending to Lady Blessington in December 1842 the lines, "Where Malvern's verdant ridges gleam"—which she published in the *Keepsake* for 1844—Landor wrote:

Y

The three persons mentioned in them are among the very best that ever lived. My excellent old friend Mr. Parkhurst was appointed by Lord North to be one of the commissaries to the armies in North America. On his return, he met Lord North in the Park.

"What, Parkhurst! you a commissary! and in your old family coach?"

"Yes, my Lord! thank God! and without a shilling more in my pocket than when I set out."

"A pretty thing to thank God for!"

He and his son-in-law Rosenhagen are the men who unite most of virtue and most of polish that I ever met with; so that I have written these verses con amore at least. Mrs. Rosenhagen, whom I remember as an infant, is the providence of her husband. Never were two persons so devoted one to the other.

Rosenhagen was blind—according to Landor, he "lost his sight by unremitted labours in the public service"—and in 1843 he was "bereft of the best and dearest wife any man ever possessed". In January 1846 Landor expressed to him delight on hearing "that you are most fortunate in finding a friend and companion so well adapted to your studious, and your social hours". This was the Rev. Rashleigh Duke, who, as Rosenhagen's secretary, read and preserved Landor's letters, of which he wrote two or three a year. Duke married Charles Landor's daughter Ellen in 1850, and they made their home with Rosenhagen till his death.

As the Rosenhagens were friends of Robert Landor, it may have been through their influence that Landor made another gesture towards reconciliation with his youngest brother. They had ceased to correspond in 1820, when Robert abused "the mean & selfish proposals of Walter" regarding his income; in 1832 Landor had vainly awaited a visit from Robert, and in the summer of 1839, when he proposed to accompany their cousin Sophia Shuckburgh to Birlingham, Robert had apparently contrived to evade a meeting. On his return to Bath in late October 1840 Landor completed *Fra Rupert*, the third play of his trilogy, and commissioned its publication by Saunders & Otley, sending a copy to Robert in December.

Torpid in the security of a country benefice, Robert had made no effort for many years to display his literary talent; living on his private income and dispensing his stipend in charity among his parishioners, he indulged freely in the pleasures of "a capitally good table" and amused himself by gardening. Now, witnessing the celebrity of the brother he had despised as a failure after the flight from Llanthony, he was stimulated to competition. "I must say that it appears a far greater work than *Count Julian*," he wrote in acknowledgment of *Fra Rupert*, and while "I cannot say that anything which you have written since has given me more pleasure than *Pericles and Aspasia* . . . I rejoice nevertheless at the publication of these dramas as fresh evidence that your powers are increased by time". He went on to remark the "strange coincidence" that he was himself printing three dramas, two of which "have been written many years". By an even stranger coincidence his three dramas, *The Earl of Brecon, Faith's Fraud*, and *The Ferryman*, were published in one volume by Landor's own publishers, Saunders & Otley, the following February; if the publishers proceeded as expeditiously with this volume as with *Fra Rupert*, the commission may well have reached them after Robert had received his copy of *Fra Rupert*.

Sending a consignment of his tragedies to his sister Elizabeth towards the end of February, Robert directed that their niece Sophy should send "one to her father, and one to Walter Landor". Landor immediately wrote of "the delight and wonder" with which he had read the tragedies; there had been nothing like *The Ferryman* "in this century or the last". He sent a copy to Lady Blessington, assuring her that his brother's poetry "appears to me to surpass, by many degrees, the best our country has produced in the present century or the last"; praising Robert's personal character, he remarked of how they had "lived without any correspondence" for over twenty years, "Neither of us is good-tempered—I am perhaps the worse of the two."

§ 3

"My body, and my mind more especially, requires strong exercise," wrote Landor to Forster in December 1840; he was "sensible to the curse of climate", and as "I cannot walk through the snow and slop . . . lately, from the want of sun and all things cheerful, my saddened and wearied mind has often roosted on the acacias and cypresses I planted". If Forster went to Bath for Landor's birthday on 30th January, Dickens presumably did not accompany him, for his wife was then expecting to be confined any moment of the son to whom Dickens invited Landor to be godfather.

Dickens must have been the more glad to pay this compliment to Landor as compensation for an embarrassment caused by the publisher Colburn. For the benefit of the widow of his former publisher, Macrone, he engaged with Colburn to edit a miscellany called *The Pic-Nic Papers*, and Landor was among those he invited to contribute. Three years before Landor had remarked to Lady Blessington that Colburn was "by no means of a friendly disposition towards me", and the publisher now gave expression to his grievance by refusing to print Landor's contribution, which Dickens—despite a threat of withdrawing his own contribution—was eventually compelled to return to its author.

Whatever explanation was made to him, Landor attached no blame to Dickens for the rejection, as in the following April he praised Dickens

to Crabb Robinson "as being with Shakespeare the greatest of English
writers, though indeed his women are superior to Shakespeare's".
Robinson was at Bath to meet Wordsworth, who was staying with Miss
Fenwick at her house in the North Parade, but he found time to call on
Landor and to breakfast with him two days later. After breakfast "he
took me a beautiful walk to Weston and pointed out sweet scenes to me
with great interest". "His sense of beauty of all kinds is his most enviable quality," thought Robinson; "Were his moral as well as his
aesthetical judgment equal to the strength of his feelings he would be
an estimable man." Landor was "full of anecdotes", and related how
a French Catholic girl, though legally divorced from her husband, preferred to live with another man as his mistress rather than commit a
breach of the sacrament by marrying him. He "praised his brother
Robert's tragedies" and lent them to Robinson, who decided that
Robert was "a man of genius certainly, but like his brother, wild and
odd".

Robinson stated that Landor, "in high spirits, declared himself to
be the happiest of men". The reason—which Robinson did not record
—was Landor's having heard that his son Walter was keeping the
promise implied in his letter of regret the previous June and coming to
England. He was to meet the boy in Paris and arrived at Gore House
in the early evening of 5th May—"my kind hostess and D'Orsay were
walking in the garden and never was more cordial reception." After
dinner with them and Lord Pembroke—whom he had not seen for
twelve years and found "grown old, and almost plain", though sixteen
years younger than himself—he accompanied them to the opera, where
"nothing could be worse than" Balfe's *Siege of Rochelle* except the
operetta that followed it.

The following morning "immediately after breakfast I went to introduce myself personally to Colonel Stopford", the husband of his wife's
sister Laura. As Landor told Mrs. Paynter, "we had been long
acquainted by correspondence; and if there is not too much pride in
me to say it, with mutual esteem." Stopford had served many years as
adjutant-general to the army of Colombia under Bolivar; though they
had never met, Landor dedicated to him the first volume of *Imaginary
Conversations*.

A more gentlemanly or more noble-minded man I never conversed with.
His wife was overjoyed at our meeting, talked to me of Llanthony, and of the
walk I took her over the hills, and of the grouse we started. Presently came
in the Minister of Caraccas and General Millar, who took over the command
of the armies of Columbia on the retirement of Bolivar. . . . Neither of these
men think highly of Bolivar as a soldier; both of them like all his family, and
were pleased with the gracefulness of his manners. And now appeared my
niece Teresita. She struck me as being very like my dear Julia, rather less
beautiful, but more intellectual.

He called again the next day on the Stopfords and "missed seeing Mademoiselle Rachel, who had just left" but met "Miss Strickland, authoress of the 'Queens of England', " and then went to call on "my old acquaintance", Jane Porter the novelist, whom he had apparently known in his youth at Bath.

Each evening he went with Lady Blessington to the opera. "On the opera nights nobody is received here," he told Mrs. Paynter, and he dined alone with Lady Blessington, D'Orsay, and his fellow guest, Lord Pembroke. He never heard Malibran, but thought the voice, expression, and acting of her sister, Pauline Garcia, better than Grisi's, and "never liked any singer so well except Pasta", whom he must have heard at Florence. Remarking now that "Madame Schodel" (? Wilhelmine Schröder-Devrient) sang "divinely" in Beethoven's *Fidelio*, and her acting was "only inferior to Pasta's", he added:

> Grisi never quite satisfied me excepting in *Norma*. There nobody can surpass her. I have seen enough of viragos in real life—they no longer can interest or even amuse me.

Lady Blessington tried to persuade him to stay over the week-end to see Rachel's London *début*, especially as he found he was "too late for my passport, which I cannot have before Monday", but "as the steamer sails on Sunday I shall go without one".

Meeting his son Walter in Paris on 11th May, he related the events of his journey in a rhymed letter to Rose Paynter, concluding:

> And now a few words of my Florentine guest,
> Who is gone, as I wish'd, rather early to rest.
> I find my poor Walter as thin as a lath,
> And wish he were quietly with me at Bath,
> At morning and evening taking his fill
> Of health and fresh air upon your Primrose-hill.
> He would find, I suspect, even health and fresh air
> The sweeter for one certain nymph being there.
>
> Tho' here is brave Walter, methinks I would rather
> My Julia, dear Julia, were now by her father,
> With her fair open forehead, eyes modest and mild
> And a voice, I do think, like my own, when a child:
> I fancy her (what will not fathers suppose?)
> As beauteous, and nearly as graceful as Rose.

To Forster he expressed surprise that "any among the literary men knew even of my existence", but "I have never anywhere received so much kindness and civility". The historian Mignet invited him to a sitting of the Institute, where Victor Cousin took the chair and Thiers —whose "countenance is like a mangy rat's"—was present. Here he met Charles Ledru, "the Erskine of France", who "conducted Lady Bulwer's case, and has undertaken the defence of the wretched fools who conspired against Louis Philippe". Through Ledru he was interested to meet the famous detective Vidocq—who seemed "about sixty years old; wonderfully strong and of a physiognomy mild and intelligent"—for two years before he had been so impressed by reading Vidocq's memoirs that "if I took any great interest in two such people as the great thief and the great thief-taker, I would compose a parallel, inch by inch", between Napoleon and Vidocq—"one of them frightened all the good, the other all the bad—one betrayed all his employers, the other all his accomplices—one sacrificed the hopeful to ambition, the other the desperate to justice".

He appears to be a man of somewhat the same stamp as Buonaparte, but much above him both in policy and courage. Fortune cast him into another galley among less voluntary and less versatile slaves. . . . He has as much of the fox as Talleyrand, and more of the lion than his master. . . . Where is the use of being great, supposing one can be? Was not this fellow great? Was not Pitt great? Is not everybody great who can do a great deal of harm, and give away a great deal of money?

"I have been introduced to many literary ladies," he wrote, "but I neither know their works nor remember their names." He met many at the *salon* of Mary Clarke, who afterwards married Julius Mohl the orientalist and for many years entertained the *élite* of intellectual Paris. Chateaubriand lived in the same house, but "having a touch of the *grippe* . . . did not make his appearance". "I was not sorry for it," said Landor; "he is a notable charlatan." Asked his opinion of Chateaubriand by an admirer, he said he seemed "a small bottle of sugar and water, fit only to catch flies". Princess Czartoryski, whose husband had been lately proclaimed king of Poland—"knowing my devotion to royalty", wrote Landor ironically, "he conversed with me the greater part of the evening"—invited him to meet Madame Récamier and Byron's former mistress, the Countess Guiccioli, but his impressions of these ladies were unrecorded. He was interested to hear that Count Geropski, before eloping with a Spanish princess, had proposed to the actress Rachel, "who replied that her profession was her *parti*, and that she desired no other".

This is wise; but it is a species of wisdom more likely to diminish than increase. She will change her mind when she grows old, and when nobody, not even a Frenchman, can love her. How few are aware of the right moment, men or women! Generally the choice is made too soon, and then the repentance is necessarily the longer, and usually the more poignant.

He stayed rather more than three weeks in Paris. He was disappointed to find the Louvre occupied by an exhibition of modern painting—"I hoped to pass every morning there." At Versailles he was "vext" to find four panes had been substituted for the one large pane in the window of Marie Antoinette's apartment in the Petit Trianon; he recalled the time he had spent there in 1802 as "happy days . . . the happiest and most tranquil in the whole of my existence . . . but not for memory".

With delicate courtesy he allowed young Walter to make his first visit in England to his maternal grandmother and aunts at Richmond, while he himself stayed at Forster's chambers in Lincoln's Inn Fields. Though Walter did not accompany his father to breakfast at Kenyon's on 13th June with Crabb Robinson, Milnes, and Forster, Robinson apparently met him on another occasion and found him "an interesting youth". When Landor went to fetch his son to take him to Bath, he expected "some degree of shyness", at least on the part of his mother-in-law, but "neither she nor any one of her daughters was less cordial with me than they had been formerly", and they said "not a single word on those matters which rendered my stay in Italy quite impossible, and equally so my return to the only habitation in which my heart ever delighted".

A general election following the dissolution of Parliament on 23rd June caused Landor to alter his plans. "I abhor all popular bustle," he told Mary Boyle, "and had I made the visits I intended to make, I should have been in the midst of contested elections, and what is worse, where some of my personal friends are opposed . . . I neither hear, nor will go where I can hear, anything of the matter." Cancelling his proposed visit to Ablett at Llanbedr, he allowed his son to make the round of his relatives on his own account. He made an exception only in the case of his brother Robert, fearing perhaps to cause offence by postponing this first visit since their reconciliation; he went from Bath on 28th June to the rectory at Birlingham, near Pershore, "a most delightful place", where Robert lived "like a prince-bishop".

After only a few days he returned to Bath, though nearly all his friends, except the Napiers, were away. "Solitude—retirement, rather, has the same charms for me as ever," he wrote to Rose Paynter, who was travelling abroad; "Bath is the place of rest for me—always was—always will be." He made an excursion to Clifton to visit his old friend, Lady Belmore, who amused him with her anger against "the vile wicked Radicals, who turned out Lord Powerscourt, although he has the most beautiful place in all Ireland". He was to see Lady Belmore again at Bath in October, but she died in the following December, moving him to recall how "thirty-seven years ago I began my acquaintance with her".

He spent August in his son's company at Warwick, where they were guests of his sister Elizabeth—"that greatest Aristocrat of our family", Henry Landor half-humorously called her, when writing in 1849 to decline his eldest brother's offer of their mother's tea-urn as a gift because their sister "would forbid my entering her House, if I deprived the future Owner of Ipsley of this Heir Loom: we must not offend her, who governs all of us". Having reached the age of fifty-three before her mother's death released her from the bondage of filial duty, Elizabeth succeeded to her mother's throne, keys, and personal belongings, ruling a well-ordered household and expecting homage as her mother's successor from the rest of the family. Within the narrow limits of county society she regally accepted and dispensed hospitality, arranging and approving marriages, feeding on local gossip, and taking a proper interest in current events so far as they were discreetly reported in chosen journals. Having determinedly treated her sister Ellen as an invalid till she died of it, she insured the continued visits of the family physician by developing martyrdom to chronic asthma, which provided an excuse for accepting sympathy, for declining unwelcome engagements, and for exacting attention from her brother Charles's daughters.

Still unimpressed by his genius, she was proud of her eldest brother's celebrity, though embarrassed by his shabby clothes. Their cousin Edward informed Forster how Landor wore his clothes, "like Dominie Sampson, until they would hardly hold together; and when he visited his sisters at Warwick they used to resort to the expedient practised upon the dominie, and leave new garments for him at his bedside, which he would put on without discovering the change". Probably he laughed his "tremendous" laugh on seeing the change of clothes, but delicately abstaining from comment, made it appear that he had noticed nothing. Shared memories supplied the chief subjects of communication between brother and sister, and details of the Warwick garden figured much in their correspondence; Landor expressed such grief for the loss of an old cedar that his sister had a writing-desk made from its wood as a present on his seventieth birthday.

A boy even so sedate as young Walter must have found his aunt's hospitality lacking in excitement; probably he preferred the shorter stay that followed in late September at his uncle Charles's Colton rectory, with female cousins for company. It does not appear whether Charles Landor shared either in his brother Henry's former coolness towards their eldest brother, or in Robert's long quarrel with him. Till his death he played his part as co-trustee with Henry, but his letters to Landor on business matters have not survived. Landor made several visits to Colton in the last few years before Charles's death in 1849, when he described him to Mrs. Paynter as "the finest man and almost the wittiest and most spirited I ever knew".

He returned alone to Bath about 9th October, when he wrote to apologise to Lady Blessington because "my shy Walter" called at Gore House neither on his arrival in May nor on his return journey through

London on his way to Italy. To Rose Paynter he wrote a few days later:

Walter has left me grieved and solitary, but by permitting his return I have a better chance of seeing the rest. Poor dear Julia thought that Walter might succeed in bringing me back to Italy with him. I soon found out that, anxious as he was to come to me, he came in the character of her ambassador.

There is only one thing in the world in which my sweet Julia could not prevail with me. To stand firm on some occasions requires more power and more energy than any active effort, and wrenches both the mind and body more. I think my strength and spirits are rather the worse for this resistance, and long walks are ineffectual in bringing me back sleep and appetite. I shall soon, however, be more reconciled to the absence of my sweet-tempered boy, who is much improved by his residence in England, and the last shades of gloom will have disappeared before your return. I have been to visit your flowers—they are doing well, and the roses I planted seemed glad to see me.

Though he had refused to accept dismissal from Landor, MacCarthy had by this time removed from Fiesole, for in July 1841 he called on Crabb Robinson in London to seek recommendation for employment; informed by Robinson of this application, Landor related the circumstances of his employing MacCarthy and how he had "remained in the house after my return to England, in spite of me", warning Robinson that "I believe him to be totally void of shame and principle". But MacCarthy's departure could not affect Landor's decision to live apart from his wife, since it was no guarantee of her behaviour towards himself in the presence of their children and servants—indeed her respect for him must have lessened if he had returned after believing her guilty of misconduct.

He occupied a wet October day in writing the imaginary conversation between Vittoria Colonna and Michael Angelo, and told Rose Paynter of dining in a family party with the Napiers and of accompanying the Napier girls to "excellent music" at the Pump Room. With Rose Paynter still in Paris, he expected that "December in Bath will be the longest and dullest month of the year", but Dickens, preparing to leave for America in the new year, invited him to attend the christening of his godson, and he went up to London in the first week of December, apparently dividing his stay between Gore House and Dickens's home, where Dickens remembered after five years "that steady snore of yours . . . piercing the door of your bedroom in Devonshire Terrace".

From London he returned to Bath for only a few days before passing Christmas with his sister at Warwick, where at his suggestion she invited her four brothers "to spend one more Christmas-day together". If Robert remained unresponsive, Landor now enjoyed the esteem and affection of his brothers Charles and Henry. After their father's death Landor had resented Henry's influence on their mother, and the coolness resulting from their differences over the purchase of Llanthony lasted till Landor wrote in 1825 to acknowledge Henry's fairness in carrying out their mother's wishes about her estate. After his visit to England in 1832 he recognised Henry's services as his trustee by generous gifts of pictures, and when he returned to settle in England, Henry thawed into cordiality, though with a reserve dictated by the antipathy of prudence towards improvidence. This reserve was now melted by Landor's carelessness of his own interests in consulting those of his children; recognising his disinterested generosity, his cautious brother was moved by his sense of fitness to discourage Landor's further concessions and to express indignation against his children's ingratitude.

Charles shared his brother Henry's feeling. Though Ablett still declined to take interest on the purchase of the Villa Gherardesca, he intimated that he would welcome an agreement for eventual repayment since the assignment of the property to Arnold, and Charles now wrote peremptorily to Arnold "as your near relation and trustee", advising "that now you are of age to act for yourself, you will act with honour and prudence". Arnold therefore deemed it prudent to visit his father in the following spring, and Landor "declined the invitations of my friends in town" to await his arrival. Kept in suspense till the last moment about the date of his son's coming, Landor heard "with terror and dismay" of a railway accident near Paris, torturing himself with the thought that Arnold might have travelled by the wrecked train. "I cannot quit the house even for a long walk until I hear from Arnold, or see him," he wrote to Rose Paynter:

Rarely as I have any painful or unpleasant dream, I dreamt on the morning of the sixth of May that he was dead. It is said that every man has some superstition. I have none—absolutely none. But I have always felt beforehand a fainter or stronger intimation of coming evils—in such a manner as to leave me no power of obviating them. I remain in the house all day. I stand on my feet at every knock, open my sitting-room door and turn back desperate. Old fathers, you see, and young lovers have some points of resemblance.

Arnold eventually arrived at Bath about 20th May 1842. He had not been shamed into the journey by his younger brother's example, and came frankly to settle business affairs. He was unfavourably impressed by a visit to Llanthony, for "he suffers much from cold, & it was unseasonably cold at Lanthony", reported Walter Landor of Rugeley, to whom Arnold confided that, while he had "not the slightest intention to sell his English property", he "would like to lay it all together at Ipsley". As Landor had always disliked Ipsley, Arnold was evidently disposed to little consideration of his father's wishes, and they soon parted in anger, Arnold to visit Rugeley and Ipsley, Landor to make at Gore House the stay deferred on his son's account. Quickly relenting, he wrote from Gore House to Rose Paynter:

I have written to Arnold—for where there is no dishonour there ought to be no dissention. That, and that alone, opens an impassable gulf between parent and son.

And he acceded to the proposals outlined by his Rugeley cousin to Henry Landor on 27th June, including the provision, "Mrs. Landor to be allowed 500£ a year instead of 400£, so that she may resume the carriage, & Arnold a hack, which they laid down when your Brother withdrew 100£ a year because Arnold would not come to England." A mortgage of £9,000 was raised on Ipsley to repay Ablett, to liquidate the annuity debt to Landor's mother's estate and various contract debts at Llanthony, and to settle the lawsuit with Antoir at Fiesole. Landor's life insurance was assigned to Arnold. Landor himself would "take his 400£ a year as at present", though in fact he was receiving only £25 a month in 1840 and seems to have made a practice of saving £100 a year for the benefit of his estate.

As his father had observed during his progress from boyhood to adolescence, Arnold offset a habit of indolence with a charm of manner that won favourable first impressions. Both traits had developed in the lax atmosphere of his mother's grass-widowhood, and Landor's affection was not blind: "Arnold, I doubt not, has attractions nearer the south than the north," he wrote to Lady Blessington; "Wherever they may be, it would be a sign of any man's sagacity to pull him out of bed by the heels." Arnold's ability to please when he wished appeared in the impression he made on Walter Landor of Rugeley, who wrote to Henry Landor:

Tho' he says he could not live in England, there are evidently schemes connected with England floating in his mind, & especially of making a summer residence at Ipsley. He looks forward too with pleasure to the facility of visiting this country, when continental railways are more general. . . . He has a childlike simplicity & artlessness. He knows his education was very incomplete, but I feel confident his principles are good, & that the kindness he has received & will do from his relations, will make him desirous to revisit England, & eventually to spend some time in it, though unless he gets more enured to the climate I don't think he could live altogether in it.

The climate seems to be his great attachment to Florence, for, excepting his sister, who is taken out by a family there, they appear to live almost in seclusion.

He fancies he shall never marry, and that he never can spend above 500£ a year, at least in Italy. His wants are so few, that I think he would be perplexed with a large income. So far his bringing up has been useful.

Landor's reputation for eccentricity of temper absolved Arnold from blame for the difference with his father, and he contrived to give the credulous country attorney an impression of a happy family at Fiesole, shunning society as superfluous to its self-contained pleasures—adroitly he averted any suggestion that their seclusion derived from their mother's reputation.

He has mixed so little in society, that it is painful to him. He says that his Father treated him precisely as when he was a child at Fiesole. He sat with him all the morning in the house, your brother reading, writing or *thinking*, & not allowing Arnold to open his mouth, as it interrupted his father's chain of thought.

He could not help contrasting this with the smiling faces at Fiesole. It depressed his spirits, & he felt unequal to face the evening parties, where his Father expected him to sing & exhibit himself.

No doubt Landor in affectionate pride seemed tiresomely eager that his friends should have opportunities to admire his son's accomplishments; on the other hand he was hardly exacting if he supposed that his wishes would be indulged for a few days after a separation of seven years. In the light of the reports from G. P. R. James and Aubrey Bezzi, from Francis Hare and Crabb Robinson, "the smiling faces at Fiesole" indicate Arnold's insincerity as significantly as the underlined *thinking* suggests the attorney's limitations—to sit doing nothing other than *thinking* seemed to the man of business a symptom of eccentricity.

Landor arrived at Gore House in time to hear a performance of Rossini's *Stabat Mater* on 29th June: "it would be presumption in me to say anything about the composition", but "I think it less simple, and feel it to be less affecting than some I have heard in Italy". On another evening "a German boy named Rubinstein (I think) has been playing to us on the pianoforte. Never did I hear anything so wonderful and of so pure a taste at the same time . . . He appears to be about eleven or twelve years old". With Lord Pembroke and the Duc de Guiche as guests at dinner, "D'Orsay was never in higher spirits or finer plumage". On 12th July the actor Macready "went to Dickens; found Landor, Maclise, and Forster there". On Landor's visit to that year's Academy, Maclise's "Play Scene in Hamlet" was one of three pictures that "struck me particularly", the others being "Ophelia" by Redgrave and "The Sanctuary" by Landseer. He much admired "the power of Landseer, who knows the hearts of all the brute creation". During his visit to Paris in the previous year he expressed disappointment in contemporary French painters—"the French have no Landseer, no Stanfield, no Eastlake." He thought "neither Claude nor Gaspar nor Nicolas Poussin ever painted anything equal" to Stanfield's "Island of Ischia", and "between the time of Hogarth and Eastlake we never had an artist who could draw".

By 20th July he was at Warwick, where Arnold was presumably a fellow-guest. Having accompanied the Paynters to Devon in August, he returned to Bristol without his luggage, which had to be sent after him, and spent the night at Cheltenham on his way to a week at Colton Rectory. Though he had been thus not overburdened with his father's company, Arnold elected to return home a month sooner than Walter had done, and accepting an invitation to attend the wedding on 7th

September of her daughter Teresita and Lord Charles Beauclerk, Landor wrote to his sister-in-law, Laura Stopford: "All day I have been disquieted to think of losing my dear Arnold. I wish he could have staid a few weeks longer."

Going to London for the wedding—for which Arnold did not delay his departure—Landor again stayed at Gore House, where he met at dinner the Duc de Guiche, Sir Francis Burdett, and Sir Willoughby Cotton.

I had not seen Burdett for many years, and never liked him much, he being always querulous—yet once upon a time we were in the habit of dining together daily. . . . We fell into politics, that is, he dragged me in. We did not differ in them quite as much as you imagine, only that he likes them and I detest them.

The fashionable wedding was followed by a breakfast to seventy guests "at Mivart's hotel in grand style". "Six bridesmaids are now become necessary on these grand occasions, as six horses were formerly. They were all such pretty girls, but Teresa too is very lovely, far beyond them." The bride's portrait by Hayter appeared in Lady Blessington's *Book of Beauty* for 1844 with some complimentary verses by Landor.

Before returning to Bath, Landor visited Julius Hare at Hurstmonceaux, where Hare and the Prussian ambassador, the Chevalier Bunsen, invited his collaboration in a Latin inscription to the memory of the famous headmaster at Rugby, Thomas Arnold, who died in the previous June. He complied, though he considered unseemly the application of classical Latin "to the commemoration of Christian thoughts and Christian relations"; sixteen years later he declined a request for a Latin epitaph on Monckton Milnes's father to be inscribed on a memorial in Fryston church, because "English names, titles, and occupations, are intractable to Latinity", and "in a country church the parishioners should be able to read the merits of the deceast".

The visit was tainted with sadness for both Landor and Hare, whose elder brother Francis had died in Sicily earlier that year. Francis had been Landor's devoted friend for more than twenty-six years, and through him Landor became a privileged friend of the rest of the Hare family. To Julius he owed a debt of gratitude for negotiating publication of the *Imaginary Conversations*, but apart from their common interest in classical study, old associations supplied the bond of their friendship. All the Hares except Francis suffered from a strain of priggishness and self-conscious virtue; from his deathbed Augustus could write to Lady Blessington, "How much I wish I could hope I was sure of meeting you in the place to which God is taking me." No doubt his ecclesiastical office required, when his colleague Archdeacon Manning joined the Church of Rome in 1851, that Julius should "mourn over" his "defection and desertion" and "wonder at the inscrutable dispensation by which such a man has been allowed to fall under so withering, soul-deadening a spell". But his character lost in natural generosity under the inhibitions imposed by a careerist's self-discipline; he might not have become so "nervous, dragged-looking a man" as Caroline Fox met in 1847 if he had not suffered "how bitter a sacrifice" in breaking his engagement to marry his cousin, Mrs. Dashwood, to gratify the dying wish of an aunt. His keeping the friendship of this correct churchman indicates Landor's ability for enjoying the best in his friends.

A few days after Landor's departure the young bookseller, Daniel Macmillan, visited Hare and took notes of his host's remarks on his recent guest.

Nothing delights him more than to pester his visitors, or his host, or any one he meets in company, with all manner of paradoxes. The truly amiable and lovely nature of Tiberius, or of Nero; or the great folly and cruelty of Pitt and Fox; or an examination of the question which of the two (Fox or Pitt) was the greater fool. . . . In these humours he praises what others blame, and abuses whatever is well-spoken of. . . . Julius thinks him the best of English prose writers, and is only sorry that he gives way to such strange tempers and crotchets and waywardness. . . . Notwithstanding these strange perversities, he is, they say, a most agreeable man when he chooses. The Hares enjoy his visits very much.

Carlyle told Charles Gavan Duffy that Landor "had fallen into an extravagant method of stating his opinions, which made any serious acceptance of them altogether impossible".

If he encountered anywhere an honest man doing his duty with decent constancy, he straightway announced that here was a phenomenal mortal, a new and authentic emanation of the Deity. . . . But there was something honourable and elevated, too, in his view of the subject when one came to consider it. He was sincere as well as ardent and impetuous, and he was altogether persuaded for the time that the wild fancies he paraded before the world were actual verities. But the personal impression he left on those who casually encountered him was that of a wild creature with fierce eyes and boisterous attitudes, uttering prodigious exaggerations on every topic that turned up, followed by a guffaw of laughter that was not exhilarating.

Young men like Reeve and Chorley found it "very good fun" when "Landor rode several fine paradoxes with savage impetuosity", but the spirit of fun was foreign to Carlyle, who was almost alone in feeling no warmth from Landor's boisterous laughter. Landor used paradox as a conversational gambit, striking an attitude to invite controversy; he gave what was expected of his social reputation for extravagance and exaggeration, as he evidently enjoyed playing up to Dickens's conception of him as Boythorn. Carlyle's lack of humour led him to express to Emerson the half-truth that "Landor's principle is mere rebellion", and his slight acquaintance with Landor and his works—at least before 1850—enabled him to tell Duffy that "Ianthe was probably a young girl at Bath, whom Landor counted the model of all perfection, and whom he got a good deal rallied about in London, other people forming quite a different estimate of her gifts".

Possibly Carlyle had heard Lady Blessington express impatience with Landor's admiration of Rose Paynter, for which she had some reason in Landor's several letters during 1839 about the reproduction of Rose Paynter's portrait in *The Book of Beauty*. Little over a fortnight before he received advance copies of the book, Landor quoted to Lady Blessington this extract from a letter of Rose Paynter's:

Mama tells me you have taken the trouble of offering my picture to Lady Blessington's *Book of Beauty*. It seems very ungrateful to say I am sorry for it, but, if it is not too late to suppress it, could you not omit the name, or only put the Christian name, which would be the same thing? I cannot bear to appear before the public in such a conceited way, and now remember with great annoyance having mentioned the subject, laughingly, one day in Bath, never imagining you would take it *au serieux*.

Landor invited Lady Blessington to "see the modesty and diffidence of this incomparably good girl", but a feminine understanding must have read signs of affectation.

As Milnes remarked, Landor's "feeling for female beauty was intense". His correspondence with the women of his youth has not survived, but the abundance of amatory verse indicates his preoccupation. For seventeen years after his marriage he suspended correspondence with women till Ianthe's visit to Florence in 1828 made him realise that he was denying himself in the interests of a marriage which offered no compensations. Removed by separation from the discomforts of his wife's jealousy, he was free to renew his pleasure in feminine company. While he remained constant in his devotion to Ianthe, she was now an old lady with interests concentrated mainly in her children and grandchildren and enjoyment of her company consisted largely of reminiscence; as Robinson belatedly recognised, "the beauty of early youth" attracted him, because young women provided a responsive audience while gratifying his capacity for admiration. Rose Paynter remained his favourite companion and confidante, but there were others, and when Miss Mitford visited Bath in the spring of 1843, she amused Miss Barrett "by desiring me to look at the date of Mr. Landor's poems in their first edition, because she was sure that it must be fifty years since, and she finds him at this 1843, the very Lothario of Bath, enchanting the wives, making jealous the husbands, and 'enjoying', altogether, the worst of reputations".

Apart from two brief excursions, Landor seems to have spent the entire winter of 1842-43 at Bath, where Dickens on 21st October brought Longfellow to dine with him on the last evening before the American poet sailed from Bristol. Late in November he visited Sir

John Dean Paul, the father of Francis Hare's widow, at Woodchester in Gloucestershire, and in early December he stayed with Sir Charles Elton, to whom he had performed a service by writing to the *Examiner* the previous February a protest against the unjust verdict of a naval court-martial on Elton's son—a protest which won a letter of congratulation from Count D'Orsay.

Southey's death on 21st March 1843 ended an unbroken friendship of thirty-five years. When he heard from Kenyon at the close of 1838 that Southey was marrying Caroline Bowles as his second wife, Landor thought that, as Southey was in his sixty-fifth year, "surely he might see the mellow fruit on the *espalier* without any hasty eagerness to gather it", and since he had "been married once, and happily . . . I think I should have liked him rather the better had he been contented to stop short of matrimony". Even then he added, "However, he is a more judicious and a better man than I am, and I trust his choice will be conducive to his happiness." When Southey wrote a few months later to explain that he had known Miss Bowles for twenty years, "that there is a just proportion between their ages, and that, having but one daughter single, and being obliged to leave her frequently, she wants a friend and guide at home", Landor explained, "Nothing is more reasonable, nothing more considerate and kind. Love has often made other wise men less wise, and sometimes other good men less good; but never Southey, the most perfect of mortals, at least of men mortals."

Southey never recovered from the mental illness following the death of his first wife, and Caroline Bowles's four years of married life were spent in anxious nursing of an invalid. The machinery of his fine intellect, trained to precision through years of labour to provide for his family, broke down under the burden of sorrow. Unable to work, he at first found recreation in reading, but soon his comprehension failed to grasp what he read, and he would wander up and down his magnificent library, a pathetic, decrepit figure, wistfully admiring his books, taking them down and replacing them upon the shelves. Landor wrote to him frequently, "but alas!" wrote Caroline Southey, "he no longer says, I will write soon to Landor; for when I proposed to answer in his stead, he said—Yes, yes do so, pray do. Landor had indeed a true regard for me". On Christmas Eve of 1841 Mrs. Southey wrote: "It is very seldom now that he ever names any person: but this morning, before he left his bed, I heard him repeating softly to himself, *Landor, ay, Landor.*" Immediately on hearing of Southey's release Landor wrote to Forster, "My reverence for his purity of soul, my grateful estimation of his affection towards me, are not to be expressed in words. But it would grieve me to think that any other men should have testified to the world regret at losing him, before I had done it," so he enclosed the lines which appeared in the *Examiner* of 25th March:

ROSE PAYNTER

From the portrait by William Fisher
in *Heath's Book of Beauty*, 1840

Not the last struggles of the Sun
Precipitated from his golden throne
Hold darkling mortals in sublime suspense,
But the calm exod of a man
Nearer, tho' high above, who ran
The race we run, when Heaven recalls him hence.

Thus, O thou pure of earthly taint!
Thus, O my Southey! poet, sage, and saint,
Thou, after saddest silence, art removed.
What voice in anguish can we raise?
Thee would we, need we, dare we, praise?
God now does that . . . the God thy whole heart loved.

His sense of personal loss was shown in four lines that lay unprinted for
many years:

Friends! hear the words my wandering thoughts would say,
And cast them into shape some other day.
Southey, my friend of forty years, is gone,
And, shattered by the fall, I stand alone.

Appropriately lines by Wordsworth were engraved on the memorial in
Crosthwaite Church; for the memorial at Southey's Bristol birthplace
Landor sent a subscription of twenty pounds with an epitaph published
in the *Examiner* of 4th November 1843, but, while accepting the first,
the municipal authorities rejected the second.

Southey's illness left little of his small savings. Hearing that his
widow had sacrificed half her small income by her marriage, Landor
wrote to Monckton Milnes on 4th April appealing for his influence to'
obtain her a pension; he emphasised her personal virtues, though "not
her merits, but his, call upon the nation for some testimonial—a very
small pension for a very few years (I fear I am over-rating its duration)
—would exonerate the country from its debt of honour, and save from
destitution the widow of that man who in our times has done it the
most honour . . . If you cannot obtain for the widow of the wisest and
most virtuous man in England what will defend her from poverty, I
swear to you that I, who am obliged to live on a tenth of my income,
will offer her the fifth". He asked Milnes to "exert your great and
noble faculties on behalf of a man whose principles and pursuits were
the same as yours", and "do not let my application be injurious to
him". Milnes was abroad, and by the time he received Landor's letter,
application for a pension for Caroline Southey had been rejected.
Declining Milnes's offer to renew the application, as he thought Sir
Robert Peel "an unlikely man to change a resolution when nothing is
to be gained by it beside the esteem of honest men", Landor bitterly

z

remarked, "Southey was only the best man and the best writer of the age in which he lived, and the strongest support of Peel's administration; but Southey is dead, and no edifice can stand upon a dead body."

From Caroline Southey's letters Landor derived some idea of how Wordsworth—as Wordsworth himself revealed in correspondence with Crabb Robinson—fermented the misunderstanding and mischief between those of Southey's children who opposed the second wife and those who befriended her. His resentment against Wordsworth on Southey's account was revived in the second imaginary conversation between Southey and Porson, published in *Blackwood's Magazine* for December 1842, in which Porson pays tribute to Southey as "the soundest and the fairest of our English critics" and asserts, "if Mr. Wordsworth should at any time become more popular, it will be owing in great measure to your authority and patronage; and I hope that, neither in health nor in sickness, he will forget his benefactor". On stepping into his dead friend's shoes as Poet Laureate, Wordsworth made no attempt to help his widow and even inspired the busy Quillinan to deny that Caroline Bowles had sacrificed anything of her income by marrying Southey: "Wordsworth is a strange mixture of sheep and wolf," wrote Landor to Caroline Southey, "with one eye on a daffodil & the other on a canal-share."

To Samuel Carter Hall, a Christian of the churchgoing persuasion, the friendship between Southey and Landor seemed "a mystery", as they "had nothing in common".

Southey was a Tory, Landor a Republican—or worse; the one was provident as well as just, the other reckless and utterly inconsiderate; the one was a devoted and affectionate husband, the other held matrimonial ties to be very slight; the one was patient, generous, "thinking no evil," abjuring the notion that revenge was virtue, the other petulant, irritable, passionate, ever ready to give or take offence;—in a word, the one was a Christian, the other, if not a mocker, was a despiser, of all creeds.

According to Henry Vizetelly, Hall was "the original of Dickens's Pecksniff"; in his *Memories of Great Men and Women of the Age,* published many years after Landor's death, he claimed that he "knew Landor in 1837, at Clifton, and had many walks with him over its health-giving downs; more than once I met him at the 'evenings' of Lady Blessington". Though "my lack of accordance with his political and social opinions prevented my taking notice of the matters on which he discoursed . . . he found me a willing, though certainly not a sympathetic listener", but "Mrs. Hall was not so patient with him—one day he called upon us, and spoke so abominably of things and persons she venerated that she plainly intimated a desire that he would not visit us again".

Receiving in January 1837 an application signed "S.C.H." for "some memoranda, out of which to form a brief page of biography, to accompany specimens of modern poets", Landor wrote to Lady Blessington that "my ignorance of every thing that passes in the literary world is such, that I am utterly at a loss whether this is Mrs. H., or some one else of a name distinguished for letters"; in case "your acquaintance, Mrs. H., should be the writer", he enclosed the desired memoranda in his letter to Lady Blessington, who replied that she had "furnished your note to Mr. Hall, the husband of Mrs. Hall, the authoress". Apparently Hall asked for an interview, for Landor told Lady Blessington in April 1837, "Mr. Hall has been making me a visit this morning", and presumably Hall was taken over the downs for a walk which became "many" in reminiscence. Though he avoided social calls in London, Landor may have made a courtesy call on Mrs. Hall as a friend of Lady Blessington's, but there was nothing to attract its repetition. Apart from Wordsworth's devotees—and even they, like Crabb Robinson, liked Landor personally while deploring his attitude to their idol—Hall shares with Samuel Rogers the distinction of expressing dislike for Landor; to be disliked by either was a recommendation to all who knew them.

§ 4

Having secured the financial objects of his visit, Arnold did not fulfil his promise to come again for the summer of 1843, but hearing in January that his daughter would be coming, Landor wrote the lines, "To my Daughter", published in *Blackwood* of March:

> By that dejected city, Arno runs,
> Where Ugolino claspt his famisht sons.
> There wert thou born, my Julia! there thine eyes
> Return'd as bright a blue to vernal skies.
> And thence, my little wanderer! when the Spring
> Advanced, thee, too, the hours on silent wing
> Brought, while anemones were quivering round,
> And pointed tulips pierced the purple ground,
> Where stood fair Florence: there thy voice first blest
> My ear, and sank like balm into my breast:
> For many griefs had wounded it, and more
> Thy little hands could lighten were in store.
> But why revert to griefs? Thy sculptured brow
> Dispels from mine its darkest cloud even now.
> What then the bliss to see again thy face,
> And all that Rumour has announced of grace!
> I urge, with fevered breast, the four-month day.
> O! could I sleep to wake again in May.

When Julia arrived at Bath early in May 1843, escorted by her brother Walter, her visit brought more happiness than Arnold's. Though now six years older, she was much as her mother had been at the time of her marriage; old enough to remember her father with affection, she anticipated the adventure of her first visit to England with the same ingenuous delight in novelty as inspired her mother, on her honeymoon, to interrupt Landor's reading of his poetry by exclaiming at "that dear delightful Punch" in the street outside. Landor had talked much of her to Rose Paynter, who was aware of his anxiety that there should be affectionate liking between his daughter and the girl who had supplied her absent place; whatever her private impression of Julia, she dutifully did her best to fulfil the hopes of the old man she loved and revered, introducing Julia to Bath society and joining with father and daughter in rallying "the old man Walter" on his successes with young women of fashion.

Unlike the two previous years, during this visit Landor went everywhere with his children. After three or four weeks at Bath, they spent most of June at Warwick with Elizabeth Landor before proceeding for the first three weeks of July to Ablett at Llanbedr. Julia had taken riding lessons with Rose at Bath, but the weather was so wet at Llanbedr that she was "tempted but once to mount a pony under the guidance of Walter", who enjoyed himself by riding and fishing. From Llanbedr they went for a week with Charles's family at Colton, calling again at Warwick before another week with Robert at Birlingham. After "a day or two" at Bath they spent a week in mid-August at Plymouth. Charles Brown had sailed with his son to New Zealand two years before, and had been already more than a year in his grave, but through him Landor had become friendly with a Plymouth neighbour, Colonel Hamilton Smith, with whom they now stayed. According to Landor "a man of more extensive and more accurate information than any in existence", Hamilton Smith was an antiquary and an old friend and collaborator of Sir Samuel Meyrick, who, said Landor, possessed "the finest and most complete collection of ancient armour, &c., &c., of any in the world . . . more authentic than that in the Tower". Meyrick's uncle, General George Meyrick, had been Landor's friend at Como and godfather to Arnold, but having already sacrificed his usual stay at Gore House for the sake of his children's society, Landor now deferred an invitation to Meyrick's Herefordshire seat, Goodrich Court, as "I think I shall not quit Bath again this autumn for any greater distance than Clifton".

On their return from Plymouth on 18th August Walter and Julia remained with their father at Bath for the rest of their visit. As he confided to Mrs. Paynter, Landor dreaded the end of these happy months:

Julia and Walter must leave me in the first week of October. They promised to be absent from Italy no longer than six months at the farthest. My heart sinks within me at the thought of their departure. The happy days of my existence are all past.

After hearing that they had promised to be away only six months, "I have never uttered one word, much less one complaint, against it." Nor did he express the resentment he must have felt at Julia's removal from society, like that of Rose Paynter and Hamilton Smith's daughters, which improved her manners; he remarked only on her improved appearance—"she is become a little less brown than she was, and looks much better for it. I was quite surprised and a little vext and grieved at seeing her so tanned."

Brother and sister sailed on 8th October, and two days later Landor wrote to Rose Paynter:

My Julia went by the steamer on Sunday. The weather was very boisterous. I rose several times in the night and attempted by putting my hand out of window to ascertain in which point was the wind. . . . My dear Julia wished not only to be with me but alone with me as much as possible. We parted in unutterable grief, but youth and fresh scenes will soon assuage all hers. That is enough.

He must have known that the girl's expressions of affection for himself would excite her mother's possessive jealousy to prevent another visit; if he realised this, the vision of the lonely old man, standing in his nightshirt before the open window to peer over his arm outstretched to the breeze, rises above the forlorn or the pathetic to achieve the desolation of tragedy.

16

THE BOYTHORN DICKENS KNEW

Midst all sorts of blunders, political and military, what think you of Napier in India? What think you of this elephant in the midst of jackals and monkeys? Only one battle since the creation ever equalled his—that of Poictiers. ... They will not make him a duke; perhaps they will not make him what they made such rapscallions as Abinger, &c., &c. Were I Napier, and they offered me a mere barony, I would fringe my glove with gold lace, and slap their muzzles till they bled.

—Landor to Milnes, *c.* June 1843

"By my soul, Jarndyce," he said, very gently holding up a bit of bread to the canary to peck at, "if I were in your place, I would seize every Master in Chancery by the throat to-morrow morning, and shake him until his money rolled out of his pockets, and his bones rattled in his skin. I would have a settlement out of somebody, by fair means or by foul. If you would empower me to do it, I would do it for you with the greatest satisfaction!" (All this time the very small canary was eating out of his hand.) . . .

—*Bleak House*, chap. ix

As if resigned to the idea that the happy days of his existence were all past, Landor talked increasingly of the end of life after the autumn of 1843. Proclaiming himself "an absolute cripple with the rheumatism", he declined all invitations to leave Bath before the following summer. In December he caught a feverish cold, and living on "bread and butter pudding, seltzer water, and strawberry jam", he exclaimed—with the impatience of illness usual in those who have enjoyed the health of a vigorous constitution—"Health, indeed, where is it gone?" Indisposition annoyed him as an injustice: "I have no ailments," he once said to Milnes, "but why should I? I have eaten well-prepared food; I have drunk light sub-acid wines, and three glasses instead of ten; I have liked modest better than immodest women, and I have never tried to make a shilling in the world."

After many years in Italy he keenly felt the damp of the long English winter. He wrote to Forster in the winter of 1840:

In this weather nobody can be quite well. I myself, an oddly-mixt metal with a pretty large portion of iron in it, am sensible to the curse of climate.

The chief reason is, I cannot walk through the snow and slop. My body, and my mind more especially, requires strong exercise. Nothing can tire either, excepting dull people, and they weary both at once.

"You may live in England," he said again, "if you are rich enough to have a solar system of your own, not without." When Forster was one July at Brighton, "I could not get salt-bathing quite so near at hand as yours," he wrote, "but I can get a fine fresh bath, or even swim, every day before my window . . . never had we such continued rain." And to Lady Blessington in the new year of 1845, "I am credibly informed that the sun has visited London twice in the month of December," he wrote; "let us hope, that such a phenomenon may portend no mischief to the nation."

Like most elderly men living alone, he took great care of himself. Always an abstemious drinker, he now never touched wine except in company. "If you really are resolved to send me any wine," he wrote to his brother Henry in 1846, "pray send me very little, for I myself seldom drink any, and it is not oftener than once a fortnight that any one dines with me." A few months later, remarking how his brother Robert "continues to be tormented by the gout", he told Rosenhagen, "I drink no wine now, so that I may hope to be except from this dreadful calamity."

He was always fastidious over his food. There are many variants of Milnes's story how, at Florence, "after an imperfect dinner", he had thrown the cook out of the window, and while the man lay with a broken limb, exclaimed, "Good God! I forgot the violets." As he had it from Kenyon, Lowell declared that Mrs. Landor remonstrated, "There, Walter! I always told you that one day you would do something to be sorry for in these furies of yours," to which Landor mildly replied, "Well, my dear, I *am* sorry if that will do you any good. If I had remembered that our best tulip-bed was under that window, I'd have flung the dog out of t'other." In Italy he had learned much of culinary art, and now superintended the preparation of his meals, himself seasoning the dishes and directing how they were to be cooked in wine—"he was a good cook in that way", said Mrs. Lynn Linton, "and to that extent".

He was methodical in daily routine, which he described to his sister in 1845:

I walk out in all weathers six miles a day at the least; and I generally, unless I am engaged in the evening, read from seven till twelve or one. I sleep twenty minutes after dinner, and nearly four hours at night, or rather in the morning. I rise at nine, breakfast at ten, and dine at five. All winter I have had some beautiful sweet daphnes and hyacinths in my windows.

Oddities grew upon him; especially he developed the absent-mindedness of those who live much alone. It became phenomenal for him to

arrive anywhere without having forgotten some of his luggage. Once
he suffered vexation on a visit to Warwick from having forgotten the
key of his portmanteau. On his next visit, in June 1843, he greeted his
sister by triumphantly brandishing the key in his hand, but as soon as
his peals of Boythornesque laughter had subsided, "the fatal discovery
presented itself that to bring only a key was more of a disaster than to
bring only a portmanteau". Of this mishap he wrote to Forster:

My portmanteau and all my clothes were left behind at Cheltenham,
against all my precautions. The worst is the loss of much poetry and prose
written in the last three months. I am not such a fool as to trouble my head
about the clothes, nor wise enough not to trouble it about the pages. However I never look after a loss a single moment.

On his summer visit to Warwick in 1844, he wrote from Birmingham
to Forster:

You will wonder what I had to do at Birmingham. Why! just nothing
at all. I should have changed trains at Coventry for Leamington, but the
fools never cried out a word about that station.

On his way home from a Cornish holiday in August 1848, he wrote
from Exeter:

I had no other accident but leaving my guide-book and gold spectacles.
I must disburse half my patrimony for another pair! Vexatious, as I have
six or seven pairs already, but at Bath.

And after staying with Rosenhagen at Cheltenham in September 1852,
he wrote to his late host from Bath:

Here I am again, not quite naked, but with only three shirts, and no change
of either linen or cloth. At Cheltenham Station I was hurried from a lower
to a higher Station. I saw my portmanteau deposited in the lower, and made
two distinct inquiries about it. "All right, sir" was the answer. At Gloster
I found no portmanteau. On Saturday I was advised to write to the Secretary of the Bristol and Birmingham Railroad at Cheltenham. He may
perhaps condescend to answer my application—he has not done it yet.

A story told by John Sterling to Caroline Fox suggests that Landor was
an interesting fellow-passenger to travel with. Sterling afterwards met
Landor at Julius Hare's, on one occasion hotly disputing with him the
merits of the Evangelicals, whom he considered Landor was "running
down most unfairly", but his first sight of him was as a fellow-passenger
on a coach journey. Landor began to talk, and "the strange paradoxical
style of conversation in which he indulged", led Sterling to suspect who
he was, so that he finally remarked, "Why! this sounds amazingly like
an Imaginary Conversation." Landor "started at this remark, but
covered his retreat"; his dislike of any sort of publicity prevented his
owning his identity to this too discerning young man in the presence of
a coachful of passengers.

Though each autumn, on settling for the winter at Bath, he regularly declared the likelihood of his never leaving this place again, he continued to travel every summer. Despite nursing his cold and Rose Paynter's sick spaniel, he was bright enough by Christmas 1843 to be reminded that "the word sounds like distant bells and chimney piece holly berries"; he begged Rose to "remember the fourteenth of January is Colonel Jervis's ball", for "I still enjoy the privilege of seeing you dance, which was always one of my greatest pleasures". Late in January he received a visit from Dickens and Forster, who carried away with him a document, dated on the 24th, assigning to him the copyright of all Landor's imaginary conversations. On 4th March Crabb Robinson was informed by the publisher Moxon "that Landor has given all his Dialogues to Forster, who is going to publish them at his own risk", and added complacently, "But he will not allow the attack on Wordsworth to be among them."

A change of lodgings in April may have caused Landor again to defer his visit to Gore House; he moved across St. James's Square from No. 35, where he had lived since the autumn of 1837, to No. 1, where his landlady was Miss Sydney Rance and Lady Leighton was a fellow lodger. Later he visited his sister at Warwick, but in September, after a short visit to Clifton, he was back at Bath, receiving Albany Fonblanque to lunch and expecting a visit from Forster to read to him eight letters received from Dickens during his trip to Italy—the trip that inspired the verses to Dickens published in the *Examiner* of 21st September 1844 (eight lines are quoted at the head of the previous chapter, page 328).

He had long been engaged on the task of revising all his writings for an edition of his collected works. The project was suggested by Forster, who declared that the work was already in progress when Landor sent him the biographical essay on Petrarca[1] published in the *Foreign Quarterly Review* of July 1843. Having acquired the editorship of this review, Forster invited Landor to contribute articles on his favourite classical authors, and the essay on Petrarca was preceded by "The Poems of Catullus" in July 1842 and "The Idyls of Theocritus" in October 1842.

The discipline of journalism was as alien to Landor as any form of dictatorship; he could concentrate only upon his inclination of the

---

[1] The fourth paragraph of the essay reads: "It may seem fastidious and affected to write, as I have done, his Italian name in preference to his English one; but I think it better to call him as he called himself, as Laura called him, as he was called by Colonna and Rienzi and Boccaccio, and in short by all Italy: for I pretend to no vernacular familiarity with a person of his distinction, and should almost be as ready to abbreviate Francesco into Frank, as Petrarca into Petrarch. Beside, the one appellation is euphonious, the other quite the reverse." This fastidiousness suggests that Landor must appeal even less to "the age of the common man" than to his contemporaries, for the journalist of the nineteen-fifties refers to everybody, from statesmen to footballers, by the names that should be decently the privilege of their family and intimates.

moment and regarded editorial guidance as an invitation to argument. When Forster ventured to suggest that "there are a hundred readers of Virgil and Horace to one of Catullus . . . The genius of Catullus you may think supreme, but that Horace is more of a favourite with greater numbers of people is a fact as little to be doubted", Landor rebuked him in the course of his essay:

One poet is not to be raised by casting another under him. Catullus is made no richer by an attempt to transfer to him what belongs to Horace, nor Horace by what belongs to Catullus. Catullus has greatly more than he; but he also has much; and let him keep it. We are not at liberty to indulge in forwardness and caprice, snatching a decoration from one and tossing it over to another.

Catullus had been his model and master since he wrote the hendecasyllabics in his *Poems* of 1795, and in preparation for his essay he asked his sister to look for notes he had made at Rugby and Oxford—"Anciently there were some bits of my Latin poetry and other such stuff in a chest of drawers which stood in my bedroom, now a dressing-room. Most of these were translations into Latin verse, and correcting his extravagance." But he was not in the mood for attempting an assessment of this favourite poet; after beginning in tentative appreciation, he abandoned the attempt to analyse his impressions, inserted a list of his critical and textual notes on each *carmen*, and concluded with comparative remarks on contemporary poets that are frequently cited against him as examples of his reckless judgments:

Cowper, and Byron, and Southey, with much and deep tenderness, are richly humorous. Wordsworth, grave, elevated, observant, and philosophical, is equidistant from humour and from passion. Always contemplative, never creative, he delights the sedentary and tranquillizes the excited. No tear ever fell, no smile ever glanced, on his pages. With him you are beyond the danger of any turbulent emotion, as terror, or valour, or magnanimity, or generosity. Nothing is there about him like Burns's *Scots wha ha'e wi' Wallace bled*, or Campbell's *Battles of Copenhagen and Hohenlinden*, or those exquisite works which, in Hemans, rise up like golden spires among broader but lower structures, *Ivan* and *Casabianca*. Byron, often impressive and powerful, never reaches the heroic and the pathetic of these two poems: and he wants the freshness and healthiness we admire in Burns. But an indomitable fire of poetry, the more vivid for the gloom about it, bursts through the crusts and crevices of an unsound and hollow mind. He never chatters with chilliness, nor falls overstrained into languor; nor do metaphysics ever muddy his impetuous and precipitate stream. . . . But no *large* poem of our days is so animated, or so truly of the heroic cast, as *Marmion*.

Perhaps no critic of eminence has ever obscured flashes of insight with illustrations so indicative of muddled values!

In treating Theocritus he followed the same method as with Catullus, a general appreciation being followed by notes on each idyl and a conclusion summarizing modern achievement in idyllic poetry. But the notes are generally more descriptive and illuminating, and the critical remarks on the moderns as happy as those in the Catullus were un-lucky:

Thomson, in the *Seasons*, has given us many beautiful descriptions of inanimate nature; but the moment any one speaks in them the charm is broken. The figures he introduces are fantastical. The *Hassan* of Collins is excellent: he however is surpassed by Burns and Scott: and Wordsworth, in his *Michael*, is nowise inferior to them. Among the moderns no poet, it appears to us, has written an Idyl so perfect, so pure and simple in expression, yet so rich in thought and imagery, as the *Godiva* of Alfred Tennyson. Wordsworth, like Thomson, is deficient in the delineation of character, even of the rustic, in which Scott and Burns are almost equal. But some beautiful Idyls might be extracted from the *Excursion*, which would easily split into *laminæ*, and the residue might, with little loss, be blown away. Few are suspicious that they may be led astray and get benighted by following simplicity too far. If there are pleasant fruits growing on the ground, must we therefore cast aside, as unwholesome, those which have required the pruning-knife to correct and the ladder to reach them? Beautiful thoughts are seldom disdainful of sonorous epithets: we find them continually in the Pastorals of Theocritus: sometimes we see, coming rather obtrusively, the wanton and indelicate; but never (what poetry most abhors) the mean and abject. Widely different from our homestead poets, the Syracusan is remarkable for a facility that never draggles, for a spirit that never flags, and for a variety that never is exhausted.

The subject of Petrarca was near his heart from his studies for *The Pentameron,* and detailed criticism could be banished to a brief passage in the conclusion because interpretation and appreciation were woven into the biographical narrative comprising the body of the essay. "That piece on Petrarca," wrote Carlyle, "surprises me (I beg many pardons) by its *impartiality* to that wearisome creature; and looks in my mind like a perfect Steel Engraving in the way of portraiture." The reader may find it hard to follow Mr. Super in believing that Landor was "reliving his own life" in writing the story of Petrarca's life, but his own feeling for Ianthe enabled him to gauge with moving sympathy the nature of Petrarca's love for Laura:

Perhaps it is well for those who delight in poetry that she was inflexible and obdurate; for the sweetest song ceases when the feathers have lined the nest. . . . In the bosom of Petrarca love burnt again more ardently than ever. It is censured as the worst of conceits in him that he played so often on the name of Laura; and many have suspected that there could be little passion in so much allusion. A purer taste might indeed have corrected in the poetry the outpourings of tenderness in the name; but surely there is a true and a pardonable pleasure in cherishing the very sound of what we love. If it belongs to the heart, as it does, it belongs to poetry, and is not easily to be cast aside. The shrub recalling the idea of Laura was planted by his hand; often, that he might nurture it, was the pen laid by; the leaves were often shaken by his sighs, and not unfrequently did they sparkle with his tears. He felt the comfort of devotion as he bent before the image of her name.

But he now saw little of her, and was never at her house: it was only in small parties, chiefly of ladies, that they met. She excelled them all in grace of person and in elegance of attire. Probably her dress was not the more indifferent to her on her thinking whom she was about to meet: yet she maintained the same reserve: the nourisher of love, but not of hope. . . .

Love is the purifier of the heart; its depths are less turbid than its shallows. In despite of precepts and arguments, the most sedate and the most religious of women think charitably, and even reverentially, of the impassioned poet. Constancy is the antagonist of frailty, exempt from the captivity and above the assaults of sin.

His studies inspired spasmodic bursts of creative work. When Forster sent him an edition of Pindar, Landor objected that he had too long neglected his Greek to undertake the review—"he was never more than a boy in Greek, though he grew up to adolescence in Latin, and bore a strong beard in English". But soon he informed Forster that the resumption of reading Greek was like entering a cathedral—it seemed dark at first, but the eye grew gradually accustomed by use till it discerned the magnificence of the surroundings. So he discarded Pindar and wrote about Theocritus instead, but a note in the edition of Pindar reminded him of a story that might have been suitably treated by Theocritus—of a wood nymph who saved her oak from the axe by inspiring the forester with love of her, and died when she supposed she had lost his love—and he wrote a poem of nearly three hundred lines in the hope "that it will be found of that order of simplicity which is simple in the manner of Theocritus". Swinburne rated this poem, "The Hamadryad" (nine lines are quoted at the head of the previous chapter, page 328), "as first but one among the *Hellenics*"; he thought "the crown of all the Hellenics is the divine 'Agamemnon and Iphigenia'", which appeared in *Pericles and Aspasia*.

In the course of revising his imaginary conversations Landor found for a few months a profitable market in *Blackwood's Magazine*. As the second Southey and Porson dialogue was unsuitable for Lady Blessington's *Book of Beauty*, somebody apparently suggested that *Blackwood* might welcome his criticism of Wordsworth, as John Wilson—the "Christopher North" and supposedly the "veiled editor" of the magazine—like his friend De Quincey, shared Landor's personal dislike of Wordsworth, while acknowledging his poetic genius. *Blackwood* published "Southey and Porson" in December 1842, paid £25 for it, and invited further contributions; the next three numbers included the dialogues between Tasso and Cornelia, Oliver Cromwell and Sir Oliver Cromwell, and Sandt and Kotzebue—the first and third were among the dialogues sent from Italy in 1828 for the intended sixth volume of *Imaginary Conversations*—the number for March 1843 also including the verses "To my Daughter". But, with the perversity for which the "veiled editor" had always been remarkable, the magazine welcomed satire on its own contributor by publishing Quillinan's "Imaginary Conversation between Mr. Walter Savage Landor and the Editor of 'Blackwood's Magazine'" in April 1843; Landor had no experience of the pleasantries with which Wilson and his collaborators publicised their fellow-contributors in the "Noctes Ambrosianæ" and wrote to withdraw the next contribution he had offered.

Faithfully he fulfilled his promise to offer his work to Lady Blessington for her annuals—she became editor of *The Keepsake* in 1840 as well as of *Heath's Book of Beauty*—and besides occasional verse, the two dialogues between Æsop and Rhodopè appeared in the *Book of Beauty* for 1844 and 1845. Frequently Forster published verses and letters in the *Examiner*. Visiting Llanbedr in July 1843, Landor addressed to the *Examiner* an appeal for more such lunatic asylums in Wales as Ablett had established at his own expense near Denbigh; enjoyment of his daughter's company did not prevent his joining in an attack by the *Examiner* on Lord Brougham, "this noisy chanticleer", for opposing reform of the law of libel, nor his urging support for the Greeks in their revolt against the tyranny of King Otho. On 22nd June 1844 the *Examiner* published a memorial to the Queen, written by Landor and signed by many of his friends in Bath, enumerating the wrongs of Ireland and appealing for the release of Daniel O'Connell—who had been recently sentenced to imprisonment on a charge of conspiracy— as "we attribute solely to his great exertions the tranquil state of Ireland, which no other man in six hundred years hath been able to establish".

On 5th November 1844 Landor was recovering from "a touch of the rheumatism . . . caused by my imprudence in rising up in my bed to fix a thought on paper—night is not the time to pin a butterfly on a blank leaf", when he wrote to Lady Blessington:

I have youth on my side. I shall not see seventy, for nearly three months to come. I am very busy collecting all I have written. It may perhaps be published in another eight or ten months. Once beyond seventy, I will never write a line in verse or prose for publication. I will be my own Gil Blas. The wisest of us are unconscious when our faculties begin to decay. Knowing this, I fixed my determination many years ago. I am now plucking out my weeds all over the field, and will leave only the strongest shoots of the best plants standing.

No doubt weeds were plucked from many of the unpublished dialogues, like that between Dante and Beatrice, which was placed—probably by Forster—with *Hood's Magazine* for March 1845. But the business of weeding was continually interrupted by the setting of new plants. Mr. Super has found evidence to indicate that the verse drama of *The Siege of Ancona* was written in October 1844, the account of the siege in Sismondi's *History of the Italian Republics* having inspired the belief that "no event in the history of Italy, including the Roman, is at once so tragical and so glorious", and Forster mentions that the beautiful idyl of "Enallos and Cymodameia" was written about this time. Yet, in reporting progress to Forster, Landor still thought much of his prose and little of his poetry:

The literary world is a dram-drinking world at present; but it is quite possible that the next generation will relish a cooler and better-flavoured drink. My Conversations, whatever their demerits, will exhibit more qualities and postures of the human mind than any other book published in my day. . . . But of my poetry what shall I say? In fact I care little about it, though I have always been nursing it assiduously. I go on correcting and correcting, adding and adding, all my life through, and nobody (as might be expected) is less satisfied at last.

The range of his knowledge and interests was too wide to allow concentration long enough to produce a single work worthy of his powers. The form of the imaginary conversations suited his temperament because length was dictated only by duration of mood and expression of idea; as he grew older, the capacity for concentration diminished as the butterfly of his fancy settled more briefly to rest in proportion to the brevity and frequency of its flights. He valued his verse the less as he resorted the more to its medium as a refuge from the greater concentration exacted by prose. "If ever you receive my collected works," he wrote to Browning on 10th November 1845, "pray do not say a single word about the poetry," and some years later he wrote the well-known passage in the dialogue "Archdeacon Hare and Walter Landor":

Poetry was always my amusement, prose my study and business. I have publisht five volumes of *Imaginary Conversations*: cut the worst of them thro the middle, and there will remain in this decimal fraction quite enough to satisfy my appetite for fame. I shall dine late; but the dining-room will be well lighted, the guests few and select.

§ 2

On his seventieth birthday, 30th January 1845, Landor received from his sister the gift of a writing desk made from the timber of a fallen cedar at Warwick. Forster was there to witness his pleasure, and remarking that he had risen at his usual hour of nine in spite of having stayed at the annual subscription ball the previous night till nearly three in the morning, he warned him that "to give such advantage to the enemy might bring him down some day", at which Landor laughed, "I don't invite him, but I shall receive him hospitably when he comes."

During the winter he looked forward to renewing his visits to Gore House in the spring, but Lady Blessington wrote that her sister Lady Canterbury was dangerously ill. She asked him to make his visit later in the summer, but he showed no consciousness of his age in casually deciding that he would "now defer it until another year". In August he went to Warwick and thence for "ten days without a ray of sunshine" to his brother Charles at Colton. He was invited to witness Dickens's performance in Ben Jonson's *Every Man in His Humour* on 20th September, but went instead for a fortnight to Budleigh Salterton, where he lodged near the Paynters and talked of a visit to Lynton with Kenyon and Aubrey Bezzi.

Silent this year on the subject of politics, he published in *Hood's Magazine* for April the lines inviting William Napier, as the historian of the Peninsular War, to write of his brother's military achievements in India:

> Napier! take up anew thy pen,
> To mark the deeds of mighty men.
> And whose more glorious canst thou trace
> Than heroes of thy name and race?

On 22nd November 1845 the *Morning Chronicle* published his verses "To Robert Browning":

> There is delight in singing, though none hear
> Beside the singer; and there is delight
> In praising, though the praiser sit alone
> And see the prais'd far off him, far above.
> Shakspeare is not *our* poet, but the world's,
> Therefore on him no speech; and short for thee,
> Browning! Since Chaucer was alive and hale,
> No man hath walk'd along our roads with step
> So active, so inquiring eye, or tongue
> So varied in discourse. But warmer climes
> Give brighter plumage, stronger wing; the breeze
> Of Alpine heights thou playest with, borne on
> Beyond Sorrento and Amalfi, where
> The Siren waits thee, singing song for song.

This tribute from a veteran of letters seemed to seal the recognition of the rising young poet; Browning's father had the verses reprinted on a leaflet, and Browning himself made prompt acknowledgment by dedicating to Landor the last number of his *Bells and Pomegranates*, containing "Luria" and "A Soul's Tragedy". Receiving the dedication as "the richest of Easter offerings made to anyone for many years", Landor bade Browning "go on and pass us poor devils! If you do not go far ahead of me, I will crack my whip at you and make you spring forward".

Apart from gratitude, there was hero-worship in Browning's regard for Landor. As Chesterton said, Browning "conceived himself rather as a sanguine and strenuous man, a great fighter"; he therefore admired the dauntless spirit of the septuagenarian who rebelled as insistently against injustice and the abuse of power as in his republican youth. The loyalty of his admiration flourished in defiance of Elizabeth Barrett's scepticism. Though in 1844 she contributed to Horne's *New Spirit of the Age* a handsome tribute to Landor, she never overcame her first impression of impatience on meeting him in Wordsworth's company. On Browning's expressions of enthusiasm for Landor she frequently cast the chill of disparagement: of "the crashing throat-peals of Mr. Landor's laughter", she remarked, "he laughs, I remember, like an ogre—he laughs as if laughter could kill, and he knew it, thinking of an enemy", and when Browning was momentarily piqued at Landor's depreciation of Goethe, she asked if he was not "one of the men who carry their passions about with them into everything, as a boy would pebbles . . . muddying every clear water, with a stone here and a stone there". But Browning affirmed that he liked Landor "more and more", and begged her in a love-letter to read Landor's "Tasso and Cornelia" dialogue, "with the exquisite Sorrentine scenery".

Landor's loneliness at Bath was intensified by the marriage, in February 1846, of Rose Paynter to the son and heir of Sir Joseph Graves-Sawle, who lived in Cornwall. On the eve of her wedding he wrote the lines "To a Bride, Feb. 17, 1846":

> Well hast thou chosen, after long demur
> To aspirations from more realms than one.
> Peace be with those thou leavest! peace with thee!
> Is that enough to wish thee? not enough,
> But very much: for Love himself feels pain,
> While brighter plumage shoots, to shed last year's;
> And one at home (how dear that one!) recalls
> Thy name, and thou recallest one at home.
> Yet turn not back thine eyes; the hour of tears
> Is over; nor believe thou that Romance
> Closes against pure Faith her rich domain.
>
> .   .   .   .   .
>
> Well hast thou chosen. I repeat the words,
> Adding as true ones, not untold before,
> That incense must have fire for its ascent,
> Else 'tis inert and can not reach the idol.
> Youth is the sole equivalent of youth.
> Enjoy it while it lasts; and last it will;
> Love can prolong it in despite of Years.

"Is it possible that I appeared to you sad and sorrowful on your wedding day," he asked her in self-reproach a month later:

I shall be delighted to see you at one more Master of the Ceremonies Ball. It is the only one I shall attend this season. And after this season I shall give up balls and all other amusements. It is time I should begin to feel the effects of age, and I think I do. Let me fold my arms across my breast, and go quietly down the current until where the current ends.

Preparation of his Collected Works, intended for completion by his seventieth birthday, was finished a few months after his seventy-first. "Hundreds of sentences and of paragraphs I have transcribed from the backs of letters and from old pocket books," he wrote; "Forster tells me he never saw such extremely small characters as I have employed in my interlining." Forster wanted to include his portrait as frontispiece, but "I resisted all entreaties to prefix one," wrote Landor to his son Arnold, "for it appears to me a sad piece of coxcombery." He had hoped to present the two volumes, "decently bound", to Lady Blessington when he visited Gore House in May 1846, but Forster "tells me I must wait about a fortnight". The delay was due to Edward Moxon's last-minute decision to have the credit of publishing the volumes instead of allowing them to be issued by the printers, Bradbury & Evans, at Landor's expense.

Late in May Landor arrived at Gore House, probably in time to renew his acquaintance with Prince Louis Napoleon, who was busily making use of Count D'Orsay and Lady Blessington on his escape to London from political imprisonment. On 31st May he dined at Forster's chambers; Macready called after dinner and enjoyed "much talk on Milton, Shakspeare, Virgil, Horace, Homer, etc.", but if Landor had just met Louis Napoleon as Lady Blessington's guest, it is unlikely that this was the occasion when he amused Macready with the statement, "Sir, the French are all scoundrels!" Two days later he dined at Kenyon's in Browning's company, but returned to Bath towards the end of the week on the day after he was able to present a copy of his works to Lady Blessington.

The two volumes were dedicated to Forster and Julius Hare, for, as Landor wrote to the former:

The volumes belong to you and Hare, without whom they could never have appeared, and I shall omit all the old dedications,—for Mina gave orders to kill a woman; Bolivar was a coxcomb and impostor, having been two hundred miles distant from the battle he pretended to have won; and Wilson is worse than a whig.

Forster persuaded him against insisting upon use of his reformed spelling, apart from "a few words defensible on Milton's authority", but Landor refused his cautious advice to omit the political dialogues, arguing, "If Shakespeare had written but *Othello*, the noblest of human works, he would scarcely have been half so great as the having written

AA

many dramas in addition, even inferior ones, has made him. Genius shows its power by its multiformity."

Having treated its readers to a forty-page consideration of Landor's works in 1837, the *Quarterly Review* chose perhaps to regard the *Collected Works* as a reprint, but the attitude of many reviewers was described by Browning in writing to Elizabeth Barrett on 17th July:

I can tell you nothing better, I think, than this I heard from Moxon the other day . . . it really ought to be remembered. Moxon was speaking of critics, the badness of their pay, how many pounds a column the *Times* allowed, and shillings the *Athenæum*,—and of the inevitable effects on the performances of the poor fellows. "How should they be at the trouble of reading any *difficult* book so as to review it,—Landor, for instance?" and indeed a friend of my own has promised to write a notice in the *Times*—but he complains bitterly,—he shall have to *read* the book,—he can do no less,—and all for five or ten pounds! All which Moxon quite seemed to understand —"it will really take him some three or four mornings to read *enough* of Landor to be able to do anything effectually." I asked if there had been any notices of the Book already—"Just so many," he said, "as Forster had the power of *getting done*"—Mr. White, a clergyman, has written a play for Macready, which everybody describes as the poorest stuff imaginable,—it is immediately reviewed in *Blackwood* and the *Edinburgh* "Because", continues M., "he is a *Blackwood* reviewer, and may do the like good turn to any of the confraternity".

The attitude of the reviewers to Landor foreshadows the attitude of posterity: a writer dignified by having his works collected must be important, but, like Dr. Johnson with Congreve's *Incognita*, they would rather praise than read him. Forster and Moxon were handicapped in their publicity efforts by Landor's objection to soliciting reviews by distributing review copies; he reprimanded Moxon for sending a review copy to Macvey Napier, the editor of the *Edinburgh Review*, and Forster had to write to Napier explaining that he had offered to review Landor's works for the *Edinburgh* because he had been privileged to read the proofs, but that the author knew nothing of his offer.

On 16th June Browning wrote to Elizabeth Barrett:

I called on Forster this morning: he says Landor is in high delight at the congratulatory letters he has received—so you must write, dearest, and add the queen-rose to his garland. F—— talks about some 500 copies—or did he say 300?—being sold already . . . so there is hope for Landor's lovers.

Miss Barrett duly added her queen-rose, though Landor could not read her signature and sent her letter to Forster to find out the identity of his correspondent. Browning himself wrote to Landor, "Nothing has been published that I can remember in which the display is so altogether extraordinary, of the rarest intellectual powers, I do believe, that were ever brought together in one man." Hare believed the volumes to "contain more and more various beauty than any collection of the writings of any English author since Shakespeare". Landor probably found most pleasure in the praise of William Napier, who wrote several times as he read the volumes:

You have two or three crotchets which you know I laugh at, though I never dispute with you on them; and which I believe you laugh at yourself in your sleeve, though it is a large sleeve that would hold your laugh. However, there they are, and they belong to you in the same manner that Cromwell's wart belonged to him, and he would be a fine fool that judged Oliver's genius by his wart! I do declare, notwithstanding your Napoleon wart, that your work is marvellous. . . . When I consider that the whole of these volumes is original, the pure production of your inventive brain, it is astounding. The variety and purity of your language, the vigour and wit of your thoughts, the extent of the ground you travel over, are all causes of amazement . . . you have shown that you could have talked well and wittily to the greatest men and women of every nation and of every age, since history took the place of fable, and perhaps better when fable *was* history. To the women you certainly could, you cunning knave, for you have adorned them with all the graces that poetry, the best and finest of fables, could invent. And yet you have borrowed nothing from former poets; unless it be the Olympus-shaking laugh of Homer's Jupiter, and that you keep for yourself. I would you could throw his lightnings also! I know where they would fall, and the world would soon be purged of all knaves and sneaking scoundrels.

§ 3

In July 1846 Landor visited Warwick, pausing at Birlingham on his way to travel on with his brother Robert, who was again inspired to publication by his brother's example, commissioning Longmans to publish at his own expense *The Fawn of Sertorius* only a few weeks after Landor's *Collected Works* had appeared. The publication was anonymous, but contained a reference to the author of *Pericles and Aspasia*, to which its design owed some suggestion, and the story, like *The Pentameron*, is supposed to be taken from an imaginary manuscript. Robert can hardly have failed to suspect that the authorship would be ascribed to his brother, as he complacently related to their brother Henry shortly after the publication:

Longmans have sent me fourteen or fifteen Criticisms, some in the Literary Papers, others from literary Men of their Acquaintance. The larger half of them suppose the Fawn to be Walter's and I am flattered by the assertion that only one Man living could have written it. So says the Author of Pericles in a letter, not to the Longmans, but to myself. Still more complimentary is one from Sir Edward Litten Bulwer, intended both for the Publisher and the Author. It is strange that such a resemblance should have occurred to so many, but it was observed by Southey in his Doctor ten years ago. It is not of a kind which could possibly arise from imitation, but must be constitutional and in the temperament. The same day that you were at Longmans, they received a letter from me in which I said that however flattering the supposition, I must disclaim it, that what would appear as a

compliment to me, would be an *imputation* against my Brother, and that there
was no other resemblance than such as often exists between very little people
and very great ones, or a Child and his Father. . . . A Second Edition may
be required soon, and then I shall place my Name on the Title page. The
only passage which in any degree refers to Walter is a Compliment, and such
a Compliment as no Man could pay to himself! Yet Walter's personal
Friends will ascribe the work to him.

Robert over-rated his brother's sales value, for a second edition was not
required, but two years later the remainder of the first was re-issued
under Robert's name at the same time as *The Fountain of Arethusa* was
published, in the preface to which he wrote of *The Fawn of Sertorius*:

It was instantly supposed to have been written by my brother: and several,
even among his most discerning acquaintances, might hardly be convinced
that the first page of it which he ever saw was already in print. . . . He endured so humiliating a misconception with the good-humoured complacency
which he always feels where my projects are concerned.

"Good-humoured complacency" was an ungracious description of
Landor's always generous praise of his brother's work, and on 4th
November 1848, aptly timed to advertise *The Fountain of Arethusa*, he
published in the *Examiner* the poem of eighty-five lines "To Robert
Eyres Landor on his *Fawn* and his *Arethusa*", measuring Robert's literary
achievements with his own and praising his conduct as a clergyman
before concluding:

> Thy Fancy rests upon deep-bosom'd Truth,
> And wakes to Harmony; no word is tost
> To catch the passing wind like unmade hay.
> Few can see this, whirl'd in the dust around,
> And some who can would rather see awry.
> If such could add to their own fame the fame
> Their hands detract from others, then indeed
> The act, howbeit felonious, were less vile;
> They strip the wealthy, but they clothe the poor.
> Aside thy *Fawn* expect some envious stab,
> Some latent arrow from obscure defile;
> Aside thy *Arethusa* never hope
> Untroubled rest: men will look up and see
> What hurts their eyes in the strong beams above,
> And shining points will bring fierce lightnings down
> Upon thy head, and mine by birth so near . . .
>
> .   .   .   .   .
>
> Better I deem it that my grain of myrrh
> Burn for the living than embalm the dead.
> Take my fraternal offering, not composed
> Of ditch-side flowers, the watery-stalkt and rank,

Such as our markets smell of, all day long,
And roister ditty-roaring rustics wear;
But fresh, full, shapely, sprinkled with that lymph
Which from Peneios on the olive-wreath
Shook at loud plaudits under Zeus high-throned.

Returning from Warwick, he spent a fortnight in August with Lord
Nugent—"Nugent, my friend from early years"—at Stowe in Bucking-
hamshire, "a very quiet and delightful place". Reaching Bath on 25th
August, he wrote next day to Mrs. Paynter:

Last evening, when I attempted to open my writing-desk, I found it quite
impracticable. I do not believe the people of the house are capable of any
kind of dishonesty, but it appears that my landlady was afraid of leaving
it in my room, and took it into hers. So it got shaken and a good deal injured. She is unwell, and wrote me a note telling me that her nerves will
never be right again while she has the charge of such precious things in her
house, and that (at my convenience) she hopes I will resign her lodgings.
On this, I went instantly and engaged rooms at No. 2 in this Square, where
I go the first of September. I hate to move, and I never can hope to live
again in any Square. This grieves me. It is now eight years within a month
that I have resided in St. James's. I have a cat-like attachment to places.[1]

In this mood of depression he wrote to Rose Graves-Sawle:

Between the hay-harvest and the corn-harvest there is a lull of nature, a
calm and dull quiescence. Autumn then comes to tell us of the world's
varieties and changes. At last the white pall of Nature closes round us. In
the last seven or eight years I seem to myself to have passed through all the
seasons of life excepting the very earliest and the very latest. I doubt whether
I have ever been so happy in any other equal and continued space of time.
Italy would sometimes flash back upon me; but the lightnings only kept
the memory awake, without disturbing it. How much, how nearly all, do I
owe to your friendship, to your music and your conversation.

He had banished from memory the miseries of the first three years after
his leaving Italy, and was resigned to seeing no more of his children
since the visit of Walter and Julia in 1843. To Lady Blessington he
wrote on 28th August:

Yesterday Colonel Jervis told me that Prince Louis Napoleon is here,
and had done me the favour to mention me to-day. I will therefore leave
my card at his hotel. . . . I feel I am growing old, for want of somebody to
tell me (charming falsehood) that I am looking as young as ever. There is a
vast deal of vital air in loving words.

Louis Napoleon returned his call and presented him with a copy of
his manual on artillery; when Landor said he would "certainly have

[1] The letter was so transcribed by Stephen Wheeler, but Mr. Super assumes from the
evidence of a letter from Landor to his brother Henry that Wheeler misprinted No. 2 for No.
42 St. James's Square. Even so, this does not explain Landor's grief that he could not "hope
to live again in any Square", and in August 1846 it was nearly nine years since he settled
at 35 St. James's Square in the autumn of 1837.

requested his acceptance of my books, only that they contained some severe strictures on his uncle the emperor", the prince replied that he knew perfectly well Landor's opinions and admired the honesty with which he expressed them—which tribute he inscribed in the presentation volume. He invited Landor to dine with him the next day in company with Lady Blessington and Count D'Orsay, and Landor related long afterwards to Mrs. Story:

> I went, finding a capital dinner and rooms most tastefully decorated with flowers. After dinner Lady Blessington and I got into the carriage for a drive, while D'Orsay sat outside with the Prince, who drove—so that, you see, I've been driven by a prince. Louis Napoleon is an extremely clever man, talking well on all subjects.

Landor's judgment of Louis Napoleon at all times was shrewder than that of the statesman, Richard Cobden, who remarked on meeting him this year that he was "a weak fellow, but mild and amiable".

About 15th or 16th September Kenyon arrived in Bath from London, and took Landor to stay with Andrew Crosse, the scientist, at Fyne Court in the Quantocks. Kenyon's "conversation and Crosse's made four days pass away delightfully," wrote Landor after his return to Bath on the 24th:

> At Taunton I met Mr Kinglake the author of "Eothen," and dined at his mother's. Never was a day spent more to my satisfaction. Indeed I may say that in seven years I have not passed seven consecutive days so pleasantly as those seven.

Kenyon had introduced Browning to Elizabeth Barrett, and this absence of his from London was chosen by the lovers as the opportunity for their elopement, since he could not be suspected of connivance.

Landor's occupation this winter was the correction of his Latin compositions. Acknowledging Forster's argument that Latin was no longer read except in schools, he had consented to the exclusion of his Latin verses from his *Works*, but persuaded Forster to superintend the publication by Moxon of his collected Latin works as *Poemata et Inscriptiones*, including all the Latin verses published between 1795 and the *Idyllia* of 1820, with about half the volume comprising compositions now first published.

Forster confessed that he "might have resisted" the publication if he had "foreseen all the troubles that attended the proper correction of its proofs". When the printers perpetrated *Angelina* for *Aufedina*, Landor asked "not at all jocosely but quite angrily", "what business the fools had to be thinking of their Angelinas of the Strand". He took as much trouble over the correction of old verses as the composition of new ones. "I left my bed this morning at six," he told Forster, "after lying awake since three, when I suddenly remembered a correction which I ought to have made fifty-four years ago." He now first began to mistrust his wonderful memory; five years later he wrote, "My memory is indeed become very imperfect; but what is wonderful, my imagination is quite as vivid as ever." So he now told Forster, "Truth is that unless I write with rapidity, I write badly, and unless I read with rapidity, I lose my grasp of the subject." His habit of composition while lying awake at night grew upon him, and Forster received illegible pencil-scrawls scribbled, for lack of a candle, in the dark.

Landor had reason to remember why he had told Lady Blessington two years before that "night is not the time to pin a butterfly on a blank leaf", for he wrote to Anthony Rosenhagen on 29th December 1846:

All the present month, from the very first day of it, I have been confined to my bed or room,—to my bed seventeen days, by a violent cold and fever. It was apprehended that the fever would become typhus, but that danger was over in two days. At the present hour I am so extremely weak that I can take only six or seven turns in my drawing room, for let it be known to you I am great man enough to have one. I should never have thought of this extravagance, but my medical adviser told me that, if I continued to live, and especially to sleep, on a ground floor, I might expect cold and rheumatism from the dampness of the area just below. I took the hint as soon as I could take it; and I am now in the same St Jameses Square at No 36. Changing my quarters, the doors were all open by necessity and that very evening I was seized with fever.

He recovered slowly during the four following months, writing again to Rosenhagen on 24th April 1847:

For five and forty years I have never been seriously ill before this winter. The whole month of December I kept my room, and the greater part of the time my bed. Age has now come upon me: years only had come upon me before. A year ago I could walk seven or eight miles without fatigue; at present I am tired after walking only two or three. But what a blessing is this discovery of inhaling ether. . . . We may die without pain—or even lose our teeth, which is a far more important thing. The last of mine that was drawn was broken three times before it came out. It was the third of my martyrdoms. . . . I read nothing but novels. Monte Christo is what I am reading now—and a wonderful work it is. I fear I shall be obliged to go to London in the beginning of May, and it cannot be until the end of July that I may promise myself the real happiness of visiting you.

He was at Gore House by 13th May, when Macready saw him among the audience at an amateur performance of *Hernani* at the St. James's Theatre—"in truth an *amateur* performance," declared Macready, though "Forster was by far the best, and with a little practice would make a very respectable actor". Two evenings later Landor dined with Macready in the company of Forster, Maclise, and others. Like Macready, who thought her "the most charming singer and actress I have ever in my life seen", Landor was impressed by Jenny Lind's performance during her first season in London, and wrote to Rose Graves-Sawle:

How perpetually I asked for your presence at the opera when Jenny Lind was singing. . . . Her acting was infinitely beyond any I conceived to be possible. One night when she performed in the Sonambula, I had the good fortune to occupy a front seat in the Russian Minister's box just over the stage. Sometimes Jenny Lind came within four paces of me. . . . I hope you are delighted with every number of Dombey and Son. Dickens looks thin and poorly. Forster fat and ruddy as usual. Macready gave a grand dinner to grand people to meet Jenny Lind. I was the only unimportant person invited, and probably the only one who declined. I wanted quiet and country air and the sight and conversation of an old kind friend.

Julius Hare was in London and invited him to travel down with him to Hurstmonceaux before Macready's dinner in Jenny Lind's honour on 30th May. After spending the morning of the 17th with Landor, Hare called on Caroline Fox, and relating examples of Landor's "intolerant" and "amusing" opinions, unfortunately mentioned that he declared "Carlyle's 'French Revolution' a wicked book, he had worn out one volume in tossing it on the floor at startling passages"; as Miss Fox was a friend and admirer of Carlyle's, she decided that Landor's "old age is an amalgam of the grotesque and forlorn".

Landor had been in London a fortnight when he went with Hare to Hurstmonceaux:

I could only stay a week with him. He has married a sweet-tempered and intelligent wife, who appears not only to reverence but to love him, which is better. He might be a bishop, but he will never leave his comfortable house and charming country. His library contains ten or eleven thousand books, and his conservatory is full of exquisite flowers. . . . My week at Hurstmonceaux has thrown several years off my shoulders. The last made me feel its weight, and perhaps the next will be as heavy or heavier. It is unwise to look forward quite so far.

On his return to Bath he found politicians campaigning for the general election of the following month. "I take no part whatever in politics," he told Mrs. Paynter, but the British fleet had been sent to Portugal to support the royal government against the Liberal revolt, and "outrageous" against "the folly and wickedness of the Ministry" in supporting the Queen of Portugal, who had "broken her oath to the constitution, to which we were guarantees", Landor drew up a petition to Parliament, which was duly presented from Bath a month later with over ten thousand signatures. At the same time he addressed a letter to the *Examiner* of 3rd July, advocating the union of Spain and Portugal and containing—as usual in his political letters—much trenchant shrewdness:

Frequently has it occurred to me that statesmen in this country are seldom to be found at the helm, and appear to think the best office is the purser's.

The guides and guardians of the public mind occupy no seat in either House of Parliament. . . . Independence has a charm in the very sound of it; the first struggles of a child and the last of a man are for independence. But there is an intermediate stage in which union is the chief blessing of existence; a state in which are sought and enjoyed mutual love, mutual succour, mutual hopes and aims. This is also the condition of nations. The true policy of Spain and Portugal is perfect union, and the true policy of England is to cement it. . . . It is high time to put an end to guarantees. But it is a pity that the Peninsula should see England a rival to France in perfidy, and more than a rival in mutability. . . . A prevarication is baser than a lie direct; there is more of craft, of subterfuge, and of insult in it. We may now withdraw from a confederacy which has lent us no assistance, and conferred on us no honour. Better let nations settle their own affairs in their own way.

Though he had sufficiently recovered from his illness to be "eating strawberries and cream, with an interlude of ices, all day long", solitude reminded him of his age and loneliness: "I continue to walk a couple of hours in the morning, and as many after dinner, but I begin to discover that the vale of years is the least pleasant of walks and the least adapted to walk in." Early in July he went to Warwick "for three weeks or a month", staying two days at Birlingham with his brother Robert on the way. For a few days all four brothers were together under their sister's roof; later Landor suffered an ear-ache and his niece Sophy—who lived at Warwick as companion to her aunt—found him a submissive patient when it fell to her to apply the treatment prescribed by a Southam physician. He was "reprehended for declining" an invitation to attend Shakespeare's birthday celebrations at Stratford, but "there could be no satisfaction to me in meeting a set of people of whom I know nothing, and who know just as little of me". Instead, he addressed a letter to the *Examiner* of 24th July, announcing that "the house in which Shakespeare was born is offered for sale" and appealing for its preservation as a national memorial: "The gentlemen of Warwickshire have never been foremost in letters, in sciences, or in arts: but if publick opinion takes an opposite direction, they have now a glorious opportunity of controverting it. . . . If the crown and parliament are so insensible to disgrace, if the English people at large are so ungrateful to the teacher of whom they have been boasting all their lives, let me exhort and implore his more immediate neighbours to protect his deserted mansion."

Returning from Warwick in the second week of August, he paused a few days at Bath to receive a visit from Forster before making his promised visit to Rose Graves-Sawle at her Cornish home, Restormel. The main object of Forster's visit was discussion of a new project about which Landor had recently written to him—a translation of "*all* the Latin Idyls" in *Poemata et Inscriptiones*, which he proposed to send to Forster at the rate of "one a week" for a small volume in which the Latin and English versions would be printed side by side.

§ 4

"Continue to write," wrote Lady Blessington after Landor's gift of his *Works*; "It is a duty you owe to your name—to posterity. There are no lees in the rich wine of your imagination, which will flow on pure, bright, and sparkling to the last, and not one drop of it should be lost." The pleasure of receiving such praise from his friends was alone an incentive for Landor to go on writing; he delighted in giving away presentation copies of his books and in receiving the letters of compliment and thanks which offered reassurance that, though lonely, he was not neglected. But, apart from this pleasure, his habit of a lifetime could not be broken, and as advancing years limited his physical activity the social engagements of the summer served as a reminder to consider an occupation for the coming winter.

The first copies of *Poemata et Inscriptiones* reached him about the beginning of July, in time for one to be presented to Sir Samuel Meyrick when he "came out of his way to dine with me" and spent a single night at Bath. Meyrick recorded in his copy that it was presented by the author "after partaking of a handsome dinner, and while in the enjoyment of his delightful conversation". Landor gave away many copies of *Poemata et Inscriptiones*, but Moxon told the Rev. John Mitford that he sold only one copy. This was to Connop Thirlwall, the Bishop of St. David's, with whom Landor had some correspondence nearly four years later about his patronage of the livings of Cwmyoy, Llanthony, and Capel-y-fyn. His attention having been drawn to the ascription of the patronage in the Clergy List to the bishop and to one of the Powells of Llanvihangel, Landor wrote in February 1851 truculently to assert his rights. The bishop replied courteously that he was investigating the error, that though he had an application from a deserving clergyman he would not make any appointment till he had ascertained the rights of the matter, and that "I take the liberty of sending you a Pamphlet, which I have lately published". Landor's reply reflects his always graceful response to courtesy:

My lord, I am greatly obliged by the early and very kind notice you have taken of my letter. Whatever may be my right of patronage, I shall be most happy to place it at your Lordship's disposal, and am, My Lord, Your very obliged

W. S. Landor

P.S. The Pamphlet with which your Lordship has favored me is not yet arrived, but my thanks are equally due.

Presentation copies of *Poemata et Inscriptiones* brought letters of praise from such scholars as William Whewell, the Master of Trinity, and Julius Hare. De Quincey also received one. In the first two numbers of *Tait's Magazine* for 1847 he had reviewed Landor's *Works*, following this comprehensive review with essays in the March and April numbers on "Orthographic Mutineers" and "Milton *versus* Southey and Landor". Forster derided De Quincey's suggestion that *Gebir* on its publication "enjoyed only two readers", Southey and himself, but there is no reason to doubt that De Quincey stumbled upon *Gebir* when, as a boy, he was reading all he could find of Coleridge, Wordsworth, and Southey. Quoting a letter of May 1819, in which Southey told Landor that the current issue of the *Westmoreland Gazette* had mentioned the author of *Gebir* as the English poet who most resembled Goethe, Forster was unaware that De Quincey then edited that newspaper.

Landor wrote to express his thanks to De Quincey for such extensive notice of his work, and when De Quincey's daughters visited their aunt at Weston Lea, near Bath, Landor called to invite them to his lodgings. They "found him delightful company", and related of him a character-istic Boythornism. When their aunt remarked of some trees he admired that they were now less beautiful than before they were recently lopped, "Mr. Landor immediately said, 'Ah! I would not lop a tree; if I had to cut a branch, I would cut it down to the ground. If I needed to have my finger cut off, I would cut off my whole arm!' lifting up that member decisively as he spoke." This manner of exaggeration, carica-tured in Boythorn, had intensified since the days when he destroyed his papers and decided to sleep away the rest of his life because Captain Vyner of the Guards had delayed in delivering the first *Imaginary Con-versations*. The most amusing example was related by Dickens of a dinner at Gore House:

His dress—say his cravat or shirt-collar—has become slightly disarranged on a hot evening, and Count D'Orsay laughingly called his attention to the circumstance as we rose from table. Landor became flushed, and greatly agitated: "My dear Count D'Orsay, I thank you! My dear Count D'Orsay, I thank you from my soul for pointing out to me the abominable condition to which I am reduced! If I had entered the drawing-room and presented myself before Lady Blessington in so absurd a light, I would have instantly gone home, put a pistol to my head, and blown my brains out!"

As Dickens recognised in recalling this example of exaggeration, Landor was acutely sensitive to the ridiculous, equally when others were the sufferers. Dickens remembered his "distress of mind in behalf of a modest young man who came into a drawing-room with a glove on his head", and with what delicacy he contrived to relieve the young man from embarrassment.

De Quincey congratulated his daughters on meeting "a man really so illustrious", and described his copy of *Poemata et Inscriptiones*—"very prettily bound in odorous Russia leather"—as "a present which gave me real pleasure", for "there is no author from whom I *could* have been more gratified by such a mark of attention". Being then ill in bed and "having no books but Mr. Landor's Latin poems . . . I read them at times with great interest", deciding "it is a pity that so many fine breathings of tenderness and beauty should perish like the melodies of the regal Danish boy, because warbled 'in a forgotten tongue'."

The grounds for De Quincey's regret were speedily removed, for Moxon published *The Hellenics of Walter Savage Landor: Enlarged and Completed* at the end of November 1847. Of the thirty-one poems in the volume, sixteen had appeared in the *Works* and three were recovered from the second volume of *Imaginary Conversations*, but twelve had never been previously published, including "The Altar of Modesty", which Rossetti rated "highest among Landor's poems", and "Acon and Rhodope", the sequel to "The Hamadryad", which Swinburne described as "a great favourite of mine—especially for its catalogue of wood-flowers". "Acon and Rhodope" did not appear in the *Works* because Landor mislaid and recovered it only when he moved his lodgings in the autumn of 1846, and some of the others must have lain long in manuscript, unfinished or unrevised, for "The Last of Ulysses" alone, a poem of more than 1,150 lines, might have represented even for Landor a creditable month's work. Any one of the poems, as Forster claimed, offers "convincing proof that up to this date Landor's powers even of fancy had not ebbed a hand's breadth on the sands of time, seventy-three years wide".

"A collection so rich and various of classical scenes and images, limiting the word as we do in sculpture and painting, and associating it with Greece and Rome, does not exist in any other single book in our literature," declared Forster. "If ever you see the *Examiner* you will see what an enthusiast he is about me and my old nonsense of poetry," wrote Landor to Rose Graves-Sawle on 18th January 1848; "I believe in his sincerity—but when others praise me, I no more heed them than I heed a plaisterer who praises the Elgin marbles." In the *Hellenics* Landor achieved his ambition, conceived fifty years before when "rambling by the side of the sea" at Swansea, of writing as "a Grecian would have written". "All are good and some great," said Swinburne, who wrote to Milnes in the year of Landor's death, "Apart from their executive perfection, all those Greek poems of his always fitted on to my own way of feeling and thought infinitely more than even Tennyson's modern versions do now."

§ 5

On his election as Pope in 1846 Pius IX excited popular enthusiasm in Italy by initiating a policy of liberal reform. "Popery," wrote Landor in "King James I and Isaac Casaubon", "is an amalgam of every religion and every institution by which mankind in all countries under heaven had been subjugated." The *Imaginary Conversations* abound in critical comment on Roman Catholicism as a political and religious system: "Religion does not call upon us to believe the fables of the vulgar, but on the contrary to correct them," Cicero tells his brother, and Tacitus informs Agricola, "Religions slip easily one into another where the priest does not lay his wand across the road." But Landor welcomed the breeze of liberalism in the Vatican by dedicating his *Hellenics* to the new Pope:

You have restored to Italy hope and happiness; to the rest of the world hope only. But a single word from your prophetic lips, a single motion of your earth-embracing arm, will overturn the firmest seats of iniquity and oppression. The word must be spoken; the arm must wave. What do we see before us? If we take the best of rulers under our survey, we find selfishness and frivolity: if we extend the view, ingratitude, disregard of honour, contempt of honesty, breach of promises: one step yet beyond, and there is cold-blooded idiocy . . . is this indeed all that Europe has brought forth, after such long and painful throes? Has she endured her Marats, her Robespierres, her Buonapartes, for this? God inflicted on the latter of these wretches his two greatest curses; uncontrolled power and perverted intellect; and they were twisted together to make a scourge for a nation which revelled in every crime, but above all in, cruelty. It was insufficient. She is now undergoing from a weaker hand a more ignominious punishment, pursued by the derision of Europe. . . . Cunning is not wisdom; prevarication is not policy; and (novel as the notion is, it is equally true) armies are not strength: Acre and Waterloo show it, and the flames of the Kremlin and the solitudes of Fontainebleau.

To correct the abuses of Louis Philippe's misgovernment he appealed to the Pope as "one honest man, one wise man, one peaceful man", who "commands a hundred millions, without a baton and without a charger".

In the following "year of revolutions", 1848, it seemed to Landor that "we are now turning over the first page of *the* Revolution", of which "the occurrences in France, at the close of the last century, are only the Preface". A few weeks after the abdication of Louis Philippe the *Examiner* of 25th March published an imaginary conversation between Thiers and Lamartine outlining the revolutionary changes that must follow the removal of Louis Philippe and Guizot: Hungary "rises both against the hungry and wolfish pack of Russia, and the somnolent and swinish herd that rubs her into intolerable soreness from overgorged Vienna", and "Poland must be Poland again", but "at the present day there is a Guizot administration in England—the same reckless expenditure, the same deafness to the popular reclamations, the same stupid, self-sufficient, subservient, and *secure* majority in Parliament". Three weeks later a letter to the *Examiner* on "Things to be Done" offered a timely reminder to western politicians that "without the co-operation of the Hungarians"—without, in fact, a means of access to Poland—"the difficulty of relieving Poland is extremely great".[1] He warned Hungary that "if she sides with Austria, she will sink again into subjection: if she sides with Italy and Poland, she stands on ground that will never give way under her".

Force hath been too generally and too exclusively opposed to force. There are various tribes of Cossacks, and several of them ill-disposed toward Russia. It would be no difficult matter to conciliate the leaders of these by presents and treaties; and very far from impossible to unite many tribes under one head, such as Platoff, and to render them the efficient allies of Poland, until they are fitted to become members of the Republic. Conciliation with them, by such measures, may shorten the last war which European nations are likely to wage against one another; a war which otherwise must continue for more years, extend over more nations, and become more sanguinary than any other in modern times. Hungary, not France, is at this hour the mistress of Europe; but France may influence Hungary, and shorten the agonies of Italy, by sending a fleet and forty thousand men up the Adriatic.

His concern for his adopted country in its struggles for liberty found expression in *The Italics of Walter Savage Landor*, a pamphlet published in London at his own expense by Reynell & Weight, including among its seven poems the moving lines "To Saint Charles Borromeo on the Massacre at Milan" and the "Ode to Sicily" beginning,

> Few mortal hands have struck the heroic string,
> Since Milton's lay in death across his breast,

and ending,

> Within the circle of six hundred years,
> Show me a Bourbon on whose brow appears
>   No brand of traitor. Change the tree,
> From the same stock for ever will there be
> The same foul canker, the same bitter fruit.
>   Strike, Sicily, uproot
>   The cursed upas. Never trust
> That race again: down with it; dust to dust.

When Ferdinand II of Sicily earned the sobriquet of Bomba by his bombardment of the revolutionaries in Messina, Landor induced Longmans to publish in a shilling pamphlet his *Imaginary Conversation of King Carlo-Alberto and the Duchess Belgioioso, on The Affairs and Prospects of Italy*, with the advertisement that "Whatever profit may arise from this impression will be given to the sufferers of Messina".

The British government, with the same obtuseness regarding south-eastern and central Europe as characterised its policy during the succeeding century, despised views like Landor's as delusions of eccentricity; when Kossuth appealed for British intervention against Austria,

---

[1] When Neville Chamberlain announced his guarantee to Poland in 1939, the present writer sent a quotation from this letter of Landor's to several leading newspapers. None published it; one offered the excuse that the time was inappropriate!

Palmerston replied that his government acknowledged the existence of Hungary only as a part of the Austrian Empire. After Kossuth had declared Hungary's independence, Landor addressed to him an open letter in the *Examiner* of 19th May 1849, excusing himself because "before you were born I was an advocate, however feeble, of that sacred cause which you are now the foremost in defending", and asking:

Do not trample on this paper for being written by an Englishman. We are not all of us jugglers and dupes, though we are most of us the legitimate children of those who crowded to see a conjuror leap into a quart bottle. . . . Be amused, but never indignant, at the spectacle of our public men; at restlessness without activity, at strides without progress, pelted from below by petulance without wit . . .

Congratulating Kossuth on having "swept away the rotten house of Hapsburg", he counselled him to lose no time in following the example of Sylla, Julius, and Augustus Cæsar, and of "Elizabeth and Cromwell and William of Nassau, our three greatest sovrans", who "distributed the forfeited estates of their enemies among the defenders of their cause". In verses "To Kossuth", published in the *Examiner* of 15th December 1849, he again lamented that England offered no help to peoples revolting against oppression:

> If Freedom's sacred fire lies quencht,
> O England! was it not by thee?
> Ere from such hands the sword was wrencht
> Thine was the power to shield the free . . .
>
> Rachael may mourn her children now . . .
> From higher source her glory springs,
> Where Shakespeare crowns Southampton's brow
> Above the reach or gaze of kings.

Of France he was even more critical than of England. He had liked Louis Napoleon and been tempted to believe in him, but when he became head of the republic, Landor recorded, "I wrote a short letter to the President, and not of congratulation. May he find many friends as disinterested and sincere." Having addressed to the *Examiner* of 23rd December 1848 his "Remarks on the Election of Louis Napoleon", he wrote on 9th January following to draw Lady Blessington's attention to his article,

deprecating the anxieties which a truly patriotic, and, in my opinion, a singularly wise man, was about to encounter, in accepting the Presidency of France. Necessity will compel him to assume the Imperial Power, to which the voice of the Army and People will call him.

You know (who know not only my writings, but my heart) how little I care for station. I may therefore tell you safely, that I feel a great interest, a great anxiety, for the welfare of Louis Napoleon. I told him, if ever he were again in a prison, I would visit him there; but never, if he were upon a throne, would I come near him. He is the only man living who would adorn one, but thrones are my aversion and abhorrence. France, I fear, can exist in no other condition. Her public men are greatly more able than ours, but they have less integrity. Every Frenchman is by nature an intriguer.

Within a few months his worst fears were realised when France sent military aid to the Pope against the Italian revolutionaries, and he wrote in the *Examiner*:

Behold the promises of a nation which declared its readiness to aid unreservedly in the deliverance of the oppressed! Behold the first public act, beyond the boundaries, of its President! What then is Europe to expect from France? what, but another link and rivet to the monarchal chain, another chin-band to the sacerdotal tiara.

In the *Examiner* he execrated the ministers who had involved the President "in this tortuous and inexplicable policy in order to accelerate his downfall"; privately he expressed the hope that "my old friend Louis Napoleon will meet with the deserts of his villainy". For the rest of his life he felt for Louis Napoleon the same hatred he had felt for the first Napoleon.

"What a mighty spirit still dwells in the heart of our friend Landor," wrote Lady Blessington to Forster on 2nd March 1848; "It is comforting to see that his genius is not tamed by time."

JULIUS CHARLES HARE
From a portrait by George Richmond, R.A.

17

OLD AGE AT BATH

We lose a life in every friend we lose,
And every death is painful but the last.
                    —*Pericles and Aspasia* (1836)

Dependent on no party, influenced by none, abstaining from the society
and conversation of the few public men I happen to be acquainted with,
for no other reason than because they are in power and office, I shall continue, so long as I live, to notice the politics and politicians which may
promote or impede the public welfare.
                    —*Examiner*, 18th November 1848

Life has much to give us, and Death has little to take away: therefore
the one is to be cherished, the other neither to be deplored nor feared.
While we retain our memory, we also retain, if we are wise and virtuous,
the best of our affections; when we lose it, we lose together with it the worst
of our calamities. Sleep, every night, deprives men of that faculty which it is
(inconsiderately!) thought an evil to lose in the last days of life. . . . I would
rather lose my memory than my teeth. One of these losses carries its own
remedy with it: we know not, or know but imperfectly, that it is gone: of the
other loss we are reminded at least twice a day, and we curse the impotence
of cookery.
                    —*Menander and Epicurus* (1856)

"Ah! these pets! these pets", wrote Landor to Rose Paynter when he
was caring for her sick spaniel during her absence in December 1843,
"when I lost my marten, I forswore all other *delizie*—and yet if Julia
sends me a yellow *can* Pomero I shall just live long enough (perhaps)
to grieve over another broken resolution." The white Pomeranian
dog, sent by his daughter, became for many years his inseparable
companion, except during his summer absences from Bath. He did not
dare to take Pomero to London, as "he would certainly be stolen, and
I would rather lose Ipsley or Llanthony". Pomero, with his feathery
tail, his busy and aggressive air, his yapping bark, became an indispensable supplement to his master as one of the sights pointed out to visitors
at Bath. S. C. Hall admitted that Landor "was a man to whom

passers-by would have looked back and asked, 'Who is that?'"; the little white dog at his heels was a mark of identification. "Everybody knows him, high and low," said Landor, "and he makes me quite a celebrity."

In Pomero he found the lonely man's more than human companionship in his dog. During an absence at Warwick he wrote to Forster:

Daily do I think of Bath and Pomero. I fancy him lying on the narrow window-sill, and watching the good people go to church. He has not yet made up his mind between the Anglican and Roman-catholic; but I hope he will continue in the faith of his forefathers, if it will make him happier.

On his return home, he described the dog's welcome:

His joy at seeing me amounted to madness. His bark was a scream of delight. He is now sitting on my head, superintending all I write, and telling me to give his love.

Habitually he spoke his thoughts aloud to Pomero, who was credited with opinions as pronounced as his master's. "His ancestors preceded the Bentivoglios, and were always staunch republicans." To Forster he described how he took the dog to hear Luisina de Sodre, Ianthe's grand-daughter, play and sing.

Pomero was deeply affected, and lay close to the pedal on her gown, singing in a great variety of tones, not always in tune. It is unfortunate that he always *will* take a part where there is music, for he sings even worse than I do.

He imagined that an "easterly wind has an evident effect on his nerves", and translated into language the dog's expressions and gestures—"he twinkles his ears and his feathery tail at your salutation. He now licks his lips and turns round, which means *Return mine*."

He suffered the increasingly recurrent sadness of bereavement inevitable in longevity. Joseph Ablett's death in January 1848 was the first of a sequence of friendships ended. Though his annual visits to Llanbedr had lapsed—apparently since 1843, when Ablett was repaid the purchase-money of the Fiesole property—Landor had intended to go that spring, with Forster as his fellow-guest, and he felt Ablett's death the more through having too late delayed this last visit. During the summer of 1848 he visited Birlingham and Warwick in July, Rose Graves-Sawle at Restormel in August, but in 1849 he once more visited Llanbedr at the request of Mrs. Ablett, who was involved in a dispute over the settlement of her husband's estate and called upon him as a friend who could testify to her husband's wishes. Assisted by an attorney, the heir to a reversionary interest in the estate was attempting to anticipate his inheritance at Mrs. Ablett's expense; as a last duty to his dead friend, Landor championed the widow's interest and printed at his own expense a *Statement of Occurrences at Llanbedr*, believing that some "benefit may be derived" from the publication, as "it is from the most sordid of matter that the earth receives much of her fertility; and it is from the most sordid of the species, thus tost about and ventilated, that mankind derives much of its instruction".[1]

During this duty visit to Llanbedr in September 1849 he wrote to Rose Graves-Sawle: "To lose so early a companion as Charles, and so kind a friend as poor Lady Blessington within so short a space of time bore heavily on my spirits." The death of his brother Charles in July 1849 deprived him of accompanying his sister from Warwick to family fraternising at Colton Rectory; Lady Blessington's death at Paris in the previous month—only a few weeks after the sale of Gore House for the benefit of her creditors—removed his most pleasant *pied-à-terre* in London. Though Dickens and Forster were his intimates, the hospitality of neither could offer the welcome he had so long enjoyed at Gore House, where his visits were like homecomings, his own room being kept for him and his own particular seat between lilac trees on the terrace, to which he referred in the lines to his hostess's memory:

> I shall not watch my lilac burst her bud
> In that wide garden, that pure fount of air,
> Where, risen ere the morns are warm and bright,
> And stepping forth in very scant attire,
> Timidly, as became her in such garb,
> She hastened prompt to call up slumbering Spring.
> White and dim-purple breath'd my favorite pair
> Under thy terrace, hospitable heart,
> Whom twenty summers more and more endear'd;
> Part on the Arno, part where every clime
> Sent its most graceful sons, to kiss thy hand,
> To make the humble proud, the proud submiss,
> Wiser the wisest, and the brave more brave.[2]

---

[1] As Landor said, "friendship and pity and all-powerful justice have impelled me throughout this troublesome exposure"; he had nothing to gain for himself. But Stephen Wheeler commented, with a naïf respect for material success, "how much fiction there may be in his story of what had happened it is impossible to decide now; but the aspersions cast on the character of Mr. John Jesse, the heir at law who was to inherit the estate when Mrs. Ablett died, are at variance with the recollection of people who knew the gentleman and with his repute as a physician and surgeon, a writer on scientific subjects, a Fellow of the Royal Society, and in 1856 High Sheriff of Denbighshire." Mr. Super remarks that "Landor was playing a most dangerous game, and in retrospect it seems marvelous that such a pamphlet did not strike terror in the hearts of his friends"—a comment which would have excited from Landor a burst of Boythorn's laughter. Apparently no reply to the pamphlet was offered by Dr. Jesse, whose attorney would improbably have neglected an opportunity for exacting damages.

[2] He was asked by D'Orsay to write a Latin epitaph: "I detest latin epitaphs, but obey," he told Rose Graves-Sawle. As his epitaph contained no pious reference to a better life beyond for Lady Blessington, it was edited for the obituary notice written by her niece for the *Athenæum*, to which periodical Landor protested that the last two lines of the amended version "would inform us that she left Gore House for a better life at Paris", and gave the English of his own version thus: "Underneath is buried all that *could* be buried of a

A long link with the past was severed by the death of his cousin Sophia Shuckburgh, on whose marriage as Sophia Venour he had written at fourteen his first original verses. The deaths of Sir Samuel Meyrick and of Lady Nugent, both in 1848, moved him to verse, and these reminders of his age inspired the mood in which he wrote, on the night of his seventy-fourth birthday, the most widely-known of all his writings, the "Dying Speech of an Old Philosopher":

> I strove with none, for none was worth my strife:
> Nature I loved, and, next to Nature, Art:
> I warmed both hands before the fire of Life;
> It sinks; and I am ready to depart.

Reading the record of his life, many have derided the first line as paradox; turbulence of temper has driven few lives along a stormier course. But while he raised his voice unfailingly against injustice and oppression, he had faithfully maintained his boyhood's resolve never to court competition; he had never striven for place or profit at another's expense.

Dickens and Forster came down to dine with him—doubtless at the then not unusual hour of three in the afternoon—on his seventy-fourth birthday, returning to London by the night train. Expecting that he and Dickens would be the only guests, Forster was apparently disgruntled on finding that the fourth member of the party was a young woman of twenty-six, Eliza Lynn, afterwards a well-known novelist and journalist as Mrs. Lynn Linton. "This", she wrote, "was my first introduction to both these men."

I found Dickens charming, and Forster pompous, heavy, and ungenial. Dickens was bright and gay and winsome, and while treating Mr. Landor with the respect of a younger man for an elder, allowed his wit to play about him, bright and harmless as summer lightning. He included me, then quite a beginner in literature, young in years and shy by temperament, and made me feel at home with him; but Forster was saturnine and cynical. He was the "harbitary gent" of the cabman's rank, and one of the most jealous of men. Dickens and Landor were his property—pocket-boroughs in a way—and he resented the introduction of a third person and a stranger.

From further experience Eliza Lynn decided that Forster was "as treacherous, too, and disloyal as he was egotistic and jealous"; when Dickens in 1869 invited her to review Forster's *Life of Landor*, he was dismayed to receive an article beginning "The Life of Walter Savage Landor has yet to be written".

Eliza Lynn was a woman of talent and brisk independence who

---

woman once most beautiful. She cultivated her genius with the greatest zeal, and fostered it in others with equal assiduity. The benefits she conferred she could conceal, her talents not. Elegant in her hospitality to strangers, charitable to all, she retired to Paris in April, and there she breathed her last on the 4th of June, 1849."

became a distinguished figure among Victorian feminists. Brought up in a country rectory, the youngest of a large family, she went to London at the age of twenty-three to live in a boarding-house and earn her living by writing. She was twenty-five and about to publish her second novel when she went to Bath to stay with Dr. Brabant, the Calne physician who attended Coleridge and had visited Landor at Florence in 1823 with an introduction from Walter Birch. With Dr. Brabant she visited the antique shop or "museum" in the Walks, kept by Charles Empson—"a noted æsthete", from whom Landor must have bought sundry pictures—and there saw

a noble-looking old man, badly dressed in shabby snuff-coloured clothes, a dirty old blue necktie, unstarched cotton shirt—with a front more like a nightgown than a shirt—and "knubbly" apple-pie boots. But underneath the rusty old hat brim gleamed a pair of quiet and penetrating grey-blue eyes; the voice was sweet and masterly; the manner that of a man of rare distinction. Dr. Brabant spoke to him, and his sister Miss Hughes whispered to me, "That is Mr. Landor."

She saw, "as if he had been a god suddenly revealed", one of her "great spiritual masters". Such fervent admiration, from a young woman of Eliza Lynn's forceful personality, only the most supercilious conceit could have damped; Landor gratefully accepted it, and gave in return affection, as well as admiration for her staunchness, courage, and independence. When her second novel, *Amymone*, appeared, a laudatory review in the *Examiner*, if not written by Landor, was inspired by him, and his influence later gained her an introduction to *Household Words*, with which she established a long connection on sheer merit, Dickens describing her on a list of his contributors as "good for anything, and thoroughly reliable".

Her devotion to Landor was such that they became father and daughter—"Mr. Landor held with me the place of a father, ever indulgent, kind and generous; I being at all times like his loving and dutiful child"—and his letters to her usually began "My dear Daughter" and ended "Your affectionate Father".

I used to stay with him at Bath for many weeks at a time, sometimes once and sometimes twice in the year. And even when I visited other dear friends in that beautiful and beloved city, it was my duty to go daily to his house punctually at twelve o'clock, and sit and walk with him until two, when he dines; also I dined with him regularly twice a week, when I was not actually staying with him, generally on Tuesday and Friday, when he always took care to give me something he knew I liked, and especially to have a bottle of his famous Malmsey Madeira on the table. This was some of a pipe laid down by his grandfather, and was over ninety years old. Sometimes the bottle was undrinkable, thick as mud and horrible to the taste; but when in good condition it was the most delicate and delicious wine.

Though he thus far sacrificed his old preference for eating alone, he never talked during dinner, and if anybody tried to engage him in conversation "he either rebuked them at the time or blazed out against them afterwards". In Eliza Lynn he found a perfect companion, for she never spoke to him unless he addressed her. Admiring and appreciative, she was an eager listener, whether on a long winter evening when, after tea, he read Milton to her for an hour or two at a stretch, or on his favourite walk round Lansdowne Crescent, which he liked for its view. He talked to her freely of her work and his own—she dedicated to him in 1851 her third novel, *Realities*—and while she noted that he rarely offered advice, she declared that she never had from anybody sounder counsel than she received from him. With her he discussed his fads about diction and orthography, but while, to the despair of Forster, he insisted on practising his theories of spelling in his own work, he never advised Miss Lynn to adopt them.

In this appears evidence both of his wisdom and eccentricity. Remarking on his oddities of pronunciation, Tom Trollope was astonished at his dropping of aspirates—"that a man who was not only by birth a gentleman, but was by genius and culture—and such culture!—very much more, should do this" seemed to Trollope incomprehensible. Angrily denouncing the "absurd calumnies" circulated about Landor after his death, Augustus Hare declared none was "so utterly absurd" as this of Trollope's, for "I lived with him in close intimacy for years, and I never once traced the slightest indication of his ever dropping the aspirate; indeed, no one was more particular in inculcating its proper use". Hare was a boy when he knew Landor, and presumably, just as Landor recognised that an established writer could afford peculiarities of spelling which would handicap a beginner like Eliza Lynn, he avoided eccentricities of pronunciation which the boy might invite ridicule by imitating. Eliza Lynn testified that Landor habitually said "woonderful", "goolden", "woorld", "srimp", "yaller", and "laylock", and pronounced "won" as in "on" instead of "wun". Such pronunciations as "yaller" and "laylock" survived from eighteenth-century fashion, but while Rosina Bulwer was amused by his use of "woonderful" as early as 1839, he seems to have increasingly indulged eccentricities of speech with advancing years, especially when excited to an impulse of mischief, as by Rosina Bulwer's affectation and by Tom Trollope's portentousness.

Eccentricity becomes exaggerated in the egocentricity of advancing age; though he never equalled the absence of mind in De Quincey, who was liable to set himself on fire when reading by candle-light, Landor's forgetfulness and outbursts of anger became increasingly comic. Eliza Lynn remarked that "his actions were always eager, half tremulous, and I must confess clumsy", and he had "no perception of small things".

He was always losing and overlooking, and then the tumult that would arise was something too absurd, considering the occasion. He used to stick a letter into a book: then, when he wanted to answer it, it was gone—and some one had taken it—the only letter he wanted to answer—that he would rather have forfeited a thousand pounds than have lost, and so on. Or he used to push his spectacles up over his forehead, and then declare they were lost, lost for ever. He would ramp and rave about the room at such times as these, upsetting everything that came in his way, declaring that he was the most unfortunate man in the world, or the greatest fool, or the most inhumanly persecuted. I would persuade him to sit down and let me look for the lost property; when he would sigh in deep despair, and say there was no use in taking any more trouble about it, it was gone for ever. When I found it, as of course I always did, he would say, "thank you," as quietly and naturally as if he had not been raving like a maniac half a minute before.

This was the veritable Boythorn—"the gentle savage", as Mary Boyle called him—the Landor who threatened never to write again when the guardsman delayed delivery of his manuscript. His brother Henry must have smiled wryly when Landor wrote to him in 1857:

Philosophy has taught me, what Christianity has failed to teach others, to suppress both malignity and anger. Nobody has seen me angry these twenty years, nor malignant ever.

Certainly he never in his life bore malice, unless so could be called his indignation against the Duke of Beaufort, the barrister Taunton, and Lord Burghersh. Nor did his temper ever cost him a friend, unless in the case of Dr. Brabant's sister-in-law, Miss Hughes, at whose house he met a foolish woman who, having seen a letter of his in the *Examiner*, remarked that he "wrote for the papers". Landor replied curtly, "I do not, madam", at which the lady playfully insisted, "Oh yes you do —I have just read something of yours", and Landor expressed himself with such fury as required a written apology to his hostess. Assuring Miss Hughes that he had "never in his life seen so impudent a woman", he wrote, "It must be because I have not acquaintance with the worst of your sex. However, if you take an interest in her, *I will return good for evil and procure her a ticket for the penitentiary.*"[1] Admitting that he was "difficult" and required "careful handling", Eliza Lynn remarked:

He would return respect for respect. He did not need, as some weak and vain men do, that a woman should be perpetually on her knees before him, worshipping; he did not require incessant flattery to keep him in good

[1] The italics are evidently Crabb Robinson's, to whom Miss Hughes showed Landor's letter when he visited Bath on 3rd October, 1851. The humour with which Landor excused his offence to an intimate friend was lost upon Robinson, who commented, after quoting this passage from the letter, "Truly he must be mad—but where does madness begin and responsibility end?" Evidently he conceived that Miss Hughes felt offended beyond forgiveness, but Mrs. Lynn Linton's biography shows that Landor continued on friendly terms with Dr. Brabant and Miss Hughes—with whom Eliza Lynn was so intimate that she called her "Aunt Susan"—till his final departure from Bath in 1858.

humour, though he liked honest praise and faithful love as well as any of us; and he respected individuality that was not aggressive; but the great thing he demanded was non-interference, and he could not brook contradiction. His wife should have been a woman of sweet temper, ready tact, and cultivated intellect; so that she would not have needlessly irritated him, and yet would have forced him to respect her. And above all she should have been able to understand when to leave a thing alone. When his passion, or madness rather, was on him, it was useless to try and reason with him. He was mad, and you might as well have tried to stop the course of a tempest as to control him. But give him time—let the fit die out—and then he would take things quietly, and perhaps laugh at himself for his fury.

Forster observed that Landor was "at his very best" in the presence of Ianthe—"in language, manner, look, voice, even in the minutest points of gesture and bearing, it was all that one could possibly imagine of the perfection of chivalrous respect". This impression was endorsed by Eliza Lynn, who often accompanied Landor on his daily visit to Ianthe when she was at Bath with her grandchildren. Now "a bright good-humoured Irish face was all her beauty, but youth still lingered in her eyes and hair"; "she was sweet and gentle, evidently very proud of her old lover's affection, very fond of him, and somewhat afraid"; seeing Landor so "tender, respectful, playful, with his old-world courtesy which sat so well on him, it was easy to understand why she had loved him so passionately in the fresh far-away past, and why she loved him still in the worn and withered present".

Ianthe's grand-daughter, Luisina de Sodre-Pereira, was "very attentive" to him; "she is like her dear mother in all things but consummate beauty, and loves me affectionately". To her he addressed verses on several occasions: after watching her dance at the Bath assembly rooms in 1850:

> A generation's faded skirts have swept
> Thro' that door opposite, since one beloved
> (Before your mother's eyes gave heaven its light,
> And made *her* mother's brighter, even hers)
> Behind these benches lean'd upon my arm,
> Nor heard the musick that provoked the dance.

Deeply he felt the warmth of tenderness, not simply nostalgic, with which age contemplates ingenuous youth, well expressing the feeling when he wrote to Rose Graves-Sawle in May 1849:

Eliza Lynn comes to see me on Saturday. What a charm it is even at the close of life to be cared for by the beautiful and gentle, and to see them come out from the warm sunshine and the sweet flowers towards us in the chilliness of our resting place. This is charity, the charity of the Graces. They are fond of walking where Love has walked before, altho' they are certain they shall not find him there again.

Since he could no longer hope to be buried beneath the mimosas Ianthe had planted at Fiesole, he fixed the site of his grave in the churchyard of Widcombe, near Bath, because she had admired the spot in his company. As her senior, he expected to die before her, but in August 1851 he wrote to Forster:

I have lost my beloved friend of half a century, Jane the Countess de Molandé. She died at Versailles on the last of July after sixteen hours' illness. . . . She will be brought over to the family vault, in county Meath . . . I hoped she might have seen my grave. Hers I shall never see, but my thoughts will visit it often. Though other friends have died in other days (why cannot I help this running into verse?) One grave there is where memory sinks and stays.

In his remaining years he often recalled in verse his love for Ianthe; the lines called "Memory", published twelve years later in *Heroic Idyls*, best reflect the prevailing mood of his loneliness:

> The mother of the Muses, we are taught,
> Is Memory: she has left me; they remain,
> And shake my shoulder, urging me to sing
> About the summer days, my loves of old.
> *Alas! alas!* is all I can reply.
> Memory has left with me that name alone,
> Harmonious name, which other bards may sing,
> But her bright image in my darkest hour
> Comes back, in vain comes back, call'd or uncall'd.
> Forgotten are the names of visitors
> Ready to press my hand but yesterday;
> Forgotten are the names of earlier friends
> Whose genial converse and glad countenance
> Are fresh as ever to mine ear and eye;
> To these, when I have written, and besought
> Remembrance of me, the word *Dear* alone
> Hangs on the upper verge, and waits in vain.
> A blessing wert thou, O oblivion,
> If thy stream carried only weeds away,
> But vernal and autumnal flowers alike
> It hurries down to wither on the strand.

§ 2

Pilfering by servants of the household compelled Landor to leave St. James's Square at Lady Day in 1849; unable to find a vacancy in the familiar square, he moved to 3 Rivers Street, adjoining Catherine Place, where one of his first guests—apart from Eliza Lynn—was his old friend Francis Hare's son Augustus, named after the uncle who had died at the time of his birth in 1834.

Augustus was the fifth child borne by Francis Hare's young wife in the first six years of her marriage; her children embarrassed her busy social life, her neglect had been blamed for the death of her eldest child, and she welcomed an offer from the childless widow of her brother-in-law Augustus to adopt his unwanted namesake. A martyr to early-Victorian piety, condemning her to self-conscious endurance of her bereavement, the widow lavished all her frustrated emotions upon her foster-son; even Proust was not more completely dominated by his mother than Augustus Hare by his foster-mother. In his fifteenth year he was unhappy in separation from her when sent to a private tutor at Lyncombe, near Bath, and never forgot the unexpected kindness received from the venerable friend of his father and uncles. In September 1848 he wrote to his foster-mother that "Mr. Landor has been here, and, thinking to do me honour, called upon" his tutor; "whilst Pomero danced about, he told numbers of stories".

Thereafter, till he left Lyncombe in December 1850, Augustus Hare went "once a week at least" to dine with Landor at Rivers Street, where the walls "were entirely covered with pictures, the frames fitting close to one another, leaving not the smallest space of wall visible".

In the evenings he would sit for hours in impassioned contemplation: in the mornings he wrote incessantly. . . . He never bought any new clothes, and a chimney-sweep would have been ashamed to wear his coat, which was always the same as long as I knew him, though it in no way detracted from his majestic and lion-like appearance. But he was very particular about his little dinners, and it was about these that his violent explosions of passion usually took place. I have seen him take a pheasant up by the legs when it was brought to table and throw it into the back of the fire over the head of the servant in attendance. . . . At the same time nothing could be more nobly courteous than his manner to his guests, and this was as marked towards an ignorant schoolboy as towards his most distinguished visitor; and his conversation, whilst calculated to put all his visitors at their ease and draw out their best points, was always wise, chivalrous, pure, and witty.

Apparently Landor still undertook his own household shopping, as at Tours thirty-five years before, for Hare wrote to his foster-mother on Easter Sunday 1849:

Yesterday Mr. Landor asked me to dine with him. First we went out to order the dinner, accompanied by Pomero in high spirits. As we went through the streets, he held forth upon their beauties, especially those of the Circus, to which he declares that nothing in Rome or in the world was ever equal. We stopped first at the fishmonger's, where, after much bargaining, some turbot was procured; then, at the vegetable shop, we bought broccoli, potatoes, and oranges; then some veal to roast; and finally a currant-tart and biscuits. Mr. Landor generally orders his own little dinners, but almost all this was for me, as he will dine himself on a little fish. He has actually got a new hat, he says because all the ladies declared they would never walk with him again unless he had one, and he has a hideous pair of new brown trousers. Pomero was put out of the room for jumping on them, but when he was heard crying outside the door, Mr. Landor declared he could not let his dear child be unhappy, and was obliged to let it in; upon which the creature was so delighted, that it instantly jumped on the top of its master's head, where it sate demurely, looking out of the window.

Hare remembered that Eliza Lynn "was by her almost filial attentions a great comfort to Landor", and also "a pretty young Bath lady, Miss Fray, who often came to dine with him when I was there. After dinner Mr. Landor generally had a nap, and would say, 'Now, Augustus, I'm going to sleep, so make love to Miss Fray'—which was rather awkward". In the summer of 1849 Landor received a visit from his son Walter, now in his twenty-seventh year, and the correct schoolboy of fifteen declared that "he was an ignorant rough youth, and never got on well with his father". Walter accompanied his father to Warwick at the beginning of July 1849 when they heard of Charles Landor's death, and from Warwick to Llanbedr in late August; leaving Landor at Llanbedr, he went alone "to spend a few days at Llanthony" before rejoining his father at Bath "only a day or two" before his return to Italy.

In May 1850 Landor went to London for the first time since his last visit to Gore House three years before; on 7th May Crabb Robinson "dined with Kenyon; only Landor with him. He and I agree tolerably well and he was boisterous and extravagant as usual and quite friendly to me". Apparently Landor spent part of his London visit with Kenyon and part with Forster at his chambers in Lincoln's Inn Fields, where James Spedding had rooms in the same building. Tennyson was staying with Spedding, and late one evening Forster fetched him in to meet Landor. Another visitor, W. J. Fox, M.P., having fallen down in leaving the building and broken his arm, was brought into Forster's dining-room, "white from pain", and Tennyson recalled to his son and biographer how "Old Landor went on eloquently discoursing of Catullus and other Latin poets as if nothing particular had happened, 'which seemed rather hard, but was perhaps better than utter silence'."[1]

Landor was back in Bath in July 1850 when Carlyle spent an evening with him on his way to Cardiff.

[1] Obviously Landor continued his talk, not from callousness, but in an attempt to ease the situation of both the sufferer and the witnesses of his pain while awaiting the arrival of a surgeon. The incident is recorded in *Alfred Lord Tennyson: A Memoir by his son* (1897) without indicating the time of its happening, but Mr. Super has discovered in an American collection (that of Professor J. Lee Harlan) a letter of 3rd August 1850 in which Landor asks Forster to "tell kind gentle Fox how much I love him and how often I have thought of him in the sad captivity of his bedroom".

Landor was in his house, in a fine quiet street like a New Town Edinburgh one, waiting for me, attended only by a nice Bologna dog. Dinner not far from ready; his apartments all hung round with queer old Italian pictures; the very doors had pictures on them. Dinner was elaborately simple. The brave Landor forced me to talk far too much, and we did very near a bottle of claret, besides two glasses of sherry; far too much liquor and excitement for a poor fellow like me. However, he was really stirring company: a proud, irascible, trenchant, yet generous, veracious, and very dignified old man; quite a ducal or royal man in the temper of him; reminded me something of old Sterling, except that for Irish blarney you must substitute a fund of Welsh choler. He left me to go smoking along the streets about ten at night, he himself retiring then, having walked me through the Crescent, Park, &c., in the dusk before.

Each felt liking and respect for the other, though Landor maintained his opinion that Carlyle was "a vigorous thinker, but a vile writer, worse than Bulwer", and declared that his "*Frederick the Great* convinces me that I write two dead languages, Latin and English!"

Forster was expecting to be invited to Aylesbury along with Landor when Lord Nugent died in November 1850. Since his wife's death two years before, Lord Nugent had apparently spent much of his time at Bath; besides feeling the bond of a friendship begun many years before, he shared Landor's views on foreign politics, especially on Kossuth's efforts for Hungarian independence, and Forster mentions their "unwearying delight in rendering service to Hungarian refugees". Landor recalled the pleasures of their companionship in the verses beginning:

> Ah Nugent! are those days gone by
> When, warm from Chaucer, you and I
> Beheld our claret's beak dip low,
> And then felt Moca's breezes blow,
> Fragrant beyond the fragrant flower
> Of citron in her dewy hour:
> We schemed such projects as we might
> In younger days with better right.

Landor's assiduity in the cause of liberty made his Bath lodgings a place of pilgrimage for revolutionary exiles. William Sandford, his friend of nearly twenty years before at Florence,[1] was "the friend also of Klapka and all the other chief Hungarians"; he visited Landor at Bath at least twice in 1850 and introduced to him Count Teleki, the former Hungarian ambassador to France, and later the assassin Orsini.

[1] Mr. Super follows Stephen Wheeler in identifying Landor's friend as William Graham Sandford, grandson of Dr. Daniel Sandford, Bishop of Edinburgh, but William Graham Sandford was born in 1834. My contemporary at Oxford, Dr. K. S. Sandford, can identify none of his forbears with Landor's friend, who may have been William Sandford (1802-63), younger son of Captain Edward Sandford and grandson of Humphrey Sandford of Isle of Rossall, though Forster inserted in the 1876 reprint of his *Life of Landor* the footnote: "Mr. William Sandford; dead since the first edition of this book was published"—*i.e.* since 1869.

Lord Dudley Stuart collaborated with Landor in raising a fund to assist exiled Hungarians in poverty; Landor esteemed him as "the truest, the most generous, the most energetick of philanthropists", and regularly corresponded with him till his death in 1854 at Stockholm on a mission in aid of the oppressed Poles.

Just as nothing is so utterly dead as a deceased statesman, no literature is more ephemeral than political writing. Perhaps for this reason— though he discreetly neglected to mention it—T. Earle Welby omitted from Landor's "Complete Works" all those political writings for the *Examiner* that Landor himself did not reprint, ignoring even the admirable selection presented in Wheeler's *Letters of Walter Savage Landor Private and Public*, which abundantly reveals the justice and the frequently prophetic wisdom of Landor's political comment. By the death of Lord Nugent, Landor lost a valuable ally, for Nugent could exercise his privilege in the House of Lords to express views published by Landor in the *Examiner*; Wheeler points out that Nugent embarrassed Lord Palmerston with a question about the government's attitude to the Austrian general Haynau's repressive measures against the Budapest revolutionaries in the same week as Landor wrote on the subject.

During 1849 he was fervent in support of the Hungarian revolution, writing week after week in an effort to stimulate movement in its support; he subscribed five guineas to a fund for the relief of the Hungarian hussars and sent thirty pounds—a lavish gift from his income—to the Hungarian Committe. When the dictator Görgei treacherously surrendered to the Russians and Kossuth was compelled to flee the country, he wrote a warning against "The Comfortable State of Europe", pointing out that "England, by timely assistance to the Hungarians, would have saved Turkey and secured Egypt" and "a long series of future wars might thus have been prevented", instead of which, "before two years are over, we must inevitably be engaged in one most formidable". In fact, not two, but four years elapsed before Russia precipitated the Crimean War by declaring war on Turkey.

On 28th July 1849 Landor's letter on "France, Italy, and the Czar" expressed the only solution remaining to repressed peoples when military power violates the laws of justice and humanity.

There springs up a virtue from the very bosom of Crime, venerably austere, Tyrannicide. The heart of Antiquity bounded before this Virtue. Religion followed Religion; new idols were worshipt; they rotted down one after another; Tyrannicide has appeared in every age, in every country, the refuge and avenger of the opprest. Can Russia have forgotten that awful vision, which hath reared its head so often over her imperial crown, and broken up, like the burst of spring, her palaces of ice?[1]

[1] Landor defended the principle of tyrannicide in the imaginary conversation, "Florentine, English Visitor, and Landor" (1828): "Far am I from the inclination of lighting up a fire to invite around it the idle, the malevolent, the seditious: I would however subscribe

As the Czar already figured as a potential enemy in the popular conception, nobody was troubled by the warning that his tyranny might invite assassination. But Landor never appreciated that principle is always governed by expediency in professional politics—that tyrants and terrorists may be styled heroes and patriots if their crimes accord with current policy. In his view Louis Napoleon and the Pope were worse criminals than the Czar because they had betrayed the liberal professions expressed on their accession to power. When the French invaded Italy to subjugate the revolution and to restore the temporal power of the Pope, he execrated Louis Napoleon as virulently as he had execrated the first Napoleon fifty years before: "Impartial History will represent not Attila nor Totila as the most devastating scourge, the most deadly plague of Italy, but Napoleon Bonaparte and his nephew Louis. The one threw her down, the other (when she had risen) strangled her . . . Thus a rat and a rabbit can undermine the architecture that has resisted ages." He now derided Pope Pius IX, whom he had applauded in his dedication of *The Hellenics*, as "an extremely weak, improvident man", who "vainly attempts to supply by cunning his deficiency of strength".

In February 1851 Chapman & Hall—to whom Forster was literary adviser—published as a pamphlet priced eighteen-pence *Popery: British and Foreign*, in which Landor repeated the appeal for church reform expressed fifteen years before in his *Letters of a Conservative* as the most positive method of allaying popular concern with papal aggression. In the previous year a papal bull had appointed in England "a hierarchy of bishops deriving their titles from their own sees", and giving effect to the decree in a pastoral letter, Cardinal Wiseman, the archbishop of Westminster, published the inflammatory statement that "Catholic England has been restored to its orbit in the ecclesiastical firmament from which its light had long vanished". The immediate popular reaction to this threat of a campaign for national conversion took the form of such demonstrations as the burning of effigies of Wiseman and the Pope instead of the usual guys on 5th November, and Lord Palmerston decided, "We must bring in a measure. The country would not be satisfied without some legislative enactment. We shall make it as gentle as possible." The gentle measure was the Ecclesiastical Titles Bill to prohibit the use by Roman Catholics of titles taken from the names of places in the United Kingdom—fairly described by John

---

my name, to ensure the maintenance of those persons who shall have lost their country for having punished with death its oppressor, or for having attempted it and failed. . . . Public wrongs may and ought to be punished by private vindication, where the tongue of Law is paralysed by the bane of Despotism; and the action which in civil life is the worst, becomes, where civism lies beneath power, the most illustrious that magnanimity can achieve. The calmest and wisest men that ever lived were unanimous in this sentence; such men were Algernon Sydney and Milton: it is sanctioned by the laws of Solon, and sustained by the authority of Cicero and Aristoteles."

Bright as "little, paltry, and miserable—a mere sham to bolster up Church ascendancy".

Landor's thesis was that "no religion hath ever done so much mischief in the world as that which falsely, among innumerable other falsehoods, calls itself the catholic", and there was no cause to fear a revival of popery if a truly religious alternative was offered.

The Church-of-England-man, at the present hour, is seen limping between two lame guides; one kicking him, the other leaning on him so heavily that he would rather be kicked than bear it. He remembers the cruelties of Popery, and how one bishop feasted his Christianity upon the stake that roasted another. Of these things he has only heard; but he has seen, with his own eyes, bishops, at the beck of Pitt, taking their seats in our House of Lords, opposite to Marat and Robespierre, on precisely the same level, and voting year after year for war. People will no longer let them sit on those benches: gouty feet must find other remedies than blood-baths. Exercise among the needy and afflicted, visits to the hospital and the school, are more healthy, and may tend to prolong their days.

At the time the Church of England was riven by the burning question, "Whether or no the Church holds it needful to be believed, that by the Blood and Merits of our Saviour Christ, Original Sin is remitted to all Infants in Holy Baptism?" Landor warned them that, while their church professed to be reformed, "the furniture seems of the same description", and though Calvinism had failed in its challenge, "Catholicism has stronger attractions and a firmer grasp". At the same time John Keble was considering the advantage of disestablishment, because "we had rather be a Church in earnest, separate from the State, than a counterfeit Church in professed union with the State", but he was concerned rather with the government of the Church's organisation than with reform of its mission. Like H. R. L. Sheppard some eighty years later, Landor counselled spirituality and principle instead of ritual and politics:

Christianity, very contrary to the intention of its blessed Founder, has almost from the beginning been the smelting-house of discords and animosities. . . . Pride has blinded those who should have been, by their special appointment, overseers and guides. . . . In the reign of James and his son, many serious and religious, and many of deep research, both jurists and divines, wrote in condemnation of Prelaty: Milton stamped the warrant. Loth am I that anything of antiquity should be so utterly swept away as to leave no vestige. It would grieve me to foresee a day when our cathedrals and our churches shall be demolished or desecrated; when the tones of the organ, when the symphonies of Handel, no longer swell and reverberate along the groined roof and dim windows. But let the old superstitions crumble into dust; let Faith, Hope, and Charity, be simple in their attire; let few and solemn words be spoken before Him "to whom all hearts are open, all desires known".[1]

[1] His lack of sympathy with Landor inspires Mr. Super to describe *Popery: British and Foreign* as "a hastily written and unsatisfactory pamphlet . . . in which his thesis was precisely what it had been fifteen years earlier in the *Letters of a Conservative*". Landor might

Fear of a recrudescence of popery undoubtedly lent an impetus to the false puritanism with which the Victorian era masked its materialism. Landor despised the fear as much as he would have deplored its result; in his first volume of *Imaginary Conversations* he had caused Isaac Casaubon thus to advise King James I:

Popery is an amalgam of every religion and every institution by which mankind in all countries under heaven has been subjugated. Not only the Egyptian and Syrian, the Brahmin and Persian, the Phrygian and Greek, but even the Druidical, was found useful in its structure; and thereupon were erected the fulminating batteries of Excommunication. This, which satisfied and satiated the ferocity of the most ferocious race among men, satisfied not the papal priesthood. They conducted their Inquisition far beyond it, extinguishing, as they went, all other lights than such as served for illusion. In Spain they succeeded perfectly; nearly so in Italy; in France the machine stuck and miscarried. The vivacity and courage of the French, and their felicity in ridicule and mimicry, kept them up from suffocation and submersion. The strong moral principle of the English, their serious temper, their habit of long reflection, their unreserved confidence one in another, their dauntless practice of delivering their opinions, their liberality in accepting and exchanging them, and, upon these, the attempering countenance of your Majesty, will deprive the papal poison of its circulation and activity. Threats are yet murmured: but if your Majesty will cease to notice them, they will die away. There is no echo but from repercussion; no repercussion but from some place higher than the voice.

Lord Palmerston might with greater advantage have considered this counsel instead of seeking to satisfy the country with his vapid measure. In the first sentence of *Popery: British and Foreign* Landor referred to *A Tale of a Tub*, and when the government launched the Ecclesiastical Titles Bill, Swift's example inspired him to address to the *Examiner* a series of *Ten Letters to Cardinal Wiseman* from "A True Believer", in which he sought to ridicule by derisive irony both the threat of papal aggression and the government's measure against it.

§ 3

During 1851, besides his concern with ecclesiastical matters, Landor produced a variety of prose and verse, beginning in *Fraser's Magazine* for January with the *Five Scenes* presenting the tragedy of Beatrice Cenci as a story of innocence betrayed and victimised. He supported his old friend Leigh Hunt by sending to his short-lived *Journal* a series of occasional verses called "Poemetti", addressed to the *Examiner* letters on subjects ranging from "Ecclesiastical Patronage" to "What to do with the Crystal Palace", and also several imaginary conversations,

---

have well retorted in a speech from his dialogue between "Æschines and Phocion": "If a thing is good it may be repeated; not indeed too frequently nor too closely, nor in words exactly the same. The repetition shows no want of invention: it shows only what is uppermost in the mind, and by what the writer is most agitated and inflamed."

LANDOR ABOUT 1854

From the sketch by Robert Faulkner
in the National Portrait Gallery. Landor
apologised for the black velvet cap, "I wear
it as an invalid."

including those between "Nicholas and Nesselrode", in which the Czar expounds his plans for expansion and indicates how Palmerston's policy was playing into his hands.

When Kossuth came to England in the autumn, Landor headed an address sent to him by the citizens of Bath, and his verses "On Kossuth's Voyage to America" were printed as a leaflet and distributed at a public meeting held in Birmingham shortly before Kossuth sailed in November. In a letter to the *Examiner*, which Landor trusted "my grandchildren will value as the highest honor that could be conferred on the best of them, and the most imperishable part of their heritage", Kossuth acknowledged his advocacy of Hungarian liberty, and on his return to England became a personal friend during Landor's visit to London in 1855. Within a few weeks of Kossuth's departure Landor published as a threepenny leaflet "for the benefit of the Hungarians in America" his poem *Tyrannicide*—beginning "Danger is not in action, but in sloth"—which was to serve as an instrument for charging him with irresponsibility not far short of madness. At the same time as he thus counselled assassination as the resort of justice against tyrants and usurpers, he continued to fulminate against Louis Napoleon and the Pope, and his friend Lord Dudley Stuart, who was closely associated with his advocacy of the Hungarian cause, protested when Landor, anticipating Louis Napoleon's assumption of the imperial dignity, wrote of him in October 1852, "His perjuries, far from excluding him, place him among the legitimate sovrans of the highest order, of whom not a single one, excepting the Emperor of Russia, is guiltless of this crime against his people, God's vicar taking the precedency." Stuart objected that the only real exception was not the Czar, "but our own venerated and beloved Queen Victoria". In the *Examiner* of 13th November following Landor acknowledged that his language was "too lenient" to the Czar:

If I have represented him as guiltless of perjury, and have placed him apart from his fellows, it was only in relation to the subjects born within his proper dominions. He swore nothing to them: he had no need for it. And indeed in regard to Poland he has done nothing worse than our administrators have done towards the Ionian Islands, Australia, Ceylon, and the Cape, by constitutions undermined, engagements broken, remonstrances derided, and the most fertile countries inundated and devastated by periodical shoals of outcast criminals.

With graceful irony he exempted Queen Victoria from his criticism of her ministers:

Yes, our gracious Queen deserves our affection and veneration. Men of your lordship's rank and proximity, whose benefactions have been followed by acclamation to the extremities of the world, may expatiate on her virtues, public and private, with equal decorousness and delight. But when the obscure and insignificant, like myself, attempt to praise a personage so elevated, there is generally a suspicion, and not always a groundless one, of an unworthy motive. Modesty on the right hand, pride on the left, admonish and coerce me to abstain.

Clearly both his faculties and his vigour were unabated in his seventy-eighth year. Finding his sister Elizabeth in August 1849 "stronger and more active than ever she has been for these last forty years", he reflected that "now poor Charles, the stoutest of us all, is gone, I trust we shall follow in due succession". With Gore House a closed chapter, he no longer looked forward to his summer excursions. Writing each year a letter of new-year greetings to Rosenhagen, he repeated annually a doubt whether he would ever leave Bath again: "Within a month I am seventy seven years old and I seldom walk beyond the Crescent, never going to parties of any kind," he wrote in December 1851, and in the following year, "Age requires rest, and even a short journey discomposes me."

Nevertheless he travelled in the summers of both 1851 and 1852. On 12th July 1851 Frederick Pollock met him at a dinner party given by Forster at Lincoln's Inn Fields, along with Kenyon, Macaulay, Sir Charles Eastlake, and the attorney-general Alexander Cockburn—"a capital dinner—turtle, venison, and the finest strawberries of the season". From London he went to Warwick, where he heard of Ianthe's death, and when he went from Warwick to stay with Kenyon at Wimbledon, Crabb Robinson found him on 7th September "in a somewhat subdued mood all day. In his judgments not at all extravagant—his laugh only as joyous and sincere as ever". From Wimbledon he went to Lymington, the Hampshire estate of Mrs. Frederick West, whose husband, owner of Ruthin Castle, was Ablett's neighbour in Denbighshire. When Dickens visited him in November, Landor told him how he had intended to give a present to his godson, ten-year-old Walter Dickens, but "Kenyon drove him about, by God, half the morning, under a most damnable pretence of taking him to where Walter was at school, and they never found the confounded house!"

Towards the end of June 1852 he spent a fortnight with Kenyon before going to Julius Hare at Hurstmonceaux. At Kenyon's he met Elizabeth Barrett Browning for the first time, apparently, since her marriage six years before; she found him "looking as young as ever, as full of life and passionate energy", and wrote to Mary Russell Mitford, like herself an admirer of Louis Napoleon:

I must tell you what Landor said about Louis Napoleon. You are aware that he loathed the first Napoleon and that he hates the French nation; also, he detests the present state of French affairs, and has foamed over in the 'Examiner' 'in prose and rhyme' on the subject of them. Nevertheless, he who calls 'the Emperor' 'an infernal fool' expresses himself to this effect about the President: 'I always knew him to be a man of wonderful genius. I knew him intimately, and I was persuaded of what was in him. When people have said to me, "How can you like to waste your time with so trifling a man?" I have answered: "If all your Houses of Parliament, putting their heads together, could make a head equal to this trifling man's head it would be well for England."' It was quite unexpected to me to hear Mr. Landor talk so.

At Hurstmonceaux he charmed both his hostess and Mrs. Alexander, the gifted widow who shared the home of the archdeacon and his wife, who wrote on 15th August:

Landor's visit has been a great enjoyment to the host, and still more so to the hostess, for I never saw Esther so animated, so amused, so drawn out. The mental vigour and effluence of Landor is indeed surprising. He gave his rich stores without stint, and was so gentle and well-bred that he seemed more pleased to receive than to bestow. He was occupied all day by his books, pen, or walking, and claimed not a moment of anybody's time; but you may suppose there was a beautiful display of summer lightning at breakfast, dinner, and in the evening! Bunsen's visit you will have heard of— curious contrast of mind and habits! I watched the two as they walked to and fro in the garden; sometimes standing still in the earnestness of discussion, Bunsen with all the action and vivacity of demonstration, Landor like a block of granite, immovable and apparently unimpressible!

From Hurstmonceaux he returned to Kenyon for a few days before going to Warwick for five weeks on 5th August, and thence to his widowed sister-in-law at Knowle, Rosenhagen at Cheltenham, and Robert at Birlingham. At Warwick the news of D'Orsay's death "fell heavily tho' not unexpectedly", as he had heard of his illness; he "felt a consolation in the loss of Lady Blessington in the thought how unhappy she would have been had she survived him". The visit to Rosenhagen was his last; in one of his last letters to him, in June 1853, he mentioned the loss of "an old acquaintance, whom I had never seen for several years, Sir Charles Elton—he was my junior by two". Rosenhagen died in the following December; the news caused Landor to reflect that "Merry Christmases . . . are mostly over with childhood", though he had the consolation of "perfectly good health" apart from his upper teeth having become "as useless as the fleets in the Euxine".

Soon after his return to Bath in the autumn of 1852 he visited Andrew Crosse at Fyne Court in the Quantocks. Andrew Crosse's second wife first visited Landor soon after his move to Rivers Street; she and her husband stayed at an hotel during their visits to Bath, but it became "a sort of institution" to spend their first afternoon with Landor. He always dined at three, and if his guests were late, he did not wait, even for women. Once he had finished his meal when Mrs. Crosse and her sister arrived; he courteously explained that it was his rule never to wait dinner, but he "had taken care that the dishes should reappear nice and hot and in every way comfortable". He dined in his drawing-room, which was his only living-room, the cloth laid on a round table; everybody enjoyed his "good and hospitable" dinners. No man of letters had less inclination to dramatise himself, but instinct had inspired his choice of these last lodgings as a setting suited to his personality—"the aspect of the old-fashioned house, and its locality, suggested the Bath of Sheridan's time".

Like Carlyle, Mrs. Crosse noticed that "even the doors, inside and out, were hung with framed oil-paintings", while "a shelf by the side of the fireplace contained the few books that Landor cared to possess". Remembering among them a Milton, a Homer, a Horace, Shakespeare's Sonnets, and a Ben Jonson, Eliza Lynn remarked that, though he received many presentation volumes, he sent every book, as soon as he had read it, to his sons in Italy or to one of his brothers.

As years passed, he grew resigned to receiving no further visits from his children, but kept as closely in touch with them as they allowed. Of all his correspondents his own children valued his letters too little to keep them. A letter to Arnold, dated 6th October 1847, was preserved because it contained a prescription—obtained from "the best aurist in England"—for the ear trouble from which Landor heard his friend Kirkup was suffering, and Arnold obeyed the injunction, "Pray take it *directly* to Kirkup with this letter". His old Florence acquaintance Mrs. Macdonell was coming to England, and Landor assured Arnold that he would "not lose a single day in waiting on her" to thank her for chaperoning his daughter Julia in Florence. He ended "with love to dearest Julia and your brothers, I remain ever, My good Arnold, your affectionate Babbo".

The household at Fiesole developed as Landor's friends had feared when they tried to induce his return. One of the sons had children by his mother's cook, and the frivolous and susceptible Julia met her inevitable fate when, in 1850 at the age of thirty, she gave birth to an illegitimate daughter. Apparently Landor was not informed of his daughter's indiscretion, as he afterwards accepted the child as her adopted daughter, but the verses he published in 1857, though conceived in another context, attribute the fault of a daughter to the crime of her mother:

> Unnatural mother,
> Who've hastened to smother
> Whatever is fairest and fondest in child;
> In Hell's bitter water
> You've plunged your own daughter,
> Nor have wept when she wept nor
> have smiled when she smiled.

In August 1855 Julia wrote that she had received an offer of marriage from a young French count; asking her father's consent, she added, "Do you think you could contrive to give me something, for that is the essential point?" On the day of its arrival Landor sent the letter on to his brother Henry, asking if a hundred pounds a year could be secured for his daughter out of the annual income from Llanthony and Ipsley.

If so, and if the inquiries I have desired to be made into the character of the young man are satisfactory, and he has something of fortune equivalent to Julia's, I think I may give my consent. Lord Normanby and the Minister of France will be applied to for information as to the Count. Arnold will have no objection to the cutting down of a little timber. Rather than that poor dear Julia should be disappointed in her affections, I would give up 100 out of my 400. I have no expenses. . . . Poor Julia I hope will now be removed from a vile mother.

Henry Landor replied on 21st August 1855:

It is not possible to secure £100 a year on your daughter from your property, the Trust Deed *must* be carried into effect. . . . You made a most indiscreet, and too liberal, arrangement of your property during your life, and in your old age, when you ought to have a House and a regular attendant, you are left to Strangers. Those in Italy have as follows:—

Mrs. Landor for herself & Household	£500
Arnold, I believe, has	£100
The House & Land worth	£150
	£750
The 2 younger sons from their Aunt each 80	£160
Your Daughter	£100
	a clear £1,010

Surely this is out of all proportion & reason, that the Owner of the Property has only £400, and thereout to pay for lodgings, no house, no servant; from which source should any Income be derived for your Daughter, I leave it to you & to your Family to decide.

Evidently Landor's family did not share his brother's view; no more was heard of the French count, and the jilted Julia evidently blamed her father for her disappointment, as her subsequent conduct was as undutiful as Arnold's.

The aunt from whom Landor's younger sons enjoyed an income was his sister Elizabeth, who died on 24th February 1854. Landor was anticipating his usual summer excursion when, in January 1853, he invited the young Irish poet, William Allingham, to visit him.

My residence is in Bath about nine months in the year, and always in the same place, 3 Rivers Street. I generally go to town about the end of June and return by the first of September. When you come again this way, I can offer you a bed, I have three spare ones—and you shall have a reading-room to yourself. You will find very few books—for I send to my sons in Italy all I buy in the course of the year, and I keep only a few Latin and Greek.

On 27th June following he told Allingham that he would be in London "within twenty days", and he must have been expected to visit that year's Academy exhibition, which included his portrait by William Boxall, completed at Bath during the previous winter. On 6th July he was still at Bath when he told his brother Henry, "I am so busy in correcting the proof sheets of a new volume for the benefit of the Madiai martyrs for their protestantism, that I have declined two invitations, and I doubt whether I shall be able to visit either Sir W. Molesworth or Archdeacon Hare." But he would not disappoint his sister, and his visit to Warwick in the following month proved to be his last.

When, at the beginning of February 1854, he heard that his sister was dying, he was suffering from bronchitis, which now attacked him every winter, and his brother Henry begged him "not to think of an attempt to make a journey here, which could not afford any relief or comfort to our afflicted Sister, and would be likely to give you increased pain, if indeed it did not lay you up". The old lady's death had been for some months expected, for Landor's verses "On the Approach of a Sister's Death" had already appeared in the volume "for the benefit of the Madiai martyrs", *The Last Fruit Off an Old Tree*. Grief at the loss of his earliest friend and playmate was intensified by the death during the same month of his "earliest Bath friend", Bess Caldwell. "Alas," he wrote to Forster, "I feel that I am gone very far down the vale of years: a vale in which there is no fine prospect on either side, and the few flowers are scarcely worth the gathering." On 24th March, a month after her death, he put into verse his thoughts of his sister:

> Sharp crocus wakes the froward year;
> In their old haunts birds reappear;
> From yonder elm, yet black with rain,
> The cushat looks deep down for grain
> Thrown on the gravel-walk; here comes
> The redbreast to the sill for crumbs.
> Fly off! fly off! I can not wait
> To welcome ye, as she of late.
> The earliest of my friends is gone.
> Alas! almost my only one!
> The few as dear, long wafted o'er,
> Await me on a sunnier shore.

He told Forster how, on the balmy evenings of early summer, he walked in the park, and watching the sun glinting on the windows, reflected how "many of my old friends lived there, and went away in like manner, one after another".

With nobody to welcome him at Warwick, he could not bring himself to leave Bath that summer, though Edward FitzGerald saw no sign of failing when he wrote from Bath on 7th May 1854:

Old Landor quoted to me "Nullus in orbe locus, etc." apropos of Bath: he, you may know, has lived here for years, and I should think would die here, though not yet. He seems so strong that he may rival old Rogers. . . . Landor has some hundred and fifty Pictures; each of which he thinks the finest specimen of the finest Master, and has a long story about, how he got it, when, etc. I dare say some are very good; but also some very bad. He appeared to me to judge of them as he does of Books and Men; with a most uncompromising perversity which the Phrenologists must explain to us after his Death.

"I have given up visiting, but many people come to see me, some of them from abroad," wrote Landor to Rashleigh Duke in October; "I would wish to see once more my old friend Archdeacon Hare, and Lord Dudley Stuart, which I had engaged to do in the present month, but the vis inertiae holds me down." He saw neither again, for Stuart died in November and Hare—who was almost exactly twenty years younger than Landor—on 23rd January 1855. In his next letter to Duke, replying to greetings on his eightieth birthday, he confessed himself "sadly deprest by the death of my dearest friend, Julius Hare, following so soon Lord Dudley Stuart's", and to Forster he lamented, "I am outliving all my friends, and it is time for me to go and join those who are gone before me. Already memory and strength are gone, and surely my days are numbered."

Yet even the sad letter to Duke, written while he was in bed with bronchitis, was enlivened by a flash of vigour:

I have been confined to my room three entire weeks by the *whooping* cough. People talk idly, who say we can have it but once. I had it above seventy years ago.

In his last letter to Landor, on receiving one of his satirical comments on current politics, Hare wrote:

The great men of England seem to be passing away, those at least of that great generation whose youth was kindled and stirred by the first French Revolution. But one of them remains, my friend Walter Landor, and may he still remain as long as his spirit is not too impatient to escape from the decay of the body! It is perhaps well that the influence which first moved you to the resentment of injustice should be with you to the end. There are still so many painful things in the actual state of the world, so much wrong and so much folly, that it may probably be the duty of those who see these evils clearly, and feel the mischief of them strongly, to do all they can to expose and redress them. But it is the very pressure of such evils that makes *me* desire more earnestly to be borne away from them by some of those visions of beauty and tenderness which you in former times raised up for me, or by more of that intercourse with sages and heroes which led me not to the treasures of antiquity alone, but to those that lie in our own native speech. The Greek and Roman dialogues you have printed separately; but I have always had a strong wish to see a selection made of the more purely poetical and dramatic dialogues, including almost all in which there are female speakers. It would be one of the most beautiful books in the language.

Though lamenting his failing faculties, Landor continued to write with effortless fertility. "He was always writing," declared Eliza Lynn: "he used to seem to be dozing, or looking out on vacancy lost in thought, when suddenly he would start up, seize a pen—one of the many blackened, scrubby, stumpy old swan quills that lay about the room—and write rapidly in his only half legible hand, throwing his paper into the ashes to dry."

In April 1853 Moxon published *Imaginary Conversations of Greeks and Romans*, a half-guinea volume containing four new dialogues, besides all the classical conversations, carefully revised, contained in the collected *Works*.[1] The book was dedicated to Dickens, who wrote on 8th September his thanks for "a great dignity", for which "the Queen could give me none in exchange that I wouldn't laughingly snap my fingers at".

In the following November Moxon published at the same price a volume of 532 pages, *The Last Fruit Off an Old Tree*, which was designed as a representative selection of his writings during the seven years since the *Works* of 1846 and included eighteen imaginary conversations, the *Popery: British and Foreign* pamphlet, the *Ten Letters to Cardinal Wiseman*, a selection of twenty of his letters to the *Examiner*, the *Five Scenes* about Beatrice Cenci, and 120 pages of miscellaneous verse, besides the three earlier essays on Theocritus, Catullus, and Petrarca.[2] It carried a dedication in Italian to the Marchese di Azeglio, an Italian patriot who opposed the Papacy, and a preface deriding "the Pio-Nonos, the Nicholases, the Louis-Philippes, the Louis-Napoleons, and their domestics in caps and hoods, in flounces and furbelows, in ribbands and cordages, in stars and crosses", and applauding the Florentine Madiai and his wife, who had been imprisoned for heresy and whose

---

[1] Mr. Super (*The Publication of Landor's Works*) describes a copy, now in Harvard College Library and inscribed "Walter Savage Landor to the worthy consort of his friend Julius Hare. July 19. 52", as "a curiosity, for its collation is identical with the book as published the following year, except for the preliminary pages". Evidently this copy was a proof which Landor presented to his hostess during his visit to Hurstmonceaux. The delay in publication may have been due, as Mr. Super suggests, to waiting for Boxall to complete his portrait of Landor, which Forster wished to include as frontispiece but was omitted at Landor's request.

[2] The "Miscellaneous Papers" comprising Volume XII of Welby's so-called edition of Landor's "complete" works presents merely a reprint of pages 141-364 of *Last Fruit* (excluding the Catullus essay, which was for some reason transferred to another volume), with the addition of *The Letters of a Conservative* and the later *Letter from W. S. Landor to R. W. Emerson*. Welby's virtually non-existent editorial labours were highly praised by reviewers, including the late Sir Desmond MacCarthy.

case against papal intolerance was stated in the imaginary conversation, "Archbishop of Florence and Francesco Madiai"—"on their behalf and for their sole emolument, I edit this volume".

On the page facing the preface were printed the four famous lines, "I strove with none, for none was worth my strife", which, together with the title, suggested that the book was Landor's *nunc dimittis*. So it was treated in *Blackwood's Magazine* for January 1854, a long and gracious review[1] deciding that "the future literary historian of our age will devote a chapter apart, and not the least interesting one, to the works of Walter Savage Landor"—which moved Landor to remark, "Blackwood, who always abused me, has said something grand about me, I hear." So, too, it was treated by Forster, who, in preparation for writing his biography, had already acquired all Landor's letters from literary friends; on 2nd March 1853, replying to Dr. Madden's request for assistance in preparing his *Literary Life and Correspondence of the Countess of Blessington*, Landor wrote, "No letters of my lamented friend Lady Blessington remain in my possession. Soon after her decease I placed them in the hands of John Forster of Lincoln's Inn."

Now too busy to apply his former patience either to propitiation or to proof-correcting, Forster paid little attention to Landor's wishes in the preparation of *Last Fruit*, and apparently immediately on receiving his copies of the book, Landor wrote angrily on 7th November 1853 to the Boston firm of Ticknor, Reed & Fields—who had published an edition of his *Popery: British and Foreign*—complaining that this "new work of mine publisht today . . . was not printed under my inspection, and the *Errata* have fresh Errata", and asking them to publish an edition with "observance of my spelling and of the order".[2] Next day, sending a copy of the book to the engraver, W. J. Linton, he apologised for the omission of his verses addressed to Linton as "the Author of 'The Plaint of Freedom'"—"I was not aware of this until the volume was bound and sent to me."

Nobody ever dealt with Forster without dispute; milder men than Landor quarrelled with him without reconciliation. But Landor's head never competed with his heart in governing impulse, nor self-interest with friendship. Sometimes he felt hurt by Forster's neglect, but the

[1] On the authority of Professor A. L. Strout, Mr. Super attributes this review to William Henry Smith (1808-72), author of the philosophical novels, *Thorndale* and *Gravenhurst*, and states that the same author wrote the article on Landor in the *Quarterly Review* of February 1837. But Sir John Murray states that the Quarterly records give the name of the author of that article as "W. Smith", and its classical erudition, as well as its conventional views on church and state, suggests that this was one of the earliest contributions by Sir William Smith (1813-93) to the *Quarterly*, of which he was afterwards editor. The review of Landor's *Pentameron* in the *Quarterly* of October 1839 was by Lockhart.

[2] In this letter, which he prints at length in *The Publication of Landor's Works*, Mr. Super finds "evidences of senility". Yet it states its business tersely, and the signs of haste and carelessness are characteristic of Landor's correspondence throughout his life—words omitted, misspelt, or illegibly written might be taken as "evidences of senility" in the letters he wrote to Baker Gabb before he was forty.

wound was healed and forgotten as soon as Forster offered an excuse of having been ill or pressed by work. When he first projected a book for the benefit of the Madiai, he was persuaded by a young admirer, Kenneth Mackenzie, to let Routledge publish it, but as soon as Forster intervened, Landor accepted his direction. He expressed indignation when Mackenzie suggested that Forster might take offence at the independent attempt to arrange publication by Ticknors, but a possible crisis was averted because Moxon had already disposed of the American rights to Harpers.

Presumably Forster supervised publication of *Letters of an American, mainly on Russia and Revolution,* by Chapman & Hall as a shilling pamphlet in June 1854. The letters were supposed to be written by an American in London, but the title page described them as "Edited by Walter Savage Landor", and a prefatory letter to Gladstone appeared over his signature. With the outbreak of the Crimean War, Landor was ardent for extirpation of the Russian menace, and having no confidence in the British Government's will to prosecute the war with energy, he hoped that Louis Napoleon would repent of his past conduct and emerge as liberty's champion:

> We Britons have resigned our heritage,
> Our ancient privilege to help opprest
> And struggling nations. In my soul's dark depths
> I grieve, with grief tumultuous, that swells o'er,
> And forces from my breast one last appeal,
> And must it, O Napoleon, be to thee?
> It must be! none hath courage, none hath strength,
> To crush the snow-colossus, to stamp down
> Into his native sands that shapeless bulk,
> But thou alone. Rise then, Napoleon,
> To greatness he who went before thee might
> (Had Honor led him onward) have attained.

Among other verse *Letters of an American* contained the epigram:

> Nations by violence are espous'd to kings,
> And men are hammer'd into wedding-rings.

As the war progressed, he abandoned hope of Louis Napoleon, whom he described as "the greatest and most powerful of living potentates— but a scoundrel like the rest". Throughout the war he poured forth enough letters and verses on politics to fill a volume. On his appointment as a commissioner for lunacy in 1855, Forster resigned the editorship of the *Examiner*, but Landor found another medium in the *Atlas*, a Radical weekly to which Hazlitt had contributed under its first editor,

R. S. Rintoul, and since controlled for many years by Robert Bell, one of the Irish journalists infesting Fleet Street in the time of Maginn. Hearing that Kossuth was engaged to write for the *Atlas*, Landor sent the paper "a couple of articles" and entered his name as a subscriber. Probably Forster would have hesitated to print either of the articles without alteration; that the *Atlas* did so emphasises Landor's prestige. Published as letters over Landor's signature and entitled "The False Politics of the War", the two articles attacked the integrity of ministers with a boldness rarely unrepressed in a country at war. The "Ministry of All the Talents" had been lately defeated, ostensibly on Roebuck's motion condemning the inept prosecution of the war, actually on Lord John Russell's resignation from pique against Gladstone. For several years Palmerston and Russell had followed each other in and out of the Foreign Office, and Landor's first letter rebuked the public for "looking at Lord Palmerston and Lord John Russell, as they played at leap-frog over each other's shoulders", while the expeditionary force at Sebastopol was suffering disease and starvation from want of supplies.

War was procrastinated in compliance with German wishes; the same wishes as induced Lord Palmerston to sacrifice the constitutionalists at Oporto and wherever else he could. Yet he and Lord John Russell are the two men especially appointed to direct our councils. Let them suggest to those who received munificent presents from the late Tzar Nicholas, that they can now without offence, bestow the value of them on our mutilated soldiers, on helpless widows and orphan children.

His second letter derided the government policy of inflaming popular opinion against Prussia for remaining neutral; in a private letter he wrote on 16th March 1855, "Could any man less of a fool than Lord J. Russell think Prussia so mad as to join our alliance, so contrary to her interests?" He pointed out that "the famishers" of "our famished soldiers . . . still direct the councils of our Sovereign, shifting from shoulder to shoulder the blame and responsibility of their misdeeds".

Such men are as incapable of ensuring an honourable peace as of conducting a successful war. Let not our eyes be turned toward the Continent for objects of reproach, but toward those nearer us, on the upper seats, awaiting condign and exemplary punishment too long delayed.

It was on reading these letters that Napier wrote: "You don't draw your ale mild, any more than I do; but if Pam or Johnny call you out, I will be your second." Readers of the *Atlas* wrote to applaud his letters, and throughout 1855 few weekly issues appeared without contributions from Landor. A minister especially despised was Sir James Graham, at one time First Lord of the Admiralty, at another Postmaster-General; the latter appointment reminded Landor that Graham, as Home Secretary in 1844, had issued a warrant for opening Mazzini's letters and communicated their contents to the Austrian government, but the *Atlas* suppressed the last two of six lines of doggerel on "Leaders and Aspirants":

> Palmerston "lies and give the lie
> With equal volubility".
> Even the "artful Dodger", little John,
> Is scarce a match for Palmerston.
> Who next? Jim Crow; he prigs our letters,
> And parries Freedom like his betters.

His prestige as a publicist was reflected when, later in the year, he successfully appealed in the *Times* on behalf of the destitute last descendant of Daniel Defoe, "a Crusoe without a Friday—in an island to him a desert"; a fund was raised, including £100 from the Queen's bounty, which provided an income sufficient to maintain the old man and, after his death, his daughter.

18

SCANDAL

Truth, it appears, is a virgin too pure to be embraced. Whatever most interests her seems most reprovable. Yet the more free our thoughts are, the nearer are they to that region where Truth resides.

—*Savonarola and the Prior of San Marco* (1860)

Little minds in high places are the worst impediments to great. Chestnuts and esculent oaks permit the traveller to pass onward under them; briars and thorns and unthrifty grass entangle him.

—*Vittoria Colonna and Michel-Angelo* (1843)

Though *vis inertiae* restrained him from leaving Bath in the summer of 1854, Landor went to London in July 1855. As he wished to see the Crystal Palace, Forster took rooms for him at a Sydenham hotel, and arranged with Sir Joseph Paxton that the fountains should play in honour of Landor's visit. As he related to Rose Graves-Sawle, Landor dined with Sir William Napier at his house in Clapham Park:

I found my old friend in better health than I expected. He had never seen the Crystal Palace. Lame as he is, he came over the following day with Lady Napier, and we went together over the whole of it. And only fancy, the great fountains were set playing for me! The beautiful N. showed me her little girl, who was very amiable with me, as little girls always were: I mean the very little ones . . . I spent some hours too with Kossuth, who could not dine with me and Forster, because he had to receive a deputation quite unexpected; and by no means the smallest part of my pleasure was the introduction to me, on the following day, of Mr. Lytton.

The son of Bulwer and Rosina, afterwards the first Earl of Lytton, then making a poet's reputation as "Owen Meredith", had written from Italy when *Last Fruit* appeared, "God bless him for what he says about the Madiai. That is a man I should greatly like to know." After their meeting Landor declared of Lytton, "None of the younger poets of the day breathes so high a spirit of poetry."

Memory of his own youthful hunger for appreciation may have

inspired his lavish praise of young writers; none appealed to him in
vain, and he was punctilious in courtesy to even the most obscure.
When he asked William Allingham to "accept thanks for a very beautiful volume of Poems, as far as I am able to judge in the first half hour
after their arrival", he knew nothing of the author, except "from the
Preface I may very pardonably believe you to be an Irishman, since
it is dated from Ballyshannon". Some two years later, in January 1853,
when he heard that Allingham was seeking employment, besides giving
him an open invitation to Bath, he introduced him to Milnes as the
most useful person he could know. Because he approved of the political
tone of Aubrey de Vere's *English Misrule and Irish Misdeeds*, he declared
on receiving a volume of his poems in 1847, "Nothing of our days will
bear a moment's comparison with them," and three years later he rated
de Vere "of a higher genius than either" Goldsmith or Tom Moore.
For such excess he became so notorious that Coventry Patmore's wife,
on the appearance of *The Angel in the House*, ungraciously mentioned a
letter from Landor "full of somewhat senile ecstasy, which I will not
quote".

   Producing political letters almost weekly, Landor found time for
what Hare called his "visions of beauty and tenderness"; on his eighty-
first birthday, 30th January 1856, Bradbury & Evans published twelve
blank-verse scenes, *Antony and Octavius: Scenes for the Study*. Forster
thought that "rarely had anything better been done by this extraordinary old man than these dozen scenes in which he had told again
the ancient story of the two gamblers in ambition and love who threw
between them for the stake of the world"; though Macready might
have likened the scenes to *Fra Rupert* as having "character and picture
without design or construction", they follow the classical design of all
Landor's dramatic writing in excluding all action that does not build
up the main characters by showing them in conflict. There are passages
of dramatic poetry equalling anything in *Count Julian*: Scopas thus
expresses affliction of conscience after murdering the boy Cæsarion:

> Away with me! Where is the door? Against it
> Stands he? or follows he? Crazed! I am crazed!
> O had but he been furious! had he struck me!
> Struggled, or striven, or lookt despitefully!
> Anything, anything but call my name
> So tenderly. O had that mild reproach
> Of his been keener when his sense return'd,
> Only to leave him ever-lastingly,
> I might not have been, what I now am, frantic.
> Upturn'd to me those wandering orbs, outspred
> Those quivering arms, falling the last of him,

> And striking once, and only once, the floor,
> It shook my dagger to the very hilt,
> And ran like lightning up into my brain.

Antony smiles when Eros remarks on his recovery of composure after hearing of Cleopatra's death:

> We can not always swagger, always act
> A character the wise will never learn:
> When Night goes down, and the young Day resumes
> His pointed shafts, and chill air breathes around,
> Then we put on our own habiliments
> And leave the dusty stage we proudly trod.
> I have been sitting longer at life's feast
> Than does me good; I will arise and go.
> Philosophy would flatten her thin palm
> Outspred upon my sleeve; away with her!
> Cuff off, cuff out, that chattering toothless jade!
> The brain she puzzles, and she blunts the sword:
> Even she knows better words than that word *live*.

At the close of the last scene Octavia replies when her brother rallies her for sadness in his triumph:

> I lack not wisdom utterly; my soul
> Assures me wisdom is humanity,
> And they who want it, wise as they may seem,
> And confident in their own sight and strength,
> Reach not the scope they aim at.
> Worst of war
> Is war of passion; best of peace is peace
> Of mind, reposing on the watchful care
> Daily and nightly of the household Gods.

Comparison of *Antony and Octavius* with *Count Julian* reveals, not only no loss of power, but no abatement of belief in the principle that "wisdom is humanity". In forty-four years the lessons of life had failed to shake Landor's fidelity to truth.

In April 1856 *Fraser's Magazine* published two new Imaginary Conversations, "Alfieri and Metastasio" and "Menander and Epicurus", and Carlyle wrote to Forster:

The first of those two imaginary conversations is really as good as anything I ever saw from Landor. Do you think the grand old Pagan wrote that piece just now? The sound of it is like the ring of Roman swords on the helmets of barbarians. An unsubduable old Roman! Make my loyal respects to him the first time you write.

Here Alfieri remarks: "Equanimity is a virtue in philosophers; it is denounced as a crime in theologians . . . lukewarmness in divinity they hold to be almost as insufferable as in venison." Again:

Rapid revolutions turn men giddy and blind. Did ever good come from that quarter? You will be cheated, robbed, plundered, torn piecemeal, and devoured. Mark my words: a century of misfortunes will confirm them. Wherever there are priests subordinate solely to a priest leader, there are snares and chains for all beyond the circle. If Piedmont falls, Italy falls: Venice will be what Naples is: and Rome will call Attila himself a beatific vision. Unhappy land of breathless hope! of enchanted heroism! of consecrated lies!

When Metastasio objects that "the turbulence of France, now dangerous to the world, arises from irreligion", Alfieri retorts:

And irreligion from false religion. Men are patient in the process of a cheat, impatient in the discovery: fools are refractory when they find themselves befooled: they shy at the first sparkle on the roadside, and swerve abruptly, and throw the rider out of the saddle.

When Alfieri remarks that "generally, to what is indelicate, and what is desirable to conceal, the English, without any maliciousness in this particular, give the French name", Metastasio comments:

False delicacy is real indelicacy. Half-educated men employ the most frequently circumlocutions and ambiguities. The plain vulgar are not the most vulgar. If there are any words which ought to be out of use, what they designate ought to be out of sight. A French duchess would not hesitate about an expression which the daughter of a convict in America might reprehend.

To charge the author of these passages with the irresponsibility of senility surely implies in his accusers the irresponsibility of prejudice!

"I retain my health and am stronger than I was two years ago," wrote Landor within a few days of his eighty-first birthday. But in March 1856 he suffered bereavement by the death of his dog Pomero. "Everybody in this house grieves for Pomero," he told Forster: "the cat lies day and night upon his grave; and I will not disturb the kind creature, though I want to plant some violets upon it, and to have his epitaph placed around his little urn." Mrs. Crosse had been no great lover of Pomero, annoyed by his yapping as an impediment to conversation, but when she visited Rivers Street for the first time after his death, the silence of the room seemed "like a reproach", and "the sight of the old man himself in his loneliness, sitting so still and quiet in his armchair, without even the distraction of his noisy little friend, was infinitely pathetic". Mrs. Lynn Linton's memories of Pomero indicate the void he left in Landor's life. The dog was his inseparable companion, trotting at his heels on his walks, lying at his feet as he sat in the park and barking at the passers-by, encouraged in noisiness by his master's boisterous manner of playing with him. When Pomero failed to return with him from a walk, Landor would refuse to eat his dinner and would stamp about the room, raving that the dog was murdered, kidnapped, or pelted with stones, that he would go out to scour the city for him, that he would give a hundred pounds—even his whole fortune—to anyone who brought him back alive. "He was always losing Pomero, and always giving some unprincipled scamp half-a-crown for his return," said Mrs. Linton; "the dog must have been a settled source of income to someone, so frequently was he lost and so regularly returned."

To sorrow was added vexation when, encouraged by the success of his appeal to charity for Defoe's descendant, Landor proposed a subscription to rescue the exiled Kossuth from indigence and the *Times* of 24th March deplored the proposal in an attack on Kossuth's political character. Kossuth was stung into denying on the 28th any knowledge of the proposal, and Landor had the humiliation of publicly withdrawing his proposal and of privately returning to the donors subscriptions already sent to him.

Significantly Landor's flow of letters to the press suddenly ceased in the autumn of 1856. Before he fell ill, he completed his *Letter from W. S. Landor to R. W. Emerson*, replying to Emerson's remarks on himself in *English Traits*, which was printed at his own expense and reviewed in the *Athenæum* of 29th November.[1] Though he described himself as "confined to the house by somewhat of a bronchitis, not so bad, however, as that which afflicted me two winters ago", he grumbled to Forster, "I have been out of doors not more than twice in fifty-nine days, a few minutes in each," adding with his old spleen against English weather, "I think I will go and die in Italy, but not in my old home— it is pleasant to see the sun about one's deathbed." Knowing the state of his health, Forster was dismayed to hear that he had been summoned to give evidence in Bath county court "upon a miserable squabble about a governess".

The action was brought by the Rev. Morris Yescombe against John Webb Roche and his mother-in-law—all Bath residents—for abducting Louise Koch, a governess, from the plaintiff's employ. Called as a witness, Landor addressed a statement to the *Bath Express* of 27th December 1856, as he had been required "to produce books, papers, writings and other documents relating to the said action":

I declare that I neither have, nor ever had, any such books, papers, writings, or documents.

I declare my belief that, therefore, this summons is litigious, vexatious, and nugatory.

I declare that I have known Mr. and Mrs. Yescombe nearly twenty years, that I first met them at the Countess of Belmore's, and frequently after.

[1] See page 263.

He had met Roche only recently at the Yescombes', where the governess was "uniformly treated as one of the family". As reported in the following week's issue of the *Bath Express*, Roche's counsel, Saunders, complained of the publication of Landor's letter that "the tendency was to undermine the foundations of justice in this case. The communication was highly disgraceful to Mr. Landor, and it could only be accounted for by his very great age, and the same want of judgment which had induced him to recommend assassination under the milder term of tyrannicide". Saunders was within his rights in protesting against publication of a statement relating to a case *sub judice*, though the editor and publisher of the newspaper were at fault equally with the author of the statement, but the references to Landor's age and to a matter of political controversy were personalities calculated to excite prejudice, and more disgraceful to both counsel and judge than Landor's statement was to him. These personal references, which the judge allowed counsel to utter, supplied the line for press comment that ruined Landor's reputation.

Against his doctor's orders Landor went to court and submitted himself to cross-examination. According to the press report, he gave his evidence tersely and plainly, but Saunders in his summing-up remarked that he was "a poor, miserable old man whom no one could respect more than he (Mr. Saunders) did, having read his *Imaginary Conversations* and other works . . . but it was a miserable exhibition to bring the poor old man into the box, to talk the twaddle he had". The jury returned a verdict against the defendants for harbouring Miss Koch, but damages were assessed at a farthing, Yescombe and Roche each paying his own costs. Though the judge drew attention to the social standing of the litigants, such a petty squabble would hardly have commanded twelve columns in the *Bath Express* of 3rd January 1857 without the news value of Landor's presence in the case.

§ 2

"I have known Mrs. Yescombe for years," wrote Augustus Hare, "and always prophesied that she would be the ruin of Mr. Landor some day." In 1834 Mary Jane, daughter of a certain Colonel Crosbie of Rusheen, Co. Kerry, married as his second wife a younger son of the third Lord Massy; her husband died eleven months after the marriage, and in 1838 she married the Rev. Morris Yescombe, retaining the style of her previous marriage as the Hon. Mrs. Yescombe. At Bath she affected smart society on the strength of her aristocratic connections, but short of "pennies", she was growing haggard in the effort to preserve a fashionable pose when she and her husband moved to

Green Park Buildings—to No. 28 between 1850 and 1852, and thence to No. 21 by 1854.

She followed fashion in cultivating Landor as a celebrity in Bath society, and realised how she might profit from the old man's generosity and his pleasure in the companionship of attractive young women. In earlier life his prudent brother Henry had been irritated by Landor's contempt for money, resenting his elder brother's demands upon resources which others sought to administer on his behalf. As late as 1845 Henry replied with sarcasm to a generous but impossible proposition by Landor to increase the settlements on his younger children, and deprecated gifts of pictures to himself. But Landor's generosity in allowing his wife and children an income sufficient to keep a carriage and to sustain their position as landed gentry, while he himself lived in lodgings and dressed like a tramp, not only dispelled his former antagonism, but excited indignation on his brother's behalf. When their sister Elizabeth left him three hundred pounds and Landor wanted to give it to his brother Charles's daughters (who already had £2,000 each from their aunt), Henry forbade their acceptance of the gift, and writing himself to express their grateful acknowledgment, suggested that if Landor wished "to give some memorial to our 2 Nieces, a Picture each from you out of the ten left by Eliz. to you would be very acceptable". Landor then insisted on surrendering his legacy to his son Arnold, whereupon Henry stated his opinion that "I think you were imprudent in giving it up, and your Son inconsiderate in accepting it", as "your age requires, & ought to have, additional attendance and comforts rather than those who are in the vigour of life & manhood". He was so concerned that he exerted himself to arrange for Landor to receive an additional fifty pounds a year from the estate, and the following year, despite lamentations that "the least additional trouble overwhelms me" and "anxiety, or over-exertion, would probably produce Paralysis", he ventured his health upon the journey to Llanthony to explore proposed repairs and development.

Receiving nothing for most of his political writings, which were published as letters to the editor, Landor gave away all proceeds from his books and magazine contributions. "Never will I benefit myself by anything I write," he assured Mrs. Andrew Crosse, when he wrote—as a last tribute to his friend, who died in 1855—a review of Crosse's *Memorials* for the *National Magazine*, for which Forster received on his behalf five pounds "and gives it to two ladies left very poor". Hearing that Eliza Lynn, by her father's will, forfeited her little patrimony on marrying W. J. Linton, he wrote:

On the first of April I shall receive my quarterly remittance, out of which I have only to pay thirty pounds for lodgings and servants, and ten to a poor pensioner of my sister. You see clearly that there will be something more

than I ought to spend upon myself, and more than I will. Therefore do not
be perverse and proud, but permit me to send you twenty in the beginning
of April. Stick it on the horn of the honey-moon before it goes: I mean the
moon, not the money.

Mrs. Linton was not well off, and he frequently helped her, saying,
"We must not either of us be too proud on these matters. We have
both something better to be proud of—I chiefly in being called by you
Father."

His benefactions among the poor of Bath, though unostentatious,
were well-known among his acquaintance, and Mrs. Yescombe saw
means of lining her slender purse with pickings. Her next-door neighbour at 20 Green Park Buildings, Thomas Clarence Hooper, had a
sixteen-year-old daughter Geraldine, whose confidence she won by
listening to the girl's tales of grievance against her mother. She
encouraged Geraldine to ingratiate herself into Landor's regard under
her chaperonage, taking her every Tuesday to dine with him and seeing
herself as an elderly Leontion with a Ternissa rather than as one of
Le Sage's duennas.

Landor was the more ready to sympathise in view of his own wife's
character as a mother, and he published the verses on the "Unnatural
mother" (quoted on page 404) in the *National Magazine* of 1857.
Curiously Geraldine's affairs became critical immediately after the
verdict in the Roche case left the Yescombes to find their own legal
costs; Mrs. Yescombe informed Landor that Geraldine "was so cruelly
treated by her mother that it was probable she might run away, and
altho she had relatives she might not take refuge with them after her
flight". Just as he had thought of his lost dog's being tortured or
stoned to death, Landor imagined this girl's meeting with such a harpy
as the procuress in Hogarth's "Harlot's Progress"; "in consternation
at the idea", he gave an order on his banker for one hundred pounds
and placed at Mrs. Yescombe's disposal a number of valuable pictures
to be sold as necessity required". A hundred pounds was the utmost
he had to give; he had so much only because his old friend Kenyon
had died in December 1856 and left him a legacy of that amount.

Soon Mrs. Yescombe told him that she had set two of his poems to
music and proposed to raise money for Geraldine's benefit by their
publication, but the music publisher wanted twenty-three pounds;
Landor "gave her instantly 15, all he had at hand, assuring her that
the merit of her composition would readily bring the remainder". A
few days later, to his surprise, Geraldine—who had never previously
visited him without Mrs. Yescombe's chaperonage—called with a
request for the eight pounds wanting; on inquiry, he found from the
music publisher that "eight pounds was the whole of his demand, and
had been paid".

Faced with this proof of deceit, Landor realised that he "ought to have been more cautious", for in the previous August, in Mrs. Yescombe's presence, he had enclosed in a letter a five-pound note intended for "a poor sick woman in Cumberland".

Captain Brickman was present and offered to put it into the post office. She snatched it up, saying she would do it. . . . Of three thousand and more letters which in 17 or 18 years he had put into the Bath post office this alone miscarried.[1]

Inquiries revealed that Mrs. Yescombe's pilfering had brought her into disrepute among local tradesmen, and a shoemaker signed a statement, witnessed by Landor's friend Brickman, that she had stolen seven shillings from his counter. Landor therefore wrote to Geraldine's parents, informing them of Mrs. Yescombe's conduct, and Hooper replied on 30th May:

I addressed two letters to the Rev. Morris Yescombe, requesting him to give me the information if possible, what my daughter had done with the 100£ given to my daughter as a new year's gift, or otherwise relieve my daughter from the obligation of her promise made to Mrs. Yescombe, my daughter having stated that she was bound to secrecy to Mrs. Yescombe not to divulge the manner in which she disposed of it. The Rev. Mr. Yescombe never even replied to either of my letters; but on the evening of Saturday, May 23, I received a letter from his wife commencing thus: "As your inquiries concern me, *not my husband*, I answer them as follows. As regard the 100£, *I never laid my eyes on it*, neither did I read *any note or letter containing such an inclosure. I know where a trifling sum was deposited*, but until your daughter sends me a note written by herself, authorizing me to do so, I shall not *divulge it*!"

Since I called in Rivers Street I have been engaged, both day and night, in trying to discover how this money has been spent, and I am still pursuing my inquiries, well aware that I had paid all my dear child's bills, up to the very day she left us to join my family at Cheltenham, altho, in consequence of the very delicate state of her health, I have not pressed matters to the greatest extremity. Yet I have so far succeeded in obtaining the confidence of the dear child as to receive her confession, by this morning's post, that she gave fifty pounds of it to Mrs. Yescombe, to pay Mr. Slack's (her solicitor) bill for the trial Yescombe versus Roche.

I dare not speak at the present moment of my feelings toward these parties, and I am too much agitated to write more than the assurance that, at the time my innocent child was imposed upon, she was only sixteen years of age, and is at this moment very, very ill.

Meanwhile, on hearing from Landor, the Hoopers had promptly removed their daughter from Mrs. Yescombe's society by sending her

[1] As appears from *Landor's "Dear Daughter"*, *Eliza Lynn Linton*, by R. H. Super (1944), the letter was addressed to Eliza Lynn, then nursing the first Mrs. W. J. Linton through her last illness at Brantwood, Coniston Water. Concerned for Miss Lynn's own health, Landor begged her to engage a second nurse, and Mr. Super quotes his letter to Forster of 24th August, 1856, saying, "I have sent five pounds for the nurse and have promist the same again next month, with strict injunctions that the highminded Linton may know nothing of the matter."

to stay with her uncle, a doctor, at Cheltenham, where Landor wrote to her, confessing his fault in advising her to trust Mrs. Yescombe and counselling her to confide in her uncle, and enclosed the letter in one of explanation to Dr. Hooper. To this Geraldine replied:

My kind, my noble friend! Rejoice and be glad: the lost sheep is found and brought back to the fold. No longer will I hold intercourse with the ungodly.

Landor commented:

Ungodly! a lady who went constantly to church! Doctor Hooper well knows the cause of his niece's deplorable state of health and spirits, and why she calls her deluder *ungodly.*

Remembering that he had invited eligible young men to dine in her company and that Geraldine had said she could think of no attachment other than her devotion to Mrs. Yescombe, he regarded the older woman as a seducer of such innocence as he had attributed to Beatrice Cenci in his *Five Scenes*.

He had ceased to meet the Yescombes, but they sought reconciliation by contriving to be present when he called on a mutual friend, Charles Stuart-Menteth, at Entry Hill House, near Bath. Falling on her knees before him, Mrs. Yescombe begged, "Don't ruin me! don't ruin me."

He abstained and shunned her: so did Mr. Hooper, who was urged as a man and gentleman to prosecute her: Both were equally reluctant to bring the unhappy girl as witness in a criminal court.

But he began to receive numerous anonymous or pseudonymous letters, repeating slanderous statements by Mrs. Yescombe and either abusing him or exhorting him to refute them. Accordingly he assembled letters and other evidence for such a pamphlet as his *Statement of Occurrences at Llanbedr*, which was printed by the publishers of the *Bath Express*, Hayward & Payne, as *Walter Savage Landor and the Honourable Mrs. Yescombe*, and issued sometime before 12th June, on which date the Yescombes' solicitor, Slack, wrote to threaten legal proceedings unless the statement was withdrawn with public apology. Landor replied with another pamphlet, *Mr. Landor Threatened*, beginning by publishing Slack's letter, with the remarks that "the writer's name is no invention by any author of farce, or comedy, or satire, but is really and truly Slack", and that "it would be unlawful to order a chairman to cudgel the fellow for his insolence". Bearing no printer's imprint, the pamphlet was described as "Printed for and Published by W. S. Landor, 3, Rivers Street, Bath", and the Yescombes thereupon started proceedings for libel, as Landor announced in an appendix written on Sunday 21st June and added in a second edition of the pamphlet.

In the previous year, following the death of their mother, Landor's nieces Sophy and Kitty—the unmarried daughters of his brother Charles—had come to live in Bath at 3 Belmont. Concern for their uncle Henry's health deterred them from informing him of the impending trouble, and they may have advised Landor in selecting a firm of Bath solicitors, Taylor & Williams, to act for him. They began by preparing a plea of justification, but this was abandoned when Forster arrived in Bath to effect a settlement with Slack on 27th July.

In his discreet account of the affair Forster was at pains to emphasise Landor's infirmity:

> The last illness of the old man, while it had left him subject to the same transitory storms of frantic passion, had permanently also weakened him, mentally yet more than bodily . . . even when anger was no longer present to overcloud his intellect, there had ceased to be really available to his use such a faculty of discrimination between right and wrong, or such a saving consciousness of evil from good, as is necessary to constitute a responsible human being. He had not now even the memory enough to recollect what he was writing from day to day; and while the power of giving keen and clear expression to every passing mood of bitterness remained to him, his reason had too far deserted him to leave it other than a fatal gift.

Landor had been so ill that on 22nd May—about ten days before he received Hooper's letter—he was persuaded by his niece Kitty to draft his will and send it to his brother Henry:

> The last three winters I have suffered much illness, and do not expect to live through another. We shall never meet again. You are now the last of my family. . . . If the Will requires altering, I do not think it worth the trouble. Throw it away or tear it up. I am quite indifferent in regard to all property, and, God knows, I do not care a straw whether I live or die . . .

The letter reached Henry when he was staying at Birlingham with Robert, who, so crippled with gout that he could "hardly walk down stairs" but proud of his fortitude in requiring his curate to take Sunday service "only six times in fourteen months", wrote on 5th June to their Rugeley cousin:

> A letter from Walter made us both merry for some minutes. It contained Walter's Will, and began by saying that he and Henry were now left alone— were the last of the Family—that all the rest were gone. Yet was the Letter sent to him *here*. I, in return, sent some flowers with my blessing—as his Uncle Robert. He has no distinct notion that I may not be his grandfather, yet can he write freshly and fiercely, and knows more about Athens as it was 2,500 years ago than you and I our knowledge together.

Though Landor was conscious of Robert's attitude of jealousy towards him and evidently meant to imply that, since Elizabeth's death, Henry was the last of the family who cared about him, Robert's letter may be regarded as endorsing Forster's estimate of Landor's mental state. Yet the drafted will is characteristic in its terseness, vigour, and contempt of hypocrisy.[1] The directions for his funeral—that, never having "indulged in maskerades or other such buffooneries", he desired "no magpie colors" on his coffin and "no rogues with staves at the side of it"—are such as he might have written at any time of his life: when, at twenty-five, he was persuaded by Mocatta to suppress the *Postscript to Gebir*; when, at thirty-seven, he exposed the Duke of Beaufort to Lord Chancellor Eldon; when, at fifty, he resented Taylor's "bowdlerising" of the *Imaginary Conversations*, or at sixty-one he published *A Satire on Satirists* and *Letters of a Conservative*. Nor could it be argued that the published expression of indignation against Mrs. Yescombe represented any deviation from lifelong habit. The writer of the Yescombe pamphlets was the same Landor who distributed handbills about Fred Betham at Usk, who printed his opinion of the attaché Dawkins, who defied the

---

[1] Dated 22 May 1857, the draft reads:

This is the last Will and Testament of
Walter Savage Landor

My estates, and all other my property, in Warwickshire, Staffordshire, Monmouthshire, and elsewhere, being in entail or in settlement, I have few articles to bequeath. Of these I dispose as follows.

The minatures of Jane Sophia Countess de Molandé, and of her daughter Maria Sodre de Pereira, and of her grandaughter Luisinha, to William Swift, Esquire of Whitechurch Lodge, Rathfarnham, Dublin.

All my books, busts, the statue of Saint Peter in maple wood by Lorenzo Ghiberti, and all my pictures to my son Arnold Savage Landor, who will preserve as heirlooms such as I may indicate, and sell the rest by auction for the benefit of these public Charities in Bath; namely

To the Bath Hospital £10.10.0
To the United Hospital £10.10.0
To the Bath Penitentiary £20.0.0
To the Refuge for the Destitute £10.10.0

I leave ten shillings to be paid yearly to the most studious boy of good conduct, in the school at Tachbrook, Warwicks.

All my writings and letters I place at the disposal of my learned and most highly esteemed friend, John Forster, Esq. of Lincolns Inn.

As I never indulged in maskerades or other such buffooneries, so I desire that nothing of the kind may be exhibited about me at the close of life. Let there be no magpie colors of black and white upon my coffin; no rogues with staves at the side of it. Death having been beforehand in the business, they cannot stave him off. Let the children play about me as they used to do, and let six chairmen carry me, on tressel or otherwise, and each receive ten shillings for his trouble, which will not be much, as I order that the coffin have no lead in it. I would lie near the tower of Widcombe Church, facing Prior Park. We all go in the same Omnibus to the same terminus: we ought all to have the same accomodation, and to pay the same fare.

In this my last Will and Testament no mention is made of my beloved and ever affectionate children, Julia, Walter and Charles, because, in addition to what is theirs already, their elder brother, Arnold, in consideration of divers farms added by me to the estates, and of farmhouses built, and of roads to the extent of eight miles made by me, and of timber trees of old growth left standing, and others to the amount of several hundred thousands planted by me, has consented to pay to each of them, on the demise of their mother, an annuity of one hundred pounds, in half yearly payments, commencing six months at farthest, after my decease.

Signed Walter Savage Landor in the presence of and in the presence of each other Catherine M. Landor, 3 Belmont, Bath. John Charles Hughes Nr 8 Edward Street Bath

I hereby appoint my brother Henry Eyres Landor to be my Executor with or without any other, as he will.

22 May 1857 C. M. Landor

J. C. Hughes.

Florence police, denied Antoir's claims to the watercourse, and denounced Wordsworth as a "detractor".

In the Yescombe affair Landor's only deviation from characteristic conduct—the only suggestion that his force was enfeebled—lay in the sole act that won Forster's approval: he allowed Forster to persuade him to sign a written apology, with an undertaking "not to repeat anything of the kind again", so inducing the Yescombes to stay proceedings. He was prevailed upon against his will, for Forster declared that only his persuasions altered Landor's resolution to defy the Yescombes, "place his property beyond seizure for damages, break up his house in Bath, sell his pictures, and return to Italy".

According to his lights, Forster acted in Landor's interest. He had become, since his wealthy marriage, as intensely respectable as he was officious; he was soon to irritate Dickens into the caricature of Podsnap in *Our Mutual Friend*. If Landor had escaped from the lawsuit unsoiled by mudslinging, he would still have been ridiculed as a credulous old man, susceptible in senility, and a target for those eager to discredit a critic of orthodoxy. He was concerned simply with saving Landor's reputation; as one of the frock-coated upper middle-class which was to rule England for the next three generations, he could not conceive that anybody sane would offend convention for a principle. That Landor wanted to do so convinced Forster that his intellect was clouded—that he was incapable of "discriminating between right and wrong".

Forster was "painfully affected" by another change in Landor: "he had so long and steadily consented to act on my advice exclusively in the publication of his writings, that here I believed I had still some efficient control", but "unhappily it proved to be not so". After his sister Elizabeth's death there were found among her papers some copies of the long-forgotten *Poems from the Arabic and Persian*, along with early manuscript verses she had treasured for more than half a century, like the lines "Written at Malvern, June 1799", "Voyage to St. Ives, Cornwall, from Port-Einon, Glamorgan, 1794", and "St. Clair" of 1796. His friends had shown so much interest in these early poems that he conceived the idea of including them in a volume along with verses he had written since the publication of *Last Fruit*. As early as the autumn of 1856 he was asking Rose Graves-Sawle and Eliza Lynn to send him verses of which he had kept no copy, but apparently Forster first heard of the projected volume when Landor informed him that he had recovered some of his manuscript verses from Mrs. Yescombe only after advertising their unauthorised detention.

As Macready's diary illustrates, Forster was rarely tactful; without discrimination he described Landor's materials for this volume as "the mere sweepings and refuse of his writing-desk", and probably he did not scruple to hint this opinion. Moreover, he was irritated by Landor's rashness, and having made up his mind that the old man's faculties were failing, he was disposed to that "supercilious tone" which Dickens resented as giving "the idea that he was the patron, or padrone". Landor was not vain of his verses, and when Rose Graves-Sawle wrote compliments after the book's publication, he replied, "For the greater part of my last poems I want pardon rather than praise." For the entertainment of Mrs. Yescombe and Geraldine he had written such verses as those addressed to "Erminine", and either from his friends or from anonymous letters he heard that Mrs. Yescombe was showing to her sympathisers not only these but other more indecent verses which she attributed to him. By publication he sought to disclaim the spurious verses by acknowledging those he had actually written, and told Forster that, while he "grieved to do anything" against his advice, "if he did not publish the poems, others would".[1]

Forster left Bath in September 1857, having refused to find a London publisher for the volume, and Landor immediately commissioned an Edinburgh publisher named Nichol to print it. At first he proposed to call the book *Dry Leaves*, but finally decided on *Dry Sticks, Fagoted by Walter Savage Landor*. With difficulty the printer persuaded him against insisting that the title should read "Fagoted by *the late* W. S. Landor", pleading that the description would give pain to his friends. Forster cited this fancy as "evidence of the strange state of Landor's mind at the moment", but Landor in fact believed that he might die before the book's publication. On 23rd October he wrote to Rose Graves-Sawle:

I was seized last Wednesday by the most inflammatory pains in the shoulder and right side . . . I was recommended to apply a mustard poultice. I never do things by halves. I kept it about me from 8 at night till 11 next day. My patience and perseverance were rewarded. I am now like one of those saints who were flayed alive and I am somewhat more of a lobster color than a man's . . . I never had rheumatism since the year I left College. I caught it lying in a damp bed after hunting. Surely I must be made of iron all but the heart.

[1] In an "anonymous contemporary manuscript" Mr. Super has seen "a few unacknowledged epigrams, not in the best taste", and "although the handwriting is not Landor's, the poems purport to be his and may well be so". In his analysis of the facts, *Extraordinary Action for Libel—Yescombe v. Landor* (1941), Mr. Super states, "Landor was the last person in the world to present a cool and impartial case in his own behalf; but, unless the illnesses which clouded his mind at this time completely altered his character, he was also the last to forge documents." In *Walter Savage Landor: A Biography* he writes, "There is obviously danger in trusting Landor too far in these matters: letters which he published over the signatures of the Hoopers or Capt. Brickman or Eliza Lynn or Mrs. Bishop, or over his own signature, were almost certainly authentic, but it is not equally certain that Landor did not himself invent the anonymous letters he claimed to have received." He records that, after Landor signed his apology, "the Yescombes began to be bombarded with anonymous letters and poems in Landor's handwriting, insulting and even indecent; or so Yescombe told the court a year later, and he was not contradicted", yet some pages later he remarks that the counsel retained by Landor's solicitors at the trial "called no witnesses and made no serious defense". There would seem obviously less "danger in trusting" the published evidence of a man with Landor's record than either the allegations of one with Yescombe's reputation or those of an "anonymous contemporary manuscript".

"My weakness is excessive," he told Forster about the same time; "with extreme difficulty do I weigh my self up from my arm-chair." When his doctor declared that his constitution would bear him through, he commented, "The same spasms, in that case, will come over again some other time, and I wish it were all at an end now."

"Age and illness had conquered him at last, and left him other than the Landor I had known," declared Forster in attempting to explain why *Dry Sticks* included verses satirising Mrs. Yescombe. He believed that Landor, having given an undertaking not to print anything further about the Yescombes, withheld from him the proofs of the book because he had broken his promise. But as Forster had refused his usual services in seeing the book through the press, Landor would naturally not wish to trouble him with the proofs, and though he had been persuaded to sign an apology for the pamphlets, it was not in his nature to understand that he was bound thereby never to speak what he believed to be the truth of the matter. Moreover, Forster had written to Landor's solicitors and to his friend Brickman, from whom he had received "an assurance . . . that everything wrong would be erased". Presumably the solicitors and Brickman passed the offending poems because they were founded on fact: Brickman himself had witnessed the shoemaker's statement that Mrs. Yescombe had stolen from his counter, the incident supplying the basis of metrical dialogue between a lady, an old woman, and a policeman in "The Modern Idyl"; Brickman had also been present when "Mother Pestcome" took the letter containing "that poor nurse's lost five-pound", mentioned in "The Pilfered to the Pilferer". Nor could Landor appreciate that fashion had changed since his youth, when he lampooned Kett, Richards, and Fellowes, and was himself libelled in the *Anti-Jacobin Review*.

Soon after the publication of *Dry Sticks* in the new year of 1858, Forster's Bath friends "heard whispers of another contemplated action for libel", though Landor in his subsequent *Defence* remarked with reason that action was taken only after he suffered an apoplectic seizure. He had the warning symptoms of blood pressure in January, when his doctor saw "no reason why I should not live another ten years" and Landor complained, "Why cannot this swimming of the head carry me to the grave a little more rapidly?" Two months later, at the end of March, his niece Kitty was sent for when he was found unconscious one morning. He remained so for twenty-four hours, and his condition was considered dangerous for about a week.

The seizure doubtless resulted from agitation caused by newspaper attacks. On 14th January Felice Orsini and three associates attempted to assassinate Louis-Napoleon by throwing bombs under his carriage, because they regarded him as a principal obstacle to the liberation of Italy; he escaped unhurt, but ten people were killed and more than a hundred and fifty injured. Landor had frequently attacked Napoleon for supporting the papal influence and repressing the Italian revolutionaries; it was known that he had received Orsini as his guest and referred to him in his *Letter to Emerson* as a refugee worthy of English hospitality; repeatedly he had asserted the principle of tyrannicide, reprinting in his *Letter to Emerson*[1] his offer to head a subscription "for the family of the first patriot who asserts by action the dignity of tyrannicide", and adding:

Abject men have cried out against me for my commendation of this ancient virtue, the highest of which a man is capable, and now the most important and urgent. Is it not an absurdity to remind us that usurpers will rise up afresh? Do not all transgressors? But must we therefore lay aside the terrors of chastisement, or give a ticket-of-leave to the most atrocious criminals? Shall one enslave millions? Shall laws be subverted, and we then be told that we act against them, or without their sanction, when none are left us, and we lay prostrate the subverter? Three or four blows, instantly and simultaneously given, may save the world many years of warfare, of discord, and of degradation.

In time of war leaders invite an opposing nation to rise against its "wicked rulers" and applaud rebels as heroes of the "resistance"; but in time of peace self-preservation requires statesmen to condemn tyrannicide as a crime and Lord Palmerston now brought in a bill to punish conspiracies to murder. His bill passed its first reading with a large majority, but members of Parliament then became aware that liberal opinion throughout the country was against it and Palmerston was forced into resignation.

Immediately on hearing of Orsini's attempt, Landor wrote to Forster:

Miserable Orsini! he sat with me two years ago at the table on which I am now writing. Dreadful work! horrible crime! To inflict death on a hundred for the sin of one! Such a blow can serve only to awaken tyranny, reverberating on the brass helmets of her satellites.

But Dr. Simon Bernard was arrested in England as Orsini's accomplice, and during his trial at the Central Criminal Court a letter was read mentioning Landor's offer to help the family of a patriot who committed tyrannicide. Newspaper comment caused Landor to write a letter to the *Times* of 17th March, denying that he had countenanced Orsini's attempt and differentiating between assassination as "the basest of crimes" and tyrannicide as "the sublimest of virtues, it being self-immolation for a man's native country", though "beyond that country it would be murder".[1] Landor declared that he had talked

---

[1] Without mentioning Landor's name, John Stuart Mill took the same line when writing of "the lawfulness of Tyrannicide" in *On Liberty* (1859): "I shall content myself with saying that the subject has been at all times one of the open questions of morals; that the act of a private citizen in striking down a criminal, who, by raising himself above the law, has

with Orsini only in the presence of his friend Sandford, who assured Forster that he had "joined Landor in advising the Italian to forbear from any declaration then against the ruler of France". But newspapers supporting the government were glad of a butt for indignation, and local opinion in Bath was conventional; the Yescombes could remember the effective play of their counsel in the Roche case on Landor's "want of judgment" in recommending "assassination under the milder term of tyrannicide", and their Mr. Slack served a writ for libel in June.

By this time Landor had made a remarkable recovery from his seizure; at the end of May his brother Henry wrote to congratulate him, and he himself wrote to Forster:

I take it uncivil in Death to invite and then to balk me. It was troublesome to walk back, when I found he would not take me in. I do hope and trust he will never play me the same trick again. We ought both of us to be graver.

He was well enough to take a drive to his proposed grave at Widcombe, and returned "less fatigued than I expected".

His solicitors, Taylor & Williams, briefed a barrister named Phinn, who advised the certainty of an adverse verdict, with damages—aggravated by breach of the undertaking dictated by Forster—likely to absorb both Landor's small personal property and his annuity for many years. Again Landor found that he had employed solicitors to act for their own profit with no advantage to himself. Taylor & Williams advised his niece Kitty that Landor must immediately leave the country and assign his annuity to her, so insuring payment of their costs.

On 12th July Forster was astonished to receive a telegram announcing Landor's imminent arrival in London, accompanied by his niece. Among friends dining with him that evening was Dickens, who went up to Landor's room to greet him. He expected to find him full of indignation against his persecutors, but returned laughing to the other guests that "he found him very jovial, and his whole conversation was upon the characters of Catullus, Tibullus, and other Latin poets."

From Boulogne on 23rd July Landor wrote to Rose Graves-Sawle:

In leaving England for ever, the heaviest of my sorrows is that I shall never see you again. I shall retain in my inmost heart the grateful memory of your kindness and compassion. How is it possible that I could ever forget

placed himself beyond the reach of legal punishment or control, had been accounted by whole nations, and by some of the best and wisest of men, not a crime, but an act of exalted virtue; and that, right or wrong, it is not of the nature of assassination, but of civil war. As such, I hold that the instigation to it, in a specific case, may be a proper subject of punishment, but only if an overt act has followed, and at least a probable connection can be established between the act and the instigation. Even then, it is not a foreign government, but the very government assailed, which alone, in the exercise of self-defence, can legitimately punish attacks directed against its own existence."

the comfort you gave me, when circumstances made it impossible for me to remain in Italy.

He felt "some vexation to part with my pictures", but the loss of these and of his friends comprised all his regret. There was grandeur in the serenity with which the unrepentant rebel faced exile in his eighty-fourth year, having pulled up his roots for the third time in his long life.

19

TWILIGHT IN ITALY

My life is closing. Private griefs (O shame! shame!) press upon and overlay public with me.

—*Alfieri and Metastasio* (1856)

If I extoll'd the virtuous and the wise,
The brave and beautiful, and well discern'd
Their features as they fixt their eyes on mine;
If I have won a kindness never wooed;
Could I foresee that . . . fallen among thieves,
Despoil'd, halt, wounded . . . tramping traffickers
Should throw their dirt upon me, not without
Some small sharp pebbles carefully inclosed?
However, from one crime they are exempt;
They do not strike a brother, striking *me*.

—Appendix to *The Hellenics* (1859)

At Bristol on 23rd August 1858, before Baron Channell and a jury, the Yescombes sued Landor on three counts for libel, and on another for breach of agreement. The libels were verses in *Dry Sticks*—"To Caina", "The Pilfered to the Pilferer", and "Canidia and Caina", the last a couplet:

Canidia shared her prey with owls and foxes,
The daintier Caina feeds from letter boxes.

In Dante's *Inferno*, Caina is a region of hell reserved for slayers of relatives; without the circumstantial evidence of the pamphlets, there was nothing to identify Caina with Mrs. Yescombe. "The Pilfered to the Pilferer", besides apostrophising "Mother Pestcome" as thief and liar, alludes to sex perversion between Mrs. Yescombe and her *protégée*:

Tho' you've made her pale and thin
As the child of Death by Sin,
When you've done with Caroline
Bid her for a night be mine;
You shall have her all the day
Following, to repeat our play.

"Child of Death by Sin" refers to Milton's allegory of Sin's incest with Death in *Paradise Lost*, and Landor told George Jacob Holyoake that the plaintiff's lawyer, being ignorant of the allusion, inserted a comma after the word "Death", so making the text suggest that Mother Pestcome had made Caroline pale and thin by her own sinfulness. Landor believed—and one juryman was reported to have said—that the correct reading "would have altered the case, and, of course, the verdict".

The jury found for the plaintiffs and damages were assessed at a thousand pounds—£750 for the three libels and £250 for the breach of agreement. Landor's counsel attempted no justification by calling witnesses to testify to the plaintiffs' reputations, from the evidence either of the Roche case or of the Bath tradesmen; as Landor remarked to Holyoake, "no action was brought against the tradesmen for their reports, which I twice published". Hazlitt asserted "as a general rule" that "all uneducated people are hypocrites"; most people in Victorian England were uneducated, newspapers sought to appeal to popular taste, and the *Times* set the tone for a press orgy of self-righteousness:

How ineffable the disgrace to a man of Mr. Landor's ability and reputation at the close of a long life to be mixed up with so disgraceful a transaction. A slanderer—and the slanderer of a lady—a writer of anonymous letters, and these letters reeking with the foulest odours of the dirtiest slums—a violator of his pledged word—who is it to whom these words must now be applied?

Forster's plea of senile irresponsibility was thus forestalled:

The old poet can scarcely lay claim to impunity on the ground of failing intellect. It must be admitted that in their own nasty way—and it is a very nasty way—the verses of Landor's old age are quite equal in point and vigour to the golden produce of his prime. But it is such filthy point—such dirty vigour! Take Jonathan Swift's impurest productions, when he sat down for a regular innings at dirt—take the obscenest off-scourings of Martial, when the Roman poet was wallowing in the very cesspool of the Muses, and you will have an idea of the nature of Landor's recent literary diversions. So far we have spoken of the old man's offence as of one against decency and morality. To describe it technically, according to the form in which it was brought the other day before the Court, we must, however, speak of it as the publication of a libel; and a fouler libel than the one brought home to him was never written by man. What made the case worse was that he had selected as the object of his attack a lady whose only fault seems to have been that she had been for many years on intimate terms with her unmanly traducer.

"Already I feel unwilling to meet any one whom I know—and after next week I shall be ashamed of my name," wrote the Rev. Robert Landor to one of his nieces at the time of the trial. "What a bombardment of indignant articles and fusillade of scandalized paragraphs he is enduring just now!" wrote Browning of Landor to Isa Blagden, and

W. S. Landor.
July 20 '59
at 85 years of age –
W W S

LANDOR AT SIENA

From the sketch by William Wetmore Story,
20th July, 1859

proceeded to a diagnosis that would have wounded Landor more than condemnation:

> Such writing is wholly indefensible on his part, no doubt: and he is no more in his dotage than you or I—but it pricks the nerve of one to feel that in some quite inexplicable way, the great old man was foolish enough to believe he did God service in so writing: I can't imagine how he fails to see the cowardice in the act of publication: if he thinks these abominations of anybody, why not be content to stand alone in his belief—why call on us to help him with our opinion and sympathy?—and yet, as a coward he certainly is *not*—one ends as one begins—by repeating . . . inexplicable. However, I—for one—am profoundly grateful to the author of the "Conversations" and would not abuse him as all these wretched catch-penny "Presses", "John Bulls", and the like, do just now—if he had libelled *me*.

Browning could not appreciate that, so far from wishing to invite sympathy, Landor was inspired by a passion for justice.

Other Pecksniffs sneered with Samuel Carter Hall at "a nasty old man tottering on the brink of the grave", and Dickens thus rebuked his sister-in-law, Georgina Hogarth:

> You must not let the new idea of poor dear Landor efface the former image of the fine old man. I wouldn't blot him out, in his tender gallantry, as he sat upon that bed at Forster's that night, for a million of wild mistakes at eighty years of age.

Dickens's warmth of heart preserved his loyalty, but even less than Browning he recognised anything beyond an unhappy aberration. "I feel certain that there is much, which the world does not know, to be said on his side," wrote Augustus Hare to his mother. "Whatever his faults are, I am sure you will feel that we who have known him well must draw a veil for ourselves over the failings of his old age, and remember only the many kind words of the dear old man, so tender in heart and so fastidious in taste, the many good and generous acts of his long life, and how many they are." Thanking Charles Empson on 11th September for his account of the sale of Landor's pictures—though "it is certainly rather mortifying to see such prices for pictures with such names"—Sophy Landor mentioned "many kind letters, showing that the late Trial has injured my Uncle's character less than might have been expected, with those who know him", but was "greatly disgusted" by Landor's request that she should forward his usual subscription to the local hospital—"ostentation at such a moment is *too* degrading".

Of all his friends Mrs. Lynn Linton alone attempted to offer a public defence. Reproaching herself that preoccupation with newly-married life had interrupted her attentions to Landor, she wrote to urge Forster's co-operation. Forster had not only inspired the disingenuous apology that made indefensible publication of the libellous verses, but he had failed to challenge Landor's solicitors in their advising him to quit the country; uneasy in conscience, he was impatient to forget an embarrassment. "It is very sad," he wrote on 26th August, "and I am as helpless as yourself, though not less anxious than yourself to do what yet I feel is hardly to be done." He promised, "if I can get any reasonable grounds on which to make a brief public statement, I will do it", and wrote accordingly to Landor's nieces and to his friend Brickman. Apparently unconscious that such appeals might be construed as admissions of guilt, he used his influence with some journals to secure promises of silence on the subject, and concluded on a note of resignation:

The saddest thing remains, that the occurrence should have taken place at all. The worst evil is nevertheless not without its admixture of good in this mystery of a world. And I pray now that our noble old Landor (from whom everything less noble than himself will soon fall off and be forgotten) may live quietly the rest of his days in Italy, and die with his children.

§ 2

Twenty years before, without any personal acquaintance with Mrs. Landor, Forster had favoured Landor's return to her. He can hardly have supposed that, after twenty-three years of bitter feelings during which they had corresponded only through third parties, Landor was likely to be warmly welcomed by his wife. At Boulogne his niece Kitty surrendered her charge of Landor to his son Walter, who evidently conveyed a mistaken impression of the welcome awaiting at Fiesole, for Landor wrote to Brickman:

You will be surprised to hear that I am returning to my old residence in Tuscany. For the first time since my honeymoon has my wife shown any affection toward me. My daughter Julia tells me that she is desirous of coming with her and meeting me at Genoa. Politeness would alone make me obviate this. The day after my arrival at that city I shall start for Florence. Never again shall I travel beyond sight of it. . . . A few of my old friends are still living at Florence, but I shall sadly miss those I must for ever leave at Bath.

Before receiving an assurance of welcome from his daughter, Landor had not intended to go to Florence. "I had designed Nervi for my residence," he wrote, "and my pictures and books were consequently directed to Genoa, near that place." But his nieces had written alarming accounts of his feeble health to his son Arnold, who doubtless expected to profit from his father's income, since Henry Landor had insisted that Landor should assign his annuity to Arnold instead of to his niece Kitty, preferring that Arnold rather than Kitty should be troubled by the lawyers' demands. Finding that the deed of assignment was likely to be set aside for payment of the Yescombes' damages and lawyers' costs, the family regretted their invitation, and after his arrival "scarcely a week had elapsed," declared Landor, "before Walter gave me to understand that the place was no longer mine."

He quickly revealed that neither age nor illness had abated his spirit. Within a few weeks he protested to Lord Normanby against "your lordship's rude reception of me at the Cascine, in presence of my family and numerous Florentines":

We are both of us old men, my lord, and are verging on decrepitude and imbecility, else my note might be more energetic. Do not imagine I am unobservant of distinctions. You by the favor of a minister are Marquis of Normanby, I by the grace of God am

Walter Savage Landor

In reply he received "a very kind note", which implied that Lord Normanby intended no slight upon Landor himself, but was not in the habit of acknowledging members of his family. During a visit to Florence earlier in 1858—some months before Landor's arrival—Augustus Hare often met "the foolish wife of our dear old Landor, who never ceased to describe with fury his passionate altercations with her, chiefly caused apparently by jealousy". Apparently Mrs. Landor was socially ostracised, for Landor remarked how "the bishop of Jamaica, Admiral Erskine, Sandford, and several others, who called on me, never enquired about her; nor did Arnold once make his appearance".

While his two younger sons were more dutiful, Arnold and Julia behaved with studied unkindness, in which Landor believed they were encouraged by their mother.

When I was extremely ill, and kept my bed, I earnestly begged that I might have put up a bell within reach. Even this was not permitted, on the plea that a picture must be removed. It was a portrait, two feet high, and the wire could run under it, or on one side. I could mention other things equally intolerable.

Repeatedly he complained to Forster of his family's conduct towards him, and asked if his brother Henry could arrange to provide him with sufficient income to live alone in lodgings. Forster ignored his appeals as confirming "the impression as to his mental state" conceived during the Yescombe trouble till, shortly before Christmas 1858, he heard that Landor had left the villa for lodgings in Florence. He then wrote to Henry Landor, but before he could conclude any arrangements he heard that Landor had returned to Fiesole. The old man had no money, and Arnold refused to make him an allowance; according to Forster, Henry Landor pointed out that Arnold, as the owner of his father's property, was the person who should properly provide for him.[1]

During these first months at Fiesole Landor was urging Mrs. Lynn Linton to secure publication by her husband and by Thornton Hunt, Leigh Hunt's son, of a "Defence" he had written in reply to the press comment on the Yescombe trial. An early trade-unionist, W. J. Linton supported the Chartist movement as "a people's protest against the misgovernment of an oligarchy", following "the example set by the middle classes in their struggle for the Reform Bill"; since applauding him as the author of *The Plaint of Freedom* in 1853, Landor had contributed to his periodicals, the *English Republic* and *Pen and Pencil*. Linton regarded the libel as one "which the quick-tempered old poet ought not to have uttered, although indeed it was not uncalled for", and declined to publish the "Defence", as "it was really a repetition of the libel, and . . . unworthy of so great a man".

Having failed with Linton, Landor applied in March 1859 to George Jacob Holyoake, another former Chartist and socialist disciple of Robert Owen, who had shared Landor's sympathies with the Hungarian and Italian refugees. He told Holyoake, "I can only offer you five pounds for 100 copies—the rest will remain yours", and "curiosity, I am assured, will induce many to purchase it, my name being not quite unknown to the public". Holyoake had already suffered imprisonment for printing seditious literature and "martyrdom was never to my taste", but he admired Landor for "his force, simplicity, directness, and the wonderful compression of his style: for his singular fearlessness, determination of thought, and his Paganism". He was flattered that Landor should esteem him as willing to take a risk in the interest of justice: "in applying to me, I supposed he had reason to believe that he could trust me in a matter where confidence might be of importance to him", and as Landor had not stipulated that he should keep the commission secret, with like generosity he undertook the printing without "any stipulation for indemnity". He had the manuscript copied at his own house, so that nobody at his office could identify the handwriting of the original; his brother set up the type and printed off the copies with his own hands; nobody else saw the pamphlet—entitled *Mr. Landor's Remarks on a Suit preferred against him, at the Summer Assizes*

---

[1] Before Landor finally left the villa, Forster asserts that "thrice during those ten months he left Fiesole to seek a lodging in Florence; thrice he was brought back". Mr. Super finds "no evidence" to support this assertion, but the fact that Landor's letters to Forster during this period have not yet been discovered does not mean that they never existed. As Landor's wife and children were still living, Forster could not print the letters, but he implied all he could by stating, "I abstain from even a mention of the character of the complaints in his letters; and from all formal expression of opinion, decided as is that which I hold, on the way in which those with whom he was now attempting to live should have discharged the duty they were under every natural and human obligation to render, and from which they could not be released by any amount of mad irritability on his part, or any number of irrational demands upon their patience."

in Taunton, 1858, illustrating the Appendix to his Hellenics—before copies were delivered by post to addresses named by Landor. These included some principal newspapers, Milnes, Forster, Kossuth, Sir William Napier, Mrs. West of Ruthin Castle, "the Judge whosoever he was" (with his usual contempt for courts of law, Landor remembered neither Baron Channell's name nor the place of the trial), curiously Lord Brougham, and ironically "Mr. Hall of Highgate"; many copies went to Bath, some to Captain Brickman, some to Empson the picture dealer.

The Yescombes offered a reward of £200 for the discovery of the printer, but the secret was kept till Holyoake published his memoirs in 1893. As Landor wrote in another draft of the pamphlet, "Justice would compare the characters of the accuser and the accused. This was not done."[1] His object was to offer such comparison by statement of the facts; Swinburne considered the statement "trenchant and conclusive . . . simply unanswerable as a vindication of the glorious old man's character from any charge but one (which it assuredly does not tend to disprove) of excess in generosity, credulity, enthusiasm of open-handed charity and open-hearted—alas! also open-mouthed indignation". But the surreptitious manner of the publication frustrated the effect desired by Landor; the Yescombes could indicate their advertised reward as evidence that they repudiated the accusations, and most of Landor's friends deplored a method of justification involving "contempt of court".

Meanwhile the Yescombes had instituted proceedings to set aside the deed transferring Landor's annuity, and the court of chancery granted an injunction against payment of rents from the estate till the damages and costs were paid. When this news reached Fiesole in June 1859 and Arnold saw no alternative to complying with the injunction, Landor— as his wife related to Tom Trollope—tried to stab himself. The imposition of financial sacrifice aggravated Arnold's hostility towards him, and Landor described—in a letter to Arthur Walker of 23rd February 1860—how he finally left Fiesole in July 1859:

You will not much wonder that I have been driven from my villa, now for the third time. I am too forgiving (you will blame this expression) and too credulous. . . . My feet are tender, as old men's are generally, and I proposed to give him a roller to smoothen the loose and sharp gravel. He and his mother told me that the rain would not then run off. Yet you know it lies twenty five feet above the ground below. But he ordered the only walk I could use to be broken up. On this I left the house the day after, without a single word of remonstrance and without obtaining permission to remove the whitewash from the lions' heads over the garden gate, which a few days before had partly covered them, to annoy me; as I must see them from my study table, ten paces off.

[1] This draft—presumably that given by Landor to the Boston publisher, James T. Fields— is described in an *Addendum* by Robert F. Metzdorf to R. H. Super's *Extraordinary Action for Libel—Yescombe v. Landor* (1941).

He "left without a word of reproach, but was assailed by Mrs. L. in language such as a prostitute could scarcely assail a thief with". He left as suddenly, following a tirade by his wife, as he had left twenty-four years before, but this time he omitted to request the use of her carriage. At noon on a hot July day, with only "some 15 pauls in his pocket", he stumbled along the burning lane to Florence and was near exhaustion when he had the luck to meet Robert Browning, then living at Casa Guidi. As Landor resolutely refused to return to Fiesole, preferring "any two rooms, with simple board, to living with his family", Browning took charge of him and wrote to Forster. Though Landor suggested a resort to "the good offices of the Commissary of Police", Browning wrote "in a mildly-gruff way" to Mrs. Landor for "clothes, books, plate, pictures, residue of cash", and was "favoured by a visit" from her, "all butter and honey (save an occasional wasp's sting overlooked in the latter when she occasionally designated our friend as 'the old Brute!')", before she duly surrendered the required belongings. Apparently Henry Landor and his nieces had attributed Landor's complaints to his character for irascibility, for Forster told Browning that "they have all been under the delusion that the Fiesole people used the greatest kindness to our poor friend", but on hearing Browning's report Forster could give the assurance that Landor's brothers were "noble, honourable gentlemen, and wealthy to boot, and will never bear indignity to their family's head".

While Browning negotiated on his behalf, Landor was reluctant to remain indefinitely an encumbrance on him. Reminded that the American sculptor, William Wetmore Story, owed him a debt of hospitality, having been entertained by him at Bath some years before on Kenyon's introduction, he wrote to him:

My friends the Brownings tell me that you are residing in Siena. This is a great inducement for me to take a house for a year in that city. My family are in possession of the most charming villa and grounds within two miles of Florence, which I very imprudently gave entirely up to them, with a large income, reserving for myself extremely little, so I am constrained to be economical.

Story invited him to be his guest till he settled on a home of his own, and Mrs. Story recalled how "he arrived one sultry morning with Browning, looking very old, and almost as shabby and dusty and miserable as a beggar". Having heard "the whole story of ingratitude . . . which Browning fully confirmed", Story "felt as if he were really Lear come back again".

Concerned after only a few days lest he should outstay his welcome with the Storys, Landor talked of finding a lodging at Viareggio, but Browning, who had returned to his sick wife at Florence, begged Story to "prevent him doing anything so foolish" and the Storys persuaded him to remain as "our honoured and cherished guest". "During the time he was with us," wrote Mrs. Story, "his courtesy and high breeding never failed him; he was touchingly pleased and happy with our life, and so delightful and amusing that we ourselves grieved when it came to an end." Every morning he rose before even the servants were astir, and was found seated in the garden, writing Latin verses, which he read to Story at breakfast. After breakfast he gave Story's daughter her first lessons in Latin and recited passages from his favourite poets; he inspired her with enthusiasm for Keats, whom he declared "the greatest poet the world ever saw". With Story he strolled about the garden, discussing its beauties—"both had the same feeling about not plucking flowers".

He entertained Mrs. Story with reminiscences of which she kept a record. "His memory for the far distant time was extraordinary . . . while the 'middle distance' was lost in a cloud and the foreground, the present immediately about us, appeared to make little impression on him." He had long worried over the failings of his once marvellous memory: "he was the most impatient man with himself I ever saw," said Story; "he was furious if he did not remember at once any passage of a book, or any name, or date, and would immediately begin to abuse himself, crying out in his sharp, high voice, 'God bless my soul! I am losing my mind, I am getting old!'"

When the Brownings arrived to spend the month of August at a neighbouring villa, Mrs. Browning found "the quiet of this place has so restored his health and peace of mind that he is able to write awful Latin alcaics, to say nothing of hexameters and pentameters, on the wickedness of Louis Napoleon". He was now entirely condemnatory of Napoleon, and Story's daughter remembered how "Mrs. Browning, with her face hidden under her large hat and curls, would be stirred past endurance by these assaults upon her hero who was her 'Emperor evermore', and would raise her treble voice even to a shrill pitch in protest, until Mr. Browning would come into the fray as mediator".

Browning brought with him to Siena a rough linen bag containing the clothes left by Landor at Fiesole, and, as Landor requested, he had obtained from Arnold "whatever may remain out of the £110 left with him, after paying what he proposed I should pay for my board and other expenses, of which his mother told me he kept an account to a *quadrino*!" Landor's old friend Kirkup assisted Browning in negotiations with Fiesole, and, among "sundry flowers of language" about the account, told Browning that "such a beastly mess he never saw!" On 6th August Landor moved into a cottage near the Brownings' villa and wrote to Forster of his gratitude to Browning, "who made me the voluntary offer of the money I wanted, and who insists on managing my affairs here, and paying for my lodgings and sustenance. Never was such generosity and such solicitude as this incomparable man has shown in my behalf".

Browning wrote reassuring reports of Landor to Forster. The Storys told him that, while they noted "inequalities of temper in him", these were "not affecting themselves", and "he may be managed with the greatest ease by 'civility' alone". At the end of Landor's stay with him, Story's comment conveyed an impression that might have been recorded at any period of Landor's life: "We have found him most amiable and interesting, with certain streaks of madness running through his opinions, but frank and earnest of nature and a hater of injustice." Remarking on his moderate wants, his evenness of temper, and his gentleness and readiness to be advised, Browning described his conduct as "faultless"; "his thankfulness for the least attention, and anxiety to return it, are almost affecting", and "he leads a life of the utmost simplicity". Apart from the hours spent writing in his garden, he divided his time between the Brownings and the Storys. The women of both households were charmed by him; he delighted Story's daughter by wearing in honour of her birthday a flowered waistcoat given to him by D'Orsay, and even Mrs. Browning wrote affectionately of "how well he looks in his curly white beard!" He allowed his beard to grow at Siena, and Story sketched him before and after the growing; later he sent Rose Graves-Sawle's little daughter "a kiss thro' a beard as long as a Jew's".

Advised by Forster of the happenings at Fiesole, Landor's brothers agreed to allow him two hundred pounds a year, with a further fifty held in reserve for special expenses. Henry Landor showed his displeasure at the conduct of Landor's children towards their father by revoking a legacy of £2,000 he had intended for Julia. Browning decided that Landor was "wholly unfit to be anything but the recipient of the necessary money's worth, rather than the money itself"; as Landor fortunately professed the same conviction, Browning agreed to administer the allowance, submitting a quarterly account "duly examined and certified by Kirkup". Before leaving for Rome at the end of November 1859 the Brownings settled him in a small house in the Via Nunziatina at Florence; believing that he needed a trustworthy and tactful attendant, Browning engaged his wife's former maid Wilson, who was married to an Italian named Romagnoli. So, within two months of his eighty-fifth birthday, the head of his family came to live in cheap lodgings within an hour's walk of his children's home at the beautiful villa of which Ablett's generosity had made him master twenty-eight years before.

§ 3

At No. 2671 Via Nunziatina, Landor had a sitting-room, bedroom, and dining-room, all communicating, on the first floor. Below were rooms for Mrs. Romagnoli and a maidservant; there was a small garden. Browning reported that Landor seemed to like Mrs. Romagnoli,

but there is some inexplicable fault in his temper, whether natural or acquired, which seems to render him very difficult to manage. He forgets, misconceives, and makes no endeavour to be just, or indeed rational; and this in matters so infinitely petty that there is no providing against them.

Mrs. Story related that "on the very day of his arrival he in a fit of anger with his landlady threw his dinner, plates and all, out of the window", but, as Henry James commented, this was related of so many of Landor's dinners and of so many windows that "he must often have fasted, apart from his bill for crockery".

The root of his irritability appears in a letter he wrote to Forster at Christmas 1859:

Bath has no resemblance on earth, and I never have been happy in any other place long together. If ever I see it again, however, it must be from underground or above. I am quite ready and willing to go, and would fain lie in Widcombe churchyard, as I promised one who is no more. It may cost forty pounds altogether. I cannot long survive the disgrace of my incapacity to prove the character of those who persecute me, and this you only can relieve me from. When I think of it, I feel the approach of madness.

To this letter Forster "found it absolutely necessary" to reply "without any kind of doubt, that what he desired could not be done"; thereafter "I continued to write to him for some time," said Forster, "but my letters were unanswered".

Landor had reason for grievance. Forster had placed him in a false position by persuading him to apologise to the Ycscombcs, abandoned him to victimisation by the Bath solicitors, and attributed all his subsequent actions to senile irresponsibility. His neglect of the appeals from Fiesole must have seemed callous to Landor. Finally, in contrast with his former energy in supervising Landor's publications, he was now careless in regard to an enlarged edition of the *Hellenics*, with a dedication to Sir William Napier, which had been undertaken by Nichol of Edinburgh before Landor left England. Landor had expressed annoyance in December 1858 at the delay in publication, yet a year later, though the book had been printed and proofed, he still had no news of its publication. When Forster attributed the delay to the death of the publisher's brother, Landor wrote angrily to Browning:

Mr. Forster could give a better reason—so can I. Much was I averse, as I told him, to his undertaking the revisal, when two learned friends had made the offer. He however persisted, and I suspected the consequence. It was intended that Napier should never be gratified by the dedication.

Sir William Napier survived just long enough to receive his old friend's compliment, for he died in February 1860 and the book was actually published when Landor wrote to Browning in the previous December. Landor's resentment was unabated when he found, besides numerous misprints, that a libellous passage in the Appendix had been necessarily deleted by the publisher; in reply to Browning's attempt to defend Forster, he wrote:

I have never given Mr. F. the slightest cause of offence. Like another great man recorded in the Bible, "he hath waxed fat and prospered". Prosperity seems to have spoilt him. . . . I never play at fast and loose. Let him play at it with others, never more with

W. Landor.

"Pray never write to him on my account," he begged Browning in another letter; "I never shall."

At the same time he was irritated by further friction with his family, who had neglected to restore to him some of his books, and he told Browning:

I have less sleep, and consequently less appetite, than ever. I shall have been as much murdered as if I had been shot or poisoned. They who robbed an indulgent and helpless father are capable of either.

He expressed his indignation against Arnold in verses entitled "Ingratitude":

> Can this be he whom in his infancy,
> Hour after hour, I carried in my arms,
> When neither nurse nor mother could appease
> The froward wailing? . . .
> All, all I gave; and what is the return?
> Not even a bell-rope at my sick-bed-side.
>   O thou of largest, wisest, tenderest heart,
> Truly thou sayest that a serpent's tooth
> Wounds not so deeply as a thankless child.

Drafted at Siena in the previous August, these verses were now amended and enclosed in a letter to Arthur Walker.

As a boy, Walker had been a playmate of Arnold Landor's at Fiesole. After serving as an army officer in India and China, he returned to England to study medicine, visited Landor at Bath, and received in February 1847 a presentation copy of his *Works*. For some years he was a welcome visitor at Rivers Street, and when he volunteered as an army surgeon in the Crimean War, Landor corresponded with him. He remained a faithful friend, and after breaking with Forster, Landor entrusted him with many of his publishing projects.

Landor's first letter to the press since his leaving England, on "Garibaldi and the Italians", appeared in the *Times* on 29th November 1859. Another letter, on "The State of Italy", followed a month later, but during his irritability on settling at the Via Nunziatina, he informed Browning that "politics have little interest for me now Garibaldi is no longer in arms, and Italy is parcelled out by Napoleon, Francis and the Holiness of our Lord". He was annoyed by the staircase at his lodgings, which he declared inferior to a mason's ladder and "down which, had I not clung to the rail, I should have fallen and have broken my back or neck"; when Walker's sister, the Countess Baldelli, was "determined to mount my stairs", he thought "no stronger proof of friendship could be given". "We have had some such fogs in Florence as I never saw but once in London"; confined to his room with a cold, he was convinced that he must die soon, and wrote the verses beginning,

> The grave is open, soon to close
> On him who sang the charms of Rose.

In the new year of 1860 he settled more cheerfully in his new home. He was well enough to drink three glasses of Chianti on Rose Graves-Sawle's birthday (19th January), and felt "better than I was two years ago", though he could not alight from a carriage without help and hoped he would not fulfil his Bath doctor's prediction that he was "good for another ten years". He began to write English again, as well as Latin; after reading Abelard's letters, he wrote an imaginary conversation between Abelard and Heloise, and during the three months following, four verse dialogues, "Sappho, Alcæus, Anacreon, Phaon", "Theseus and Hippolyta", "Homer, Laertes, Agatha", and "The Trial of Æschylos". The first begins with Sappho saying,

> I wonder at the malice of the herd
> Against us poets. O what calumnies
> Do those invent who can invent nought else!

To which Alcæus replies:

> Idlers show no idleness
> In picking up and spreading false reports.
> Nay, 'tis said also (thing incredible)
> That women carry them from house to house,
> And twirl and sniff them as they would a rose.
> Nothing is lighter than an empty tale,
> Or carried farther on with fresh relays;

No ball do children leap at with more glee,
Catch, and look more triumphant, than do men
At lies.

When he heard of Macaulay's death, he wrote:

His *Lays of Rome* are clever, but the word lays is inapplicable to the poetry of antiquity. His history is partial, his criticism superficial, his style fantastic. I once sat at table between him and Lord Northampton, whom I knew at Rome. . . . At this dinner Lord Northampton chattered, Macaulay was silent. I never talk when I am eating, and I took no notice of either.

He was reading Balzac, as well as novels by James, Trollope, and Harriet Beecher Stowe. Impressed by Schlegel's *Dramatic Art and Literature*, he recalled his personal dislike of Schlegel but rated him and Southey as the only two critics of poetry "worth rubbing the ear and touching the brow for". Schlegel led him to reading "regularly through" all Shakespeare's dramatic works, though not his sonnets, as "I cannot feast on mince-pies and rich puff-paste". Reading an article on Milton, he was interested to find that "his children robbed him as mine have robbed me, but they had it not in their power, if in their will, to be so ungrateful".

Kirkup called on him frequently, and he made many new friends. Isa Blagden, the Brownings' friend, regularly visited him; to her villa on the hills he made in April his first excursion beyond the city gate since his coming to the Via Nunziatina. Through the Storys his lodgings became a resort for American tourists, among them Senator Winthrop and the Boston publisher, James T. Fields, who not only delighted him by promising to have his "Defence" inserted in an American periodical, but proposed to publish a new volume of his poetry and an edition of his collected works. Fields was not a maker of empty promises, but the civil war broke out in America soon after his return and suspended his publishing plans. But the proposal provided an incentive to work, and by April Landor had accumulated enough unpublished verse for a volume of two hundred pages.

Walker's sister, the Countess Baldelli, came often with her two little daughters, remaining till his death so devoted in her attentions that two years later he spoke of her as "my dear old friend the Countess Baldelli". The last young woman to satisfy his pleasure in feminine beauty was Kate Field, the American girl who won the devotion of the brothers, Tom and Anthony Trollope. At the age of twenty she had arrived in Italy from America with an uncle and aunt early in 1859, met Isa Blagden and through her the Brownings, with whom she came to stay at Siena in August 1859, and so met Landor. The Storys told her that "I always put him into a good humor", and Browning wrote to Forster, "Whatever he may profess, the thing he really loves is a pretty girl to talk nonsense with; and he finds comfort in American visitors, who hold him in proper respect."

When she came to Florence to lodge with her mother and to be chaperoned socially by Tom Trollope's wife Theodosia—whom Landor had known twenty years before as Theodosia Garrow—he undertook to teach her Latin. Though she "went each day for her Latin lesson", her lodgings were within walking distance and he called on her several times a week, usually with a bouquet—a nosegay he called it, disdaining the word *bouquet*, "which the French, who distort and abuse everything, have formed out of *boschette*"—of camellias or roses, grown in his own garden, "in which he took great pride". He read Latin with a "majestic flow, and sounding, cataract-like falls and plunges of music". Kate Field, like Mrs. Story, was fascinated by his reminiscences: she "looked with wonder upon a person who remembered Napoleon Bonaparte as a slender young man". Few octogenarians retain a talent for entertaining talk, but Landor had "ready wit and even readier repartee" to embellish "his great learning, varied information, extensive acquaintance with the world's celebrities". Kate Field endorsed Story's admiration for his marvellous memory, which failed him only occasionally in recalling names, when he would exclaim in annoyance, "God bless my soul, I forget everything!"

She relates stories of his tenderness for his Pomeranian dog, Giallo, similar to those told by Mrs. Crosse and Mrs. Lynn Linton of Pomero. Giallo was a present from Story on Landor's return from Siena to Florence, and yapping at the old man's heels, became a sight almost as familiar in Florence as Pomero had been at Bath. He was taught habits like Pomero's, jumping into his master's lap to lay his head against his neck and being indulged in boisterous play after dinner. Landor would break off conversation to address the dog: "no matter upon what subject conversation turned, Giallo's feelings were consulted". He composed doggerel epigrams "to please Giallo", and commemorated their affection in the verses:

> Giallo! I shall not see thee dead,
> Nor raise a stone above thy head,
> For I shall go some years before,
> Where thou wilt leap at me no more.

He was right in thinking that he would suffer no repetition of his grief at losing Pomero; Giallo was still a young dog when his master died, and survived another eight years in the care of the Countess Baldelli. Asked if he thought dogs were admitted to heaven, Landor replied, "Why not? They have all the good and none of the bad qualities of man."

In the first week of July 1860 Landor accompanied the Brownings to Siena for the hot summer months. According to Kate Field and

Mrs. Story, he was "full of wit and sense and all sorts of noble things". Charmed by his company, a lady expressed the hope of meeting him again the following season; Landor replied, "Ah, by that time I shall have gone farther and fared worse!" Told that Pope Pius IX was likely to die, erysipelas having settled in his legs, he remarked, "He has been on his last legs for some time, but depend upon it they are legs that will last—the Devil is always good to his own, you know!" "How surprised St. Peter would be," he said again, "to return to earth and find his apostolic successors living in such a grand house as the Vatican. Ah, they are jolly fishermen!" Mrs. Browning was "often convulsed with laughter at his scorching invective and his extraordinary quick ejaculations, perpetual God-bless-my-souls, &c.". He retained the violence of expression caricatured in Boythorn on such subjects as Louis Napoleon, of whom he wrote to Holyoake on 2nd July, "This wretch, and his uncle, have been the two greatest scourges of Italy," and to Rashleigh Duke the following January, "Of all the conquerors that ever infested Italy the two Napoleons are the most perfidious. The one bartered Venice for a vile woman who deserted him in his adversity, and the other kept the chain on her neck."

As fervent in admiration of Garibaldi as in execration of Napoleon, he expressed the hope, in the same letter to Holyoake, that "Sicily may become independent, and that Garibaldi will condescend to be its king, under the protection of Italy and England". In the previous February, sending to the *Athenæum* his verses on the death of Arndt, he asked, "What would this patriot have thought of the proposal to annex Savoy, and even Nice, to France?" Having no money to subscribe to the fund raised for Garibaldi's Sicilian expedition, he gave Browning his watch to present to the fund. When after a few days Browning persuaded him to take back his watch, he set about writing in Italian an imaginary conversation between "Savonarola and the Prior of San Marco", which was published at Florence as a pamphlet for the benefit of the wounded Tuscans. This Italian version, reminiscent of his *Poche Osservazioni* of nearly forty years before, "gave me some trouble to compose", and he was helped in its revision by Arthur Walker, who came to visit him during the summer. The English version he sent to Mrs. Lynn Linton, who secured its publication in the *London Review* of 22nd September; two other dialogues, in which Garibaldi himself figured, were printed in the *Athenæum*.

On his return to Florence in October he asked Browning for twenty franasconi, as the printing of the Italian pamphlet cost "about twelve franasconi" and he owed "seven or eight" for gilding picture-frames; he wanted besides "only a dozen more for Christmas boxes—and none whatever for all the remainder of next year". As usual, he was too optimistic about the modesty of his requirements. He spent nothing on clothes—"it is my glory to be in rags, in order to help a little the necessitous and the deserving"—but he had no sooner given all he had to one charity than he was asking for an advance to give to another. He was fastidious about comfort and service in his lodgings, and during the winter, when weather kept him much indoors, his letters to Browning in Rome abounded in complaints. "As my teeth are gone . . . I told Mrs. Romagnoli that I would be glad if she would *twice or thrice* in the week dress a chicken or a lamb's head for me"; when "she would not undertake it, pretending she was quite sure that she would never please me", he decided that she had a grievance against him and "after this day I will begin to give a proof how little will content me. A cup of milk and another of chocolate will be my whole maintenance for the remainder of my life". Later he protested that he had "never complained of Mrs. Romagnoli's cooking", and "we continue good friends". He was unable to use his drawing-room because the chimney's smoking "affected my lungs no less than my eyes", and he feared "the landlord will not alter the stove or chimney". When Browning told him that Mrs. Romagnoli had "very little latitude allowed her" as "strict economy is enjoined on us" and "one must be content with one's restricted means", he exclaimed:

My dear Browning, this *shocks* and overthrows me. It makes me fear that I have caused you to assist me in money matters out of your limited means. I did believe and never doubted that my brother Henry, with whom you were in correspondence, had offered to advance the very little I wanted. In an extremely short time I shall want nothing, and my brother would receive from my rents what he had sent for me here in Italy. In the many years since my mother's death there must have been some savings.

Still unable to appreciate that law is unconcerned with equity, he supposed that, as lawyers could obtain damages and costs from his rents, his brother could recover from the same source a debt incurred by himself. He asked Browning to inform his brother that "I am resolved to confine my expenses to £120 a year", being apparently unaware that he was already receiving more than that amount.

French successes made him vexed with politics: "I tremble for Garibaldi in his little island." Reminding Browning of his published opinion that "nothing is so glorious as tyrannicide, nothing so base as assassination", he exclaimed, "O Orsini, Orsini! how glorious, how beneficent to the world would thy achievement have been, if the guilty had fallen and the innocent had not." He grumbled at such "severe and comfortless weather as there can have been in England". When he had his photograph taken and Browning ordered a dozen for his use, he declared, "I have not a dozen friends surviving upon earth . . . In nine days I enter on my eighty-seventh year, and all my contemporaries have left the world." To Kate Field he said, "I have lived too long."

Yet he was still writing. A verse dialogue between "Joan of Arc and Her Judge" was sent to Mrs. Lynn Linton in January, when he asked Walker if he knew of an editor who would give "a few crowns" towards helping Garibaldi's wounded for an imaginary conversation between Virgil and Horace. When this appeared in the *Athenæum* of 9th March 1861, he complained that "Printers are properly called Devils", since "*Virgil* and *Ovid* are made Englishmen", though "they called one another Virgilius and Ovidius". On receiving two guineas for this contribution, he offered the money to Kate Field, who was not well off; for years he had presumed on his age to offer such presents to women friends—with disastrous results in the cases of Mrs. Yescombe and Miss Hooper—and he still sought to assist Mrs. Lynn Linton, reminding her in June 1860 that her letters to him "must never be prepaid, for I am the richer of the two". Kate Field declined the gift, so he broke his rule never to profit from his writings and told Browning, "This will cover all my expenditure, beyond for board and lodging, these two years, excepting for picture frames."

In May 1861 Kate Field moved her lodging to "the new square, a mile distant", and Landor resigned himself sadly to the loss of her society, "for I doubt whether I shall be able to go beyond my short street". Valuing herself on an "artistic temperament" besides her beauty, Kate Field took herself more seriously than even the average young woman of her age, and a letter to her aunt indicated that she did not share Landor's regret for loss of their daily meetings:

Mr. Landor comes to see me every day, bringing me flowers, books, etc.; and although I have the very highest respect for his intellect and derive advantage from his visits, yet I do grudge passing every morning to such comparatively small profit. I console myself by thinking that I am pleasing an old man, and therefore making myself useful. He sent me yesterday all the manuscript scraps in his possession, which I am to edit and publish after his death. What will Mr. Forster's biography say to this? I endeavoured to persuade him otherwise; but he insisted, and I was obliged to accept them in self-defence. . . . Mr. Landor is a great man, the cleverest mind I have ever encountered, as well as being the most wayward,—wayward in temper and fancies. There is much good in him. His latest donations to me are a Virgil, a fine Latin dictionary, and Aubrey de Vere's poems, that I fancy greatly.

Relating her difficulty in refusing gifts from the old man, she remembered "looking over his large collection that once belonged to Barker, the English artist, which Landor had purchased to relieve him of certain debts, and particularly admiring four original sketches by Turner—two in oil and two in india ink—that had been given to Barker by his brother painter: no sooner had I spoken than Landor went in search of the scissors and, had I not earnestly protested, would have cut out the Turners and given them to me".

Though he complained that Giallo "grows horribly fat, because I

LANDOR AT SIENA

From a drawing by William Wetmore Story, July 1859

am unable to walk out with him", Landor had always contrived, even when his cough was bad, to walk the length of the street to Kate's lodging. After she moved, he found some solace in regular visits from his two younger sons. "Good, grave Walter" seems to have behaved little better than Arnold while Landor was at Fiesole, but he and Charles were both sufferers from their elder brother's selfishness and may have been not disinterested in becoming decently attentive to their father. When Landor assigned his estates to his eldest son, Arnold undertook to pay, on his mother's death, an annuity of £150 each to his brothers and sister, but "he now refuses to do it", Landor told Browning, "altho' I gave him everything, and could have disposed of nearly £40,000". Landor asked his brother Henry to write "a line of remonstrance to Arnold on his ingratitude and dishonesty", and Browning to obtain from Forster the letter from Arnold to himself "by which his brothers may legally claim the £150 annuity".

Of old friends few came to remind him of the past—Gibson the sculptor, Sandford, who called in the course of his travels, and Kirkup, "deafer than a post now", who tried "in vain to convert him to the spiritual doctrine", at which, wrote Mrs. Browning, "Landor laughs so loud in reply that Kirkup hears him". He was deprived of a third summer at Siena by Mrs. Browning's death on 29th June, when he wrote:

My dear Browning: Of all your friends who lament your irreparable loss, not one grieves more deeply than I do. I will not say more, I can say nothing more true. Let these few lines, if they can be but of small or no comfort to you, at least manifest the affection of your affectionate

W. Landor.

In such matters his sense of delicacy never failed. For three weeks he avoided intrusion on Browning's sorrow; before accompanying Kate Field to Isa Blagden's, where Browning was staying, he wrote a note of warning lest Browning might think "a visit from an old friend unseasonable".

On 1st August 1861 Browning left Florence, and Landor never saw him again. In the same month Kate Field returned to America. Since the Latin lessons ceased in May, Landor had driven out frequently in a hired carriage with Kate and her mother. Once they drove to Fiesole; as they came within sight of his villa, he "gave a sudden start . . . tears filled his eyes and coursed down his cheeks". As the horses were turned back to Florence, he sighed, "I have seen it probably for the last time," and finished the drive in silent dejection. On their last drive together Kate tried vainly to cheer him: "I shall never see you again," he said, "I cannot live through another winter, nor do I desire to. Life to me is but a counterpart of Dead Sea fruit, and now that you are going away, there is one less link to the chain that binds me."

When she called to say good-bye, he insisted on returning with her to her own door, and staggered down to the waiting carriage with the heavy album that once belonged to Barker "of Bath", as a parting gift to make her "think of the foolish old creature occasionally".

With Kate Field gone, he had no incentive to muster energy for walks. "A walk of a hundred paces tires me out, so that I confine it to my room." As his landlord would not make the alteration—though "to him the advantage will be permanent—to me (God knows) it must be very temporary", he substituted for his bedroom window a glass door, opening upon a terrace, on which he proposed to spend all his October days. Florence was full of visitors for an exhibition, but he declined Countess Baldelli's invitation to escort her there: "I abhor all crowds, and am not fascinated by the eye of kings. I never saw him of Italy when he was here before, and shall not now." He re-read the romances of G. P. R. James; though retaining his high opinion of his old friend's work, he confessed "I doze twenty times in the day when I am reading, which I continue nine hours in the twenty-four".

With approaching winter he developed rheumatism and sciatica; he could not go out, and after keeping his room from November to January, found it painful even to bend over his writing-table. In November he wrote to Browning that his grave was being prepared at Widcombe in the place "fixt upon sixty years ago by a Lady who loved me to her last hour". The parson at Widcombe was retiring, and informed Landor that the grave must be made before the new incumbent came. His friend Sandford, who was living at Bath, paid the bill of ten pounds five shillings for digging and bricking the grave, and for four months Landor worried over the means of repayment. He asked Browning to apply to Arnold for the money, but knowing the futility of appeal in that quarter, Browning applied to Henry Landor, who refused. This news "so affected me that I could not rest one moment in the night".

I hope to live long enough to know that Arnold has sent you the ten pounds. I knew that he, being my heir, must pay the expenses of my funeral, and I supposed he would repay my brother the money advanced for my support. I hope Henry will oblige him to do so. . . . Offer my thanks to my brother Henry for all past kindnesses, and assure him that I will beg Mrs. West to *give* me ten pounds. This is humiliation—but what humiliation have I not undergone.

Lest Browning should think odd that he "thought of asking a lady, altho' an old friend, to *give* me £10", he explained that "I would not ask anyone to *lend* me what I might not be able, and my son Arnold would certainly not be willing, to repay", and he had given to Mrs. West his bust by Gibson and his daughter's by Bartolini.

He was spared this humiliation when his son Walter paid the debt.

Determined "never to receive anything from my family", he was unwilling to accept the gift from Walter; to reimburse him, he gave Walter "pictures which have cost me forty-odd pounds". Once Charles brought him a meat pie, which he refused to accept till he was assured that he could pay the woman who made it. Walter and Charles evidently intended to secure the few personal valuables remaining to their father, at the expense of dutiful attentions which could not be long protracted. Though Landor found "something funny in my making a will . . . all my disposable property not being worth twenty pounds—without the pictures", he was persuaded to make one. As the witnesses were Walter and Charles, the principal beneficiaries, this will was illegal according to English law, but on Landor's death his niece Sophy, deputising for her uncle Henry as executor of the previous will, sought as far as possible to carry out the wishes of both wills. Three valuable pictures, including a Salvator and a Guido, were left to Browning, but he declared himself "more than rewarded for my poor pains by being of use for five years to the grand old ruin of a genius, such as I don't expect to see again", and the three pictures went to Landor's brother Robert, who shortly confided to Forster such charitable memories of the donor.

Probably Landor cherished no illusions about the dutiful attentions of his younger sons; after expressing to Browning, on Christmas Eve 1861, the hope that "I may live long enough to see you once more", he added:

Latterly my son Walter fancied that he found me in worse health than usual. This is not the case. However, he sent Dr. —— to visit me and prescribe. He made me a second visit, and found me well. In fact I did not take his medicine. This perhaps accounts for it.

Apart from crippling sciatica, which prevented his climbing into a carriage even with assistance, he wintered well, his cough being less troublesome than in the previous year. Kirkup, Theodosia Trollope, and Countess Baldelli were his regular visitors, and he received numerous American callers. He believed—apparently wrongly—that James T. Fields had published his "Defence", and Fields put him in correspondence with one or two American editors, to whom he sent copies of the prose and verse which Mrs. Lynn Linton and Arthur Walker received in England.

Commissioned to find a publisher for a small volume of unpublished verse, Walker engaged the services of T. C. Newby. Mainly a publisher of fiction, Newby was found unsatisfactory by the Brontë sisters as publisher of *Wuthering Heights* and *Agnes Grey*; he had published Anthony Trollope's first novel, and Landor may have had his name from Trollope, who was introduced to him by the Tom Trollopes during his visit to Florence in the winter of 1860. The printing was slow; in February 1862 Landor had received "only five long slips—perhaps enough for a sheet", and "only forty-eight pages" reached him by the end of May. Walker was "diligent in their revisal", and Landor hoped soon to send Browning a copy of the volume, to be called *Sweepings from Under the Study Table*.

While awaiting the proofs, he delivered his last words on politics. His American friendships inspired interest in the Civil War; as always, he favoured the cause of the under-dog, an attitude so shocking to Kate Field, a Northerner, that she regarded his letters as evidence of "how a mind once great was tottering ere it fell". He believed the "South-rons" to be "fighting for their acknowledged rights, as established by the laws of the United States", and "the North had no right to violate the Constitution", for "slavery was lawful, execrable as it is"; it was better that "the blacks should be contented slaves than exasperated murderers or drunken vagabonds", as many might become on sudden emancipation, and he suggested an "accomodation", by which slaves should be freed after ten years' service, none should be imported or sold or separated from wife and children, and adequate grants of land should be given to the liberated. He sensed the danger of war between England and America when, in February 1862, he warned her that "France and England will not permit their commerce with the Southern States to be interrupted much longer", citing the "great discontent in Manchester and Leeds" from unemployment, of which he probably heard from Holyoake.

The idea of an "accomodation" inspired a pamphlet of "twenty or more pages", which he sent to Walker to be printed:

My poetry will find but little favor with the public, but I am confident that this will be red eagerly. . . . If Mr. Newby is so occupied that he cannot bring it out within the week after he receives it, throw it [away], for, like fish and venison, it must not stay on the table to get cold.

Pamphlets were not in Newby's line, so Walker took it to Pickering, who excited Landor's indignation by requiring payment for the printing on publication. "I am astounded at the impudence of such publishers," he told Walker:

In England I always paid at the termination of the current year for any trifle I ordered to be printed. It does not become me to make bargains and stipulations with such people. Were I to live a century, instead of a few months, I would never write another line for publication.

But he promised that "the printing of the Letters shall be paid within six weeks after. If only 100 are sold, little will be left owing". He received his copies by 5th June, and asked Walker to send copies to Monckton Milnes, Kenneth Mackenzie, and Mrs. Lynn Linton, but not even the assiduity of such a collector as Thomas J. Wise succeeded in finding a copy of the pamphlet called *Letters of a Canadian.*

His last letter to the press appeared in the *Times* of 26th June 1862. His contempt for royalty inspired disappointment that Garibaldi, instead of establishing a federal republic, had presented the fruits of his successes to King Victor Emmanuel, and he sent Walker a satirical letter, purporting to be written from Leghorn on the return journey from an imaginary visit to Rome. Walker sent it to the *Times* in good faith, but Browning was furious. When Landor explained that he had intended the letter to be anonymous, Browning told Isa Blagden that, since Landor admitted the letter to be a lie, he regarded the explanation as another, and "anything more disgraceful to him or to Walker I cannot easily fancy". His anger probably arose from the embarrassment of explaining to Henry Landor how his brother, represented as living with strict economy at Florence, came to be travelling as far as Rome. His dislike of Walker, to whom he referred derisively as "Hookey", may have been personal, but may have derived from jealousy because Landor entrusted his publishing negotiations to Walker rather than to himself. In the previous February he had offered to correct the proofs of the *Sweepings*, but Landor replied, "I owe you much, but I must not be indebted to you for revising the proof sheets of the volume which is now under the press." He accepted the services of admirers like Julius Hare, Forster, and Walker, but shrank from troubling those whom he regarded as his equal in genius; two years before he had told Browning, "I am ready to dash my head against the wall on reading that you have taken the trouble to transcribe my poetry, while you could be writing much better yourself."

Walker was an unsatisfactory agent. Months passed in awaiting proofs of the *Sweepings*. When they arrived, they contained so many errors that Landor complained how "Doctor Walker, who undertook to revise the proofs, left it to me, week after week, until I had a brain fever for four days and nights, and in my impatience I threw 732 letters and all my papers under the grate". This reminder of the vexation caused by the guardsman's carelessness with the manuscript of the first *Imaginary Conversations* recalls Julius Hare's difficulties in preparing Landor's copy for the press. Probably Landor had contributed to the delay by sending additions and emendations; in correcting errors an army surgeon could hardly be expected to compete in classical scholarship with Julius Hare, and the poems included nearly seventy pages of Latin, which Landor—who had revived his zeal for Latin of forty years before—told Browning were "the best of them".

He had neither health nor patience for proof-correcting. Walter and Charles, who visited him daily, seem to have continually discussed his impending end; like Charles II, Landor might have apologised for taking an unconscionable time over dying. Having paid Walter in pictures for the cost of preparing his grave, he proposed to sell the rest of his pictures to pay the charges for transporting his corpse to England. He ordered an enormous case to contain the pictures, but encountered difficulties with the shippers, who required a valuation of the consignment. By November 1862 he was persuaded by Browning to abandon hope of burial at Widcombe and "to rest my bones at Florence, where my two sons, Walter and Charles, will defray the expenses of my funeral".

Renunciation of his arrangement with Ianthe was likely to inspire sad reflections, and despondency deepened in December, when he told Browning "the chances are against me living thro' the winter". He thought his cough "will carry me off"; "it is high time for me to go too", he wrote to Rose Graves-Sawle on her birthday in January 1863, "nothing I wish more". News of the death of Rose's mother, Mrs. Paynter, came from his niece Kitty with greetings on his eighty-eighth birthday, and he recalled how "I first saw her, when she was only six years old, walking on the burrows at Swansea, led by her sister Rose Aylmer, ten years older".

In the following April he seems to have suffered such a seizure as that of five years before, for on the 27th he wrote to his brother Henry:

Being on my last legs, or rather on no legs at all, I think it right and proper to write to you, and to give you this very unimportant intelligence. For three days and nights I have been insensible. This morning, as you perceive, I can write. It is for the last time I shall take up the pen.

The Honble Mr. Twisleton came yesterday to visit me, and brought to me a letter from my friend Browning.

My sons Walter and Charles have visited me last two evenings. Mrs. L. and her daughter have never come near me nor inquired for me. The Countess Baldelli has come to sit with me every evening, and has brought her three little children with her. She is the daughter of Admiral Walker my old friend.

Adieu, dear Henry, and believe me ever

Your affectionate brother Walter.

On the same day he wrote at greater length to Browning, thanking him for introducing Edward Twisleton, a younger brother of Lord Saye and Sele and a pioneer of educational reform. Ten days later he wrote again to Browning of the pleasure he derived from Twisleton's visits: "Mr. Twisleton adds good sense to good humour and sound scholarship ... he has tolerated my half-deafness, and has nearly cured the other half." During his convalescence in May, Twisleton called "almost every evening", and Landor expressed appreciation of his attentions in the dedication of *Heroic Idyls*: "All my old friends are dead, let their place continue to be supplied by Edward Twisleton."

As he recovered strength, he renewed preparations for impending death. He had promised to give Walker his writing-desk—the desk in which Stephen Wheeler found much material for his *Letters and other Unpublished Writings of Walter Savage Landor*—and on 15th May he sent the desk to Countess Baldelli to be kept for her brother, "as in a little while I must take a long journey, and I shall not be able to take London in my way". He urged Walker to proceed with the printing of the *Sweepings*, now to be entitled *Hellenic Idyls*; "finding myself extremely ill the whole of this week, I do not think it prudent to wait for the last proof-sheet". A few days later he wrote again to Walker:

Above all things I am anxious that no copy of the book be sent to me. God grant me patience to recover from what I have suffered already. The sight of anything relating to this accursed book might drive me distracted for another four days of the delirium it caused.

Countess Baldelli found him on 17th May "apparently better than usual but persuaded that he will not live many days"; by the end of May he was "recovering from my total deafness, and I can write a little, but not long together, nor perhaps very legibly". His son Walter took him for drives in his carratella, and he visited Casa Guidi to see the white slab commemorating the residence of Mrs. Browning. The treachery of his memory for names intensified; though he had been for weeks in daily conversation with Twisleton, he wrote of him to Browning as "our friend Thistlethwaite" and two months later as "Thisleton". His letter to Walker of 15th May was dated, perhaps with deliberate irony, 1st April. But he still went on writing; regularly during the next few months he sent manuscripts to Twisleton and Browning—mostly of verse, like "The Marriage of Helena and Menelaos" and the dialogues, "Endymion and Selene" and "Pythagoras and a Priest of Isis", which Forster printed in his biography from manuscripts supplied by Twisleton. In August he sent Browning "an article for the *Times*", which either Browning suppressed or the *Times* ignored in displeasure at the Leghorn hoax.

He fretted at the continual delay in publishing *Hellenic Idyls*. "I entrusted them to a friend who I believed would have attended to the printing," he wrote in July; "it seems he was too occupied in things more important." His son Walter—probably with no intention of carrying out a commission so expensive—sought to appease his agitation by employing a Florentine printer to publish the book. In September he promised Browning the first bound copy, as Newby was publishing the volume, finally entitled *Heroic Idyls*, during the following month. Walker ignored the injunction that no copy should be sent to him, and Landor fell into a passion over the printer's corrections of his spelling. Browning exaggerated in telling Isa Blagden that Landor "and Walker are at daggers-drawn—he accusing Walker of various delinquencies, quite forgetting his own stupidity,—if these be truly charged,—in getting into a passion of wonder over the perfection of the man": in fact Landor complained to Walker of being made to write "endurated" for "indurated", "spread" for "sprad", and "Ptolemies" for "Ptolemais", but concluded in gentle reproach, "God has preserved me from cutting my throat after this . . . May you be happier than your affectionate W. L."

Aware that his sons would appropriate everything on his death, he gave away such of his belongings as he thought his friends would value. Frequently he sent parcels of books to Browning, mostly for Browning's son; he also sent books to Mrs. West. He sent pictures to London to be sold by Christie's, intending the proceeds for Mrs. Lynn Linton; when her husband churlishly refused to let her accept the gift, Landor found a way to evade the veto—he asked Browning, "When you have repaid yourself for the carriage, let me have the rest," and writing at Christmas to console his "dear daughter" on the death of her stepson, he enclosed two banknotes, as "I happen to have more than I want".

During the autumn he was well enough to enjoy the visits of Walker, Sandford, and Mrs. West, but in November his cough became so troublesome that he did not care "whether I was to live or die". In December he was rid of bronchitis but "so tortured by rheumatism and sciatica" that for nearly the whole month "I have been so helpless as to be unable to get into my bed without the laborious help of two persons".

Annoyed at receiving "a most insolent letter" from somebody proposing to write his biography, he consulted Twisleton, who pointed out that his career and personality were bound to attract biographers, that he might have thought himself fortunate in the offer by a man of letters so distinguished as Forster, and that it was a pity he had quarrelled with Forster. Landor replied:

Do not think I bear any malice towards Mr. Forster. I forget, and have long forgotten, what caused my correspondence to cease. Certainly I saw reason for it at the time, and he must also have seen it, otherwise he would have come to an explanation. Both quarrels and explanations are too troublesome for me. What is dropt I never stoop to pick up. Of all things difficult to bear is malice. . . . It gives an unwholesome warmth and exposes to ridicule the wearer.

On Twisleton's advice he wrote to Forster:

Well do I know the friendship you had for me, and have grieved over its interruption. I would not now write but for the promise you once held out to me that you might consent to be my biographer.

Relating the proposal of the undesirable aspirant, he asked, "If you still retain a thought of becoming my biographer, I hope you will protect me from this injustice," and ended with a hint of reproach for Forster's desertion in the Yescombe trouble:

> How often have I known you vindicate from unmerited aspersions honest literary men! Unhappily no friend has been found hitherto who takes any such interest in
> Walter Landor.

Within three weeks he was enabled to write "instantly on receiving your generous and manly letter" that "sciatica has deprived me both of locomotion and of sleep, but not of gratitude", and thenceforward Forster received regular bulletins about the old man's declining health.

His sons Walter and Charles came each evening to undress and put him to bed; soon he insisted that both should sleep at his lodgings because he feared "their returning at night to the villa on account of brigands". In January he sent his brother Henry birthday greetings and "hearty thanks for the continual acts of your kindness to me".

> I do not expect to live many days beyond my birthday, so that what I am now writing to you is probably for the last time. It will be a great comfort to me to hear that you suffer less than I do. Sciatica cramps me sadly. It is late and with difficulty that I creep out of my bed. Many friends, English and strangers, come to visit me, but I can receive few. My earing [*sic*] and sight are almost gone.

His old friend Kirkup called regularly till he heard that Landor did not enjoy his visits, because "we are both as deaf as posts, and it brings me the bronchitis to speak audibly". Kirkup then "went just enough to show that I did not take offence, and I made my visits short", but finally ceased his visits after meeting Landor in the street, wheeled in a chair by his son Charles; the son stopped to speak, but the old man "hardly noticed" him.

In such a querulous mood young Algernon Swinburne found him in March 1864, when, bringing a letter of introduction from Milnes, he "hunted out the most ancient of the demi-gods". Perhaps Landor was disconcerted by the young man's exaggerated mannerisms; perhaps he supposed that Swinburne was the undesirable aspirant-biographer. Swinburne "found him, owing I suspect to the violent weather, too much weakened and confused to realise the fact of the introduction without distress . . . he seemed so feeble and incompatible that I came away in a grievous state of disappointment and depression". Back at his hotel, he wrote "a line of apology and explanation . . . expressing (as far as was expressible) my immense admiration and reverence in the plainest and sincerest way I could manage", and received in reply an invitation to come again. This time he found Landor "as alert, brilliant, and altogether delicious as I suppose others may have found him twenty years since", and wrote to Milnes:

I have got the one thing I wanted with all my heart. If both or either of us die to-morrow, at least to-day he has told me that my presence here has made him happy; he said more than that—things for which of course I take no credit to myself but which are not the less pleasant to hear from such a man. There is no other man living from whom I should so much have prized any expression of acceptance or goodwill in return for my homage, for all other men as great are so much younger, that in his case one sort of reverence serves as the lining for another. My grandfather was upon the whole *mieux conservé*, but he had written no *Hellenics*. In answer to something that Mr. Landor said to-day of his own age, I reminded him of his equals and predecessors, Sophocles and Titian; he said he should not live up to the age of Sophocles—not see ninety. I don't see why he shouldn't, if he has people about him to care for him as he should be cared for. I should like to throw up all other things on earth and devote myself to playing valet to him for the rest of his days. I would black his boots if he wore any—*moi*. He has given me the shock of adoration which one feels at thirteen towards great men. . . . I told him, as we were talking of poems and such things, that his poems had first given me inexplicable pleasure and a sort of blind relief when I was a small fellow of twelve. My first recollection of them is *The Song of Hours* in the *Iphigenia* . . . I could hardly tell you what pleasures I have had to-day in a half-hour's intercourse with him.

As Landor died before he could receive the dedication of *Atalanta in Calydon*, Swinburne added an elegy in Greek while retaining the dedicatory inscription, so "that though losing the pleasure I may not lose the honour of inscribing in front of my work the highest of contemporary names".

Landor told Swinburne that he "had no belief or opinion whatever" on the "doctrine of a future state", but "was sure of one thing . . . that whatever was to come was best—the right thing, or the thing that ought to come". Among his papers was a letter from Anaxagoras to Pericles, evidently intended for insertion in a future edition of *Pericles and Aspasia*:

It is part of your wisdom, O Pericles, to abstain so totally, as you tell me you do, from all disquisitions on theology. . . . It is better to be idle than to run after what never can be reacht. We take the gods as we find them, and there we leave them. Morals are not to be improved by the tongue turning them over. Our conscience teaches them and is their best interpreter.[1]

A draft of one of his last verse dialogues, "Pythagoras and a Priest of Isis", concludes:

> We priests of Isis
> Acknowledge duly our progenitor
> Whose moral features still remain unchanged
> In many, thro' all times.
>   Did ever Ape
> (As kindred nations have been doing since)
> Tear limb from limb his brother, grin to see

[1] Printing the letter in *Some Landor Waifs*, 1932, Dr. M. F. Ashley-Montagu deduced from the handwriting that it was written between 1850 and 1855.

His native bush and his blue babes enwrapt
In flames about the crib for winding sheet?
There live in other lands, from ours remote,
The intolerant and ferocious who insist
That all shall worship what themselves indite.
We never urge this stiff conformity.
Forms ever present are our monitors,
Nor want they flesh and blood, nor shed they any.
No creed is it of ours that Gods descend
In human shape and substance to beget
Another God who leaves no trace behind,
No likeness of himself, no kept command.
Ours teach us silently; let ev'ry man
Leave each man his choice, whether he incline
To worship sculptured block or pictured plank.
But only let him rise from his knees,
Abstain from sprinkling blood around the base
Nor drive his kindred from parental door.[1]

In religion, as in politics, he retained his early faith unshaken by life experience—a faith as simple as that of the ancient Greek philosophers or of Llewelyn Powys's *Damnable Opinions*.

Mrs. Romagnoli related how Landor rang for her at two in the morning on May Day, and asked for his room to be lighted, for the windows to be thrown open, and for pen, ink, paper, and the date. Having written a few lines of verse, he leaned back and said, "I shall never write again. Put out the lights and draw the curtains." Beyond a few brief notes to friends, he kept his word.

During May he received visits from Augustus Hare and Aubrey de Vere; Hare reported, "He is terribly altered, has lost the use of his hearing and almost of his speech, and cannot move from his chair to his bed." He could still read; Aubrey de Vere found him with a volume of Dickens in his hand, and perhaps the last book he read was Forster's *Life of Sir John Eliot*—a present from the author. He sent his "love to noble Dickens"—once even wrote a note to him, enclosed with one to Forster.

To Browning he wrote on 22nd August:

I am nearly blind and totally deaf. My son Charles undres[ses] me, and I do not give any trouble. I dine on soup. What can you think of the enclosed! I am unable to step from stair to another, nor have I for several months.

The "enclosed" was a statement of grievances against the owner of his lodgings, set out with the same terse precision as his letters to Baker

[1] The last eleven lines, as given by Dr. Ashley-Montagu, differ from the version printed from Twistleton's manuscript in Forster's biography.

Gabb about his Llanthony tenants fifty years before. To Forster he wrote on 9th September:

I lost my senses for five days and nights in consequence of a verdict obliging me to pay so vast a sum for exposing [Mrs. Yescombe]. I must leave off. My head is splitting. You will print what I sent you.

Eight days later, on 17th September 1864, he died. For three days he had refused to eat, so weakening himself that a bout of coughing stopped his heart.

He was buried in the English cemetery at Florence; as Browning reported, "he was followed to the grave by two of his sons, and nobody else—the grand old solitary man, beset by weaknesses just as, in his own words, 'the elephant is devoured by ants in his inaccessible solitudes'." So his plans went astray to the last; Ianthe had chosen two resting-places for him, but he lay neither at Widcombe nor under the mimosas she had planted at Fiesole. All his life it had been so: his early ambition as a poet, his projected marriage with Dorothy Lyttelton, his love for a married woman, his luckless marriage, his plan for a model estate, his paradise at Fiesole, his devotion to his children—worst irony of all, one of the most lucid thinkers of his time was disparaged as an eccentric.

Of Catullus he wrote: "there is little of the creative, little of the constructive, in him: that is, he has conceived no new varieties of character; he has built up no edifice in the intellectual world; but he always is shrewd and brilliant; he often is pathetic; and he sometimes is sublime". So much might be said of Landor as a poet. "Without the sublime," he said, "there can be no poet of the first order." His poetry was too lavish in quantity to be even in quality, but he achieved the sublime more often than any outside the inner circle of supreme masters, though his gems may be found sometimes in unworthy settings.

Of his prose it is impossible to turn a page without being impressed by the presence of the sublime; no writer has ever possessed more confidently the genius for the telling phrase, the illuminating image, the reverberating melody of just expression. "A writer as great as Shakespeare surely," wrote George Moore in *Confessions of a Young Man.* "The last heir of a noble family. All that follows Landor is decadent." Landor himself declared, "I shall dine late, but the dining-room will be well lighted, the guests few and select." But the march of materialism leaves the humanities more than ever unheeded; dust and cobwebs cluster the chandeliers while Landor's dining-room is ignored for scrambles in the cafeteria.

"The best thing is to stand above the world; the next is, to stand apart from it on any side," he wrote in "Barrow and Newton"; "you *may* attain the first: in trying to attain it, you are certain of the second".

Apart and above he still stands, as he stood in life, though, as Swinburne said, "he had won for himself such a double crown of glory in verse and in prose as has been worn by no other Englishman but Milton".

And with that special object of his lifelong veneration he had likewise in common other claims upon our reverence to which no third competitor among English poets can equally pretend. He had the same constancy to the same principles, the same devotion to the same ideal of civic and heroic life; the same love, the same loyalty, the same wrath, scorn, and hatred, for the same several objects respectively; the same faith in the example and kinship to the spirit of the republican Romans, the same natural enjoyment and mastery of their tongue.

Swinburne, too, supplies his biographer with a fitting conclusion in the fiftieth and last stanza of his *Song for the Centenary of Walter Savage Landor*:

> Poet whose large-eyed loyalty of love
>   Was pure toward all high poets, all their kind
> And all bright words and all sweet works thereof;
>   Strong like the sun, and like the sunlight kind;
> Heart that no fear but every grief might move
>   Wherewith men's hearts were bound of powers that
>   bind;
> The purest soul that ever proof could prove
>   From taint of tortuous or of envious mind;
>   Whose eyes elate and clear
>   Nor shame nor ever fear
>   But only pity or glorious wrath could blind;
>   Name set for love apart,
>   Held lifelong in my heart,
>   Face like a father's toward my face inclined;
>   No gifts like thine are mine to give,
> Who by thine own words only bid thee hail, and live.

CHRONOLOGY OF EVENTS IN LANDOR'S LIFE

1775	30th January	Born at Warwick.
1779–1782		School at Knowle.
1783	January	Goes to Rugby School.
1791	December	Removed from Rugby.
1792		At Ashbourne with Rev. William Langley.
	13th November	Matriculates at Trinity College, Oxford.
1793	January	Begins residence at Oxford.
1794	June	Rusticated from Oxford.
	Autumn	At Tenby.
1795	January–May	Lodging at Beaumont Street, Portland Place, London.
	May	*Poems* published by Cadell & Davies.
		Returns to Tenby (? living with Nancy Jones).
1796	October	Meets Rose Aylmer at Swansea.
1797	Early months	Writing *Gebir* at Swansea.
	Late autumn	Electioneering at Warwick.
1798	July	*Gebir* published.
1798–1801		Between London, Swansea, and Warwick.
1800	May	*Poems from the Arabic and Persian* published.
1801	Early months	In London and Oxford.
1802		*Poetry by the Author of Gebir* published.
	July–August	Visits Paris.
1803–1807		Mainly at Bath.
1803	February	New edition of *Gebir* published.
		Meets Ianthe (Sophia Jane Swift).
1805	3rd November	Death of his father.
1806	Spring	*Simonidea* published.
1807	Summer	Visits the Lakes.
1808	April	Meets Southey at Bristol.
	May	*Guy's Porridge Pot* published.
	Summer	Purchases Llanthony Abbey and sells his Rugeley estate.
	August	Goes to Spain as a volunteer.
	November	Returns from Spain.
1809	January	*Letters to Riquelme* published.
		Living at Bath (? in South Parade).

1810		*Ode ad Gustavum Regem* published by Valpy.
	April	Defends freedom of the press.
	Autumn	Begins writing *Count Julian.*
1811	January	Meets Julia Thuillier at Bath.
	24th May	Marries Julia Thuillier.
	June	Goes to live in rooms adjoining Llanthony Abbey.
1812	January	Charles Betham arrives at Llanthony.
	February	*Count Julian* published.
	March	*Commentary on the Memoirs of Fox* suppressed.
	August	Application for magistracy refused.
	October	Canvasses against Tories at General Election.
	November	Baker Gabb becomes his attorney.
1813	Spring	Quarrels with Betham.
	Summer	Moves into new house at Llanthony.
	October	Leaves Llanthony for Swansea.
	December	*Letters of Calvus* published.
1814	31st March	Last letter to Gabb from Swansea.
	April	Sued for libel by the Bethams.
	27th May	Sails from Weymouth for Jersey.
	October	Arrives at Tours.
1815	April	Meets Francis Hare at Tours.
	Autumn	*Idyllia* published.
	2nd October	Robert Landor arrives at Tours.
	Late October	Leaves Tours for Como.
	December	Suspected as a spy on the Princess of Wales.
1817	June	Southey's visit to Como.
1818	5th March	His eldest son Arnold born at Como.
	September	Ordered by the authorities to leave Como.
	October	At Albaro, near Genoa.
	November	Settles at Pisa.
1819	Spring	Leaves Pisa for Pistoia.
		Sponsalia Polyxenae published.
	Autumn	Returns to Pisa.
1820	6th March	His daughter Julia born at Pisa.
	Summer	*Idyllia Heroica* published at Pisa.
	4th December	Refuses to reveal "bedchamber secrets" of Queen Caroline.
1821	March	Publishes *Poche Osservazioni.*
	April	Southey's *Vision of Judgment* published.
	Summer	Leaves Pisa for Palazzo Lozzi, Florence.
		Writing *Imaginary Conversations.*
	November	Moves to Palazzo Medici, Florence.
	December	Byron's Appendix to *The Two Foscari.*
1822	March	First *Imaginary Conversations* sent to Longmans.
	August	Julius Hare undertakes publishing negotiations.
	13th November	His second son Walter born at Florence.

1823	April	John Taylor undertakes to publish *Imaginary Conversations.*
	July	Southey-Porson dialogue in *London Magazine.*
		Begins friendship with Charles Brown.
		Meets Leigh Hunt at Florence.
1824	March	First two volumes of *Imaginary Conversations* published.
	Autumn	At Castel Ruggiero for two months.
1825	March	Hazlitt at Florence.
	6th March	Death of Dr. Parr.
	April	Quarrel with Taylor—publication of third volume of *Imaginary Conversations* suspended.
	5th August	His third son Charles born at Florence.
	September	Takes three years' lease of Villa Castiglione as summer residence.
	November	Jefferson Hogg's visit.
1826	January	Visits Rome with Francis Hare.
	May	Second edition of *Imaginary Conversations* published by Colburn.
	September	Portrait by William Bewick.
1827	June	Meets the Blessingtons and Count D'Orsay.
	July	At Villa Castiglione.
	August	Visits Naples with Lord Blessington.
	Late autumn	Moves from Palazzo Medici to Casa Cremani, Florence.
1828	February	At Casa Castellani, Florence.
	Spring	Meets Joseph Ablett.
	May	Colburn publishes third volume of *Imaginary Conversations.*
	June	Bust modelled by Gibson.
	Autumn	Moves to Palazzo Giugni, Florence.
		Begins friendship with Sir Robert Lawley (Lord Wenlock).
1829	April	Threatened expulsion from Florence.
	May	At the Baths of Lucca—Duncan publishes fourth and fifth volumes of *Imaginary Conversations.*
	25th May	Death of Lord Blessington.
	7th June	Returns to Florence.
	Autumn	Leaves Florence for Villa Gherardescha, Fiesole.
	8th October	Death of his mother.
		Ianthe visits Florence.
1830	August	Crabb Robinson at Florence.
1831	Spring	Duel with Antoir averted.
	April	*Gebir, Count Julian, and Other Poems* published.
		Writing *High and Low Life in Italy* (published in Leigh Hunt's *Monthly Repository*, August 1837 to April 1838).
	Autumn	Trelawny's *Adventures of a Younger Son* published.

GG

1832	May	Visits England.
	June	Visits Southey and meets Wordsworth.
	28th September	Visits Lamb at Edmonton.
	29th September	Visits Coleridge at Highgate.
	October	Sails to Rotterdam with Julius Hare—meets Schlegel and Arndt at Bonn.
	30th November	Arrives back at Fiesole.
1833	May	Emerson visits Fiesole.
	Summer	Monckton Milnes at Fiesole.
		Friendship with G. P. R. James
1834	April	N. P. Willis at Fiesole.
	May	MacCarthy employed as tutor.
	23rd July	Death of Coleridge.
	Autumn	*Citation and Examination of William Shakspeare* published.
	29th December	Death of Charles Lamb.
1835	March	Mrs. Paynter at Fiesole.
	April	Leaves Fiesole and his family.
	Summer	At Florence and Lucca, writing *Pericles and Aspasia*.
	September	Returns to England.
1836	February	Settles at Clifton to write *Letters of a Conservative*.
	March	*Pericles and Aspasia* published.
	April	*Letters of a Conservative* published.
	May	First stay at Gore House—meets John Forster.
	26th May	First night of Talfourd's *Ion*.
	June	Returns to Clifton by Oxford and Cheltenham.
	July–September	At Heidelberg.
	21st August	First contribution to the *Examiner*.
	September	*Terry Hogan* issued.
	October	Settles at Penrose Cottage, Clifton.
	November	Visited by Southey.
	December	*A Satire on Satirists* published.
1837	June–November	At Torquay with Kenyon and at Plymouth with Brown.
	November	Settles at 35 St. James's Square, Bath—friendship with Napier.
	December	*The Pentameron and Pentalogia* published.
1838	May	At Gore House—meets Carlyle, Macaulay, etc.
	27th June	In London for the coronation.
	17th July	Death of his sister Ellen.
	August	At Southampton and Isle of Wight.
	September	Visits G. P. R. James at Petersfield.
	Oct.–Nov.	Writing *Andrea of Hungary* and *Giovanna of Naples* (published April 1839).
1839	March	Lady Bulwer's proposed dedication of *Cheveley*.
	May	At Gore House—meets Louis Napoleon.
	June	At Warwick—attacks Lord Brougham in the *Examiner*.

	Sept.–Nov.	Letters on Middle-Eastern politics.
1840	January	At Gore House—meets Henry Reeve and R. H. Horne.
	27th February	Dickens and Forster at Bath.
	March	Crabb Robinson at Bath.
	June	At Warwick, where his sons fail to arrive from Italy.
	Aug.–Sept.	At Torquay and Exmouth.
	October	At Llanbedr and Cheltenham.
	December	*Fra Rupert* published.
1841	April	Crabb Robinson at Bath.
	5th May	Arrives at Gore House.
	11th May	Meets his son Walter in Paris.
	28th June	Visits his brother Robert at Birlingham.
	Aug.–Sept.	At Warwick and Colton.
	December	Stays at Gore House and with Dickens.
	Christmas	At Warwick.
1842	15th January	Death of Francis Hare.
		Contributes to *Foreign Quarterly Review* and *Blackwood's Magazine*.
	May	His son Arnold arrives at Bath.
	June–September	Visits Gore House, Warwick, Devon with the Paynters, Gore House again, and Julius Hare at Hurstmonceaux.
	21st October	Dickens and Longfellow at Bath.
	Nov.–Dec.	Visits Sir John Dean Paul and Sir Charles Elton.
1843		Writes essay on Petrarca and begins preparation of collected *Works*.
	21st March	Death of Southey.
	May	Walter and Julia at Bath.
	June–August	With Walter and Julia to Warwick, Llanbedr, Colton, Birlingham, and Plymouth.
1844	January	Dickens and Forster at Bath—assigns copyrights to Forster.
	April	Moves from 35 to 1 St. James's Square, Bath.
	September	Returns to Bath from visits to Warwick and Clifton.
		Writing verse dramas, idylls, and imaginary conversations.
1845	30th January	Forster at Bath.
	August	Visits Warwick and Colton.
	September	At Budleigh Salterton.
	22nd November	Verses to Browning in *Morning Chronicle*.
1846	18th February	Rose Paynter's marriage.
	May	At Gore House.
	June	*The Works of Walter Savage Landor* published in two volumes.
	July	Visits Birlingham and Warwick.

	August	Stays with Lord Nugent at Stowe.
	September	Moves from No. 1 to 2 or 42 St. James's Square, dines with Louis Napoleon, and visits Andrew Crosse.
		Collecting Latin verses for *Poemata et Inscriptiones* (published July 1847).
	December	Moves to 36 St. James's Square—illness.
1847	May	At Gore House.
	June	Visits Julius Hare at Hurstmonceaux.
	July	Advocates union of Spain and Portugal and an end of guarantees—visits Birlingham and Warwick.
	August	Visits the Graves-Sawles at Restormel.
	November	*Hellenics* published, with dedication to Pope Pius IX.
1848	9th January	Death of Joseph Ablett.
	February	*The Italics of Walter Savage Landor* published.
	March–April	Letters on Poland and Hungary.
	May	*Imaginary Conversation . . . on the Affairs and Prospects of Italy* published.
	July	Visits Birlingham and Warwick.
	August	Visits Restormel.
	Oct.–Dec.	Letters on foreign affairs in *Examiner*.
1849	30th January	Eliza Lynn meets Dickens and Forster.
	March	Leaves St. James's Square for 3 Rivers Street.
	19th May	Open letter to Kossuth.
	4th June	Death of Lady Blessington.
		Third visit of his son Walter.
	July	Death of his brother Charles.
	August	At Warwick.
	September	Visits Llanbedr and publishes *Statement of Occurrences at Llanbedr*.
	May–November	Letters on foreign affairs in *Examiner*.
1850	Jan.–Feb.	Political letters in *Examiner*.
	May	In London, staying with Kenyon and with Forster.
	July	Carlyle at Rivers Street.
	July–August	Appeals for the Hungarians.
	Aug.–Sept.	Attacks the Pope and predicts war with Russia.
	26th November	Death of Lord Nugent.
1851	January	*Five Scenes* of Beatrice Cenci in *Fraser's Magazine*.
	February	*Popery: British and Foreign* published.
	June–August	"Nicholas and Nesselrode" and "Antonelli and Gemeau" in *Examiner*.
	July	In London.
	31st July	Death of Ianthe.
	August	At Warwick.
	September	Visits Kenyon at Wimbledon and Mrs. West at Lymington.

	Sept.–Dec.	"Letters to Cardinal Wiseman" in *Examiner*.
	December	*Tyrannicide* published.
1852	June–October	Visits Kenyon at Wimbledon, Hare at Hurst-monceaux, Warwick, Knowle, Cheltenham, Birlingham, and Andrew Crosse at Fyne Court.
	23rd October	"The Coming Empire" in *Examiner*.
1853	19th February	"Archbishop of Florence and Madiai" in *Examiner*.
	April	*Imaginary Conversations of Greeks and Romans* published.
	Summer	Working on *Last Fruit Off an Old Tree* (published November).
	August	Last visit to Warwick.
	December	Letters on Czarist aggression in *Examiner*.
1854	24th February	Death of his sister Elizabeth.
	June	*Letters of an American, mainly on Russia and Revolution* published.
1855	23rd January	Death of Julius Hare.
	17th March	Begins series of political letters to the *Atlas*.
	July	In London—visits Sir William Napier.
1856	January	*Antony and Octavius* published.
	March	Death of his dog Pomero.
	April	"Alfieri and Metastasio" and "Menander and Epicurus" in *Fraser's Magazine*
	November	*Letter from W. S. Landor to R. W. Emerson* published.
	Nov.–Dec.	Illness.
	27th December	Statement in *Bath Express* on *Yescombe v. Roche*.
1857	22nd May	Makes his will.
	30th May	Letter from Geraldine Hooper's father.
	Early June	*Walter Savage Landor and the Honourable Mrs. Yescombe* published.
	Late June	*Mr. Landor Threatened* published.
	27th July	Forster's settlement with the Yescombes.
	September	Forster at Bath.
1858	January	*Dry Sticks, Fagoted by Walter Savage Landor* published.
	14th January	Orsini's attempted assassination of Napoleon III.
	17th March	Letter to the *Times* denying countenance of Orsini.
	28th March	Suffers a seizure.
	May	Convalescent.
	June	The Yescombes issue writ for libel.
	12th July	Arrives at Forster's London chambers.
	23rd July	At Boulogne.
	23rd August	Convicted of libel at Bristol Assizes.
	27th August	Arrives at Fiesole.
1859	May	*Mr. Landor's Remarks* issued by Holyoake.
	June	Tries to stab himself.

GG*

	Early July	Leaves Fiesole to be sheltered by Browning.
	July–October	At Siena.
	November	Established by Browning at 2671 Via Nunziatina, Florence.
	December	New edition of *Hellenics* published.
		Ceases communication with Forster.
1860	12th February	Death of Sir William Napier.
		Writing "Homer, Laertes, Agatha" and other verse dialogues.
	July–October	With the Brownings at Siena.
		Writing for Garibaldi's cause.
1861	29th June	Mrs. Browning's death.
	August	Browning and Kate Field leave Italy.
	November	His grave dug at Widcombe.
1862	February–May	Preparing "Sweepings from Under the Study Table".
	May	*Letters of a Canadian* published.
	26th June	Last letter to the *Times*.
	Winter	Illness.
1863	April	Another seizure.
	Summer	Resumes writing verse, "Pythagoras and a Priest of Isis," and "The Marriage of Helena and Menelaos".
	October	*Heroic Idyls* published.
	December	Resumes correspondence with Forster.
	Winter	Crippled by rheumatism and sciatica.
1864	March	Swinburne's visit.
	1st May	Writes verse for the last time.
	May	Augustus Hare's last visits.
	9th September	Last letter to Forster.
	17th September	Death at Florence.

BIBLIOGRAPHY OF AUTHORITIES

Author's Note.—In my *Savage Landor* (1941) I expressed gratitude to Miss Blanche Baker-Gabb, of The Chain, Abergavenny, for the use of over fifty unpublished letters from Landor to her ancestor, together with other letters and documents relative to Landor's affairs at Llanthony; to Mr. Walter Noble Landor, of Chadscroft, Rugeley, for his transcripts of the correspondence between Landor and members of his family, as well as for much miscellaneous information; to Dr. M. F. Ashley-Montagu for generously placing at my disposal materials he had collected for a projected biography of Landor; and to Mr. J. Alex. Symington, of Leeds, for supplying transcripts of Landor manuscripts and letters formerly in the possession of T. J. Wise, including a manuscript draft of Landor's "Defence" (quoted in Chapter 18 of the present book). I have since been indebted to many correspondents for details of information, such as that about Alfieri from Sir Henry McAnally noted on page 61; to them I record here collectively the gratitude I have already expressed to them personally, as also to members of the staffs of many libraries and newspapers. Particularly I am grateful for the courtesy extended to me and to my representatives by the Bodleian Library, the British Museum, the Victoria and Albert Museum, the Bath City Library, and the filing department of the *Bath Chronicle*, and for assistance in research to Miss Sally Connely and Mr. Derek Portman.

My greatest debt—as must be the debt of all future biographers of Landor—is to Mr. Robert H. Super, of the University of Michigan, who began his researches more than twenty years ago as an undergraduate at Oxford. To his work I have referred at the end of Chapter 1 and frequently in footnotes; while I often disagree with his interpretations of Landor's character and conduct, and lament his limited sympathy with his subject, I have nothing but admiration for the pertinacity and precision of his research, evidence of which appears in the meticulous source-references that occupy more than a hundred closely-printed pages of his *Walter Savage Landor: A Biography* (New York University Press, 1954) and in his bibliographical study, *The Publication of Landor's Works* (London, The Bibliographical Society, 1954).

Owing to his long life and his having been a literary celebrity during its last forty years, Landor figures in innumerable memoirs and reminiscences of his juniors. The appended list makes no attempt to enumerate all the works consulted in the preparation of this book, but includes those authorities either quoted or referred to in the narrative, here given under subject-headings to obviate the disfigurement of textual notes.

AINSWORTH: *William Harrison Ainsworth and His Friends*, by S. M. Ellis, 2 vols., 1911.

ALLINGHAM: *Letters to William Allingham*, ed. H. Allingham and E. Baumer Williams, 1911.

APPERLEY: *My Life and Times*, by "Nimrod" (Charles Apperley) in *Fraser's Magazine*, January to December 1842.

ASHLEY-MONTAGU: "Three Unknown Portraits of Walter Savage Landor", by M. F. Ashley-Montagu, *The Colophon*, vol. ii, no. 2; "Some Landor Waifs", by M. F. Ashley-Montagu, *Review of English Studies*, January 1932.

BETHAM: *A House of Letters*, ed. Ernest Betham, n.d.

BEWICK: *Life and Letters of William Bewick*, ed. Thomas Landseer, 2 vols., 1871.

BIRCH: "Some Unpublished Letters of W. S. Landor" (to Walter Birch), ed. Rev. E. H. R. Tatham, *Fortnightly Review*, February 1910.

BLACKWOOD: *William Blackwood and His Sons*, by Mrs. Oliphant and Mrs. Gerald Porter, 3 vols., 1897–98; *Blackwood's Magazine*, January 1854.

BLESSINGTON: *The Idler in Italy*, by the Countess of Blessington, 3 vols., 1839; *Literary Life and Correspondence of the Countess of Blessington*, by R. R. Madden, 3 vols., 1855; *The Blessington Papers*, ed. Alfred Morrison, 1895; "Landor-Blessington Papers" in *Literary Anecdotes of the Nineteenth Century*, ed. W. Robertson Nicoll and T. J. Wise, 1895; *The Most Gorgeous Lady Blessington*, by J. Fitzgerald Molloy, 2 vols., 1896; *Blessington-D'Orsay: A Masquerade*, by Michael Sadleir, 1933; *Count D'Orsay: The Dandy of Dandies*, by Willard Connely, 1952.

BLOXAM: *Companion to the Rugby School Register*, by T. L. Bloxam, 1871.

BOYLE: *Mary Boyle: Her Book*, 1901; "Some Letters of Walter Savage Landor", ed. James Russell Lowell, *Century Magazine*, February 1888.

BROOKFIELD: *Mrs. Brookfield and Her Circle*, by Charles and Frances Brookfield, 2 vols., 1905.

BROUGHAM: *Lord Brougham and the Whig Party*, by Arthur Aspinall, 1939.

BROWN: *Shakespeare's Autobiographical Poems*, by Charles Armitage Brown, 1838; *Some Letters and Miscellanea of Charles Brown*, ed. Maurice Buxton Forman, 1937; *Letters of John Keats*, ed. M. B. Forman, 2nd ed., 1935; *The Emigrants*, by Hector Bolitho and John Mulgan, n.d. (1939); *The Keats Circle*, by H. E. Rollins, 1948; *John Keats: The Living Year*, by Robert Gittings, 1954.

BROWNING: *Letters of Elizabeth Barrett Browning*, ed. F. G. Kenyon, 2 vols., 1898; *Letters of Robert Browning and Elizabeth Barrett*, 1845–46, 2 vols., 1899; *Elizabeth Barrett Browning in Her Letters*, by Percy Lubbock, 1906; *Letters of Robert Browning*, ed. T. L. Hood, 1933; *Robert Browning and Julia Wedgwood, a Broken Friendship*, ed. R. Curle, 1937; *Family of the Barrett*, by Jeannette Marks, 1938; *Poetical Works of Robert Browning*, 2 vols., 1896; *Robert Browning*, by G. K. Chesterton, 1903; *Life of Robert Browning*, by Edward Dowden, 1904; *The Immortal Lovers*, by Frances Winwar, 1950; *Robert Browning: A Portrait*, by Betty Miller, 1952.

BULWER: *Bulwer: A Panorama*, by Michael Sadleir, 1931; *Life of Rosina Lady Lytton*, by Louisa Devey, 1887; "Reminiscences of W. S. Landor," by Lady Lytton Bulwer, *Tinsley's Magazine*, June 1883.

BYRON: *Works*, 8 vols., 1831; *Works*, ed. E. H. Coleridge, 7 vols., 1898–1904; *Letters and Journals*, ed. R. E. Prothero, 6 vols., 1898–1901; *Correspondence*, ed. John Murray, 2 vols., 1922.

CARLYLE: *Correspondence of Thomas Carlyle and R. W. Emerson*, ed. C. E. Norton, 2 vols., 1883; *Thomas Carlyle: His Life in London*, by J. A. Froude, 2 vols., 1884; *Conversations with Carlyle*, by Sir Charles Gavan Duffy, 1892; *New Letters of Thomas Carlyle*, ed. Alex. Carlyle, 2 vols., 1904; *Necessary Evil: The Life of Jane Welsh Carlyle*, by Lawrence and Elisabeth Hanson, 1952.

CHORLEY: *Henry Fothergill Chorley: Autobiography, Memoirs, and Letters*, ed. H. G. Hewlett, 2 vols., 1873.

CLAIRMONT: *Claire Clairmont*, by R. Glynn Grylls, 1939.

COLERIDGE: *Unpublished Letters of S. T. Coleridge*, ed. E. L. Griggs, 2 vols., 1932.

COLVIN: *Landor*, by Sidney Colvin, 1881; *Memories and Notes*, by Sir Sidney Colvin, 1921; *The Colvins and their Friends*, by E. V. Lucas, 1928.

COTTLE: *Reminiscences of Coleridge and Southey*, by Joseph Cottle, 1847.

CROSSE: Mrs. Andrew Crosse—*Red-Letter Days of My Life*, 2 vols., 1892; "John Kenyon and His Friends," *Temple Bar*, April 1890; "Walter Savage Landor," *Temple Bar*, June 1891.

DE QUINCEY: *Collected Writings*, ed. David Masson, 14 vols., 1889–90; *Thomas De Quincey: His Life and Writings*, by A. H. Japp, new ed., 1890; *Confessions of an English Opium-Eater*, ed., with *A Life of De Quincey*, by Malcolm Elwin, 1956.

DERBYSHIRE: *Victoria History of the County of Derby*, vol. 2, 1907.

DICKENS: *Letters of Charles Dickens*, ed. by his sister-in-law and eldest daughter, 3 vols., 1880–82; *Life of Charles Dickens*, by John Forster, ed. J. W. T. Ley, 1928; *Mr. and Mrs. Charles Dickens*, ed. Walter Dexter, 1935; *Letters*, ed. Walter Dexter, 3 vols., 1938; *Charles Dickens: His Tragedy and Triumph*, by Edgar Johnson, 2 vols., 1953; "Landor's Life," *All the Year Round*, 24th July 1869.

DILKE: *Papers of a Critic*, by Charles Wentworth Dilke, 2 vols., 1875.

DONNE: *William Bodham Donne and His Friends*, ed. C. B. Johnson, 1905.

D'ORSAY: see BLESSINGTON.

DUKE: *Notes on the Family of Savage of Warwickshire*, by R. E. H. Duke, *Miscellanea Genealogica*, Dec. 1901–Sept. 1902; *Pedigree of the Paternal Ancestry of W. S. Landor*, *Miscellanea Genealogica*, June 1912.

ELKIN: *W. S. Landor's Studies of Italian Life and Literature*, by Felice Elkin, 1934.

EMERSON: *English Traits*, by Ralph Waldo Emerson, 1856.

FIELD: "Last Days of Walter Savage Landor", *Atlantic Monthly*, April–June 1866; *Kate Field: A Record*, by Lilian Whiting, 1899.

FIELDS: *Yesterdays with Authors*, by James T. Fields, 1872; *Biographical Notes and Personal Sketches*, by James T. Fields, 1882.

FITZGERALD: *Letters of Edward FitzGerald*, 2 vols., 1894.

FONBLANQUE: *Life and Labours of Albany Fonblanque*, by E. B. de Fonblanque, 1874.

FORSTER: *Walter Savage Landor: A Biography*, by John Forster, 2 vols., 1869, and revised edition 1876; *John Forster and His Friendships*, by Richard Renton, 1912; *Victorian Wallflowers*, by Malcolm Elwin, 1934.

FOSTER: *Alumni Oxonienses*, by Joseph Foster, 4 vols., 1887–88.

FOX: *Memories of Old Friends*, by Caroline Fox, ed. H. N. Pym, 1883.

FOX BOURNE: *English Newspapers*, by H. R. Fox Bourne, 2 vols., 1887.

FRANCIS: *John Francis, Publisher of the Athenæum*, ed. J. C. Francis, 2 vols., 1888.

FRERE: *Works of John Hookham Frere*, 2 vols., 1872.

GRAVES-SAWLE: *Sketches from the Diaries of Rose Lady Graves-Sawle*, 1908.

GRAY: "An Unpublished Literary Correspondence," by W. Forbes Gray, *Cornhill Magazine*, July 1926.

GRONOW: *Reminiscences and Recollections of Captain Gronow*, 2 vols., 1900.

HALL: *A Book of Memories*, by S. C. Hall, n.d.; *Retrospect of a Long Life*, by Samuel Carter Hall, 2 vols., 1883.

HARE: *The Story of My Life*, by Augustus J. C. Hare, 6 vols., 1896–1900; *Memorials of a Quiet Life*, by Augustus J. C. Hare, 2 vols., 1872.

HAZLITT: *New Writings*, ed. P. P. Howe, 1925; *Life of William Hazlitt*, by P. P. Howe, new ed., 1928; *The Fool of Love*, by Hesketh Pearson, 1934; *Born Under Saturn*, by Catherine Macdonald Maclean, 1943.

HOGG: *Two Hundred and Nine Days*, by T. J. Hogg, 2 vols., 1827; *Life of Shelley*, by Thomas Jefferson Hogg, new ed., 2 vols., 1933; *Jefferson Hogg*, by Winifred Scott, 1951.

HOLYOAKE: *Sixty Years of an Agitator's Life*, by George Jacob Holyoake, 3rd ed., 2 vols., 1893.

HORNE: *A New Spirit of the Age*, ed. Richard Hengist Horne, 2 vols., 1844.

HUBBELL: "Some New Letters of Walter Savage Landor," by Jay B. Hubbell, *Virginia Magazine of History and Biography*, July 1943.

HUNT: *Lord Byron and Some of his Contemporaries*, by Leigh Hunt, 2nd ed., 2 vols., 1828; *Autobiography of Leigh Hunt*, 3 vols., 1850; *Correspondence of Leigh Hunt*, ed. Thornton Hunt, 2 vols., 1862; *Leigh Hunt: A Biography*, by Edmund Blunden, 1930.

KNIGHT: *Passages of a Working Life*, by Charles Knight, 3 vols., 1865.

LAMB: *Life of Charles Lamb*, by E. V. Lucas, 2 vols., 1905; *Letters of Charles and Mary Lamb*, ed. E. V. Lucas, 3 vols., 1935; *The Essays and Last Essays of Elia*, ed. Malcolm Elwin, 1952.

LANDOR, R. E.: *The Count Arezzi*, 1824; *The Impious Feast*, 1828; *The Earl of Brecon. Faith's Fraud. The Ferryman*, 1841; *The Fawn of Sertorius*, 2 vols., 1846; *The Fountain of Arethusa*, 2 vols., 1848; *Robert Eyres Landor*, by Eric Partridge, 1927.

LINTON: *My Literary Life*, by Mrs. Lynn Linton, 1899; *Mrs. Lynn Linton: Her Life, Letters, and Opinions*, by G. S. Layard, 1901; "Reminiscences of Walter Savage Landor," *Fraser's Magazine*, July 1870; "Walter Savage Landor," *North British Review*, July 1869; *Memories*, by W. J. Linton, 1895.

LLANTHONY: *Hills and Vales of the Black Mountain District*, by Richard Baker-Gabb, n.d.; *A Descriptive & Historical Account of Llanthony Abbey*, 1906.

LONGFELLOW: *Life of Henry Wadsworth Longfellow*, by S. Longfellow, 2 vols., 1886.

LOWELL: see BOYLE.

MACKENZIE: *A Scottish Man of Feeling*, by H. W. Thompson, 1931.

MACMILLAN: *Memoir of Daniel Macmillan*, by Thomas Hughes, 1882.

MACREADY: *Diaries of William Charles Macready*, ed. William Toynbee, 2 vols., 1912; *Macready's Reminiscences*, ed. Sir F. Pollock, 1876.

McCARTHY: *History of Our Own Times*, by Justin McCarthy, 5 vols., 1901–3.

MARTIN: *The Secret People*, by E. W. Martin, 1954.

MEDICI: "Walter Savage Landor", by Marchesa Peruzzi di Medici, *Cornhill Magazine*, April 1915.

MILL: *On Liberty*, by John Stuart Mill, 1859, 3rd ed., 1864.

MILNES: *Monographs: Personal and Social*, by Lord Houghton, 1873; *Life, Letters, and Friendships of Richard Monckton Milnes, First Lord Houghton*, by T. Wemyss Reid, 2 vols., 1891; *Monckton Milnes: The Years of Promise*, by James Pope-Hennessy, 1949; *Monckton Milnes: The Flight of Youth*, by James Pope-Hennessy, 1951.

MINCHIN: *Walter Savage Landor: Last Days, Letters, and Conversations*, ed. H. C. Minchin, 1934.

MOORE: *Memoirs, Journal, and Correspondence of Thomas Moore*, ed. Lord John Russell, 8 vols., 1853–56.

MURRAY: *Memoir and Correspondence of John Murray*, by Samuel Smiles, 2 vols., 1891.

NAPIER: *Life of General Sir William Napier*, by H. A. Bruce, 2 vols., 1864.

PARR: *Memoirs of the Life, Writings and Opinions of the Rev. Samuel Parr*, by Rev. William Field, 2 vols., 1828; *Works of Samuel Parr, with Memoirs . . . and Correspondence*, ed. John Johnstone, 8 vols., 1828; *Parriana*, by E. H. Barker, 2 vols., 1828.

PATMORE: *My Friends and Acquaintance*, by P. G. Patmore, 3 vols., 1854; *Memoirs and Correspondence of Coventry Patmore*, by Basil Champneys, 2 vols., 1901.

PEACH: *Historic Houses in Bath*, by R. E. Peach, 2 vols., 1883–4.

POLLOCK: *Personal Remembrances of Sir Frederick Pollock*, 2 vols., 1887.

PROCTER: *Bryan Waller Procter: Autobiographical Fragment and Letters*, ed. Coventry Patmore, 1877.

QUARTERLY REVIEW: January 1824, February 1835, February 1837, October 1839, March 1850, April 1865.

REDDING: *Fifty Years' Recollections*, by Cyrus Redding, 3 vols., 1858.

REEVE: *Memoirs of the Life and Correspondence of Henry Reeve*, by J. K. Laughton, 2 vols., 1898.

RIVINGTON: *The Publishing House of Rivington*, by Septimus Rivington, 1919.

ROBINSON: *Diary, Reminiscences, and Correspondence of Henry Crabb Robinson*, ed. Thomas Sadler, 3 vols., 1869; *Correspondence of Henry Crabb Robinson with the Wordsworth Circle*, ed. Edith J. Morley, 2 vols., 1927; *Life and Times of Henry Crabb Robinson*, by Edith J. Morley, 1935; *Henry Crabb Robinson on Books and their Writers*, ed. Edith J. Morley, 3 vols., 1938.

SEVERN: *Life and Letters of Joseph Severn*, by W. Sharp, 1892.

SHELLEY: *Shelley in England*, by Roger Ingpen, 1917; *Mary Shelley*, by R. Glynn Grylls, 1938; *Shelley*, by Edmund Blunden, 1946.

SHERWOOD: *Life and Times of Mrs. Sherwood*, ed. F. J. Harvey Darton, 1910; *The State of Mind of Mrs. Sherwood*, by Naomi Royde Smith, 1946.

SOUTHEY: *Life and Correspondence of Robert Southey*, ed. Rev. C. Cuthbert Southey, 6 vols., 1850; *Letters of Robert Southey*, ed. J. W. Warter, 4 vols.,

1856; *Correspondence of Robert Southey with Caroline Bowles*, ed. Edward Dowden, 1881; *Southey*, by Edward Dowden, 1880; *Southey*, by Jack Simmons, 1945; *Memoir of the Life and Writings of William Taylor of Norwich*, by J. W. Robberds, 2 vols., 1843.

STEPHEN: "Hours in a Library—Landor's Imaginary Conversations," *Cornhill Magazine*, December 1878.

STORY: *Conversations in a Studio*, by William Wetmore Story, 2 vols., 1890; *William Wetmore Story and His Friends*, by Henry James, 2 vols., 1903.

SUMNER: *Memoir and Letters of Charles Sumner*, by E. L. Pierce, 2 vols., 1878.

SUPER: *Walter Savage Landor: A Biography*, by R. H. Super, 1954; *The Publication of Landor's Works*, by R. H. Super, 1954; "An Unknown Child of Landor's," *Modern Language Notes*, June 1938; "Extraordinary Action for Libel—Yescombe v. Landor," by R. H. Super, with "Addendum: A New Landorian Manuscript," by R. F. Metzdorf, *Modern Language Notes*, September 1941; "Landor's 'Dear Daughter', Eliza Lynn Linton", *Modern Language Notes*, December 1944; "Landor and the 'Satanic School'," *Studies in Philology*, October 1945; "The Publication of Landor's Early Works," *Modern Language Notes*, June 1948; "The Authorship of *Guy's Porridge Pot* and *The Dun Cow*," *The Library*, June 1950; "Landor's American Publications," *Modern Language Quarterly*, December 1953; " 'None was Worth My Strife': Landor and the Italian Police," *Bibliographical Society of America Papers*, 2nd Quarter 1953; "Walter Savage Landor", Chapter 8 in *The English Romantic Poets and Essayists: A Review of Research and Criticism*, ed. Carolyn W. Houtchens and Lawrence H. Houtchens, Modern Language Association of America, New York, 1957; "Landor's Letters to Wordsworth and Coleridge", *Modern Philology*, November 1957.

SWIFTE: *Wilhelm's Wanderings: an Autobiography* (by William Richard Swifte), 1878.

SWINBURNE: *Collected Poetical Works of Algernon Charles Swinburne*, 6 vols., 1919–20; *Miscellanies*, 1886; *Life of Swinburne*, by Edmund Gosse, 1917; *Letters of Algernon Charles Swinburne*, ed. Edmund Gosse and T. J. Wise, 2 vols., 1918; *Letters of A. C. Swinburne*, ed. Thomas Hake and A. Compton-Rickett, 1918; *Swinburne and Landor*, by W. Drayton Henderson, 1918; *Swinburne*, by Harold Nicolson, 1926.

TAYLOR: *Life and Letters of Bayard Taylor*, ed. M. Hansen-Taylor and H. E. Scudder, 2 vols., 1884.

TAYLOR: *Keats's Publisher: A Memoir of John Taylor*, by Edmund Blunden, 1936.

TENNYSON: *Alfred Lord Tennyson: A Memoir by His Son*, 2 vols., 1897; *Alfred Tennyson*, by Charles Tennyson, 1949.

TRELAWNY: *Adventures of a Younger Son*, 1831; *Letters of Edward John Trelawny*, ed. H. Buxton Forman, 1910; *The Friend of Shelley: A Memoir of E. J. Trelawny*, by H. J. Massingham, 1930; *Trelawny*, by R. Glynn Grylls, 1950; Trelawny's *Last Days of Shelley and Byron*, ed. J. E. Morpurgo, 1952.

TREVES: *The Golden Ring: The Anglo-Florentines 1847–62*, by Giuliana Artom Treves, 1956.

TROLLOPE: *What I Remember*, by Thomas Adolphus Trollope, 3 vols., 1887–89; "Letters by T. Adolphus Trollope to Kate Field," *Bulletin of Boston Public Library*, July 1927.

WELBY and WHEELER: *The Complete Works of Walter Savage Landor*, ed. T. Earle Welby and Stephen Wheeler, 16 vols., 1927–36 (Prose, 12 vols., ed. Welby; Poems, 4 vols., ed. Wheeler).

WHEELER: *Letters and Other Unpublished Writings of Walter Savage Landor*, ed. Stephen Wheeler, 1897; *Letters of Walter Savage Landor, Private and Public*, ed. Stephen Wheeler, 1899; *Charles James Fox: A Commentary on His Life and Character*, ed. Stephen Wheeler, 1907 (presents the suppressed *Commentary on Memoirs of Mr. Fox Lately Written*, 1812).

WHITING: *The Florence of Landor*, by Lilian Whiting, 1905. (See FIELD.)

WILLIS: *Pencillings By the Way*, by N. P. Willis, new ed., 1942.

WISE: *A Landor Library*, by Thomas James Wise, 1928.

WISE and WHEELER: *A Bibliography of the Writings in Prose and Verse of Walter Savage Landor*, by Thomas James Wise and Stephen Wheeler, 1919.

WORDSWORTH: *Life of William Wordsworth*, by G. M. Harper, 2 vols., 1916; *Letters of William and Dorothy Wordsworth: The Later Years*, ed. E. de Selincourt, 3 vols., 1939; *Wordsworth: A Re-Interpretation*, by F. W. Bateson, 1954; *Dora Wordsworth: Her Book*, by F. V. Morley, 1924. (See ROBINSON.)

LIST OF LANDOR'S PUBLICATIONS

The Poems of Walter Savage Landor, 1795.
Moral Epistle, Respectfully Dedicated to Earl Stanhope, 1795.
To the Burgesses of Warwick, 1797.
Gebir, 1798; 2nd edition, 1803.
Poems from the Arabic and Persian, 1800.
Iambi (? 1802).
Poetry by the Author of Gebir, 1802.
Gebirus, 1803.
Simonidea, 1806.
Latin Idyls and Alcaics (? 1807).
The Dun Cow, 1808.
Hints to a Junta (? 1808).
Three Letters, Written in Spain, to Don Francisco Riquelme, 1809.
Ode ad Gustavum Regem, 1810.
Letters to Sir Francis Burdett, 1810.
Count Julian, 1812.
Commentary on Memoirs of Mr. Fox, 1812.
Address to the Freeholders of Monmouthshire, 1812.
Letters addressed to Lord Liverpool, and The Parliament, on the Preliminaries of Peace, by Calvus, 1814.
Letter from Mr. Landor to Mr. Jervis, 1814.
Idyllia Nova Quinque Heroum atque Heroidum, 1815.
Sponsalia Polyxenae, 1819.
Idyllia Heroica Decem, 1820.
Poche Osservazioni, 1821.
Imaginary Conversations of Literary Men and Statesmen, 2 vols., 1824; 2nd edition, 1826.
Imaginary Conversations of Literary Men and Statesmen, vol. 3, 1828.
Imaginary Conversations of Literary Men and Statesmen, Second Series, 2 vols., 1829.
Gebir, Count Julian, and Other Poems, 1831.
Citation and Examination of William Shakspeare, 1834.
Pericles and Aspasia, 2 vols., 1836; American edition, 1839.
Letters of a Conservative, 1836.
A Satire on Satirists, 1836.
Terry Hogan, An Eclogue, 1836.
The Pentameron and Pentalogia, 1837.
Andrea of Hungary, and *Giovanna of Naples*, 1839.

Fra Rupert, 1840.
To Robert Browning, 1845.
The Works of Walter Savage Landor, 2 vols., 1846.
Poemata et Inscriptiones, 1847.
The Hellenics of Walter Savage Landor, 1847; new edition, enlarged, 1859.
Imaginary Conversation of King Carlo-Alberto and the Duchess Belgioioso, on the Affairs and Prospects of Italy, 1848.
The Italics of Walter Savage Landor, 1848.
Carmen ad Heroinam, 1848.
Savagius Landor Lamartino, 1848.
Epistola ad Romanos, 1849.
Statement of Occurrences at Llanbedr, 1849.
Two Poems, 1850 (attacking J. G. Lockhart, editor of the *Quarterly Review*).
Popery: British and Foreign, 1851.
On Kossuth's Voyage to America, 1851.
Tyrannicide, 1851.
Imaginary Conversations of Greeks and Romans, 1853.
Two Poems, 1852.
Last Fruit Off an Old Tree, 1853.
Letters of an American, mainly on Russia and Revolution, 1854.
Antony and Octavius. Scenes for the Study, 1856.
Letter from W. S. Landor to R. W. Emerson, 1856.
Walter Savage Landor and the Honourable Mrs. Yescombe, 1857.
Mr. Landor Threatened, 1857; 2nd edition, 1857.
Dry Sticks, Fagoted by Walter Savage Landor, 1858.
Mr. Landor's Remarks on a Suit preferred against him, 1859.
Savonarola e Il Priore di San Marco, 1860.
Letters of a Canadian, 1862.
Heroic Idyls, 1863.

Note: Landor's works were first collected posthumously by John Forster in *The Works and Life of Walter Savage Landor,* 8 vols., 1876. In this edition Forster omitted several imaginary conversations previously published in periodicals, and deliberately excluded much verse published in *Last Fruit, Dry Sticks,* and *Heroic Idyls.* An edition in ten volumes by Charles G. Crump, 1891–3, closely followed Forster, though including useful notes and textual emendations; the two volumes of poetry were frankly a selection. In 1927 Chapman and Hall, the publishers of Forster's edition, commenced the issue of a handsomely printed edition of *The Complete Works of Walter Savage Landor.* They might have been more fortunate in the choice of an editor, for the late T. Earle Welby, though scrupulous in providing passages appearing in the original editions of the *Imaginary Conversations* but cancelled, at Forster's suggestion, in the 1846 edition, apparently lacked a sufficient knowledge of Landor's life and times to supply fully informative footnotes worthy of such an ambitious undertaking. Between 1927 and 1931, twelve volumes of the prose works were issued under Welby's editorship; *High and Low Life in Italy* was reprinted for the first time since its serial publication in Leigh Hunt's *Monthly Repository,* but the single volume of "Miscellaneous

Papers" merely reprinted those letters to the press which Landor himself reprinted in *Last Fruit Off an Old Tree*, omitting all subsequent letters except the separately published *Letter to Emerson*. The omission of the important *Commentary on Memoirs of Mr. Fox* alone nullified the edition's aspirations to completeness. After Welby's death the publication was concluded with four volumes of the *Poems*, admirably edited by Stephen Wheeler, whose work was also issued in a three-volume edition by the Oxford University Press.

INDEX